UNDERSTANDING CANADIAN BUSINESS

UNDERSTANDING CANADIAN BUSINESS

William G. Nickels
University of Maryland

James M. McHugh
St. Louis Community College—Forest Park

Susan M. McHugh
Learning Specialist

Paul D. Berman
McGill University and John Abbott College

IRWIN

Burr Ridge, Illinois
Boston, Massachusetts
Sydney, Australia

IRWIN
Concerned About Our Environment

In recognition of the fact that our company is a large end-user of fragile yet replenishable resources, we at IRWIN can assure you that every effort is made to meet or exceed Environmental Protection Agency (EPA) recommendations and requirements for a "greener" workplace.

To preserve these natural assets, a number of environmental policies, both companywide and department-specific, have been implemented. From the use of 50% recycled paper in our textbooks to the printing of promotional materials with recycled stock and soy inks to our office paper recycling program, we are committed to reducing waste and replacing environmentally unsafe products with safer alternatives.

Cover model builder: George E. Slye
Cover photographer: Paul Avis Photographer, Inc.

Senior sponsoring editor: Roderick T. Banister
Developmental editor: Elke Price
Project editor: Lynne Basler
Product manager: Murray Moman
Production manager: Bob Lange
Designer: Heidi J. Baughman
Art coordinator: Mark Malloy
Photo Research Coordinator: Patricia A. Seefelt
Compositor: Carlisle Communications, Ltd.
Typeface: 10/12 Bembo
Printer: Von Hoffmann Press

ISBN 0-256-10 800-5
Library of Congress Catalog Card No: 93–61413

Printed in the United States of America
2 3 4 5 6 7 8 9 0 VH 1 0 9 8 7 6 5 4

To my students—who taught me so much

Paul D. Berman

Dr. William G. Nickels is an associate professor of business at the University of Maryland, College Park, Maryland. He has over 20 years of teaching experience. He teaches introduction to business and marketing principles to large sections (250 students) each semester. Bill won the Outstanding Teacher on Campus Award at the University of Maryland in 1985. He has also won teaching excellence awards in the Division of Behavioral Science and in the College of Business and Management. He was again nominated for the Outstanding Teacher on Campus Award two out of the last three years.

Dr. Nickels received his M.B.A. degree from Case Western Reserve University and his Ph.D from The Ohio State University. He has written a principles of marketing text and a marketing communications text in addition to many articles in business publications. Bill is a marketing consultant and a lecturer on many topics.

Jim McHugh is an associate professor of business at St. Louis Community College—Forest Park. Jim holds an M.B.A. and has broad experience in both education and business. In addition to teaching several sections of Introduction to Business each semester for 14 years, Jim has maintained adjunct professorships at Lindenwood College and Fontbonne College, teaching in the marketing and management areas at both the undergraduate and graduate level. Jim has conducted numerous seminars in business and maintains several consulting positions with small and large business enterprises in the St. Louis area. He is also involved in a consulting capacity in the public sector. Jim authored several textbook supplements, including study guides and test banks.

Susan McHugh is an educational learning specialist with extensive training and experience in adult learning and curriculum development. She holds an M.Ed. and A.B.D. in education administration with a specialty in adult learning theory. As a professional curriculum developer, she has directed numerous curriculum projects and educator training programs. Susan designed and developed the instructor's manual, test bank, and computer simulation program.

Paul D. Berman founded a firm of chartered accountants and was actively engaged in the fields of management consulting, auditing, and taxation for 35 years. These activities involved considerable time overseas. He then went on to John Abbott College near Montreal, where he continues to teach a variety of business courses. Since 1988 he has been teaching an international business policy course at McGill University.

Paul's academic work has also taken him overseas. He has taken students to Denmark and the former East Germany to study these countries' education systems and how they do business. In the late 1980s, he spent considerable time in China, under a CIDA program, teaching, lecturing, and doing management consulting. This led to a special award from China's highest economic body, the State Economic Commission. Paul has also spent time in Japan, where he engaged in a joint research project with Japanese colleagues.

PREFACE

As we move through the last decade of the 20th century, we are witnessing a high degree of doubt and uncertainty, as well as many difficult problems, in Canada and around the world. A new and complex world is slowly and painfully taking shape. Change dominates the global economic environment as rapid and significant political and technological developments are changing the nature of how we live, prepare for careers, and do business with each other. New challenges and opportunities are emerging as we move toward the 21st century.

Understanding Canadian Business has been designed to help students understand and cope with the sometimes bewildering array of information they face in learning about business. It also provides insight into career choices and opportunities.

This book marks the first Canadian edition of one of the most popular introductory business texts in the United States. Hundreds of colleges and universities in both countries have adopted that text, currently in its third edition. *Understanding Canadian Business* is a complete revision with substantial changes in every chapter to properly reflect the Canadian scene. Chapters 1, 3, 16, and 19 were completely rewritten. Nearly all the examples cited are Canadian companies or transnational companies operating in Canada, as are the cases and statistics. Reviewers have commented very favourably about this feature. The number of chapters, 19, was decided on after careful thought and discussion. This number takes into consideration the limitations of the 13-week semester or term (commonly found in Canada) and student capacity to absorb information.

MAJOR THEMES

There are four major themes in the book, exemplified by the boxes that appear in each chapter: Spotlight on Small Business, Reaching beyond Our Borders, Making Ethical Decisions, Spotlight on Big Business. This conforms to the vital importance of these factors in the Canadian economy and society.

Small businesses are the major creators of new jobs in the 1990s; they provide numerous goods and services for both big business and consumers. They create livelihoods for hundreds of thousands of Canadian men and women who want to run their own businesses. Many of these entrepreneurs operate businesses out of their own homes, which is a rapidly growing phenomenon in this decade. Small business is responsible for a great deal of computer software and other technological innovations. In addition, a large and growing number of women are setting up small businesses and achieving great success. Spotlight on Small Business focuses on this important sector of the Canadian economy.

Reaching beyond Our Borders underlines the importance of international business in today's world. Major pacts, such as the Free Trade Agreement with the U.S. and the North American Free Trade Agreement have emerged. These pacts have had a major impact on Canada; the need to be internationally competitive has permeated every aspect of Canadian business. This is particularly important since over one-third of our economy is dependent on exports. This need has led to an unprecedented restructuring of companies and has stimulated major technological developments. On the downside, these developments have aggravated the massive layoffs and unemployment caused by the ongoing recession.

Business Ethics have received a great deal of attention lately in both the media and in academic research. Canadian society's expectations about the standards of behaviour of managers of business, government, and other organizations have changed significantly in recent years. Managers, executives, and businesses in general are now expected to be concerned with the effect of their decisions and actions on society. In addition, they are expected to apply ethical standards in decision making and in dealing with employees, minorities, and other countries. The environment has become a major concern in the 1990s, and businesses are expected to do their utmost to protect the environment, and in some cases, to bear the costs of cleaning up past misuses. Most large companies have set up departments to ensure that ethical and environmental standards are set and maintained. Making Ethical Decisions provides scenarios where students must think about ethical standards in decision making.

Spotlight on Big Business highlights the crucial role big businesses play in Canada. They produce most of the products we consume or export and they employ many people. Big businesses are essential in many industries, such as automobile and airplane manufacturing, pulp and paper mills, telecommunications, and pharmaceuticals, where large amounts of capital are required to start up and operate.

REAL WORLD EMPHASIS

The Canadian author has applied his extensive practical experience to ensure that the book portrays the real business world. Thus, most chapters contain new material not usually found in other texts. Not only is it very current, but the impact of technological change is clearly noted in every aspect of business—accounting, marketing, information systems, finance, production, human resources, and management in general. In accounting, computers have forever changed the traditional sequential nature of recording transactions and producing reports and financial statements. Production and operations have been revolutionized by computers. In addition, the emphasis on quality and employee participation in management are changing the nature of how we manage.

Many of these chapters contain text, figures, and illustrations that highlight information in a way not previously seen. In Chapter 5, a comparison of the pros and cons of each form of ownership is an example. A comparison of the different modes of financing in Chapter 18 is another example. Realistic guidelines for increasing chances of success when starting and operating a small business are illustrated in Chapter 6. A great deal of new and empirically based material is introduced in this important chapter.

HISTORICAL PERSPECTIVE

A historical perspective has been provided in many chapters to help illustrate the source of certain developments so they can be projected into the future. This applies to the first chapter on trends affecting business—how technology is a prime mover of change, the rapid growth of home-based businesses, the growing importance of environmental issues and sustainable development, and so forth. It also applies to Chapter 16 on labour/management issues, where a knowledge of the history of the union movement is important in understanding the difficulties in that relationship today. Current conditions require a major change in attitudes of both labour and management: cooperation between management and labour is critical for the future. Similarly, the role of government (Chapter 3) and ethical issues (Chapter 19) can be best understood if we know where we are coming from so we can more readily move into the future.

It is the Canadian author's belief, based on his business and teaching experience, and on the reviews of the manuscript, that students and instructors will find *Understanding Canadian Business* informative, thought provoking, and challenging.

SPECIFIC PEDAGOGICAL FEATURES

- The book's four themes mentioned above—small business, big business, internationalization of business, and ethical issues—are highlighted in the boxes in each chapter. These help unify the book and give students a feel for the dominant components of the Canadian business scene.
- Learning Goals at the beginning of each chapter are repeated as marginal notes in the chapter summary and are tied to questions and answers that review the main elements of that chapter.
- Key Terms for each chapter are listed after the Learning Goals. They appear in bold type and are defined in the text where they first appear. In addition, the Key Terms and definitions appear as marginal notes alongside the text. They are also repeated in the Glossary that follows the last chapter. Only Key Terms are shown in bold in the text. This makes it easier for students to note Key Terms and their meaning, thus building their business vocabulary.
- Each chapter starts with a Profile and a picture of a Canadian whose activities highlight the main content of that chapter.
- Scattered throughout each chapter are two elements entitled *Progress Check* and *Thinking It Through*. *Progress Check* contains three or four questions reviewing the chapter material to that point. *Thinking It Through* contains questions that encourage students to think about the issues relating to the chapter material and how these issues relate to their lives.
- Each photo or illustration has a short paragraph that shows its relevance to the text material.
- The end-of-chapter materials provide students the opportunity to participate in individual or group projects or to engage in class discussion. They also encourage students to think through various issues, to do critical analysis, and

to learn that many decisions must be made under uncertain conditions that managers face on a daily basis. These materials include:

1. Two cases followed by decision questions.
2. Getting Involved exercises.
3. Let's Talk Business questions.

To further stimulate students' involvement, where controversial issues are discussed, their opinions or further thought is asked for.

SUPPLEMENTS: AN INTEGRATED TEACHING AND TESTING SYSTEM

The resource package for instructors is unique in Canada. It is a very comprehensive set of tools that gives instructors a wide choice. No other introductory business text package is as easy to use and as fully integrated. To accomplish this integration, the authors of the text prepared the *Instructor's Manual,* the *Test Bank,* and *Computest III.* They also prepared the *Transparency Masters.*

1. Instructor's Manual

This detailed manual gives close guidance for each chapter lesson. It provides a topic outline, key terms, lecture outline, a detailed planning table, application exercises, answers to case questions, lecture enhancers, and other helpful material.

2. Test Bank

One part of the integrated teaching and testing system always receives more attention than the rest—the Test Bank. The success of a course depends on tests that are comprehensive and fair. Tests should measure a student's ability to remember and use the material in real-world situations. So the Test Bank must have questions that measure both recall and the ability of students to apply the material. Furthermore, there must be enough questions to change them each semester and still have high-quality tests.

The Test Bank to accompany *Understanding Canadian Business* is like no other. It tests three levels of learning: knowledge of key terms, understanding of concepts and principles, and application of principles. Each item has a unique rationale for the correct answer as well as the corresponding text page and identifies objective and learning level. There are over 4,000 test questions.

One helpful tool, unique to this package, is a Test Table. This chart helps you develop balanced tests by identifying items by objective and level of learning. You can then easily choose items that test objectives at your selected level of learning. For the ultimate in ease, each chapter concludes with a Quick Quiz. The 10-item tests are ready for reproduction and distribution for testing or for outside assignments.

3. Study Guide

The Study Guide reinforces what is learned in the text. It is not merely a synopsis of the text nor a collection of multiple-choice questions. The exercises contain various forms of questions that require students to write their answers so that the material becomes part of them. It is not an easy study guide; it is an effective one that demands active participation. If your students use this guide, they will be fully prepared for class discussions and exams.

4. Transparency Masters

Judiciously selected charts, graphs, and tables from the text are reproduced as transparency masters for your easy use in the classroom. These masters are in the Instructor's Manual.

ACKNOWLEDGEMENTS

Many people have made important contributions, in different ways, to *Understanding Canadian Business*. There are too many to be able to thank them all individually. I would like to single out the reviewers from across the country, who on several occasions, while the book was in progress, took the time to review different versions of the manuscript. They made invaluable suggestions to improve the quality and coverage and also noted any inaccuracies or weaknesses. I would like to extend my deepest thanks to all of these people, whose names are listed below:

Jim Alsop–Seneca College
Barry E. C. Boothman–University of New Brunswick
Brad Davis–Brock University
Jane Doyle–Sheridan College
Stephen Drew–McMaster University
Sean Hennessey–University of Prince Edward Island
Ray Klapstein–Dalhousie University
George Knight–Grant MacEwan Community College
Lionel Lustgarten–Vanier College
Mike Manjuris–Ryerson Polytechnical Institute
Blane McIntosh–Camosun College
Richard C. Powers–University of Toronto
John Redston–Red River Community College
Gerry Stephenson–Okanagan College

I would also like to thank the staff at Richard D. Irwin, Inc., in particular Elke Price, developmental editor; Rod Banister, senior sponsoring editor; and Lynne Basler, project editor for their help and patience. Thanks go also to Michael Polselli, who did a great job on many of the photographs used in the text. To my children, Victor, David, and Judith, I owe a great deal for their patience and cooperation as I plied them with questions and requests relating to their various fields of expertise. Finally, I would like to express my deep appreciation to my wife, Esther Berman, whose patience and direct and indirect assistance in so many ways, over an extended period of time, really made this book possible.

Paul D. Berman

CONTENTS IN BRIEF

CONTENTS

▶ PART V

▶ PART VI

ACCOUNTING AND FINANCE 539

CHAPTER 17 ACCOUNTING FUNDAMENTALS 541

CHAPTER 18 FINANCIAL MANAGEMENT 577

PART I

CANADIAN BUSINESS: TRENDS AND ISSUES

ST 100

MAJOR TRENDS AFFECTING CANADIAN BUSINESS

LEARNING GOALS

After you have read and studied this chapter, you should be able to:

1. Explain the importance and impact of technological developments.
2. Describe what is meant by the *information age* and what its implications are.
3. Discuss the globalization of business and why it is important for Canadian companies.
4. Identify the methods used by big business to become more competitive and the pressures to do so.
5. Show how the Canadian economy has shifted so that manufacturing remains vital but has been replaced by the service sector as the principal provider of jobs.
6. Explain the trend towards, and the importance of, small business and why home-based small businesses have become so popular.
7. Understand how Canadian business has rediscovered the importance of high-quality goods and services.
8. Explain how population trends have a major impact on business and what the current trends are.
9. Describe how environmental and other ethical issues play a major role in all business planning and actions.
10. Show how jobs and careers are affected by all of the trends discussed in the chapter.

KEY TERMS

customer-driven p. 15
decentralized p. 14
empowerment p. 14
globalization p. 9
goods-producing sector p. 17
information age p. 7
joint ventures p. 10
lean and mean p. 13
restructuring p. 13
service sector p. 17
strategic alliances p. 10
sustainable development p. 24

Judith Aston

PROFILE WOMEN AND MEN WHO STARTED BUSINESSES AT HOME

In 1986, after completing the professional translation program at McGill University, Judith Aston started a French–English translation service working out of her home. She emphasized high quality and fast service. At first she supplemented her income with a part-time job at a translation service, but as her billings grew, she was able to devote all her time to her own business. Now she has a fully equipped set-up—high-capacity computers and modem, a laser printer, and a fax machine. This enables all work to move rapidly from client to her to client, including billing by fax. Her volume has grown to the point that her husband John has given up his consulting work to assist her. Working at home kept the overhead low and made it easier for Judith to raise her son, who was 10 when she started. High quality and fast service have resulted in rapid growth that shows no sign of slackening.

In five years, Architech Microsystems Inc., a systems integrator, has built sales from $275,000 to more than $9 million. Cofounders Michael Trueman and Frank Gerencser, both 31, are the engines behind the Architech success story. As engineering students at university, they shared a fascination with computers and a dream of launching their own company. It was the classic bootstrap start-up. Architech operated out of the basement. The two partners lived upstairs with "three roommates, a dog, two birds and a for-sale sign on the lawn," recalls Gerencser. "Our marketing prof said keep it lean—and we took him to heart."

Working out of their home, Jan Williams and Rick Forsythe became the first domestic distributors of recycled stationery products in Canada when they launched The Paper Source. Start-up financing was limited: a $7,000 loan from the Ontario government's New Ventures Program and $8,500 from savings. Their only hard asset: a $3,500 computer. When their first fiscal year ended in September 1989, sales totalled $140,000—quadruple their initial projection. By September 1990, they were at $250,000.

Sources: Shaun McLaughlin, "Competition Heats Up in the Recycled-Paper Chase," *Small Business* 9, no. 3, March 1990, p. 12. Personal interviews.

TRENDS

These are a few examples of a trend to home-based business that has become a major factor in Canada and in the United States. This is only one of many important trends that affect the business environment in Canada. In this chapter we will explore some of the significant trends, many of which nourish each other, that are determining the nature of the business world today and in which you will find yourself when you have completed your studies.

The two most important universal trends are the rapid developments in technology—often called the *technological revolution*—and the *globalization* of business, which has become totally international in nature. Computers, robots, lasers, fibre optics, satellites, and many other significant advances in technology have radically altered the way we produce and what we produce, the way we buy and sell things, the way people and businesses communicate with each other, the manner and speed with which goods and information are sent and received, the way funds are obtained, and just about everything else in the business world.

Advances in communication and transportation technology have made the planet into a much smaller place and made it possible for business to operate on a global basis. Uptown and downtown may now be, and often are, thousands of kilometres away without any great inconvenience.

These two dominant trends will be found in various chapters in the book, as they are in the world of business. In this chapter we examine these and other trends that interact with, and are mainly the result of, technological change and the globalization of business.

THE TECHNOLOGICAL REVOLUTION

Human history is characterized by a steady flow of improvements in how work gets done and how life is made easier for people. Every time somebody finds a new way of doing something, using a better or new tool, device, or machine, we have an advance in technology. Sometimes the advance is a revolution. The first animal-drawn plow was such a revolution. Figure 1–1 lists some other important inventions. All these advances made significant changes in how we lived, worked, and produced.

If you look carefully at this list, which is far from complete, you will note that many inventions took place within the last two centuries. Since then the process of

Prior to 1700	The wheel, writing, bronze, iron, the arch, printing, gunpowder, clocks
Late 1700s	Steam power
1800s	Railways, telegraphy, photography, telephones, phonographs, steel-making, typewriters, oil and gasoline, rubber, automobiles, electricity, light bulbs, x-rays, and a vast array of machinery for agriculture and industry
1900s	Motion picture cameras, radio, refrigeration, airplanes, computers, plastics, rocketry and space exploration, satellites, television, photocopiers, atomic energy, robots, telefaxes, cellular phones, fibre optics

Figure 1–1 Revolutionary technological advances that radically altered how societies functioned.

The Royal Hudson is a steam-engine train that still transports tourists from North Vancouver to Squamish along beautiful Howe Sound.

REACHING BEYOND OUR BORDERS

Small Canadian Firm Has Big International Clout

From his home office in Toronto, consultant Uriel Domb has played a role in more than half the satellite projects launched in the 1980s and the early 1990s around the world. Domb, once an engineer at the U.S. National Aeronautics and Space Administration (NASA), has built a team of 20 consultants for his company, Telespace Ltd.

The firm has an enviable track record for complicated international communications contracts. It operates without the sophisticated marketing efforts, office bureaucracy, and centralized operations of large satellite consulting firms.

"My basic philosophy is it's important to serve our clients where they are," Domb says. And since Canada's satellite-communications market is already mature, Telespace has pursued contracts around the world. Telespace has an international reputation for excellent work, says Keith Rowe, ground-control manager of Inmarsat in London, who has worked with the firm on several projects. "Domb's strength is overall knowledge of satellite operations. But we have used their systems and people in every area."

Most clients learn of Telespace by word of mouth, Domb says. Certainly that was the case with Thaicom, which chose Telespace over at least four bigger competitors for a large consulting project in 1991. A consultant is always on hand for any problem Thaicom can't handle, Domb says. He attributes Telespace's winning of the Thai contract to this commitment always to be there—and to the smaller scale of the company.

"Thailand is a developing country moving into the telecommunications field for the first time," Domb says. "They didn't want to be overwhelmed. They preferred someone who would give them first priority." Telespace bid only after receiving a request for proposal from Thaicom, which had heard about Telespace from another small country that had launched a satellite.

Telespace is cost effective, partly because it doesn't spend money on expensive marketing efforts, Domb says. Its resources have instead gone into hiring the right people. Thailand needed a consultant who could provide expertise in all areas of satellite communications, but the Thais wanted to develop their own expertise so they wouldn't remain reliant on consultants. "We found this through our work with Brazil," Domb says. "Developing countries put a high priority on transferring technology and training people."

Domb, an Israeli-born, U.S.-educated aerospace engineer, worked at NASA in Washington, D.C. from 1967 to 1970. In 1970, he was recruited by Telesat Canada, then establishing its satellite-communications program, to direct ground-control systems. He spent a year at Bell-Northern Research Ltd., Toronto, then left to start Telespace.

Initially, Domb acted as a consultant on ground-control systems. As business grew, he recruited experts from international organizations to work alongside him. They have expertise in satellite-control systems, spacecraft design, mission software, launch campaigns, ground control, and station keeping.

Source: Susan Noakes, *Financial Post,* May 1, 1992, p. 1. ▼

technological advance has been speeding up, especially in the last decade. Most commentators on technology expect that the rate of change will accelerate even more in the next decade or two.

The most significant change in our era has been the advent of the computer. The computer and other electronic marvels—CDs, communication satellites, faxes, modems—as well as fibre optics, have helped to speed up the rate of technological change. They have had three major effects on business:

1. Operations have been revolutionized.
2. The information age has been ushered in.
3. Our large planet has been made into a small globe.

Throughout this book, we examine each of these three phenomena and their spinoffs. In Chapter 9 we look at the impact of technology on production and operations. These developments have such sweeping ramifications that the operation of modern business cannot be understood unless they are taken into account.

THE INFORMATION AGE

Towards the end of the 18th century, the invention of steam power in England led to the Industrial Revolution, which started in Europe and quickly spread across the Atlantic Ocean. For the first time in history, it became possible to set up factories employing many people under one roof to produce large quantities of a given product. Prior to that time only limited amounts of consumer and other goods were produced, by hand, at home or in small workshops by various craftspeople. Trade was slow and very limited.

Continual inventions expanded production until we reached the almost limitless capabilities we now have. The vast improvements in transportation facilitated trade and speeded up distribution of the now much greater supply of goods. The 19th century and the early 20th century were the era of production—trying to produce enough of everything from food to cars to meet people's needs. It is obvious that today, at least in Canada and in the rest of the developed world, there is no longer a shortage of goods and services. Many individuals may be unable to afford them, but they are certainly available.

Today producers of goods and services compete fiercely for buyers. Any edge gained by a company gives it a competitive advantage. Information has become a very important edge. That is why our time is called the **information age**—an era in which information is a crucial factor in the operation of organizations. (Perhaps inaccurately, we are often said to be living in the post-industrial information society.)

information age
An era in which information is a crucial factor in the operation of organizations.

Computers and the whole range of electronic gadgets—faxes, modems, portable phones, and more—have made the information age possible. One key to competitiveness is access to information about your operations. You require a similar information flow about your competitors, your markets, government activities, and technological developments that may affect your business.

To achieve this, businesses require good communication systems—especially the giant corporations with operations and facilities around the world. That is where computers and information systems play a critical role. (The appendix on

This is the information age. Over half of the work force is involved in teaching and other aspects of the information industry. These trends are likely to continue, so you need to learn to work with computers, fax machines, and the other information technology of the 1990s.

Management Information Systems at the end of Part III examines this in some detail).

Information has become a crucial element for competitiveness, and competition has become fiercer as it has become global. How can the CNR or CPR know exactly where each of their tens of thousands of rail cars is located, loaded or empty, anywhere in Canada or the United States? How can a courier service like Federal Express promise next-day delivery to any major city in the world from almost any other city? A computerized information system makes it possible. Every Federal Express unit, truck, and plane has a computer that is tied to the main computer system, so at any given moment the system knows where any parcel is.

The electronically fed information age also makes possible home-based businesses and home-based employees. How could they function without the battery of modern gadgetry?

HOME-BASED BUSINESSES

> Already considered the fastest-growing small business trend in Canada, the home-based business movement is expected to expand even more rapidly in the 1990s and beyond. An estimated 20 percent of the work force already toil out of their houses. And some studies forecast that by 2000 up to 40 percent of the labour force—mostly self-employed people—will be working at home.[1]

Why do people start such businesses? Some dislike their jobs or find them unfulfilling; some had jobs that disappeared or were threatened; others have a dream or strong passion; some want to be their own boss; still others want a change in lifestyle. Many women welcome this opportunity because they find their career path blocked because they are women. Or, they are mothers and find that a home-based business is a good way of earning income and being your own boss, and being home to look after their children. The common threads are:

1. Workers are prepared for a major shift from employment to self-employment for reasons noted above.
2. The new technology of computers, modems, cellular phones, and faxes makes home business more feasible.
3. Home-based businesses require little capital to start, and operating expenses demand minimal additional cash outlays.
4. There is a growing market for services to fill business needs.

Here are some examples from the *Globe and Mail:*[2] Terry and Nancy Belgue, aged 53 and 40, "dropped out of the Toronto corporate rat race to move to Victoria and set up an advertising agency in the basement of their home" in the Oak Bay area. They "wanted a slower pace of life and to spend more time with their young boys."

Louis Garneau, "a former Quebec and national cycling champion, started his successful sportswear company bearing his name, in St. Augustin, Quebec, by making cycling shorts in his parents' garage."

Bill Ross, 51, set up "a home-based consulting business, which focuses on sales training seminars for technical support people in computer companies."

James Bradley, 40, of Hamilton was laid off in November 1991 by the small engineering firm where he had worked as a drafter for five years. He had also lost a full-time job during the recession in 1982. Now, says the father of two boys, aged 9 and 12, "I'm getting too old to be laid off every five years, every time the economy goes down." With his wife working, he is able to take "a small-business management course hoping to turn a hobby into a videotaping and photography business. If you're going to take a gamble, you might as well enjoy it."

Home Inc., The Canadian Home-Based Business Guide (McGraw-Hill Ryerson, 1990), and the National Home Business Institute are resources to help budding home entrepreneurs start and operate their own home businesses.

Working at home is not confined to the self-employed. Many large companies are experimenting with having employees in certain departments work out of their homes. The idea is to cut down on expensive office space and employees' time and costs of travelling to and from work, without sacrificing efficiency. Various tests have also shown that employees who arrive at work after a frustrating commute do not function at their best for about an hour, until they settle down. IBM is thinking about letting its marketing people operate out of their homes.[3]

It is clear that the work-at-home trend is well established and growing in importance. Later we will look at the broader question of the rapid growth of the number of small businesses, especially in services, in Canada and at other developments that are nourishing small business and its home-based aspect.

We look next at the previously referred to globalization of business. Except for the smallest companies, the geographic area of competition has widened to encompass the whole world.

PROGRESS CHECK

- Why does technology have so much impact on business today? Give some examples. What advance has singlehandedly revolutionized how business operates? How?
- What is meant by the *information age?* How is it connected to technology? Why is information so important to business?
- Why are home-based businesses so popular? What conditions favour this trend?

THE GLOBALIZATION OF BUSINESS

From the earliest days, countries have traded with each other. Sailing vessels criss-crossed many of the oceans, seas, lakes, and rivers of the world. In Canada, aboriginal peoples and settlers travelled by canoe through the Great Lakes and the thousands of rivers and lakes that span North America. What is different about the globalized world of business—an expression that has become almost a cliché? There is no comparison between doing business today and yesterday.

globalization
A globally integrated system of production, marketing, finance, and management.

When we refer to the **globalization** of business, we are talking about a globally integrated system of production, marketing, finance, and management. All of these functions are carried out with little regard for borders or distances. Companies that operate globally are now called transnational companies (TNCs). Two prominent Canadian TNCs are Northern Telecom (Nortel) and Bombardier, who have operations scattered around the world. They may raise funds in Toronto, New York, London, or Tokyo. Some of these funds may be provided by the Royal Bank of Canada, which has agencies and branches around the world to service Canadian and other TNCs.

A telephone or switching equipment, a plane or a train, may have components from a dozen different countries. Nortel and Bombardier do far more business

Caterpillar sells over half its equipment to overseas buyers.

Here Caterpillar equipment is being used on a major project in South Korea.

outside Canada than in their home market. They both have international boards of directors. A so-called Canadian, American, or Japanese car may be designed, engineered, and tested in various countries. It certainly has components made on every continent. That's what globalization means.

Companies scour the world for the most reliable, lowest-cost, highest-quality locations to produce all or parts of their products. That means that all countries are in a globally competitive market. Tokyo vies with New York for financing, Mexico with Brazil or South Korea for production, and Canada with the United States or Germany to provide computer software. Toyota and Honda are producing cars in Ontario and Hyundai in Quebec. This trend towards companies investing and producing in countries outside their home base is a basic aspect of globalization.

A logical extension of this trend includes General Motors getting together with Toyota to manufacture cars in the U.S. GM has a joint venture with Suzuki to produce cars in Ontario. Ford and Volkswagen have also combined their efforts to produce their cars in the same assembly plant in South America. These are **strategic alliances** or **joint ventures**—arrangements whereby two or more companies cooperate for a special or limited purpose.

strategic alliances or joint ventures
Arrangements whereby two or more companies cooperate for a special or limited purpose.

A joint venture in the service sector was exemplified recently when two Canadian Companies, the BCL Group and Imax Corporation, teamed up to produce a feature-length film of the 1989/90 Rolling Stones's Steel Wheels/Urban Jungle Tour. *At The Max* was the first concert film in the IMAX® format. It attracted 1.4 million viewers in Canada, the U.S. and Europe. The film followed on the success that the BCL Group had in producing the Stones's tour of three continents. In one year, the tour shattered all existing records for live music events, drawing 6.2 million fans to 117 shows.

Rolling Stones "At the Max" was produced by two successful Canadian Companies: The BCL Group and Imax Corporation. Filmed over five nights in London, Berlin, and Turin, the film captures the world's greatest rock 'n' roll band with the world's largest film format.

Peter Drucker, a world-famous management consultant, expects the trend to international investment in manufacturing and financial services to grow in importance.[4] (Chapter 2 is devoted to this important topic.)

This means that Canadian, American, Japanese, or Korean firms are losing their clearcut identities as pure companies of one national origin. As one Harvard economist put it recently, it is getting increasingly harder to answer the question (in the industrial sense): Who is us?[5]

THINKING IT THROUGH

Do you think the trend to home-based business improves the quality of life? Why? How about the reduction in interaction with people?

Some people are concerned that technology is "taking over." Do you see it as a threat or as an opportunity? What about the job market?

Can you suggest what a business should be doing to make it more competitive globally? How do you feel about the prospect of working in a global environment?

The Trend towards the Pacific Rim: B.C. Takes the Lead[6]

Globalization also means that the difference in time zones around the world has been removed. Although half the world is sleeping while the other half is awake, stock exchanges are moving to 24-hour operations and some businesses are operating outside regular hours. The end of the business day in Canada is the start of the next business day in the Pacific Rim countries of the Far East.

This area contains some of the most dynamic economies in the world. Led by Japan, the *Four Dragons*—South Korea, Taiwan, Singapore, and Hong Kong—and the *Three Mini-Dragons*—Indonesia, Thailand, and Malaysia—offer tremendous opportunities for investment and trade. China, with one-fifth of the world's population, looms on the horizon as a rapidly developing country with endless similar opportunities.

British Columbia leads the country in trade and investment with the Pacific Rim. Consider this: "Nationwide, more than 75 percent of Canada's trade is with the United States, but in B.C. the figure is 40 percent and falling. Southeast Asia, meanwhile, now accounts for 40 percent of B.C.'s trade and is rising." (See Fig. 1–2).

This difference is not simply because the province is on the Pacific Ocean and faces the Pacific Rim countries. It is also because the influx of immigrants from Taiwan and Hong Kong has created a process that shows no sign of letting up.

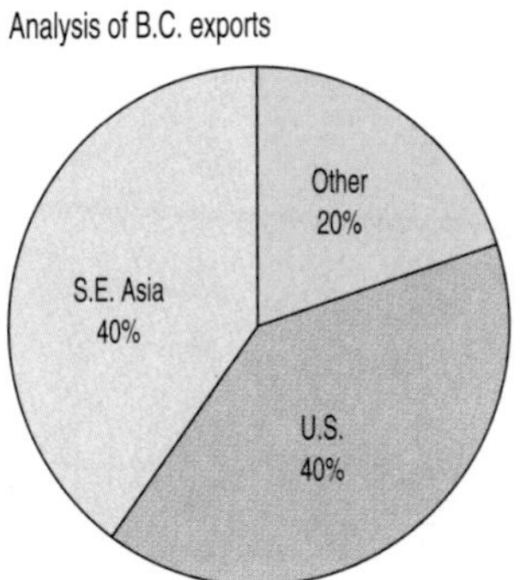

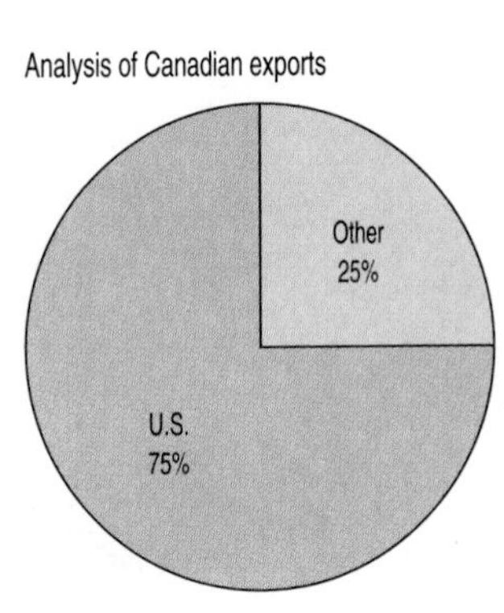

Figure 1–2 A comparison of the trading patterns of British Columbia and the rest of Canada shows British Columbia is much less reliant on the U.S. It is strongly turned towards the Pacific Rim.

Effect of Chinese Immigration on B.C. Business[7]

Consider what is happening to Vancouver (and the lower mainland):

> Thousands of newcomers, led by affluent Hong Kong and Taiwanese immigrants, including members of some of Asia's richest families, are injecting new vitality and a sharper edge into the city's once parochial business culture. "The hierarchy of the Hong Kong business establishment is being transplanted here in Vancouver," says Andrea Eng, a Colliers Macaulay Nicolls Inc. vice-president, who has sold $650 million worth of commercial property, mostly to Asians, in the past three years.

At first most of the investments were in real estate developments led by Li Ka-shing, Hong Kong's wealthiest industrialist, who bought one-sixth of downtown Vancouver in 1988 and announced his $2 billion Pacific Place development. More recently, entrepreneurial money began to flow into start-up ventures in electronics, apparel, and other industries. As the *Financial Times* puts it, "First came the mega-project billionaires and the fast-buck real estate investors. Now Canada's thriving West Coast jewel is being powered by entrepreneurial Asians who are building the economy one small business at a time." The *Financial Times* continues:

> Asian investments worth upwards of $1.5 billion a year are helping British Columbia set the pace for economic growth. While Canada's economy shrank . . . [in 1991] and the manufacturing heartland (Ontario) continues to struggle, Vancouver emerged relatively unscathed. B.C.'s economy shrank by a modest 0.5 percent in 1991 to set the pace in 1992 with growth of about 2.5 percent. It's hard to overstate the growing importance of Asian investment and immigration to the Vancouver area's 1.6 million residents.

According to Joachim Knauf, an Employment and Immigration Department economist,

> Between 1975 and 1991 Vancouver's employment base grew by 50 percent, three times the rate for Montreal and nearly 1.5 times the rate for Toronto. Job growth came in . . . engineering, tourism, and manufacturing. Vancouver added 30 percent more manufacturing jobs between 1988 and 1991 (Toronto lost 15 percent), thanks partly to Asian investment.

Scenic Vancouver has become a hub of foreign investment. Its proximity to the Pacific Rim has sparked an increase in trade, investment, and immigration with and from Asian countries.

This entire picture of people and investments coming to British Columbia and then developing significant trade with the Pacific Rim is a good example of one aspect of the globalization of business. The rest of Canada is well behind B.C. in turning its face towards Asia. Its outlook is still dominated by the Free Trade Agreement with Canada's largest trading partner, the United States, and its traditional ties to England.

The latter is illustrated by a comparison of the size of our embassies in Tokyo and London. According to Professor Charles MacMillan of York University, in an interview on CTV's "Question Period," January 18, 1992, the London embassy has a staff of 600 and the Tokyo embassy 40 people. We do a lot more business with Tokyo, our second-largest customer, than we do with Great Britain. MacMillan tried to have this huge disproportion rectified when he was an economic adviser to the Prime Minister but was unsuccessful.

BIG BUSINESS SHARPENS ITS COMPETITIVE POSITION

A major phenomenon of the last few years involved Canadian companies becoming **lean and mean**—the severe process of cutting all possible costs of operations. This was part of a greater global trend whereby companies sought to become more competitive by reducing costs. Management, office, and factory personnel all felt the weight of the axe. The recession at the beginning of the 1980s gave strong impetus to this movement. The deepening of the recession into the early 1990s, as global competition heated up, extended the trend into the current decade.

lean and mean
The severe process of cutting all possible costs of operations.

It is not an exaggeration to say that without computers it would have been impossible to engage in such wholesale cutbacks in staffing. Senior managers use computers instead of middle managers to get information and to keep on top of operations. Factory personnel, secretaries and assistants have been let go as the ubiquitous computer takes up a lot of the slack. Technology paved the way for these massive changes, called **restructuring.** This is the process of reorganizing the structure of companies to make them more efficient.

restructuring
The process of reorganizing the structure of companies to make them more efficient.

As a result of these policies, and despite growth in production and sales during the decade, there was no increase in the number of people working for large companies during the 1980s. Yet the total number employed in Canada rose by 2 million. (See Figure 1–3). Who employed them? While governments and

Year	People Working (000s)
1950	5,163
1955	5,610
1960	6,411
1965	7,141
1970	8,395
1975	9,974
1980	11,573
1985	12,532
1990	13,681
2000	16,500 (estimate)

Figure 1–3 Number of people working in Canada from 1950 to 2000.

Source: *Canadian Social Trends,* Spring 1991, no. 20, StatsCan, Cat. no. 11–008E.

non-profit organizations increased their employment rolls, small business took up the lion's share. (See Chapter 6.)

It is not certain whether the trend of staff reduction will, or can continue. It would seem as if there is very little fat left to trim after the extensive restructuring of the last few years. However, other means are also being sought to improve competitiveness. One of these ties in with the reduction of personnel because it leads to a significantly different managerial style.

Towards a More Effective Management

As companies trim the numbers of managers and reduce the size of the work force that they manage, those employees and managers who remain are given more responsibility. This delegation of power downward from the top of the hierarchy is a complex process that simultaneously achieves many desirable effects.

One aid to greater effectiveness is a more rapid response to the demands of the market and to challenges from competitors. The more decision making is **decentralized** (spread downward from the top), the quicker the reaction time to these demands and challenges. This obviously improves the company's ability to compete.

decentralized
Decision making is spread downward from the top of an organization.

A second advantage is that employees and lower-level managers feel a greater sense of participation in important decisions, which makes their work more meaningful and fulfilling. This, in turn, boosts morale and therefore performance. There is a growing trend towards the empowerment of employees. **Empowerment** means that the leaders of organizations give their workers the freedom, the incentives, and the training to be decision makers and creative contributors to the organization.

empowerment
The leaders of organizations give their workers the freedom, incentives, and the training to be decision makers and creative contributors to the organization.

A third advantage complements this point: employees who are involved in making decisions carry them out more enthusiastically. This *participative management* leads to more suggestions for improvement of procedures and thus to greater efficiency. All of these advantages are illustrated in the Chrysler story in the next section on quality.

Finally, many surveys have shown that a more satisfied work force means fewer accidents, less absenteeism, and a lower turnover of personnel. This substantially reduces costs of operations. In Parts III and IV you will see a more detailed discussion of these important issues.

All of these advantages are a normal feature of large Japanese companies and are one reason Japan occupies the top rungs of international competitiveness. Another major feature of Japanese (and German) competitive strength is the high quality of their products and customer satisfaction.

Quality: A New Interest in an Old Value

An old concept has recently gotten a lot of attention in Canadian (and American) business circles—*quality*. Why is this? Hasn't quality always been a normal way of doing things? Unfortunately, that has not been true since the 1960s. Before that, things were made to last. It didn't matter whether it was a pot, a chair, a car, or a house.

Then a strange new scenario took over. The throw-away philosophy of management gradually became the norm. Perhaps it was meant to boost sales and profits by ensuring a steady flow of replacement purchases. It was also partly based on the belief that quality work costs more, so no more quality would be provided than was necessary to keep the customers buying.

At about the same time the Japanese (and the Germans) were going in the opposite direction. Led by an American, Edwards Deming, who was ignored in his own country, the Japanese proved that quality is not more costly. Furthermore, it gave them a wonderful competitive edge, which they exploited to the utmost. That is how their autos and electronic products made such headway in North America and all over the world. Their quality programs were **customer-driven.** Customer satisfaction became the driving force that permeated companies.

customer-driven
Customer satisfaction becomes the driving force that permeates the company.

We finally got the message, a little late for the electronics industry but not too late, we hope, for the important auto industry. Deming, now in his nineties, and a few others have been avidly courted in the United States since the mid-1980s. Their quality message is sweeping through North America, but companies are finding that it is a lot easier to talk about it than to put it into practice.

Chrysler is one company that has gotten into quality seriously. In June 1992, its chairman, Lee Iacocca, was in Ontario at the Chrysler plant in Bramalea. Talking about why Canadians are buying so many imported cars, he said to workers and guests at the official launch of production of the new LH models:

> The only question in the mind of the import buyer is quality. Is our quality going to be first class? You bet it is. But we're going to get it right from the start. That's why we've got a slow launch . . . . Quality will drive the daily schedule.

He noted that there is a normal temptation to ease standards and crank up output, but "we've had that in the past and it doesn't work." This represents a significant shift of philosophy and shows that the quality message has finally gotten through to Chrysler. The movement to quality production also requires that the work force get more involved in the whole process, which ties in with the trend to greater employee empowerment and decentralization of management.

The plant manager, John Franciosi, said that the workers at Bramalea began building the new cars and got involved in the development process much earlier than at any Chrysler assembly plant in the past. Previously, cars were handed over to the plant only 22 weeks before production, but this time workers were involved in assembly nearly a year and a half before start day. At the one-year mark, all preproduction vehicles were being built by the employees. "Decision making at Bramalea has been moved to the lowest levels," said Franciosi. "So far [workers] have identified many improvements in the product and production processes—and they have been encouraged to continue to do so."[8]

PROGRESS CHECK

- What is meant by the *globalization of business?* How is it different from what came before? Can you give some Canadian examples of globalization?
- Why is there so much pressure on business, especially big business, to be more competitive? Can you name three things it is doing to meet that challenge?
- What effect do these actions have on the Canadian economy? Why is so much importance attached to quality? What demands are being placed on the new work force?

SPOTLIGHT ON QUALITY

There's No Substitute for Quality

Despite widespread business claims that customer satisfaction is of the highest importance to success in today's global marketplace, current practices often fail to reflect those claims.

German and Japanese firms place far more importance on incorporating the customer's voice into the design of new products and services than do North American firms. While 58 percent of Japanese and 40 percent of German businesses almost always translate customer expectations into the design of new products and services, only 22 percent of U.S. and 14 per cent of Canadian businesses do so.

Today, firms can no longer rely on low-cost labour for their competitive advantage. National boundaries no longer define market niches, and economic nationalism has given way to consumers' unrelenting demand for access to the best possible products and services regardless of country of origin.

Global leaders recognize that there is no substitute for quality as the foundation of their success. By building customer information into the design of every product or service, they capture today's global markets.

A survey by the University of Toronto's Institute of Market-Driven Quality of 336 Canadian companies with quality programs showed how important these programs are to them. Despite the recession and two-thirds of the companies having their sales "under pressure," only 10 percent reported reducing their investment in such programs.

The survey also shows that the quality programs are showing results. Of companies reporting more satisfied customers over a two-year period, 70 percent had clearly defined quality management strategies. Of those with unhappier customers, only 43 percent had such strategies.

Source: John Raymond, "Worth Repeating" (quoting chairman Ray Groves of Ernst & Young), *Report on Business, Globe and Mail,* July 8, 1992, p. B4.
Niches, "Quality Time," *Report on Business, Globe and Mail,* July 14, 1992, p. B24.

SMALL BUSINESS: A GROWING IMPACT ON THE CANADIAN ECONOMY

We are now in a period when entrepreneurship—the undertaking to form and operate a business—is flourishing. By 1993, 150,000 new businesses were being started annually in Canada; most of these new companies are small businesses. There are some 1 million small businesses in Canada. While many do not last long and a

Approximately 150,000 small businesses are started each year in Canada. Many jobs are created by small businesses and their contribution to the Canadian economy is very important.

SPOTLIGHT ON SMALL BUSINESS

A Global Matchmaker

President Carolyn Cross of tiny Brukar International Ltd. of Toronto has a different specialty. "Global, specialized, and intermediary . . . it is a service business for the '90s." Her business is "a classic example of the trend toward what economists call *intermediation.* The company's product is the information and communication that brings together far-flung buyers and sellers."

Examples of the products she locates and sells are software from Halifax and hardware accessories from B.C. for Apple computers. Cross is "particularly proud of a 'supermouse' made by Advanced Gravis Computer Technology Ltd., and a disk drive made by Aristotle Industries Inc., both of Burnaby, B.C., which she sells in Japan."

She is very proud of a compact printer for Apple computers that is made by Eastman Kodak. The inside of the printer is made in Japan and shipped to Kodak's main plant in Rochester, New York. There it is paired with software and Brukar then sells the completed printer back to Japan to the 180 retailers in the distribution network connection that Cross's company has established.

Source: "Selling Computer Products to Japan," *Financial Post,* 3 no. 183, Dec. 18, 1990. p. 118. ▼

large number go under regularly, the number of active small businesses continues to increase. What exactly is a small business? A *small business*

1. is independently operated.
2. is not dominant in its field.
3. meets certain size limits in terms of number of employees and annual sales. Various organizations, laws, and regulations use different size limits. The number of employees can range from zero to 100, sales up to $10 million and profits up to $200,000 annually.

Frequently these companies provide some service like computer consulting or auto repair or are restaurants or bars, retail stores such as clothing shops, or construction firms. Many are also manufacturing companies. Most of them provide jobs to employees as well as a livelihood for the owners. More recently, a growing number of these start-ups are home based. They usually offer a variety of consulting and professional services, as will be seen in many of the profiles, cases, and spotlights in various chapters.

The vast majority of new small businesses are in the service sector, discussed in the next section. Small business created most of the jobs for the additional 2 million people working in Canada in the 1980s. Many people regard the small business sector as vital for the continuing success of big business. These entrepreneurs are adventurous and innovative and provide many essential services for big business.

Because this is such an important and growing area of our economy, Chapter 6 devotes considerable space to small business.

THE SERVICE SECTOR[9]

goods-producing sector
The sector that produces tangible products, things than can be seen or touched.

service sector
The sector that produces services, not goods. Examples are financial, information, marketing, health, recreational and repair services.

The service sector of society is distinct from the goods-producing sector. The **goods-producing sector** produces tangible products that can be seen or touched, like clothes, oil, food, machines, or automobiles. The **service sector** produces services rather than goods, like financial, information, marketing, health, recreational, or repair services. In the last 25 years, the service sector in Canada has grown dramatically.

The Economic Council of Canada reports that between 1967 and 1988, service employment increased at an average annual rate of 3.2 percent, compared with 0.9 percent in the goods-producing sector—three and a half times as fast. In fact, the shift in Canada's employment make-up away from goods-producing industries began early in the century and has accelerated rapidly since the 1950s. The trend is expected to continue, although perhaps at a reduced rate. By the year 2000, the service sector could account for 78 percent of all jobs in Canada. This growth is due to a complex series of factors.

First, technological improvements have enabled businesses to reduce their payrolls while increasing their output. This accounts for the fact that despite the huge increase in gross domestic product (GDP) between 1960 and 1990, manufacturing still accounts for the same 19 percent of GDP (Figure 1–4), while its percentage of total work force has been cut in half—from 30 to 15 percent—in the same period. At the same time, because staffing has been sharply pruned and business has become more complex and specialized, companies rely more heavily on outside service firms.

For example, lumber and resources giant Macmillan Bloedel relies on Karo Design Resources, a small Vancouver-based industrial and marketing firm, to investigate how parallel strand lumber could best be manufactured from weeds in Georgia (U.S.A.), and marketed to customers for building doors and windows. Employment in this type of business-oriented service grew 20 percent between 1961 and 1986.

Canada has a large number of such specialized companies that service the manufacturing sector and other businesses. In a study of the service sector for the Institute for Research on Public Policy, economist William Empey showed that the service component of Canadian products has been growing steadily since 1971. He argues that "competitiveness in manufacturing depends critically on access to efficient producer services." He mentioned banking, insurance, transportation, and communication as such important services.

Figure 1–4 The role of manufacturing in the economy. Despite the growth in GDP, the manufacturing sector has maintained a constant share of GDP. The *number* of people employed in manufacturing has hardly changed, but its *percentage* of total employed has been cut in half, from 30 percent to 15 percent.

	1960	**1990**
Total employed in Canada	6,400,000	13,700,000
Number employed in manufacturing	1,920,000	2,055,000
Percentage	30%	15%
Manufacturing share of GDP	19%	19%

Sources: Terence Corcoran, *Report on Business, Globe and Mail,* May 2, 1990, p. B2. Madeleine Drohan, *Report on Business, Globe and Mail,* April 18, 1990, p. B1.

Molly Maid started as a small maid service and has grown to become the world's largest housekeeping company.

Because employee-benefits planning and sophisticated data-processing techniques are very complicated, they have contributed to the proliferation of service specialists. Canada has a large number of computer components and software specialist companies scattered across the country from Halifax, N.S., to Burnaby, B.C., whose products are in demand in Canada as well as Hollywood, Europe, and Japan. They produce everything from computer games to movie special effects. For example, the magic carpet in *Aladdin* was modelled on software created by Alias Research Inc. of Toronto.

Other service firms have risen or expanded rapidly to provide traditional or personal services that used to be done by women at home. So many women have entered the work force that there is a greater demand for food preparation, child care, and household maintenance. An additional boost for this type of service was the rise in wages that occurred in the 1950s, 1960s, and 1970s.

An interesting example of a home-cleaning service that met such needs is Molly Maid. It started as a small maid service in suburban Toronto in 1979. At the end of 1990, now known as Molly Maid International Inc., it was the world's largest housekeeping company with annual revenue of $45 million and franchises in Germany, England, Scotland, the U.S., and Japan. The total number of franchises was 345, of which 180 were outside Canada.

THINKING IT THROUGH

Can you see yourself setting up your own business? In the service sector? Does a home-based business attract you? Why or why not?

How has technology led to the mushrooming of the service sector? Give specific examples.

A third area that has contributed to the rise in service sector jobs is the government or quasi-government area, which includes public administration (federal, provincial, and municipal), health, and education. The post-war baby boom, the installation of Medicare in 1970, and the large growth in immigration to Canada all stimulated the demand for such services.

PROGRESS CHECK

- Why is big business no longer a creator of new jobs? Why is small business creating so many jobs? In what sector of the economy are these new companies and jobs to be found?
- How does small business stimulate big business? How does it complement big business?
- What exactly is the service sector? Why is it so essential to the Canadian economy?
- What role has technology played in stimulating the growth of the service sector? What other factors have contributed to its growth?

HOW IMPORTANT IS MANUFACTURING TO CANADA?

The serious recession of the early 1990s saw about 600,000 jobs lost in Canada, a large portion of them in manufacturing. As indicated in Figure 1–4, manufacturing employed just under 2 million people in 1960; that number increased 7 percent by 1990. Since then, because of these massive job losses, the number appears to have fallen for the first time in more than three decades. Manufacturing gross output has also declined steadily from 1989 to 1991, from $96 billion to $85 billion (as measured in 1986 dollars) for an 11.5 percent drop.[10]

This decline raises important questions on which there are divergent views. One person who has strong opinions is Akio Morita, the world-famous founder and chief executive of Sony Corp. He spoke in Ottawa in May 1989, warning Canada and the United States about the danger of a shrinking manufacturing sector and reliance on the service sector for growth and stability. Morita continued:

> If Canadians ignore manufacturing, while thinking of themselves as information technicians in a service-based economy, they might find themselves on the sidelines of international business. It is only manufacturing that creates something new, which takes raw materials and fashions them into products which are of more value than the raw materials they are made from.[11]

Sony is a giant transnational corporation with plants, subsidiaries, and operations on all continents, and Morita has been the guiding light in its very successful history—a true rags to riches story. So perhaps we should pay close attention to what he says. He may be biased towards manufacturing, but he should not be ignored.

Various opinions and data on this important question were examined in a detailed article in the *Globe and Mail*.[12] Michael Walker, director of an ultraconservative think tank, The Fraser Institute, stated that "the service sector could account for 99.9 percent of economic output without damaging the economy."

The opposite opinion was voiced by Todd Rutley, senior economist of the Canadian Manufacturers' Association (CMA). He maintained that it was "ridiculous" not to realize the importance of the manufacturing sector. He pointed out that Canada was running a $20 billion annual deficit in its trade and investment with other countries. Exports of manufacturing goods, he noted, play a significant role in reducing that deficit.

Developments in 1992 and 1993, as reported by Statistics Canada, indicate that manufacturing exports are also helping to lead the economy out of the deep recession of the last few years. This issue is discussed in some detail in the next chapter.

Economic Council of Canada economist Gordon Betcherman supports Rutley's position. He suggests that "too much emphasis on one sector at the expense of the other is bad." He pointed out that a recent study by the Council, based on a model of the Canadian economy, determined that:

> When you stimulate the goods sector, the whole economy does well. If you stimulate the services sector, there's basically no payoff. Both goods and services are extremely important to a healthy economy.

The article also reports a "forceful" speech by CMA chairman David Vice, vice-chairman of Northern Telecom, outlining why manufacturing is essential to Canada's future. It further notes that this debate is heating up in the U.S., where there is great fear of "the United States losing its competitive edge along with its manufacturing jobs to the Japanese." Echoing Morita's ideas, Betcherman says:

> Japan is the only major industrialized country where employment in manufacturing increased before, during, and after the 1981–82 recession. In both Japan and West Germany manufacturing output and employment is higher as a proportion of the overall economy than in the other industrialized countries. Could there be a link between the size of their manufacturing sector and their continued economic success?

Finally, the article notes, Statistics Canada believes that some aspects of what manufacturing companies used to do have shifted to service companies. Tasks such as accounting, payroll, legal work, and advertising are commonly contracted out to service companies specializing in these fields. This accounts for some of the shift in jobs from manufacturing companies, although they were really service jobs all along.

Another voice downgrading the importance of manufacturing is that of Canadian economist Nuala Beck, who argues:

> A new knowledge economy is rapidly replacing the old mass-manufacturing economy. "Knowledge workers" now make up 30 percent of North America's work force, while only 10 percent are actually involved in production. What's more, knowledge-intensive new industries are creating most of the jobs and driving the economy.
>
> Old industries are shrinking year after year. Significantly, the old industries, like logging, don't use many knowledge workers. But the old industries still employ a lot of people, and by force of habit we still define our prosperity by the number of people toiling in factories, mines, and fisheries. We fret about the inroads of the Japanese auto industry and the number of housing starts.
>
> . . . [But] the auto industry has passed its peak. Housing is now less than 4 percent of the U.S. economy. The cookie industry is nearly twice as big as the machine-tool industry.[13]

If we look at the significant international competitors (in addition to Japan and Germany) such as South Korea, Taiwan, Singapore, and Hong Kong, their strength was and continues to be manufacturing. Are there any lessons there for us? Should we be paying more attention to the importance of manufacturing to our continuing economic health? Or are these the success stories of yesterday, as Nuala Beck and many others claim? The answers to these questions will influence the kind of economy that you will be living in during the decades to come.

POPULATION TRENDS[14]

Demographic (population) trends have a significant effect on business planning and activities. For example, in the 20 years following World War II (1946 to 1966), Canada witnessed an unusual phenomenon. Large numbers of war veterans, aided by government grants, got married and acquired housing for their families. In addition, the hundreds of thousands of immigrants who were entering Canada annually also needed housing. Four children per family was the norm. This explosive growth in population and family formation led to a 20-year boom in many industries.

Construction of houses, cottages, apartments, and other dwellings—as well as schools, colleges, CEGEPs, and universities for the hundreds of thousands of children—took off with a bang. Home furnishings and appliances, children's clothing, sports and school supplies also flourished. To accommodate this vast growth in retail business, new stores, malls, and shopping centres sprang into being. Companies expanded rapidly, new firms mushroomed, and all required additional space, so office towers and factories began appearing everywhere. These in turn needed furniture, equipment, and supplies.

The explosion of the construction industries fueled tremendous growth in all the allied industries and services that feed upon new construction: banks, trust and insurance companies, lawyers and notaries, lumber, concrete, brick, electrical, paving, plumbing, landscaping, carpentry, painting, roofing, telephone and hydro, and heating. All these businesses and many more experienced great expansion in employment, sales, and profits. As suburbs developed to accommodate all this population and business growth, cars and busses were needed for transportation and new roads were built.

Those businesses that analyzed what was happening and prepared for the effect of these demographic trends became very profitable. Today, other important demographic trends have emerged that will have a great impact on the next few decades. Those individuals and companies who correctly analyze these trends and

As the population ages, businesses targeting older people will incease. Recreation activities will be in great demand.

Year	Under 6	6–19	20–34	35–64	65 and Over
2001	1,639	4,862	5,759	11,673	3,684
	5.9%	17.5%	20.7%	42.0%	14.0%
1991	2,097	5,088	6,749	9,506	3,173
	7.9%	19.1%	25.4%	35.7%	11.9%
1986	2,174	5,142	6,780	8,514	2,698
	8.6%	20.3%	26.8%	33.6%	10.7%
1981	2,139	5,657	6,560	7,626	2,361
	8.8%	23.2%	26.9%	31.3%	9.7%
1971	2,228	6,267	4,779	6,550	1,744
	10.3%	29.1%	22.2%	30.4%	8.1%
Percent change					
1981–1991	−2.0	−10.1	2.9	24.7	34.4
1992–2001	−21.8	−4.4	−14.7	22.8	22.4

Figure 1–5 Population distribution by age group, selected years, 1971–2001 (000s)

Source: Statistics Canada. *Population Projections for Canada. Provinces and Territories.* 1984–2006. Cat. 91-520 (Ottawa: Ministry of Supply and Services, May 1985).

their impact on future business obviously will do very well. What are these current population trends? You may already be familiar with some of them.

The population of Canada is aging. More people are living longer, due in part to better medical knowledge and services, proper nutrition and exercise, and avoidance of cigarettes and alcohol. By 2011, the portion of the population over 65 and 75 will be about double what it was in 1981. More than 16 percent will be over 65 and 7.5 percent over 75. By the year 2001, it is estimated that there will be about 1 million people over 75. Figure 1–5 shows some interesting statistics on these population trends.

At the same time, the portion of the population that is very young continues to decrease because of declining birth rates since the mid-1960s. While the rate is low, the actual number of children being born is still large because of the echo-boom. The echo-boom is the result of the so-called baby boomers, born in the 1946–1966 period, starting families.

In addition, we have had steady immigration into Canada. In the 1980s more than 1 million immigrants entered Canada. More than half of these were under 30, so many are likely to have children. The 1990s may see some 2 million immigrants enter Canada.

What does all this add up to regarding needs of the population? Businesses that cater to older people should prosper, everything from health care to recreation, from education to travel. Smaller apartments should be in greater demand. More grandparents with more money in their pockets will be buying more gifts for more grandchildren. The continuing large number of births assures prosperity for those businesses supplying children's needs. There should be many opportunities for existing and new businesses to explore.

ENVIRONMENTAL ISSUES

One of the most important ethical and social issues of our times is the serious deterioration of the physical environment of our planet. The unlimited expansion of population and industry has so altered the air, water, forests, insect and plant life,

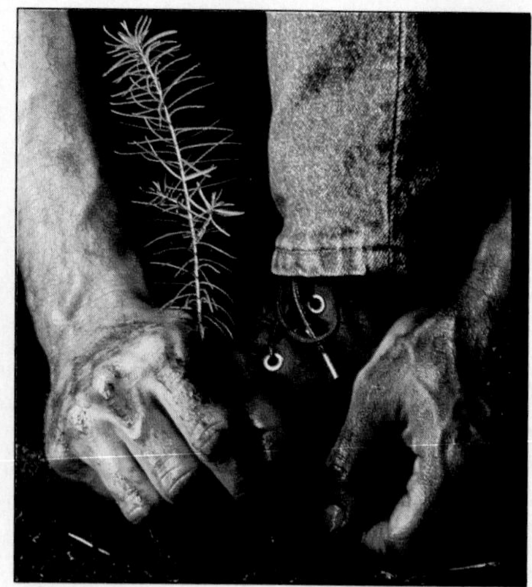

These photos show a site that was seeded after lignite mining by the Dolet Hills Mining Venture. After it is mined, most of the land is planted in timber as shown, but some areas are preserved specifically for wildlife habitats. Concern for the air, water, and land is a central part of responsible management.

and soil that we face grave threats to our very existence. We are all familiar with the problems of too much waste—much of it highly toxic—and how it pollutes our air, rivers, lakes, oceans, and soil. We have learned about the emission of vast quantities of gases that are heating up the atmosphere and what this greenhouse effect will do to our climate, agriculture, and ocean levels. We have become aware of the chemicals we put on the food we grow, the indiscriminate destruction of tropical forests, soil erosion, and silting up of rivers. And there are many more problems that will not be solved unless we begin to live and think in a new, more socially responsible way.

In Canada we are confronted by many of these problems and are seriously affected by acid rain. Thousands of our lakes are completely dead, with no plant or fish life remaining. Our maple trees are dying off, paint peeling from houses, and bricks disintegrating. The polluted rain and snow from factory chimneys thousands of kilometres away continues to cause hundreds of millions of dollars in damage to Canada each year. The whole world, from the Arctic to the Antarctic, is affected by this problem.

Companies can no longer make decisions based only on their immediate economic interests. This new input into the planning and thinking of management involves a major shift and will continue to grow in importance. Governments have passed many new laws requiring industries to observe ever more stringent environmental standards. This often involves greater costs, which inevitably find their way into the prices consumers have to pay. Are these costs any higher than the damages caused by unrestricted operations?

New industries and professions are being spawned from the new awareness of environmental issues. Recycling and waste management companies have sprung up, and alternative materials and processes are being explored. This leads to new discoveries, jobs, and investment opportunities. The movement towards conservation has had the same effect. Businesses have discovered ways to reduce costs, making them more competitive.

sustainable development
Economic development that meets the needs of the present without endangering the external environment of future generations.

The concept of **sustainable development** was promoted in 1988 at a major international conference on the environment in Toronto. Sustainable economic development meets the needs of the present without endangering the external environment of future generations. In the Brundtland report, the Prime Minister of

SPOTLIGHT ON BIG BUSINESS

A Constructive Approach to Environmental Problems

Some giants that are household names in Canada, like Mobil Oil, Shell, and Nova Corp., are typical of Alberta's industry in that they are starting to make safe air, land and water instead of just talking about it.

"The environment ranks with international competition as a key force affecting business behaviour," says Firman Bentley, Nova Corp.'s senior vice-president and chairman of the Canadian Chemical Producers' Association.

Alberta's business establishment is making moves that are beginning to add up financially and have significant results. Mobil Oil spent $1.5 million on the first Canadian trial of a new process for tapping sour natural gas, at Lone Pine Creek northeast of Calgary. When the plant cut emissions of acid-rain-causing sulphur dioxide by 60 percent "the site's yield of sulphur, which fetches up to $125 U.S. per tonne, rose by 122 tonnes per month."

Others are falling into step. "Shell's $825 million Caroline project northwest of Calgary is studded with new measures. They range from the world's longest pipeline for liquid sulphur (to bury the flow safely and out of sight) to elaborate emergency procedures and additions of hardened equipment."

This industry program is called Responsible Care: A Total Commitment. [It] was devised with help from a national committee of environmentalists. After gestating since the early 1980s . . . this program . . . voluntarily enacts controls on making, handling, shipping, and distributing all products." Adds Bentley, "This is not a public relations exercise. We have got our house in order."

Source: Gordon Jaremko, "Environment Seen More as a Key Force Affecting Business," *Calgary Herald,* April 17, 1991, p. B5.

Norway made it clear that, in her committee's opinion, the only way for the world to survive is to abandon unlimited development for the socially responsible alternative.

Because of the importance of these ethical and environmental issues, Chapter 19 is devoted to these topics.

CROSS-BORDER SHOPPING: A SERIOUS CONCERN

A new factor has been introduced into the Canadian economic climate: cross-border shopping. A large portion of the Canadian population lives within a short drive of U.S. cities, so shopping in the U.S. is not a new phenomenon. Prices are traditionally lower there for a wide variety of goods. January 1991, when the Goods and Service Tax (GST) came into effect, saw a tremendous increase in the numbers of Canadians flocking south to shop. This ongoing trend continues to drain significant dollars from Canadian retail, service, and manufacturing companies, aggravating the recession. As companies' sales drop, government sales and income tax revenues show a similar decline. Everybody lays off employees as business declines, further reducing consumer purchasing power in Canada.

This growth in cross-border shopping may be due to an unusual combination of economic and psychological factors. The federal government told Canadians that the Free Trade Agreement (FTA) with the U.S. (effective January 1, 1989) would bring us lower consumer prices, but consumers were not aware of reduced prices after two years of the FTA. The severe recession that hit Canada in 1990 forced people to stretch their dollars as far as possible. The Canadian dollar was high against the U.S. dollar. American gasoline prices are much lower and cigarette prices are a fraction of Canadian prices. After the GST was imposed, border towns and cities in the U.S. made a concerted marketing drive aimed at Canadian shoppers. Large

To combat cross-border shopping, some stores advertise no GST, no PST. In fact, these taxes have already been built into the purchase price of the good or service.

shopping malls have sprung up in small American towns near the Canadian border mainly for Canadian customers.

Many observers see this trend as a consumer tax revolt. The unpopular GST seemed to be the straw that broke the camel's back. This revolt seems to have caught our business and government leaders by surprise. There is concern that the continued drain of billions of dollars out of the Canadian economy will endanger social services such as Medicare, which Canadians want and which cost many billions of dollars annually.

Various strategies are attempting to reduce the $6-billion annual drain from our economy and bring the consumer dollar back home. Some provinces permitted retailers to be open on Sundays and the federal government tightened its customs procedures to cut down on unreported purchases. It is collecting duties, the GST as well as the provincial sales tax in some provinces, which makes it less economical to shop in the U.S. It also reduced tariffs on a wide range of imported goods to make them less expensive in Canada.

In addition, many local Canadian municipalities in conjunction with retailers have embarked on marketing efforts to halt the flow of dollars south. This was helped along by the fact that some U.S. retailers have raised their prices while Canadian retailers have been lowering theirs and the Canadian dollar has been declining in value, making shopping in the U.S. more expensive.

The cumulative effect has been a steady slippage of cross-border vehicle crossings, according to StatsCan figures. But in early 1993, 5 million Canadian vehicles are still making one-day trips *every month* to the U.S. That's not counting those who go for longer periods. If we assume an average of two persons per car, that may add up to some four times our total population, on an annual basis![15]

CAREERS AND JOBS FOR THE FUTURE[16]

What is the effect of all of the trends discussed in this chapter on jobs and careers into the next century? First, 3.7 million more people were working in Canada in 1990 than in 1975. An additional 3 million people are expected to be working by the year 2000. (See Figure 1–3.) Most of these jobs will be in the service sector and many will be filled by women, young people, and minorities. Opportunities should be growing for all segments of the population.

THINKING IT THROUGH

Should Canadians strengthen the manufacturing sector? What can they do? Is there a role for government in this effort?

How do you feel about the challenge of a safer environment? Do you see it as an opportunity or a threat to Canadian business? Do you think we can develop environmental expertise that will create new industries? What, specifically, needs doing?

Can you think of any type of service or product not currently on the market that would appeal to the growing number of seniors? Would you be interested in trying to develop that item? Why or why not?

Have any of the trends discussed in the chapter given you any ideas for a career? Explain. Are you thinking about whether the rest of your education should be broader or more specialized? Review the pros and cons of each choice.

Of course, there will also be significant job losses from plant closings, bankruptcies, and other business closures due to such factors as changes in demand, new technology, and competition from outside Canada. In the early 1990s we have heard mostly bad news on the job front. There have been plant closings and layoffs due to decline in business, mergers, or companies moving to the United States or Mexico. Staff has been reduced due to automation or restructuring and to governments and the non-profit sector reducing operating expenses.

In the past, the number of people working in Canada increased every five years despite recessions. But given the very heavy job losses in the early 1990s, the 1995 figures may not show an increase over 1990.

One thing is certain. Of the new jobs being created, more than half will require college or university education. Figure 1–6 shows how the trend in jobs is estimated to shift by the year 2000. Jobs that require little education continue to dry up while those demanding college education continue to expand. This is in keeping with the increasing importance of technology, the stress on quality, the tougher competitive environment, and the growing empowerment of the work force.

All of these developments require managers and employees who have more advanced education. They must be able to grasp mathematical concepts and reason logically. This preparation develops the confidence to make decisions as authority is decentralized and the entire work force adapts to the quick response time that is required in today's fast-moving business world.

The companies mentioned in this chapter (Chrysler, Telespace, Nortel, Bombardier) and many other successful firms all require that their employees have these

Years of Schooling Needed for Job	Current* Jobs	Future† Jobs
8 years or less	6%	4%
1–3 years of high school	12	10
4 years of high school	40	35
1–3 years of college or university	20	22
4 or more years of university	22	29
Total	100%	100%

Figure 1–6 Demand for education in the future. Note the decline in jobs for those with less than college education and the increase for those with college education.

*1989

†Between 1989 and 2000.

Source: *Jobs and Education,* Economic Council of Canada, 1991.

qualities. If their staff cannot carry out their responsibilities properly and quickly, the companies will be unable to compete. Employees must have the education to meet the requirements of their jobs.

Dulcie Richards is a good example of what is now expected of employees. The *Globe and Mail* reports that in 11 years at Toronto Plastics Ltd., she was "rarely asked to think on the job." But 1991 marked a major change in her job demands. The company had applied for certification under ISO 9000, an international quality assessment program. This quality scorecard was adopted by the International Standards Organization (ISO) in 1987 and is "fast becoming a prerequisite for selling to the European Community," the huge market of 12 European countries led by Germany, France, England, and Italy.

Her new job description

> seems more appropriate to a statistician than a low-skilled production worker. Several times a day she reads a digital display indicating measures of her machine's performance. She punches data into a calculator, works out averages, and charts them on a graph. If the plotted line lurches off its normal path, she must make quick decisions in case the machine starts spitting out defective [units].

It was difficult at first for Richards, who did not finish high school, to adapt to the new requirements of her job. But she put a lot of effort into it and is finding it easier now.

This is a good example of how the drive for quality is changing the nature of even the lowest production job. And "it is only the first rung up the quality ladder," according to Larry Rogers, president of the Quality Management Institute, a division of the Canadian Standards Association (CSA), which is affiliated with the ISO. The CSA audits companies seeking the ISO 9000 certification.[17]

If we add to the demands for quality, constant technological changes, a downsized work force, and relentless global competitive pressure, it becomes clear that managers and employees of the future will require excellent preparation. If a production worker like Dulcie Richards now has to *think* on the job, imagine how much more is demanded from people who have greater responsibility. That is why the stress is now on higher education and a more general education.

Nuala Beck is one of a growing number of economists, academics, and managers who maintain that

> The new economy . . . offers more jobs, better pay, and more intellectual interest. But to take advantage of knowledge work, we need to look again at our

MAKING ETHICAL DECISIONS

In every chapter you will find a box like this with an ethical question relating to that particular chapter. Ethics is concerned with doing what is right or morally acceptable. Throughout life we are often confronted with decisions to be made where there are various options. This certainly applies to the business world. Managers and employees are commonly faced with difficult decisions where the choices may range from the morally repugnant to the highly desirable. The whole issue of ethics itself has become a modern trend in business. In the past, the business community came under fire for shady or environmentally bad practices. The result has been a heightened awareness by companies that the community expects a stronger ethical approach to decision making.

In the succeeding chapters you will have the opportunity to examine some typical tough decisions that managers have to make involving careful consideration of ethical issues. ▼

> education system. We should stop training people for jobs in dead or dying industries. The real jobs, today and tomorrow, demand three basic skills.
>
> Students need computer and print literacy. They need to know how to use telecommunications equipment like faxes and modems. And they need basic numerical skills. . . . Education ought to be a "smart" industry but too often it's dumb. Either it's training students for yesterday's jobs or it's hindering both teachers and students from mastering the skills they need for the new economy.[18]

Are you preparing yourself for the new job market?

PROGRESS CHECK

- Why are environmental issues so important now? What effect does this have on business plans and actions? What opportunities does it open up for business?
- Why are population trends significant? What are some major current trends that are important to business? Why are they important?
- Why did cross-border shopping become a serious problem? What effect is it having? What is being done about it?
- What is the effect on careers and jobs of current business trends? What should students be doing to meet these requirements?

SUMMARY

1. Technology leads to new products and services being developed and existing methods, products, and services becoming obsolete.

   How does this affect business?

   Technological developments—including more efficient and automated equipment, photocopiers, computers, faxes, and robots—lead to a reduction in the number of employees and managers, thus reducing costs. Employees must be trained to cope with the new technology. Companies and individuals that do not keep up with these developments cannot compete in the job and business market.

   1. Explain the importance and impact of technological developments.

2. The *information age* refers to the fact that rapid, reliable, and relevant information has become a vital component of effective competition.

   Why has this development taken place?

   Computers and ever-improving communication technology have developed information to a high level. They have shrunk the planet into a small world. Information has become as important a component of operations as finance, materials, and labour. It enables management to plan better and to react more quickly to favourable or unfavourable developments.

   2. Describe what is meant by the *information age* and what its implications are.

3. Big business now operates on a global basis.

   What accounts for this development and what are its implications?

   The technological revolution in transportation and communication has made possible buying, selling, borrowing, staffing, investing, and manufacturing as if the world were one country. Canadian companies search for the lowest costs and markets and opportunities wherever they exist.

   3. Discuss the globalization of business and why it is important for Canadian companies.

4. Canadian companies must participate in the globalized world of business and meet world competitive standards.

4. Identify the methods used by big business to become more competitive and the pressures to do so.

▼ *How do companies improve their competitiveness?*

Becoming more competitive means adopting the latest and most efficient means of production, financing, distribution, and management information systems as technology and experience make them available. This search is done internationally as are investment decisions. Alliances and joint ventures are sought on a global basis. The pressures arise from competitors who are engaged in a similar process.

5. The manufacturing component of the Canadian economy has remained unchanged in the last decade at about 19 percent of GDP.

5. Show how the Canadian economy has shifted so that manufacturing remains vital but has been replaced by the service sector as the principal provider of jobs.

▼ *Despite this, why has the service sector become much more important?*

The manufacturing sector employs fewer people and its labour force is a much smaller percentage of the total labour force as the service sector has grown enormously, employing some 75 percent of the work force. Manufacturers contract out many service aspects of their business and also require new services in the information age. Nevertheless, many people believe that an efficient competitive manufacturing sector is the motivator of the entire economy.

6. There has been an explosion in the number of small businesses in Canada. A growing number of these are home-based.

6. Explain the trend towards, and the importance of, small business and why home-based small businesses have become so popular.

▼ *What factors led to these developments?*

Some of the factors are new technology (computers, faxes, modems); the rise in the number of women and single parents in business, who find working at home easier and less costly; women finding their career paths blocked due to sexism; the rising number of professionals and managers who found themselves laid off and had poor prospects for re-employment; and people opting out of the rat race or seeking more control over their lives.

7. Emphasis on total quality management has become a key aspect of business in recent years.

7. Understand how Canadian business has rediscovered the importance of high-quality goods and services.

▼ *What has led to this development?*

Successful competition by companies from Japan and Germany, where concern with quality is an obsession, has led to the quality revolution in the thinking and operations of Canadian managers.

8. Shifts in the make-up of the population of Canada have been a constant feature. We have had the baby boom period and now the composition of our population is shifting again.

8. Explain how population trends have a major impact on business and what the current trends are.

▼ *What is the significance of the latest demographic trend for business?*

Demographic changes create new markets as old markets diminish. They also determine whether there will be an adequate supply of labour. Current trends are for a gradually aging population and a declining percentage of younger people. Businesses must look for opportunities in the new markets being created by the large number of older people.

9. People are increasingly concerned by the actions of business that affect society. This applies to a wide range of activities, including ethical behaviour in general and the environment in particular. Businesses and government have had to deal with this.

9. Describe how environmental and other ethical issues play a major role in all business planning and actions.

▼ *Why have these questions come to the fore recently?*

A whole series of scandals in different industries has drawn attention to the need for ethical procedures and behaviour of managers. The serious deterioration of the environment has forced business and government to examine closely every element of operations to ensure that these problems are not being aggravated.

10. So many trends are changing the way businesses operate that jobs and careers are being greatly affected.

▼ *How is the nature of jobs and careers moving in new directions?*

The impact of technology is to require better educated, more skilled employees. Decentralization means that managers and employees must be prepared to undertake more responsibility. Everyone has to have wider horizons to encompass global business, which means a broader education. More young people have to think seriously about working for small businesses or starting their own business, perhaps at home.

10. Show how jobs and careers are affected by all of the trends discussed in the chapter.

GETTING INVOLVED

1. Go to the library and see what small business magazines you can find. Scan through a few back issues for some stories of successes and failures. See if you can get a few ideas that might inspire you to consider a small business venture. Make sure you examine the possibility of a home-based business.
2. This chapter and the appendix on management information systems (Part III) indicate how much the computer has revolutionized what organizations do and the way managers function. You want to become mentally geared to this new age, where information is a key to cost reduction, rapid response, and managers' method of keeping on top of things. If you do not already have a personal computer, consider buying one as an investment in your future.
3. Population trends noted in the chapter indicate the growing proportion of seniors. See if you can discover any needed services for them that are not being provided in your area.
4. Look for evidence in your area of the effect of the globalization of business—for example, businesses that are being hurt or businesses that are growing because they are taking advantage of finance, marketing, purchasing, investment, or other international opportunities.
5. Try to get interviews with senior management officials in large companies in your area to find out how technological developments have affected their operations. Take notes during the interviews and use them as a basis of discussion in class.
6. See if you can find a significant growth in certain types of businesses or new types of businesses, due to some trends that are not discussed in the chapter (for example, an increase in crime).

PRACTICING MANAGEMENT DECISIONS

Case One Applying the New Management Techniques

Tom Peters writes and lectures extensively on management. You may have seen his lively lectures on TV. He also does special on-the-spot programs showing how companies have successfully changed management techniques to become more efficient.

In a video on the importance of speeding up reaction time to consumer demands and product development time, Peters quotes a book called *Competing against Time.* The authors state that firms spend 95 to 99.5 percent of their time doing nothing to add value to their products or services. That is why it takes an insurance company 22 days to process an application that only takes 17 minutes to read. The rest of the time is lost to paper shuffling, bureaucratic delay (rules and regulations), faulty management procedures, and a lack of proper planning.

Peters gives examples of many American companies that are learning to cut product development time from years to months. Camco, the Canadian appliances subsidiary of Canadian General Electric, and Chrysler Corp. are two other such examples. Companies are learning that a timely response to technological developments and to consumer demands is a major competitive tool.

What is amazing is that improvements are made without adding any employees or equipment, or spending any more money. The only changes made were in managerial procedures and organizational structure. Managers were formed into cross-functional teams—marketing with engineering, purchasing with manufacturing—so that they worked together right from the start of any action or plan. The entire team would go out to talk to customers to find out what needed improvement and what customers' needs were. The cross-functional teams enabled various departments to work together to create what the customer wanted—fast.

Employees were empowered to make decisions on the spot without having to wait for a request and reply to move slowly up the chain of command and back down again. The latest in information technology was used. Management systems were simplified and everyone was made to feel part of a smoothly running team. Speed was emphasized. (It's much like the two-minute drill in football, where the team must score quickly. You do what has to be done to accomplish this goal. There is no time for meetings or schedules.) That is the formula for success in the 1990s, whether you are a business, a non-profit organization, or a government.

Decision Questions

1. The Canadian author of this text sent a letter to a large trust company requesting information about the processing procedure of the monthly credit card statement. Two months later he got a printed card apologizing for the delay in answering and promising a reply in the near future. It never came. What does this reveal about the company? What should they be doing to improve the situation? How can they prevent such poor customer service from being repeated?
2. Note how often direct mail companies say, "allow 6 to 8 weeks for delivery." Why does it take so long to process an order and mail an item? Do you think a company would gain a competitive advantage if it promised to send out the article within one week of receiving the order? Why don't more companies do that?
3. From your own work or school experience, have you noticed any procedures or policies that result in long delays in what seems like a simple process to you? Discuss how this can be avoided without incurring additional costs.
4. Many companies still resist changes in organization and procedures discussed in the chapter. Why do you think there is so much resistance? What should be done to overcome it?

Case Two New Technologies Threaten Canada Post

For some time, Canada's postal service has been feeling the creeping effect of various modern technologies. Faxes, courier services, shopping by telephone and credit card, direct deposit of cheques to bank accounts—all of these technological advances have revolutionized how business, government, and individuals communicate and do business. Canada Post has been a significant loser because of these developments. The bulk of its revenue comes from first-class mail, and this is the area that has been particularly hard hit.

This trend gives every indication of an explosive expansion in the near future. Every business and government is busy trying to adopt new technology to reduce the cost of communications and other operations. Individuals can already receive directly into their bank accounts: pensions, their regular pay, dividends, interest on bonds, income tax refunds, annuities, and other items. This avoids the need to write, and mail, tens of millions of cheques monthly.

Banks and other businesses are continually seeking procedures that reduce the need for documents—cheques, deposits, and correspondence. As the postal service relies on business for 85 percent of its revenues, this trend is obviously quite a threat. In June 1993, Macy's, the giant New York department store, announced "a 24-hour-a-day cable service, offering its merchandise to its U.S. customers. The technological upgrade of Canada's system would allow shoppers to select and pay for products from similar systems without using the telephone or the post office."

Canada Post has responded to the decline in traditional letter mail by buying control of Purolator Courier Service Ltd., Canada's largest courier service. Says Georges Clermont, president of Canada Post, "We have been in the small-parcel business for over a century. Things change and today the overnight package-delivery service has become increasingly important."

Decision Questions

1. What do you think of Canada Post's decision? Is there anything else it might do to adapt to these new conditions? Do you think mail service will disappear entirely and be replaced by other services made possible by technology?
2. This is one example of a large organization trying to cope with new technology. Can you think of any other company that has made some major change in policy or operations for similar reasons? Are you aware of what specific developments caused this change?
3. Do you think that the schools and colleges of your experience have responded to the technological revolution? What have they done that you think is successful or at least a step in the right direction? What should they be doing now?
4. How are you personally responding to the technological era? How is it affecting the selection of your program of study? The courses you choose? The careers you are thinking about?

Sources: Murray Oxby, "Canada Post Buys 75% Stake in Purolator," *The Montreal Gazette,* June 5, 1993. p. C1; Ian Austen, "New Technologies Taking Away Business from Canada Post," ibid., p. C2.

LET'S TALK BUSINESS

1. Demographic trends point to certain population changes. What types of businesses stand to gain from these shifts? Which will lose? What should they be doing about their situation?
2. Can you see any trends that might encourage you to think about starting your own business? Why? Would you opt for a service company? What type of service?
3. What evidence do you see that businesses are thinking and acting globally? Scan the financial pages of newspapers or financial papers and magazines for current evidence and discuss.
4. The recent stress on quality is slowly changing business operations. Do you think your education is preparing you to function in a quality-conscious business atmosphere? Where is it succeeding? Where is it failing? How can it be improved?
5. What do you see as the most significant impact quality will have on Canadian business? How are you preparing yourself, in terms of career planning, for this situation? Is there anything special you should be doing?

LOOKING AHEAD

The business world extends beyond the borders of Canada. The future of Canadian business is directly tied to the future of world business. International trade and investment directly affect the economies of individual nations and are particularly important for Canada. Chapter 2 is devoted to an examination of international business.

CANADIAN EXPLORER
TORONTO

CANADA AND THE GLOBAL BUSINESS ENVIRONMENT

LEARNING GOALS

After you have read and studied this chapter, you should be able to:

1. Discuss the increasing importance of the international market and the role of comparative advantage in international trade.
2. Explain how the marketing motto "Find a need and fill it" applies to international business.
3. Apply the terminology used in international business.
4. Describe the status of Canada in international business.
5. Illustrate the strategies used in reaching global markets.
6. Discuss the hurdles of trading in world markets.
7. Debate the advantages and disadvantages of trade protectionism.
8. Describe the role of transnational corporations in a globalized world economy.
9. Identify and describe international trade organizations and trade agreements.
10. Discuss the future of international trade and investment.

KEY TERMS

balance of payments, p. 44
balance of trade, p. 44
bartering, p. 51
common market, p. 57
comparative advantage theory, p. 39
consortium, p. 50
countertrading, p. 51
dumping, p. 44
embargo, p. 56
exchange rate, p. 45
foreign subsidiary, p. 48
General Agreement on Tariffs and Trade (GATT), p. 56
import quota, p. 55
international joint venture, p. 49
International Monetary Fund (IMF), p. 57
licensing, p. 47
mercantilism, p. 54
multinational or transnational corporation (MNC or TNC) p. 37
producers' cartels, p. 57
protective tariffs, p. 54
revenue tariffs, p. 55
trade protectionism, p. 45
World Bank, p. 57

Paul Stern

PROFILE PAUL STERN, FORMER CEO OF NORTHERN TELECOM

In 1987, Northern Telecom stuck its corporate neck out by publicly announcing a bold and perhaps impossible dream. Called *Vision 2000,* its aim is to make Canada's largest telecommunications-equipment manufacturer the world leader in its industry by the year 2000. This is an industry dominated by giants like Alcatel of France, AT&T of the U.S., and Siemens of Germany.

"Yeah, it's a tall order," conceded Paul Stern, then chairman and CEO of Northern Telecom. "Can we do it? Hell yeah, we can do it. Why not?" Indeed, there is evidence Northern Telecom's dream is coming true. Sales for 1991 are expected to top $8 billion U.S., with about two-thirds coming from foreign markets. The company's operating empire stretches through 40 nations and has more than 60,000 employees. It has also moved into second place in world market share behind its much larger American competitor, giant AT&T.

But Stern was after more than leadership in simply dollars and market share. "I'm not a subscriber to the concept that size equals leadership." What Stern had in mind was something more subtle and more challenging. He was seeking a "journey to perfection" that started with Northern Telecom's employees and encompassed suppliers, customers, and communities around the world.

"I see the day . . . that if anyone was to go to the employment market in the countries we operate in, they'd say, 'I want to go to work at Northern Telecom.' When customers prefer us [and] make us the company of choice; when suppliers want to work with us because we're ethical, we're trustworthy, we're a good partner; and, finally, when communities want Northern Telecom in their midst . . . then we are the leader. That is Vision 2000."

As one analyst put it: "Northern wants to be the Honda or BMW of the industry." It's an ambitious goal. Twenty years ago the company, then known as Northern Electric, was little more than the manufacturing arm of Bell Canada, selling virtually all of its $500-million-a-year output to its lone customer. How did Northern Telecom emerge from Ma Bell's cottage to make a challenge for global leadership?

One of the answers is smart technology. The company bet early on digital technology (the heart of computers and all modern communication systems) replacing analogue technology (the heart of telephones and phonographs). Digital has become the standard of the industry, and Northern has benefitted immensely from its pioneering work. (Note: In 1993, after five successful years, Northern Telecom (Nortel) suffered a huge loss and decided to replace Paul Stern as CEO. As part of this change Nortel also decided to abandon Vision 2000 as a grand strategy.)

Source: Dominique Lacasse, "Taking On the World," *The Montreal Gazette,* October 26, 1991, p. D2.

THE GLOBALIZATION OF BUSINESS

In the previous chapter, we referred to the globalization of business. Because of developments in communications and transportation, our planet has become a small place. We noted how products and services are marketed to, and provided from, the whole world. World barriers to trade and investment have been dropping steadily. If

Northern Telecom (Nortel) has become a world player in the telecommunications field. It is an excellent example of a Canadian-based company that has transformed itself into a transnational company.

we look at some facts about this world market, we will see why this trade is so important:

- There are 27 million customers in Canada but over *5.5 billion* potential customers worldwide.
- Every year, the world's population increases by some 95 million people. That's three and a half times the total Canadian population.
- Combined world trade exceeds $4 *trillion* each year.

Northern Telecom has become a world player in a big way. This type of globalized, or transnational (TNC), company is very different from the old-style multinational (MNC) company that has been engaged in world trade for a long time. Both **TNC** and **MNC** are often used interchangeably to refer to an organization that does manufacturing and marketing in many different countries and has international stock ownership and multinational management.

TNC or **MNC**
An organization that does manufacturing and marketing in many different countries; it has international stock ownership and multinational management.

The MNC did business in various countries and had plants in a number of countries. The TNC has gone from that stage to organizing management, investment, production, and distribution as if the world were one country or even one city. Goods can be designed in one country, raw material shipped to or from a second country, partially or completely manufactured in a third country, and then shipped to the ultimate customer. The company thus makes maximum use of the competitive advantage (discussed in the next section) of each country in order to be the most efficient producer. Top management and boards of directors have an international component to reflect the new nature of operations.

More and more, TNCs seem not to have a home base at all. Robert Reich of Harvard University has written extensively on this topic. His articles in the *Harvard Business Review* have such provocative titles as "Who Is Us?" and "Who Are Them?" The implication is that it is becoming impossible to distinguish between an American company and a Japanese company. If, say, IBM produces more computers in Japan than in the

U.S. and Honda has more employees in the U.S. than in Japan, how should we classify these companies? This growing phenomenon is part of the globalization of business.

Nortel is a good example of a Canadian company that has been completely transformed by this globalization. As the profile shows, it has employees and plants all over the world specializing in various aspects of production. It also has an international board of directors. Some of the technological advances that Nortel pioneered helped produce the revolutionary changes in communications that, in turn, contributed to the globalization of business. Other large Canadian players in the world of TNCs include Alcan Aluminium, Seagrams, International Nickel (INCO), MacMillan Bloedel, Bombardier, Hees International, and Nova Corp.

WHY COUNTRIES TRADE WITH EACH OTHER

There are several reasons why a country trades with other countries. First, no country, no matter how advanced, can produce all the products that its people need or want. In Canada, we must import those products that our climate does not allow us to grow. This includes tropical fruits, citrus fruits, and indeed all fruits and vegetables during the winter season. We also cannot grow cotton.

Second, some nations have an abundance of natural resources and lack technological know-how. Others, like Japan, have very few natural resources but may be world leaders in technology.

Third, some countries produce a lot more of certain products than they can consume, so they must export these surpluses. Canada has a small population but produces vast quantities of grains, autos, auto parts, lumber, newsprint, metals, minerals, and other products. Thus we rank very high among nations that export. In fact, we depend upon exports to maintain a substantial segment of our standard of living, somewhere in the 35 percent range.

Figure 2–1 shows that in 1991 Canada exported U.S. $141 billion. This ranks Canada seventh amongst exporting nations of the world. The six countries ahead of us had much larger populations, but we edged out the former Soviet Union, whose population was 10 times that of Canada.

Finally, some countries are better than others at producing certain products in terms of quality and/or price, so they have what is called a comparative advantage. Japan has shown this ability with cars and electronic items. Canada has such an advantage with certain forestry products, aluminum, and various minerals.

Figure 2–1 Analysis of Canadian exports and imports of merchandise for 1991.

Exports	(billions)	Imports	(billions)
Autos, trucks, and parts	$ 32	Autos, trucks, and parts	$ 32
Industrial goods	29	Industrial goods	25
Machines and equipment	29	Machines and equipment	43
Forest products	20	Forest products	1
Energy products	15	Energy products	7
Agricultural and fish products	13	Agricultural and fish products	9
Consumer goods	3	Consumer goods	17
Total	$141	Total	$134

Source: *Canadian Economic Observer,* StatsCan, Cat. No. 11–010, June 1992.

The Theory of Comparative Advantage

International trade is the exchange of goods and services across national borders. Exchanges between and among countries involve more than goods and services, however. Countries also exchange art, athletes (for international competition and friendly relations), cultural events (plays, dance performances), medical advances, and space exploration (for example, the U.S./Russian space programs). The guiding principle behind international economic exchanges is supposed to be the economic **comparative advantage theory.** This theory states that a country should produce and sell to other countries those products that it produces most effectively and efficiently and should buy from other countries those products it cannot produce as effectively or efficiently.

comparative advantage theory
Theory that a country should produce and sell to other countries those products that it produces most efficiently and effectively and should buy from other countries those products it cannot produce as effectively or efficiently.

In practice, this theory does not work out quite so neatly. There are many countries that, for various reasons, decide to produce certain agricultural, industrial, or consumer products despite a lack of comparative advantage. This means that they restrict imports of competing products from countries that can produce them at lower costs. For example, Japan and South Korea ban all imports of rice. Similarly, countries of the European Community heavily subsidize their farmers so that their expensive grains can compete with those from countries such as Canada and the U.S., which have a significant comparative advantage.

Many countries institute policies from time to time to restrict the import of various goods. Canada has done this with cars, textiles and shoes. The result of such restraints is that the free movement of goods and services is inhibited. We shall return to the topic of trade protectionism throughout this chapter.

GETTING INVOLVED IN INTERNATIONAL TRADE

Students often wonder which firms are best for finding a job in international business. Naturally, the discussion focuses on *large* multinational firms that have large overseas accounts. But the real secret to success in overseas business may be with *small* businesses. Getting started is often a matter of observation, determination, and risk. What does that mean? First of all, it is important to travel overseas to get some feel for the culture and lifestyles of various countries in order to better understand how to do business with people and companies in foreign countries. You will notice that many developing countries lack certain goods and services that are widely available in Canada.

For example, a traveller in one part of Africa noticed that there was no ice available for drinks, for keeping foods fresh, and so on. Further research showed that, in fact, there was no ice factory for hundreds of miles, yet the market seemed huge. The man returned to North America, found some venture capital, and went back to Africa to build an ice-making plant. Much negotiation was necessary with the authorities (negotiation best done by locals who know the system), and the plant was built. Now the man is indeed wealthy.

Lyle Fox was in Japan working as a journalist. He discovered that there were no bagels in the part of Japan in which he lived. Using an old family recipe, Fox and his Japanese wife began producing bagels and selling them in the local market.

Mike Solomko bought a franchise to sell West Bend Cookware in Japan. Today, his company has 400 salespeople selling pots and pans door-to-door in Japan. He appears on Japanese TV as "Super Solomko." You can see that international business is something like domestic business in that the goal is to find a need and fill it. The

This photo shows a soybean farmer. Soybeans are an important crop in international markets.

difference is that one has to do much more preparation to buy and sell in foreign markets.

Importance of Exporting Goods and Services

As mentioned previously, there are many reasons why nations trade with each other. Countries are always importing and exporting products and services. However, all countries favour exporting over importing because exports create many more jobs and also help to give the country a favourable balance of trade and balance of payments account. (These terms are discussed later in this chapter.)

Because exports are particularly important to the economic well-being of Canada, we have a very large and elaborate government apparatus to assist companies in their exporting and foreign investment activities. Not only the federal government but most provincial and all large municipal governments have various ministries, departments, and agencies that provide a wide variety of services, including information, marketing, financial aid, insurance and guarantees, publications, and contacts. All major trading countries provide similar support to their exporters.

The federal government departments that have the main responsibility for international business are External Affairs and International Trade Canada. These ministries combine their efforts under EAITC, which has trade commissioners in Canadian embassies abroad and in Canada. EAITC also maintains "one-stop" international trade centres in Canada. This federal organization engages in a wide variety of activities that are shown in more detail in the next section. Any business that is contemplating going international can get almost any information and help it requires from EAITC. Further information may be obtained from InfoExport's toll-free line: 1–(800)–267–8376.

Competitiveness as a Factor in Exporting

In the 1990s an old word became a new buzzword in Canada: *competitiveness*. Business leaders, politicians, academics, and business journals have all been saying Canadian companies are losing their ability to compete on the international scene. In Chapter 1 we referred to the current trends that affect business. One of these is the increasing importance of technological developments. Businesses that do not keep up with advances in their fields of activity become less competitive.

Historically, Canadian companies have been weak in the amount of research and development (R&D) they do. Some people attribute this to the fact that

SPOTLIGHT ON SMALL BUSINESS

Mall King Takes Message to Moscow: Location Is Key

In a country in which the market system is more dream than fact, a Winnipeg real estate developer is teaching the last word of consumerism: shopping mall development.

Sandy Shindleman, who owns and operates 33 strip malls in Manitoba, as well as large apartment buildings, makes periodic visits to Moscow to teach real estate development for the Certified Commercial Investment Member program sponsored by the construction trust of the Moscow city council, Moscapstroi.

"The first day, the students, who are all managers for the construction project management department of the city of Moscow, are working with supply-and-demand concepts for the first time. They resist what they regard as capitalism. A few weeks later, we are working on advanced cost accounting, cash flow analysis, and annuity principles," explains Shindleman.

Moscapstroi, he notes, has been in charge of 90 percent of the building starts in Moscow since the 1917 revolution. Getting from building for a command-allocation system to building for a market-driven economy will not be easy, Shindleman says.

"Lending money against the security of a building, which is the basis of mortgage finance, can't be done in Russia now. They do not have the necessary accounting, the real estate title registration, insolvency and bankruptcy systems. So the concept of money being invested in property can work only at a theoretical level.

There is a great shortage of equipment and they use slow labour instead. They are building today the way Canadians built in 1950. So a 30,000-square-foot mini-mall that would take 150 days in Canada would take a year in Moscow and even longer in rural areas."

At the age of 35, Shindleman is regarded as a local phenomenon in Winnipeg. He gets respect in an industry the public often considers a form of legal plunder. He has come a long way from his youth, when he helped out in his parents' grocery store and slaughterhouse in the town of Portage la Prairie an hour's drive west of Winnipeg.

"What I do here for a living and what I teach in Moscow emphasize site selection. I show how to find markets for development in the free market for consumer products. I show how to use demographics and to map where people work and live in order to find definitive sites for development. For example, until now, they have put food stores in irrelevant places, sometimes near where people work, sometimes not." Shindleman thinks it will take two decades for Moscow to get to the level of consumer accessibility that is typical of comfortable Eastern European cities such as Budapest.

"I don't think that Russian cities will get to look like the worst of commercial strips of Canadian cities. The Russian people are now so far from access to services that highways lined with shopping malls and billboards and franchise food stores won't be a problem within my lifetime.

"Anyway, if the state organizes to serve the people, it would be a good thing. In Moscow on Red Square, where McDonald's has its largest store in the world, people line up for four hours to buy Big Macs. You can't tell these people that a street of franchise food joints is a bad thing."

Source: Andrew Allentuck, *Globe and Mail,* May 5, 1992, p. B24.

Canada has a *branch-plant economy.* That is, many of our companies are branches of foreign (mainly U.S.) parent companies who do their main R&D outside Canada. Many of these company names are well known: Canadian General Electric, General Motors Canada Ltd., ESSO-Imperial Oil Ltd. (subsidiary of Exxon). By contrast, Northern Telecom is an outstanding example of a Canadian-owned company that has consistently invested heavily in R&D and has thus become a world leader in its field.

Similarly, educating, training, and retraining the work force has taken on great significance. Modern sophisticated technology demands a skilled work force with a higher educational level than before. In Canada and the United States there is a great preoccupation now with drastically improving the educational systems. A lot of emphasis is being placed on upgrading math education and making it compulsory to enable future graduates to cope with the demands of high-tech jobs.

Some business leaders complain that wages and social benefits are too high and as a result Canadian goods are priced too high to compete in the global market.

One way to participate in international exchange is to import fine products from other countries. This picture shows an Irish Imports store that sells quality goods from Ireland. No doubt you have seen similar stores selling shoes from Italy, small appliances from all over Europe, and so on. If not, shop around and see if such stores might be an interesting career possibility.

Other prominent people, notably Lester Thurow, dean of the School of Management at the Massachusetts Institute of Technology, point out that our fiercest competitors, Japan and Germany, pay higher wages than Canada and have very extensive social benefits. Germany, Thurow says, has more holidays, longer vacations, and other benefits. The trick is to work *smarter,* not harder. This requires better education, better management, better equipment, better training, and better government input. We will return to the important topic of competitiveness towards the end of this chapter.

ACCESSING THE GLOBAL MARKET: SERVICES OF THE CANADIAN GOVERNMENT

Because exports have traditionally been such an important issue for Canadians, the federal government has always maintained a high profile in this regard. Recently its main efforts have been channelled through EAITC, which has absorbed previous agencies and developed a comprehensive basket of aid and support for Canadian companies wishing to export or to engage in investment outside Canada. This advice and aid is administered through some 800 trade commissioners—500 in over 100 Canadian embassies, 300 in Ottawa, and more in 12 trade centres across the country. Here is a *partial* list of some of their important activities:[1]

Trade Counselling and Assistance

- International trade centres in 12 Canadian cities for one-stop information services.
- Geographic trade divisions dividing the world into five regions.
- Sectoral trade divisions dividing marketing, investment, and financing opportunities into 14 product/services sectors.
- Advice about Canadian regulations restricting exports and imports.

Programs

These all offer financial assistance.

- Information and aid on providing military services and supplies to U.S. and European governments under various mutual agreements.
- Export/orientation programs to help small and medium-sized companies expand into the U.S. and overseas.
- Investment development program to help foreign corporations bring new capital and technology into Canada. Also helps to set up joint ventures with Canadian companies.
- Program for export market development to facilitate a variety of marketing activities such as attending or setting up booths at trade fairs, setting up permanent sales offices abroad, and arranging visits by foreign buyers to Canada.
- Technology inflow program to sponsor group missions or individual companies' visits abroad and visits to Canadian companies by foreign technical experts.

Export Financing/Foreign Sales Procurement:

- Industrial Cooperation Program of Canada International Development Agency helps Canadian companies seeking investment opportunities and transfer of technology abroad.
- Export Development Corporation provides a full range of financing, insurance and guarantees to Canadian companies investing or doing business abroad.
- Canadian Commercial Corporation acts as the prime contractor when foreign governments or international agencies wish to purchase goods or services from Canada through the government.
- World Information Network for Exports (WINS) lists over 30,000 Canadian exporters and would-be exporters offering approximately 23,000 products and services. This constantly updated information is used by the trade commissioners mentioned above to find potential buyers for these products. Foreign importers can also access WINS to find products they are seeking.

Trade Data and Publications:

- *CanadExport* is a trade newsletter published twice monthly and sent to 56,000 readers. Contains a variety of useful information for Canadian companies who export or invest outside of Canada.
- A variety of directories and special studies of use to actual or potential exporters.
- An International Trade Data Bank that stores a wide range of information from the United Nations and various trade blocs about international trade.

TERMINOLOGY OF INTERNATIONAL TRADE

When you read business periodicals or listen to news reports, you will see and hear terms relating to international business. Many of these terms may be familiar to you, but it will be helpful to review them before we discuss international business in more detail.

balance of trade
The relationship of the amount of exports to the amount of imports.

Balance of trade. The **balance of trade** is the relationship of exports to imports. A *favourable balance of trade* or trade surplus occurs when the value of exports exceeds imports. An *unfavourable balance of trade* or trade deficit occurs when the value of imports exceeds exports. It is easy to understand why countries prefer to export more than they import. If I sell you $200 worth of goods and buy only $100 worth, I have an extra $100 available to buy other things. However, I'm in an *unfavourable* position if I buy $200 worth of goods and sell only $100. For many years Canada has had a favourable balance of trade (see Figure 2–2), although the gap has narrowed recently.

balance of payments
The difference between money coming into a country (from exports) and money leaving the country (for imports) *plus* money flows from other factors such as tourism, foreign aid, investments, and interest and dividend payments.

Balance of payments. The **balance of payments** is the difference between money coming into a country (from exports) and money leaving the country (for imports) *plus* money flows from other factors such as tourism, foreign aid, investment, and interest and dividend payments. The amount of money flowing into or out of a country from these and other factors may offset a trade imbalance. The goal is always to have more money flowing into the country than flowing out of the country. This is called a *favourable balance of payments.* For the latter half of the 1980s, Canada had an unfavourable (deficit) balance of payments.

dumping
Selling products to foreign countries for less than you charge for the same products in your own country.

Dumping. The practice of selling products to foreign countries for less than you charge for the same products in your own country is called **dumping.** In Canada, as in other countries, this is illegal. When proven, it results in heavy penalties to the importer. The problem is that it is very difficult to prove. Nevertheless, charges of dumping have been proven in the past. Sometimes the charge of dumping is used to keep out foreign goods by making them too costly. Industries that are hurt by cheaper imports often raise the cry of dumping even when it is not true. This is especially true in the United States.

A recent report showed that three of Canada's largest bicycle manufacturers have asked the federal government to place stiff anti-dumping tariffs on frames and complete bicycles being imported from Taiwan and China. They claimed the bicycles were being sold below cost, which meant they were being dumped in Canada.[2]

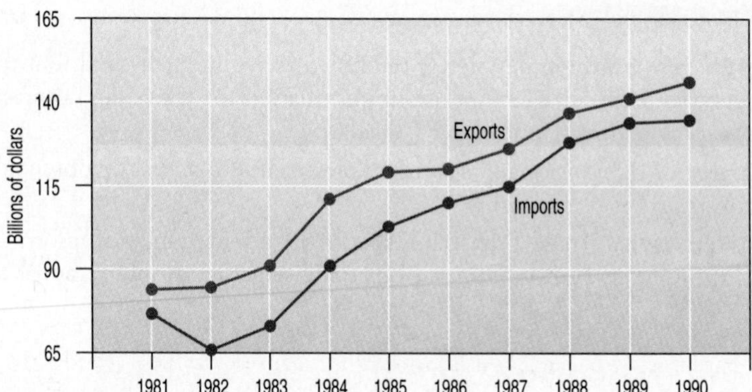

Source: *Canadian Economic Observer, StatsCan,* June 1991, Cat. No. 11-010.

Figure 2–2 Balance of trade. Exports exceeded imports during the entire period.

Trade protectionism. **Trade protectionism** is the use of government regulations to limit the import of goods and services. Countries often use trade protectionism measures to protect their industries against dumping and foreign competition that hurts domestic industry. Protectionism is based on the theory that such practices will help protect domestic producers from foreign competition, allowing them to survive and grow, producing more jobs. We shall discuss trade protectionism in detail later.

trade protectionism
The use of government regulations to limit the import of goods and services, based on the theory that domestic producers should be protected from competition so that they can survive and grow, producing more jobs.

Exchange rate. The **exchange rate** is the value of one currency relative to the currencies of other countries. Raising the *value of the dollar* means that a dollar would buy more foreign goods (or would be traded for more foreign currency) than normal. *Lowering the value of the dollar* means that a dollar can buy less overseas than it once did. That makes foreign goods more expensive because it takes more dollars to buy them. It also makes Canadian goods cheaper to foreign buyers because it takes less foreign currency to buy them. The net effect is to export more and buy fewer foreign products, improving the balance of trade but increasing inflation as imported goods now cost more.

exchange rate
The value of one currency relative to the currencies of other countries.

For many years, the U.S. dollar has played the role of the international currency, so most international transactions are quoted in U.S dollars. Movements in the exchange rate of this dollar relative to other currencies affect nearly all international trade and investments. This is particularly important for Canada, because about three-quarters of all our imports and exports are with the U.S. Since 1980, the value of the U.S. dollar has fluctuated greatly, creating ups and downs for many trading nations. In addition, as the U.S. dollar fluctuates against other currencies, it affects Canada's competitiveness with other countries because it makes our exports more or less expensive.

Now that you understand some terms, we can begin discussing international trade in more depth. The first question to address is how Canada is doing in world trade. First let's check your progress.

PROGRESS CHECK

- Can you cite statistics to show why international trade is so vital for Canadian business (population, size of market, growth of market)?
- What is comparative advantage?
- What is the difference between balance of trade and balance of payments?
- Can you explain how changes in the value of the dollar affect imports and exports?

TRADING IN WORLD MARKETS: THE CANADIAN EXPERIENCE

Statistics have to be examined very closely to make sense of them. This is especially true in the case of Canada's foreign trade statistics. Looked at in total, they are impressive. For a country with only 27 million people in 1992, we ranked seventh in volume of world trade. However, if we look carefully at the figures we see that 75 percent of this exporting and importing is with one country, the U.S. No other modern industrialized country is so dependent on one country for trade and investments. The controversial Canada–U.S. Free Trade Agreement (discussed in detail in Chapter 4) that came into effect in 1989 is designed to facilitate and further increase trade between the two countries.

An even closer look at what we export to the U.S. showed that the largest single item—some 25 to 30 percent—is "autos, trucks, and parts" and has been so for some time. This is offset by a roughly similar amount that we import, although we usually export more than we import from the U.S. annually. All of this stems from the Auto Pact between Canada and the U.S. signed in the mid-60s that was designed to stimulate the auto industry in both countries. This trade is subject to the vagaries of the demand for the autos of the Big Three (Chrysler, Ford, and General Motors) in Canada and the U.S. The growing success of Japanese cars severely reduced demand for Big Three cars in 1990 and 1991. This had a serious impact on business and employment in Canada, especially in Ontario, which relies heavily on auto parts and auto manufacturing.

A traditional major area of Canadian exports is natural resources, which are abundant across the country. Pulp and paper products and lumber from our forests and forest industries, combined with agricultural products, fish products, energy (natural gas, coal and electricity from water power), minerals, and metals, constitute almost half our exports. Developing countries are now giving Canada stiff competition in the natural resource area.

Where Canada is still weak is in the high-tech "glamour" industries of the 1990s and into the next century. Biogenetics, telecommunications, computers, air and rail transport, and materials technology are some of the areas where the high-skilled jobs and exports are expected to be. There are some Canadian stars that have a strong international posture in some of these areas. For example, Northern Telecom and Bombardier are making substantial gains in exports—but there are not enough of these.

Exports are often referred to as the lifeline of Canada because a large percentage of our standard of living depends on our ability to export. Canada is a country with a small home market but a large productive capacity. This means we must be able to produce what world markets demand, and we must be competitive with other countries that produce competing products. We face a serious challenge in this regard.

A number of smaller but successful firms have made an impact globally. SPAR Aerospace, maker of the robotic Canadarm on the U.S. space shuttle; CAE Industries, one of the few makers of flight simulators in the world; Rolls Royce

UTDC Bi-Levels (a division of Bombardier Inc.) in the Tri-Rail system move Florida commuters between West Palm Beach, Fort Lauderdale, and Miami.

(Canada) Ltd., a leader in aircraft and industrial engine repair and maintenance; and Phoenix International Life Sciences Inc., one of the top drug-testing labs in North America are but a few of dozens of small companies with excellent records outside of Canada.

THINKING IT THROUGH

You have read that there are 5.5 billion people in the world but only a small percentage of Canadian companies engage in world trade. Why is that? What do such figures indicate about the future potential for increasing Canadian exports? What do they say about future careers in international business?

In thinking about other countries you should be asking yourself: What languages do they speak? What are the trade possibilities? Are you missing out on an opportunity by failing to take other languages in school and courses in international business?

STRATEGIES FOR REACHING GLOBAL MARKETS

An organization may participate in international trade in many ways, including exporting, licensing, creating subsidiaries, franchising, joint venturing, and counter-trading. These topics represent careers that will be both challenging and rewarding for the future graduate.

Exporting

The simplest way of going international is to export your products. As you will see in the chapters on marketing, many decisions have to be made when a company markets a new product or goes into new markets with existing products. Often the first export sales occur as a result of unsolicited orders received. Regardless of how a company starts exporting it must develop some goals and strategies for achieving those goals.

Other decisions include what distribution channels are appropriate: for example, direct sales, sales to wholesaler, or an exporting and/or importing agency. Each route has its pluses and minuses. Important decisions about pricing policy must also be made.

Success in exporting often leads to licensing a foreign company to produce the product locally, in order to better serve the local market.

Licensing

A firm may decide to service a growing overseas market by **licensing** the manufacture of its product by a foreign producer on a royalty basis. The company sends representatives to the foreign producer to help set up the production process and may provide a variety of services such as marketing advice.

licensing
Agreement in which a producer allows a foreign company to produce its product in exchange for royalties.

A licensing agreement can be beneficial to a firm in several different ways. Through licensing, an organization can gain additional revenues from a product that it would not have normally generated domestically. In addition, foreign licensees often must purchase start-up supplies, component materials, and consulting services from the licensing firm. In some instances, these services extend beyond the start-up stage and become an ongoing source of additional revenue. Coke and Pepsi often enter foreign markets through licensing agreements that typically extend into

Coke has licensing agreements in several countries. This is a Coke can as sold in China.

long-term service contracts. One final advantage of licensing worth noting is that licensors spend little or no money to produce and market the product. These costs come from the licensee's pocket. Therefore, licensees generally work very hard to see that the product succeeds in their market. The greater the sales, the greater the royalties that are paid to the licensor.

Unfortunately, licensing agreements may provide some disadvantages to a company. One major problem is that often a firm must grant licensing rights to its product for an extended period, maybe as long as 20 years. If a product experiences remarkable growth in the foreign market, the bulk of the revenues go to the licensee. Perhaps even more threatening is the fact that a licensing firm is actually selling *its* expertise in a product area. If a foreign licensor learns the technology, it may break the agreement and begin to produce a similar product on its own. If legal remedies are not available, the licensing firm loses its trade secrets, not to mention the agreed-upon royalties. This problem is avoided when the technology changes rapidly, because the licensor can keep several jumps ahead of the licensee.

Creating Subsidiaries

foreign subsidiary
A company owned by another company (parent company) in a foreign country.

As the size of a foreign market expands, a firm may want to establish a foreign subsidiary. A **foreign subsidiary** is a company that is owned by another company (parent company) in a foreign country. Such a subsidiary would operate much like a domestic firm with production, distribution, promotion, pricing, and other business functions under the control of the foreign subsidiary's management. Of course, the legal requirements of both the home and host country would have to be observed. As you might suspect, the primary advantage of a subsidiary is that the company maintains complete control over any technology or expertise it may possess. Additionally, after tax obligations are paid, profits generated belong exclusively to the parent firm.

You will see Marriott hotels in a number of countries around the world. Franchising is popular in both domestic and international markets.

Canadian subsidiaries of American companies played a major role in developing the Canadian economy. More and more countries are welcoming such investments as a way of developing their economies.

Franchising

Franchising is popular both domestically and in international markets. Firms such as McDonald's, Ramada Inn, Avis, Hertz, and Dunkin' Donuts have many overseas units operated by franchisees. In Canada there are thousands of franchise units in many categories of business. This topic will be discussed in detail in Chapter 6.

Franchisers have to be careful to adapt in the countries they serve. For example, Kentucky Fried Chicken's first 11 Hong Kong outlets failed within two years. Apparently, the chicken was too greasy and messy to be eaten with fingers by the fastidious people of Hong Kong. McDonald's also made a mistake when entering the Amsterdam market. It originally set up operations in the suburbs, as it does in North America, but soon learned that Europeans mostly live in the cities. Therefore, McDonald's began to open outlets downtown. There are now thousands of franchises operating internationally. McDonald's franchises now serve beer in Germany and wine in France.

Joint Ventures

An **international joint venture** is a partnership in which companies from two or more countries join to undertake a major project or to form a new company. This has become a very popular avenue for companies that want to go into business in foreign countries. There are obvious advantages to having a partner who shares in the financial investment and risk, knows the local market, understands local ways of thinking, has good government connections and access to local skilled labour or supplies, and/or is acquainted with the laws and regulations affecting business in the country. The Canadian or other foreign company brings additional assets to the

international joint venture
A partnership in which companies from two or more countries join to undertake a major project or to form a new company.

joint venture. These usually include the technology, management skills, specialized equipment and material, and financing necessary to commence and continue operations.

consortium
A temporary association of two or more companies to bid jointly on a large project.

Sometimes companies that may or may not be competitors form a **consortium,** a temporary association, to submit a joint bid on a very large or complex construction project such as a dam, bridge, tunnel, or large building project. This may make it easier for the government or company that asked for bids, since it deals with only one entity instead of many different groups. If the consortium gets the contract, the work is divided up according to the specialties of each member company.

Sometimes two or more competitors make a joint bid. For example, Bombardier teamed up with Alsthom of France to bid successfully for the subway car contract for New York City.

Thousands of joint ventures of different types exist around the world and are constantly being formed. Many such deals are being set up in the former communist countries of Eastern Europe and in the former Soviet Union, now called the Commonwealth of Independent States. The hope is that these ventures will help revive and reorganize the economies in these countries as they move from centrally planned operations to a free market economy. The local participants also learn modern management skills.

The difficulty in joint ventures usually relates to having management or control divided between two or more partners who may disagree on policy, strategy, and tactics. This may be avoided by spelling out at the beginning how management responsibilities will be divided.

Another form of competing internationally is a strategic alliance between companies, which is less comprehensive than a joint venture but usually longer lasting than a consortium. Two or more companies might pool some of their human and financial resources to engage in some very complex and expensive basic research

SPOTLIGHT ON BIG BUSINESS

Journey's End Expands Market by Joint Venture

Journey's End Corp. is expected to announce today that it is entering into a joint venture with a major U.S. hotel company, **Choice Hotels International Inc.**

There have been rumours in recent weeks that Journey's End of Belleville, Ont., which operates 120 properties across Canada, may be the target of a takeover. In the past month, its stock price has run up to $6.12 from $3.75.

However, a source close to Journey's End said yesterday that the motel and hotel company has struck a deal that will give it perhaps 50 more properties to manage in Canada as well as access to the international reservation system of Choice Hotels, the world's fourth-largest hotel company.

"It's no takeover," the source said, "To the contrary, it's a great coup."

Choice Hotels, formerly known as Quality Inns International, operates about 2,300 properties in 26 countries under banners such as Clarion, Quality and Comfort. It is based in Silver Springs, Md.

International ambitions are not new for Journey's End. During the 1980s, as it was gobbling up properties in Canada, the company was also seeking to expand into Europe and the United States.

In 1990, however, the economy began to falter and by the beginning of 1992 Journey's End had stopped developing properties, halted dividend payments and divested almost all of its foreign interests.

It is now primarily a management company, an aspect of the business it believes to be the most profitable and the least risky.

Source: Scott Feschur, "Journey's End Plans Joint Venture," *Globe and Mail,* April 21, 1993, p. B9.

programs. Each company then goes on to develop its own products from the knowledge gained.

Countertrading

One of the oldest forms of trade is called **bartering,** the exchange of merchandise for merchandise with no money involved. **Countertrading** is more complex than bartering in that several countries and companies may be involved, each trading goods for goods.

bartering
The exchange of merchandise for merchandise.

countertrading
Bartering among several countries and companies.

Examples of countertrade and bartering agreements are many. Chrysler traded its vehicles in Jamaica for bauxite. McDonnell Douglas traded jets in Yugoslavia for canned hams. General Motors has traded vehicles with China for industrial gloves and cutting tools. Telelex Media has traded television shows for advertising time in several foreign countries. Westinghouse sold an air defense radar system to Jordan in trade for phosphate.

Barter is especially important to poor countries that have little cash available for trade. Such countries may barter with all kinds of raw materials, food, or whatever resources they have. Pepsi-Cola took vodka in exchange for Pepsi in the former Soviet Union and then sold the vodka. Colombia has traded coffee for buses. Romania traded cement for steam engines. The Sudan pays for Pepsi concentrate with sesame seeds. Tanzania uses sisal, and Nicaragua uses sesame seeds and molasses. Sometimes more complex deals involve three parties.

With many world economies still in a state of flux, there is no question that countertrading will grow in importance in the 1990s. Trading products for products helps avoid some of the problems and hurdles experienced in global markets.

PROGRESS CHECK

- What does a trade deficit mean?
- Can you name four ways to enter foreign markets?
- What are the major benefits a firm may gain from licensing its products in foreign markets? What are the primary drawbacks?
- What are the major benefits of a joint venture in global markets?
- How does countertrading work?

HURDLES OF TRADING IN WORLD MARKETS

Succeeding in *any* business takes work and effort due to the many hurdles you encounter. Unfortunately, the hurdles get higher and more complex in world markets. This is particularly true in dealing with differences in cultural perspectives, societies and economies, laws and regulations, and fluctuations in currencies. Let's take a look at each of these hurdles.

Cultural Differences

Anyone who travels to different countries cannot help noticing that there are peculiarities of life in each country that are different from how we live in Canada. Every company that engages in international trade or investment must take these cultural differences into account if it wants to succeed in these operations.

In Canada and the U.S., we like to do things quickly. We tend to call each other by our first names and try to get chummy even at the first encounter. In Japan, China, and other countries these actions would be considered surprising and even rude. Canadian negotiators will say *no* if they mean *no,* but Japanese probably say *maybe* when they mean *no.*

Religion is an important part of any society's culture and can have a significant impact on business operations. For example, in Islamic countries, dawn-to-dusk fasting during the month of Ramadan causes workers' output to drop considerably. Also, the requirement to pray five times daily can affect output. For example, an American manager in Islamic Pakistan toured a new plant under his control in full operation. He went to his office to make some preliminary forecasts of production. As he was working, suddenly all the machinery in the plant stopped. He rushed out expecting a possible power failure and instead found his production workers on their prayer rugs. He returned to his office and lowered his production estimates.

Cultural differences can also have an impact on such important business factors as human resource management. In Latin American countries, managers are looked on by workers as authoritarian figures responsible for their well-being. Consider what happened to one participative American manager who neglected this important cultural characteristic. This manager was convinced he could motivate his workers in Peru to higher levels of productivity by instituting a more democratic decision-making style. He even brought in trainers from the United States to teach his supervisors to solicit suggestions and feedback from workers. Shortly after his new style was put in place, workers began quitting their jobs in droves. When asked why, Peruvian workers said the new production manager and supervisors did not know their jobs and were asking the workers what do to. All stated they wanted to quit and find new jobs, since obviously this company was doomed because of incompetent managers.

Without question, culture presents a significant hurdle for global managers. Learning about important cultural perspectives toward time, change, competition, natural resources, achievement, even work itself can be a great assistance. Today, firms often provide classes and training for managers and their families on how to adapt to different cultures and avoid culture shock. Your involvement in courses in cultural variations and anthropology can assist you in your career in global business.

Societal and Economic Differences

Certain social and economic realities are often overlooked by North American businesses. General Foods squandered millions of dollars in a fruitless effort to introduce Japanese consumers to the joys of packaged cake mixes. The company failed to note, among other factors, that only 3 percent of Japanese homes were then equipped with ovens. Similarly American automakers tried to sell their cars in Japan without providing right-hand-drive vehicles for a country that drives on the left side of the road. Since Japan is such an important trading partner, you would think that businesspeople would know such important information about the Japanese market, but often that is not so.

It's hard for us to imagine buying chewing gum by the stick instead of by the package. However, in economically oppressed nations like the Philippines, this buying behaviour is commonplace because consumers have only enough money to buy small quantities. Factors such as disposable and discretionary income can be critical in evaluating the potential of a market. What might seem like an opportunity of a lifetime may in fact be unreachable due to economic conditions.

Technological constraints may also make it difficult or impossible to carry on effective trade. For example, some less developed countries have such primitive transportation and storage systems that international food exchanges are ineffective because the food is spoiled by the time it reaches those in need. These constraints are further complicated by the tremendous geographic distances that separate some countries.

Exporters must also be aware that certain technological differences affect the nature of exportable products. For example, how would the differences in electricity available (110 versus 220 volts) affect an appliance manufacturer wishing to export?

Legal and Regulatory Differences

In any economy, the conduct and direction of business are firmly tied to the legal and regulatory environment. As we know, business operations are heavily affected by various federal, provincial, and local laws and regulations. In global markets, there is naturally a wider variation in such laws and regulations. This makes the task of conducting world business even tougher.

What businesspersons find in global markets is a myriad of laws and regulations that are often inconsistent. Important legal questions related to antitrust, labour relations, patents, copyrights, trade practices, taxes, product liability, and other issues are written and interpreted differently country by country. In many countries, bribery is acceptable and perhaps the only way to secure a lucrative contract. How do you think Canadian business and government leaders should handle this ethical dilemma?

To be a successful trader in foreign countries, one might choose to begin by contacting local businesspeople and gaining their cooperation and sponsorship. The problem is that foreign bureaucracies are often stumbling blocks to successful foreign trade; to penetrate those barriers, often one must find a local sponsor who can pay the necessary fees to gain government permission.

Hong Kong is one of the busiest cities in the world, with many successful businesses. It is not always easy to become established in such markets, but there are people who can help in every country. Businesspeople are a little cautious about doing business in Hong Kong today because of the unrest in China and the upcoming return of Hong Kong to China in 1997.

MAKING ETHICAL DECISIONS

As a top manager of Nightie Nite, a maker of children's sleepwear, you are required to be aware of all the new government regulations that affect your industry. A recently passed safety regulation prohibits the use of the fabric that you have been using for girl's nightgowns for the past 15 years. Apparently the fabric does not have sufficient flame retardant capabilities to meet government standards. In fact, last week Nightie Nite lost a lawsuit brought against it by the parents of a young child severely burned because the nightgown she was wearing burst into flames when she ventured too close to a gas stove. Not only did you lose the lawsuit, but you may lose your nightshirt if you don't find another market for the warehouse full of nightgowns you have in inventory. You realize that there are other countries that do not have such restrictive laws concerning products sold in their borders. You are considering exporting your products to these countries. What are your alternatives? What are the consequences of each alternative? What will you do? ▼

Problems with Currency Shifts

As you are probably aware, the global market does not have a universal currency. Mexicans shop with pesos, Germans with deutsche marks, South Koreans with won, the British with pounds, and Japanese with yen. One thing that makes world trade difficult today is the widely fluctuating values these currencies undergo. For example, one month a dollar may be exchanged for 1.5 deutsche marks, but the next month you may get 1.4 or 1.6 deutsche marks for your dollar. These changes can cause many serious problems.

In the example of the deutsch marks, there is a 7 percent fluctuation in the exchange rate with the dollar. Over a year or two a currency may rise or fall 20 percent or more in relation to the Canadian dollar. This makes it 20 percent more expensive or less expensive for foreign companies to buy Canadian goods or services.

TRADE PROTECTIONISM

As we said in the previous section, cultural differences, societal and economic factors, legal and regulatory requirements, and currency shifts are all hurdles to those wishing to trade globally. What is often a much greater barrier to international trade is the overall political atmosphere between nations. This barrier is best understood through a review of some economic history of world trade.

Business, economics, and politics have always been closely linked. In fact, economics was once referred to as "political economy" indicating the close ties between politics (government) and economics. For centuries, businesspeople have tried to influence economists and government officials. Back in the 16th, 17th, and 18th centuries, nations were trading goods (mostly farm products) with one another. Businesspeople at that time advocated an economic principle called **mercantilism.** Basically, the idea of mercantilism was to sell more goods to other nations than you bought from them; that is, to have a favourable balance of trade. This results in a flow of money to the country that sells the most. Governments assisted in this process by charging a tariff (basically a tax) on imports, making it more expensive to import goods.

mercantilism
The economic principle advocating the selling of more goods to other nations than a country buys.

protective tariffs
Import taxes designed to raise the price of imported products so that domestic products are more competitive.

There are two different kinds of tariffs: revenue and protective. **Protective tariffs** are designed to raise the price of imported products so that domestic products will be more competitive. These tariffs are meant to save jobs for domestic workers and to keep industries from closing down entirely because of foreign competition. Without such a protective tariff, the Canadian shoe and textile industries, for example, would have been almost totally taken over by imports. **Revenue tariffs,** on the other hand, are designed to raise money for the government. Revenue tariffs are commonly used by developing countries.

revenue tariffs
Import taxes designed to raise money for the government.

Today, there is still much debate about the degree of protectionism a government should practice. For example, the government is concerned about protecting domestic auto producers and workers from Japanese producers. The government convinced Japanese producers to voluntarily limit the number of Japanese cars sold here. The term that describes limiting the number or value of products in certain categories that can be imported is **import quota.**

import quota
A limit on the number or value of products in certain categories that can be imported.

James Thwaits, president of international operations of the 3M Co., says that as much as *half* of all trade is limited by *non-tariff* barriers. In other words, countries have established many strategies that go beyond tariffs to prevent foreign competition. For example, France tried to protect its video cassette recorder (VCR) industry by requiring that all imported VCRs be sent through an undermanned customs post that was 100 miles from the nearest port. Denmark requires that beverages be sold in returnable bottles; this effectively cut off French mineral water producers, who found the cost of returning bottles prohibitive. Margarine must be sold in cubes in Belgium, closing the market to countries that sell margarine in tubs.

Other non-tariff barriers include safety, health, and labelling standards. In 1992, the U.S. stopped some Canadian goods from entering because it said the information on the labels was too small. Canada has stopped American cattle or beef from entering because of hormone and antibiotic injections that violated our health standards. Canadian electrical standards have prevented certain appliances from being imported on the basis that they were not safe.

Sometimes, as in the French VCR case, the intent is clearly to put difficulties in the way of imports. Other times it is not so clear whether the barriers are deliberate or are a normal part of a reasonable set of standards. Of course, when a country is in a protectionist mode, it will exploit these standards to try to reduce imports.

Protectionism Backfiring

Sometimes attempts to keep out foreign goods or restrict their entry into a country lead to strange results. A good example of this occurred in the 1980s with Japanese cars, which had become very popular in Canada and the United States. They were of better quality, offered better warranties, used less gas, had better trade-in values, and cost less than the Big Three North American products. Instead of competing on value, the Big Three pressured the Canadian and U.S. governments to restrict the entry of Japanese autos. Both governments negotiated deals with the Japanese government and their automakers to "voluntarily" not increase the number of vehicles they would export to Canada and the U.S. for three years. These quotas were based on the number of units, not total dollar value.

The Big Three, feeling less pressure, raised their prices. The Japanese carmakers proceeded to do the same so that their prices were still competitive. They wound up exporting the same number of cars but making a lot more profit. They used this excess profit to build auto plants in Canada and the U.S., which ultimately led to Japanese cars capturing an even greater share of the North American market (about 35 percent).

Other Restrictions on International Trade

embargo
A complete ban on all trade with or investment in a country.

Sometimes countries restrict trade for purely political or military reasons. For example, for some years Canada and many other countries had an embargo on doing business with South Africa because of its racist laws and policies. An **embargo** is a complete ban on all trade with or investment in a country. The U.S. has strict restrictions or complete embargoes on exporting what it classifies as secret or very high-tech parts or equipment that could be used for military purposes by its enemies. The U.S. also bans all trade with Cuba because it doesn't like Cuba's communist government. All these restrictions are of a purely political or military nature and should not be confused with trade protectionism, which is of an economic nature.

Consequences of Protectionism

Today, nations throughout the world are debating how much protectionism they should use to keep foreign competition from driving their firms out of business. You can read about this trend in current business periodicals. As you do, keep in mind that the severity of the Great Depression of the 1930s was attributed by some people to the passage of the highly protectionist Smoot-Hawley Tariff Act of 1930 in the U.S. Economists were almost unanimous in opposing the bill. Nonetheless, believing it would protect American business, the government put tariffs on goods from England, France, and other nations. The result was that other countries raised tariffs in return. This hurt businesses in all countries badly, as world trade dropped sharply.

In the U.S. by 1932, exports to England were at one third the 1929 level, exports to France were only one fourth of 1929, and exports to Australia were one fifth of 1929. Wheat exports fell from $200 million to $5 million, and auto exports fell from $541 million to $76 million. In short, some economic theorists contend that protectionist policies of governments (based on old mercantilist thinking) helped create the greatest depression in the history of modern capitalism. Unemployment soared in Canada and most countries, with serious economic consequences.

PROGRESS CHECK

- What are the major hurdles to successful international trade?
- Identify at least two cultural and societal differences that can affect global trade efforts.
- What are the advantages and disadvantages of trade protectionism?
- What is an embargo? Can it be applied for non-economic reasons?

INTERNATIONAL TRADE ORGANIZATIONS

General Agreement on Tariffs and Trade (GATT)
Agreement among trading countries that provides a forum for negotiating mutual reductions in trade restrictions.

The major trading nations learned an important lesson from the terrible effects of trade protectionism. After World War II, they got together and formed the **General Agreement on Tariffs and Trade (GATT),** an agreement among trading countries that provides a forum for negotiating mutual reductions in trade restrictions. For almost half a century it has gotten all nations to agree on a gradual reduction in tariffs and non-tariff barriers to international trade. This has not been a smooth road and there are still glitches, but the trend and goals are clearly established and agreed to by all countries.

As these words are being written, one serious bottleneck has existed for several years. The Uruguay Round of negotiations is stalled because of several major disagreements, mainly about the European Community's huge subsidies to farmers, which create unfair advantages or non-tariff barriers. As we will see in Chapter 3, Canada's marketing boards are a form of non-tariff barrier to the importation of certain agricultural products. That is why they are also under attack in this round of negotiations.

The success of these negotiations is considered critical to the continued existence of GATT. Opinion is divided as to whether this serious hurdle will be overcome. Everyone agrees that failure would lead to a new round of trade protectionism that would undo much of the work of the last few decades of GATT.

Even before GATT, the **International Monetary Fund (IMF)** was signed into existence by 44 nations at Bretton Woods, New Hampshire, in 1944. The IMF is an international bank that is supported by its members and usually makes *short-term* loans to countries experiencing problems with their balance of trade. Its basic objectives are to promote exchange stability, maintain orderly exchange arrangements, avoid competitive currency depreciation, establish a multilateral system of payments, eliminate exchange restrictions, and create standby reserves. The IMF makes *long-term* loans at interest rates of just 0.5 percent to the world's most destitute nations to help them strengthen their economies. This makes the function of the IMF very similar to that of the World Bank.

International Monetary Fund (IMF)
An international bank that makes short-term loans to countries experiencing problems with their balance of trade.

The **World Bank** (the International Bank for Reconstruction and Development), an autonomous United Nations agency, is concerned with developing the infrastructure (roads, schools, hospitals, power plants) in less-developed countries. The World Bank borrows from the more prosperous countries and lends at favorable rates to less developed countries. Figure 2–3 lists some of the major international bodies that impact on trade.

World Bank
An autonomous United Nations agency that borrows money from the more prosperous countries and lends it at favorable rates to less-developed countries.

Some countries felt that their economies would be strengthened if they were to establish formal trade agreements with other countries. Some of these agreements involve forming producers' cartels and common markets.

Producers' Cartels

Producers' cartels are organizations of commodity-producing countries. They are formed to stabilize or increase prices, optimizing overall profits in the long run. The most obvious example today is OPEC (the Organization of Petroleum Exporting Countries). Similar arrangements have been made to manage prices for copper, iron ore, bauxite, bananas, tungsten, and rubber. These are all contradictions to unrestricted free trade and letting the market set prices.

producers' cartels
Organizations of commodity-producing countries that are formed to stabilize or increase prices to optimize overall profits in the long run. (An example is OPEC, the Organization of Petroleum Exporting Countries.)

Common Markets

A **common market** is a regional group of countries that has no internal tariffs. Common markets have a common external tariff and a coordination of laws to facilitate exchange. Notable are the European Community (EC), the Central American Common Market (CACM), and the Caribbean Common Market (CCM).

common market
A regional group of countries that has no internal tariffs, a common external tariff, and a coordination of laws to facilitate exchange. (An example is the European Community.)

Figure 2–3 Who's minding the economic store? International alliances formed to set policies on trade, debt, and aid to developing nations steer the course of the world's economy. The leader of the pack is the Group of Seven, economic powerhouses that hold the greatest sway over global money matters.

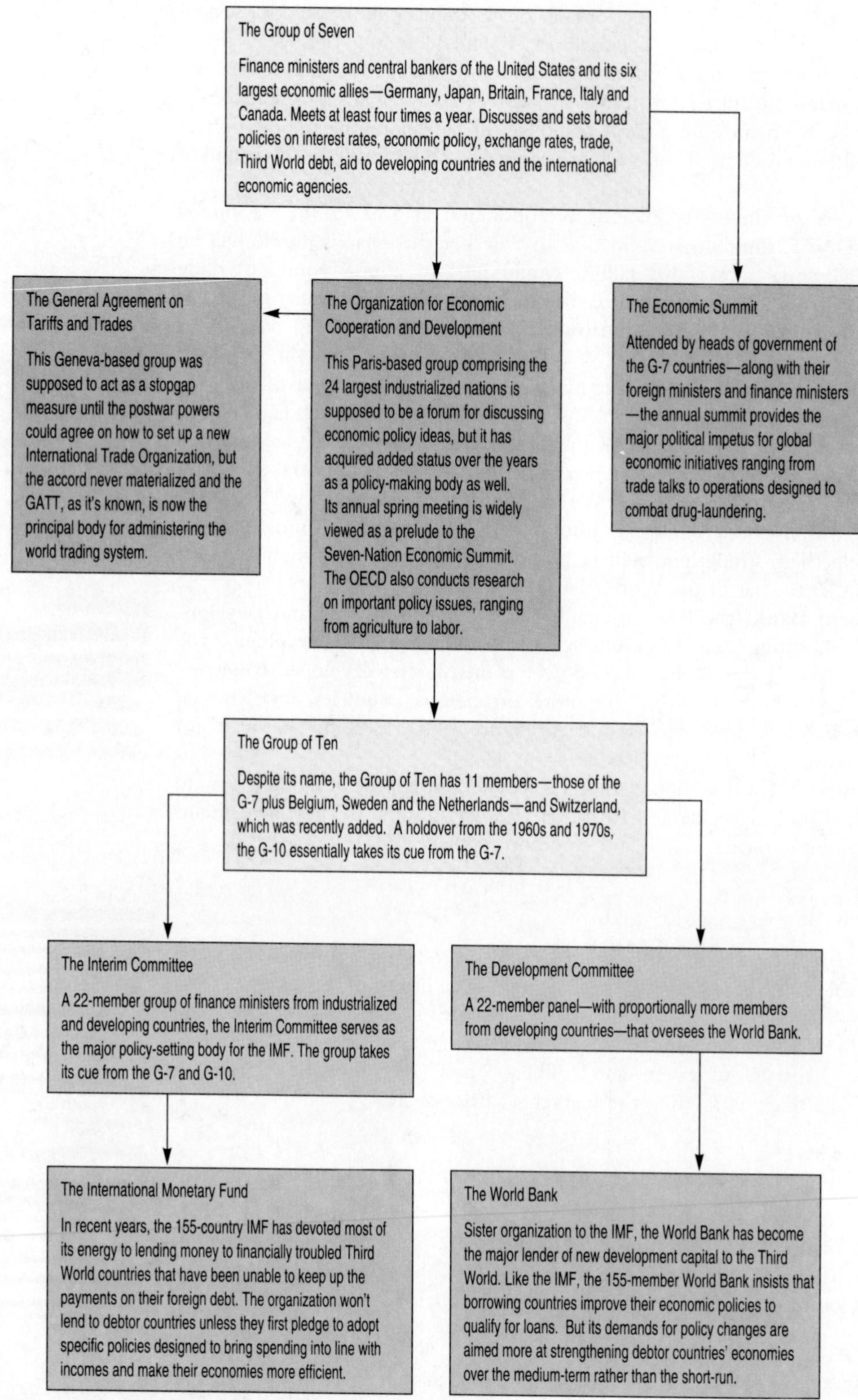

Source: *Los Angeles Times,* May 7, 1991, p. H5.

The Canada–U.S. Free Trade Agreement[3]

A form of common market was established between Canada and the United States, when the Free Trade Agreement (FTA) came into effect on January 1, 1989. It affected nearly all goods and services traded between Canada and the United States as well as intercountry investments. These two countries are each other's largest trading partners. Over 75 percent of Canada's imports and exports are with the U.S. The Canada–U.S. trading bloc has the largest two-country trade in the world.

The formal purpose was to phase out most tariffs and other restrictions on free trade between the two countries over a period of 10 years. The FTA made it easier for cross-country investments and buyouts to take place. It guaranteed the U.S. access to our energy resources. The movement of professionals and certain other categories of people across the border was also eased. For various reasons, each side kept certain items outside the FTA. For example, Canada insisted that beer and cultural industries and products be excluded. The U.S. insisted that shipping be excluded.

These aspects of the FTA were not really the key features as far as Canada was concerned. After all, the international GATT has been successfully reducing trade barriers and tariffs among all countries for the past 40 years. Some 80 percent of our trade with the U.S. was already duty-free, and the average U.S. tariff on the rest of our exports was about 5 percent. In addition, most cross-country investments proceeded with little difficulty. But for Canada, there were three much more important goals to be achieved.

First, because of the political structure and practice in the U.S., there was a historic problem of protectionist policies and regulations that created uncertainty in trade relations. Canadian, and other, exporters could never feel secure that their access to the U.S. market would not be interrupted. In fact, Canadian companies had experienced many such problems in the past.

Furthermore, there were fears that this problem was worsening because the United States was increasingly concerned about the flood of imports from Japan, Korea, China, and other Asian countries. This could lead the U.S. to embark on a protectionist course, creating problems for all exporting countries. There was no real recourse to combat such restrictions.

Therefore, one major goal of the Canadian negotiating team was to provide relief from unilateral U.S. actions in this regard. A binational panel would adjudicate on disputes between the two countries. Unfortunately, this has not stopped the U.S. from continuing what many Canadians feel is harassment of our exporters (three examples are B.C. lumber, Honda cars, and steel from Ontario.) Some cases were so frivolous (for instance, uranium from Saskatchewan) that they were easily won. But the process involves Canadian exporters in heavy legal costs and draws executives' time away from productive efforts. It also makes foreign companies wary of investing in Canada.

Both Simon Reisman, who was our chief negotiator of the FTA, and his deputy, Gordon Ritchie, were extensively quoted in the media in early 1992 as criticizing the U.S. for continuing actions they deemed not to be in keeping with either the spirit or letter of the agreement.

The second aim of the FTA was to expose Canadian companies to greater competition from American companies to force them to become more competitive. This was deemed essential for Canada to be able to compete in the tough, globalized business world. The thinking was that, since the world has now become one market, only the best can survive in that fiercely competitive global marketplace. The problem was that the Canadian government gave no aid to help certain industries through what it admitted would be a very difficult transition period, despite promises to do so.

Other countries, such as Japan, Singapore or Korea, that wanted to raise certain industries to world-class competitiveness followed a different path. They gave them three years to shape up while they protected them from foreign competition. They aided them and monitored them closely to see that they were moving forward. They helped to retrain workers whose jobs were disappearing.

So far the deterioration in Canadian manufacturing has been enormous. Hundreds of companies have closed plants, moved to the U.S. or Mexico, or gone bankrupt. The heartland of Canadian industry in Ontario and Quebec has been decimated, and unemployment has soared to well over 11 percent. About 600,000 people have lost their jobs. The deep and still worsening recession has compounded this very bad situation. There is very little sign of the new-job creation promised by the FTA.

The third aim was to give the vast American market better access for Canadian goods and services. This was closely related to forcing Canadian companies to become more competitive, since they would have to compete with American companies. But U.S. protectionism against Canadian companies and industries continues to be a problem. Further signs that the FTA is not producing easier access are the increasingly successful campaigns to lure Canadian companies to set up operations in the U.S. Many states in the U.S. are waging aggressive campaigns to woo Canadian industry to relocate there. The FTA agreement was supposed to make that unnecessary because of easier access to the American market. The CBC "Sunday Morning" radio show (March 8, 1992) indicated that at least 300 companies had moved south, causing the loss of 100,000 jobs.

In the 1988 election, when the FTA was the main issue, Prime Minister Mulroney and the Conservative party got only 43 percent of the vote but managed to win a majority of the seats in the House of Commons. By mid-1992, polls and other data made it clear that fewer than 30 percent of Canadians support the FTA.

PROGRESS CHECK

- What were the objectives of Canada that led it to sign the FTA?
- What is the primary purpose of the International Monetary Fund (IMF) and the General Agreement on Tariffs and Trade (GATT)?
- How does a common market work? Why do countries enter into common market agreements?
- How does the future for international trade appear? What might be some important factors that will have an impact on future global trading?

A United Europe

On December 31, 1992, 12 nations of the European Community (EC) (see Figure 2–4) dissolved their economic borders. Most of the advanced part of Europe is now one vast market of some 340 million inhabitants with the free movement of people, goods, services, and capital. Centuries-old regional characteristics will remain a strong force for many, many years, but economic, political, and social differences are beginning to narrow. Many EC structures now in place are helping the movement in that direction, including a European Parliament.

There are two major goals the EC hopes to achieve by the end of the century: monetary and political union. That means one currency—the *ecu* (European

REACHING BEYOND OUR BORDERS

The North American Free Trade Agreement

In the first half of 1992, there was a spate of news reports and government announcements concerning a proposed free trade agreement among Mexico, Canada, and the United States. Negotiations had been under way for about 18 months, and by late June 1992 it seemed as if the three parties had almost reached agreement on all outstanding items. Why another free trade agreement? What impact could it have on Canada?

The motivators for the North American Free Trade Agreement (NAFTA) are to be found basically in the needs of the U.S. and Mexico. Mexico's population continues to explode and its economy cannot provide jobs for large numbers of its people. For many years they have been pouring across the long U.S. border, mostly illegally. These uncounted millions of Mexicans are having a major, rapid impact on American society that is disturbing many Americans. The U.S. government seeks to stop this flow by helping the Mexican economy grow fast enough to provide jobs in Mexico.

The Mexican government is of course interested in developing its economy and sees access to the vast American market as the way to spur growth, provide jobs for its people, and raise the low standard of living in Mexico. The U.S. demands that Mexico undertake to provide oil to America, with conditions similar to those imposed on Canada in the FTA. It also wants Mexico to remove restrictions on foreign ownership and on imports.

Canada is really a minor player in this deal. It is concerned that it may be left out or penalized indirectly unless it sits at the table. We do have something to gain by having freer access to the growing Mexican market, but it is still a minor customer for Canada. The U.S. is seeking to modify the FTA in its favour as the price for letting Canada be a part of the NAFTA. We do not have many bargaining chips.

There is great concern in Canada and the U.S. that even more manufacturing jobs will be lost to Mexico because of the NAFTA. Wages and general conditions are very much lower in Mexico. This time around (unlike with the FTA), many Canadian businesspeople are opposed to the NAFTA because they do not like the details that have leaked out. In addition, Mexico has a poor policy on environmental problems, bad working conditions, and a dubious record on human rights. It has repeatedly been condemned by many organizations in North America and abroad for serious flaws on all of these counts.

The U.S. has announced a broad strategy of creating one vast free-trade area of the entire western hemisphere. It sees itself as dominating this bloc, which will give it important leverage in trading with the rest of the world. With Europe moving to a single market and Japan becoming the linchpin of a huge East Asia bloc, the U.S. wants to be sure it has the strength to compete with these upcoming major trading blocs.

There has not yet been a major public policy discussion in Canada as to where we fit into all of this. Do we really want to cast our lot with U.S. strategy? Perhaps we are being swept into this without adequate consideration of our options. Many people are concerned about our very independence being threatened.

Sources: *Financial Times, Financial Post, Globe and Mail,* various issues March/June 1992.

[On February 25, 1993, Canada's Minister of International Trade deposited the 4,000-page NAFTA agreement in Parliament. It was passed in the House of Commons on May 27, 1993, and by the Senate on June 23, 1993. The U.S. Congress also approved the NAFTA agreement on November 18, 1993. Approval of the agreement is still required by the Mexican Congress. ▼

Germany	Spain
France	The Netherlands
Portugal	Italy
Greece	Denmark
Britain	Belgium
Ireland	Luxembourg

Figure 2–4 The 12 countries in the European trade community, formerly the European Community (EC), now the European Union (EU).

The flags of the European Community (EC) remind us that the business environment of the 1990s will be more competitive than ever before. There will be more opportunity and challenge than ever before in history to create world markets. There is also the potential for trade wars. The path to peace and prosperity worldwide is through free trade in global markets.

currency unit)—and an EC government. You can see how having a single currency avoids all the trade problems of currency fluctuations discussed earlier. One government will also make a common trade policy much easier to fashion for the 12 countries. This will be a historic movement towards countries giving up their sovereignty, which is a major reversal of the past few hundred years' evolution towards the modern independent nation–state.

This complex and very difficult process began with six countries in 1957 led by some farsighted statesmen in France and Germany. They felt that the only way to avoid even more devastating wars in Europe than the two world wars was to unite in a common destiny.

Gradually, other reasons emerged for strengthening this unity movement. More and more people began to see such integration as the only way to raise their standard of living while at the same time improving their ability to compete with Japan and the U.S. in both European and world markets.

The free movement of people, money, goods, and services and shared social programs, new tax systems, and shared professional standards was extremely difficult to achieve. This movement is now seen by the rest of Europe as the wave of the future, and most of the countries that are not in the EC now are eager to join. This will eventually produce the largest unified market in the world, packing a powerful economic punch.

One advantage for Canadians is that English will be the common language of the EC. This should help Canadian companies compete in this giant market, as it will be one less barrier to international trade and investment. Some observers fear that a European protectionist superstate, "Fortress Europe," may emerge, but others see no danger of this happening. One of the most significant international developments of the next decade will be the progress of this newly united Europe. In late 1993 this integrating process was in serious disarray. It remains to be seen whether this is just another of the many stumbling blocks previously overcome or is a more serious threat.

This development is part of a worldwide movement towards unified, giant, economic trading blocs. The three main areas—Europe, dominated by Germany, North America (with South America joining later) dominated by the United States, and East Asia, dominated by Japan—have been called the *triad* that will dominate world trade. The question is, will these blocs cooperate or will they engage in fierce competition with each other? Only time will tell.

THINKING IT THROUGH

Many countries in the world are called less-developed countries. Why are they less developed? Is it the lack of natural resources? Then how do you explain the success of Japan, which has few natural resources? Does lack of free markets keep countries from developing? Why would a government restrict free trade? What could happen to the world's standard of living and quality of life if all countries engaged in free trade? What is keeping that from happening? What would it take to eliminate such barriers?

HOW DOES CANADA SHAPE UP AS AN INTERNATIONAL COMPETITOR?

The Porter Report

The 1990s have seen a torrent of complaints in Canada that our competitiveness has been sliding steadily. One of the most influential sources assessing Canada's competitiveness is the Porter report, commissioned by the Canadian government. It is called *Canada at the Crossroads: The Reality of a New Competitive Environment*. This year-long study by a team headed by Michael E. Porter, the guru of competition from the Harvard Business School, was released in January 1992. It is a very comprehensive analysis; the summary is 101 pages long. It is based on concepts and techniques elaborated in Porter's influential book *The Competitive Advantage of Nations*.

What are Porter's conclusions? According to the analysis by Professor Donald N. Thompson of York University, "Drastic and immediate action . . . [is] required by Canada." He continues:

> It is hard to overstate the urgency of the problem highlighted by Porter. Canada is behind in the technology race, and has shown almost no productivity growth in a decade. Its 30 percent high school dropout rate is the highest in the western world. In training effectiveness Canada ranks 20th of 24 countries rated by the OECD (Organization for Economic Cooperation and Development). A government that should be taking the lead in research, technology, and training has spent almost two terms pursuing noninterventionist policies such as deregulation, privatization, and free trade. Reversing that policy and finding initiatives that are affordable is difficult.

Porter "is unrelenting in . . . [his] criticism of government, business, and labour for Canada's failure to abandon old ways of thinking and to embrace a new economic order of continual productivity growth and innovation."

He believes governments should concentrate on education, employee training, developing "closer links between government, universities, and industry research bodies," and specialized regional development policies. Business must "treat labour as a partner and act in a less authoritarian way," be "innovative-driven," spend more on training, "transform foreign subsidiaries into home bases" and "rely more on advanced technologies and methods," and "focus on products, markets and businesses that provide a lasting competitive advantage." Labour's "priorities must become encouragement of technological change and skills upgrading, and more cooperative labour–management relations" as "the best guarantee of good wages" and jobs in the long term.

Porter, the American, notes that "one of Canada's competitive problems is the high concentration of foreign-owned firms that perform little sophisticated production or R&D." Not mentioned by Porter is that these are nearly all subsidiaries of U.S. firms. Nearly half (45 percent) of Canada's manufacturing sector is foreign owned. Thompson points out that "most academics and government officials maintain that the level of foreign ownership is not significant in determining the competitiveness of" Canada. Porter disagrees, arguing:

> It matters a lot where a multinational calls home, because a company's home base is where the best jobs exist, where core R&D is undertaken, and where strategic control rests. . . . Home bases are important to an economy because they support high productivity and productivity growth.

Thompson notes that in this difference of opinion, Porter takes a position "closer to economic nationalists" than to the more conventional economic wisdom.

Finally, concludes Professor Thompson, the message is "that we must move quickly or risk a real loss in standard of living."[4]

Evidence Contradicting Porter and Conventional Wisdom

Two reports in the *Globe and Mail* seem to be somewhat at odds with all the bad news about Canada's competitive ability. The first, a Statistics Canada study, shows that exports of Canadian manufacturing products accounted for 47 percent of all our merchandise exports in 1990 (compared to only 32 percent in 1980). They began increasing in the latter half of the 1980s, despite the rise of the Canadian dollar against the U.S. dollar making our exports more expensive. Later StatsCan figures showed the percentage continued to rise in 1991–1993, despite the recession.

Even when automotive trade with the U.S. is excluded, manufacturing exports still increased from 20 percent to 37 percent of overall exports in the 1980s. According to Philip Cross, StatsCan's director of current analysis, the big losses in manufacturing appeared to occur in the domestic market. Such industries as textiles, furniture, appliances, food products, printing, and publishing were hit.

The big gains were in aircraft and parts, where we are one of the top five exporters, and in railway rolling stock, where we ranked first in the world in 1989. (Bombardier played a big role in both items.)

Cross's statistics are borne out by the comments of J. Myers, economist of the Canadian Manufacturers Association. He says that "the real weakness in manufacturing has not been in exports . . . but on the domestic side." He notes that Canadian manufacturers' share of the domestic market slipped from 73 percent in 1980 to 55 percent in 1991. Perhaps even more impressive, Cross says:

> Manufacturing output has declined at a slower pace than has manufacturing employment during the recession as companies have continued to make productivity gains even as output fell, *which is highly unusual* (authors' emphasis). Productivity is defined as real output per person-hour worked.

These statistics are almost startling in view of all the gloomy statements by Porter and so many others about the poor productivity of Canadian manufacturers.[5]

The second report from the *Globe and Mail* covers a study by a University of Toronto political science professor, Joseph Fletcher, about Canadian attitudes to capitalistic and entrepreneurial ideologies. "Canadians, it turns out, are more American than the Americans." On a long list of questions designed to compare Canadian and American attitudes, we seem to be waving ideological business banners "even more zealously" than our cousins to the south.

While it is rather surprising to discover that we are really so different from the image usually projected of Canadians there is something even more surprising. This study, entitled *Canadian Attitudes towards Competitiveness and Entrepreneurship,* was commissioned by the federal government. But it was held up by the Department of Industry, Science and Technology for nearly a year, until well after the delivery of the Porter report in October 1991. The lengthy delay is understandable, since the study conflicts with a basic premise in Porter's report. The article notes that

> Mr. Porter concluded in his report that the biggest barriers to improving Canada's competitiveness are attitudinal. He said that if his study had only one impact, he hoped it would be the way Canadians think about competitiveness. Although there was not a shred of attitudinal research in the Porter report, big business and government quickly picked up the theme.

The *Globe and Mail* article then quotes Michael Wilson and the president of the Royal Bank of Canada, John Cleghorn, on the need to change attitudes. The reporter concludes: "But Canadians had already embraced competitiveness, even before the government was converted to the cause, according to data in the Fletcher survey.[6]

More research is required to explain these contradictions, but it is clear that no one has all the answers to the important question: How does Canada shape up as an international competitor?

PROGRESS CHECK

- What is the EC? What is it trying to achieve?
- What is the *triad?* What is its significance?
- What is the Porter report? What are its main conclusions according to Professor Thompson?
- What is the evidence contradicting some of its conclusions?

SUMMARY

1. Discuss the increasing importance of the international market and the roles of comparative advantage in international trade.

1. The world market for trade is huge. Some 95 percent of the people in the world live outside Canada and the United States.

- *Why should nations trade with other nations?*

  (1) No country is self-sufficient, (2) other countries need products that prosperous countries produce, and (3) there is a world imbalance of natural resources and technological skills.

- *What is the theory of comparative advantage?*

  The theory of comparative advantage contends that a country should produce and sell those products it produces most efficiently and buy those it cannot produce as efficiently.

2. Students can get involved in world trade through importing and exporting. They do not have to work for big transnational corporations.

2. Explain how the marketing motto "Find a need and fill it" applies to international business.

▼ *What kinds of products can be imported and exported?*

Just about any kind of product can be imported and exported. The most important thing for a potential importer or exporter to remember is to find a need and fill it.

3. In order to understand international business, you must first understand the terminology.

3. Apply the terminology used in international business.

▼ *What terms are important in understanding world trade?*

Exporting is selling products to other countries.
Importing is buying products from other countries.
Balance of trade is the relationship of exports to imports.
Balance of payments is balance of trade plus other money flows such as tourism, foreign aid, and investments.
Dumping is selling products for less in a foreign country than in your own country.
Trade protectionism is the use of government regulations to limit the importation of products. See other terms in the Key Terms section to be sure you know the important ones.

4. Canada has only 27 million people, yet it ranks seventh in the world in volume of international trade. Canadian companies also invest large sums of money in the U.S. and in other countries.

4. Describe the status of Canada in international business.

▼ *What made Canada's success in international trade possible?*

Canada is an efficient, modern industrialized country with a well-trained work force. It has developed high levels of expertise in agricultural, energy, and other natural resource production. It thus produces huge quantities of these products as well as automotive vehicles and parts, which are exported to the U.S. under the special Auto Pact. More recently, electronic and telecommunication products and transportation equipment have become major exports.

5. A company can participate in world trade in a number of ways.

5. Illustrate the strategies used in reaching global markets.

▼ *What are some ways a company can get involved in international business?*

Ways of entering world trade include exporting and importing, joint venturing, licensing, creating subsidiaries, franchising, and countertrading.

6. There are many restrictions on foreign trade other than protectionism.

6. Discuss the hurdles of trading in world markets.

▼ *What are some of the other hurdles that can discourage participation in international business?*

Potential stumbling blocks to world trade include cultural differences, societal and economic differences, legal and regulatory differences, and fluctuations in values of different currencies.

7. Political pressures are often the most difficult hurdles to international trade.

7. Debate the advantages and disadvantages of trade protectionism.

▼ *How does trade protectionism reduce international trade?*

Trade protectionism is the use of government regulations to limit the import of goods and services, based on the theory of favouring domestic producers to survive and grow and generate more jobs. Some tools of protectionism are tariffs and quotas.

▼ *What are tariffs?*

Tariffs are taxes on imports. There are two kinds of tariffs. Protective tariffs are used to raise the cost of imports, and revenue tariffs are used to raise money for the government.

▼ *How does a quota differ from a tariff?*

A quota limits the quantity of particular imports.

▼ *Is trade protectionism good for domestic producers?*

That is debatable. Trade protectionism hurt all countries badly during the Great Depression of the 1930s, because other countries responded to foreign tariffs with tariffs of their own.

▼ *Why do governments continue such practices?*

Pressure from industries and their associations, unions, and communities affected by imports nurtures the practice of trade protectionism.

8. Transnational corporations have a huge impact on world trade.

▼ *How do these corporations differ from other corporations that participate in international business?*

Unlike companies that are involved in just exporting or importing, transnationals have international manufacturing facilities. They also do financing, marketing, and management on an international basis.

8. Describe the role of transnational corporations in a globalized world economy.

9. There are many organizations and trade agreements that facilitate world trade.

▼ *What are some of these organizations and trade agreements?*

Among the most important are the World Bank, the International Monetary Fund (IMF), and the General Agreement on Tariffs and Trade (GATT). The first two help fill various needs of developing countries by a variety of financial programs. GATT works to reduce or remove tariff and non-tariff barriers to trade between all countries.

9. Identify and describe international trade organizations and trade agreements.

10. One of the most significant developments for the future of world trade is the formation of twelve European countries into one trading bloc, called the European Community (EC).

▼ *What trading partnership may be more important to Canada than the EC?*

The U.S. and Canada have signed a Free Trade Agreement (FTA) and are in the process of approving a North American Free Trade Agreement (NAFTA), which will include Mexico and replace the FTA.

10. Discuss the future of international trade and investment.

▼ *Will future growth in world trade be with large developed nations?*

Yes, but more growth will likely be with the rapidly developing Pacific Rim countries such as China and other countries in Southeast Asia. The former communist countries in Eastern Europe and what was the Soviet Union also offer great potential for investment and trade.

GETTING INVOLVED

1. Visit an Oriental rug dealer or some other importer of foreign goods. Talk with the owner/manager about the problems and satisfactions involved in international trade. Visit several such organizations and compile a list of advantages and disadvantages. Then get together with others in the class and compare notes.
2. Let's dream for a minute. Imagine yourself living in an exotic country where the weather is great, the living easy, and the people friendly. Have you ever visited such a place? Well, picture yourself living there. What language would you have to learn, if any? What could you import there that would be fun to sell? Share your vision with others. What's keeping you from making that dream come true?
3. Some countries are rich and have an overabundance of food. Some countries are poor and people are starving. Some countries have few natural resources, but are prosperous (for example, Japan, Singapore). Others are relatively rich in natural resources, but are poor (for example, Ghana). Do trade barriers cause such disparities to continue? Is the problem economic, social, political, or some combination? Discuss.
4. Write a short essay describing the benefits and disadvantages of trade protectionism. Have your class divide into two sides and debate this issue: "Resolved that Canada should increase trade protection to save Canadian jobs and Canadian companies."
5. Many firms have made embarrassing mistakes selling overseas. Sometimes the product is not adapted to the needs of the country, sometimes the advertising makes no sense, sometimes the colour is wrong, and so forth. Discuss the steps Canadian businesses should follow to be more responsive to the needs of foreign markets. Discuss your list with others, and together form a plan for improving trade overseas.

PRACTICING MANAGEMENT DECISIONS

Case One International Expansion: Two Cautionary Tales

Canada has seen many entrepreneurs develop huge multinational holdings in the last few decades. Examples are Conrad Black and Pierre Peladeau, with giant holdings in publishing and printing, and Paul Desmarais and his financial and conglomerate empire. These are just a few of the many who have achieved remarkable international growth. But let us look at two cases where things are somewhat different.

Robert Campeau emerged from northern Ontario and made a fortune in real estate development. However, he was aiming much higher. He set his mind on controlling the largest retail empire in the world. In the 1980s, when the merger and takeover mania was at its peak in the U.S., he acquired some vast retail holdings there. These units included some of the most prestigious department stores and chains in the U.S. His acquisitions were financed by huge borrowings running into the billions of dollars, and banks seemed only too willing to lend him these vast sums. Of course, all his other holdings were pledged as collateral security to the lenders.

Within two years his entire empire began to totter. It eventually collapsed and he lost everything. The huge cash flow from the retail stores, not as large as expected, was insufficient to meet the very large interest and capital payments on his borrowings. It ended in total disaster for Robert Campeau.

This brings us to the second special case. In his desperate attempts to stave off defeat, Campeau was helped by the Reichmann brothers of Olympia and York Development (O & Y), of Toronto. They lent Campeau $250 million. O & Y was reputed to be the largest real estate development company in the world, with multibillion dollar holdings in Toronto, New York, and London. The three brothers started a small tile company in the 1950s and 30 years later they had become giant real estate operators. They also had a controlling interest in some very large Canadian corporations.

Before getting involved in London, theirs was one of the outstanding success stories in recent Canadian history. They were reputed to be one of the wealthiest families in the world. But they could not resist the lure of a blockbuster deal that would make them kingpins of their field. They devised a plan for redeveloping the huge, derelict dock area of London. They would build a multitower office, apartment, and commercial development, the largest in Europe and perhaps in the world. The daring Canary Wharf plan received the enthusiastic backing of the then Prime Minister of England, Margaret Thatcher. It was backed by financing from banks around the world, including Japan and Canada.

Unfortunately, the recession that started in England in 1990 grew deeper and took hold in Canada, the U.S., and other countries. Real estate values plunged and the demand for space in Canary Wharf fell to almost zero at the same time that cash flow from O & Y's other vast holdings was declining because of the recession. Meanwhile, the cash demands from their involvement in the huge Hibernia oil development off Newfoundland forced them to withdraw from that partnership.

The combined pressure from all of these events led to stories in financial papers in March 1992 about the serious cash squeeze that O & Y was facing. Because their debts were rumoured to amount to some $20 billion, there was great concern about the effect of a default on the many banks that were creditors. There was also concern about the possible effect on the stability of the Canadian dollar.

Stopgap measures were found for delaying payments by restructuring the debt and by other short-term arrangements. Day after day the newspapers followed this incredible drama as the giant firm struggled to remain alive, but in May 1992 O & Y was forced into bankruptcy proceedings in Canada, England, and the U.S. The collapse of the hitherto unshakeable Reichmann rock of Gibraltar sent shivers through the world financial community and the Canadian government.

Decision Questions

1. Should a successful company be very cautious about international expansion that is based on extensive borrowings? Should it ever pledge all its assets to back one giant venture?

2. Given the globalization of business, how can a company avoid going international with its attendant risks? How are the opportunities balanced with the threats (the reward/risk ratio)?
3. Is risk taking a normal activity that cannot be avoided? What is an acceptable level of risk?
4. Rather than going it alone, is it more prudent to enter into major projects with partners to share the investment, risk, and profits?

Case Two To Bribe or Not to Bribe: That Is the Question

Condor Manufacturing has a joint venture with a local company in an African country we shall call Lorino. Condor sent you out to be the general manager for three years in order to train a Lorinese to take over from you. You are facing certain problems that you do not know how to resolve.

Bribery and kickbacks are normal methods of getting things done in Lorino. This applies to dealings with other companies and with the government. Salaries are very low and bribes are expected to make up the shortfall so that people can get by.

The vice-president of international operations for Condor is not very keen about this way of doing business, especially as it violates the company's ethical code. However, he informs you that these are decisions that you will have to make as the general manager. You have tried to pass the buck and it has been passed right back to you.

You have had to bribe people to get certain licenses, to get supplies, to have a road repaired, and to get sales contracts signed. You know that other local companies have learned to live with these conditions. Now you are negotiating to buy a piece of land adjacent to the factory because Condor will have to expand in the near future. A substantial bribe is being demanded and you are trying to resist it.

Decision Questions

1. Should you go along with this demand since it is a one-time issue?
2. Should you hold your nose and go along with this "normal" way of doing things?
3. Should you try to get a transfer out of Lorino even if you have to cook up some medical or personal reason?
4. Do you have any other alternatives? What are the likely results of each of the previous choices?

LET'S TALK BUSINESS

1. What aspect of international business interests you most: importing, exporting, investment, production, finance, marketing, or franchising?
2. How seriously have you explored working in a global economy? What courses might you take to better prepare yourself?
3. What do you see as the greatest barriers to open world trade and investment? Should those barriers be removed? How could that be done? What organizations may help?
4. How is the impact of the Canada–U.S. Free Trade Agreement being assessed now? Are you aware of any effect on jobs, exports and imports, business expansion or closings?
5. What is happening now with respect to the European Community? To the North American Free Trade Agreement? To other global trade agreements?

LOOKING AHEAD

In this chapter we saw that government actions have a significant impact on the international activities of Canadian companies. In Chapter 3, we look at the major role that government plays in the functioning of business in general in Canada.

THE ROLE OF GOVERNMENT IN BUSINESS

LEARNING GOALS

After you have read and studied this chapter, you should be able to:

1. Explain the historical role of government in the Canadian economy.
2. List some of the major crown corporations in Canada and understand their role in the economy.
3. Understand how the start-up and operations of companies take place within a framework of government reporting requirements.
4. Describe how the various types of taxation affect business.
5. Identify some major legislation affecting competition in Canada.
6. Discuss the role of government in stimulating or restraining the economy.
7. Understand the role of government in consumer and investor protection.
8. Outline some major government incentives to business.
9. Identify the role of government in environmental protection.
10. Understand the controversy about a government industrial policy.

KEY TERMS

articles of incorporation, p. 78
crown corporation, p. 73
economies of scale, p. 80
fiscal policy, p. 79
industrial policy, p. 74
marketing boards, p. 94
monetary policy, p. 87
National Policy, p. 74
privatization, p. 73
prospectus p. 90
securities commission p. 90

Gérald Tremblay

PROFILE GÉRALD TREMBLAY: A QUEBEC CABINET MINISTER WHO WORKS CLOSELY WITH BUSINESS

Gérald Tremblay has been minister of industry, trade, and technology in the Quebec government since 1989. A lawyer with an M.B.A. from Harvard Business School, he has had an active business career. Starting as a financial analyst and business consultant, he played a key role in turning around a major Quebec credit co-operative, protecting the savings of tens of thousands of members as well as hundreds of small businesses. Before becoming a member of the Liberal government, he was on the board of directors of the mammoth Quebec fund, the Caisse de dépôt et placement. He was also a board and executive committee member of Hydro-Quebec.

With such a background in business prior to his major cabinet portfolio, it is not surprising that Tremblay is well received in the business community. He has played an important role in stimulating business enterprises and innovation through a wide-ranging series of programs involving financial and other aid to new and established entrepreneurs and companies.

He has gotten a lot of attention with his newest program, the industrial clusters initiative. This is based on a concept elaborated by noted Harvard professor Michael Porter, who is an acknowledged authority on international competitiveness. Porter has written a preface to a recent book on Quebec industry that analyzes industrial clusters in detail.

Porter notes that:

> Countries, provinces, or even cities are rarely competitive in a single industrial sector but rather in "industrial clusters," often concentrated geographically or connected by common suppliers or clientele, or by other kinds of relationships. . . . Colleges, universities, and [other] public bodies adapt themselves to the needs of these groups.

It is this concept that Tremblay is promoting energetically to help Quebec companies become more competitive internationally. In general, most of his energy is devoted to close co-operation between his department and business. He is an excellent example of how government can play a significant role in helping business and the economy to move forward.

Sources: "Industrial Clusters," *The Montreal Gazette,* December 21, 1992, p. C8; April 10, 1993, p. E1; April 13, 1993, p. C1; various publications of the Ministere de l'industrie, du Commerce et de la Technologie; *L'Atlas industriel du Québec,* ed. Pierrette Gagné et Michel Lefèvre (Montreal: Publi-Relais, 1993), pp. 1–25.

GOVERNMENT INVOLVEMENT IN THE ECONOMY

The Canadian economic system is often described as a mixed economy—that is, a capitalist economy where government plays an important role. If you look at the Government of Canada section (and equivalent provincial government sections) in the blue pages in a city telephone directory, you will get some idea of the degree of involvement of the government in our economy. There are so many such services that federal and provincial governments issue publications listing them in detail. For example, the 12th edition of the *Guide to Federal Programs and Services,* published in 1992, is a 450-page book. It lists programs and services for 140 government-owned companies, departments, and agencies, with addresses and toll-free phone numbers across the country and much other information.[1] Companies owned by the federal or provincial governments are called **crown corporations.**

crown corporation
A company set up and owned by the federal or a provincial government.

How Government Affects Business

Government activities can be divided into five categories, as shown in Figure 3–1. This chapter will look at all of them.

All countries' governments are involved in the economy, but the extent of involvement and the specific ways they participate varies a great deal. In Canada there are particular historical reasons why we developed into a nation where government plays a very important role. Before looking at this history and the many ways that governments affect business, let us look at the current trends of government involvement.

A Smaller Role for Government

The 1980s ushered in a period that began to reverse the long-standing trend of growth in size of governments. This growth was the result of ever-expanding services to, and regulation of, business and consumers. The prime minister of England, Margaret Thatcher, and the president of the United States, Ronald Reagan, represented a new approach aimed at reducing the role, and therefore the size, of government in the economy. When the Progressive-Conservative Party won the 1984 election in Canada, the new prime minister, Brian Mulroney, allied himself with this movement.

In Canada we saw governments embark upon a whole series of measures whose net effect was to reduce the role of government in the economic life of the country. Crown corporations like Teleglobe Canada, Air Canada, and Alberta Government Telephone were sold off; others, like Petro-Canada, are no longer 100 percent owned by the government. The process of government selling crown corporations is called **privatization.**

privatization
The process of government selling crown corporations.

Industries that had been regulated, such as airlines and trucking, were partially or completely deregulated—no longer subject to certain regulations. Similar activities were undertaken by provincial governments.

1. **Laws and regulations.** These cover a wide range, from taxation and consumer protection to environmental controls, working conditions, and labour–management relations.
2. **Crown corporations.** There are hundreds of such companies, and they play an important role in the economy. They sometimes compete with regular businesses.
3. **Services.** This includes a vast array of direct and indirect activities, among them helping specific industries go international, bringing companies to Canada, training and retraining the work force, and providing a comprehensive statistics service.
4. **Financial aid.** All levels of government provide a host of direct and indirect aid packages as incentives to achieve certain goals. These consist of tax reductions, tariffs and quotas on imports, grants, loans, and loan guarantees.
5. **Purchasing policies.** Governments are very large purchasers of ordinary supplies and services and materiel for military purposes. Because the federal government is the single largest purchaser in Canada, its policies regarding where to purchase have a major effect on particular businesses and the economy of specific provinces and regions.

Figure 3–1 Government involvement with business

Some people believe this trend should be reversed to get the economy moving again and to deal with the unprecedented structural changes (discussed in Chapter 1) that have occurred in the early 1990s. They believe that the lack of a comprehensive, coordinated government plan to guide and revitalize the economy, called an **industrial policy,** will undermine our ability to recover from the very severe recession of the early 1990s. Others are strongly opposed in principle to such government action. We will return to this issue at the end of the chapter.

industrial policy
A comprehensive, coordinated government plan to revitalize the economy and lay out a path for the future.

A Historical Review

When Canada was formed as a country in 1867, the federal government was given the power to "regulate trade and commerce." As the western provinces later joined this confederation, it became clear that it would take special efforts to build a united Canada. The very small population was scattered across a huge country and there was no railway connecting them. Trading patterns were in a north-south configuration because, like today, most people lived near the U.S. border. (We can see that the current cross-border shopping phenomenon is not new, although it now takes on special significance.)

The U.S. was developing much faster, with a much larger population and a bigger economy that provided products that were not available in the provinces, either because they were not made here or there was no transportation to distribute them.

This led Canadian governments, starting with our first prime minister, Sir John A. MacDonald, to evolve what was called the **National Policy.** It placed high tariffs on imports from the U.S. to protect Canadian manufacturing (which had higher costs). In addition, the government began to grapple with the difficult question of building a costly rail line to the west coast.

the National Policy
Federal government policy imposing high tariffs on imports from the United States to protect Canadian manufacturing.

These two issues set the tone for the continuing and substantial involvement of Canadian governments in developing and maintaining the Canadian economy. The same type of mixed economy can be found in many countries: advanced, like Germany and Japan; newly developed countries, like Taiwan and South Korea; and developing ones, like Brazil and Thailand.

Air Canada was one of many crown corporations affected by privatization. The airline is no longer owned by the federal government.

THINKING IT THROUGH

The issue of how much government should be involved in the economy has been the subject of much debate in Canada. In the United States, ideology has played a major role in influencing Americans to believe that, in principle, government should "butt out." This ignores the significant role the U.S. government has played and continues to play in its economy. In Canada, we are less negative and perhaps more pragmatic: If it works, let's do it. But where do we go from here? Do we need less or more government involvement? Is it a question of the quality of that involvement? Could it be *smarter* rather than just *less?* What are your thoughts?

CROWN CORPORATIONS

In Canada an important aspect of the role of government is expressed through crown corporations. Some major federal ones are Canada Post Corporation, Atomic Energy of Canada Ltd., Canada Mortgage and Housing Corporation, Canadian National Railways (CNR), the Canadian Broadcasting Corporation (CBC), the Canadian Wheat Board, and the Export Development Corporation. There are many more large and small federally owned crown corporations.

Each province also owns such corporations. Typically, a crown corporation owns the province's electric power company. New Brunswick Electric Power, B. C. Hydro, Ontario Hydro, and Hydro-Quebec are some examples. Some of the telephone systems in the western half of Canada are owned by provincial crown corporations. The provinces also own other specialized corporations.

Governments set up crown corporations either to provide services that were not being provided by businesses (which is how Air Canada came into being in the 1930s), to bail out a major industry in trouble, (how the Canadian National Railways was put together in 1919) or to provide some special services that could not otherwise be made available, as in the case of Atomic Energy of Canada Ltd. or the Bank of Canada. Two important examples in Alberta and Quebec are discussed below.

One of the major crown corporations owned by the federal government is Canada Post. This corporation provides the mail service throughout Canada.

SPOTLIGHT ON SMALL BUSINESS

Federal Business Development Bank

One crown corporation that is particularly helpful to business is the Federal Business Development Bank (FBDB). The bank has been in operation since the mid-1940s and has been invaluable for small and medium-sized businesses. It originally functioned only as a lender—the bank of last resort—but over the years it has developed into a multi-service organization.

The FBDB not only lends money to businesses that cannot get loans from commercial banks, but it also invests in enterprises that are just starting up or expanding. The owners have the right to buy out the FBDB holdings in their companies any time in the future at the value then prevailing. When the FBDB takes an equity position (buys shares in a company), this often encourages other investors or lenders who might otherwise have been reluctant participants.

In addition, the bank provides management services through its Counselling Assistance to Small Enterprises (CASE). CASE uses the services of retired businesspeople and experts as consultants to smaller companies. This large group of people with every conceivable background in business is made available at reasonable rates. It is a useful service, since many entrepreneurs are weak in some aspect of management—marketing, finance, production, or planning. Over the years, thousands of CASE consultants have helped tens of thousands of businesspeople to prosper.

Another service provided by the FBDB is the Automated Information for Management (AIM). This large database contains useful information for small and medium-sized businesses. It lists all assistance programs available from all levels of government in Canada, sources of information, and various business opportunities all over the country.

Among FBDB's publications is a quarterly publication, *Profits,* with useful articles and information for entrepreneurs and small businesses. The autumn 1991 issue highlighted Small Business Week in Quebec. This annual event started in British Columbia in 1979 and takes place in a different province each year. It includes "business fairs, exhibits, workshops, conferences, luncheons, award ceremonies, and much more."

Sources: Various publications of FBDB; *Profits,* Federal Business Development Bank, Autumn 1991, vol. 11, No. 2. ▼

Special Financial Role of Two Provincial Crown Companies

The Alberta Heritage Savings Trust Fund was established in the 1970s, when the Alberta economy was prospering as a result of the oil boom and the government set aside part of its oil royalty revenue to start the fund. At the end of 1992 it was worth $15 billion. It must operate on a sound financial basis but, as much as possible, it makes investment decisions that will benefit Alberta.

Quebec has the Caisse de dépôt et placement du Québec, a giant fund that was established to handle the funds collected by the Quebec Pension Plan. At $41 billion, it is one of the largest pools of funds in North America. This plan was set up parallel to the Canada Pension Plan in 1966. The fund also handles other Quebec government funds. It is a very powerful investment vehicle that is used to guide economic development in Quebec. While it too must operate on a sound financial basis, it has a lot of scope to make decisions that will benefit the Quebec economy.

A closer look at what Quebec has been doing reveals some important initiatives of government, in close cooperation with business.

Quebec Inc.: A Model for Other Governments to Follow?

"It's Working, It's Working." A couple of 1992 headlines pointed to some interesting developments taking place in Quebec. "Quebec Inc. Called Model for Canada" (*Financial Post,* March 11, 1992) and "Enthusiasm Is Brimming at Quebec

Inc." (*Globe and Mail,* January 31, 1992) refer to a province where government has adopted a very interventionist policy as far as the economy is concerned. Here is how the vice-president of the Canadian Institute for Advanced Research describes it:

> If there is anything good to be said about this recession, it is that English Canada is being forced to re-evaluate the mindless laissez-faire theology of Ronald Thatcherism," said historian John Godfrey in a speech to the Chambre de Commerce de Montréal. Godfrey said Ronald Thatcherism is the model of savage capitalism championed by former U.S. president Ronald Reagan and former British prime minister Margaret Thatcher.
>
> The system maximizes competition among small and medium-sized industries to the benefit of consumers but to the detriment of smaller nations like Canada. "We tend to produce dynamic and enterprising economic dwarfs to do battle with equally dynamic and enterprising economic giants abroad," said Godfrey, former editor of the *Financial Post.*
>
> Godfrey argued that the federal government is obsessed with the American model of capitalism, which lets the marketplace decide what's good for the economy but ignores the need for central planning from government. "The notion that we must *let the market decide* has been seriously challenged by both the recession and the difficulties we have experienced with the U.S. since the implementation of the free-trade agreement.
>
> Godfrey argued there is a solution to Canada's economic woes—more government involvement. What Canada needs now is "goals and vision," Godfrey said, and one vision is already evident today—the concept known as Quebec Inc. "Alone in North America, Quebec has developed a group competitive economy," said Godfrey. "Like Japan, Quebec has a long-term outlook." Quebec Inc. is not perfect, as it produced such huge business failures as the Lavalin Group, he said. "But the country would do well to develop a unique Canada Inc. based on our own model rather than somebody else's.[2]

Another report mentions that despite some "illustrious" failures and a raft of serious economic problems and the "shaky status" of some well-known corporations in the province, the Quebec Inc. experiment is alive and well.

Basing itself on the German model and on ". . . the theories of strategy guru Michael Porter," Quebec believes that it can "serve as a model for the rest of Canada and certainly for division-racked Ontario." The article goes into detail on the long-term strategy adopted by the Quebec minister of industry, trade and commerce, (profiled at the beginning of this chapter) who says enthusiastically, "It's working! It's working!"[3]

Or is it? A very different viewpoint is expressed in the *Financial Times,* which says, "Quebec Inc. has got to change." The article observes that the province's powerful economic partners are shifting away from their traditional emphasis on state control." It reviews the battering that a lot of Quebec stars, companies and individuals, have suffered. Bernard Lamarre and Lavalin (engineering giant that went bankrupt), Domtar (pulp and paper company controlled by the Caisse de dépôt and in poor circumstances), McNeil Mantha (brokerage firm taken over by RBC Dominion Securities after sustained losses), Michel Gaucher's Socanev ("which was crippled by the government-assisted takeover of Steinberg's" supermarket chain, which is now bankrupt)—these are all examples of major shocks to Quebec Inc.

As a result, notes the report,

> Bloodied and humbled by the recession, Quebec Inc.—shorthand for an informal partnership between the province's business, labour, and government—is regrouping. . . . Now it's time to shift gears. There's an emerging agreement on the need for change. Quebec's bosses now want to shift away from their previous emphasis on direct government intervention, towards better cooperation between the partners.

The article elaborates on new plans afoot to carry out this shift in policy. It notes that

> Quebec's business fraternity, small, close-knit, and unified by language and culture, will never completely cut its ties to government. It's just that now, Quebec Inc.'s managers want to make its investments in a more rational, utilitarian way.

A severe critic of the centrally directed aspects of Quebec's economy is Léo-Paul Lauzon, a chartered accountant and accounting professor at the Université du Québec à Montréal. He says that reform is overdue.

> After 30 years of coddling by the state, Quebec's entrepreneurs have to learn to stand on their own. Here in Quebec, the private sector is private in name only. A lot of Quebec companies are on artificial life support, and if the government pulled the plug they would die.[4]

The last section of the chapter will look at this important issue in more detail.

PROGRESS CHECK

- What are three of the five categories of government intervention in the economy?
- What does privatization refer to? Can you cite any examples?
- What are crown corporations? Why are they set up? Can you name three?
- What is Quebec Inc.?

REGISTRATION, REPORTING, AND INFORMATION

Registration

Governments need to know what businesses are in operation in order to ensure that a wide range of laws and regulations are being followed. It is also important to ensure that names of businesses are not duplicated to avoid confusion. In addition, they have to be sure that all taxes are being paid. To achieve these and other goals, every company must register at the appropriate provincial authority when it commences business. This is a simple, routine, and inexpensive procedure.

articles of incorporation The legal documents, obtained from the federal or provincial governments, authorizing a company to operate as a corporation.

In addition, all corporations must obtain **articles of incorporation.** This is legal authorization from the federal or a provincial government permitting a company to use the corporate format. This is usually done through a legal firm and is discussed in detail in chapter 5. Governments, and the public at large, thus have a record of the existence of every corporation in Canada.

Reporting and Information

Businesses receive many documents from governments during the course of the year. Some are just information about changes in unemployment insurance, Canada or Quebec Pension Plan, or tax legislation as it affects them and their employees. Then there are various statistics forms that all companies must complete so that governments can compile reports that businesses, individuals, research organizations, and governments need in order to operate more effectively.

Statistics Canada maintains vast databases that it accumulates from these reports and from many other sources, including international databases. StatsCan issues many quarterly, semi-annual, or annual reports on a host of topics. It also publishes a variety of special reports at irregular intervals. Some of them are quoted in this text.

All corporations must also file annual reports containing basic data about themselves: for example, how many shares have been issued, who the officers and directors are, and where the head office is located. Of course, every company must also file annual tax returns containing financial statements and pay the necessary income and other taxes during the year.

THE TAXATION OF COMPANIES

Each level of government collects some kind of taxes from companies to give it the income it needs to discharge its legal obligations. The main source of income for municipalities is taxes on property, but there are a variety of other taxes and fees as well. Federal and provincial governments rely mostly on income taxes on individuals and corporations. Provincial sales taxes are also an important source of revenue for the provinces (only Alberta has no sales tax), while the Goods and Services Tax (GST) brings very substantial monies to the federal government. In some provinces, Medicare is financed by a tax on the total wages and salaries paid by companies.

Taxes on businesses are considered part of the cost of doing business and thus are included in the prices they charge. Small corporations get a tax break; they pay about half the normal tax rates. Manufacturing corporations also get a reduced rate. Various other fiscal (taxation) devices are discussed in the next section.

Fiscal Measures to Influence The Economy

One purpose of taxation, as we have just seen, is to raise funds for government needs. Governments also use taxation to help the economy move in a desired direction. For example, taxes may be lowered when the economy is weak, in order to stimulate it. Similarly, taxes may be raised when the economy is booming along to cool it off and slow down inflation.

Taxation is often used in more subtle ways to stimulate or restrain various aspects of the economy or the whole economy. This is called **fiscal policy.** For example, to stimulate the economy government may ease the taxation load of the construction industry, a basic industry that affects many others. When that industry begins to move, the spin-off effect means more equipment, vehicles, and material supplies purchased. More homes, offices, and factories built and sold leads to more sales of furniture and appliances and new mortgages and insurance, thus stimulating a wide range of industries and services. When government deems the economy to be overheated and inflation is a problem, it implements the reverse policy.

fiscal policy
The use of taxation to stimulate or restrain various aspects of the economy or the economy as a whole.

Federal and provincial governments constantly use the lever of fiscal policy to stimulate specific geographic and industrial areas. It offers special tax credits to companies that open plants in areas of chronically high unemployment, such as Cape Breton, the Gaspe, or Newfoundland. All companies that invest in specific activities that are considered desirable (a term which varies from time to time but usually includes manufacturing, processing, or scientific research) receive an investment tax credit that reduces the income tax they would normally have to pay.

HOW GOVERNMENTS SPEND TAX DOLLARS TO HELP BUSINESS

Governments in Canada disburse tens of billions of dollars annually in old age pensions, various allowances to low-income families or individuals, unemployment insurance, welfare, workers' compensation, and various other payments to individuals. These vast sums put a lot of consumer buying power into the hands of Canadians. As they spend these dollars, large numbers of Canadian companies and their employees benefit. Governments, in turn, collect taxes on the profits of these companies and on the salaries and wages of their employees. Increasing or lowering the rates or eligibility for these payments results in further fine-tuning of the economy.

Government Purchasing Policies

Most governments are very large purchasers and consumers of goods and services; indeed, in Canada they are the largest buyers. The federal and provincial governments use this enormous purchasing power to favour Canadian companies. The provinces favour those companies in their own territories. They have even set up important trade barriers between provinces (discussed below). When advanced technology items, civilian or military, must be obtained from foreign companies, our governments usually insist that a certain minimum portion must be manufactured in Canada. This enables Canadian companies to acquire advanced technology know-how.

Contracts are awarded most often to help Canadian businesses even if they are sometimes more expensive than bids by non-Canadian companies. This is particularly true in the significant military acquisitions programs. Whatever can be produced or serviced in Canada—ships, electronics, trucks, artillery, personal weaponry, ammunition—is acquired from Canadian companies.

These federal and provincial policies are being modified as a result of the Free Trade Agreement with the U.S. and recent rulings by GATT as part of the general movement to freer trade. Oddly enough, in many cases, it is easier to trade with foreign countries than between provinces. We look at this anomaly next.

No Free Trade between Provinces

The provincial governments have erected walls between the provinces that practically rule out interprovincial government acquisitions. The municipal governments within a province also follow this procedure. These protectionist policies favour the companies in each province but almost eliminate normal free trade and competition. They also create other distortions by insisting, for example, that a beer company must have a plant in the province if it wants to sell beer there. This prevents the normal cost savings that could be achieved with fewer but larger plants. Larger-scale production would result in lower costs, called **economies of scale,** and therefore lower prices to consumers. This would make many Canadian companies more competitive on the international scene, especially with American firms.

economies of scale
The cost savings that result from large-scale production.

A case that drew a lot of attention a few years ago was a paving job in the town of Aylmer, Quebec, near the Ontario border. The town bought bricks from an Ontario company but was forced by the provincial government to pull them up and replace them with Quebec bricks. This is an extreme example of a common problem in Canada. "By one estimate there are more than 500 trade barriers between provinces," according to an article in *The Montreal Gazette*.

> For a country that was supposed to have eliminated barriers to trade 125 years ago, Canada in some ways behaves more like a collection of warring principalities than a single economic unit. Ontario consumers can't buy milk from Quebec or Manitoba. Quebec wouldn't buy busses from an Ontario plant until the plant moved to Quebec. A phone company in one province won't buy telephone wire from another. Nova Scotia's Moosehead beer is readily available in the U.S. but not in other provinces. . . .

At the time of writing, there is mounting pressure for the provinces to end this uneconomic behaviour, which is estimated to cost the Canadian economy up to $6 billion annually. When we are in a severe recession and Canada's ability to compete on the international scene is in doubt, many people believe that we can no longer afford such additional costs.

The question of protectionism comes up regularly at annual meetings of ministers from the provinces. Everybody agrees that something must be done, but as each year passes no detectable changes take place. The reason is clear: removal of barriers would mean a difficult period of adjustment as each province loses jobs due to closing of uncompetitive operations.[5]

PROGRESS CHECK

- What is Statistics Canada? How is it useful to Canadian businesses?
- What is fiscal policy? What are two purposes of the federal taxation system?
- How do government expenditures affect business? What are three broad categories of such expenditures?
- Are there any barriers to trade between the provinces? What developments are going to have an effect on this situation?

Other Government Expenditures

Governments spend huge sums of money on all levels of education, on health, on roads, ports, waterways, airports, and on various other services required by businesses and individuals. They also provide direct aid to business.

There are many direct and indirect government programs that are designed to help businesses. Governments also intervene on an ad hoc (special, unplanned) basis in important cases. The Chrysler and de Havilland cases, discussed later in the chapter, are examples of this. Aid to Saskatchewan farmers and Newfoundland fishermen when their industries faced severe hardships are other examples.

Direct Intervention

All levels of government offer a variety of direct assistance programs to businesses. These include grants, loans, loan guarantees, consulting advice, information, and other aids that are designed to achieve certain purposes. One of the largest special cases occurred early in the 1980s, when a combined Canadian and U.S. government loan guarantee to banks in excess of $1 billion was required to save Chrysler Corp. from collapsing. Had it gone bankrupt, many companies that were creditors of Chrysler would have been dragged down as well and hundreds of thousands of jobs would have been lost in both countries.

Government aid can be provided when industries face hardship. Farmers sometimes receive aid when struck with droughts, floods, or other hardships.

In areas of persistent high unemployment, all levels of government co-operate to attract industries and offices by offering various financial inducements. A municipality may offer reduced or zero property taxes for up to ten years. Federal and provincial governments may allow many kinds of special reductions of income taxes for businesses involved in certain activities or in certain geographic areas. Often long-term interest-free loans are negotiated. Sometimes outright grants are given, based on the number of jobs to be created.

It is common for major companies to hint or even announce outright that they are planning to close a large plant that they claim is not efficient enough to be competitive. They often suggest they will consolidate operations with other plants in Canada or the U.S. This naturally results in a flurry of efforts by all affected parties to attempt to prevent the closure. Unions, municipalities, and provincial and federal governments all work to save the jobs and economies of the area. There are many examples of such cases in the last decade.

Auto plants, pulp and paper mills, food processing plants, oil refineries, shipbuilding yards, meat-packing plants, steel mills, and other industries across the country faced such closures. In many cases this could not be prevented. But the General Motors plant north of Montreal and the de Havilland plant north of Toronto, among others, were saved by such concerted action. (See Spotlight on Big Business.)

A newspaper report shows how the Ontario and federal governments combined with the steelworkers' union, banks, and shareholders to prevent the Algoma Steel mill in Sault Ste. Marie, Ontario, from closing. This involved government aid and employee purchase of the plant.[6] A similar rescue of the troubled Sydney Steel complex in Sydney, Nova Scotia, in 1981 ended with the Nova Scotia government buying the company. In Alberta, the government intervened to keep some meat-packing plants alive.

Many of these rescue efforts end in costly failures. For example, the Nova Scotia government announced in February 1992 that it will have to sell or close Sydney Steel, after having spent almost a billion dollars over a decade to modernize it and to make it competitive. Was it worth it to spend such a sum to provide hundreds of jobs in chronically depressed Cape Breton? Was it the best way to help the unemployed in this area of high unemployment? These types of questions are constantly being asked in Canada.

SPOTLIGHT ON BIG BUSINESS

A Rescue Package for an Ailing Giant

In January 1992, in a joint scheme, the Ontario and federal governments announced a $490 million aid package to facilitate a deal whereby Bombardier Inc. of Montreal bought 51 percent and the Ontario government 49 percent of the shares of de Havilland Aircraft in Toronto to save the company from closing. There were many reasons why saving this company was considered vital. It is the largest employer in the Toronto area, with some 4,500 employees still working there after several reductions in work force. It had the potential to compete globally since the previous owner, giant Boeing Aircraft Co. of the U.S., had spent huge sums acquiring, modernizing, and updating production facilities (with generous grants from both levels of government in Canada). Unfortunately, the deep recession and other factors led Boeing to throw in the towel after several cuts in the work force.

Bombardier had earned a solid reputation with its successful acquisition of similar troubled companies in the U.S. and Northern Ireland in the previous few years. As a result it had become a world leader in the small-aircraft field, which many believe is one of the high-tech industries of the future. In addition, the recession and other factors had seen hundreds of plant closings and hundreds of thousands of jobs lost in Ontario. This combination of social, political, and economic factors led the Ontario and federal governments to ask Bombardier to continue its string of successful takeovers. Bombardier, with its record of sound financial analysis and management, insisted on the substantial aid package from the governments to lay a sound basis for the future of de Havilland.

Sources: Various issues of *The Montreal Gazette* and the *Globe and Mail Report on Business,* January 1992. ▼

In addition to direct intervention, governments are active in aiding various sectors of the economy. Another initiative of note is the establishment of the National Networks of Centres of Excellence program. The minister for science, William Winegard, joined with university, industry, and government researchers, and the presidents of the federal granting councils, to sign the first official agreement for a network. The MicroNet Network on ultra-large scale integration (ULSI) is expected to become the mainstay of the next generation of telecommunications and computer systems.

> The MicroNet agreement reflects a commitment to establish research linkages between academia, industry, and government, a strong determination to expeditiously exploit intellectual property, and a desire to manage research resources in effective and innovative ways.[7]

Other Federal Programs to Help Small Business

The Ministry of Small Business and Tourism has a variety of programs going. There are three to promote entrepreneurship:

- The National Policy on Entrepreneurship supports a range of activities to improve the climate for small business.
- The National Entrepreneurship Awareness Project works to raise public awareness of the social, cultural, and economic benefits of entrepreneurship by helping non-profit organizations undertake activities to promote entrepreneurship.
- The National Entrepreneurship Development Institute is a non-profit body created "to foster entrepreneurship education, to develop entrepreneurship curriculum for all levels of education, and to promote entrepreneurship across the country."[8]

The Ministry of Industry has started a Prosperity Initiative designed to make Canadian business more competitive on the world stage. It has nominated

REACHING BEYOND OUR BORDERS

Aid to High-Technology Companies

The importance of high technology to a modern economy is repeatedly stressed in this book. Governments in Canada are concerned with the progress of companies in these fields. Three ministries play important roles in assisting such companies: International Trade, External Affairs, and Industry, Science and Technology. Together with Investment Canada and in co-operation with research and technology associations, they publish many informative brochures and listings of Canadian companies active in specific fields. They distribute these to companies overseas and arrange meetings with Canadian company representatives.

High Technology Opportunity: If Software Is Your Business, Canadian Partners Can Make the Difference is a glossy, multicoloured brochure with a multilingual introduction. Included in this attractive package is detailed information on 60 software companies with good track records. The aim is to promote joint ventures and other tie-ins in Canada. This is of great benefit to the hundreds of smaller high-tech companies that cannot afford such expenditures themselves.

Sources: Various publications of Investment Canada; Departments of International Trade and Industry, Science and Technology.

prominent people to head up its steering group. Their assignment "is to advance the debate about Canada's strategy for gaining a global competitive advantage."[9]

Chapter 2 listed the many ways governments aid Canadian businesses that wish to export or invest outside of Canada. This extensive aid package plays a major role in helping internationally minded Canadian companies.

Specialized Government Incentive Programs

For many years, the federal government has had some major form of incentive program, under different names and departments, to encourage industrial development in Canada. Currently, this program is under the Department of Industry, Science and Technology (DIST). The heart of this department is the Industrial and Regional Development Program (IRDP).

Canada is a very large country with uneven resources, climate, and geography. This has led to uneven economic development. Ontario and Quebec, which had large populations, proximity to the U.S., an abundance of all kinds of natural resources, and excellent rail and water transport, were the earliest to develop industrially.

Nova Scotia and New Brunswick began to suffer when wooden ships gave way to metal ships in the last century and their lumber industries declined. The west was sparsely populated until well into this century. Alberta and British Columbia became strong industrially only in the last 30 years as oil, gas, coal, hydro-electric power, and forestry became significant competitive resources for them. Saskatchewan and Manitoba are essentially tied to the volatile agricultural industry. Newfoundland, which became part of Canada in 1949 and was far behind the average Canadian living standard, has relied mainly on fisheries and pulp and paper. The Yukon and the Northwest Territories are very lightly populated and have a difficult climate.

A long-standing system of payments (transfers) to poorer provinces, which was financed by the wealthier ones (Ontario, B.C., Alberta), is being gradually reduced by the federal government.

The populated regions that are industrially underdeveloped have high unemployment and lower standards of living. One purpose of DIST is to help those areas by encouraging industries to establish or expand there. We have mentioned Cape

MAKING ETHICAL DECISIONS

You own a small manufacturing company in Ontario. You have recently installed some costly modern equipment. After much effort, you succeeded in getting substantial grants from both the Ontario and federal governments to pay for this equipment as part of a government program to help make Canadian companies more competitive. You will now have greatly reduced production costs, which will allow you to be more competitive internationally.

Your industry association, of which you are an active member, has a policy of urging less government involvement in the economy. You have been asked to speak on this topic at an upcoming association luncheon. You are in a quandary as to what to do because of the contradiction between the benefits you actively sought from government actions and the association's policy. What should you do? What alternatives do you have? ▼

The wide body Canadair Challenger 601-3A business jet features a 3.365 nautical-mile range, fuel-efficient General Electric CF34–3A turbofan engines, and low noise levels that permit it to operate during airport curfew hours. It is suitable for a variety of other roles, such as air ambulance, flight inspection, airborne early warning, maritime surveillance/SAR, and electronic surveillance.

Breton Island in Nova Scotia and the Gaspe in Quebec as two such areas. Regions in other provinces and in Newfoundland, which has a chronically high unemployment rate, have also been targeted.

DIST has four levels of support, each tier offering different amounts of support. It also has a wide range of other programs, among them help to the tourist industry, economic assistance to native Canadians and to residents of remote areas, and small business assistance.

THINKING IT THROUGH

Advances in technology are extremely important in keeping a country globally competitive. Since governments do not have unlimited amounts of money to spend, they may have to focus on a few areas. Would it be wise for Canadian governments to concentrate on advanced technology? Should they, in conjunction with business, pick some high-tech industries and give them substantial support? Should this include a major effort to get more students to pursue scientific and engineering careers?

THE EFFECT OF OTHER LAWS AND REGULATIONS ON BUSINESS

We have seen how provincial and federal governments carry on a wide variety of government activities that affect business. We will now take a closer look at some of the major departments of the federal government that handle these activities. There are corresponding departments in many of the provinces, especially the four largest, most developed ones: Ontario, Quebec, B.C., and Alberta.

Department of Consumer and Corporate Affairs

The Department of Consumer and Corporate Affairs has a major role in regulating business in Canada. It administers a wide variety of acts passed by Parliament. Companies wanting to incorporate federally must apply to this department for articles of incorporation. It maintains a complete registry of all corporations incorporated under federal law. Corporations that do not plan to do business outside of a province apply to that province. Annual reports are required to keep the register up to date; it is open to public inspection.

The department also administers the Competition Act, which aims to make sure that mergers of large corporations will not restrict competition and that fair competition exists among businesses. The act covers discriminatory pricing, price fixing, misleading advertising, and refusal to deal with certain companies, among other activities.

Department of Communications

The Department of Communications is responsible for the Canadian Radio-Television and Telecommunications Commission (CRTC). The CRTC grants licenses to radio stations, TV stations, and cable companies for limited periods, usually one to three years. Public hearings are held at license granting and renewal times so that anyone can criticize or voice opposition to such renewal. The CRTC also regulates the types of programs and the minimum percentage of Canadian content. It must approve at public hearings all rate and service changes of cable and federally incorporated telephone and telegraph companies.

Department of Transportation

The Department of Transportation administers a number of acts, including the Motor Vehicle Transportation Act and the National Transportation Act. These cover all modes of interprovincial transportation in Canada. The National Transportation Agency grants licenses, hears complaints, and makes sure safety regulations are being followed. It has inspectors on the road. (You can sometimes see their cars beside trailer trucks stopped for inspection.)

Finance Department

One of the most influential ministries is the Finance Department. It has overall responsibility for setting tax and financial policy and thus has a major impact on Canadian business. The annual budget presented to Parliament, usually every spring, by the minister of finance is a major event. The budget is a comprehensive document that reveals government financial policies for the coming year. It shows how much revenue the government expects to collect, any changes in income and other taxes, and whether expenditures will exceed income (resulting in a deficit).

The budget speech is usually broadcast live and followed by many interviews and commentaries. The speech is scrutinized carefully by a host of economists, businesspeople, managers, trade unionists, academics, consumer and women's associations, and newspeople to see what impact the budget will have on specific areas of business and on consumers.

Bank of Canada. A major agency of the Finance Department is the Bank of Canada, an independent body run by a board of governors appointed by the government. The minister of finance (or his or her deputy-minister) attends board meetings but has no vote. The Bank of Canada has two main responsibilities. One is to oversee the operations of all federally chartered banks, which means nearly all the banks in Canada. They all report to the Bank of Canada regularly. Some reports are required daily, some weekly, and some monthly.

The second responsibility is to set **monetary policy,** which means to control the supply of money in the country and influence the level of interest rates. (You will remember that another government tool that has a major impact on business is taxation, or fiscal policy). Controlling the supply of money in Canada is very complex and involves a variety of methods. You may be most familiar with the determination of the appropriate level of interest rates at any particular time.

monetary policy
The Bank of Canada's exercise of control over the supply of money and the level of interest rates in the country to influence the economy in a desired direction.

Every Tuesday, the bank announces the rate it will charge commercial banks for borrowings. It is mostly symbolic, as these banks do not do much in the way of borrowing from the Bank of Canada. The bank rate mainly gives the banks guidelines as to whether they should be raising or lowering their interest rates.

Interest rates were a hot topic in Canada in the latter part of the 1980s and the early 1990s. Governor John Crowe of the Bank of Canada had been pursuing a firm policy of trying to reduce inflation by keeping interest rates high. The unpleasant side effects—high costs of business borrowings and a high Canadian dollar relative to the U.S. dollar—translated into high unemployment and other serious problems. There was strong pressure from many premiers of the provinces, various business and union leaders, and other prominent Canadians to soften his policy.

The Bank of Canada, in the nation's capital of Ottawa, Ontario, oversees the operations of all federally chartered banks and sets monetary policy for the country.

The controversy was aggravated by the uneven nature of the problem in different parts of this vast country that is Canada. The main inflationary pressure was coming from southern Ontario, where the economy was booming. But in many other parts of the country, the effects of the 1980–81 recession were still being felt and recovery had not yet really taken place. The Prairies, Atlantic Canada, and parts of Quebec and Ontario were still depressed. To make matters worse, the economy began to deteriorate in 1990 and by the end of 1991 was in a serious recession. Bankruptcies, plant closings, and layoffs were dominating the news as almost daily occurrences.

The high Canadian dollar was a particular irritant because the Free Trade Agreement with the U.S., which came into force in 1989, was supposed to give a big boost to Canadian exports to the United States. By far our largest trading partner, the U.S. accounts for some three-quarters of Canadian exports. The high interest rates were driving the Canadian dollar up, making Canadian goods more costly for Americans to buy.

All of these issues led to demands for a change in policy. Crowe refused to budge and patiently explained why he had to stick with his plan. The minister of finance and the prime minister supported his policy, declaring it necessary to defeat inflation, which they saw as a greater long-term threat to economic stability in Canada. The annual inflation rate dropped to below 3 percent in early 1992 and fell to under 2 percent by late 1992. It remained under 2 percent in 1993. History will have to judge the soundness of Crowe's policy and determine whether costs of unemployment and bankruptcies will be balanced by long-term benefits to the economy of a low inflation rate.

While the Bank of Canada operates independently from the government, if there is ever a wide divergence from broad government policy, the governor of the bank would have to resign. In fact, this has happened only once in the 60 years of the bank's existence.

PROGRESS CHECK

- What are three forms of direct government aid to business? Two forms of indirect aid?
- What are four large companies that owe their existence to such aid? Why was such aid extended?
- How do governments help poorer regions of Canada?
- Why is the Department of Finance so important? What is the annual budget it prepares and why does it attract so much attention?
- What were the effects of the high interest policy of the Bank of Canada? What was the main reason for following this policy?

PROTECTING CONSUMERS

The Department of Consumer and Corporate Affairs administers many laws designed to protect consumers. These laws have a great impact on companies, which must make sure their policies and operations conform with legal requirements. Some of the major consumer protection laws are shown in Figure 3–2.

Canadian Agricultural Products Standards Act covers a wide range of farm products, such as meat, poultry, eggs, maple syrup, honey, and dairy products.

Consumer Packaging and Labelling Act applies to all products not specifically included in other acts.

Food and Drug Act covers a whole range of regulations pertaining to quality, testing, approval, packaging, and labelling.

Hazardous Products Act covers all hazardous products.

National Trademark and True Labelling Act includes not only labelling but also accurate advertising.

Textile Labelling Act includes apparel sizing and many other special areas.

Weights and Measures Act applies to all equipment that measures quantities (scales, gas pumps, etc.).

Figure 3–2 Some major consumer protection laws

All of these acts, and others under the jurisdiction of other federal or provincial departments, are designed to protect and inform consumers. Every time you buy an agricultural product, you are assured that someone has inspected it or a sample of the batch it came from. The list of ingredients and expiration date are there because of a regulation. The same applies to the clothes you wear, which have a label showing country of origin, size, type of fabric, and washing instructions.

Similarly, you are assured that all the food, drugs, toys, and other products you buy do not contain anything hazardous. Whether you buy a kilo of grapes or 25 litres of gasoline, you can feel confident that you have gotten a true measure because there is a sticker on the equipment showing when it was last inspected. The provinces have various laws giving consumers the right to cancel contracts or return goods within a certain time of signing or purchase. It is just about impossible to get through a day without being helped in some way by legislation or regulation. Similarly, a company cannot get through a day without being affected by various laws.

Canada Deposit Insurance Corporation

Another body that plays an important role in protecting the consumer is the Canada Deposit Insurance Corporation. (CDIC). It insures individual deposits in banks and trust companies against these institutions' failure or collapse. The CDIC guarantees deposits up to $60,000. It is funded by annual premium payments from all banks and trust companies that wish to have their customers' deposits insured, which in practice means just about all such financial institutions. The CDIC reports to the chairman of the Treasury Board, who is a minister of state in the government.

The Impact of Municipalities on Business

Municipalities also play a role in consumer protection. They all have regulations and laws regarding any establishment that serves food. Inspectors regularly examine the premises of all restaurants for cleanliness. If you look carefully in your local newspapers, you will see lists of restaurants fined for not maintaining required standards.

There are similar laws about noise, smells, signs, and other activities that may affect a neighbourhood. These are called zoning laws because certain zones are restricted to residences only and others permit only certain "quiet" businesses to operate.

Zoning requirements also limit the height of buildings in certain zones and how far back they must be set from the road. Most Canadian cities require that all high-rise buildings have a certain ratio of garage space so that cars have off-street parking places. Parking problems in residential areas due to overflow of vehicles from adjacent businesses have led to parking being limited to residential permit holders on certain streets, so stores and other places of business must offer commercial parking lots for their customers.

All businesses must usually obtain a municipal licence to operate so the appropriate department may track them to make sure they are following regulations. Many municipalities also have a business tax and charge for water consumption.

Provincial Regulation of Business

The consumer as investor is protected by various laws that lay down the procedures companies must follow to attract investors or lenders by public offerings. Companies seeking public financing must issue a **prospectus,** which provides minimum specified information about the company and its officers and directors to better inform potential investors. This document must be approved by the **securities commission** in the province where public funding is being sought. This is the official body set up by a province to regulate the stock exchange and to approve all new issues of securities.

prospectus
A document, which must be prepared by every public company seeking financing through issue of shares or bonds, that gives the public certain information about the company. It must be approved by the securities commission of the province where these securities will be offered for sale.

securities commission
The official body set up by a province to regulate the stock exchange and to approve all new issues of securities in that province.

It is expensive to produce a prospectus because it requires a lot of input from legal and accounting firms before it can be approved. This cost must be borne by the company that is seeking public financing. There are five stock exchanges in Canada: Toronto, Montreal, Calgary, Vancouver, and Winnipeg and a securities commission in each of the provinces where these cities are located. One of their aims is to ensure that the small investor is not taken advantage of by powerful or unscrupulous companies or individuals. All companies whose shares are listed on the stock exchanges must issue quarterly reports to their shareholders, as well as annual reports. There are many other provisions in these regulations, which vary somewhat from province to province.

One common regulation makes it illegal for *insiders*—those with inside or private information not yet available to the public—to take advantage of that information. They cannot engage in securities transactions (the sale or purchase of stocks and bonds and related instruments), based on inside information, for their personal gain.

For example, suppose your sister told you that her company was about to announce that it had had an unusually profitable period, which would likely send the price of the company's shares up sharply. You rushed to buy some shares; when they rose quickly after the announcement, you sold them and made a nice profit in a few days. This is insider trading and is illegal.

All businesses must comply with the consumer protection requirements that affect them. While this may add to the costs of doing business, everybody is in the same boat, so no company has an edge over any competitor. Furthermore, similar conditions exist in most industrialized countries, so the level playing field extends beyond the borders of Canada. This means that the international competitiveness of Canadian companies is not weakened because of such regulations.

LABOUR STANDARDS AND WORKING CONDITIONS

In later chapters, you will learn about the many federal and provincial laws and regulations that affect companies' conditions of employment. Perhaps we tend to take for granted minimum wages, vacation pay, and a host of other working conditions. Figure 3–3 lists some of the major issues that are affected by legislation.

Figure 3–3 is only a partial list of the legal requirements that employers must meet. The many laws across Canada that protect workers have accumulated over more than 100 years. As the standards of civilized or acceptable behaviour evolved in Canada, laws were passed to reflect these rising expectations. It is a continuing process that sees new developments every few years. One of the most recent issues to evolve is pay equity for women (discussed in Part V).

ENVIRONMENTAL REGULATIONS

Chapter 19 reviews the importance of concerns with the impact of production activities on our physical environment. These concerns have led to regulatory requirements that are changing how companies operate.

We are all well acquainted with many of the serious consequences to our environment of the uncontrolled operations and growth of industry. We are now faced with the huge problems caused by certain dirty industrial processes and the mountains of waste that are an inevitable result of many business operations.

Some environmental problems are product-related. For example, cars are major contributors to pollution, inefficient users of energy, and increasingly less useful for commuting to and from work due to traffic jams. This is what led governments to create ministries of the environment. Now many companies face heavy expenditures of money and managements' energy to become *green,* or environmentally responsible. Some far-sighted companies are developing technology for waste

Figure 3–3 **Aspects of employment affected by legislation**

Banning of child labour.
Minimum wages.
Overtime pay after a normal work week.
Specified number of paid holidays.
Paid vacations of not less than two or three weeks (or equivalent pay if employed less than one year).
No firing without cause after a specified period of employment.
No discrimination by sex, nationality, colour, or religion in hiring, remuneration, promotion, or firing.
Unpaid or paid maternity/paternity leave.
No unhealthy or unsafe working conditions.
No sexual or racial harassment.
Unemployment insurance contributions.
Canada/Quebec Pension Plan contributions.
Workers' compensation for employees injured at work.

Industrial waste is a major problem faced by nations around the globe. The federal and most provincial governments have ministries of the environment that set policy on environmental standards and regulations.

management and energy-efficient operations that will give them important competitive advantages.

EMPLOYMENT AND IMMIGRATION IN CANADA

Another department of the federal government that has a major impact on business is the Department of Employment and Immigration, which has a direct impact on the nature, size, and skills of the work force in Canada. A coherent immigration policy helps to ensure a good inflow of required skills for employers. After all, Canada became a modern industrial country with the aid of the skills and financial capital that immigrants brought here.

Students in community colleges, CEGEPs, and universities are familiar with the employment centres on their campuses. There are many more such centres in cities and towns across Canada where the unemployed register and search for jobs. Employers list their job openings and requirements with the centres, which try to match people with available jobs. One of the anomalies of recent times is that despite the very high number of people who are unemployed or working at part-time or temporary jobs, there are still many jobs that cannot be filled because of the lack of applicants with the necessary skills.

Federal and provincial ministries are involved in manpower training and retraining schemes designed to overcome this problem. Such programs encourage unemployed people to enroll in colleges to upgrade their skills and support them financially during their retraining period. Other manpower programs to train or retrain workers are joint efforts of governments, unions, and employers in varying combinations. Some will be discussed in more detail in later chapters.

Education and training are becoming increasingly important as low-skilled jobs disappear due to automation and to companies moving to the U.S. or Mexico. Rapid changes in technology mean that long-term employment in one job or skill is becoming rare. This issue is forcing increased attention to the whole question of education and training and is capturing a lot of headlines.

Controlling the flow of immigrants to Canada is another major responsibility of the Department of Employment and Immigration. There is much pressure from people in many parts of the world who would like to live in Canada. The department tries to ensure that immigrants have the proper skills or finances to fit into the needs of the Canadian economy. Immigrants have always been a vital factor in the development of Canada and will continue to play an important role. The department must try to find that delicate balance between admitting too many, faster than the economy can absorb, and not admitting enough.

NATIONAL RESEARCH COUNCIL

One of the best-kept Canadian secrets concerns the National Research Council (NRC), a federal agency which came into being in 1916. This organization of some 3,000 scientists, researchers, and technicians is Canada's principal science and technology agency. It plays a significant role in research that helps Canadian industry to remain competitive and innovative. Its Canadian Institute for Scientific and Technical Information (CISTI) has the largest international collection of information on science, technology, and medicine in Canada. CISTI gets about half a million requests for information annually. Subscribers to its online system can access this vast worldwide database directly from their own computer terminals.

The NRC operates the Industrial Research Assistance Program (IRAP) and 16 specialized institutes in some major industries of tomorrow, including biotechnology, industrial materials, environmental science and technology, information technology, automated manufacturing, and microelectronics. Eleven of the institutes are in Ottawa and the other five are spread out from St. John's, Newfoundland, to Vancouver, B.C. Every year thousands of Canadian firms receive technical and financial help through the NRC's industry development programs. Its specialized equipment allows companies to do tests and experiments that would otherwise not be possible. This is especially useful for many smaller high-tech firms.[10]

In 1990, the NRC announced a new industrial R&D group to develop computer-integrated injection moulding technologies.

> The Special Interest Group in Injection Moulding (SIGIM) links NRC's Industrial Materials Institute in Boucherville, P.Q. (outside Montreal), with eight industry partners, two universities (McGill and Ecole Polytechnique), and the Society of the Plastics Industry (SPI). The group will combine NRC's industrial manufacturing expertise with its diverse fields of interest to develop, apply, and transfer new technologies needed by the plastics industry.[11]

During the last few years, the budget and staff of the NRC have been consistently cut. It is unfortunate that funding has been reduced for such an important organization in an era when technological know-how is one of the major competitive tools for business. There are constant complaints that the amount of spending on R&D in Canada is lower than that of any other advanced industrial country. The federal government has repeatedly committed itself to raise the level of R&D spending, which makes it difficult to understand the reduction in NRC funding.

GOVERNMENT IMPACT ON FARMING BUSINESS

marketing boards
Organizations that control the supply and/or pricing of certain agricultural products in Canada.

In Canada we have a special system of **marketing boards,** which control the supply and pricing of certain agricultural products. This supply management is designed to give some stability to an important area of the economy that is normally very volatile. Farmers are subject to conditions that are rather unique and have a great effect on their business and on our food supply. Weather and disease are major factors in the operation of farms that are beyond the control of the individual farmer.

We have experienced periods of severe drought, flooding, severe cold, and disease that affect crops, livestock, and poultry. The situation regarding international markets and supply has a serious impact on Canada's grain farmers, since we export much more wheat than we consume domestically. This market fluctuates greatly depending on the supply in other major grain-exporting countries like the U.S., Argentina, and Australia. It also depends on demand from major importers like China and Russia, whose ability to meet their own requirements is subject to wide variation. Often the Canadian government (like other governments) grants substantial loans with favourable conditions to enable these countries to import our wheat.

As we export some $14 billion of agricultural products annually, ability to hold our own in international markets has a major impact on the state of the Canadian economy. When prairie farmers are flourishing, they buy new equipment and consumer goods and their communities feel the effects of ample cash flow. So does the transportation industry. Conversely, when farmers are suffering—which unfortunately has been the case for most of the 1980s and well into the 1990s—all these sectors hurt as well.

To smooth out the effect of these unusual conditions on this sector of our economy and to ensure a steady supply of food to consumers at reasonable prices, six government agencies have been set up to control poultry, dairy products, and wheat and barley. The Canadian Wheat Board operates in the three prairie provinces and is the sole legal exporter of wheat and barley. It is also the sole sales agent domestically for industrial use of these products. The Canadian Dairy Commission controls the output and pricing of milk and other dairy products. (Both of these boards are crown corporations.)

The Canadian Egg Marketing Agency, Canadian Chicken Marketing Agency, Canadian Turkey Marketing Agency, and Canadian Broiler Hatching Egg Marketing Agency consist of representatives from the provinces that produce these items.

All of these bodies except the Wheat Board control the amount of production for the products under their supervision by allocating quotas to each province that

Marketing boards control the supply and/or pricing of certain agricultural products.

produces them. Provincial agencies administer these quotas and set prices for their province. Each of them controls products that are sold only in its province.

Unless you have a quota, you cannot produce these products for sale to the public. Quotas are purchased from farmers who are willing to sell them. A certain percentage of the quota allocation of each province is usually set aside for new entries.

In the late 1980s and early 1990s, large subsidies by Western European governments allowed their grain farmers to undercut other exporters. The U.S. and Canadian governments were forced to provide similar subsidies to maintain their share of their traditional markets. This effort, which cost the Canadian government billions of dollars, is still a major source of friction between governments.

Supply Management under Attack

A system to manage the supply of agricultural products can be found in many countries, although not necessarily in the same format as in Canada. Various subsidy and indirect support methods can be found almost everywhere. Supply management of farm products is an effective barrier to their entry into Canada, because imports are also subject to the quota system.

The Canadian system of marketing boards has been under attack by various organizations because it does not permit normal competitive conditions to operate in this field. This, they argue, distorts the whole industry and raises prices to Canadian consumers. Defenders of the system argue that other countries, including the U.S., have different systems that have the same effect as our marketing boards but are just less visible.

We referred earlier to the General Agreement on Tariffs and Trade, whose main purpose is to reduce barriers to trade between countries. Many trade experts believe the whole Canadian system of marketing boards may be threatened by the most recent negotiations among the 108 GATT members.

We end the chapter with a closer look at the very important issue of a national industrial policy referred to earlier.

DOES CANADA NEED AN INDUSTRIAL POLICY?

In 1993, Canada was still suffering from a very severe recession that had begun in 1990. Unemployment had passed 11 percent, bankruptcies were at record levels—over 75,000 in 1992—and plant closings and layoffs were regular occurrences. In the 400 days from the end of 1990 to the beginning of 1992, 1,000 jobs per day had been lost—400,000 in all. Manufacturing had been particularly hard hit. And the carnage continued unabated into 1993.

Many companies had asked their remaining employees to take pay cuts so they could continue operating. Shopping malls and downtown shopping streets, suffering from the combined effects of unemployed consumers and consumers stretching fewer dollars by cross-border shopping, displayed an unusual number of vacant storefronts. Many farmers and rural communities were in desperate straits after years of very depressed world prices for grains. Canada's two major airlines were posting record losses and the CNR announced major layoffs, as did other large companies, crown corporations, and governments.

These economic conditions led to continual pressure on governments to do something. In fact, they undertook various ad hoc palliative measures—special payments to farmers and bailouts of certain companies—but more was demanded.

Many experts outside and inside governments, including cabinet ministers, were commenting that Canada was losing its competitive edge.

The solution to all of these problems, according to many people, is for the federal government to develop a long-term industrial policy to lead the country out of its existing problems. An industrial policy means government leadership to develop, in close consultation with business and labour, a comprehensive, long-term program for sustainable industrial development.

Many people are opposed in principle to such government involvement. As mentioned earlier, the 1980s witnessed a movement towards deregulation and less government involvement in Canada and in other countries. But the seriousness of the current economic situation in Canada may bring this issue to the forefront once more.

Those who want government to fashion a strategy to lead us back to prosperity and improve Canada's competitive edge point to other countries where this has worked. The best examples are to be found, they say, in Germany, Japan, and the so-called Four Dragons of East Asia: South Korea, Taiwan, Hong Kong, and Singapore. All of these countries are extremely competitive, have trade surpluses, and developed rapidly economically in the last two decades.

In all of these cases, except for Hong Kong, there is no denying that strong government leadership in planning, prioritizing, and direction has contributed to their success. The question is: Can it work in Canada? We have a different culture; we are a large, dispersed, very diverse, low-density population that rarely unites to pull in the same direction. We have a different history and political structure, so much power is dispersed to provincial centres. We are also a democracy, while the four dragons have a history of dictatorships (ranging from the brutal to the benign in Singapore).

Germany, however, the country with the greatest exports per capita in the world, is a democracy. So is Japan, second only to the U.S. in the size of its economy. Is there anything we can learn from these and other successful countries about the major role of government in the economy? We have seen how Quebec has moved strongly in this direction but, although it worked well in the 1980s, there is now some division of opinion about that path. This question is being increasingly discussed in Canada and even in the U.S., where the concept of *laissez-faire,* or do-nothing, *capitalism* is very strong. But President Clinton seems to be favouring a stronger role for government.

THINKING IT THROUGH

You have seen many examples of government initiatives to aid business in Canada. Do we need an overall strategy to plan where our economy should be going? If so, where is the leadership from our major business organizations? Is this a responsibility of government? How relevant are the successful East Asian countries whose governments pursued such a course?

The prestigious *New York Times* carried an article reviewing the diverse opinions of three economists. Despite their different backgrounds and approaches, and for different reasons, they all conclude that the U.S. government will have to become much more involved in solving the country's serious economic and social problems. They all found that the free market has not been able to solve these problems and, in fact, has contributed to them. Further, they do not agree that such government involvement is necessarily desirable. They simply see no other solution.[12]

Back in Canada, the *Financial Post* also disputes that the free market is the best medium for solving society's economic woes. It says, "The only problem with this laissez-faire notion of the world is that it denies history and reality." It also notes that the management of technology on an international scale is long term, large scale, complex, difficult, and risky—and very costly. That is why governments must be involved.

It gives examples of different countries to show that historically, governments have played an essential role in most major developments.

> The driving force behind many U.S. achievements—from computers to semiconductors to lasers to aerospace—has been military procurement. In Japan it is the government, through the Ministry of International Trade and Industry, which has orchestrated industrial research and development in certain crucial high-tech areas such as super-conductivity. In France the government played a critical role in the development of high-speed trains, the supersonic Concorde, and the commercial jet aircraft Airbus.
>
> It would be difficult to find a major technology company in the world which did not depend on direct or indirect government support and involvement. Whether it's Boeing or Airbus, the "market" has hardly been operating in a free and unfettered manner.

The article ends by reminding readers that Canadian history is replete with many successful "examples of government stepping in to produce solutions when the market couldn't," such as the Canadian Pacific Railway, the trans-Canada pipeline, Ontario Hydro, Polysar, and our wartime industries during World War II.[13]

So we end the chapter where we started it, by looking at the extent of the role that government plays in business. But now we are asking whether it is time to deepen government involvement. What do *you* think?

PROGRESS CHECK

- Can you name four laws that are important for consumer protection? What does the CDIC do? How do all of these affect businesses?
- What is a prospectus? What purpose does it serve? How does it affect companies?
- What are two important functions of the Department of Employment and Immigration? How does that affect businesses in Canada?
- How does the NRC help technology advancement in Canada? Can you give three specific examples?
- What are marketing boards? What area of business is affected by them?

SUMMARY

1. Explain the historical role of government in the Canadian economy.

1. The Canadian government played a key role from the beginning of the country in 1867 in protecting young manufacturing industries and getting the railroad built to the west coast, helping to bind the country together.

- *Why did the government have to do what it did?*

  It had the legal power and responsibility. The U.S. threatened to overwhelm our industry, which was not strong enough by itself to resist or to build the railway.

2. Crown corporations were one way government did its job.

2. List some of the major crown corporations in Canada and understand their role in the economy.

▼ *Why were crown corporations necessary?*

Companies were not willing or able to assume certain responsibilities or fill some needs in the marketplace. The CNR, Air Canada, Hydro Quebec, and Atomic Energy of Canada Ltd. are some important examples.

3. Companies must be properly registered to have a public record of all businesses.

3. Understand how the start-up and operations of companies take place within a framework of government reporting requirements.

▼ *Why is registration necessary?*

Those who do business with a company may want to know who are the owners, when the business started, and other basic information. Governments need to know who is in business to ensure that taxes are paid, statistical data collected, and information supplied.

4. All levels of government impose taxes.

4. Describe how the various types of taxation affect business.

▼ *How do they divide the taxation pie?*

The federal government relies mainly on income taxes and the GST, the provincial on income and sales taxes, and the municipal on property, business, and water taxes and licence fees.

5. Many laws and regulations affect competition in Canada.

5. Identify major legislation affecting competition in Canada.

▼ *What is the major piece of federal legislation?*

The Competition Act is probably the most important act governing competition in Canada.

6. Governments have various methods for stimulating or restraining the economy as they deem it necessary.

6. Discuss the role of government in stimulating or restraining the economy.

▼ *What are their principal tools?*

The two main methods are fiscal policy, which adjusts taxation, and monetary policy, which adjusts interest rates and money supply. Monetary policy is the domain of the Bank of Canada.

7. Canadian society demands a certain level of consumer and investor protection.

7. Understand the role of government in consumer and investor protection.

▼ *How is this achieved?*

Each level of government has legislation designed to give such protection. There is a wide range of laws and regulations supervised by consumer protection divisions in government. Investors are protected by provincial security commissions and the CDIC.

8. All our governments provide incentives to businesses to start up, expand, export, locate in certain areas of high unemployment, or enter high-tech industries.

8. Outline some major government incentives to business.

▼ *What are some of these incentives?*

They include tax holidays, tax reductions, grants, loans, loan guarantees, free consultations, and contacts with potential customers.

9. Protection of the environment has become a major issue today.

9. Identify the role of government in environmental protection.

▼ *How do governments carry out that responsibility?*

Each level has a department concerned with the environment. They set goals and policies, get laws passed to achieve them, and have inspection procedures to ensure implementation. They establish deadlines to give industry time to conform with laws. They also provide information to business and the public at large.

10. Many countries have established industrial policies to guide their development.

10. Understand the controversy about a government industrial policy.

▼ *Why is there controversy in Canada about the desirability of establishing such a policy?*

Most large businesses lean towards a laissez-faire ideology. They are supported in this thinking by some segments of the population. On the other hand, large segments of the country, lean towards greater government participation and direction to resolve Canada's economic woes.

GETTING INVOLVED

1. Scan your local newspapers, the *Financial Times,* the *Financial Post,* or a Canadian magazine like *Canadian Business* for references to government programs of help to Canadian business or a specific company. Bring these articles to class and discuss.
2. At your school library, see if you can find any book or guide that lists all government departments and agencies and what aid they offer to businesses. Can you spot some programs designed to help small businesses?
3. Using the information that you got in the previous suggestion, check out your neighbourhood for businesses that have benefitted from one of those programs. Find out what the reaction has been to the program.
4. Ask your parents, relatives, instructors, and any business owners or managers that you know how they feel about government intervention in the economy. Take an informal poll and see what results you get. This might be a group project where you could compare results with your classmates.
5. Do some research to see how many points you can find to support each side of the argument concerning a government industrial policy.

PRACTICING MANAGEMENT DECISIONS

Case One Max Ward: A Sad Fable of Clipped Wings

The federal government, in partnership with the Business Council on National Issues, spent $1 million or so to fund a study on the sorry state of the Canadian economy by celebrity professor Michael Porter of Harvard University. This lucrative spinoff of Porter's *The Competitive Advantage of Nations* astonished no one with its warnings that Canada's rate of productivity growth is abysmally low and that we scrimp on R&D, fail to search out new markets, and need to set higher standards of quality.

Ottawa then rolled out its own consultation paper on prosperity, which repeated the aforementioned criticisms of business while absolving government for this country's inability to be a global competitor. The government says magic prescriptions will eventually derive from all this costly navel gazing, but only after the expenditure of some $15 million on further consultations. Ottawa might better invest in a few copies of *The Max Ward Story: A Bush Pilot in the Bureaucratic Jungle.*

Max Ward claims that government bureaucrats rather than the hazards of being a bush pilot in the north caused his hair to turn white by the age of 45. His memoirs are a readable, spirited account of life spent wrestling against cold weather in the Northwest Territories and the cold shoulders of regulators and politicians in Ottawa.

His bitterness in the aftermath of the collapse of Wardair, one of Canada's great entrepreneurial adventures, leads to some exaggeration and simplification. Part of his early financing, for example, came from government sources. But Ward scores heavily and entertainingly against our myth of benign big government. He started as a bush pilot in the north, scraping together $10,500 for his first plane in 1946. During the following 40 years he built up a flourishing international charter business carrying almost 1.6 million passengers, with revenues of $474 million in 1985.

He did all this by following all the business and marketing procedures that Porter lists as essential for success, making him an outstanding example of successful entrepreneurship in Canada. He details his endless, frustrating battles with the federal government over many years as he tried to enter the then lucrative and expanding field of regularly scheduled flights as Air Canada and Canadian were biting into the charter business. He claims that Ottawa was out to protect Air Canada and Canadian Airlines from real competition. His attempts to go it alone proved too costly and he was forced to sell his Wardair to Canadian Airlines, which absorbed it, thus losing its identity. He walked away with $70 million.

The real builders of Canada have not been civil servants and their pampered monopolies. They have been hard-working, brilliant individualists like Max Ward. Small consolation that Wardair will fly high in Canadian history books.

Decision Questions

1. Air Canada was a crown corporation at the same time as the government was the regulator of the airline industry. Does the Max Ward story point to a conflict of interest? Can government regulate an industry where it has a major crown corporation?
2. Crown corporations began because business was not prepared to undertake operations in those fields. Are crown corporations still necessary today? Are they essential for a smaller economy to get a start in certain important areas of business activity? Do they help or weaken our competitive ability as a country?
3. Assuming Max Ward's claims are justified, is his an isolated incident or a common story? Does government only hinder business or does it have a positive role to play? Are there any lessons to be learned from other countries?
4. Deregulation of the airline industry has not produced more competition, lower fares, or better service. Should government deregulate other industries? Where is the evidence that less regulation would produce the expected results?

Sources: David Olive, "The Icarus Factor," *Report on Business, Globe and Mail,* February 1992, p. 7; "Max Ward—A Sad Fable of Clipped Wings," *Globe and Mail,* March 1992, p. 58.

Case Two Missing the Market

A few years ago, Randy Powell couldn't have located Kuala Lumpur on the map if his job depended upon it. Today, his job does depend on it and Powell, executive vice-president of BC Gas Inc., not only knows where the capital of Malaysia is, he travels there every year.

Although most BC Gas employees still toil in places like Kamloops and Kelowna, a growing number can be spotted in Southeast Asia and South America. "We have plenty of opportunities in Canada," says Powell, "but this gives us a window on new markets and a chance for employees to broaden their horizons."

In this parochial world of Canadian business, Randy Powell and BC Gas are rare commodities. In recent years Canada has sold a mere 9 percent of its exports to developing countries—about $13 billion a year—compared with 35 percent to 40 percent sold by the Europeans. In 1990, Canada exported about eight times as much to the U.S. as it did to the entire developing world, where four-fifths of the world's population lives. "Canadian companies, by and large, aren't interested in these markets," sighs one federal trade official. "They're so preoccupied with the U.S."

In every developing region in the world, Canada ranks dead last among the G7 countries. In 1990, a paltry 1.62 percent of Canadian exports went to Latin America and the Caribbean; more went to New York State. And only 4.7 percent of our exports went to all of continental Asia, where a young population is driving what is expected to be the world's fastest-growing economic region over the next 20 to 30 years.

Decision Questions

1. Canadian business has been slow to move into the large and very dynamic markets outside of the U.S. Is there a special role here for the Canadian government to direct companies' efforts to these lucrative markets? What exactly could the government do? Is it already doing some of these things?
2. Some people think the problem is due largely to the high percentage of Canadian business that is foreign-owned, mostly by American parent companies. It is these parents that do the exporting to foreign markets. Should government be doing anything about this? What can it do?

3. Is the Free Trade Agreement with the U.S. a factor in turning Canadians' attention more to that country? In the long run, is it healthy to be doing 75 percent to 80 percent of Canada's trade with one country? Won't the FTA drive that percentage even higher? Should the government be doing anything about this problem?
4. A North American Free Trade Agreement is currently being negotiated among the governments of Canada, Mexico, and the U.S. Do you think this will help to make Canadian business reach out more? How may it encourage efforts towards doing business in those other areas referred to above?

Source: John Stackhouse, "Missing the Market," *Report on Business, Globe and Mail,* January 1992, p. 38.

LET'S TALK BUSINESS

1. Canada is constantly subject to pressure of all kinds from our neighbour to the south. Many American states have strong marketing campaigns to attract Canadian businesses. They also offer many inducements, financial and others, to lure businesses to move there. Should anything be done about this? Should our provincial governments be making similar or better offers to keep them here?
2. Cross-border shopping has become a popular activity. Many Canadians regularly head south to buy gas, cigarettes, clothing, and other consumer goods. This drains billions of dollars from the Canadian economy, hurting businesses, jobs, and government tax revenues. What, if anything, should be done about this problem? What can government do?
3. While unemployment remains very high, especially among young people, businesspeople complain that they cannot find trained employees to fill existing vacancies. Job candidates lack math and science backgrounds and their written English language skills are weak. (In Quebec there are similar complaints, but the language problems are French.) Further, too many are high school dropouts. What can be done about this serious problem? Should business or government be working on it? What exactly should they be doing?

LOOKING AHEAD

To understand the language of business, you will have to understand some basic economics. Further, it is important to understand the roots of the Canadian business system. For Canada to prosper in the future, its businesspeople will need a clear understanding of world economic developments. Chapter 4 discusses how economic issues affect business.

HOW ECONOMIC ISSUES AFFECT BUSINESS

LEARNING GOALS

After you have read and studied this chapter, you should be able to:

1. Define economics.
2. Draw a diagram showing the circular flows of money in the international economy and discuss the increasing importance of international economic flows relative to national economics.
3. Discuss Adam Smith's strategy for wealth creation and his basic principles.
4. Outline the basic rights of capitalism.
5. Describe how free markets work, using the terms *supply, demand,* and *prices.*
6. Discuss some limitations of the free market system and what countries are doing to offset those limitations.
7. Show how socialism attempts to solve some of the limitations of capitalism but creates new problems.
8. Describe the effects of the economic system in communist countries and what they mean for world economic development.
9. Examine the mixed economy in Canada and explain its strengths and weaknesses.
10. Define inflation and describe one major measure of inflation.
11. Define recession.
12. Discuss the issues surrounding the national debt.

KEY TERMS

capitalism, p. 110
capitalist system, p. 105
communist system, p. 106
consumer price index (CPI), p. 130
cyclical unemployment, p. 127
demand, p. 112
demand curve, p. 112
depression, p. 131
economics, p. 105
equilibrium point, p. 112
factors of production, p. 105
free market system, p. 110
gross domestic product, p. 124
inflation, p. 129
market price, p. 112
mixed economy, p. 123
monopolistic competition, p. 114
monopoly, p. 115
national debt, p. 132
oligopoly, p. 115
perfect competition, p. 114
productivity, p. 124
recession, p. 131
seasonal unemployment, p. 127
socialist system, p. 106
structural unemployment, p. 127
supply, p. 111
supply curve, p. 111

PROFILE JOSEPH A. SCHUMPETER, ECONOMIST

Joseph A. Schumpeter

Joseph A. Schumpeter (pronounced *Shoom-pater*) was one of the first economists to give a clear explanation of business profits. His doctoral dissertation, "The Theory of Economic Development," became popular and was published in Europe when Schumpeter was only 28. That was back in 1911. The year is significant, because way back then Schumpeter anticipated the rapid structural changes the economy is now experiencing; that is, the rise of innovative small businesses and service organizations.

Schumpeter felt that an expanding economy needed more and more capital investment. The source of that investment was *profit.* Schumpeter felt profits were the only way to maintain jobs and create new ones. He built on the theories of Adam Smith, the father of modern economics, who lived 200 years ago. (You will read more about Smith later in this chapter.)

Later, Schumpeter wrote *The Tax State* to describe the government's power to redistribute income from the productive to the unproductive. He felt such power would lead to political irresponsibility and inflation.

The best-known work of Schumpeter is *Capitalism, Socialism, and Democracy,* published in 1942. In this book, he argued that capitalism would be destroyed by its own success. He felt that, to be popular, a freely elected government would cause the nation to become more and more like the "welfare state." Eventually the government burden and the inflation it caused would destroy both democracy and capitalism.

These questions are still the subject of much debate in many countries. In England, led by former Prime Minister Margaret Thatcher, and in the U.S. under former President Reagan—two politicians who dominated the 1980s—steps were taken to reduce tax rates and to cut government aid to the needy. These policies were often grouped under the name "Reaganomics." While they seemed to give the economies a boost for a while, both countries now have serious problems. England in particular has very high unemployment rates. Although Schumpeter saw the trend toward a welfare state, he did not anticipate the recognition by world governments that such a trend was counterproductive and that major changes would be introduced to reverse the trend. We shall discuss economic trends throughout the world in this chapter, because the nature of the economy has a direct bearing on businesses and consumers.

Source: For a good review of the ideas of Schumpeter, see Peter F. Drucker, "Schumpeter and Keynes," *Forbes,* May 23, 1983, pp. 124–32.

THE IMPORTANCE OF ECONOMICS TO BUSINESS

The success of the Canadian and American systems is based partially on an economic and political climate that allows business to operate freely. Any major change in the economic or political system has a major influence on the business system. The *world* economic situation and world politics also have a major influence on businesses in Canada. Therefore, to understand business, one must also understand basic economics and politics. Most universities require students to take economics courses *before* they take business courses, because economic concepts are the basis for most major business decision making. If you have already studied economics, you will find this chapter an excellent review of how economics affects business.

WHAT IS ECONOMICS?

Economics, says Nobel Prize winner Paul Samuelson, is the study of how society chooses to employ scarce resources to produce goods and services and distribute them for consumption among various competing groups and individuals. You know what it means to "economize" in your own life. We learn to "make do" because we do not have all that we want. The world is in a similar situation.

economics
The study of how society chooses to employ scarce resources to produce various goods and services and distribute them for consumption among various competing groups and individuals.

Allocation of Resources

Economists use the term *factors of production* to refer to the resources used to create wealth. **Factors of production** are the five basic inputs of a society: (1) land (and natural resources), (2) labour, (3) capital (money, machines, tools, and buildings), (4) entrepreneurship (the ability and willingness of business owners and managers to take risks to produce goods and services), and (5) information. In this computer age, businesses cannot operate efficiently or compete globally without a rapid, reliable flow of internal information about costs, sales, and finances, as well as external information about markets, financial conditions, technological advances, competitors' activities, and other important factors affecting business.

factors of production
The basic inputs of a society: land and natural resources, human labour, capital, entrepreneurship, and information.

These factors of production are used to produce goods and services to satisfy our need for food, shelter, clothing, transportation, education, health, recreation, and other wants and needs. The economic questions are "*Who* decides how to allocate those resources?" and "*How* should they be allocated?"

The economic system. Regardless of whether resources are allocated by free markets or government forces or both, the goal is the same—a high standard of living and good quality of life. The question is: What form of allocation creates the best *overall* results?

Different Economic Systems

capitalist system
System in which resources are allocated by consumers and businesses bargaining freely in the marketplace and trading goods and services.

communist system
System in which resource allocation is largely government controlled.

socialist system
System in which resources are allocated partially by the market (the free trade of goods and services) and partially by the government.

How a country answers these questions is what gives a particular name to its economic system. A **capitalist system** is one in which resources are allocated by consumers and companies bargaining freely in the marketplace and then trading their goods and services. Such is the system that prevails in Hong Kong, Switzerland, the U.S., Canada, and many other countries.

In a **communist system,** resource allocation is largely government controlled. That is what we find in Cuba, North Korea, Vietnam, and China. These are sometimes called *command economies* because of the extent of government control.

A **socialist system** is one in which resources are allocated partially by the free trade of goods and services in the market and partially by the government. Sweden and the other Scandinavian countries are in this category. They are sometimes called *welfare states* because of the extent of government involvement in the welfare of its people.

There are two important qualifications to the discussion of economic systems. First, these different types of economic systems are more a matter of degree than a question of absolute differences. Second, each type of system moves constantly along the continuum between pure capitalism and pure communism. England, for example, has moved from a socialist towards a free enterprise system. Russia is completely abandoning the communist system, while China is allowing much more private enterprise. Figure 4–1 shows one version of this spectrum of countries.

There are no pure capitalist, socialist, or communist countries; it is really an issue of the extent of government involvement versus the extent of private ownership and the degree of freedom of the marketplace. Another defining quality of economic systems is the degree to which individuals' health, education, jobs, pensions, and general welfare are provided by the government free or at low cost. In capitalist Canada, we provide higher education at low cost to individuals and medical and hospital facilities at no direct cost to users. Socialist and communist countries provide even more of these services or facilities, usually at no direct cost to individuals.

Even the largest free-enterprise, capitalist country, the United States, has a great deal of government intervention in the workings of the economy. Agriculture, aerospace, aircraft manufacturing, and other major industries could not function without vital direct and indirect government financing and other inputs. Military contracts often contain a disguised form of government subsidies to American industry. It is prudent to look beyond formal names of economic systems to see what the reality is.

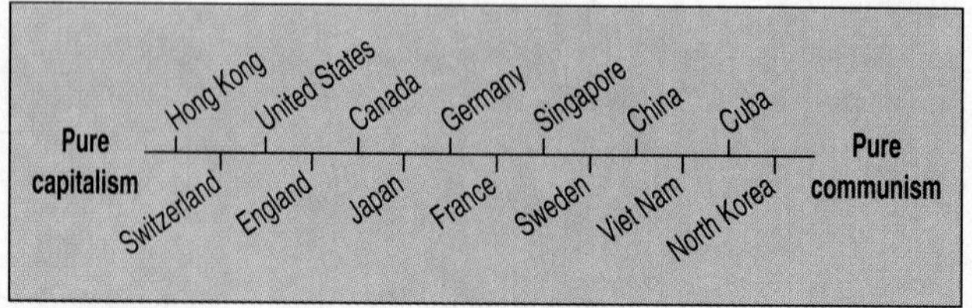

Figure 4–1 One distribution of countries along the capitalist–communist continuum.

Broadly speaking, most countries have recently moved towards less direct government control and ownership and towards a freer marketplace. The former communist Soviet Union has become a series of independent countries determined to establish capitalist-type economies. The same applies to a half-dozen former communist countries in eastern Europe. Communist China and Vietnam are also allowing a freer marketplace and private enterprise.

The Canadian system is closer to the American model but has many features of the welfare state, such as universal old age pensions and a national health system popularly known as *Medicare*. The Canadian model is often called a mixed economy and is typical of that found in many countries towards the centre of Figure 4–1. It is discussed in more detail later in the chapter.

ECONOMIC FLOWS

You and I and all the other people in the world provide businesses with the factors of production we mentioned earlier: land, labour, capital, entrepreneurship, and information. In return, businesses provide us with the goods and services we want and need. Businesses receive money from companies and individuals who become owners. Profits the businesses make belong to the owners and flow back to them through dividends. Thus, there is a circular flow of inputs, outputs, and money between businesses and the public (see Figure 4–2). In addition to the circular flow

Figure 4–2 The three major economic flows

This figure shows the exchange of land, labour, capital, entrepreneurship, and information by the public for wages, goods, services, and profits from business. Businesses also provide the government with goods and services and tax revenues in exchange for government services such as education, and medical services, highways, ports, and so on. The government provides similar services to the public in exchange for taxes. Canadian businesses trade with foreign businesses, and the Canadian public also trades with foreign businesses. Altogether there are three major economic flows: (1) business–consumer flows, (2) government trade with businesses and consumers, and (3) international trade and investment among businesses and between businesses and the public.

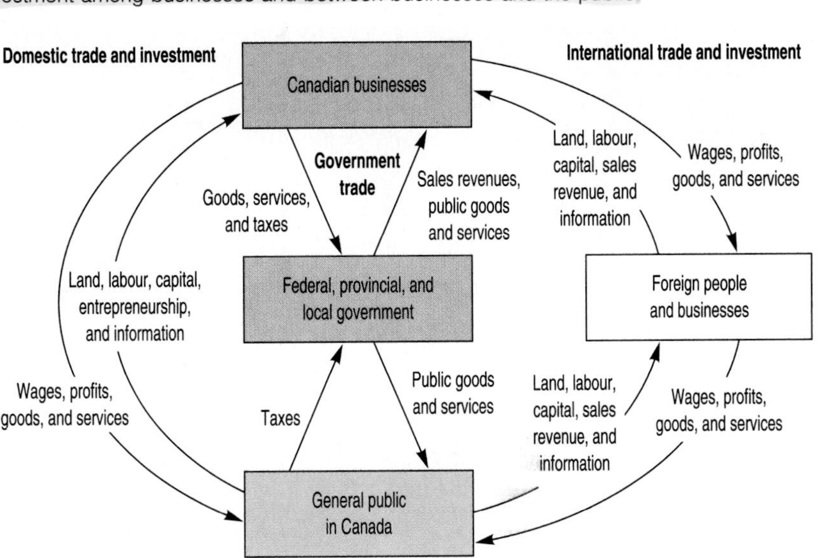

between businesses and the public, there is a flow of money and other resources to the government from the public and businesses that is returned in the form of public goods and services such as roads, schools, military establishments, and hospitals.

Today the Canadian economy is an integral part of the world economy. Business firms use labour from other countries, buy land in other countries for their facilities, and receive money from foreign investors. To understand events in the Canadian economy, therefore, one has to understand the world economy. Figure 4–2 also shows the circular flows between Canadian businesses and businesses of nations throughout the world.

From 1985 to 1990, $125 billion in foreign capital flowed into Canada. Foreign investors have been buying land, companies, and luxury hotels, as well as setting up new companies. They have also been building new factories and financing a large part of the national debt by buying government securities (bonds and treasury bills).[1]

For various reasons, companies find it advantageous to expand outside their home country. Many Canadian assets are cheaper for foreigners to buy because their currency is high in relation to our dollar and because prices for these assets are much higher in their own countries. For example, the famous Chateau Whistler Resort in British Columbia has been bought by a Japanese company, Yamanouchi Pharmaceuticals. A French company bought the very successful Connaught Laboratories in Toronto.

Another reason that foreign investors like to come into Canada is because we have a stable economic and political environment. Investing is risky enough without having to worry about unpredictable dictatorial regimes, massive corruption, and a weak rule of law. The country with the largest investment in Canada by far is the United States. British, Dutch, Japanese, and French companies are also significant investors in Canada. At the same time, billions of dollars are invested outside Canada by Canadian companies.

When Canadians buy Japanese cars, videocassette recorders, and other products, money flows out of the country. It flows back in when Japanese businesspeople buy property such as the Chateau Whistler Resort. Such international flows of money show the importance of international economics.

SPOTLIGHT ON BIG BUSINESS

A Canadian Company Rocks the World of Business

It's not often that a Canadian company sends jitters through world financial markets. But that's what happened with Olympia & York Developments Ltd., the huge holding company for the secretive Reichmann family. The Toronto-based billionaires have been going through tough times lately. Their giant multibillion-dollar empire, invested primarily in real estate in Canada, the U.S. and England, but also in energy, pulp-and-paper, and financial services, has been squeezed by the recession and by huge interest payments on its multibillion debt.

When those troubles caught up with the Reichmanns, the Canadian dollar plunged below 84 cents U.S. Currency traders blamed part of the dollar's decline on rumours that Olympia & York has been having trouble selling commercial paper—short-term IOUs that companies routinely use to finance their operations.

These, and other rumours of possible bankruptcy, spread to the Toronto and New York stock exchanges. Despite company denials, bank shares dropped because of fears that O & Y might not be able to pay the interest on billions in loans to major Canadian and U.S. banks.

Last month, Dominion Bond Rating Service, an agency that gauges the credit risk of corporate securities, downgraded some of Olympia & York's commercial paper, further spooking investors. The Reichmanns' troubles are not new. Over the last couple of years, they've suffered a series of setbacks, including a collapse in the North American real-estate market, a decline in oil and newsprint prices, and a disastrous $635-million loan to failed developer Campeau Corp.

The biggest problem remains the $3 billion U.S. they've sunk into Canary Wharf, the largest commercial development in Europe, being built in London's decayed Docklands area. The Reichmann brothers have bet the company on Canary Wharf, and it could be a very expensive roll of the dice. The project is just now starting to generate some cash flow.

The real-estate market in London is "extremely weak," the rating agency said. Canary Wharf could still be a winner. It's close to downtown London and it's much more modern and efficient than most London office towers. Over the longer term, Canary Wharf could become one of Europe's premier office complexes. But the Reichmanns will have to survive a difficult period first.

Source: Peter Hadekel, *The Montreal Gazette,* March 7, 1992, p. D1.

[Since this article appeared O & Y has been forced into bankruptcy in Canada, the U.S., and England. It is one of the largest international bankruptcies ever, and creditor bankers from many of the world's largest banks are trying to untangle a very complex situation. The Reichmann story dominated the world financial press for many months.] ▼

PROGRESS CHECK

- What are the factors of production?
- What are the three major circular flows that together make up the Canadian economic system?
- What are the main differences between the capitalist, socialist and communist systems?

CAPITALIST ECONOMICS: A FREE MARKET SYSTEM

The year was 1776. A Scotsman named Adam Smith published his book *An Inquiry into the Nature and Causes of the Wealth of Nations.* He espoused the importance of freedom and the power of *economic* freedom.

Smith felt the freedom to compete was vital to the survival of any economy. He believed that people would work hard if they knew they would be rewarded for doing so. He made the desire for money (*capital*) the foundation of his theory. According to Smith, as long as farmers, labourers, and businesspeople could see economic reward for their efforts, they would work long hours. As a result of these efforts, the economy would prosper, with plenty of food to eat and products of all kinds available to buy. As people try to improve their *own* situation in life, like an *invisible hand* the economy grows and prospers through the production of needed goods, services, and ideas. The invisible hand turns self-directed gain into social and economic benefits for all.

The name used to describe Smith's powerful new economic system, based on economic freedom and incentives, was capitalism. **Capitalism** is an economic system in which all or most of the means of production and distribution (for example, land, factories, railroads, and stores) are privately owned and operated for profit. Wealth is distributed by the workings of the market.

capitalism
Economic system in which all or most of the means of production and distribution are privately owned and operated for profit.

Individuals living in a capitalist system have certain basic rights. These include:

- The right to private property. This is the most fundamental of all rights under capitalism. It means that people can buy, sell, and use land, buildings, machinery, inventions, and other forms of property, and pass the property on to their children.
- The right to make and keep all profits, after taxes, of a business.
- The right to freedom of competition. Within certain guidelines established by the government, a company is free to compete with new products, promotions, and other strategies.
- The right to freedom of choice. People are free to choose where they want to work and whether or not they will join a union.
- Other freedoms of choice include where to live and what to buy or sell.

One of the most important features of capitalism is free markets. Let's see why in the next section.

How Free Markets Work

A **free market system** is one in which decisions about what to produce and in what quantities are decided by the market, that is, by buyers and sellers freely negotiating prices for goods and services.

free market system
System in which decisions about what to produce and in what quantities are decided by the market; that is, by buyers and sellers freely negotiating prices for goods and services.

You and I and other consumers in Canada and other free market countries send signals to tell producers what to make, how many, in what colour, and so on. The way we do that is by going to the store and buying products and services. For example, if all of us decided we wanted more fish (rather than red meat), we would signal fishermen to catch more fish. The message is sent by the *price*. As the demand for fish goes up, the price goes up as well, because people are willing to pay more. Fishers notice this price increase and know they can make more money by catching more fish. Furthermore, more people go fishing. These are people who previously could not make a profit fishing but now can because of the higher price. The kind of fish they go for depends on the kind of fish we prefer (request in the store).

The same process occurs with all products. The *price* tells producers how much to produce. As a consequence, there is rarely a long-term shortage of goods in Canada. If anything were wanted but not available, the price would tend to go up until someone would begin making or importing that product or sell the ones they already had, given free markets.

How Prices Are Determined

Prices are not determined by sellers alone. Rather, they are determined by buyers and sellers negotiating in the marketplace. A seller may want to receive $10 a pound

A simple supply line showing the quantity of fish supplied at different prices. The supply line rises from left to right. Think it through. The higher the price of fish goes (the left margin), the greater the quantity that the fish industry will be willing to supply.

Figure 4–3 Supply line for fish quantities

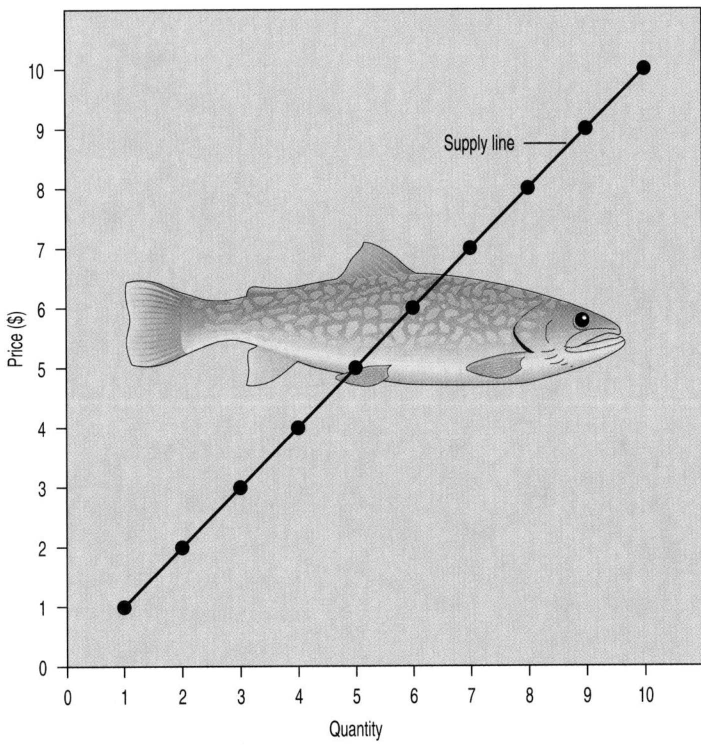

for fish, but the quantity demanded at that price may be quite low. The lower the price the seller charges, the higher the quantity demanded is likely to be. Many more people can and will buy fish at $1 a pound than at $10 a pound. How is a price determined that is acceptable to both buyers and sellers? The answer is found in the economic concepts of supply and demand.

Supply. The quantity of products that manufacturers or owners are willing to sell at different prices at a specific time is called **supply.** Generally speaking, the amount supplied will increase as the price increases. Economists usually show this relationship between quantity supplied and price on a graph. Figure 4–3 shows a simple supply curve. The various points on the graph indicate how many fish a fisher would provide at different prices. For example, at a price of $2, a seller would provide only two fish, but at $8, he or she would supply eight fish. The line connecting the dots is a supply line or **supply curve.*** It indicates the relationship between the price and the quantity supplied. All things being equal, the higher the price, the more product sellers will be willing to supply.

supply
The quantity of products that manufacturers or owners are willing to sell at different prices at a specific time.

supply curve
Line on a graph that shows the relationship between price and the quantity supplied.

*Such lines are usually curved but are shown straight to keep the example easier to understand.

Figure 4–4 Demand line for fish prices

A simple demand line showing the quantity of fish demanded at different prices. The demand line falls from left to right. It is easy to understand why. The higher the price of fish, the lower the quantity demanded. As the price falls, the quantity demanded goes up.

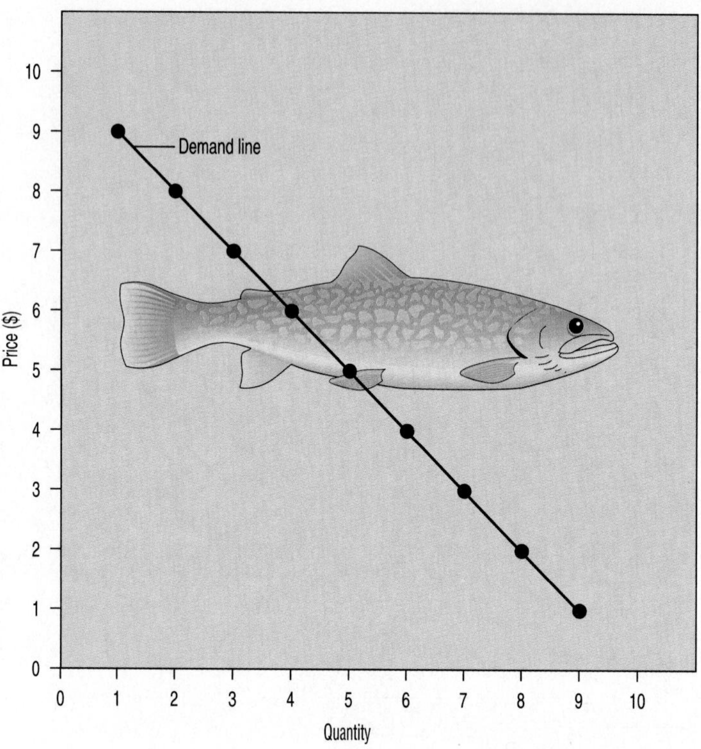

demand
The quantity of products that people are willing to buy at different prices at a specific time.

Demand. The quantity of products that people are willing to buy at different prices at a specific time is called the **demand.** Generally speaking, the quantity demanded will decrease as the price increases. Again, the relationship between price and quantity demanded can be shown in a graph. Figure 4–4 shows a simple demand line. The various points on the graph indicate the quantity demanded at various prices. For example, at a price of $8, the quantity demanded is just two fish. But if the price were $2, the quantity demanded would increase to eight. The line connecting the dots is a **demand curve.** It shows the relationship between quantity demanded and price.

demand curve
Line on a graph that shows the relationship between quantity demanded and price.

Equilibrium point. It should be clear to you after reviewing the graphs that the key factor in determining supply and demand is price. Sellers prefer a high price and buyers prefer a low price, all other things being equal. If you were to lay the two graphs on top of one another, the supply line and the demand line would cross. At that crossing point, the quantity demanded and the quantity supplied would be equal. Figure 4–5 illustrates that point. At a price of $5, the quantity demanded and the quantity supplied are equal. This **equilibrium point** will become the market price. **Market price,** then, is determined by supply and demand.

equilibrium point
Point at which supply and demand are equal.

market price
Price determined by supply and demand.

What would happen if the seller moved his or her price up to $6? At that price, the buyer would be willing to buy only four fish, but the seller would be willing to

Figure 4–5 Equilibrium point

The interaction of quantity demanded and supplied at the equilibrium point. When we put supply and demand lines on one graph, we find that they intersect at a price where the quantity supplied and the quantity demanded are equal. This is therefore called the equilibrium point. In the long run, the market price will tend towards the equilibrium point.

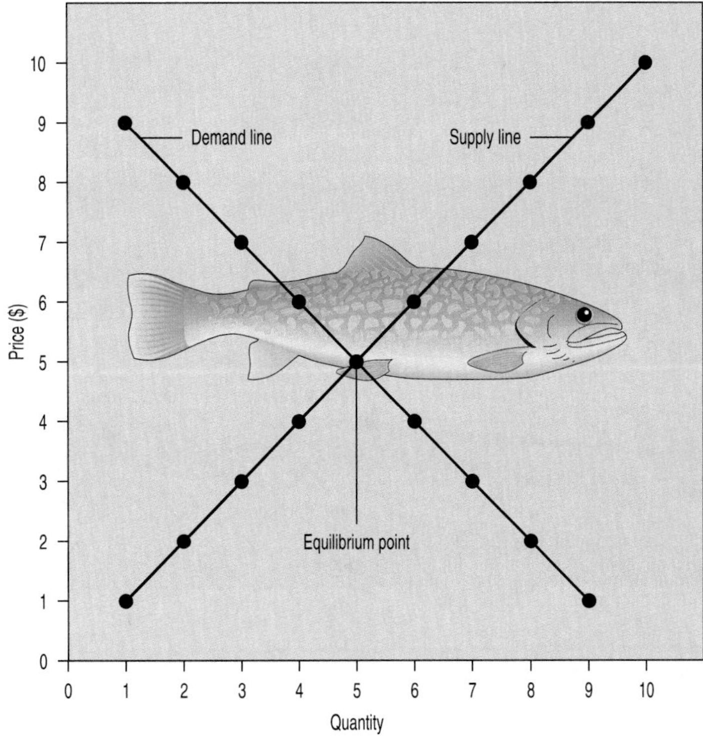

sell six fish. Similarly, if the price were cut to $4, then buyers would be willing to buy six fish, but sellers would be willing to sell only four. In a free market, prices will always tend toward the equilibrium price.

In theory, it is the interaction between supply and demand, then, that determines the market price in the long run. Proponents of a free market would thus argue there is no need for government involvement or government planning. If surpluses develop, a signal is sent to sellers to lower the price. If shortages develop, a signal is sent to sellers to increase the price. Eventually, supply will again equal demand if nothing interferes with market forces. In practice, large-scale government intervention is often required to keep the economy operating without undesirable side effects. (This was discussed in detail in Chapter 3.)

Competition in a Free Market System

Competition is a cornerstone of the free market system. In Canada, the Competition Policy Division of the Consumer and Corporate Affairs Department serves as a watchdog to ensure that competition among sellers flows freely and new competitors have open access to the market. However, competition exists in different degrees, ranging from perfect to nonexistent. Economists generally agree on four

The focus of supply and demand ultimately sets the price you see at the fish market. When there is a huge oil spill in Alaska, you can expect the supply of fish to fall and the price to rise. The high demand for fish today has pushed the price rather high. I'm sure you've noticed.

classifications of competition: (1) perfect competition, (2) monopolistic competition, (3) oligopoly, and (4) monopoly.

perfect competition
The market situation where there are many buyers and sellers and no seller or buyer is large enough to dictate the price of a product.

Perfect competition is said to exist when there are many buyers and sellers in a market and no seller or buyer is large enough to dictate the price of a product. Under perfect competition, sellers produce products that appear to be identical. Agricultural products are often considered to be the closest examples of perfect competition at work. For example, a consumer would be content to buy cucumbers from either farm A or farm B, since there is little or no difference between cucumbers and the prices are the same. Why are the prices the same? Remember, no seller or buyer is large enough to dictate the price of a product. Price is determined according to the principles of supply and demand. Under perfect competition, the market is guided by Adam Smith's invisible hand theory.

There are few examples of perfect competition. Today, government price supports and drastic reductions in the number of farms make it hard to argue that even farming is an example of perfect competition. Can you think of any products or services in your area where perfect competition exists?

monopolistic competition
The market situation where a large number of sellers produce similar products, but the products are perceived by buyers as different.

Monopolistic competition exists when a large number of sellers produce products that are very similar but are *perceived* by buyers as different. Under monopolistic competition, product differentiation (the attempt to make buyers think similar products are different in some way) is a key to success. Think about what that means for just a moment. Through tactics such as advertising, branding, and packaging, sellers try to convince buyers that *their* product is different from competitors'. Actually, the competitive products may be similar or even interchangeable. Jeans are a good example of this. One seller may inform consumers that wearing its product gives the right image, a competitor promises better quality, still

In competitive markets, some businesses succeed and some fail. Going-out-of-business sales are common, but so are new start-ups. The market rewards those who provide the best value and ignores those who do not.

another competitor offers the best price. The buyer selects a particular brand as superior even though any of the three products would do the job well. Prices are set by individual sellers.

An **oligopoly** is a form of competition in which a market is dominated by just a few sellers. Generally, oligopolies exist in industries such as steel, automobiles, aluminum, gasoline, and aircraft. One reason some industries remain in the hands of a few sellers is that the initial investment to enter an oligopolistic industry is tremendous. Think what it would cost to build a steel mill or an automobile assembly plant. In an oligopoly, prices are generally similar rather than competitive. The reason for this is simple. Intense price competition would lower profits for all the competitors, since a price cut on the part of one producer would most likely be matched by the others. Product differentiation rather than price difference is usually the major factor in market success.

oligopoly
A form of competition where the market is dominated by just a few sellers.

A **monopoly** occurs when there is only one seller for a product or service. Both the price and supply of a product are controlled by the single seller. In Canada, laws prohibit the creation of monopolies. However, the legal system does permit approved monopolies such as public utilities that sell gas and electric power or telephone service. These utilities' prices and profits are usually regulated by public service commissions that protect the interests of buyers.

monopoly
A market in which there is only one seller.

World Markets: Supply and Demand

Every day, billions of consumers throughout the world are sending signals to millions of producers throughout the world telling them what they want. The signals are sent by the amount of goods and services being bought. The signals are sent very quickly, so there should be little delay in ending surpluses and shortages. In the real world, there are many interferences to the free exchange of goods and services among countries. Consequently, some countries have surpluses (for example, Canada has a surplus of many crops) and others suffer from scarcity (many countries do not have sufficient food). A free market system would seem to be the best system for improving the world's economic condition. Given the advantages of such a system, there must be offsetting disadvantages or else the world would consist only of united free market countries.

Limitations of the Free Market System

The free market system, with its freedom and incentives, was a major factor in creating the wealth that some advanced countries now enjoy. Some even talk of the free market system as a true economic miracle. On the other hand, certain inequities seem to be inherent in the system. Rich people can buy almost everything that they need, and poor people cannot. We shall explore how this happens and then we'll discuss what can be done about it.

Picture a market with buyers all willing to *buy* one unit of a commodity (for example, a large steak), but with each person willing to pay a different *price*. Picture also 10 sellers who are calling to *sell,* but at different prices. Figure 4–6 shows how this market might look.

As you can see, the price where supply equals demand (the equilibrium point) is $6. If the steak were priced at $6, there would be no excess supply nor any excess demand. But notice this also. At the price of $6, there are some buyers who want steak but are shut out by the market. All the buyers willing to pay from $1 to $5 (the majority) don't get what they want. Similarly, all the sellers who were willing to sell at prices from $7 to $11 are effectively shut out from the market. The market thus *excludes* buyers with too little money and sellers that cannot survive at low prices.

Thus, we have the situation where many people cannot afford enough food or adequate housing. The same thing is true with health care, clothing, and other goods and services. The wealthy seem to get all they need, and the poor get less than they need. Furthermore, there is rising crime in Canada, including white-collar crime by business executives. There seem to be problems controlling pornography, prostitution, and drugs. The hunger for *economic* freedom may lead to too much negative *social* behaviours. Many people feel that free markets do not foster moral and ethical behaviour. This is not true to the same extent in all capitalist countries, however. It is possible to have economic freedom and tight controls on social behavior. Such actions are usually dependent on the particular culture.

When people criticize the results of capitalism, they are saying, in effect, that they do not approve of the price mechanism (free markets) as the *only* means for allocating resources and regulating the economy. This is because of the unpleasant side effects in society—poverty, unemployment, discrimination, environmental damage, and lack of ethics in decision making.

Figure 4–6 Buyers and sellers at different prices

						Equilibrium Point					
Price	$11	$10	$9	$8	$7	$6	$5	$4	$3	$2	$ 1
Number willing to buy a steak at this price	0	1	2	3	4	5	6	7	8	9	10
Number willing to sell a steak at this price	10	9	8	7	6	5	4	3	2	1	0

The number of buyers and sellers at different prices. Five people are willing to buy or sell a steak for $6. Most people prefer bargain prices.

Free markets brought prosperity to Canada, but they also brought inequality. That inequality has caused much national tension. In the search to achieve more equality, the government has intervened in the free market system to create more social fairness and a more even distribution of wealth.

Governments at the local, provincial, and federal levels take a large share of total national output and reallocate it to create more equality. Some money goes to build and maintain roads, bridges, and ports, some to health care and schools, some to help those who are unemployed, some to disabled people, and so on. The economic question becomes how much money should be available to the government to allocate for the defense of the country and for social welfare and how much should be left to free market forces to provide incentives for more output. If more is left to business, then the economic pie may grow and there will be more money to spread around. But if too much money is allocated by free markets, then some people may suffer.

What is the proper blend of government and free markets and freedom of behaviour? That is the question. We shall discuss such issues in greater depth later in the chapter. Before we do, let's review what other countries have done to allocate scarce resources. One alternative system is socialism. Socialism is an interesting contrast, because it is a combination of free market allocation and government allocation.

THINKING IT THROUGH ▼

How much government involvement should there be in an economy? How important is freedom versus equality? How much control should the government have over ownership and operation of production and distribution facilities? How much of the wealth of a nation should go to support those in need? Should government give direct aid to the poor, or should it provide incentives to businesses to provide jobs—or both? Should government regulate sensitive activities such as banking, insurance, the stock market, and airlines? What should the role of government be in regulating pornography, music, movies, and the moral and ethical behaviour of its citizens? These are the issues that businesses and governments face throughout the world.

PROGRESS CHECK

- What did Adam Smith believe were the two keys to economic success?
- What are the basic foundations of a free market system?
- Can you explain how supply, demand, and the price system tell producers how much to make and what to make? What happens if a producer makes too many items? What happens if a producer makes fewer items than are needed?
- What are three negative consequences of basing an economy totally on a free market system?

SOCIALISM: ALLOCATION OF RESOURCES BY THE MARKET AND THE GOVERNMENT

The United States could be the economic model for the rest of the world. Adam Smith's free market economic principles are clearly a means to prosperity. How is it, then, that many countries, rich and poor, have adopted socialism as their economic model? If free market capitalism is to expand worldwide and create prosperity for all the world's citizens, capitalism will have to prove itself a better system *overall.*

What is capitalism's weak point in the eyes of the world? One answer is *equality.* Capitalism needs to meet the needs of *all* people, especially the poor, the sick, the old, and the unemployed, if it wants to win the hearts and votes of citizens in other countries. Socialist systems have tried to address these problems. However, some argue they may go too far in letting government allocate resources. Let us look at a few examples.

Denmark

In Denmark during the 1980s, two-thirds of the population were sustained by the state. A breadwinner with a meagre salary paid at least 55 percent in taxes and top tax *rates* were as much as 73 percent. A plumber who charged $20 for a job paid $4 in sales taxes, $5 in income tax, and $8 for expenses, leaving him or her $3.[2] That was perceived as unfair for the people who worked hard to make a living in Denmark. One-third of the people were supporting two-thirds. As a consequence, tax rates were recently lowered from a top rate of 73 percent to 68 percent. Denmark feels that certain functions such as health care are better provided by the state. Thus, the government needs more money to provide such services.

Denmark does not like to call its system socialist because most businesses are still privately owned. Nonetheless, the government is highly involved in allocating resources, as it would be under socialism. Danes prefer the term *welfare-state capitalism* to describe their system. It is basically a capitalist system with a socialist component. Whatever term is used the result is a country with much more of its resources allocated by the government. This is one definition of socialism.

Sweden

In Sweden, the government benefits seem good. To minimize unemployment, the government pays $5.25 per hour towards the wages of workers who would otherwise be laid off. Hospital care is just $4 a day. Dental care for children is free. But, as they say, "There's no such thing as a free lunch." A person who makes more than $31,000 in Sweden pays 50 cents of each additional dollar he or she earns to the government. For those Swedes who make $26,000 or less, the top tax rate is 30 percent.[3]

In socialist countries, the government sometimes gets the bulk of the money people make and allocates that money back to people in the form of social services. You are usually given more care by the government than under capitalism, but you have less discretion in how you spend your money. This, of course, is a good deal to those who are in the bottom half of society, but is not nearly as attractive to people who make a lot of money.

The goal of socialist countries, therefore, is to provide enough freedom to stimulate initiative and still provide social benefits that are more generous than in capitalist countries. The problem is in finding the right balance between government and private industry.

Sweden and Denmark continue to be efficient, competitive countries with a very high standard of living. But like many other countries, they are finding it harder to compete in the tougher, globalized business climate.

Africa

Many African countries, from Algeria in the north to Tanzania, Mozambique, and Angola in the south, chose the socialist route for development. Most are now abandoning this approach because it did not work too well due to a series of complex reasons. These included inefficient and corrupt dictatorships, lack of experience, wars, badly thought-out, large-project, world-aid plans, and tribal and religious differences. These African governments are moving to a freer market, more like a capitalist economy, but will probably differ from the Canadian and U.S. models.

COMMUNISM: ALLOCATION OF RESOURCES MOSTLY BY THE GOVERNMENT

Karl Marx, the 19th-century economist, wrote that capitalism would lead to the economic exploitation of the working class by an elite class that would control the factors of production. He forecasted a worldwide class struggle that would eventually do away with all traces of private property. The result would be all people sharing a nation's resources under the direction of strong central government. He called this system of state control of industry and resources communism.

The first communist country, the Soviet Union, was established in 1917. Others, in Europe and Asia, came into being after World War II in the late 1940s. The most important of these was China. Communism made some important initial improvements in the quality of people's lives because their living standards were deplorably low in nearly all respects, including health, housing, food, and education. However, these gains were achieved at a terrible cost of many lives in ruthless, dictatorial rule.

At the beginning this was accepted by most of the people because they finally had peace, food, and an end to revolutions, civil wars, invasions, and gross corruption. There was also no unemployment because everybody had a job whether they did much work or not. Costs and profits were not a consideration. Gradually, however, the negative aspects of communism began to outweigh the positive. Since nearly all major activities, from business to health, were run by the government, a massive civil service was created to do this work. Such a vast government bureaucracy crushed all initiative and also led to tremendous corruption and cynicism as the elite at the top reserved the best of everything for themselves.

The improvement in peoples' living standards in capitalist countries in Europe and North America gradually became known to the people of China and the Soviet Union through TV, films, books, magazines, computers, and faxes. As more and more officials, scientists, students, and others travelled to the U.S., Canada, or other capitalist countries, they saw with their own eyes the vast differences between conditions in their own country and the outside world.

The shock was all the greater because for years they had been fed propaganda that conditions were terrible in capitalist countries. Their controlled media had played up all the negative features of U.S. society: crime, drugs, homelessness, poverty, a declining educational system, and more. They totally ignored such positive aspects as the general standard of living, democracy, and freedom to travel.

In addition, conditions were deteriorating in communist countries. Ordinary consumer goods were becoming harder to find. Communist countries had always stressed industrial development, education, and health rather than consumer goods. The Soviet Union, like the U.S., spent untold trillions of dollars on military hardware, supplies, personnel, and bases. But unlike the U.S., it could not also supply a vast array of consumer goods. There were shortages of all sorts—food, clothing, housing, to say nothing of luxuries. Bribery and corruption to obtain goods and services were rampant. It was also becoming clear that the communist countries were not keeping up with the technological changes that were rapidly transforming capitalist countries into advanced producing countries.

Changes in China

The combined effects of these and other factors led to a major change in policy of some Chinese leaders in the late 1970s. They openly admitted that their country had to adopt some capitalist features, such as private ownership of factories and farms, producing for private profit, and more freedom. Significant changes began to occur in China. However, traditional communist leaders fought these radical changes, so progress was slow and uneven.

Eventually these hard-line leaders won out, and in June 1989 they brutally suppressed a month-long student-led demonstration in the capital, Beijing, that was demanding more democracy and an end to corruption. For the moment, the political clock has been turned back in China, but major reforms are still proceeding on the economic front. How long economic freedom can grow without coming into conflict with lack of political freedom remains to be seen.

A Quiet Revolution in the Soviet Union

In the Soviet Union, radical changes were proposed in the mid-1980s by a new generation of leaders led by a bold president, Mikhail Gorbachev. He proposed both political and economic reforms to democratize the Soviet Union and move to a free market economy. He described conditions in his country at the time:

> The Soviet Union, the world's biggest producer of steel, raw materials, fuel and energy has shortfalls in them due to wasteful or inefficient use. . . . We have the largest number of doctors and hospital beds per thousand of population and, at the same time, there are glaring shortcomings in our health services.[4]

Decay began in public morals. Alcoholism, drug addiction, and crime were growing. One major problem, as in all communist countries, is that prices for goods and services were set arbitrarily without regard to the cost of producing them. The ideology dictated that necessities should be priced low enough that everybody would have access to them. So rent, electricity, gas, food, and all transportation costs were very cheap.

While people approved of making the basics available to all, there was no incentive to produce enough of these and other services and products. The huge bureaucracy and the lack of democracy gave rise to tremendous corruption and crushed all initiative, so the economy went backwards while the needs of the population grew. The result was a breakdown. People had to wait years to get an apartment, so if they married they had to live with parents or in-laws in a small apartment. Many families had to share kitchens and telephones. There was an interminable wait for plumbers and electricians. To get a car might take six years.

In 1991, the old rulers were overthrown and the Soviet Union ceased to exist, so Gorbachev lost his job. The various republics are now independent countries and are firmly set on the road to a free market economy, though this historic conversion will doubtless be rocky.

When asked whether most Soviets understand the link between high prices and more plentiful supply, Leonid Abalkin, the man in charge of restructuring the Soviet economy, said:

> No, they don't. In the coming two to three years, we will reform the entire pricing system. It will certainly involve increases in prices of meat and dairy products. There will be some confusion. We hope to convince our people of the need for price reform, but this is a problem that will take some time to resolve.[5]

REACHING BEYOND OUR BORDERS

Opportunities for Canadian Business

The collapse of the communist system in Eastern Europe and in the former Soviet Union has opened up a vast market for investment and exports. The people are in such a hurry to develop modern industry and to obtain food and consumer goods that the demands are almost limitless. Add to this the widespread environmental mess that was left behind and a weak infrastructure—transportation, financial, and communication systems—and the total capital investment required is staggering.

For perspective, look at the amount of money West Germany has had to pour into the former communist East Germany. A small area of some 18 million people has already sucked in hundreds of billions of dollars in a couple of years and will continue to require such infusion for some years. German officials, economists, bankers, and industrial leaders admit they underestimated the vast amounts of capital that would be required to bring the former East Germany up to the high standards of the rest of the country.

The other former communist countries have a population of 400 million people, with a huge territory that stretches from Europe across the huge expanse of new republics to the Pacific Ocean. There we encounter China and Vietnam (1.2 billion and 55 million people, respectively), two communist countries that are very open to investment from and trade with capitalist countries. All in all, some one and three-quarter *billion* people have a great thirst for our capital investments, our know-how, our products, and our services!

The great barrier to trade is their inability to pay for imports. Recently the Russians were having trouble paying for Canadian wheat imports despite large Canadian government loans. Even their ships that arrive at Canadian ports to take delivery of the wheat are seized by other creditors for non-payment of bills. In June 1992, President Boris Yeltsin asked for more aid from Canada, which was agreed to by the government.

The barriers to investment are many and complex. Laws relating to ownership, taxation, environment, working conditions, contracts, legal actions, and withdrawals of profit are either non-existent or just being formulated. The attitudes of people to working hard, to private profit, to accumulation of wealth will have to undergo a significant shift. Management has no experience and knowledge of such basic concepts as *costs, efficiency, profits, competition,* and so on.

Another major roadblock to investment is the question of political stability. Companies shy away from investing in uncertain political climates. The news media have carried many reports of the difficulty these countries are having in establishing democratic governments that have good support from their people. Poland has had about a dozen governments in three years. In former Yugoslavia, violent military conflicts have caused thousands of deaths and destroyed much property. Transportation, communication, and economic life in general are almost at a standstill. Several of the former Soviet republics are experiencing civil wars.

Canadian companies have started to nibble cautiously at this vast, complex, challenging market, and so far they are showing mixed results. It will not be an easy road to travel, but the opportunities for trade and investment are so great that an increasing number of companies will probably venture into these countries. Other countries are doing the same, and we do not want to be left behind. ▼

The very unstable political and economic climate in Russia in late 1993 makes Abalkin's comment about "some confusion" one of the great understatements of recent times.

Communism Disappears in Eastern Europe

The former communist countries in Eastern Europe—Hungary, Poland, Czechoslovakia, Romania, Bulgaria, Yugoslavia, and Albania—all face the same problems as they start down the slow, complex, uncharted paths towards a mixed economy type of capitalism. These countries will likely undergo massive unemployment and high inflation as they painfully adjust to a market-driven economy. Czechoslovakia has split into two republics and Yugoslavia is going through a tragic civil war that has torn that country apart.

Figure 4–7 compares the various economic systems. These descriptions are more theoretical than real. In practice there are wide variations. The most common format is the mixed economy.

Figure 4–7 Comparison of economic systems.

	Capitalism	Mixed Economy	Socialism	Communism
Social and economic goals	Private ownership of land and business. Liberty and the pursuit of happiness. Free trade. Emphasis on freedom and the profit motive for economic growth.	Private ownership of land and business with government regulation. Government control of some institutions (e.g., health care). High taxation for the common welfare. Emphasis on balancing freedom and equality.	Public and private ownership of major businesses. Private ownership of smaller businesses and shops. Government control of education, health care, utilities, mining, transportation, and media. Very high taxation. Emphasis on equality.	Little private property. Public ownership of factories. Centralization of communication and transportation with the state. No rights of inheritance. Free education and health care. Emphasis on equality.
Motivation of workers	Much incentive to work efficiently and hard because profits are retained by owners. Workers are rewarded for high productivity.	Incentives are similar to capitalism except in government-owned enterprises, which have few incentives. High marginal taxes can discourage overtime work.	Capitalist incentives exist in private businesses. Government control of wages in public institutions limits incentives.	Worker incentives come largely from within. The idea is "To each according to his or her need." Some incentives are being introduced by the state and some free enterprise is encouraged.
Control over markets	Complete freedom of trade within and among nations. No government control of markets.	Some government control of trade within and among nations (trade protectionism). Government regulation to assure fair trade within the country.	Some markets are controlled by the government and some are free. Trade restrictions among nations vary and include some free trade agreements.	Central control of markets and production.
Choices in the market	A wide variety of goods and services are available. Almost no scarcity or oversupply exists for long because supply and demand control the market.	Similar to capitalism, but scarcity and oversupply may be caused by government involvement in the market (e.g., subsidies for farms).	Variety in the marketplace varies considerably from country to country. Choice is directly related to government involvement in markets.	Often very limited variety in the market. Scarcities common. Response to market demand and market changes very slow.
Social freedoms	Freedom of speech, press, assembly, religion, job choice, movement, and elections.	Similar to capitalism. Separation of church and state may limit religious practices in schools.	Similar to mixed economy. Governments may restrict job choice, movement among countries, and who may attend upper-level schools (i.e., college).	Government control of press. Limited freedom of speech, religion, and assembly. Often difficult to emigrate or to move from one district to another—restricted travel. Almost no free elections.

MIXED ECONOMIES: ALLOCATION OF RESOURCES BY FREE MARKETS WITH GOVERNMENT REGULATION

Canada is not a purely capitalist nation. Rather, it has a **mixed economy;** that is, a combination of free markets plus government allocation of resources. As a mixed economy, Canada falls somewhere between a pure capitalist state and a socialist state. This is probably the most common economic system in the world today. The degree of government involvement in the economy is a matter of some debate.

mixed economy
An economy that combines free markets with some government allocation of resources.

Several features have played a major role in Canada's becoming an independent economic entity with a high percentage of government involvement in the economy.

First, we are one of the largest countries in the world geographically, but we have a small population (27 million in 1992). This means we have one of the lowest population densities in the world.

Most important, our neighbour to the south has 10 times our population and an economy even greater than that proportion, speaks our language, is very aggressive economically, and is the most powerful country in the world. This means the U.S. exerts a very powerful influence on Canada. To control our own destiny, Canadian governments have passed many laws and regulations to make sure significant economic institutions such as banks, insurance companies, and radio and TV stations remain under Canadian control. (Even powerful countries like the U.S. and Japan have similar regulations.)

All of these factors led to the Canadian capitalist system taking on many characteristics of a mixed economy. Massive government support was necessary to build our first national rail line, the CPR, in the 1880s. When air transport was beginning in the 1930s, no company wanted to risk investing in it in such a large country with only 10 million people spread thinly across the land. So the government set up Air Canada (then called Trans Canada Airlines) to transport mail, people, and freight. There are many such examples of government action to protect the national interest.

In the 1980s, many countries, including Canada, began to reduce government involvement in and regulation of the economy. This trend towards deregulation is widespread. In Canada, airlines, banks, and the trucking industry have all seen a marked reduction in regulatory control. Even in Communist China there have been movements in this direction.

We have seen how the former communist countries of Europe and the republics of the former Soviet Union are moving rapidly in this direction as well. It may not be an exaggeration to say that communism is disappearing as it moves towards mixed economies, socialist countries towards less mixed economies, and mixed economies towards purer capitalist systems.

PROGRESS CHECK

- What are some of the potential negative social consequences of introducing freer markets into countries such as China and the former Soviet Union?
- What is a mixed economy? What are its advantages over a free market economy?
- What does deregulation mean and how is it affecting the economy of Canada?

ECONOMICS AND BUSINESS

The strength of the economy has a tremendous effect on business. When the economy is strong and growing, most businesses prosper and almost everyone benefits through plentiful jobs, reasonably good wages, and sufficient revenues for the government to provide needed goods and services. When the economy is weak, however, businesses are weakened as well, employment and wages may fall, and government revenues may decline as a result.

Because business and the economy are so closely linked, business newspapers and magazines are full of economic terms and concepts. It is virtually impossible to read such business reports with much understanding unless you are familiar with the economic concepts and terms being used. One purpose of this chapter is to help you learn additional economic concepts, terms, and issues—the kind that you will be seeing daily if you read the business press, as we encourage you to do.

Gross Domestic Product[6]

gross domestic product (GDP)
The total value of a country's output of goods and services in a given year.

Almost every discussion about a nation's economy is based on **gross domestic product (GDP),** the total value of a country's output of goods and services in a given year. It is good for GDP to grow, but not too fast or too slow.

From 1979 to 1989, Canada's GDP grew about 3.2 percent annually. That compares with 4.3 percent in the 1970s and 5.2 percent in the 1960s. Clearly growth is slowing, but the country is at the end of one of the longest periods of economic growth in its history. We started the 1990s in a period of recession, but average GDP growth rate for the 1990s is forecast to be 2.7 percent annually.

One way to increase the GDP is to increase productivity. To stay competitive with other countries, Canadian companies must increase their productivity. In 1989, productivity grew by 1.5 percent—about the same as the previous four years. The predicted annual rate of growth for the 1990s is about 0.7 percent, which is not enough to get the economy booming again.

Distribution of GDP

The money that is earned from producing goods and services goes to the employees who produce them, to the people who own the businesses, and to governments in the form of taxes. The size of the share that goes to governments has a major impact on the economy as a whole. The general trend worldwide is for governments to reduce their share of GDP. There is a constant debate in Canada (and other countries) as to what percentage of the GDP pie should go to governments to most favourably affect the economy.

It is difficult to make comparisons between countries, because the right percentage depends on what services each government provides. For example, in Canada our national health care system is financed by taxes. In the U.S. there is no such universal plan, so taxes are lower but individuals and companies must pay these costs themselves.

Productivity And Labour Cost

productivity
The total output of goods and services in a given period of time divided by work hours (output per work hour).

Productivity is measured by dividing the total output of goods and services of a given quality by the total hours of labour required to produce them. A similar calculation is done for countries to compare their rates of productivity. An increase in productivity is achieved by (1) producing a *greater* quantity of a certain quality for a *given* amount of work hours or (2) producing the *same* quantity with *fewer* work hours.

Workers in manufacturing are highly productive because of machinery like this. In the service sector, workers are not as productive because they have fewer machines. As service workers get more robots, computers, and other machinery, their productivity will increase. Nonetheless, it will be important to measure service quality as well as quantity.

Labour cost measures the same equation in dollars. The dollar value of the output is divided by the dollar value of the work hours to arrive at the labour cost per unit. Anything that increases productivity or reduces labour cost makes a business, and a country, more competitive. The great gains in productivity that have occurred during the last century, especially in the last few decades, are due mainly to the introduction of increasingly efficient machinery, equipment, and processes. The 1980s in particular saw computers and robots play a major role in this development.

Any country that does not keep up with the international level of technological improvements falls behind in the fierce global competitive battle. In Canada this is a major problem, because our businesses are spending less on research and development than many advanced countries.

Of course, technological advances usually lead to people being replaced by machines. This often contributes to unemployment. We will now examine this important question.

- Can you define gross domestic product? Productivity? Labour cost?
- How can productivity be improved and labour cost decreased?
- Why is productivity so important to a country's ability to compete?

PROGRESS CHECK

The Issue of Unemployment

For more than a decade, Canada's official unemployment rate has ranged from 7.5 to 11.8 percent. (See Figure 4–8.) This means that officially 1 million to 1.5 million

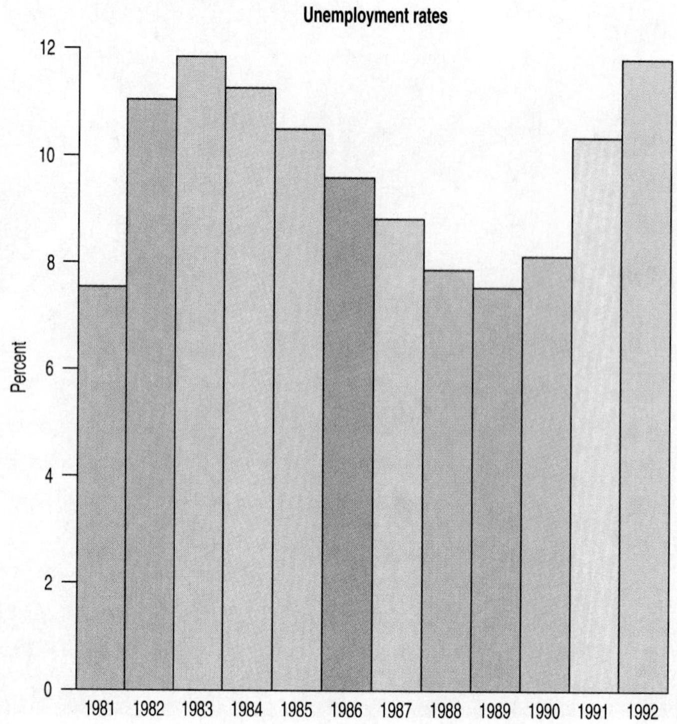

Figure 4–8 Unemployment rates fluctuated between 7.5% and 11.8% from 1981 to 1992.

people were constantly out of work. The real rate is much higher because Statistics Canada does not include people who have given up looking for jobs, those who are working at part-time or temporary jobs or who stay in or return to school because they cannot find full-time work, and various other categories of people. If you work at least one hour per week, you are classified as employed.

People are unemployed in Canada for various reasons. Perhaps their employer goes out of business or their company cuts staff because sales are down. Young persons enter the job market looking for their first job and employees quit their jobs but have trouble finding new ones. Companies merge and jobs are consolidated or trimmed. Companies transfer their operations to another country or a branch of a foreign company is closed down. There are many reasons people may be out of work. Of course, in a period of economic recession (for example, the early 1980s or early 1990s), unemployment increases.

An important cause of unemployment is technological advances. When a company acquires a new machine that replaces five existing machines, each tended by one person, then four of the employees may no longer be required. When computer terminals are installed at the desks of senior managers, they may need fewer middle managers and secretaries. They can now access and send information directly. This creates *technological unemployment.*

Technology can lower costs for companies, making them more competitive and perhaps able to expand and hire more people in the future. In fact, while we are now more automated than ever before, we also have more people working than ever before. So while people are constantly being displaced by machines, eventually new jobs are created. And somebody has to make and service those new machines.

From the economic point of view, unemployment is a great waste of resources. It means that labour that could be producing goods or services is producing

This art student tries to earn tuition fees during a jobless summer by creating street art. Unemployment rates in Canada were in the 12 percent range in 1993.

nothing—and receiving unemployment insurance or welfare. This reduces GDP. The terrible human cost of continued unemployment—the lack of funds and the demoralization that can destroy individuals and families must also be considered. Retraining our unemployed citizens to become more skilled and thus help the country become more competitive is a necessity.

Categories of Unemployment

Cyclical unemployment is caused by a recession or similar downturn in the business cycle. Unemployment fluctuates with the economic cycles of boom and recession that occur regularly in capitalist economies.

cyclical unemployment
Unemployment caused by a recession or similar downturn in the business cycle.

Seasonal unemployment arises in those industries where the demand for labour varies with the season. For example, ski hills employ very few people in summer. Summer resorts and children's camps do not employ anyone in winter. The Christmas season sees an increase in retail jobs. Summer is a much bigger tourist season in Canada than winter.

seasonal unemployment
Unemployment that occurs where the demand for labour varies over the year.

Structural unemployment results from changes in the structure of the economy that phase out certain industries or jobs. Employees of fish plants in the Atlantic provinces are laid off when fish catches are reduced or fishing banned to rebuild cod stocks. Our shift from a manufacturing-based economy to a service-dominated one is a major structural cause of unemployment. This is further aggravated as manufacturers restructure to meet strong international competition. In general, Canada is moving from a resource-based to a knowledge-based economy.

structural unemployment
Unemployment caused by people losing jobs because their occupation is no longer part of the main structure of the economy.

Employees laid off in a tire plant in Ontario do not have the skills to be employed in a forestry company in B.C. that is trying to hire more staff. There is an unfilled demand for knowledge workers in computer software and other aspects of information technology. Retraining programs may help unemployed people to acquire new skills.

Regional differences. Finally, since Canada is such a large country with regional economies, there are always major regional differences. For example, when the auto and related businesses were booming in Ontario in the mid-1980s, the Atlantic provinces were enduring unemployment rates in the 15 percent range. The rate was much higher in Newfoundland and in specific areas such as Cape Breton. When B.C. was booming in the early 1990s, Quebec and Ontario underwent a serious decline and high unemployment. Saskatchewan has been suffering a decade-long problem of unfair foreign competition in the grain market due to massive government subsidies of competing countries' farmers. The regional unemployment picture can be seen in Figure 4–9.

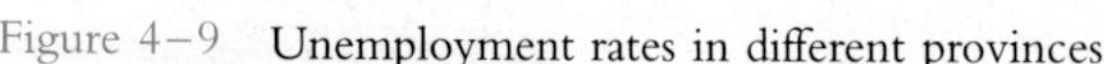

THINKING IT THROUGH

Would Canada be better off today if we had not introduced modern farm machinery? There would be more people employed on the farm if we had not. Would the world be better off in the future if we did not introduce new computers, robots, and machinery? They do take away jobs in the short run. What happened to the farmers who were displaced by machines? What will happen to today's workers who are being replaced by machines?

Unemployment Insurance (UI)

In Canada, the Unemployment Insurance Commission administers the system of compensation to unemployed people. Nearly all employees and all employers must contribute to the fund. Employers pay 40 percent more than employees. When you are unemployed, you qualify to receive payments for almost a year if you meet certain conditions. The fund is really designed to tide you over between jobs. You are also paid while you attend an approved retraining program.

In times of recession, the fund gets depleted; in prosperous times, it gets built up again. Because Canada has had two substantial recessions since 1981, the fund has been emptied—$18 billion was paid out in 1991 alone. So the government has

Figure 4–9 Unemployment rates in different provinces

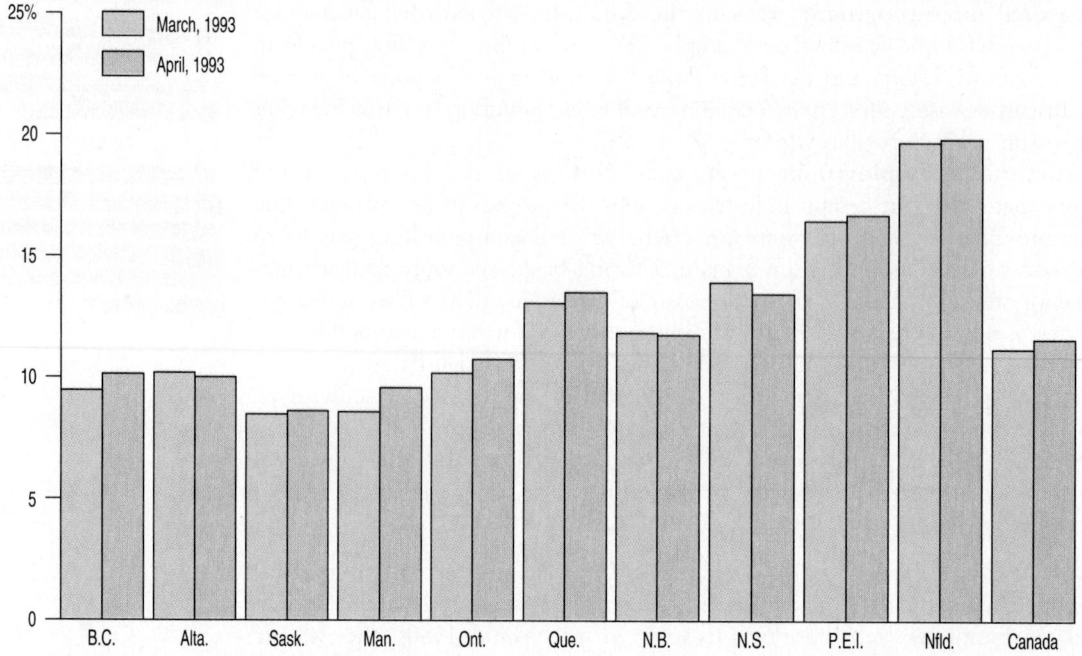

several times been forced to raise the amounts that employees and employers pay to finance the fund. In 1992 and 1993 it also had to lend the fund billions of dollars to meet the shortfall, thus increasing the national debt. To reduce payouts, the government has made it harder to qualify for UI. It also pays less and for shorter periods. The rules are more generous in areas with persistent high unemployment.

There is an ongoing controversy as to whether UI payments discourage people from taking jobs, especially low-paying ones. Another issue is the question of UI fraud (people drawing benefits illegally). Many polls and statistics show that both of these issues are greatly exaggerated. The ratio of fraud to payments is extremely small, and most people would rather work than draw UI.

PROGRESS CHECK

- Can you explain the differences between seasonal, structural, and cyclical unemployment? Which is causing the largest unemployment today?
- What are regional differences in unemployment? Why do they exist?

Inflation and the Consumer Price Index

One of the measures of how an economy is doing is its ability to control inflation. **Inflation** refers to a general rise in the price level of goods and service over time. Since the early 1970s, Canada's inflation rate has been substantially above 3 percent. The rate peaked in 1981 at 12.5 percent. It then hovered in the range of 4 to 6

inflation
A general rise in the prices of goods and services over time.

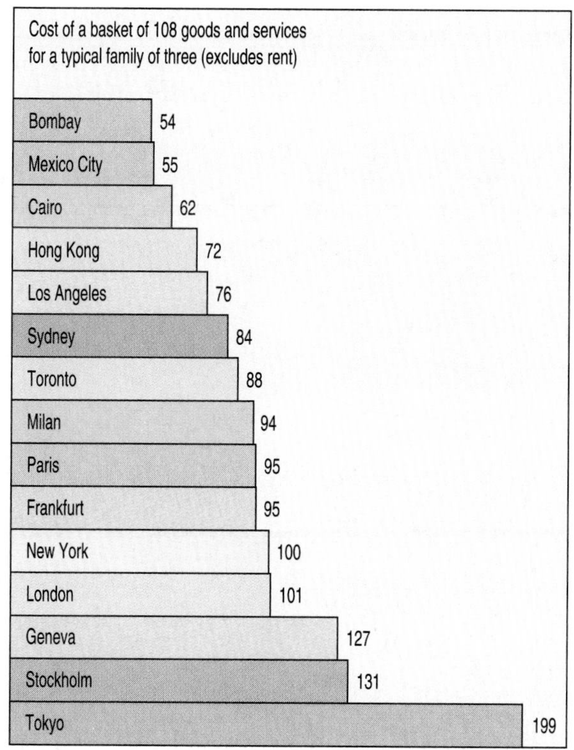

Source: Reprinted from November 7, 1988, issue of *Business Week* by special permission, copyright © 1988 by McGraw-Hill, Inc.

Note that living costs are more than twice as high in Tokyo, Japan, as they are in Toronto. On the other hand, living costs in Bombay, India, and Mexico City are less than two thirds of Toronto.

percent until 1992, when it dropped below 2 percent. The question of inflation has been a central issue in Canada for almost 20 years. Economists do not agree about the causes of inflation, the specific cures, or whether the cures might be worse than the disease.

Why is the issue of inflation so important? Imagine you have $10,000 and you are considering buying a Ford Escort. Instead of buying the car you buy Canada Savings Bonds and earn interest every year, which you use for some cash income while you are at school. Five years later you get a job and decide to cash in your bonds to buy that Ford Escort. You take your $10,000 and go to the car dealer, but you are shocked to find that this same car now costs $13,000 because of inflation over the last five years. One serious effect of inflation is the reduction in the value of a country's currency.

Inflation raises the cost of doing business. When a company borrows money, interest costs are higher, employees demand increases to keep up with the rise in cost of living, suppliers raise their prices, and as a result the company is forced to raise its prices. If other countries are successful in keeping their inflation rates down, then Canadian companies become less competitive on the world market.

consumer price index (CPI) Monthly statistics that measure changes in the prices of a basket of goods and services that consumers buy.

One popular measure of price changes over time (inflation indicators) is the consumer price index (CPI). The **consumer price index** measures changes in the prices of a basket of goods and services for an average family over time. Such an index gives a vivid picture of the effects of inflation on consumer prices. If the cost of the "market basket" is $1,000 one month and goes up to $1,006 the next, it is said that the inflation rate was 0.6 percent for the month, or roughly 7.2 percent annually. At that rate, the cost of consumer goods would double in about 10 years. Figure 4–10 shows the whole CPI picture from 1981 to 1991.

The consumer price index is calculated monthly by Statistics Canada and published widely. It is very closely followed because many companies and government programs base their salary and payment increases on it.

Figure 4–10 These figures indicate that a Canadian's income had to rise by 67 percent from 1981 to 1991 just to keep up with the rise in the CPI.

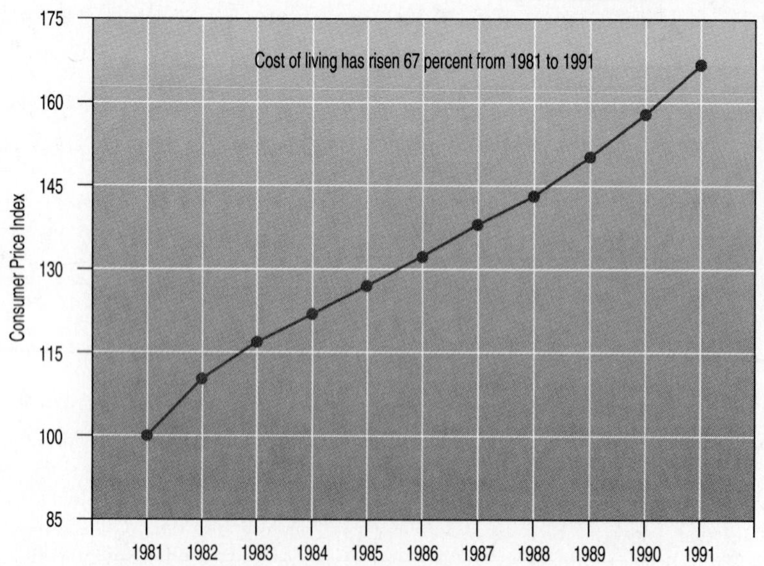

Sources: *Bank of Canada Review,* Table H11, July 1991 *Consumer Price Index,* Cat. no. 62-001, Statistics Canada, December 1991, p. 7.

Inflation and the Rule of 72

No formula is more useful for understanding inflation than the rule of 72. Basically, the idea is to compute quickly how long it takes the cost of goods and services to double at various compounded rates of growth. For example, if houses were increasing in cost at 9 percent a year, how long would it take for the price of a home to double? The answer is easy to calculate. Simply divide the annual increase (9 percent) into 72 and you get the number of years it takes to double the price (eight years). If houses go up in price by 12 percent, it takes only 6 years for the price to double (72/12 = 6), and so on. Of course, the same calculation can be used to predict how high food prices will go or the price of a car 10 years from now.

THINKING IT THROUGH

If annual tuition fees are $2,500 today, how much will it cost today's 4-year-old to go to school 14 years from now, if college or university costs go up 10 percent a year? The answer is that college or university costs will quadruple, so the cost will be $10,000 a year! Are you ready for that?

Recession versus Inflation

A **recession** is defined as two consecutive quarters of decline in the GDP. When unemployment climbs, prices fall, and businesses begin to fail, a recession has begun. A recession has severe consequences for an economy: high unemployment, business failures, and an overall drop in living standards. For years (since the 1930s, when the Great Depression occurred), the government has put much effort into preventing another recession or depression. A **depression** is a severe recession. Whenever business has slowed or unemployment increased, the government has pumped money into the economy to revive it.

recession
Two consecutive quarters of decline in the GDP.

depression
A severe form of recession.

The Canadian government becomes concerned when inflation exceeds 4 or 5 percent. However, these figures must be put in some perspective. In 1988, inflation in Brazil was 1,000 percent; in Peru, it was over 10,000 percent[7]; and in Nicaragua it was 20,000 percent.[8] Inflation rates like these can destroy a country's economy and businesses. Such rates also set the stage for major revolutions. In Germany, inflation rates in 1923 were unbelievable. The price of coffee or bread often doubled in an *hour!* At the height of the problem, a loaf of bread cost 200 *billion* marks. People had to carry baskets filled with money to buy groceries. Is it any wonder that Germany today is *very* concerned about preventing inflation?

GOVERNMENT INTERVENTION IN THE ECONOMY

Prior to the 1930s, governments in capitalist countries, including Canada, generally followed a policy of interfering as little as possible in the operations of their economies. But as the decade wore on, it became clear that a very serious economic depression had gripped most of the world. It was the worst economic crisis in modern times. Hundreds of millions of people were out of work, factories closed, farmers were desperate, most of the world was going to bed hungry every night. Something had to be done. The situation in Canada has been referred to as the Hungry Thirties and the Dirty Thirties.

Keynesian Economics

It was at this time that governments began to turn to John Maynard Keynes (pronounced *Canes*) for advice. He, like his father before him, was an economist at Cambridge University in England. His theories were a radical departure from those of Adam Smith, which had served as a basic guide for capitalist countries for over 150 years. Keynes's policies made him one of the most famous economists of this century.

John Maynard Keynes

You will recall that Adam Smith believed that the economy would automatically function at its best with *minimal* government intervention. This seemed to work more or less for about 150 years. But it was obviously no longer working, given the severe crisis that showed no signs of letting up. In fact, things were getting worse every year.

Keynes wanted to stabilize the economy by careful government intervention on a regular basis. He said government must use *fiscal policy* to achieve this. That is, he believed that inflation could be slowed by increasing taxes and/or lowering government spending. If unemployment got too high—which was now the main problem—he proposed the reverse policy: cutting taxes and/or increasing government spending. This latter policy is called *deficit financing* because governments must borrow to finance their spending. These loans would be repaid in good times when governments had a surplus of funds from higher taxes and lower spending.

These strategies, which became known as *Keynesian economics,* seemed to work. They became the guiding philosophy for many governments—England, Canada, and the U.S. included—for half a century. Keynes still has many supporters, but some say he is outdated. They advocate less government intervention, which seems to be the current trend.

The National Debt

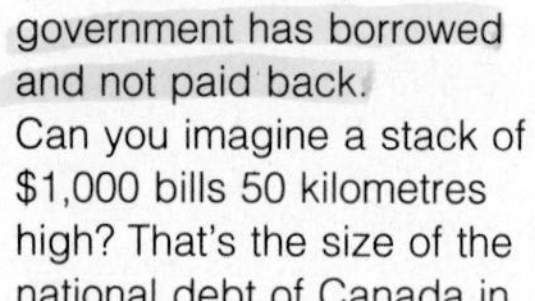

national debt
The sum of money the government has borrowed and not paid back.

Can you imagine a stack of $1,000 bills 50 kilometres high? That's the size of the national debt of Canada in 1994.

Canadian government policies for many years followed only one of Keynes's suggestions. The government borrowed heavily for many years, but it forgot to reduce spending when times were good in order to pay back these loans. The result is a large **national debt,** the accumulated amount owed by the Canadian government from its past borrowings. It will surpass $500 billion by 1994. The interest alone on this debt amounts to approximately $100 million every day of the

MAKING ETHICAL DECISIONS

Imagine that you have been out of school for a while and you and your spouse are now self-employed and earning $50,000 a year. To get to that point, you both paid your way through college. Now you can each afford to put the maximum allowable amount into a Registered Retirement Savings Plan (RRSP), which in your case amounts to $9,000 each. These payments are deductible from your income for tax purposes.

You also feel that you should give some money to charities. This too is deductible for tax purposes. You read in the paper that you and other people who give money to charity and can save for retirement are receiving unfair tax breaks. After all, poor people can't afford to give to charity or save for retirement. They feel that you should not receive a "government subsidy" for these payments. You think you are paying enough in taxes so that you are entitled to these deductions.

Is it ethical for the government to give tax breaks to people who have more money than others? Such people can buy RRSPs and give to charity and reduce their taxes while doing so. Businesses can write off some luncheons, travel expenses, and more. What percentage of a person's income should go to the government? Should everyone pay the same percentage, or should the rich pay more? What are the moral and ethical reasons for your position? ▼

year. This means that 20 to 25 percent of the total revenues the government receives goes to pay interest on the national debt.

The result is that when tough times hit the economy, as in the early 1990s, the government cannot follow the recipe of Keynes—reduce taxes and spend more—to help the economy out of recession. Consequently, taxes remain high just when individuals and businesses need as much income as possible to help boost the economy.

Canada is not alone in this situation. The U.S. has the same serious debt problem, which hampers efforts by its government to help its economy out of recession. However, in relation to the size of both economies, Canada's debt problem is much more serious.

OTHER ECONOMIC FACTORS

There are other important factors that affect the Canadian economy, government policy, and the climate in which Canadian business operates. They include the level of interest rates, imports and exports, and the exchange rate of the Canadian dollar with the U.S. dollar. These factors were discussed in great detail in Chapter 3, where we looked at the role of government in the economy, and in Chapter 2, on the major effect of international business.

The Outlook for the Canadian Economy

Most economists, think tanks, business journals and magazines, business associations, and major business and government officials are forecasting a slowly improving economy over the next few years as Canada emerges from the depths of the most serious recession in 50 years. Interest rates and inflation are expected to remain down, which is good news. But unemployment rates will probably stay up in the 10 to 11 percent range. Figure 4–11 shows how Canada stood in comparison with 11 other countries in late spring 1992 with regards to inflation and unemployment. We had the lowest inflation rate but the second highest unemployment rate.

The deep recession forced many companies to cut costs to the bone. A major casualty was the labour force. Most companies have learned to operate with fewer bodies, and this may become a permanent style of work. The electronic revolution has helped to make this possible.

Those who seek employment will need to be well educated and skilled in the information and technology areas, in science, engineering, and maths. Computer literacy will be as necessary as reading and writing—skills that still remain essential. Marketing will continue to be a major area of employment as competition becomes ever keener. You should be aware of these demands as you plan the rest of your academic education.

PROGRESS CHECK

- Why is the issue of inflation so important?
- What is a recession? How does it differ from a depression?
- What is the size of the national debt? Why is it so important?
- According to Keynes, how should the government use fiscal policy to manage the economy?

Figure 4–11 Economic snapshot

An economic snapshot of how Canada compared to 11 other countries in late spring 1992.

	Inflation Annual Change, %		Unemployment Rate, %	
	Latest	Year Ago	Latest	Year Ago
Canada	**1.3**	**6.3**	**11.2**	**10.2**
Australia	1.7	4.9	10.6	9.4
Belgium	2.8	3.2	8.2	7.6
Britain	4.3	5.8	9.5	7.7
France	3.1	3.2	9.9	9.1
Germany	4.5	3.0	6.5	6.3
Italy	5.6	6.8	9.9	10.2
Japan	2.4	3.0	2.0	2.1
Netherlands	4.2	3.3	6.9	7.6
Spain	6.8	5.9	16.5	15.7
Sweden	2.4	10.0	4.2	2.3
United States	3.2	4.9	7.5	6.8

Source: *The Montreal Gazette*, June 21, 1992, p. 88 [from *The Economist*].

SUMMARY

1. Define economics.

1. Economics is the study of how society chooses to use resources and to distribute goods and services to competing groups and individuals.

▼ *How do capitalist, socialist, and communist economic systems allocate resources?*

In capitalist systems, resources are allocated by individual consumers, bargaining in the marketplace. In socialist systems, the market and the government allocate resources. The government allocates the resources in communist systems.

2. Draw a diagram showing the circular flows of money in the international economy and discuss the increasing importance of international economic flows relative to national economics.

2. There is a circular flow of inputs, outputs, and money and other resources between the Canadian economy and the economies of other nations (see Figure 4–2).

▼ *Why is it important for you to understand the various economic systems and how they work?*

Economic flows among nations in the future will be determined by how each economy allocates scarce resources and how they view international trade.

3. Discuss Adam Smith's strategy for wealth creation and his basic principles.

3. The foundation of Adam Smith's economic theory was man's desire for money.

▼ *What did Adam Smith mean by an invisible hand?*

Adam Smith's invisible hand referred to the idea that countries prosper as individuals within the country prosper because the way to make money is to provide needed goods and services to others through trade. The invisible hand turns self-directed gain into social benefits for all.

▼ *What were the two keys to economic success identified by Adam Smith?*

Smith's keys to economic success were freedom and incentives.

4. Outline the basic rights of capitalism.

4. People living in capitalist systems enjoy certain basic rights.

▼ *What are the basic rights of capitalism?*

The basic rights of capitalism are the rights to (1) private property, (2) keeping all profits, (3) competition, and (4) choice.

5. Describe how free markets work, using the terms *supply, demand,* and *prices.*

5. A free market system is one in which decisions about what to produce and in what quantities are decided by the market.

▼ *How do supply and demand affect what kind and in what quantity products are produced in a free market system?*

The price of a product tells producers to make more or less of a product. The more money producers make from higher prices, the more they are likely to produce the product. Price is determined by supply and demand. The higher the quantity demanded, the higher the price. In turn, the higher the supply, the lower the price.

6. In spite of the wealth that countries with a free market system enjoy, the system suffers from certain inequities.

▼ *What are some limitations of the free market system?*

In countries with free market systems, the rich can buy almost everything, and the poor often cannot buy what they need. There may be much crime and much tolerance of negative social behaviour. That is, economic freedoms and social freedoms often go hand in hand.

6. Discuss some limitations of the free market system and what countries are doing to offset those limitations.

7. Socialism attempts to avoid some of the limitations of capitalism.

▼ *How do socialist countries try to avoid the problems of capitalism?*

In socialist countries, the government provides many social services such as health care and care for the elderly. The government distributes the wealth more evenly.

▼ *What problems are created by a socialist system?*

In a socialist system, you may earn plenty, but you must give most of your salary to the government in the form of taxes in order for it to provide social services for others.

7. Show how socialism attempts to solve some of the limitations of capitalism but creates new problems.

8. The governments of countries with communist systems decide how their nation's resources will be allocated.

▼ *What effects have their economic systems had on communist countries?*

People in communist countries have few incentives to create the wealth needed to fund the governments' projects. As a result, there are often shortages of food and basic household goods.

8. Describe the effects of the economic system in communist countries and what they mean for world economic development.

9. Canada does not operate under a pure capitalist system but a mixed economic system.

▼ *What does it mean to say Canada has a mixed economy?*

Canada falls somewhere between a pure capitalist state and a socialist state. Its economy is a combination of free markets plus government allocation of resources.

9. Examine the mixed economy in Canada and explain its strengths and weaknesses.

10. A general rise in the price of goods and services over time is called *inflation.*

▼ *How is inflation measured?*

The government measures the increase in the cost of consumer items with the consumer price index (CPI).

10. Define inflation and describe one major measure of inflation.

11. When real GDP declines for two quarters, an economy is said to be in a recession. A deep recession is known as a depression.

▼ *What happens in a recession or depression?*

Unemployment increases, prices fall, and businesses fail.

11. Define recession.

12. Because the government is spending more than it is receiving in taxes, the national debt is going up.

▼ *What is the national debt?*

The national debt is the sum of money the government has borrowed and not paid back.

▼ *How did the national debt get so high?*

Most government programs have automatic increases built into them, so spending goes up automatically each year. Revenues from taxes have not gone up as fast as spending, so a deficit has been created.

▼ *What can be done about the national debt?*

Some people feel the government is spending too much money. They want to cut back on government programs. Others feel that taxes are too low. They want to keep or increase government programs. To increase government revenues, some people propose putting more money into the economy and lowering interest rates. That is supposed to increase production and thereby increase government income. But that could also cause inflation.

12. Discuss the issues surrounding the national debt.

GETTING INVOLVED

1. Go to your local or school library and find a couple of introductory economics texts. Look through the tables of contents and briefly leaf through the books. What are the major topics? How hard are the books to read? Share your findings with others in the class.
2. What are some of the disadvantages of living in a free society? How could such disadvantages be minimized? What are the advantages? Write a short essay describing why a poor person in India might reject capitalism and prefer a socialist/communist state. How could Canada overcome this situation to broaden the base of the free market system? Perhaps two students could debate capitalist versus communist societies to further reveal the issues.
3. Democratic capitalism is said to be based on Judeo-Christian ethics. Write a short essay discussing whether or not the moral and ethical foundation of our country is weakening. What would you recommend? Discuss with your class.
4. Have some fun using the rule of 72 to anticipate future prices. For example, calculate how much a new car will cost a child now 5 years old when he or she reaches age 17 if car prices go up by 6 percent a year. Assume the cost of a new car is now $15,000. How much will a textbook cost if prices go up by 12 percent a year and the book now costs $50? These exercises will teach you about the problems of inflation!
5. Everyone is for peace, but nobody seems to know how to create it. Discuss the proposition that some percentage of the world's military expenditures should go to help develop poor countries. Would that be a step towards peace? How would you promote such a step? Discuss both sides of the issue, including a defense for high military spending in Canada, to understand both sides.
6. Discuss other current economic issues with your classmates and instructor. Pick two issues of general concern and discuss various viewpoints. Be ready to defend your position by finding facts and figures to support it. Have you set up a file system yet to keep such figures?

PRACTICING MANAGEMENT DECISIONS

Case One Mixing in a Mixed Economy

Canada may now be said to have a mixed economy. In addition to the reasons for government involvement noted previously is the fact that capitalism has negative consequences. Those consequences include old people who cannot afford decent housing or nourishing food, many single mothers with children living in poverty, persistent and significant unemployment, millions of illiterate citizens, hungry children, and large powerful businesses that dominate the economy. This led to a whole series of government efforts and agencies to try to achieve fairness, equality, and a higher level of general welfare.

Some agencies, such as the federal Competition Tribunal and various provincial bodies, try to ensure that adequate competition will exist between businesses in the same field. Other federal and provincial departments look after the health and welfare of citizens. The provincial departments of education concern themselves with schooling. In spite of all these efforts, serious problems persist and many are getting worse.

Decision Questions

1. What can be done in Canada to solve these problems of poverty, hunger, and illiteracy? Is big business power something to worry about? Who should be doing something about these issues? What are the alternatives? Are there any business opportunities?

2. Are other countries solving these problems better than we are? Are there any negative consequences from focusing on them? Any positive consequences?
3. Why should business owners and managers be particularly concerned about how governments attempt to find solutions? Should businesses play a more active role?
4. One negative consequence of the strong emphasis on financial success in capitalist society is the unethical or immoral behaviour of owners or managers. What can be done about this? Is this kind of behaviour less prevalent in communist or socialist countries? Why or why not?

Case Two Let's Just Tax the Rich and Pay Off the Debt

For years, economics has been defined as the allocation of scarce resources among competing groups and individuals. No two groups would seem more in competition in Canada than the rich versus the poor. The feeling among many people is that the rich got rich by exploiting the poor (labour). In their search for more equality, such people suggest increasing taxes on the rich and giving the additional money to the poor. Such was the thinking behind most socialist governments until the early 1990s, when socialism lost its glow, even in Sweden, the model socialist country for many people.

The problem with such thinking is that there simply aren't enough rich people making enough money so that taxing them more will allow the government to pay for all its programs. Rich people make most of their money from investing in real estate and businesses. If the government increased their taxes, that investment money would no longer be there, and the whole economy would slow down. Therefore, it is clear that "taxing the rich" is not a solution to the government's problems. The tax burden always falls on the middle class, those people who are struggling to pay their mortgage, send their kids to school, and so forth. Increasing their taxes makes them poorer, and nobody feels better off.

The only long-term solution to meeting government needs is for the economy to grow. That increases the size of the pie and makes it possible for everyone to have more without taking it from someone else. The problem is that growth strategies directly conflict with goals of more equality. Growth often comes from cutting taxes on the rich, encouraging them to invest more and make the economy grow. The rich get richer and the poor get richer too, but at a slower rate. The net result is a bigger gap between rich and poor. It is interesting to note, however, that half of the families in the bottom 20 percent of income are not there seven years later. In other words, there is a good chance that people on the bottom will become middle-income earners sometime in their lives. The persistently poor make up only about 3 percent of the population.

Most businesses in the 1980s cut workers from their payroll because competition and a failing economy forced them to do so. At the same time, the number of government workers climbed greatly in some cities. There is some room, therefore, for government spending cuts. There is also the potential for less spending on the military as tensions relax in the world. In short, there is an opportunity to cut taxes, spur growth, and still increase some necessary social programs.

Decision Questions

1. Recently, Sweden joined many of the other nations in the world in cutting taxes. The Swedish people also voted against a socialist government. Taxing the rich is no longer the preferred way to balance government budgets. What are the alternatives?
2. There are thousands of millionaires and a few billionaires in Canada. What are the advantages and disadvantages of taxing such people at much higher rates than now prevail?
3. There is a notion that "a rising tide lifts all ships." That is true in Canada for all but 3 percent of the population. What can be done to help raise those people as well?

4. Every year, there seems to be a call for a cut in "government waste and corruption." Years pass, and no such cuts appear to be made. What steps would you recommend for making local, provincial, and federal government agencies more efficient and effective?

Sources: Thomas Sowell, "Lies, Damn Lies and Politicized Statistics," *Forbes,* July 8, 1991, pp. 777–79; Warren Brookes, "Stomping the Rich, Producing an Old Whine," *The Washington Times,* October 17, 1990, pp. G1 and G4; and Clayton Yeutter, "When 'Fairness' Isn't Fair," *The New York Times,* March 24, 1992, p. A21.

LET'S TALK BUSINESS

1. You have seen that business continues to automate and install ever more productive equipment requiring fewer and fewer employees. Do you think that is good for the work force in the long run? What is in it for employees? Doesn't it keep the unemployment rate high?
2. Many African countries are shifting their economic systems to a kind of mixed economy, sometimes called welfare capitalism or democratic socialism. Why is this shift occurring? What do they expect to gain? What do they expect to avoid? Do you think it is a good development? Why or why not?
3. There are many opportunities for Canadian businesses to branch out into Europe and Asia, where the economies are expected to grow rapidly. When interest rates are low, would you favour extensive borrowing to finance the necessary R&D, production, and marketing costs to expand into these new areas? What are the risks if you do it? What are the risks if you do not do it?
4. The European Community has a huge, rich consumer and industrial market and is very stable. The former communist countries in Eastern Europe are hungry for investment and trade and need everything, but their future is uncertain as they move to a free market economy. However, the early bird stands to reap great rewards. Canada is rich in millions of multilingual people who speak the languages of Europe. Which market would you go into? What facts should help you make your decision? Does it depend on your product or service? On your financial strength? On your human resources?

LOOKING AHEAD

Now that you are familiar with some economic terms you should know when you read business literature, we can focus our attention on business itself. Chapter 5 looks at the different forms of business ownership. You have no doubt heard of partnerships and corporations. How about sole proprietorships? These formats and their advantages and disadvantages are examined in detail in the next chapter.

PART II

BUSINESS FORMATION

SPRINGRIDGE
FARM
Welcome
OPEN WEEKDAYS 8-8
WEEKENDS 8-5
Strawberry Picking Now
Pies · Preserves · Country Gifts

FORMS OF BUSINESS ORGANIZATION

LEARNING GOALS

After you have read and studied this chapter, you should be able to:

1. List the three basic forms of business ownership.
2. Compare the advantages and disadvantages of:
   1. Sole proprietorships.
   2. Partnerships.
   3. Corporations.
3. Explain the differences between limited and general partnerships.
4. List the contents of a partnership agreement.
5. Describe the process of incorporation.
6. Define and give examples of three types of corporate mergers.
7. Summarize the advantages and disadvantages of private corporations.
8. Explain the role of co-operatives.
9. Describe the purpose of joint ventures.

KEY TERMS

conglomerate merger, p. 155
co-operative, p. 155
corporation, p. 142
general partner, p. 147
horizontal merger, p. 154
limited liability, p. 147
limited partner, p. 147
merger, p. 154
partnership, p. 142
partnership agreement, p. 149
private corporation, p. 151
public corporation p. 151
sole proprietorship, p. 142
unlimited liability, p. 146
vertical merger, p. 154

Armand Bombardier

PROFILE ARMAND BOMBARDIER, FOUNDER OF BOMBARDIER INC.

Born in 1907 in Quebec, J. Armand Bombardier was only 15 when he built his first propeller-driven snow vehicle from the wreck of an old Ford. His mechanical abilities led him to numerous experiments, resulting in the invention of a revolutionary new sprocket wheel and track system in 1935. In 1937 he started a company to mass produce the snowmobile based on his inventions.

Over the next two decades, he designed numerous all-terrain vehicles. In 1959 Bombardier began marketing the first small Ski-Doo snowmobile. He thus not only solved the problem of individual transportation on snow but created a new sport. Armand Bombardier died in 1964 without an inkling of the market success his invention was to enjoy.

Today Bombardier Inc. is a giant transnational company with production facilities in Canada, the U.S., and five European countries. It has 17 subsidiaries with activities in all forms of rail transport, aerospace and defence, motorized consumer products, financial services, and real estate development.

Source: *Annual Report,* January 31, 1991, and other documentation from Bombardier Inc.

FORMS OF BUSINESS OWNERSHIP

Like Armand Bombardier, tens of thousands of people start new businesses in Canada every year. Chances are you have thought of owning your own business or know someone who has. One key to success at a new business is knowing how to get the resources you need to start. You may need to take on partners or find other ways of obtaining money. To stay in business, you may need help from someone with more expertise than you in certain areas or you may need to raise more money to expand. How you form your business can make a tremendous difference in your long-run success. The three major forms of business ownership are: (1) sole proprietorships, (2) partnerships, or (3) corporations.

It is easy to start your own business. For example, you can begin a word processing service out of your home, open a car repair centre, start a new restaurant, or go about meeting other wants and needs of the community on your own. An organization that is owned directly, and usually managed, by one person is called a **sole proprietorship.** That is the most common form of business ownership (over one million firms in 1992).

sole proprietorship
A business that is owned directly, and usually managed, by one person.

Many people do not have the money, time, or desire to run a business on their own. They prefer to have someone else or some group of people get together to form the business. When two or more people legally agree to become co-owners of a business, the organization is called a **partnership.**

partnership
A legal form of business with two or more owners.

There are advantages to creating a business that is separate and distinct from its owners. A legal entity that has an existence separate from the people who own it is called a **corporation.** Owners hold shares in the corporation. There are about 100,000 corporations in Canada, but they have the largest share of business by far. (See Figure 5–1.)

corporation
A legal entity with an existence separate from its owners.

As you will learn in this chapter, each form of business ownership has its advantages—and disadvantages. It is important to understand these advantages and disadvantages before starting a business. Keep in mind that just because a business starts in one form of ownership, it doesn't have to stay in that form. Many

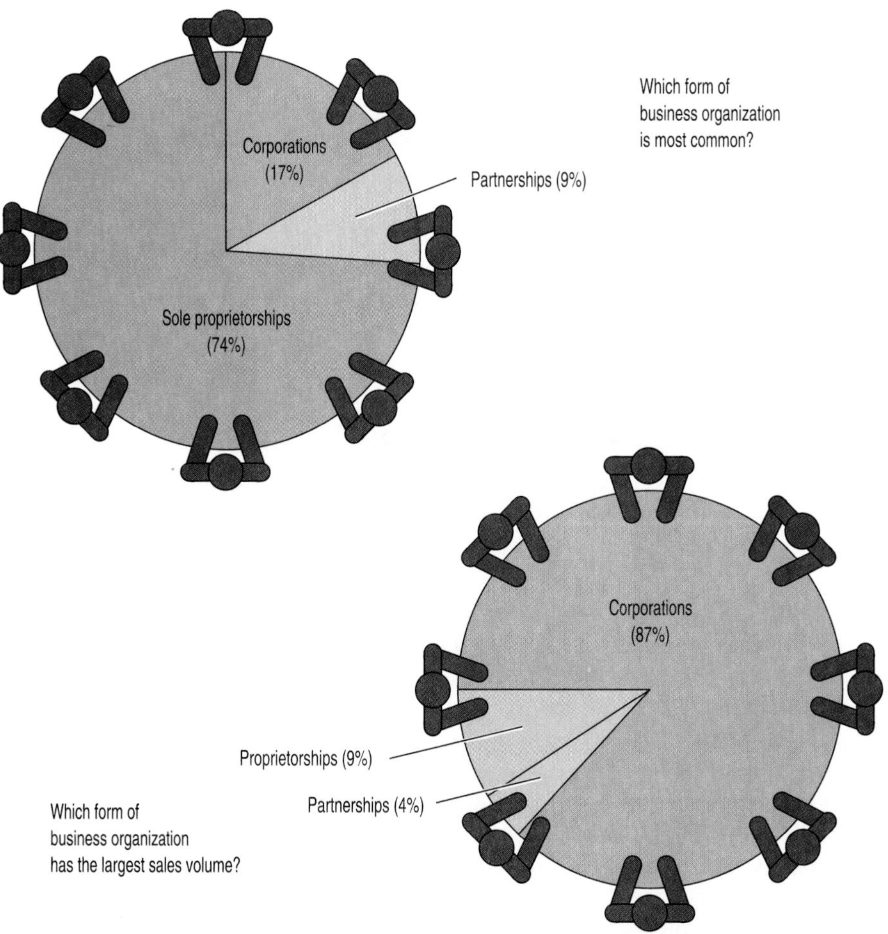

Figure 5–1 Forms of business organizations. Although corporations make up only 17 percent of the total *number* of businesses, they have 87 percent of the sales volume. Sole proprietorships are the most common form of ownership (74 percent), but they have only 9 percent of sales volume.

companies, like Armand Bombardier's, started out as "one-man shows," added a partner or two, and eventually became corporations.

ADVANTAGES AND DISADVANTAGES OF DIFFERENT FORMS OF OWNERSHIP

Before examining the possible types of ownership of businesses in Canada, it is important to see how the *size* of a business affects its advantages and disadvantages. This is often not well understood.

Small Businesses

A small business that is owned by one person may be set up as a sole proprietorship or a corporation. Similarly, a small business that is owned by two or more people may be organized as a partnership or a corporation. In each case, the owner(s) have complete freedom to choose the route they wish to follow. Regardless of the choice, a small business has all the advantages and disadvantages of a small-size operation as well as the advantages and disadvantages of the corporate or non-corporate form selected.

A small business, such as this souvenir shop, may be set up as a sole proprietorship or a corporation. There are advantages and disadvantages to both forms of ownership.

This means that a sole owner has the *advantages* of having no boss, making all the decisions, not having to share the profits, and having all the pride and satisfaction of ownership and success. But he or she has the *disadvantages* of not being able to share responsibility or the heavy workload or losses and financing needs. These conditions exist *whether or not the business is incorporated.*

When two or more persons form a small business partnership or corporation, the workload, decision making, losses, and financial responsibility are shared. But there may be differences of opinion and conflicts, profits must be shared, and it is complicated if one owner wishes to leave or dies. Again, this holds true whether or not the business is incorporated.

Large Businesses

When it comes to big businesses the situation is quite different. As you will see when you examine the corporate form of ownership all large companies must adopt this form of ownership. They regularly require substantial investing or borrowing from the public and this can only be done in the corporate form. In addition, the large number of owners (shareholders) means that the limited liability feature of corporations is also necessary. So, while small business owners have a choice of form of ownership large companies really have no such choice.

Various publications regularly compile lists of the largest 50, 500 or 1,000 companies in Canada and they are all corporations. In Figure 5–2 you will see a list of the ten largest companies in 1992, ranked by sales.

Sole Proprietorships

Advantages of Sole Proprietorships

There must be some major advantages to being a sole proprietor. After all, hundreds of thousands of people in Canada have formed this kind of business. Sole proprietorships are also the easiest kind of businesses to explore in your quest for an interesting career. Every town has some sole proprietorships that you can visit. There's the local produce stand, the beauty shop, the auto repair garage and the

Rank '92	Rank '91	Company	Sales (million dollars)	Assets (million dollars)	Employees
1	1	BCE Inc.	20,784	48,312	124,000
2	2	General Motors of Canada Ltd.	18,347	6,231	39,237
3	3	Ford Motor Co. of Canada Ltd.	14,443	3,882	19,784
4	4	George Weston Ltd.	11,599	3,965	62,000
5	6	Imasco Ltd.	9,957	48,519	75,000
6	7	Alcan Aluminium Ltd.	9,654	12,895	46,000
7	11	Chrysler Canada Ltd.	9,454	3,142	13,800
8	9	Loblaw Cos. Ltd.	9,262	2,474	47,000
9	8	Imperial Oil Ltd.	9,127	13,192	10,152
10	5	Canadian Pacific Ltd.	8,964	20,224	63,300

Figure 5–2 Canada's ten largest companies in 1992*

Source: "The Corporate 500," *Canadian Business,* June 1993, p. 70.
*Ranked by volume of sales and comparison to their position in 1991.

accountant. If you look closely, you'll find sole proprietors who do income taxes, repair appliances and television sets, and provide all kinds of local services. (Ascertain that they are not corporations.) Talk with them about the joys and frustrations of being on their own. Most people will mention the benefits of being their own boss and setting their own hours. They may also mention the following advantages:

1. **Ease of starting and ending the business** All you have to do to start a sole proprietorship is buy the needed equipment (for example, a saw, a computer, a tractor, a lawnmower) and put up some announcements saying you are in business. It is just as easy to get out of business; you simply stop. There is no one to consult or to disagree with about such decisions. You may have to get a permit or license from the government, but that is usually no problem. The profiles of the people who started sole proprietorships in their own homes (see Chapter 1) give you some feel for how such businesses can start small and grow rapidly.
2. **Being your own boss** "Working for others simply does not have the same excitement as working for yourself." That's the way sole proprietors feel. You may make mistakes, but they are *your* mistakes—and so are the many small victories each day.
3. **Pride of ownership** People who own and manage their own businesses are rightfully proud of their work. They deserve all the credit for taking the risks and providing needed goods or services.
4. **Retention of profit** Other than the joy of being your own boss, there is nothing like the pleasure of knowing that there is no limit to how much money you can make and you do not have to share that money with anyone else (except the government, in taxes). People are often willing to start working early in the day and stay late because the money they earn is theirs to keep.

For these and other reasons, there are more sole proprietorships than any other kind of business in Canada. Tens of thousands of new businesses are formed every year. Most of these are very small companies, so the total amount of business they do is a small fraction of the total business done by a much smaller number of very large corporations. And thousands of small businesses fail. Many people dream of owning their own business, but there are also disadvantages to sole proprietorships.

Disadvantages of Sole Proprietorships

Not everyone is cut out to own and manage a business. It is difficult to save enough money to start a business *and* keep it going. Often the cost of inventory, supplies, insurance, advertising, rent, utilities, and other expenses is simply too much to cover alone. There are other disadvantages of owning your own business.

unlimited liability
The responsibility of a business's owners for all of the debts of the business, making the personal assets of the owners vulnerable to claims against the business; sole proprietors and general partners have unlimited liability.

1. **Unlimited liability—the risk of losses** When you work for others, it is their problem if the business is not profitable. When you own your own business, you and the business are considered one. You have **unlimited liability;** that is, any debts or damages incurred by the business are *your* personal debts and *you* must pay them, even if it means selling your home, your car, and so forth. This is the most serious disadvantage of a sole proprietorship. It requires careful thought and discussion with a lawyer and an accountant.
2. **Limited financial resources** Funds available to the business are limited to the funds that the one (sole) owner can gather. Since there are serious limits to how much one person can do, partnerships and corporations have a greater probability of recruiting the needed financial backing to start a business.
3. **Overwhelming time commitment** It is hard to own a business, manage it, train people, and have time for anything else in life. The owner must spend long hours working. The owner of a store, for example, may put in 12 hours a day, six or seven days a week. That is almost twice the hours worked by a salaried labourer, who may make more money.
4. **Few fringe benefits** If you are your own boss, you lose many of the fringe benefits that come from working for others. For example, you have no disability insurance, no sick leave, no vacation pay and so on.
5. **Limited growth** If the owner becomes incapacitated, the business often comes to a standstill. Since a sole proprietorship relies on its owner for most of its funding, expansion is often slow. This is one reason why many individuals seek partners to assist in a business.
6. **Limited life span** If the sole proprietor dies, the business ceases to exist legally. Practically, unless arrangements have been made to pass the ownership/management on to others, the business comes to an end.

Talk with a few small business owners about the problems they have faced in being on their own. They know more about the situation in your area than anyone else does. They are likely to have many interesting stories to tell about problems getting loans from the bank, problems with theft, and problems simply keeping up with the business. These problems are the reason that many sole proprietors discourage their children from following in their footsteps, although many would have it no other way. These problems are also reasons why many sole proprietors choose to find partners to share the load. Remember, though, partnerships have disadvantages, too.

THINKING IT THROUGH

Have you ever dreamed of opening your own business? If you did, what would it be? What talents or skills do you have that you could use? Could you start a business in your own home? About how much would it cost to start? Could you begin part-time while you worked elsewhere? What could you get from owning your own business in the way of satisfaction and profit? What would you lose?

Partnerships

A partnership is a legal form of business with two or more owners. It is not difficult to form a partnership, but it is wise to get the counsel of a lawyer experienced with such agreements. Lawyers' services are expensive, so would-be partners should read all about partnerships and reach some basic agreements before calling in a lawyer. It is often easier to *form* a partnership than to operate or end one, and many friendships have ended after friends became partners.

Advantages of Partnerships

There are many advantages of having one or more partners in a business. Often, it is much easier to own and manage a business with one or more partners. Your partner can cover for you when you are sick or go on vacation. Your partner may be skilled at inventory-keeping and accounting while you do the selling or servicing. A partner can also provide additional money, support, and expertise. Some of the people who are enjoying the advantages of partnerships today, more than ever before, are doctors, lawyers, dentists, and other professionals. They have learned that it is easier to take vacations, stay home when they are sick, or relax a little when there are others available to help take care of clients. With some care, partnerships can have the following advantages:

1. **More financial resources** Naturally, when two or more people pool their money and credit, it is easier to have enough cash to start and to pay the rent, utilities, and other bills incurred by a business. A concept called limited partnership is specially designed to help raise capital (money). A **limited partner** invests money in the business but cannot legally have any management responsibility and has limited liability. **Limited liability** means that limited partners are not responsible for the debts of the business. Their personal property is *not* at risk. The worst that can happen is that they will lose their investment.
2. **Shared management** It is simply much easier to manage the day-to-day activities of a business with carefully chosen partners. Partners give each other free time from the business and provide different skills and perspectives. Many people find that the best partner is a spouse. That is why you see so many husband/wife teams managing restaurants, service shops, and other businesses.

limited partner
Owner who invests money in the business but does not have any management responsibility or liability for losses beyond the investment.

limited liability
The responsibility of a business's owners for losses only up to the amount they invest; limited partners have limited liability.

Disadvantages of Partnerships

Any time two people must agree on anything, there is the possibility of conflict and tension. Partnerships have caused splits among families, friends, and marriages.

1. **Unlimited liability** Each general partner is liable for all the debts of the firm, no matter who was responsible for causing those debts. Like a sole proprietor, partners can lose their homes, cars, and everything else they own if the business fails or is sued by someone. Such a risk is very serious and should be discussed with a lawyer and an insurance expert. A **general partner,** then, is an owner (partner) who has unlimited liability and is active in managing the firm. (As mentioned earlier, a limited partner risks an investment in the firm but is not liable for the business's losses beyond that investment and cannot legally help to manage the company.) As with sole proprietorships, this is the most serious disadvantage of partnerships.

general partner
An owner (partner) who has unlimited liability and is active in managing the firm.

Many of the disadvantages of owning your own business are taken care of when you find a business partner. When one partner is not there, the other can take over operations. Although the funding for partnerships is easier than for sole proprietorships, it is harder than for corporations.

2. **Division of profits** Sharing the risk means sharing the profit, and that can cause conflicts. For example, two people form a partnership: one puts in more money and the other puts in more hours. Each may later feel justified in asking for a bigger share of the profits. Imagine the resulting conflicts.
3. **Disagreements among partners** Disagreements over money are just one example of potential conflict in a partnership. Who has final authority over employees? Who hires and fires employees? Who works what hours? What if one partner wants to buy expensive equipment for the firm and the other partner disagrees? Potential conflicts are many. Because of such problems, all terms of partnership should be spelled out in writing to protect all parties and to minimize future misunderstandings.
4. **Difficult to terminate** Once you have committed yourself to a partnership, it is not easy to get out of it. Questions about who gets what and what happens next are often very difficult to solve when the business is closed. Surprisingly, law firms often have faulty partnership agreements and find that breaking up is hard to do. How do you get rid of a partner you don't like? It is best to decide that up front, in the partnership agreement.[1]

Again, the best way to learn about the advantages and disadvantages of partnerships is to interview several people who have experience with such agreements. They will give you additional insights and hints on how to avoid problems.

Categories of Partners

Several different types of partners can be involved in a partnership. The most common types are the following:

- *Silent partners* take no active role in managing a partnership, but their identities and involvement are known by the public.
- *Secret partners* take an active role in managing a partnership, but their identities are unknown to the public.

- *Nominal partners* are not actually involved in a partnership but lend their names to it for public relations purposes.
- *Dormant partners* are neither active in managing a partnership nor known to the public.
- *Senior partners* assume major management roles due to their long tenure or amount of investment in the partnership. They normally receive large shares of the partnership's profits.
- *Junior partners* are generally younger partners in tenure who assume a limited role in the partnership's management and receive a smaller share of the partnership's profits.

How to Form a Partnership

The first step in forming a partnership is choosing the right partner. The importance of this step cannot be overemphasized. Many partnerships dissolve because of disagreements between partners. One should choose a business partner as carefully as a marriage partner.

For your protection, be sure to put your partnership agreement in writing. The following should be included in a **partnership agreement:**

partnership agreement
Legal document that specifies the rights and responsibilities of the members of a partnership.

1. The name of the business. All provinces require the firm name to be registered with the provincial officials if the firm name is different from the name of any partner.
2. The names and addresses of all partners.
3. The purpose and nature of the business, the location of the principal offices, and any other locations where the business will be conducted.
4. The date the partnership will start and how long it will last. Will it exist for a specific length of time or will it stop when one of the partners dies or when the partners agree to discontinue?
5. The contributions made by each partner. Will some partners contribute money, others real estate, personal property, expertise, or labour? When are the contributions due?
6. The management responsibilities. Will all partners have equal voices in management or will there be senior and junior partners?
7. The duties of each partner.
8. The salaries and drawing accounts of each partner.
9. Provision for sharing of profits or losses.
10. Provision for accounting procedures. Who will keep the accounts? What bookkeeping and accounting methods will be used? Where will the books be kept?

MAKING ETHICAL DECISIONS

Imagine that you and your partner own a construction company. You receive a bid from a subcontractor that you know is 20 percent too low. Such a loss to the subcontractor could put him out of business. Accepting the bid will certainly improve your chances of winning the contract for a big shopping centre project. Your partner wants to take the bid and let the subcontractor suffer the consequences of his bad estimate. What do you think you should do? What will be the consequences of your decision? ▼

11. The requirements for taking in new partners.
12. Any special restrictions, rights, or duties of any partner.
13. Provision for a retiring partner.
14. Provision for the purchase of a deceased or retiring partner's share of the business.
15. Provision for how grievances will be handled.
16. Provision for how to dissolve the partnership and distribute the assets to the partners.

One of the fears of owning your own business or having a partner is the fear of losing everything you own if the business loses a significant amount of money or someone sues the business. Many businesspeople try to avoid this and the other disadvantages of sole proprietorships and partnerships by forming corporations.

PROGRESS CHECK

- Most people who start a business in Canada are sole proprietors, and most of them are no longer in business after 10 years. What are the advantages and disadvantages of this form of business?
- What are some of advantages of partnerships over sole proprietorships?
- Unlimited liability is one of the biggest drawbacks to sole proprietorships and general partnerships. Can you explain what that means?
- What is the difference between a *limited* partner and a *general* partner?

Corporations

Although the word *corporation* makes people think of big businesses like Imperial Esso, the Royal Bank, or Bell Canada, it is not necessary to be big in order to incorporate (start a corporation). Obviously, many corporations are big. However, incorporating may be beneficial for small businesses also.

A corporation is a federally or provincially chartered legal entity with authority to act and have liability separate from its owners. This means the corporation's

Size and money are just two of the advantages of corporations such as Canada Trust. They have about 85 percent of total business sales, with a little over 15 percent of total number of businesses. Corporations have many advantages over other forms of business, but there are disadvantages too.

owners (shareholders) are not liable for the debts or any other problems of the corporation beyond the money they invest. Owners no longer must worry about losing their houses, cars, and other property because of some business problem—a very significant benefit. A corporation not only limits the liability of owners, it enables many people to share in the ownership (and profits) of a business without working there or having other commitments to it.

In Canada, commercial corporations are divided into two classes, public and private. **Public corporations** have the right to issue shares to the public, which means their shares may be listed on the stock exchanges. This offers the possibility of raising large amounts of capital.

public corporation
Corporation that has the right to issue shares to the public, so its shares may be listed on the stock exchanges.

Private corporations are not allowed to issue stock to the public, so their shares are not listed on stock exchanges and are limited to 50 or fewer shareholders. This greatly reduces the costs of incorporating. All small corporations are in the private category. This is the vehicle employed by individuals or partners who do not anticipate the need for substantial financing but want to take advantage of limited liability. Some private corporations have grown to be very large. For example, the T. Eaton Co. Ltd. is still owned by the Eaton family.

private corporation
Corporation that is not allowed to issue stock to the public, so its shares are not listed on stock exchanges and it is limited to 50 or fewer shareholders.

There is one important advantage Canadian-owned private corporations have over public corporations: the income tax rate on the first $200,000 of annual business profits is half the normal corporate tax rate. It is also about half of what individuals pay when they are not incorporated. This is another feature that leads individuals and partners to incorporate.

Advantages of Corporations

The concept of incorporation is not too difficult, even though the procedures for incorporating are often rather complex. Most people are not willing to risk everything to go into business. Yet, for businesses to grow and prosper and create abundance, many people would have to be willing to invest their money in business. The way to solve this problem was to create an artificial being, an entity that exists only in the eyes of the law. That artificial being is called a *corporation*. It has a separate legal identity from the owners—the shareholders—of the company. The corporation files its own tax returns. This entity is a technique for involving people in business without risking their other personal assets.

The first three advantages listed here apply only to large public corporations. The last three apply to all corporations.

1. **More money for investment** To raise money, a public corporation sells ownership (shares) to anyone who is interested. (We shall discuss shares in Chapter 18.) This means that thousands of people can own part of major companies like INCO, Bombardier, and MacMillan Bloedel. If a company sold 1 million shares for $50 each, it would have $50 million available to build plants, buy materials, hire people, build products, and so on. Such a large amount of money would be difficult to raise any other way. Laws regulate how corporations can raise this money. The types of shares and the amount of debt that can be incurred vary from province to province.
2. **Size** Because they have large amounts of money to work with, corporations can build large, modern factories with the latest equipment. They can also hire experts or specialists in all areas of operation. Furthermore, they can buy other corporations in other fields to *diversify their risk*. (When a corporation is involved in many businesses at once, if one fails, the corporation will survive.) In short, large corporations have the size and resources to take advantage of opportunities anywhere in the world. However, corporations do

not have to be large for their shareholders to enjoy the benefits of limited liability and access to more capital.

3. **Separation of ownership from management** Public corporations are able to raise money from many different investors without getting them involved in management. The corporate hierarchy is shown in Figure 5–3. The pyramid shows that the owners/shareholders are separate from the managers and employees. The owners elect a board of directors. The directors select the officers, who in turn hire managers and employees. The owners thus have some say in who runs the corporation.
4. **Limited liability** Corporations in Canada have Limited, Incorporated, or Corporation after their names, as in T. Eaton Co. Ltd. The Ltd. stands for *limited liability* and is probably the most significant advantage of corporations. Remember, limited liability means that the owners of a business cannot lose more than their investment in that business. The corporation itself is fully liable for all of its debts. Banks and other financial institutions usually require the personal guarantee of the owners of small corporations before making loans to these companies. These owners therefore lose the limited liability protection for those debts.
5. **Perpetual life** Because corporations are separate legal entities from the people who own them, the death or departure of one or more owners does not terminate the corporation. This makes corporations a better risk to bankers and other lenders, so it is easier to get loans.
6. **Ease of ownership change** It is easy to change the owners of a corporation simply by selling the stock.

Other Types of Corporations

When reading about corporations, you may find many confusing terms. A *non-resident corporation* does business in Canada but its head office is outside Canada. Examples are most foreign airlines. A *personal service corporation* is set up by an athlete,

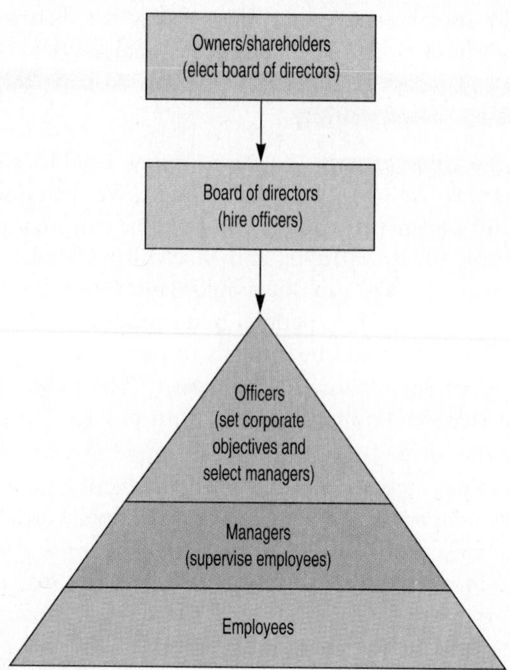

Figure 5–3 Owners influence how a business is managed by electing a board of directors. The board hires the top managers (or fires them). It also sets the pay for top managers. Top managers then select other managers and employees with the help of the human resources department.

entertainer, or some other high-earning, self-employed person to access some advantages of corporate ownership.

A *non-profit corporation* is formed for charitable or socially beneficial purposes. It is not run for personal profit. It has many of the features of business corporations, but it pays no income taxes and does not issue shares. Therefore it has no owners/shareholders. The number of non-profit corporations runs into the tens of thousands. In some towns, much of the property is tax exempt because it belongs to non-profit organizations such as churches, hospitals, colleges, museums, YMCAs, or athletic, artistic, or charitable organizations.

Figure 5–4 compares different types of ownership.

Figure 5–4 Comparison of types of ownership.

		Partnerships		Corporations	
	Sole Proprietorship	General Partnership	Limited** Partnership	Public Corporation	Private Corporation
Documents needed to start business	None (may need permit or license).	Partnership agreement, oral or written.	Written agreement. Must file certificate of limited partnership.	Articles of incorporation, bylaws.	Articles of incorporation, bylaws. Must meet criteria.
Ease of termination	Easy, just pay debts and quit.	May be difficult, depending on agreement.	Same as general partnership.	Difficult and expensive to terminate.	Not difficult: pay off debts, sell off assets, withdraw cash, and pay taxes.
Life span	Terminates on death, sale, or retirement.	Terminates on death or withdrawal of a partner*.	Terminates only on death or withdrawal of general partner*.	Perpetual life.	Perpetual life.
Transfer of ownership	Sale terminates sole proprietorship.	Requires agreement of partner(s) (per partnership agreement).	Agreement usually allows for such transfers.	Easy—just sell shares.	Easy—just sell shares*.
Financial resources	Limited to owner's capital and loans.	Limited to partners' capital and loans.	Same as general partnership.	May issue as many shares and bonds as market will absorb.	Owners' capital and loans. No public stock issue allowed.
Personal risk of losses	Unlimited liability.	Unlimited liability.	Limited liability.	Limited liability.	Limited liability.
Income taxes	Taxed as personal income.	Taxed as personal income.	Taxed as personal income.	Corporate income tax plus lower personal tax on dividends.	Low corporate rate plus lower personal tax on dividends.
Management responsibilities	Owner manages all areas of the business.	Partners share management.	Cannot participate in management.	Management separate from ownership.	Owners usually manage all areas.

*Unless agreement specifies otherwise.

**There must be at least one general partner who manages the partnership and has unlimited liability.

PROGRESS CHECK

- What are the major advantages and disadvantages of the corporate form of business?
- What is the role of owners (shareholders) in the corporate hierarchy?
- If you buy shares in a corporation and someone gets injured by one of the corporation's products, can you be sued? Why or why not? Could you be sued if you were a general partner in a partnership?

THINKING IT THROUGH

What would Canada be like without major corporations? What products would be hard to get? What would be the benefits? Now that you've read about sole proprietorships, partnerships, and corporations, which sounds like the best place for you to work? Why? Which calls for taking the most risks? Which would be most fun? Most profitable? What part of your personality most determines where you fit in best?

CORPORATE EXPANSION: MERGERS AND TAKEOVERS

The 1980s was a decade of considerable corporate expansion. It seemed nearly every day you heard a new corporate merger or acquisition announced in the news. A **merger** is the result of two firms forming one company. An *acquisition* is when one company buys another company. Figure 5–5 highlights several important corporate deals that occurred in the '80s.

merger The result of two firms forming one company.

There are three major types of corporate mergers: vertical, horizontal, and conglomerate. A **vertical merger** is the joining of two firms involved in different stages of related businesses. Think of a merger between a large soup company and a company that produces aluminum cans. Such a merger would ensure a constant supply of aluminum cans needed by the soup company. It could also help ensure quality control of the soup company's product. A **horizontal merger** joins two firms in the same industry and allows them to diversify or expand their products. An

vertical merger The joining of two firms involved in different stages of related businesses.

horizontal merger The joining of two firms in the same industry.

Figure 5–5 The 1980s' largest mergers and acquisitions.

Rank	Value 1989 ($ million)	Purchase Price ($ million)	Acquiring Company	Acquired or Merged Company
1	$6,930	$6,600	Campeau Corp.	Federated Dept. Stores, U.S.
2	6,241	4,133	Dome Petroleum	Hudson's Bay Oil & Gas
3	5,775	5,500	Amoco Petroleum, U.S.	Dome Petroleum
4	5,707	5,004	Campeau Corp.	Allied Stores, U.S.
5	4,960	4,960	Imperial Oil	Texaco Canada
6	4,668	3,091	Seagram	duPont, U.S. (partial ownership)
7	3,421	3,000	Gulf Canada	Hiram Walker Resources
8	3,383	2,850	Olympia & York	Gulf Canada
9	2,965	2,600	Allied Lyons, U.K.	Hiram Walker-Gooderham
10	2,931	2,570	Imasco	Genstar

Source: *Financial Post,* Summer 1990, p. 165.

SPOTLIGHT ON SMALL BUSINESS

Selecting an Appropriate Form of Ownership

How does an individual decide on the best form of ownership for a new enterprise? It really depends on several factors. If you are starting a service business, say computer software design, you will not be buying and selling raw material or finished goods, you will not be incurring major debts. Also, if you are starting small you do not need much capital. Under these circumstances, the advantage of limited liability that the corporate form offers is not very important, because proper insurance can avoid major liabilities that could arise from accidents or from product liability. This means that you can start as a sole proprietorship and avoid the disadvantages of incorporating. The same holds true if two partners start a business. If the business expands and conditions change, you can incorporate later.

If you are starting a manufacturing, wholesale, or retail business it is a different story. Once you start selling goods, you will be buying on credit and therefore accumulating debts. At any one time, the business will normally owe at least one or two months' purchases. There may be a long and expensive lease commitment and perhaps a substantial balance owing for equipment and improvements to the premises. Under these circumstances, it would be prudent to incorporate from the start to avoid the possibility of having to assume personal liability for all of these debts. ▼

example is the merger of a large milk company with a soft drink producer. The milk company can now supply a variety of beverage products. A **conglomerate merger** unites completely unrelated firms. Its primary purpose is to diversify business operations and investments. The acquisition of a movie studio by a soup company would be an example of a conglomerate merger. Some 2,785 mergers and acquisitions took place in the U.S. in 1988.[2] More such deals are expected in the 1990s. Many such mergers have also occurred in Canada.

conglomerate merger
The joining of completely unrelated firms.

CO-OPERATIVES

Some people dislike the notion of having owners, managers, workers, and buyers as separate individuals with separate goals. They envision a world where people co-operate with one another more fully and share the wealth more evenly. These people have formed a different kind of organization that reflects their social orientation: a co-operative, or co-op.

A **co-operative** is an organization that is owned by members/customers, who pay an annual membership fee and share in any profits (if it is a profit-making organization). Often the members/customers work in the organization a certain number of hours a month as part of their duties. In Canada there is a wide range of co-ops. There are *producer co-ops*. Fishermen on both coasts and farmers on the prairies, in Ontario, and in Quebec each produce their own product, but part or all of their marketing is done through these jointly owned co-ops. Any *profit* is distributed to the co-op members in proportion to the quantity supplied by each. It is regarded as additional payment for produce provided.

co-operative
An organization owned by members/customers, who pay an annual membership fee and share in any profits.

Producer co-ops use their combined purchasing power to buy equipment, seeds, and other items at reduced prices. This enables them to have some bargaining power with the large companies they often deal with.

At *consumer co-ops* in cities, consumers get together and establish a food store in the hope of reducing their food costs. The members/owners/employees/customers work in the store, buy their food there, and share any profits as a reduction of their cost of food.

Co-operatives are important in agriculture. They enable farmers to purchase seed and equipment at reasonable prices. They also provide an outlet for farm products. Co-operatives do not pay taxes as corporations do and they also have other advantages.

There are also many *financial co-ops,* called credit unions and Caisses Populaires. These serve the purpose of banks, but they have no shareholders. Instead, they distribute their profits annually to their member/owners in various ways. The Caisses Populaires in Quebec have become very large and have a significant share of financial business there.

Because co-ops distribute their profits to members as a reduction in members' costs, these profits are not subject to income tax. From time to time various business organizations assert that many co-ops are now more like large businesses and should be taxed. So far this viewpoint has not been successful as it does not appear to have much support. Figure 5–6 lists some of the largest co-operatives in Canada. Some co-ops are also becoming corporations.

JOINT VENTURES

One of the latest trends in business is for two or more corporations (often from two different countries) to form strategic alliances to accomplish some objectives. A joint venture, then, is an effort by two or more business firms to capture new markets through cooperation and shared investment risk. This enables world markets to benefit from the expertise of all nations' businesspeople working together. For example, GM joined with Toyota to assemble Geo Prizms and Toyota Corollas in Fremont, California. Such agreements are taking place all over the world. Britain's state-owned car company, BL, formed a joint venture with Japan's Honda to build cars in England. In 1988, Chrysler joined with Mitsubishi Motors to make a sporty car code-named X25.

Non-Financial Co-operatives*	Revenue ($000)	Assets ($000)	Employees
1. Saskatchewan Wheat Pool	$2,063,599	$ 823,958	2,100
2. Federated Co-operatives	1,540,576	648,249	1,938
3. Alberta Wheat Pool	1,069,165	446,141	1,520
4. Agropur Co-operative	1,030,320	369,098	3,112
5. Calgary Co-operative Assn.	522,158	126,718	3,640
6. United Co-ops. of Ontario	488,767	170,523	1,822
7. Co-op Atlantic	424,979	87,151	1,000
8. United Farmers of Alberta Co-op.	320,480	119,267	595
9. CSP Foods	187,249	81,089	N.A.
10. Manitoba Pool Elevators	150,931	212,629	798
Financial Co-operatives			
1. Co-operators Group	$1,396,495	$2,630,271	5,182
2. Co-operators General Insurance	954,782	1,488,113	2,960
3. Desjardins Life Assurance Co.	745,243	2,910,738	1,320
4. Caisse Centrale Desjardins	436,851	5,087,096	154
5. Vancouver City Savings C.U.	292,335	2,970,159	728
6. Co-operators Life Insurance	277,475	942,695	N.A.
7. Credit Union Central (Sask.)	205,983	1,992,352	354
8. B.C. Central Credit Union	186,405	1,860,096	207
9. Credit Union Central of Ontario	134,102	1,413,339	270
10. Surrey Metro Savings C.U.	114,283	1,014,540	473

Figure 5–6 This is a list of Canada's 10 largest financial and 10 largest non-financial co-ops.

Source: Report on Business, *Globe and Mail,* July 1992, p. 119.
*All are agricultural or food related.

The Moscow McDonalds is a joint venture between McDonalds Canada Ltd. and a Russian government agency. Its opening attracted worldwide media attention.

REACHING BEYOND OUR BORDERS

Canadian Joint Ventures

An example of joint ventures and strategic alliances involving Canadian companies is Bombardier Inc., whose rail car division has various agreements with companies from France, the U.S., and other countries for bidding on contracts to build subway systems and high-speed rail lines and equipment. Northern Telecom is another giant Canadian company that has joint ventures and alliances with telecommunication companies in other countries. One of the best-known Canadian joint ventures abroad is the huge McDonald's restaurant in Moscow, which is jointly owned by McDonald's Canada Ltd. and a Russian government agency. ▼

WHICH FORM IS FOR YOU?

As you can see, you may participate in the business world in a variety of ways. You can start your own sole proprietorship, partnership, corporation, or co-operative. There are advantages and disadvantages to each. However, the risks are high no matter which form you choose. The miracle of free enterprise is that the freedom and incentives of capitalism make such risks acceptable to many people, who go on to create the great Canadian corporations.

One of the best known is the giant department store chain, the T. Eaton Co. Ltd. It was founded 125 years ago by Timothy Eaton in Toronto as a small store. Canadian Tire is another success story. So is Magna International, the large auto parts manufacturer. Bombardier, Canadian Airlines, CAE, and Steinberg's are only a few of the many companies whose success was due to the confidence, hard work, and abilities of the individuals who founded them. They all started small, accumulated capital from profits, grew, and became leaders in their fields. It is still being done today. Could you do the same?

Many students prefer to take the more cautious route of working for a corporation. The advantages are many: a fixed salary, paid vacations, health coverage, limited risk, job security, promotional possibilities, and more.

The disadvantages of working for others are also significant: limited income potential, fixed hours, repetitive work, close supervision, and limited freedom. Sometimes it is fun to work for others while starting your own business on the side. Apple Computer was started in a garage. Many firms have started in people's basements and attics. Business offers many different opportunities for tomorrow's graduates.

SPOTLIGHT ON BIG BUSINESS

Bombardier Inc.: From Snowmobiles to Trains and Planes

The profile at the beginning of this chapter highlighted the career of Armand Bombardier. From his tiny, tentative beginnings more than half a century ago with a vehicle to provide mobility on the snow, his company has now become a giant transnational.

In 1991, Bombardier had 25,000 employees, assets exceeded \$2 billion, and sales totalled just under \$3 billion. From 1986 to 1990 the company made several major acquisitions in Europe and in North America. Perhaps the best known are Canadair in Montreal, de Havilland in Toronto, and Learjet in the U.S. It has become a technological leader in its fields of operation.

This is what *Time* magazine said: "[Bombardier's] 254 train cars and loaders [manufactured for the English Channel tunnel] will be among the world's most technologically advanced rolling stock when they go into service in 1993."* Armand Bombardier's little company has come a long way since 1937.

*November 12, 1990, p. 27.
Annual Report, January 31, 1992 and other sources. ▼

PROGRESS CHECK

- What is the major benefit of a private corporation?
- Why do companies enter into joint ventures?
- Suppose you want to start a day care centre where you and your friends can send your children. You do not want to make it a profit-making organization and you want all your friends to help in running the organization. What form of organization will you use?

SUMMARY

1. A business can be formed in several ways.

1. List the three basic forms of business ownership.

- *What are the three major forms of business ownership?*

  The three major forms of business ownership are sole proprietorships, partnerships, and corporations.

2. Each form of business ownership has advantages and disadvantages.

2. Compare the advantages and disadvantages of:
   1. Sole proprietorships.
   2. Partnerships.
   3. Corporations.

- *What are the advantages and disadvantages of sole proprietorships, partnerships, and corporations? Is there some way to review them quickly?*

  See Figure 5–4 on page 153.
- *Which form of business is the most popular?*

  Sole proprietorships are most popular.
- *Which form of business does most of the business in Canada?*

  Corporations do most of the business in Canada.

3. Not all partners have the same roles and responsibilities.

3. Explain the differences between limited and general partnerships.

- *What are the main differences between general and limited partnerships?*

  General partners are owners (partners) who have unlimited liability and are active in managing the company. Limited partners are owners (partners) who have limited liability and are not active in the company.
- *What does unlimited liability mean?*

  Unlimited liability means that sole proprietors and general partners must pay all debts and damages caused by their business. They may have to sell their houses, cars, or other personal possessions to pay business debts.
- *What does limited liability mean?*

  Limited liability means that corporate owners (shareholders) and limited partners are responsible for losses only up to the amount they invest. Their other personal property is not at risk.

4. The first and most important step in forming a partnership is choosing the right partner.

4. List the contents of a partnership agreement.

- *How do you form a partnership?*

  The most important step in forming a partnership is choosing a partner wisely. Then, no matter how good friends you and your partner may be, put your partnership agreement *in writing* (see pp. 149–50).

5. Forming a corporation is more complex than forming a partnership.

- *How do you form a corporation?*

  Two major steps are needed to form a corporation. You must file articles of incorporation (the articles include the name, purpose, and duration of the corporation). You must also write bylaws telling how the firm will operate (authority of directors and officers, etc.).

5. Describe the process of incorporation.

▼ *Why do people incorporate?*

Two important reasons for incorporating are ease of transfer of ownership and limited liability.

6. The 1980s seemed to be the decade of corporate mergers.

6. Define and give examples of three types of corporate mergers.

▼ *What is a merger?*

A merger is the result of two firms forming one company. The three major types of mergers are vertical mergers, horizontal mergers, and conglomerate mergers.

7. Private corporations have some advantages and disadvantages.

7. Summarize the advantages and disadvantages of private corporations.

▼ *What are the advantages?*

Limited liability and ease of transfer of ownership are the main advantages. There is also a lower income tax rate.

▼ *What are the disadvantages?*

The principle disadvantage is that shares cannot be sold to the public.

8. People who dislike organizations in which owners, managers, workers, and buyers have separate goals often form co-operatives.

8. Explain the role of co-operatives.

▼ *What is the role of a co-operative?*

Co-operatives are organizations that are owned by members/customers. Some people form cooperatives to give members more economic power than they would have as individuals.

9. One of the latest trends in business is for two or more companies to participate in a joint venture.

9. Describe the purpose of joint ventures.

▼ *What is the purpose of joint ventures?*

Joint ventures enable firms to capture new markets by co-operating and sharing investment risk.

GETTING INVOLVED

1. If you look around, you will be able to find people who are involved in sole proprietorships, partnerships, and corporations in your area. Since your career depends on such information, spend some time interviewing people from each form of ownership and get their impressions, hints, and warnings. How much does it cost to start? How many hours do they work? What are the specific benefits? Share the results with your class.
2. Find out how much it costs to incorporate a company in your province. Then compare it to the cost of a federal incorporation. Is there a significant difference?
3. Have you ever thought of starting your own business? What kind of business would it be? Think of a friend(s) who you might want for a partner in the business. List the capital and personal skills you need for the business. Then make separate lists of the capital and personal skills you might bring and those your friend(s) might bring. What capital and personal skills do you need that neither of you have?
4. Look in the Yellow Pages and find a co-operative in your community. Visit the co-operative to find out how it was formed, who may belong to it, and how it operates.
5. Get an annual report of a large corporation from the library or by writing the company. What are the firm's annual sales? Net income (profit)? Number of common shareholders? Profit shareholders received in dividends?
6. Debate the following statement with fellow students: "It is better for a college or university graduate to go to work for a large corporation than to start his or her own business because there is less risk, the salary is secure, fringe benefits are ample, and the chances for promotion are good."

PRACTICING MANAGEMENT DECISIONS

Case One Should the Partnership Incorporate?

Helen and Dimitri have worked hard at their business for three years. Their wholesale beauty supplies partnership has come a long way from the early days when they were working in the basement of their home. Last year, sales exceeded $1 million, and this year they are running well ahead of last year. They expect their profit this year to be about $100,000 after deducting their own salaries, which amount to $60,000. They expect sales and profits to rise dramatically in the next three years.

Most of their friends who are in business are incorporated and Helen and Dimitri have been wondering if they should go that route too. Their accountant has been urging them to take this step because of the many advantages of the corporate form of ownership.

They are somewhat reluctant to do this because they like the simplicity of their partnership format. They are also concerned about the costs of making the switch, the more complex structure, and the ongoing additional legal and accounting costs of operating as a corporation.

Decision Questions

1. What are the major advantages and disadvantages of each type of ownership?
2. Do you think that in this case the advantages of incorporation outweigh the partnership form? Why?
3. Will it be easier for Helen and Dimitri to obtain funding in the future if they make the switch? Explain.
4. If they incorporate, will they run a greater risk of a hostile takeover? Why?

Case Two Going Public

George Zegoyan and Amir Gupta face a difficult decision. Their private auto-parts manufacturing company has been a great success—too quickly. They cannot keep up with the demand for their products. They must expand their facilities but have not had the time to accumulate sufficient working capital, nor do they want to acquire long-term debt to finance the expansion. Discussions with their accountants, lawyers, and stockbrokers have confronted them with the necessity of going public to raise the required capital.

They are concerned about maintaining control if they become a public company. They are also worried about the loss of privacy because of the required reporting to various regulatory bodies and to their shareholders. Naturally, they are also pleased that the process will enable them to sell some of their shareholdings to the public and realize a fair profit from their past and expected future successes. It will also let them raise substantial new capital to meet the needs of their current expansion program.

The proposed new structure will allow them to retain 60 percent of the outstanding voting shares, so they will keep control of the company. Nevertheless, they are somewhat uneasy about taking this step, because it will change the whole nature of the company and the informal method of operating they are used to. They are concerned about having "partners" in their operations and profits. They are wondering whether they should remain as they are and try to grow more slowly even if it means giving up profitable orders.

Decision Questions

1. Are George and Amir justified in their concerns? Why?
2. Do they have any other options besides going public? What are they?
3. Do you think they should try to limit their growth to a manageable size to avoid going public, even it if means forgoing profits now? Why?
4. Would you advise them to sell their business now if they can get a good price and then start a new operation? Explain.

LET'S TALK BUSINESS

1. Pick a small-business area in your neighbourhood and survey how many are owned by women or men alone and how many by partners (women, men, or mixed). Do your results indicate whether there is any gender preference for a particular form of company ownership? If so, why do you think this is the case?
2. In doing the survey above, ask whether there were any reasons one form of ownership was chosen over another (sole proprietorship, partnership, or corporation). Does it relate to the type of business or to the personalities of the owners? Is it a question of raising the required amount of cash? Of long hours?
3. Speak to a lawyer, accountant, or stockbroker to find out how popular limited partnerships are. Inquire under what circumstances limited partnerships are used.
4. Look at a listing of all the Toronto Stock Exchange transactions for a week. You can find this in the *Financial Post, Financial Times,* or perhaps your local newspaper. Look at the column called "Vol" for number of shares of a particular company that were traded that week. Make some reasonable dividing line between very active trading and low-volume trading shares (say, 100,000). Count how many high-volume and low-volume stocks are listed. What does that tell you about large and small Canadian public companies? What useful information does this yield?
5. Why are joint ventures becoming more common, especially for foreign activities? What are their main advantages?

LOOKING AHEAD

If you are excited about the idea of starting your own business someday, join the crowd. Entrepreneurship is the in thing for the near future. Entrepreneurs are starting the new high-tech firms that will be the IBMs and Xeroxes of tomorrow. Chapter 6 will discuss such entrepreneurs. Also, you will learn about the response of large corporations to competition from small firms: *intrapreneuring,* or creating small entrepreneurial areas within the large company.

One area of strong interest today is franchising, a way of getting into business with less risk and more certain managerial assistance. Chapter 6 also describes opportunities and pitfalls to watch out for in starting a franchise.

After that, the text will introduce the use of business functions in small business. Later chapters will go into much greater detail about these business functions—marketing, accounting, personnel, finance, and so forth.

TRY OUR
SOFT DRINKS
COFFEE
CHOCOLATE
CHIPS
MAPS
CIGARETTES
JUICES
CIGARETTES
LARGE
$4.95
plus taxes
WELCOME
PETRO-CANADA
FAST FRIENDLY SERVICE
2L COKE PRODUCTS
$149
CHIPS 140G
99¢

SMALL BUSINESS, ENTREPRENEURSHIP, AND FRANCHISING

LEARNING GOALS

After you have read and studied this chapter, you should be able to:

1. Define small business and discuss its importance to the Canadian economy.
2. Summarize the major causes of small-business failures.
3. Explain why people are willing to take the risks of entrepreneurship.
4. Describe the attributes needed to be a successful entrepreneur and explain why women have a higher success rate than men.
5. Identify ways you can learn about small businesses.
6. Explain what a business plan is and outline the general areas of information it should include.
7. Explain what a market is and why it is important for a businessperson to know the market.
8. Describe intrapreneuring and its benefits for big businesses.
9. Define franchising and compare the advantages and disadvantages of franchising.
10. Outline the areas you need to analyze when evaluating a franchise.

KEY TERMS

business plan p. 179
entrepreneur p. 167
franchise p. 186
franchise agreement p. 186
franchisee p. 186
franchising p. 186
franchisor p. 186
intrapreneur p. 167
skunkworks p. 167
small business p. 173
venture capitalist p. 183

Bob Dickie

PROFILE BOB DICKIE, PLUGGED IN

Bob Dickie just doesn't get it. When this country started to sniff the cold wind of recession, Dickie stripped his savings and started his own company. When the nation's talk turned to retrenchment and rationalization, Dickie turned to the high cost, high risk of research and development. When consumers stopped spending, Dickie launched a new product at a higher price than that of competitors. Initial assessment (of Bob): severely impaired judgment, possibly due to a previous lifestyle with fast boats and motorcycles.

So how come Bob Dickie now seems so self-satisfied? How is it that, having put everything on the line, he has come to possess a Mercedes and a Ferrari at his fabulous country home north of Toronto? Most important, how has he managed to create a successful research and development hothouse in a onetime dance hall, bustling with cheerful gnomes who proclaim themselves Dickie devotees? Doesn't Dickie understand that these are sombre days of sinkhole despair?

Bob Dickie has thumbed his nose at the economy. He has done this by doing what others only dream of: He invents and adapts things, he makes things better. He has 42 patents, with 10 more pending.

Dickie's greatest accomplishment so far is a wall plug, a subject that usually excites little interest. Nevertheless he has designed his very own, which, in the world of electrical extrusions, is revolutionary. To those who sneer, he points out that Canadian Tire Corp. Ltd., which started selling his FlatPlug extension cords before Christmas with zero advertising, can't keep them on the shelves. Peter Stephens, who buys things electrical for Canadian Tire, says the chain sold 25,000 in four months. At $4.99 compared to $1.99 for the conventional plug, Canadian Tire will increase its profit. It plans to feature FlatPlug in its spring catalogue.

In the U.S., Ace Hardware (with 5,300 stores) placed an order for 30,000 units. A large California lighting fixture manufacturer has started affixing them to its lamps and plans to use 25,000 weekly soon.

In a small but significant way, Dickie's efforts speak to the nation's need to rediscover R&D in order to embrace a new prosperity. "I think creating something is step one in making value," he says simply, echoing the regular dose of *Business Week* that he has taken since his teens. "There are a lot of people on Bay Street who are hustling deals, but they are not creating anything. They're only hanging off something that somebody else created, be it a piece of real estate or stock in a company. . . . If we lose Canada's manufacturing base, then it's over," he continues. "You're nothing—you're Iceland."

Source: "Plugged In," *Report on Business Magazine, Globe and Mail,* May 1992, p. 60.

THE IMPORTANCE OF ENTREPRENEURSHIP TO AN ECONOMY

Entrepreneurship is accepting the calculated risk of starting a business to make a profit. At one time, entrepreneurship was not included in the factors of production. Economics texts tended to focus on land, labour, and capital. It became clear over time, however, that a country that had little land and few other natural resources could prosper *if* it had brilliant entrepreneurs. The best examples today are

Singapore, Japan and South Korea. Canada has both natural resources and entrepreneurs, but its success in the future is more dependent on entrepreneurs than on natural resources. An **entrepreneur** is a person who organizes, manages, and assumes the risks of starting and operating a business to make a profit.

entrepreneur
A person who organizes, manages, and assumes the risks of starting and operating a business to make a profit.

One definition of an entrepreneur is "someone who undertakes to do something." Successful entrepreneurs are usually bold, determined innovators obsessed with an idea that drives them to put up with all sorts of difficulties and discouragement to achieve their goal. Nearly all the modern conveniences and technological advances that we now take for granted are due to the efforts of such entrepreneurs.

The sewing machine, the radio, transistors, TV, telephones, cars, computers—all were the ideas of various geniuses whose work has been put to practical use by entrepreneurs. Some inventors have also been good entrepreneurs, but that is quite rare. Many entrepreneurs just find better ways to produce or distribute existing products. That's how chain and department stores and supermarkets developed.

Entrepreneurs played a major role in developing the early Canadian economy in fur trading, lumber, shipbuilding, fishing, farming, retail trade, and transportation. Some became giant companies like the Hudson Bay Co., CPR, and MacMillan Bloedel.

Since entrepreneurship is still the major driving force in the Canadian economy, we are going to examine its implications for you and your future career. We will be looking at entrepreneurship in large corporations and in small business, and we will examine the franchising aspect of large and small businesses.

Entrepreneurial Teams

Large organizations are cautious, bureaucratic, and slow to react to changes in the markets they serve. Many companies have set up teams of managers from different areas within the company to overcome such difficulties. Entrepreneurial teams help the company function efficiently and ensure better co-operation and co-ordination among different functions of the business.

To encourage the entrepreneurial spirit, employees and managers from different areas of the business who have shown such spirit are organized into special teams. A team can be better than an individual because it brings together people with a variety of skills and experience to bounce ideas off each other.

Such teams are said to consist of intrapreneurs. An **intrapreneur** is a person with entrepreneurial skills who is employed in a corporation to launch new products. Such people take hands-on responsibility for innovation in an organization.

intrapreneur
A person with entrepreneurial skills who is employed in a corporation to launch new products and who takes hands-on responsibility for innovation in an organization.

Some groups become more daring and enterprising and work on what seem like way-out projects. These are known as *skunkworks* (the name comes from the Li'l Abner comic strip) because no one knows what outlandish ideas they may come up with. **Skunkworks** is a highly innovative, fast-moving entrepreneurial unit operating at the fringes of a corporation.

skunkworks
A highly innovative, fast-moving entrepreneurial unit operating at the fringes of a corporation.

Many companies have benefitted enormously from intrapreneurial teams and from skunkworks. An example is the development of the Avro–Arrow military plane by de Havilland, the most advanced of its kind. Do some research in your library to see what other examples you can find.

One of the most famous examples of intrapreneurial success is the "Post-it"™ gummed note pad, developed at the 3M Company. Despite its many obvious uses, intrapreneurs had to persist for years before it became a major product.

Intrapreneurs develop new products for the corporations that employ them. One product, the Post-it note pad, is widely used by people in business and academic settings. The development of this product generated new profits for the 3M Company.

SPOTLIGHT ON BIG BUSINESS

Intrapreneurs at Work

One exciting new company that developed in the 1980s was Compaq Computer. It was started by three senior managers at Texas Instruments: Bill Murto, Jim Harris, and Rod Canion. All three were bitten by the entrepreneurial bug and decided to go out on their own. They debated starting a Mexican restaurant, a company to produce hard disks for computers, or a business built around a beeping device for finding car keys. However, they finally decided to build a portable personal computer compatible with the IBM PC.

The key to Compaq's success was that it was built around this "smart team" of experienced managers. The chief executive officers in such firms are not order givers but co-ordinators whose main task is to tap the potential of their teams. A study of 90 West Coast companies found that a strong management team was the top priority for success. At Compaq, the team wanted to combine the discipline of a big company with an environment where people could feel they were participating in a successful venture. The trio of corporate entrepreneurs recruited seasoned managers with similar desires. They recruited a 14-year veteran from Texas Instruments to set up a state-of-the-art accounting system. A senior vice president from Datapoint became operations manager, and an IBM veteran became the sales and resource manager.

All the managers work as a team. That is, the company's treasurer and top engineer contribute to production and marketing decisions. Everyone works together to conceive, develop, and market products. In its first year, Compaq generated $11 million in sales, the hottest performance in the history of American business. Sales soared 950 percent to $1.2 billion, and soon Compaq ranked fifth in *Fortune* magazine's list of the 25 fastest-growing U.S. corporations. The success of Compaq can be traced to its entrepreneurial team.

Sources: Joel Kotkin, "The Smart Team at Compaq Computer," *Inc.*, February 1986, pp. 48–56; Stuart Gannes, "America's Fastest-Growing Companies," *Fortune,* May 23, 1988, pp. 28–40.

THE ENTREPRENEURIAL CHALLENGE

There have been many surveys asking people why they opened their own businesses. Thousands of new businesses are started every month, and most of these are small, owner-managed enterprises. Statistics indicate that the number continues to increase, and women are playing an ever-increasing role. This occurs despite a very high failure rate. Why do so many men and women, young and old, newly arrived immigrants and long-settled residents undertake this difficult, risky task? Here are some of the reasons.

New idea, process, or product. Some entrepreneurs are driven by a firm belief, perhaps even an obsession, that they can produce a better widget, or the old widget at a lower cost, than anybody else. Perhaps they have gotten hold of a new widget or have conceived of an improvement that they are convinced has a large potential market. That's how Apple Computers started. Three young engineers led by Steve Jobs left good positions with Digital Equipment to develop the personal computer. Bob Dickie, profiled at the start of this chapter, is another example. Sometimes you just "know" that you can run that business better than your boss or company.

Independence. Some employees who have imagination and/or confidence in themselves find their jobs too restrictive. They need breathing space and a little elbow room! Perhaps their company does not encourage intrapreneurism in their operations, so at the right time they make the break. Many people cannot conceive of working for someone else. They like doing things their own way without someone standing over them. This type of person gets a great deal of satisfaction out of what he or she achieves. Do you know anybody who feels that way?

Challenge. Closely related to the previous factors are the excitement and the challenge of doing something new or difficult. Many people thrive on overcoming challenges. These people welcome the opportunity to run their own businesses.

Family pattern. Some people grow up in an atmosphere where family members have started their own businesses—perhaps going back several generations. The talk at the dinner table is often about business matters. This background often predisposes young men or women to think along the same lines. Sometimes there is a family business, and the next generation grows up expecting to take its place there in due course.

Profit. It's natural for people to want to benefit monetarily from their ideas and dedication and to be rewarded for the money they risk when they run a business. Yet long after a business has produced substantial profits and amassed personal fortunes for its owners, many continue to enjoy the challenge of overcoming the endless problems that every business faces and the satisfaction of continued success.

Job insecurity or joblessness. A recent phenomenon is the downsizing policy in many large and medium-size companies since the serious recession of the early 1980s. Companies have been on a decade-long campaign of paring staff to the bone to reduce costs. In combination with the significant inroads made by computers in the same period (the technological unemployment referred to in Chapter 4), many employees, including middle-level and even senior-level managers, have been laid off. This has forced many of them to change their orientation from employee to self-employed. The accelerating movement to home-based operations has made this transition easier.

Immigrants. Many immigrants who come to Canada lack educational skills. This, combined with no Canadian job experience and weak language skills in English or French, makes it difficult for them to find employment. However they often have the drive and desire to succeed, and if they can obtain the capital, they can start their own business. We see this in the many immigrants who run convenience stores (dépanneurs in Quebec), as well as other types of businesses, such as importing and manufacturing.

On the average, entrepreneurial activity is higher among immigrants and their average income is 9 percent higher than other Canadians'.[1] Figure 6–1 shows wide variations in rates of self-employment for different ethnocultural groups.

What Does It Take to Be a Successful Entrepreneur?

How do you know if you have the qualities necessary to make a successful businessperson? There is no foolproof formula. Likely winners have proven to be losers and predicted losers have been big winners. External conditions play a major role in determining the success or failure of a business venture. Wars, recessions, inflation, changes in government policies, competitors' actions, technological developments—all can have a significant effect on businesses, especially new companies.

Nevertheless, certain personal qualities are necessary to start and, more important, to operate a small business. Many skills can be learned through work experience and formal education, but the kind of person you are may be the most important factor. Here are some major qualities that will increase your chances of succeeding as an entrepreneur.

1. **Self-direction.** You should be a self-starter, with lots of confidence in yourself. You do not hesitate to step in "where angels fear to tread." Doing your own thing should seem like the *only* way. Furthermore, you are the boss and everything really rests on your shoulders.
2. **Determination.** Closely related is the drive you need to see you through all the obstacles and difficulties that you will encounter. You have to keep going where others would give up. This often accompanies the high degree of self-confidence mentioned above.
3. **High energy level.** You must be able to put in long hours every day, six or seven days a week, for the first few years at least. You must be able to take hard work, physically and mentally.
4. **Risk orientation.** Because there is a high risk of failure, you must be able to live with uncertainty. You must accept the fact that all your hard work and money may go down the drain. On a day-to-day basis, you must make decisions that involve varying degrees of risk.

Figure 6–1 Self-employment by self-identified ethnocultural groups (per 1,000)

Group	Rate	Group	Rate
Black	26.5	Italian	64.5
British	59.1	Japanese and Korean	109.7
Chinese	72.9	Jewish	149.6
Czech/Slovak	91.3	Latin American	34.3
Dutch	107.9	Polish	69.0
Filipino	17.6	Portuguese	30.8
Finnish	64.1	Russian	81.0
French	48.6	Scandinavian	103.1
German	103.0	Spanish	48.4
Greek	124.2	Ukrainian	88.1
Hungarian	95.1	West Asian/Arab	99.9
Indo-Pakistani	50.7	Yugoslavian	71.4

Source: *Highlights of Self-Employment of Ethnocultural Groups in Canada, Report I.* (Multiculturalism Canada, March 1986).

5. **Vision.** Many successful entrepreneurs had some dream or vision they were impelled to realize. Perhaps it was to make that product better than anyone else or to provide a new product or service.
6. **Ability to learn quickly.** Making errors is inevitable. Only those who do nothing make no mistakes. What is important is what you learn from them. Good entrepreneurs are quick to learn such lessons. They adapt and shift gears as required instead of letting their pride stand in the way of admitting their mistake.

How do you stack up as a potential entrepreneur? You can take the entrepreneurial readiness questionnaire at the end of this chapter to see how you rate. Remember, these are only guidelines. The only rule about starting a business is that there *is* no rule. Some people have had an entrepreneurial bent since they were children. They were always promoting something—delivering papers, organizing other kids to collect bottles or plastic containers, selling, or doing other part-time work at an early age. As adults, they don't ask people if they should go into business for themselves—they do it!

A 17-year-old composer once asked Mozart's opinion about the quality of his compositions. After examining the works, Mozart told him they lacked maturity and that he should wait until he was a little older. The visitor, somewhat exasperated, replied that Mozart himself had started composing when he was 5! Mozart replied, "That's true, but I didn't ask anybody."

Others are a little more cautious. They get some education—perhaps even a bachelor of commerce (B.Com.) or master of business administration (M.B.A.) degree or a professional designation such as chartered accountant (C.A.), as well as some work experience before they decide to venture into business. Some follow this procedure as part of a deliberate plan; others make the decision to go off on their own later, as a result of business experience they have accumulated.

Women Entrepreneurs

A major phenomenon of the 1980s was the large number of women who went into business for themselves. Throughout this book, you will see many examples of such enterprises. Between 1975 and 1990, the number of male entrepreneurs grew by 50.4 percent. But over the same period, the number of female entrepreneurs grew 172.8 percent. In 1990, 29.8 percent of all self-employed Canadians were women, up from 19 percent in 1975.[2] Women who start their own business have tended to concentrate in certain industries. In 1990, 58 percent of self-employed women worked in the service sector, 28 percent in retail trade, 10 percent in agriculture, and approximately 7 percent in manufacturing, construction, transportation, or communications. A very small number of self-employed women were involved in such primary industries as fishing, logging, or mining.[3]

Catherine Enright is applying her entrepreneurial (SeaFarm Venture), educational (M.B.A. in international business and Ph.D. in marine biology), and networking (World Aquaculture Society, vice-president) skills to the development of a new and growing industry in Nova Scotia: oyster farming.

Studies and surveys have come up with a variety of reasons for this significant emergence of female entrepreneurs.

Financial need. The 1980s saw average real incomes of Canadian employees dropping, and unemployment has remained high for the past decade. This has forced many wives to support the family budget by starting a business, sometimes part-time, sometimes with their husbands.

Lack of promotion opportunities. Most positions in higher management are still dominated by men. While the situation is improving, the rate is extremely slow. Many women who are frustrated by this take the entrepreneurial route.

Women returning to the work force. Many women who return to the job market after raising a family find that their skills are outdated. They also encounter subtle age discrimination. These factors encourage many to try self-employment.

Feminism. The feminist movements of the last three decades have given many women the confidence to strike out on their own.

Family and personal responsibility. The high divorce rate in recent years has created a situation where many divorced women found themselves with children and little or no financial support from their ex-husbands. Some even refused such support to be more independent. The development of affordable personal computers and other modern technology has made it possible for women to start businesses based at home. There are many examples in this book of home-based enterprises run by women.

Public awareness of women in business. As more and more publicity highlights the fact that growing numbers of women have started their own ventures, the idea catches on and gives others the confidence to try. Often two or more women will team up to form a partnership.

Part-time occupations. Often, married women with some particular talent—publicity, writing, designing, making clothes, cooking, organizing, human relations—are encouraged to develop their hobby or skills on a part-time basis to see how far they can go with it. This procedure has produced many notable success stories, some of which are reported in this book.

Couples in partnership. Some ventures are started by couples who cannot find jobs. Or sometimes one member of a couple joins his or her partner whose business is growing and needs more help.

Higher Rate of Success for Women

Women entrepreneurs seem to have a better success rate than men. Various factors may account for this. Women feel less pressured than men to achieve quick results. They are a little more cautious, less apt to "shoot from the hip," so they make fewer mistakes. They also accept advice more readily than men, who may have a macho image of having to know it all. It will be interesting to follow this process in the 1990s to see if women continue to start ventures at the same rate and maintain their remarkable track record.

THINKING IT THROUGH

Do you know anyone who seems to have the entrepreneurial spirit? What about him or her makes you say that? Are there any similarities between the characteristics demanded of an entrepreneur and those of a professional athlete? Would an athlete be a good prospect for entrepreneurship? Why or why not? Could teamwork be important in an entrepreneurial effort? If you are a woman, are you motivated by women's success rate?

Entrepreneurs of the 1990s

Many people believe that future entrepreneurs will need better education and preparation than in the past. Business has become much more complex. A complicated mass of governmental laws and regulations, the rapid rate of advances in technology, international competition, and concerns with environmental and ethical issues have all combined to make it far more difficult to start and operate a business now.

International management guru Peter Drucker feels that, in the future, people with college and university training and some corporate experience will do much better as entrepreneurs in the long run. Of course this will not—and should not—discourage those who are strongly determined to start their own company. Such determination and self-confidence are major requirements for success in business. It is important to remember that there is no formula that guarantees success.

PROGRESS CHECK

- What are the advantages of entrepreneurial teams?
- Can you give five reasons why entrepreneurs go into business themselves?
- Why are so many women becoming entrepreneurs? Why do they have such a high success rate?

WHAT IS A SMALL BUSINESS?

It would be helpful to try to define what we mean by the term *small business*. If you are a giant company like Esso or General Motors, you look at nearly all companies as small. Governments have various size guidelines for different aid programs. In the definition we have previously used, a **small business** is "independently owned and operated, not dominant in its field, and meets certain standards of size in terms of employees or annual receipts."

small business
Business that is independently owned and operated, not dominant in its field, and meets certain standards of size in terms of employees or annual receipts.

By this definition, the vast majority of businesses in Canada are small—under 10 employees and with annual sales under $500,000. This volume of sales, less than $10,000 per week, might be further analyzed as follows (in round numbers):

Number of Days Open Each Week	Sales per Day Less than
5	$2,000
6	1,700
7	1,500

Of course, many small businesses have sales in the millions and up to 50 employees.

There is constant movement as far as individual businesses are concerned. Many are closing up while larger numbers are starting. Many are steadily growing larger, and some eventually become very large companies. Some merge with others or are sold as owners retire or die.

It is estimated that at the beginning of the 1990s there were about 900,000 businesses in Canada. For this purpose, a business is defined as having at least one paid employee plus the owner. The number of businesses that have no employees may reach into the tens of thousands. Of all these businesses, only a tiny fraction, perhaps 2 to 3 percent, had more than 100 employees.[4]

This bagel shop in Montreal is an example of many of the small businesses in Canada. A large number of small businesses are started each year by entrepreneurs seeking the challenge of fulfilling a dream.

Importance of Small Business

The small business sector is a very dynamic part of the Canadian economy. It provided nearly all the new jobs that were created in the 1980s and is expected to repeat this process in the 1990s. Small business also is responsible for a big share of innovation and initiative over a wide spectrum of business activities.

Small businesses continue to be feeders for future large businesses. As they prosper and develop new services or products, they are often bought out by large companies, which thus become more competitive. The founders usually profit handsomely from the transaction while retaining a managerial position and acquiring shares in the larger entity. Alternatively, after small businesses establish a good track record, they convert from private to public companies, enabling them to obtain significant financing and become larger companies.

Nearly all small businesses are Canadian-owned and -managed, in contrast to large businesses, many of which are foreign-owned and -managed. Small business thus plays a big role in helping to maintain the Canadian identity and Canadian economic independence.

Small-Business Categories

Another significant aspect of small business is the wide diversification of its activities. If you look about, you will find small businesses in:

1. **Service businesses** You are already familiar with the services provided by dry cleaners, travel agencies, lawn care firms, beauty parlours, and other services that cater to you and your family. In your career search, be sure to explore services such as hotels/motels, health clubs, amusement parks, income tax preparation organizations, employment agencies, accounting firms, rental firms of all kinds, management consulting, repair services (for example, computers, robots, VCRs), insurance agencies, real estate firms, stockbrokers, and so on.

SPOTLIGHT ON SMALL BUSINESS

Hard Times Make More Entrepreneurs

The hours are endless, the pay is meagre and the headaches are common. But Paul Nolan, president of Acton, Ontario-based Wicklow Hills Publishing Co., wouldn't trade his two publications, five employees, and 100-hour work weeks for a nine-to-five corporate grind.

"I like being my own boss," says the 27-year-old Nolan, who publishes *The Standardbred,* a bi-weekly tabloid for the Canadian harness racing industry, and the *Acton Tanner,* a weekly community newspaper. Projected sales this year are $300,000. "It's a thirst for new challenges, a belief that what you do with your life's work should always be fresh and dynamic and never stale and regimented." Nolan is one of a small but growing number of young entrepreneurs who are bypassing the tight job market that awaits college and university graduates, and setting up shop on their own.

"This has ruled my life for four years and has taken everything I've got," says Nolan, who bought *The Standardbred* with a $10,000 personal loan and a $50,000 vendor-financed loan upon completing his bachelor of arts degree from the University of Western Ontario in 1988. Nolan averages 14 hours a day, seven days a week, and didn't start collecting a regular salary until his third year. "You have to make sure your family and friends are aware of what this means in terms of a change in lifestyle."

Then it's time to do some homework, says Julie Smyth, manager of the Ryerson Business Consulting Service, a low-cost consulting group at Toronto's Ryerson Polytechnical Institute that prepares feasibility studies and business plans. Grads who are unable to pay for this kind of research can do it on their own.

Before arranging financing, it's necessary to complete a detailed business plan, which describes the overall picture of the operation. "This includes sales forecasts, information about the product and how it will be marketed, and information on management," Smyth says.

"Entrepreneurship is growing among students, partly [due to] the recession," says Sharon Lee, co-ordinator of student placement services at the counselling and career development centre at the University of Western Ontario in London. She estimates on-campus recruiting by employers at the school has dropped 35 percent since 1989.

"We used street vending as a way of test marketing," explains Lynda Eng, 29, who co-owns Toronto-based Manushka Designs Inc. with Manon LeBlanc, 28. Four years ago, the Ryerson fashion graduates sold their line of sarongs—wraparound skirts that double as halter tops—on the streets of downtown Toronto and developed a customer profile through surveys. Today, they rent a downtown studio where they do most of their design work and a boutique in the upscale Queens Quay Terminal. Sales last year were $250,000.

Take Rob French. The 28-year-old owner of Markham, Ontario-based Forever New Clothing Care Products Ltd. developed his own niche market by taking detergent out of the traditional grocery and drugstore markets and selling it to clothing and lingerie retailers. "We positioned ourselves as 'clothing care experts', so retailers look to us not only for the product but also for advice on how to take care of fine fabrics. When a salesperson sells an expensive silk outfit, we provide them with the means to tell the customer how to take care of it."

As part of its education component, the six-year-old distributing and manufacturing company sends a quarterly newsletter to retailers that explains how to wash everything from sweaters to swimsuits. Sales for the economics grad, who got his business idea from his lingerie retailer mother, were about $1 million last year.

For help in preparing a business plan and securing a loan, the federal or provincial government is a recent grad's best bet. The Federal Business Development Bank and the provinces of Ontario, Saskatchewan, and Prince Edward Island offer a variety of education programs and term and start-up capital loans. Ontario's industry ministry runs 26 self-help business offices that are stocked with publications on every facet of business development. This includes how to write a business plan, how to manage a business, and how to handle regulations, incorporation, taxation, and patents. [All provinces have similar programs.]

The Ontario Ministry of Industry, Trade & Technology made 259 ministry-arranged, start-up capital loans to college and university grads in fiscal 1991–92, 24.5 percent more than in 1990–91.

The Youth Venture Loan Program provides up to $7,500 to applicants age 18 through 29 who can match 20 percent of the loan with cash or equipment, and is interest-free for one year. "We provide business financing that might not normally be available to the new graduate because of age and lack of experience," says Patricia Hamilton, co-ordinator of this program.

Source: Louise Kinross, *Financial Post,* Sept. 23, 1992, p. C16.

2. **Retail businesses** You have only to go to a major shopping mall to see the possibilities in retailing. There are stores selling shoes, clothes, hats, skis, gloves, sporting goods, ice cream, groceries, and more. Much more. Watch the trends, and you will see new ideas like fancy popcorn stores, T-shirt shops, videotape rental stores, and yogurt shops.
3. **Construction firms** Drive through any big city and you will see huge cranes towering over an empty lot where major construction is taking place. Would you enjoy supervising such work? Visit some areas where construction firms are building bridges, roads, homes, schools, buildings, and dams. There is a feeling of power and creativity in such work that excites many observers. How about you? Talk to some of the workers and supervisors and learn about the risks and rewards of small construction firms.
4. **Wholesalers** Have you ever visited a wholesale food warehouse, jewellery centre, or similar wholesale firm? If not, you are missing an important link in the small-business system, one with much potential. Wholesale representatives often make more money, have more free time, travel more, and enjoy their work more than similar people in retailing. Check it out.
5. **Manufacturing** Of course, manufacturing is still an attractive career for tomorrow's graduates. Surveys show that manufacturers make the most money among small-business owners. There are careers for designers, machinists, mechanics, engineers, supervisors, safety inspectors, and a host of other occupations. Visit some small manufacturers in your area and inquire about such jobs, so that you can get some experience before starting your own manufacturing business. The high-tech world of today opens up many opportunities if you are interested.

SPOTLIGHT ON SMALL BUSINESS

Young Businesspeople in Small Business

Twelve winners of the Federal Business Development Bank's (FBDB) Young Entrepreneur Award were revisited recently, with interesting results. Three of these winners are Caroline Houle, 30, Jeff Golfman, 24, and Jon Manship, 30.

Caroline Houle, along with partners Christian and Charles Comas, both 31, founded Les Boulangeries Comas Inc., of Montreal in 1984. The company makes frozen bakery products, which have been sold in the past to supermarket chains and delis with ovens on their premises. They have recently increased their sales staff from three to five and are aggressively pursuing corporate cafeterias, hotels, and restaurants. For the year ending September 30, 1992, they had a 40 percent increase in sales.

Jeff Golfman owns Plan-It Recycling Inc. of Winnipeg. It collects and sells 13 kinds of recyclable trash, ranging from milk cartons and glossy flyers to tin cans. The company offers a private blue-box pickup and has about 9,500 customers. Because he charges $70 a year, Golfman is feeling the pinch of the recession, but he is now engaged in marketing tactics to maintain his level of operations.

Jon Manship asks "Recession, what recession?" His company, Spielo Manufacturing Inc., of Moncton, N.B., makes video lottery terminals. His sales jumped from 6 million in 1991 to 15 million in 1992.

Some of the winners of the Young Entrepreneur Award met at the FBDB Awards ceremony in Montreal in 1992. They have continued to meet and set up a network linking young entrepreneurs across the country. The non-profit Young Entrepreneurs of Canada wants to develop and support young entrepreneurs through regional chapters. The group has several membership levels, ranging from $10 a year for students to $100 for associates or experienced entrepreneurs under the age of 30.

For information, contact YEA Canada at P.O. Box 124, Moncton, N.B., E1C 8R9, or fax 506-852-9324.

Source: Shirley Won, "Young Business Pioneers Continue to Succeed," *Globe and Mail,* classroom edition, January 1993, p. 11.

There are also thousands of small farmers who enjoy the rural life and the pace of farming. Small farms have been in great trouble for the last few years, but some that specialize in exotic crops do quite well. Similarly, many small mining operations attract college and university students with a sense of adventure. People who are not sure what career they would like to follow have a busy time ahead. They need to visit service firms, construction firms, farms, mines, retailers, wholesalers, and all other kinds of small and large businesses to see the diversity and excitement available in Canadian business.

THINKING IT THROUGH

Imagine yourself starting a small business. What kind of business would it be? How much local competition is there? What could you do to make your business more attractive than competitors'? Would you be willing to work 60 to 70 hours per week in such a business?

Learning About Small-Business Operations

In spite of overwhelming odds against them, entrepreneurs set out to conquer the business world, confidently and enthusiastically. How hard do they work? Almost half of the owners work 56 hours a week. In addition to the long hours working the new business, nearly 20 percent of the new owners keep up full-time or part-time jobs as well. Clearly, the job as owner of a new small business calls for considerable stamina.[5] Only 11 percent work less than 40 hours; 86 percent put in extra hours on weekends.

Thousands of would-be entrepreneurs of all ages have asked the same questions: How do I get started? How can I learn to run my own business? Many of these people had no idea what kind of business they wanted to start; they simply wanted to be in business for themselves. That seems to be a major trend among students today. As you will see shortly, you have to understand business practices or you'll go broke in your own business. Here are some hints for learning about small business.

One of the best ways to learn retailing is to get a job at a bustling retail store and learn from the owner/manager. You will gather many insights about how to run a successful store.

Learn from Others

There are a few courses available that teach small-business management well. You might begin by investigating your local schools for such classes. The best thing about these courses is that they bring together entrepreneurs. *That* is how to learn to run a small business—talk to others who have done it.

The starting place for budding entrepreneurs is talking with small-business owners and managers. Learn from their experience, especially their mistakes. They will tell you that location is critical for retail business. They will caution you not to be undercapitalized. They will warn you about the problems of finding and retaining good workers. And, most of all, they will tell you to keep good records and hire a good accountant and lawyer before you start. Small-business owners can give you hundreds of good ideas, ranging from how to get bank loans to how to design creative advertising. This free advice is invaluable.

Get Some Experience

There is no better way of learning small-business management than becoming an apprentice or working for a successful entrepreneur. In fact a high percentage of small-business owners got the idea for their businesses from their prior jobs. The prior jobs of almost half of new business owners were in small businesses. The rule of thumb is: get three years' experience in a comparable business.

We noted earlier that new entrepreneurs of the 1990s could come from corporate management. Many corporate managers are tired of the big-business life and are quitting to start small businesses. They bring their managerial expertise and enthusiasm.

Starting and Running a Small Business

There are several ways to get into your first business venture.

1. Start your own company,
2. Buy an existing business, or
3. Buy a franchise unit.

Franchising will be discussed in the last segment of this chapter. Let us first look at some common procedures you should follow regardless of which path you pursue.

1. Gather information. The Federal Business Development Bank (FBDB) publishes some useful, free material for new entrepreneurs. So do most of the larger banks in Canada. The Canadian Federation of Independent Business (CFIB) is also a useful body for entrepreneurs. It has branches across Canada. Read through some CFIB booklets and you will get important clues as to what you should be doing before starting a business. Other useful federal sources are regional offices of the National Research Council, the Patent Office of the Ministry of Consumer and Corporate Affairs, the Small Business Administration, and the Small Business Data Base of Statistics Canada. This database is backed by the federal and provincial governments. It provides information on how competitors or potential competitors are performing. Most provincial governments provide a lot of information, assistance, and financing for small business. This is reviewed in some detail in Chapter 3.

2. Obtain professional advice. Find a good accountant or equivalent professional who will be your most important adviser for starting and running a business. Ask friends, other entrepreneurs or family to recommend someone. An experienced accountant

Source	Percentage Using Source	Importance Rank of Source
Accountant	78%	1
Other business owners	77	3
Friends/relatives	76	5
Bankers	72	2
Lawyers	63	6
Books/manuals	62	7
Suppliers	59	4
Trade organizations	47	9
Seminars	41	8
Government sources	33	10

Figure 6–2 Information sources

Small-business managers turn to accountants and bankers for important advice. They also question other business owners and friends for ideas.

will be able to give you invaluable advice and help you through all the procedures of getting your company organized and running. (See Figure 6–2.)

Don't fret about the cost. Remember that you are planning to invest (and borrow) thousands of dollars and a long period of hard labour. It is wise to protect that investment by spending a small portion of those dollars at the start for experienced counsel. Your accountant will also be invaluable on an ongoing basis. He or she will organize your accounting system and your office procedures, produce monthly figures, analyze results, advise on taxation matters, and free you up to concentrate on those functions that only you can and should attend to: buying, selling, servicing customers, collecting payments, and more.

3. Prepare a business plan. It is amazing how many people are eager to start a small business but have only a vague notion of what they want to do. Eventually, they come up with an idea for a business and begin discussing the idea with professors, friends, and other businesspeople. It is at this stage that the entrepreneur needs a **business plan,** a detailed written statement that describes the nature of the business, the target market, the advantages the business will have over competitors, the resources and qualifications of the owner(s), and much more.

business plan
A detailed written statement that describes the nature of the business, the target market, the advantages the business will have over competitors, the resources and qualifications of the owners, and much more.

A business plan forces potential owners of small businesses to be quite specific about the products or services they intend to offer. They must analyze the competition, the money needed to start, and other details of operation. A business plan forces the entrepreneur to translate hopes and dreams into concrete reality: to see how much cash is required, how much sales and profit must be generated to break even, how much profit will be made if all goes well, whether the target market is there, and what the competition is doing. It gives the entrepreneur a good look at what he or she may be walking into.

A business plan also enables investors, bankers, or other lenders to evaluate your proposal properly. You cannot expect to ask for financing without presenting a full picture of what you are all about. A well-prepared business plan provides the vital information these people require before they can make a decision. It also makes an excellent impression, because it shows that you have gone to a lot of trouble and expense and are very serious about your project.

To prepare a thorough plan, you will most likely need the assistance of a good accountant. In general, a business plan should include the following:

1. A cover letter summarizing the major facets of your proposed business.
2. A brief description of the industry and a detailed explanation of the products or services to be offered.

3. A thorough market analysis that discusses the size of the market, the need for the new product (service), and the nature of the competition.
4. A marketing plan that includes location, signs, advertising, and display.
5. An operating plan that includes a sales forecast, financial projections, accounting procedures, and human resource requirements.
6. A comprehensive capitalization plan describing how much money the owner(s) is committing. Few banks or investors will support a new firm unless the owner(s) has a substantial financial commitment.
7. A description of the experience and expertise of the owner(s). This may include résumés, letters of recommendation, and financial statements.

Unless you spend adequate time and effort preparing your business plan, it may end up like thousands of others—in a wastebasket, unread! Of 1,200 proposals received in a few months, the Aegis Partners, a Boston venture capital firm, read 600, researched 45, and funded only 14. Why? Because most entrepreneurs don't spend enough time preparing a good business plan but expect potential lenders to spend several hours reading it.[6]

A proper business plan takes months to prepare, as you and your accountant gather information and organize it into the proper format. Unfortunately, you have to convince your busy readers in just a few minutes that it is worth their while to continue reading. For them to do that, the plan has to be a real plan, not something cooked up to justify a decision to go into business made on intuition or some other basis.

Many books and articles have been written on how to prepare and write a good business plan. A sample outline of a business plan is provided in the following Spotlight on Small Business. Your accountant will be well informed on these matters. By working closely with him or her, you will find out what part of the job is yours.

This man is busy planning for his future. He is working on a business plan that will be the foundation for success. It will spell out who the market will be, how much capital will be needed, and how the business will meet and beat the competition.

SPOTLIGHT ON SMALL BUSINESS

Outline of a Comprehensive Business Plan

Cover Letter Only one thing is for certain when you go hunting for money to start a business: You won't be the only hunter out there. You need to make potential funders want to read your business plan instead of the hundreds of others on their desks. Your cover letter should summarize the most attractive points of your project in as few words as possible. Be sure to address the letter to the potential investor by name. "To whom it may concern" or "Dear Sir" is not the best way to win an investor's support.

Section 1—Introduction Begin with a two- or three-page management overview of the proposed venture. Include a short description of the business, and discuss major goals and objectives.

Section 2—Company background Describe company operations to date (if any), potential legal considerations, and areas of risk and opportunity. Summarize the firm's financial condition. Include past and current balance sheets, income and cash-flow statements, and other relevant financial records. (You will read about these financial statements in Chapter 17.) It is also wise to include a description of insurance coverage. Investors want to be assured that death or mishaps do not pose major threats to the company.

Section 3—Management team Include an organization chart, job descriptions of listed positions, and detailed résumés of the current and proposed executives. A mediocre idea with a proven management team is funded more often than a great idea with an inexperienced team. Managers should have expertise in all disciplines necessary to start and run a business. If they do not, mention outside consultants who will serve in these roles and describe their qualifications.

Section 4—Financial plan Provide five-year projections for income, expenses, and funding sources. Don't assume the business will grow in a straight line. Adjust your planning to allow for funding at various stages of the company's growth. Explain the rationale and assumptions used to determine the estimates. Assumptions should be reasonable and based on industry/historical trends. Make sure all totals add up and are consistent throughout the plan. (It will be necessary to hire a professional accountant or financial analyst to prepare these statements.)

Stay clear of excessively ambitious sales projections; rather, offer best-case, expected, and worst-case scenarios. These not only reveal how sensitive the bottom line is to sales fluctuations but also serve as good management guides.

Section 5—Capital required Indicate the amount of capital needed to commence or continue operations and describe how these funds are to be used. Make sure the totals are the same as the ones on the cash-flow statement. This area will receive a great deal of review from potential investors, so it must be clear and concise.

Section 6—Marketing plan Don't underestimate the competition. Review industry size, trends, and the target market segment. Discuss strengths and weaknesses of the product or service. The most important things investors want to know are what makes the product more desirable than what's already available and whether it can be patented. Compare pricing to the competition's. Forecast sales in dollars and units. Outline sales, advertising, promotion, and PR programs. Make sure the costs agree with those projected in the financial statements.

Section 7—Location analysis In retailing and certain other industries, the location of the business is a crucial factor. Provide a comprehensive demographic analysis of consumers in the area of the proposed store as well as a traffic-pattern analysis and vehicular and pedestrian counts.

Section 8—Manufacturing plan Describe minimum plant size, machinery required, production capacity, inventory and inventory-control methods, quality control, plant personnel requirements, and so on. Estimates of product costs should be based on primary research. (See Chapter 13).

Section 9—Appendix Include all marketing research on the product or service (off-the-shelf reports, article reprints, etc.) and other information about the product concept or market size. Provide a bibliography of all the reference materials you consulted. This section should demonstrate that the proposed company won't be entering a declining industry or market segment.

Sources: Eric Adams, "Growing Your Business Plan," *Home-Office Computing,* May 1991, pp. 44–48; R. Richard Bruno, "How to Write a Business Plan for a New Venture," *Marketing News,* March 15, 1985, p. 10; Ellyn Spragins, "Venture Capital Express," *Inc.,* November 1990, pp. 159–60.

One of the most common mistakes new small-business owners make is waiting too long to talk to bankers. You would be surprised how long it takes to review and process loans. Another common mistake is to ask for too little money.

Next, we will discuss some of the many sources of money available to new business ventures. All of them call for a comprehensive business plan. The time and effort invested *before* a business is started pays off many times later. With small businesses, the big payoff is survival.

Funding a Small Business

The problem with most new small businesses is that the entrepreneurs have more enthusiasm than managerial skills and capital. Our economic system is called capitalism for a reason. It is capital (money) that enables entrepreneurs to get started; buy needed goods, services, labour, and equipment; and keep the business going. Some of the *financial* reasons cited for failure are:

- Starting with too little capital.
- Starting with too much capital and being careless in its use.
- Borrowing money without planning how and when to pay it back.
- Trying to do too much business with not enough capital.
- Not allowing for setbacks and unexpected expenses.
- Extending credit too freely.

Entrepreneurs, like most people, are not highly skilled at obtaining, managing, and using money. Inadequate capitalization or poor financial management can destroy a business even when the basic idea behind it is good and the products are accepted in the marketplace. One secret of finding the money to start your business is knowing where to look for it.

PROGRESS CHECK

- Can you name the five different classes of small businesses?
- What factors are used to classify a firm as a small business?
- What advice would you give a friend who wanted to learn more about starting a small business?

- We gave you six reasons why small businesses fail financially. Can you name three?
- There are many sections in the business plan. This plan is probably *the* most important document a small-business person will ever make. Can you describe at least four of those sections?

One of the major problems of new entrepreneurs is misinformation or lack of information about capitalization and financial management. A new entrepreneur has several sources of capital: personal savings, relatives, former employers, banks, finance companies, venture capital organizations, and government agencies.

In Canada, the most common sources of commercial financing are the chartered banks. Since they rarely make unsecured loans for new business ventures, entrepreneurs may turn to the federal or provincial governments, which have a variety of agencies or programs to aid new or existing businesses. For example, the Small Business Loans Act authorizes the federal government to guarantee up to 85 percent of loans by authorized lenders, usually banks. The Federal Business Development Bank is also available for those unable to obtain bank loans. There are also venture capital companies, whose purpose is to seek out worthwhile new ventures and back them. Investors known as **venture capitalists** may finance your project—for a price. Venture capitalists ask for a hefty stake (frequently 60 percent) in your company in exchange for the cash to start your business. Experts recommend that you talk with at least five investment firms and their clients to find the right one for you.

venture capitalist
Individuals or organizations that invest in new businesses in exchange for partial ownership.

Venture capital companies are interested only in equity positions—buying shares in the company. The FBDB may take an equity position or make a loan. Both will insist on seats on the board of directors to keep an eye on the company's operations. In practice, the venture capitalists play a more active role than the FBDB. They also will not usually consider a request for less than $500,000. By contrast, the majority of FBDB loans are under $100,000. The FBDB plays a crucial role because it will invest in businesses with no track record, making it possible for them to obtain additional financing from other sources.

The financing agreement usually provides that, after a certain period of time, the entrepreneurs may buy back the shares held by these institutions at their current value.[7]

Most new businesses are started with personal savings. Many entrepreneurs turn to their families for the needed funds. Watch out if you plan to tap your relatives for a loan. Such a plan can backfire. Be sure to cover an intrafamily loan with a letter of agreement just in case a silent partner becomes outspoken.

You may want to consider borrowing from a potential supplier to your future business. Helping you get started may be in the supplier's interest if there is a chance you will be a big customer later.

As you may have guessed, technology-minded entrepreneurs have the best shot at attracting start-up capital. Such potential businesses are more attractive to venture capitalists and the federal and provincial governments have grant programs that provide funds for such ventures.

Personal Considerations Before Going into Business

You have been advised several times that owner/managers must work long hours and perhaps seven-day weeks, especially for the first couple of years. If you are unattached, then you are free to devote all your time to your business. If you want to sleep on a cot in your office there's nothing to stop you.

But what if you are married and have a child or two? Is your spouse ready to back you by undertaking to play daddy and mommy? Will you be torn between your family and business demands? Suppose you have no kids but you have a spouse or companion. How will she or he react to your constant absence? Have you considered what it may do to your relationship? These questions are often overlooked by entrepreneurs until they crop up and create havoc.

Finally, think about what kind of support system you can draw on when required. You may need some no-cost bodies like family members or friends to pitch in sometimes—to answer the phone, do some bookkeeping, help pack or ship. Do you have a shoulder to cry on when things get rough from time to time, as they certainly will?

Once you have passed all these hurdles—business plan, financing, and personal factors—you're ready. So far we have discussed starting a new business. Let us now look at buying a business.

Buying a Business

There are many legitimate reasons for owners of a business to want to sell their company. They may want to retire, they may be ill, or they may have other interests that have become more important. Sometimes partners cannot get along or a company wants to divest itself of a subsidiary that does not fit into its core business.

On the other hand, the main reason for selling might be negative business factors. You must be very careful about this. A business whose profits have been declining for a couple of years may be sick. Or perhaps the business seems to be doing all right but the owners know of some new factor that threatens its viability. This might be a change in a highway route that would result in a loss of vehicle traffic that is the lifeblood of the business. Perhaps a new competing franchise unit is scheduled to be built nearby. Or maybe the area has become run down and regular customers are turning away.

A new technological advance might threaten to make the company's processes, equipment, or product obsolete. (For example, plastic might replace steel and glass.) Imported competing products might be taking away the company's traditional markets (TVs, autos, jeans, and shoes are good examples). The company may be on the verge of losing a major customer. Or perhaps some new environmental regulations are due to kick in shortly that will involve a substantial outlay for new equipment.

To get the real story, do two things. Engage a professional accountant to examine the books and financial statements for the last three to five years. He or she will assess whether the financial statements give you a reliable picture of the company's operations during this period.

While this audit is being conducted, do some intensive investigation of your own. Check out every possible source of information in the municipality or area. Chambers of commerce, business development bodies, local newspapers, adjacent businesses (especially if you are considering a retail business), real estate agents, and local banks are all good sources of information. Drop in on the company unannounced at different hours to see what the operations look like. You might get a chance to speak to employees and customers. Get information from the trade association and trade publications of the particular industry about problems, trends, and developments.

When the audit and your investigation are both done, it is time to sit down with your accountant and review all the facts. (In effect, you have both been assembling some of the data necessary to prepare a business plan.) If you decide to go ahead, there still remains the question of determining a fair price. A business valuation expert can be very useful at this point. Often your accountant can do the job. If you require financing in addition to your own investment, it is time to prepare the formal business plan.

Causes of Small-Business Failure

Statistics show that most new businesses will fail within five years. There are many reasons for this. Most are avoidable weaknesses, what you might call personal or internal mistakes. They are usually lumped together as signs of poor *management*. (Part III of this book contains a thorough discussion of management.)

1. **Lack of finances** Due to any one or a combination of the following:
   Insufficient capital at start.
   Extending too much credit.
   Allowing customers to continually pay late.
   Carrying too much inventory.
   Not making sufficient allowance for slow beginning.
   Inadequate reserve for the unexpected.
   Initial overhead too high.
2. **Lack of experience**
   Inadequate experience in that line of business.
   No previous work experience at all.
   Poor marketing: pricing, products, and/or promotion.
3. **Poor allocation of time**
   Allotting time according to pressure of events.
   Not prioritizing according to importance of activity, such as selling, customer service, and collections.
4. **Weak or no professional guidance**
   Poor planning.
   Inadequate accounting system and misleading or outdated information.
   Lack of outside objective assessment.
5. **Lack of necessary personal qualities**

Often external or objective causes that are not subject to the individual's control play an important role in the collapse of a business. For example, if one or two of your major customers go bankrupt while they owe you substantial sums, as often happens in a recession, you may be dragged down with them. If Chrysler had not been saved by U.S. and Canadian government backing, it would have gone bankrupt in 1980 and would have dragged down many small businesses.

Similarly, changes in government policy sometimes have a major impact on business. The Free Trade Agreement has hit many sectors of business in Canada since 1988—wine producers, fruit growers, furniture manufacturers, and more. Some other external factors are the rate of inflation, recession or boom, high or low interest rates, fluctuation in value of the Canadian dollar, and technological advances. The entrepreneur has no control over any of these.

This brings us to the last option, buying a franchise unit.

PROGRESS CHECK

- Why do so many people continue to start new businesses when the majority of them will be out of business in five years?
- What are three common causes of business failure?

FRANCHISING

Not everyone is cut out to be an entrepreneur, or an intrapreneur, either. The personality called for is that of a risk taker and innovator. Some people are more cautious or simply want more assurance of success. For them, there is a vastly different strategy for operating a business; that is the opportunity of franchising. Business students often mistakenly identify franchising as an industry. **Franchising** is a method of distributing a product or service, or both, to achieve a maximum market impact with a minimum amount of investment.

Entrepreneurship and franchising are actually complementary processes. Entrepreneurs develop ideas and build a winning product or service that they attempt to exploit through a franchise agreement. Basically, a **franchise agreement** is an arrangement whereby someone with a good idea for a business (the **franchisor**) sells to others (the **franchisees**) the rights to use the business name and sell a product or service in a given territory. As you might suspect, both franchisors and franchisees have a stake in the success of the **franchise.** There are over 1,000 franchisors in Canada and the number of franchise outlets exceeded 50,000 in 1988, with sales of over $69 billion or 27 percent of total retail sales. With so many retailers now operating as franchises, you shouldn't have much difficulty finding places to visit where you can get more information from franchise owners/managers.[8] (See Figure 6–3)

franchising
A method of distributing a product or service, or both, to achieve a maximum market impact with a minimum amount of investment.

franchise agreement
An arrangement whereby someone with a good idea for a business sells the rights to use the business name and sell its products or services in a given territory.

franchisor
A company that develops a product concept and sells others the rights to make and sell the products.

franchisee
A person who buys a franchise.

franchise
The right to use a specific business's name and sell its products or services in a given territory.

Advantages of Franchises

Franchising has penetrated every aspect of Canadian and global business life by offering products and services that are reliable, convenient, and cost effective. Richard Ashman, chairman of the International Franchise Association (headquartered in Washington, D.C.), probably put it best when he commented, "You name it and there is a good chance that someone out there is franchising it." Obviously, the growth in franchising throughout the world was not accomplished by accident. Franchising clearly has many advantages.[9]

Management assistance A franchisee (the person who buys a franchise) has a much greater chance of succeeding in business than an independent because he or she has an established product (for example, McDonald's hamburgers), help with choosing a location and with promotion, and assistance in all phases of operation. It is like having your own business with full-time consultants available when you need them. Furthermore, you have a whole network of peers facing similar problems who can share their experiences with you.

Personal ownership A franchise operation is still *your* business and you enjoy most of the freedom, incentives, and profit of any sole proprietor. You are still your own boss, although you must follow more rules, regulations, and procedures than with your own privately owned store.

Figure 6–3 Checklist for evaluating a franchise[10]

The Franchise

Did your lawyer approve the franchise contract you are considering after he or she studied it paragraph by paragraph?
Does the franchise give you an exclusive territory for the length of the franchise?
Under what circumstances can you terminate the franchise contract and at what cost to you?
If you sell your franchise, will you be compensated for your goodwill?
If the franchisor sells the company, will your investment be protected?

The Franchisor

How many years has the firm offering you a franchise been in operation?
Has it a reputation for honesty and fair dealing among the local firms holding its franchise?
Has the franchisor shown you any certified figures indicating exact net profits of one or more going firms that you personally checked yourself with the franchisee?
Will the firm assist you with:
 A management training program?
 An employee training program?
 A public relations program?
 Capital?
 Credit?
 Merchandising ideas?
Will the firm help you find a good location for your new business?
Has the franchisor investigated you carefully enough to assure itself that you can successfully operate one of its franchises at a profit to both the franchisor and you?

You, the Franchisee

How much equity capital will you need to purchase the franchise and operate it until your income equals your expenses?
Does the franchisor offer financing for a portion of the franchising fees? On what terms?
Are you prepared to give up some independence of action to secure the advantages offered by the franchise?
Are you ready to spend much or all of the remainder of your business life with this franchisor, offering its product or service to your public?

Your Market

Have you made any study to determine whether the product or service that you propose to sell under franchise has a market in your territory at the prices you will have to charge?
Will the population in the territory given you increase, remain static, or decrease over the next five years?
Will the product or service you are considering be in greater demand, about the same, or in less demand five years from now than today?
What competition already exists in your territory for the product or service you contemplate selling?

Nationally recognized name It is one thing to open a new hamburger outlet or ice cream store. It is quite another to open a new Burger King or a Baskin-Robbins ice cream shop. With an established franchise, you get instant recognition and support from a product group with established customers from around the world.

Financial advice and assistance A major problem with small businesses is arranging financing and learning to keep good records. Franchisees get valuable assistance in these areas and periodic advice from experts. Some franchisors will even provide financing to potential franchisees they think will be valuable parts of the franchise system.

Disadvantages of Franchises

It may sound as if the potential of franchising is too good to be true. Indeed, there *are* costs associated with joining a franchise. Be sure to check out any such arrangement with present franchisees and discuss the idea with an experienced franchise lawyer. The following are some disadvantages of franchises:

Large start-up costs Most franchises demand a fee just to obtain the rights to the franchise. Fees for franchises can vary considerably. The very successful ones demand a fee that will place them out of range of a small business venture.

Shared profit The franchisor often demands a large share of the profits, or a percentage commission based on *sales,* not profit. This share is generally referred to as a *royalty.* Often, the share taken by the franchisor is so high that the owner's profit does not match the time and effort involved in owning and managing a business. The royalty demanded by a franchisor is an important factor to consider in your involvement. (See Figures 6–4 and 6–5.)

Management regulation Management assistance has a way of becoming managerial orders, directives, and limitations. Franchisees may feel burdened by the company's rules and regulations and lose the spirit and incentive of being their own boss with their own business.

Beckers stores are found throughout cities and towns in Ontario. These convenience stores are a popular choice of franchise for potential small business owners. Many people apply for franchises each year, but only a few get them.

Figure 6–4 Benefits and drawbacks of franchising. The start-up fees and monthly fees can be killers. Ask around. Don't by shy. This is the time to learn about opportunities and risks. (This schedule applies to well-established franchises.)

Benefits	Drawbacks
▼ Nationally recognized name and established reputation.	▼ High initial franchise fee. Monthly fees for advertising.
▼ Help with finding a good location.	▼ A monthly percentage of gross sales to the franchisor.
▼ A proven management system.	▼ Possible competition from other nearby franchisees.
▼ Tested methods for inventory and operations management.	▼ No freedom to select decor or other design features.
▼ Financial advice and assistance.	▼ Little freedom to determine management procedures.
▼ Training in all phases of operation.	▼ Many rules and regulations to follow.
▼ Promotional assistance.	▼ Coattail effect.
▼ Periodic management counselling.	
▼ Proven record of success.	
▼ It's your business!	

Coattail effects What happens to your franchise if fellow franchisees fail? You might be forced out of business even if your particular franchise were profitable. This is often referred to as a coattail effect. The actions of other franchisees have an impact on your future growth and level of profitability. Remember, franchising is a team effort. If you play with a bad team, chances are you will lose.

Buying a Franchise

As we have seen, there are many advantages *and* disadvantages you need to explore before buying a franchise. Nonetheless, it *is* an excellent way to enter business as an owner or a manager and make a nice salary plus profit.

A good source of information about franchise possibilities is Franchise Watchdog in Burlington, Vermont. It compares what franchisors have to offer, including fees and support services, and also rates franchisors by sampling franchisees.

Be careful of franchises that grow too fast or whose ownership changes often. For example, Mother's Restaurants changed hands three times between 1986 and 1989, and its debt grew substantially as a result. In 1989, the 15-year-old, 90-unit franchise went bankrupt, dragging many franchisees down with it.[11] Be sure to check out the financial strength of a company before you get involved.

Figure 6–5 Some of the largest franchises in Canada in 1988–89

Rank by Sales	Company	Sales (millions)	No. of Units	Royalties (Percentage of Sales)	
				Profits	Ads
1	Shopper's Drug Mart	$2,356	612	varies	0–2
2	Uniglobe Travel	830	124	0.75–1	$616/mo.
3	McDonald's	681	322	N.A.	N.A.
4	Jean Coutu (Drugstore)	680	139	4–5	N.A.
5	Beaver Lumber	597	123	2	none
6	Tim Horton Donuts	240	396	3	3.5–4
7	Tilden Car Rental	178	365	4–8	N.A.
8	Couche-Tard (convenience store)	175	117	10–13	N.A.
9	Dairy Queen	153	406	4	3–6
10	Hartco (Computers)	150	85	N.A.	varies
11	Pizza Hut	130	94	5	4–5
12	St. Hubert BarBQ	125	82	4	5.5
13	A & W	108	231	2.5	3.5

Source: *Canadian Business,* June 1989, p. 19.

1. N.A. means that information was not available.
2. It is difficult to obtain reliable figures, and they change from year to year. Those who compile such information use different definitions of a franchise. For example, Canadian Tire is not included and McDonald's data excludes franchisor-owned units. Thus, these figures should be regarded as giving a broad picture.
3. Many franchises are owned by larger companies. Pizza Hut is owned by Pepsi, Beaver Lumber by Molson's, Shopper's Drug Mart by Imasco, and so on. Some franchises do not disclose information, so they are excluded from this list. Among such exclusions are Burger King, Harvey's, and Swiss Chalet (owned by Cara). U.S. laws require disclosure of all information, but in Canada, only Alberta has such laws.

There are many things to do before jumping into a franchise. First, get an accountant. Then, have a lawyer review the contract. Remember, you are making a sizeable financial investment. Furthermore, you have to analyze yourself, the franchise, and the market. Take some time to go over the checklist in Figure 6–3; it will help you understand many of the questions that franchisees should ask if they want a successful venture.

THINKING IT THROUGH

Is it fair to say that franchisees have the true entrepreneurial spirit? Can you think of any franchise opportunities that may grow in the future? What about the future of franchising—continued growth or a gradual slowdown? Could you see yourself as a franchisee or franchisor? Which one?

INTERNATIONAL ASPECTS OF ENTREPRENEURSHIP

Our planet has become a smaller place in recent years. We can no longer do business without considering the international market as both an opportunity and a challenge. Foreign companies come in to compete with domestic companies, and we must broaden our horizon to think international.

If you are contemplating becoming a franchisor, be aware of the ultimate potential of franchise outlets in other countries. We have all seen the attention paid to two of the largest foreign fast-food franchises, McDonald's (Canada) in Moscow and Kentucky Fried Chicken (now KFC) in Beijing. These successful ventures took many years of patient planning, heavy cost, and much frustration. Smaller franchisors have similar opportunities but will need to build a solid management team, reputation, and strong financial resources before they can move in that direction.

If you start your own business, be alert to international investment and export possibilities. As shown in Chapter 3, the Canadian and provincial governments offer extensive financial aid, information, and other support concerning exports. As you grow, you may consider opening branches, sales offices, or even plants in other countries. You might license a patent to, or enter into a joint venture with, a foreign company. See Chapter 2 for more about doing business internationally.

Small business plays an important role in Canada's export trade. The *Globe and Mail* reports that two such companies, Bloemhof Industries Ltd. and Merfin Hygienic Products Ltd., continue to thrive in the export market. Bloemhof is still a small company with annual sales of $500,000, but it depends on exports for 60 percent of its sales. Bloemhof has six full-time and three part-time employees. Merfin, which manufactures special absorbent paper for sanitary pads and diapers, has grown from small beginnings a few years ago to 1992 sales of almost $31 million. Thirty percent of its sales are to Europe, 15 percent to the Pacific Rim, and the rest to the United States and South America. In fact, Merfin has only one significant customer in Canada, reports president Ivan Pivko.[12]

PROGRESS CHECK

- What is a franchise? A franchisor? Or franchisee?
- What are the advantages of going into business by acquiring a franchise? What are the disadvantages?

REACHING BEYOND OUR BORDERS

The Next Move at Speedy

Fred Karp, an intensely private fellow, is one of Canada's least-known retailing heroes. In the past two years, Karp, president and CEO of Speedy Muffler King Inc., has pulled off a great business coup—repatriating the company from its U.S. owners and subsequently leading a campaign of international expansion, all in the face of the recession.

But first a bit of background. Speedy is Karp's baby. He was there at Speedy's birth, when it was a single garage located in downtown Toronto. He stuck with the company as it expanded, first across Canada, and then ultimately into the United States under the *Car-X* name. "We never dreamed it would get so big," says Karp.

By the late 1960s, the need for capital prompted Karp and his partners to invite Tenneco Automotive, a division of Tenneco Inc., to buy into the fledgling muffler chain. In 1977, Tenneco went all the way and bought out Karp and his friends. Karp stayed on and became president in 1985. In the late 1980s, things began to unravel for Tenneco. That was Karp's cue. In June 1989, with the backing of Goldfarb Corp. of Toronto, Karp paid an estimated $140 million U.S. for Speedy, then consisting of 709 muffler shops.

Since the buyout from Tenneco, Speedy has grown from an undermanaged division in a faltering conglomerate to an 825-store chain with operations in the U.S., Germany, France, and Belgium. Twenty more stores are due to open in 1991, says Karp. But Karp and the Goldfarbs bought in at a bad time. In a recession, drivers drive less. And the automotive aftermarket has become intensely competitive, both from other heavily advertised chains—such as Midas Muffler & Brake Shops, Canada's biggest chain—and from upstart operators. However, fewer new cars are being bought in the recession, which means more older cars requiring repairs.

In the first half of 1991, on sales estimated at more than $200 million, Speedy lost about $1.5 million. No problem, says Karp. As proof, he points to Speedy's continued expansion in North America and its recent acquisition of an 81-shop chain in France (price unspecified). "All our capital expansions were financed through our cash flows, not bank loans," he says.

Karp believes that Speedy can hold on to its number two spot in the Canadian market (it also has 7 percent of the huge U.S. market). Unlike many Canadian retailers, he has had enough successful experience in the U.S. to make a reasonably well-informed estimate of growth opportunities. Speedy's Car-X stores hold the number one or two spot in several northeastern U.S. cities, a fine base for further expansion.

Source: Michael Harrison, "The Next Move at Speedy," *Financial Times,* October 21, 1991, p. 8. ▼

MAKING ETHICAL DECISIONS

You are considering buying a small paint factory. In the course of your examination of company operations, an employee informs you that it has been dumping hazardous waste illegally instead of disposing of it properly. The additional expense of legal dumping would add to the company's production costs. Competition is quite fierce, and any edge you have will give you an important advantage.

When you raised the issue with the owner, he was a little surprised but said that the problem was minor and that, in any case, he has been planning to do something about it next month. He also said the approved disposal method was quite new and not yet proven.

The accountant you engaged reports that the company is operating at a small but steady profit. You are satisfied with the overall scene, so you are about to make an offer. What will you do about the pollution question if you buy the business? What will you do if you don't buy it? What will be the consequences of either decision? ▼

SUMMARY

1. Define small business and discuss its importance to the Canadian economy.

1. Of all the non-farm businesses in Canada, over 95 percent are considered small.

▼ *Why are small businesses important to the Canadian economy?*

Small business accounts for a significant portion of the national economy. Perhaps more important to tomorrow's graduates, 90 percent of the nation's new jobs in the private sector are in small businesses.

▼ *What does the "small" in small business mean?*

A small business is independently owned and operated, not dominant in its field of operation, and meets certain standards of size in terms of employees (fewer than 100) or sales. (That depends on the size of others in the industry. For example, American Motors was considered small in the auto industry before it merged with Chrysler.)

2. Over two-thirds of the small businesses started this year will not survive to celebrate their fifth anniversary.

2. Summarize the major causes of small-business failures.

▼ *Why do so many small businesses fail?*

Many small businesses fail because of managerial incompetence and inadequate financial planning.

3. There are many reasons why people are willing to take the risks of entrepreneurship despite the high risks of failure.

3. Explain why people are willing to take the risks of entrepreneurship.

▼ *What are a few of the reasons people start their own businesses?*

Reasons include profit, independence, opportunity, and challenge.

4. Successful entrepreneurship takes a special kind of person.

4. Describe the attributes needed to be a successful entrepreneur and why women have a higher success rate than men.

▼ *What does it take to be an entrepreneur?*

A person must be self-directed, self-nurtured, action-oriented, tolerant of uncertainty, and energetic.

▼ *Why are women more successful than men?*

Women are less pressured to achieve quick success, they are more cautious and accept advise more readily.

5. Most people have no idea how to go about starting a small business. They have some ideas and the motivation; they simply don't have the know-how.

5. Identify ways you can learn about small businesses.

▼ *What should you do before starting a small business?*

First, learn from others. Take courses and talk with some small-business owners. Second, get some experience working for others. Finally, consult with an accountant experienced in small business.

6. Begin with a plan. The more effort you put into a business plan, the less grief you'll have later.

6. Explain what a business plan is and outline the general areas of information it should include.

▼ *What goes into a business plan?*

See the box on p. 181.

▼ *Should you do it all yourself?*

Most small-business owners advise new entrepreneurs to get outside assistance in at least two areas: you need a good lawyer and a good accountant. Also, seek help from government publications and any other sources you can find. The more knowledge you can gain early, the better.

7. It is important for a small-business person to "know the market."

7. Explain what a market is and why it is important for a businessperson to know the market.

▼ *What is a market?*

A market consists of a group of people with unsatisfied wants and needs who have both the resources and the willingness to buy.

▼ *Why must a businessperson know the market?*

The goal of a businessperson is to find a need and fill it. One must first identify the wants and needs of potential customers.

8. *Intrapreneuring* is a big business's answer to the entrepreneur.

8. Describe intrapreneuring and its benefits for big businesses.

▼ *What is intrapreneuring?*

It is the establishment of entrepreneurial centres within a larger firm where people can innovate and develop new product ideas internally.

9. A person can participate in the entrepreneurial age by buying the rights to market a new product innovation in his or her area.

9. Define franchising and compare the advantages and disadvantages of franchising.

▼ *What is this arrangement called?*

A franchise is an arrangement to buy the rights to use the business name and sell its products or services in a given territory.

▼ *What is a franchisee?*

A *franchisee* is a person who buys a franchise.

▼ *What are the benefits and drawbacks of being a franchisee?*

The benefits include a nationally recognized name and reputation, a proven management system, promotional assistance, and pride of ownership. Drawbacks include high franchise fees, managerial regulation, shared profits, and the coattail transfer of adverse effects if other franchisees fail.

10. One should not jump blindly into franchise ownership.

▼ *What areas should you analyze when evaluating a franchise?*

Before you buy a franchise, analyze yourself, the franchise, the franchisor, and the market.

10. Outline the areas you need to analyze when evaluating a franchise.

GETTING INVOLVED

1. Select a type of small business that looks attractive as a career possibility for you. Talk to at least three people who manage such businesses. Ask them how they started their businesses. Ask about financing, personnel problems (hiring, firing, training, scheduling), accounting problems, and other managerial matters. Pick their brains. Let them be your instructors. Put together a rough business plan of how you would start a particular business. Discuss it in class.
2. Go to the library and get some business magazines for the last couple of years. Look through the table of contents and briefly review several articles in each issue. What kind of information is available? Make copies of interesting articles for your career file. Share what you found with the class.
3. Put together a checklist of factors that might mean the difference between success and failure of a new business. Discuss the checklist in class.
4. In the library reference section, find the *Franchise Opportunities Handbook* or a similar listing. Look for the cost of a franchise, the variety of franchises available, and other interesting information. If several people each write down two entries, the class will have enough information to give them a good feel for franchising opportunities.
5. Visit a franchise other than a fast-food restaurant and see what the owners have to say about the benefits and drawbacks of franchising. Would they buy the franchise again if they could start all over? What mistakes did they make, if any? What advice would they give a student interested in franchising?

PRACTICING MANAGEMENT DECISIONS

Case One Two Canadian Hot Shots in the Paging Industry

Shlomo Friedman, an Israeli Army-trained electronics technician, and Nils Eriksson, a Swedish-born electronics engineer, are proven winners in the brutally competitive paging industry. Now they're out to do it again. This time around, their First Security Corp. of Vancouver is marketing a sophisticated paging service that sets a new national—and international—standard.

Among the features are a single fax and phone number, fax forwarding to remote locations, and a "meet me" feature, which allows a caller to wait briefly while a mobile subscriber is paged. The subscriber can use any nearby phone, dial his or her line and talk to the waiting caller. If the chat is long distance, the meet-me feature forces the caller to pay (in contrast to other pagers where the subscriber, once alerted, places a return call and pays the long-distance fee).

These services are available in Toronto and several other Canadian cities as the first steps towards developing a nationwide paging service that will be operated by a subsidiary, Canadian Telelink Ltd. Telelink owns one of seven valuable nationwide paging frequencies awarded by Ottawa in 1989.

Another First Security unit, Ralco Electronics Inc., will develop and assemble special switching terminals for sale to Telelink and competing service companies. A prototype is already in operation.

"The worldwide potential is enormous," says Friedman. Brave talk, given that First Security is a start-up, with little financial backing and annual revenue of maybe $500,000. It is competing with Glenayre Electronics Ltd. of Vancouver, the world's biggest paging-equipment manufacturer, which isn't sitting still. But First Security is primed for a scrap. "Glenayre will have a very serious problem at some point," says Friedman.

Gibberish? Consider the past accomplishments. Friedman and Eriksson established their first Canadian company in 1979. Each invested $500 to create a pager-switching terminal that they fabricated in a garage in Montreal. By 1983, after capturing most of the Canadian market, they sold their hot company to Glenayre for $2.5 million and moved to Vancouver to help Glenayre improve it. In 1986, Friedman and Eriksson did it again. They bought a failing Vancouver-based paging-service company for $400,000. Two years later, Motorola Canada Ltd. bought them out for $6 million.

Decision Questions

1. What do you think of the partners' strategy of developing companies and then selling them off at a handsome profit? Why do you think they do that?
2. Given the great importance of rapid and reliable communications in business today, do you think they should take a more long-range view? Will such a strategy yield higher returns in the long run?
3. Here is another case of two young people developing a new product in their garage. Does this example encourage you to try a pet scheme? What should you do to get started?
4. Can you see any franchise possibilities for this paging equipment or service? Is there any international potential here? Discuss both of these expansion ideas.

Source: Alan Bayless, "First Security: One Call Away from a National Paging Service," *Financial Times*, December 9, 1991, p. 3.

Case Two Opportunities in Home-Based Franchising

You are toying with the idea of starting your own business but are a little nervous about going it on your own. You like the help you would get with a franchise and that you could still run your own show—almost. The problem is that well-known names demand an investment of $150,000 to $1 million, which is much too rich for your blood.

You have heard recently about home-based franchises that require anywhere from $10,000 to $50,000 to start up. Sheldon Adler, who heads a franchising consulting company, says they are pretty easy to get into. He points out that they have been growing steadily in the U.S. for the last 15 years and are making headway in Canada. He provides you with a sample listing:

Heels on Wheels, a mobile shoe-repair business operating out of a van. Staff members go directly into offices to fix and polish the shoes of businesspeople. Women often bring three or four pairs to work for repair.

Location Lube, which provides a similar service for automobile lube jobs. Technicians service the cars in office parking lots, saving car owners the trip to a service station.

Colour Your Carpet, a rug-dyeing business that restores your carpet at a fraction the price of buying a new one.

Other home franchises that have appeared recently include cleaning services, computer training, personnel services, and travel and interior design agencies. In most cases, the franchisee starts off actually doing the work but soon hires staff and takes on a management role.

Nevertheless, Adler warns that home-based franchises demand people who are much more outgoing and marketing oriented than salespeople in retail-shop outlets. "You've got to go out and knock on a lot of doors, because you don't have a storefront for people to walk through," he says. "If you're inhibited, forget it."

Gary Shulz of Victoria is a recent convert to home franchising. Three months ago, he became Canada's master franchiser for Foliage Design Systems, a Florida-based chain that installs and maintains tropical plants in hotels, restaurants, offices, and homes.

"Most businesses have plants," Shulz says. "But they need someone to install and maintain them." A plant lover, he was attracted to the Florida-based franchise chain because the company has 20 years of expertise, enough time to kick the bugs out of the system. Foliage Design Systems gave Shulz horticultural training, marketing assistance, and time-tested business manuals.

The financial returns on home franchises can be lucrative, but Adler cautions would-be owners not to expect overnight success. "It takes a while to build up, because you have to go out and sell," he explained. "It's not like retail."

Vicky Telycenas, coordinator of franchise operations for Trend Tidy's Ltd. of Markham, Ontario, says owners can expect a gross weekly income of up to $4,800 after 30 months by managing two or three cleaning teams. She estimates net income at 20 percent, or $960 weekly. Some of the 21 franchisees are ex-housewives who tried returning to the work force but found their skills were obsolete.

Most are earning more money than they would have in traditional office jobs. They also have more responsibility. Trend Tidy's other franchise operators include former bankers, teachers, and accountants. "In each case, they reached a crisis point in their jobs and decided to leave the rat race," Teleycenas said. "They took control of their lives."

Decision Questions

1. What kinds of questions should you ask before buying a franchise?
2. Are the lower risks of franchise organizations worth giving up the freedom of ownership and total control? How would you find information to answer such a question?
3. Look around your town or area and see which franchises seem to be successful. (Do not think only of retail operations.) Why do you think they are successful?
4. Do any of the franchises you found in answer to the previous question interest you? Would you consider operating one? Why or why not?

Source: *Globe and Mail,* Sept. 30, 1991, p. B6.

LET'S TALK BUSINESS

1. When you work for a large or medium-size company, such employee benefits as pensions; vacation and holiday pay; group medical, accident, and life insurance; paid maternity leave; low-cost meals; sick leave; and unemployment insurance can be worth an additional one-third of your salary. When you are self-employed at a small operation, you will have none of these benefits. Does this make running your own business seem less attractive? Do you think the advantages outweigh these and other disadvantages (long hours, hard work, worry, high risk)? What are the advantages?
2. What kind of experience do you already have in business? Has it encouraged you to start a small business of your own? What are the pros and cons of taking over a business from a successful older person who wants to retire?
3. Why do small businesses have so much trouble finding people to lend them money? How can this be overcome? What role can a business plan play in the search for funding?
4. Would you rather operate a franchise or "do your own thing"? Why? Which is likely to require more initial capital? Why is this so?

LOOKING AHEAD

Part III of this book will look at management and leadership principles that are needed to guide organizations in the future. This part also reviews what it takes to manufacture and to operate a business in Canada, including some of the latest production techniques and equipment.

But first, take a few minutes to fill out the entrepreneurial readiness questionnaire in the appendix. It will help to determine whether or not you are the entrepreneurial type.

ENTREPRENEURIAL READINESS QUESTIONNAIRE*

Not everyone is cut out to be an entrepreneur, but all kinds of people with all kinds of personalities have succeeded in starting small and large businesses. There are certain traits, however, that seem to separate those who will be successful as entrepreneurs from those who may not be. The following questionnaire will help you determine into which category you fit. Take a couple of minutes to answer the questions and then score yourself at the end. **A low score doesn't necessarily mean you won't succeed as an entrepreneur.** It does indicate, however, that you might be happier working for someone else.

Each of the following items describes something you may or may not feel represents your personality or other characteristics. Read each item and then circle the response (1, 2, 3, 4, or 5) that most nearly reflects the extent to which you agree or disagree that the item seems to fit you.

	Response				
Looking At My Overall Philosophy of Life and Typical Behaviour, I Would Say That . . .	**Agree Completely (1)**	**Mostly Agree (2)**	**Partially Agree (3)**	**Mostly Disagree (4)**	**Disagree Completely (5)**
1. I am generally optimistic.	1	2	3	4	5
2. I enjoy competing and doing things better than someone else.	1	2	3	4	5
3. When solving a problem, I try to arrive at the best solution first without worrying about other possibilities.	1	2	3	4	5
4. I enjoy associating with co-workers after working hours.	1	2	3	4	5
5. If betting on a horse race, I would prefer to take a chance on a high-payoff long shot.	1	2	3	4	5

*Source: Kenneth R. Van Voorhis, *Entrepreneurship and Small Business Management* (New York: Allyn and Bacon, 1980).

Looking At My Overall Philosophy of Life and Typical Behaviour, I Would Say That . . .	Response				
	Agree Completely (1)	**Mostly Agree (2)**	**Partially Agree (3)**	**Mostly Disagree (4)**	**Disagree Completely (5)**
6. I like setting my own goals and working hard to achieve them.	1	2	3	4	5
7. I am generally casual and easygoing with others.	1	2	3	4	5
8. I like to know what is going on and take action to find out.	1	2	3	4	5
9. I work best when someone else is guiding me along the way.	1	2	3	4	5
10. When I am right, I can convince others.	1	2	3	4	5
11. I find that other people frequently waste my valuable time.	1	2	3	4	5
12. I enjoy watching football, baseball, and similar sports events.	1	2	3	4	5
13. I tend to communicate about myself very openly with other people.	1	2	3	4	5
14. I don't mind following orders from superiors who have legitimate authority.	1	2	3	4	5
15. I enjoy planning things more than actually carrying out the plans.	1	2	3	4	5
16. I don't think it's much fun to bet on a sure thing.	1	2	3	4	5
17. If faced with failure, I would shift quickly to something else rather than sticking to my guns.	1	2	3	4	5
18. Part of being successful in business is reserving adequate time for family.	1	2	3	4	5
19. Once I have earned something, I feel that keeping it secure is important.	1	2	3	4	5
20. Making a lot of money is largely a matter of getting the right breaks.	1	2	3	4	5
21. Problem solving is usually more effective when a number of alternatives are considered.	1	2	3	4	5
22. I enjoy impressing others with the things I can do.	1	2	3	4	5
23. I enjoy playing games like tennis and handball with someone who is slightly better than I am.	1	2	3	4	5
24. Sometimes moral ethics must be bent a little in business dealings.	1	2	3	4	5
25. I think good friends would make the best subordinates in an organization.	1	2	3	4	5

Scoring: Give yourself one point for each 1 or 2 response you circled for questions 1, 2, 6, 8, 10, 11, 16, 17, 21, 22, 23, 24. Give yourself one point for each 4 or 5 response you circled for questions 3, 4, 5, 7, 9, 12, 13, 14, 15, 18, 19, 20, 25.

Add your points and see how you rate in the categories below:

21–25 Your entrepreneurial potential looks great if you have a suitable opportunity to use it. What are you waiting for?

16–20 This is close to the high entrepreneurial range. You could be quite successful if your other talents and resources are right.

11–15 Your score is in the transitional range. With some serious work, you can probably develop the outlook you need for running your own business.

6–10 Things look pretty doubtful for you as an entrepreneur. It would take considerable re-arranging of your life philosophy and behaviour to make it.

0–5 Let's face it. Entrepreneurship is not really for you. Still, learning what it's all about won't hurt anything.

PART III

FUNDAMENTALS OF MANAGEMENT

MANAGEMENT AND LEADERSHIP

LEARNING GOALS

After you have read and studied this chapter, you should be able to:

1. Explain how and why the role of managers is changing in the 1990s.
2. Identify the four functions of management.
3. Distinguish between goals and objectives and among strategic, tactical, and contingency planning, and explain the relationships of goals and objectives to the various types of planning.
4. Describe the significance of an organization chart and explain the role of each management level in the corporate hierarchy.
5. Describe the directing function of management and illustrate how the function differs at the various management levels.
6. Summarize the five steps of the control function of management.
7. Explain the differences between managers and leaders and compare the characteristics and use of the various leadership styles.
8. Describe the skills needed by top, middle, and first-line managers.
9. Illustrate the six skills you will need to develop your managerial potential and outline activities you could use to develop these skills

KEY TERMS

conceptual skills, p. 219
contingency planning, p. 208
controlling, p. 206
delegating, p. 219
directing, p. 206
goals, p. 207
interpersonal skills, p. 219
leadership, p. 214
management, p. 206
management by walking around, p. 204
middle management, p. 210
objectives, p. 207
organizing, p. 206
participative management, p. 202
planning, p. 206
rational decision-making model, p. 220
strategic planning, p. 207
supervisory (first-line) management, p. 210
tactical planning, p. 208
technical skills, p. 219
top management, p. 209

Walter Shawlee

PROFILE WALTER SHAWLEE OF NORTHERN AIRBORNE TECHNOLOGY

There are no dividing lines at Northern Airborne Technology (NAT) in Kelowna, B.C. President Walter Shawlee has no executive parking space; every morning he jockeys for space right along with the guy from the shipping department. No executive secretary defends his office against intruders. The office itself, for that matter, differs little from the others in the building and employees flow in and out with a casualness that would smack of disrespect in most companies grossing $1.62 million in 1989 and projecting double that in 1990. (1993 sales exceeded $5 million).

When Shawlee walks by any of the 30 employees who are constructing or supporting the construction of the company's avionics communications equipment, they mostly ignore him. This slightly unnerves the casual observer; company presidents never pass unnoticed. Usually a visible tightening occurs in a room when a president strolls in. A hush falls gradually, shoulders tense and rise slightly, busy becomes busier.

This morning at NAT two computer software programmers are leaning back in their chairs shooting the bull. One waves casually to Shawlee without even pausing in his sentence. There is no tension here.

What's up? Has Shawlee lost control of this privately owned company that is considered a world leader in the field of building communications equipment for use in emergency situations? Just who is in charge here? The employees?

Back in his office, Shawlee finds these questions amusing. The truth is, he says, no one is in control at NAT because the idea of control by any one person in any company is false. A company is the sum of all its people. What he is really saying is that NAT does not follow any of the normal North American corporate rules.

What is happening at NAT is a symbol of significant changes that have been sweeping through management in large and small companies. We will explore some of these concepts and practices in Chapters 7, 8 and 9.

Source: Mark Zuelke, "Who Is In Charge Here?," *B.C. Business* 18, no. 1, January 1990, p. 51.

THE MANAGEMENT CHALLENGE OF THE 1990s

Walter Shawlee is just one of the many managers who have adopted a modern management style. His work force lends itself admirably to this style of management. His employees are highly skilled and need guidance and support, not the old-fashioned tight control and an order-giving boss that are still widespread. This type of management has been advocated for many years by various experts.

participative management Management style that involves employees in setting objectives and making decisions; democratic and laissez-faire leadership are forms of this type of management.

This approach, called **participative management,** involves employees in setting objectives and making decisions. Later in the chapter you will read about leadership styles based on the philosophy of participative management.

Walter Shawlee's style will become more common as companies continue to reduce their work force and those that remain or are newly hired are better educated and more highly skilled. Such restructuring will require a participative style if companies are to get the best results from their staff. Many commentators say the day of the strong individual leader is giving way to team efforts with decision-making power more widely distributed. We look at this important development in more detail later in the chapter.

A major factor in the reorganization of businesses is *the need to respond better to customers.* Corporations had to give more authority and responsibility to lower-level managers who could respond to consumer requests more quickly. Foreign competitors were known for being more responsive to the market and for bringing in innovations more quickly. Canadian firms had to restructure and change their management styles to become equally responsive and able to produce new products quickly.

Accelerating technological change also brought in a new breed of workers, more educated and with higher skill levels. They demanded more freedom of operation and a different managerial style as well.

Perhaps the greatest challenge to managers in the 1980s was global competition. The major impetus behind the restructuring and refocusing of corporations in this period was the need to compete with foreign producers. Chief executives in the year 2000 will likely have experience abroad. Meanwhile, the executive of today must learn how to deal in global markets and in a global economy.

In short, the late 1980s and early 1990s were an era for corporate housecleaning—time to get rid of the old divisions and managerial styles that had been accumulating and introduce a whole new way of operating. Naturally, this caused much disruption in business. Many managers were fired and had to find new jobs. The same was true of blue-collar workers. Hundreds of firms went through sweeping organizational and managerial changes. Now Canadian firms are leaner and meaner and ready to take on world competition. That will call for great managers.

The Changing Role of Managers

An early management scholar, Mary Parker Follett, defined management as "the art of getting things done through people." At one time, that meant that managers were called *bosses,* and their job was to tell people what to do and watch over them to be sure they did it. Bosses tended to reprimand those who didn't do things correctly, they generally acted stern and "bossy." Many managers still behave that way. Perhaps you have witnessed such managers yelling at employees at fast-food restaurants or on shop floors.

Today, management is changing from that kind of behaviour. Managers are being educated to *lead, guide,* and *coach* employees rather than boss them around. Modern managers emphasize teamwork and co-operation rather than discipline and order giving. Managers in some high-tech and progressive firms dress more casually, are more friendly, and generally treat employees as partners rather than unruly underlings. Walter Shawlee is a good example.

Here are a few other examples of the changing role of managers: Groupe Innovation was formed by three prominent Quebec executives who are each presidents of major corporations. David Culver of CAI Capital Corp., Claude Beland of Mouvement des Caisses Desjardins, and Gaetan Lussier of Weston Bakeries (Quebec) Ltd. agreed that "time has run out on traditional management techniques." The goal of this non-profit consulting organization "is to analyze new trends in management and share information with its Quebec members."[1]

Alan Webber, former editorial director of the prestigious *Harvard Business Review,* writes:

> Time was, if the boss caught you talking on the phone or hanging around the water cooler, he would have said, "Stop talking and get to work!" Today if you're not on the phone or talking with colleagues and customers, chances are you'll hear, "Start talking and get to work!" In the new economy, conversations are the most important form of work.

In the same article Webber, quoting from Tom Peters's new book *Liberation Management,* explains why conversation is such an important management technique. Today's information age means that diffusing knowledge rapidly and thoroughly has become crucial in making companies competitive. He cites numerous examples of how American companies have adopted this procedure.[2]

An article in the *Financial Post* magazine carries the title "The New Breed," referring to chief executive officers (CEOs). This article quotes a number of Canadian business consultants and CEOs on the new kind of management thinking and behaviour that is required today.

> [I]t's clear that many of the country's top CEOs are also fans of the team play. For most, working with others is a matter of both logistics and common sense. "The issues and responsibilities are just too much for one person to adequately handle alone," says (president John) Morgan, who spends the majority of working hours in the company of (his) senior management team at Labatt Breweries. Similarly, (Matthew) Barrett (CEO of Bank of Montreal) devotes three mornings every week to discussing "everything from strategy to policy to consensus building (with senior executives)." (John) Cassaday (CEO of CTV), too, expresses allegiance to the collegial approach. "One of the first things I did when I came to CTV was to organize a management team that I expected to share responsibility for running the business with me," he says.[3]

The Most Effective Managers

What the most effective managers have in common is that they are action oriented. A manager today has to be able to manage change effectively. A second characteristic of such managers is the ability to build a sense of shared values, an ability to motivate and generate loyalty.

Nine attributes were listed by one executive recruiter: an advanced degree; profit and loss experience; steady progress through the ranks, with an occasional detour to a staff position; some background in international business; excellent communications skills; a vision that can be imparted to others; self-confidence; the ability to take risks without undue worry; and high integrity.

These are the traits that make top executives attractive to other firms. The favourites typically have a healthy ego, a fondness for competitive sports, and a lot of experience moving from city to city or country to country.

Management is experiencing a revolution. Books like *The One Minute Manager* encourage supervisors to actively praise employees (see Case Two at the end of the chapter). A concept called **management by walking around** (MBWA) encourages managers to get out of their offices and mingle with workers and customers. This does not mean that managers are becoming mere cheerleaders. It does mean that they are working more closely with employees in a joint effort to accomplish common goals.

management by walking around
Managers get out of their offices and personally interact with employees and customers.

Henry Mintzberg, the well-known author and professor in the faculty of management at McGill University, has written extensively about what managers actually do and what they should be doing. His speech to the Canadian Club was titled "Message to Managers: Get Out of Your Offices."

> Management expert Henry Mintzberg had some pointed advice for an audience of blue-chip Montreal business leaders yesterday: don't sit in your office and try to manage by remote control. He said Canadians have picked up a few bad habits from our American neighbours, and one of them is the prevailing management style. Business leaders and decision makers can't spend their days

Management by walking around means talking with employees on the job. This woman is going over plans with one of her employees so he can visualize just what she is talking about.

> sitting in offices poring over numbers and flow charts, he said. They have to get out and meet people, be they workers or customers.
>
> Numbers and words are important elements in decision making, but they must also be balanced with the insightful elements of images and feeling. Those insights can't be obtained by having somebody report to you, Mintzberg said. They have to be sensed by the individual. Aloof management based only on cold calculations of numbers and words is partly responsible for the current round of cutbacks and layoffs in workplaces.
>
> While some of the layoffs may be needed, he said, cutbacks have become akin to medieval bloodletting. Whenever there appears to be something wrong with a patient, we cut and bleed him. Mintzberg said there may be more creative ways of dealing with the problem, like shorter working hours. And a manager must also assess other elements, such as whether the damage to staff morale is worth the savings any layoffs might bring.[4]

What this means for tomorrow's graduates is that managerial careers demand a new kind of person. That person is a skilled communicator as well as a planner, coordinator, organizer, and supervisor. Many managers today believe that they are part of a team and enjoy the new responsibility and flexibility that comes with more open and casual management systems. These trends will be discussed in the next few chapters to help you decide whether or not managing is the kind of thing you would like to do.

Henry Mintzberg of McGill University is one of the world's authorities on management. He has written extensively on organizational structure and strategy.

The Definition and Functions of Management

One reason people go to college or university is because college or university prepares them to become managers. Students have told us, "I don't know *what* I want to do, really. I guess I would like to be in management." Management is attractive to students because it represents authority, money, prestige, and so on. But few students are able to describe just what it is that managers do. That is what this chapter is for: It describes what managers are, what they do, and how they do it.

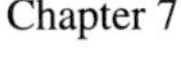

management The process used to accomplish the goals of the organization through planning, organizing, directing, and controlling organizational resources.

planning Anticipating future trends and determining the best strategies and tactics to achieve the goals and objectives of the organization.

organizing Designing the organizational structure, attracting people to the organization (staffing), and creating conditions and systems that make sure everyone and everything works together to achieve the objectives of the organization.

directing Guiding and motivating others to achieve the goals and objectives of the organization.

controlling Checking to determine whether or not an organization is carrying out its plans, and taking corrective action if it is not.

As we noted earlier, management could be called the art of getting things done through people and other resources. A well-known management consultant, Peter Drucker, says managers give direction to their organizations, provide leadership, and decide how to use organizational resources to accomplish goals. Both definitions give you some feel for what managers do. **Management** is the process used to accomplish the goals of the organization through planning, organizing, directing, and controlling people and other organizational resources.

This definition spells out the four key functions of management: (1) planning, (2) organizing, (3) directing, and (4) controlling. (See Figure 7–1.)

1. **Planning** involves anticipating future trends and determining the best strategies and tactics to achieve the goals and objectives of the organization.
2. **Organizing** includes designing the organizational structure, attracting people to the organization (staffing), and creating conditions and systems that ensure that everyone and everything works together to achieve the goals and objectives of the organization.
3. **Directing** is guiding and motivating others to work effectively to achieve the goals and objectives of the organization.
4. **Controlling** is checking to determine whether or not an organization is carrying out its plans, and taking corrective action if it is not.

You have some familiarity with management tasks already: You have *planned* to go to college or university to learn something about business. You have *organized* your time and materials to do that. You may also have experienced *directing* in a sports team or a social group. Periodically, you will have to evaluate and *control* your progress to decide whether or not you are meeting your objectives. You know how important it is for a manager to set goals, inspire others, and establish strong values that will enable the organization to succeed.

You might also know that managing is much more complex than doing a few tasks. A good manager must know about the industry the firm is in and all the technological, political, competitive, and social factors affecting that industry. He or

Figure 7–1 What managers do.

Planning

Setting organizational goals.
Developing strategies to reach those goals.
Determining resources needed.
Setting standards.

Organizing

Allocating resources, assigning tasks, and establishing procedures for accomplishing goals.
Preparing a structure (organization chart) showing lines of authority and responsibility.
Recruiting, selecting, training, and developing employees.
Placing employees where they will be most effective.

Directing

Leading, guiding, and motivating employees to work effectively to accomplish organizational goals and objectives.
Giving assignments.
Explaining routines.
Clarifying policies.
Providing feedback on performance.

Controlling:

Setting clear performance standards.
Monitoring and recording actual performance (results).
Comparing results against plans and standards.
Communicating results and deviations to the employees involved.
Taking corrective action when needed.

she must also understand the kind of people who work in the industry and what motivates them. Finally, a manager must be skilled in performing various managerial tasks, especially technical tasks, human relations tasks, and conceptual tasks. These will be discussed shortly.

PROGRESS CHECK

- What were some of the factors that forced executives to change their organizations and managerial styles in the 1980s?
- What are the four functions in the definition of management?
- What is the purpose of managing by walking around?

PLANNING

Planning is the first managerial function used to pursue organizational goals. Many people believe it is the most important, since it sets the path the other functions must follow. Planning involves the process of setting objectives. It is important to understand what goals are and how they differ from objectives. **Goals** are the broad, long-term accomplishments an organization wishes to attain. **Objectives,** on the other hand, are specific, short-term tasks that must be completed to achieve the organizational goals. One of your goals for reading this chapter, for example, may be to learn basic concepts of management. One objective you could use to achieve this goal is to plan to answer correctly the Progress Check box. Another example of a goal is to make Fiberrific, a hypothetical cereal, the number one cereal in Canada. One objective might be getting Fiberrific on the shelves of 85 percent of the supermarkets in Ontario by the end of the year. What is important to remember is: goals are broad, long-term statements of what the organization wants to achieve, whereas objectives are specific, short-term statements of how to meet those goals.

goals
Broad, long-term accomplishments an organization wishes to attain.

objectives
Specific, short-term tasks that must be completed to achieve the organizational goals.

Planning is an ongoing process that never ends. A plan developed last year, last month, or even last week is affected by events that are usually different from those forecast when the plan was prepared. That means plans must constantly be updated to make them more realistic and thus more effective.

Does this mean the original plans were a waste of time? Not at all. Planning gives direction and guidelines that are necessary for a business or any organization to function effectively. Planning answers three fundamental questions:

1. *What is the situation now?* What is the state of the economy? What opportunities exist for meeting people's needs? What products and customers are most profitable? Why do people buy (or not buy) our products? Who are our major competitors?
2. *Where do we want to go?* How much growth do we want? What is our profit goal? What are our social objectives? What are our personal development objectives for employees?
3. *How can we get there from here?* This is the most important part of planning. It takes three forms (see Figure 7–2).
   a. **Strategic** *(long-range)* **planning** determines the major goals of the organization and the policies and strategies for obtaining and using resources to achieve those goals. In this definition, *policies* are broad guides

strategic planning
Process of determining the major goals of the organization and the policies and strategies for obtaining and using resources to achieve those goals.

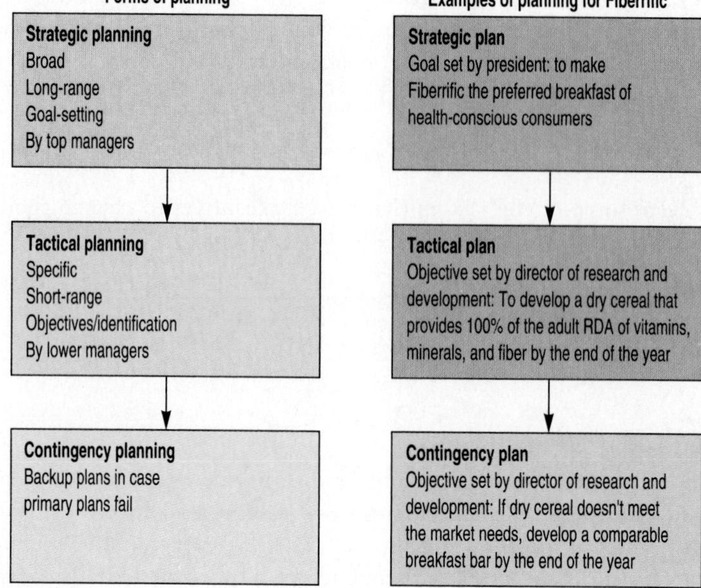

Figure 7–2 Planning functions: Very few firms bother to make contingency plans. If something changes the market, such companies are slow to respond. Strategic planning and tactical planning are practiced in most firms.

to action, and *strategies* determine the best way to use resources. The time frame may be three years or even longer. In Japan, large companies have very-long-range plans—ten years or more. The larger the firm, the longer range the planning. At the strategic planning stage, the company decides which market segments to serve and what products or services to sell.

tactical planning
Process of developing detailed, short-term decisions about what is to be done, who is to do it, and how it is to be done.

b. **Tactical** *(short-range)* **planning** is the process of developing detailed, short-term decisions about what is to be done, who is to do it, and how it is to be done. Just as objectives are specific plans to meet broad goals, tactical planning involves defining *specific* plans to achieve *broad* strategic plans. Tactical planning is normally done by managers at lower levels of the organization, whereas strategic planning is done by the top managers of the firm (for example, the president). Tactical planning involves setting annual budgets and deciding on other details of how to meet the strategic goals.

contingency planning
Process of preparing alternative courses of action in case the primary plans do not achieve the objectives of the organization.

c. **Contingency planning** is the preparation of alternative courses of action that may be used if the primary plans do not achieve the objectives of the organization. The economic and competitive environments change so rapidly that it is wise to have alternative plans of action.

Planning versus Seizing Opportunities

Robert Waterman, co-author of the best-selling *In Search of Excellence* (see Case One at the end of this chapter), has since written *The Renewal Factor: How the Best Get and Keep the Competitive Edge*. He says that leaders of renewing companies set *direction,* not detailed strategy. They are the best of strategists precisely because they are suspicious of forecasts and open to surprise. They think strategic planning is great—as long as no one takes the plans too seriously. The problem is that strategy is needed, but the future is uncertain. The answer is to stay flexible, listen for opportunities, and seize them when they come, as long as they fit into your overall strategy.

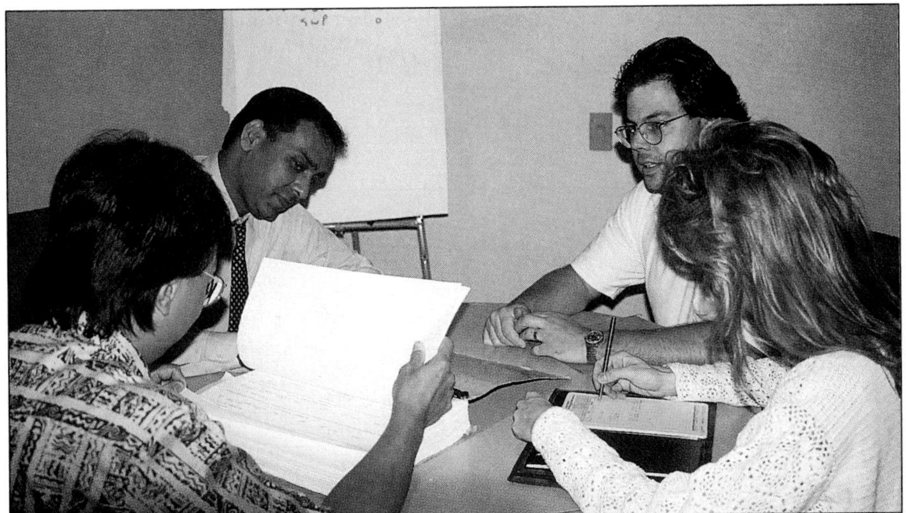

Planning is a critical part of a manager's job. It consists of setting goals and objectives. Objectives are the steps one must accomplish to reach the long-term goals.

PROGRESS CHECK

- What are the differences between strategic, tactical, and contingency planning?
- Contrast planning and seizing opportunities.
- Why might many organizations today be less concerned with strategic planning? Could it slow down response time to today's rapidly changing market conditions?

ORGANIZING

How often have you heard the comment, "One of these days we'll have to get organized"? Clearly, organization is an important managerial task. Basically, organizing means allocating resources, assigning tasks, and establishing procedures for accomplishing the organizational objectives. The basic concepts are easy to understand because you already have some experience organizing. For example, to play baseball, you have to gather together some materials: gloves, ball, bat. Then you have to find people to play the various positions. (In business, this is called *staffing*.) Someone must decide who bats first, who second, and so on.

When organizing, a manager develops a structure that relates all workers, tasks, and resources to each other. That framework is called the organization structure. Most organizations draw a chart showing these relationships. A very simple organization chart would look like Figure 7–3.

The organization chart pictures who reports to whom and who is responsible for each task. The problem of developing organization structure will be discussed in more detail in Chapter 8. For now it is important to know that the corporate hierarchy illustrated on the organization chart includes top, middle, and first-line managers.

Top management is the highest level of management and consists of the president, vice-presidents, and other key company executives who develop strategic

top management
Highest level of management; consisting of the president, vice-president, and other key company executives who develop strategic plans.

Figure 7–3 This organization chart (or organogram) shows what an organizational structure might look like for a small company.

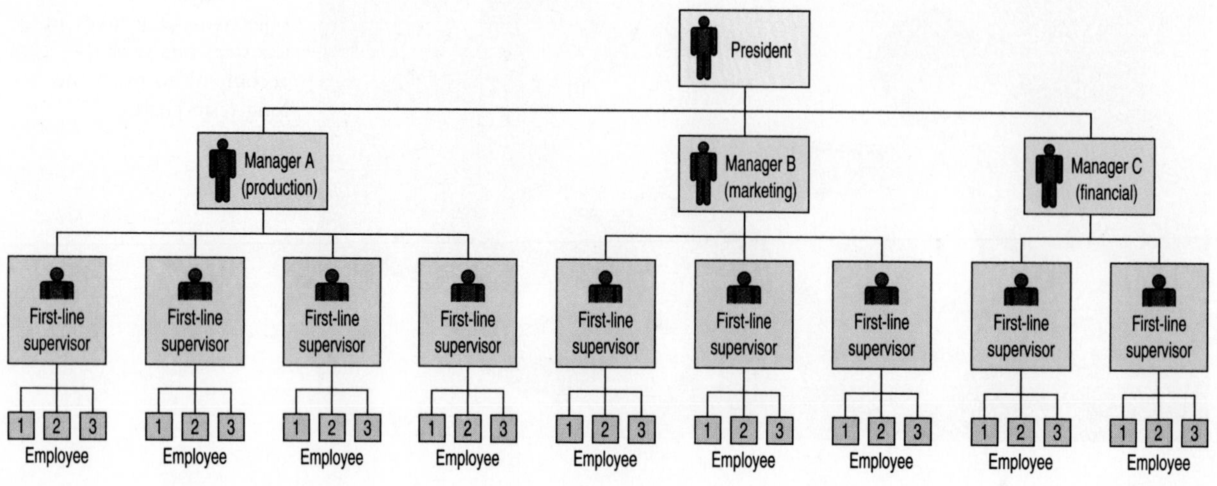

plans. Three terms you are likely to see often are chief executive officer (CEO), chief operating officer (COO), and chief financial officer (CFO). The CEO is often the president of the firm and is responsible for all the top-level decisions. CEOs are responsible for introducing changes into an organization. COOs are responsible for putting those changes into effect. Their tasks include structuring, controlling, and rewarding to ensure that people carry out the leader's vision.

middle management
Level of management that includes plant managers and department heads who are responsible for tactical plans.

supervisory (first-line) management
First level of management above employees; includes people directly responsible for assigning specific jobs to employees and evaluating their daily performance.

Middle management includes branch and plant managers, deans, and department heads who are responsible for tactical plans. **Supervisory (first-line) management** includes people directly responsible for assigning specific jobs to workers and evaluating their daily performance. They are known as first-line managers because they are the first level above workers (see Figure 7–4).

All of this work of gathering materials and people together and assigning tasks is organizing. If you drew a baseball field to show everyone where to stand, you would have an organization chart. A list of who bats in what order could be part of the chart. Managers call that scheduling. In short, organizing is a necessary part of all human effort.

An important part of organizing is staffing, getting the right people on the business team. You are probably familiar with the term *personnel* to describe that function. Today it is called *human resource management* because it is as important to develop the potential of employees as to recruit good people in the first place. We will discuss human resource management in Chapter 15.

Making Organizations More Flexible

Tom Peters was a co-author of *In Search of Excellence*. Like Robert Waterman, he wrote a follow-up book, *Thriving on Chaos* (see Case One at the end of this chapter). He emphasized the need for organizations to become more flexible. That usually means that the organization should be smaller, have fewer levels of management, and adapt more quickly to changes in the market, including the international market.[5] We shall talk more about organization in Chapter 8.

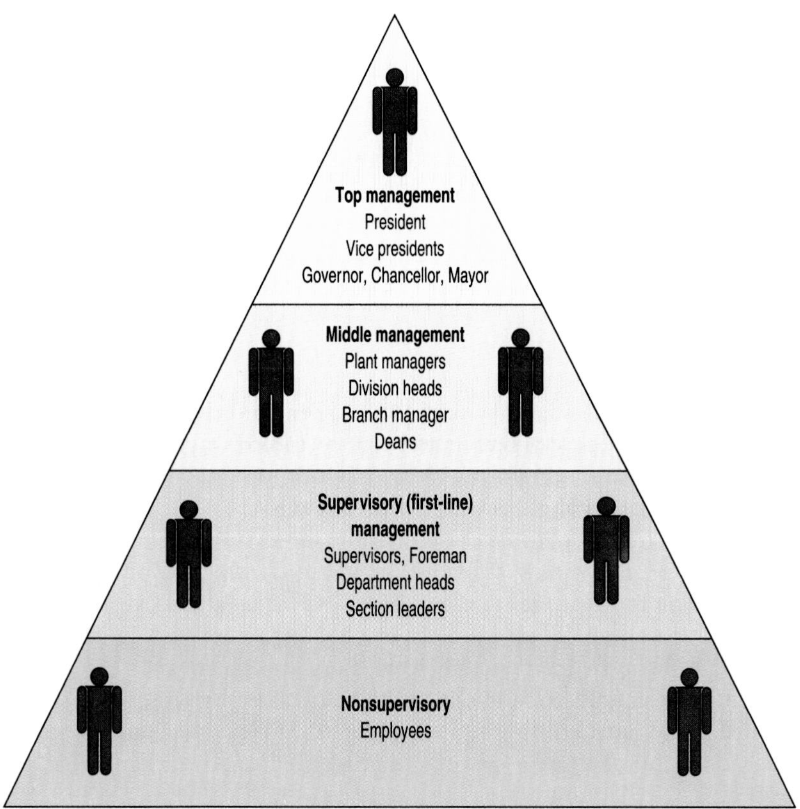

Figure 7–4 Levels of management. This figure shows the three levels of management. In many firms, there are several levels of middle management. Recently, however, firms have been eliminating middle-level managers to cut costs. This is aided by the widespread use of computers, which sometimes makes the role of middle manager redundant.

It is easier to understand the functions of management if you can relate them to your own experiences or observations. For example, it is easier to understand what organization is all about when you imagine the process of organizing players for a baseball team.

MAKING ETHICAL DECISIONS

As a first-line manager, you assist in the decisions made by your department head. The department head retains full responsibility. If the plans succeed, it is his success; if the plans fail, it is his failure. You have new information that the department head hasn't seen. The findings in this report indicate that your manager's recent plans are sure to fail. If the plans do fail, the manager will probably be demoted and you are the most likely candidate to fill the vacancy. Will you give him the report? What will be the consequences of your decision? ▼

DIRECTING

After the plans are made, the organization designed, and the standards established, managers must direct the workers in activities to meet the goals and objectives of the organization. Directing involves giving assignments, explaining routines, clarifying policies, and providing feedback on performance.

All managers, from top managers to first-line supervisors, direct employees. The process of directing is quite different, however, at the various levels of the organization. The top managers are concerned with the broad overview of where the company is heading. Their immediate subordinates are middle managers who are responsible, in turn, for directing workers to meet company objectives. The directions of top managers to subordinates, therefore, are characteristically broad and open-ended. The farther down the corporate ladder, the more specific the manager's directions become. First-line managers allocate much of their time to giving specific, detailed instructions to employees.

The effective manager today works closely with the people he or she supervises in more of a team effort and less of a boss–employee relationship. Understanding the firm's goals and objectives allows the employee to play a greater role in decision making. This permits greater flexibility in operations and also results in more motivated employees. Employee motivation is the subject of Chapter 14.

A critical step in managerial decision making is choosing the right ethical solution. It is important that moral and ethical behaviour be an integral part of the system. This manager is weighing the benefits and costs of such a decision.

CONTROLLING

Often managers get so involved with the planning process and the day-to-day crisis management of the firm that they tend to shortchange the control function. Control involves measuring performance relative to objectives and standards and taking corrective action when necessary. The control function is the heart of the management system, because it provides the feedback that enables managers to adjust to any deviations from plans and to changes in the environment that have affected performance (see Figure 7–5).

Controlling consists of the following steps:

1. Setting clear performance standards.
2. Monitoring and recording actual performance (results).
3. Comparing results against plans and standards.
4. Communicating results and deviations to the employees involved.
5. Taking corrective action when needed.

Setting Standards

The control system's weakest link tends to be the setting of standards. To measure results against standards, the standards must be specific, attainable, and measurable. Goals and standards such as "better quality," "more efficiency," and "improved performance" are too vague. It is also important to establish a time frame in which goals are to be met. Examples of useful goals and standards are:

- Cutting the number of finished product rejects from 10 per 1,000 to 5 per 1,000 by March 31.
- Increasing the times managers praise employees from three times per week to 12 per week by September 30.
- Increasing the sales of product X from 10,000 in the month of July to 12,000 in that same period.

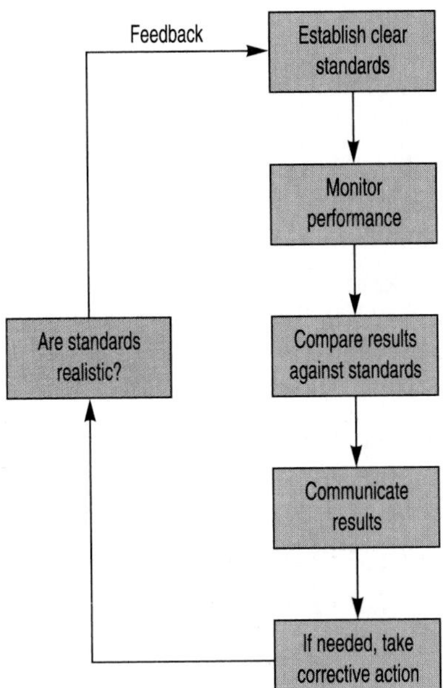

Figure 7–5 The control process. The whole control process is based on clear standards. Without such standards, the other steps are difficult, if not impossible. With clear standards, performance measurement is relatively easy and the proper action can be taken.

One key to making control systems work is establishing clear procedures for monitoring performance. Naturally, management should not be burdened with such control procedures unless the goals are important enough to justify such reporting. Most managers have seen, for example, elaborate accident reports that took hours of management time simply to report, "All is well." To minimize paperwork, such reports could be limited to exceptions.

Many companies have too much reporting of trivial details and too little reporting of significant performance results. To assure a free flow of communication on performance results versus standards, the number of elements measured should be kept to a minimum; those elements measured must be written; and management must provide feedback, to those reporting, that action is being taken on deviations. Sometimes this action requires adjusting unrealistic standards.

LEADERSHIP

Business, and all organizations, require both managers and leaders. Managers ensure the orderly carrying out of all plans and activities; leaders have vision and create change.

Leaders also plan, organize, direct, and control, but their vision is broader. As they carry out these functions, they are aware of the global competitive challenge. **Leadership** consists of creating a vision for others to follow, establishing corporate values and ethics, and transforming the way the organization does business so it is more effective and efficient. Leaders know how vital it is to harness the energies and ideas of all their employees.

leadership
Creating a vision for others to follow, establishing corporate values and ethics, and transforming the way the organization does business so it is more effective and efficient.

The difference between managers and leaders might be shown as follows:

Managers	Leaders
Do things right	Do the right thing
Command and control	Inspire and empower
Seek predictability	Seek flexibility, change, and stability
Are internally focussed	Are externally oriented

Leaders should:

1. Have a vision and rally others around that vision. Rather than manage, the leader should be openly sensitive to the concerns of followers, give them responsibility, and win their trust.
2. Establish corporate values. These values include concern for employees, for customers, and for the quality of the products the company makes. When companies set their goals today, they are going beyond just business goals and are defining their values as well.
3. Emphasize corporate ethics. This means an unfailing demand for honesty and an insistence that everyone in the company get a fair shake. (That is why we have stressed ethical decision making throughout this text.)
4. Not fear change, but embrace and create it. The most important job may be to transform the way the company does business so that it is more effective and efficient.

Managers work within organizational boundaries. Leaders set those boundaries and constantly change the organization to meet new challenges. Today's excellent corporations, more often than not, are reflections of their leaders. The leaders of successful corporations have had a vision of excellence and have led others to share that vision. Walt Disney's leadership can still be seen in Disney amusement parks and movies. Isadore (Issy) Sharp has created a corporate culture that spells excellence in the Four Seasons hotels and restaurants.

Leadership Styles

Nothing has challenged researchers in the area of management more than the search for the "best" leadership traits, behaviours, or styles. Thousands of studies have been made just to find leadership *traits;* that is, characteristics that make leaders different from others. Intuitively, you would conclude much the same thing the researchers found; the findings were neither statistically valid nor reliable. You and I know that some leaders seem to have traits such as good appearance or tact while others are unkempt or abrasive.

Just as there is no one set of traits that can describe a leader, there is no one best style of leadership. Let's look briefly at a few typical leadership styles.

Autocratic. Autocratic leadership involves making managerial decisions without consulting others, and implies power over others. Many businesspeople who are sports leaders seem to use rather successfully an autocratic leadership style that consists of issuing orders and telling players what to do. Motivation comes from threats, punishment, and intimidation of all kinds. Such a style is effective only in emergencies and when absolute followership is needed (for example, on army maneuvers).

Democratic. Democratic or participative leadership consists of managers and employees working together to set objectives and make decisions. Many new, progressive organizations are highly successful at using this style of leadership, where traits such as flexibility, good listening skills, and empathy are dominant. This is the current trend among most top-performing companies.

The best workers in the world still need leadership to set goals and values. A brilliant orchestra leader blends the sounds of many different musicians into a beautiful concert. That is the role a top manager plays in a firm.

Laissez-faire. Laissez-faire leadership is an extension of participative management and involves setting objectives jointly with employees who are relatively free to do whatever it takes to accomplish those objectives. In organizations where managers deal with doctors, engineers, and other professionals, the most successful leadership style is often laissez-faire or free-rein leadership. The traits needed by managers in such organizations include warmth, friendliness, and understanding.

Individual leaders rarely fit neatly into just one of these categories. Researchers Tannenbaum and Schmidt illustrate leadership as a continuum with varying amounts of employee participation ranging from purely boss-centred leadership to subordinate-centred leadership. (See Figure 7–6.) How would you determine which style is most appropriate to a specific company?

When to Use Various Leadership Styles

Research supports the idea that effective leadership depends on the people being led and the situation. It also implies that different leadership styles, ranging from autocratic to employee controlled, may be successful depending on the people and the situation.

In fact, any one manager may use a variety of leadership styles depending on whom he or she is dealing with and the situation. A manager may be autocratic but friendly with a new trainee; democratic with an experienced employee who has many good ideas that can be fostered only by a manager who is a good listener and flexible; and laissez-faire with a trusted, long-term supervisor who probably knows more about operations than the manager does. To summarize:

- No leadership traits are effective in all situations, nor are there leadership styles that always work best.

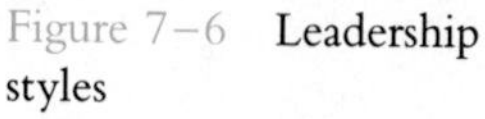
Figure 7–6 Leadership styles

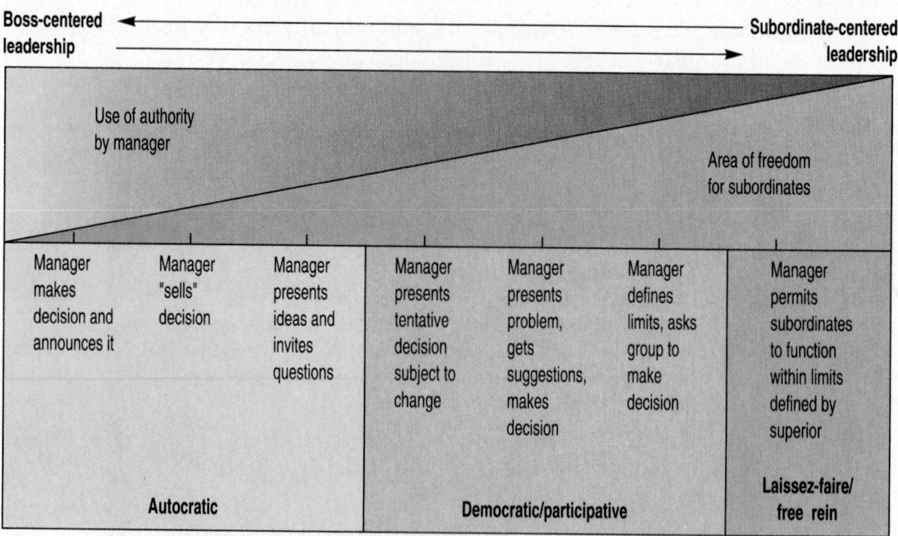

Source: Reprinted by permission of the *Harvard Business Review.* An exhibit from "How to Choose a Leadership Pattern" by Robert Tannenbaum and Warren Schmidt (May/June 1973). Copyright © 1973 by the President and Fellows of Harvard College; all rights reserved.

SPOTLIGHT ON SMALL BUSINESS

How Far Can You Go with Participative Management?

Participative management involves employees in setting objectives and making decisions; democratic and laissez-faire leadership are forms of participative management.

Some firms have had difficulty implementing participative management because some managers hesitate to give up what they feel are their rights. That includes, as they perceive it, the right to be bossy, to tell others what to do, and to punish them if they don't. It certainly does not mean working with people as partners. "Why call me a boss if I am just another worker?" is their attitude. Such people must change if the organization is to develop the teamwork that is necessary to compete in today's changing environment.

On the other hand, some managers have welcomed participative management with open arms and have gone much further than imagined in implementing the concept. In the profile at the beginning of this chapter, we saw how Walter Shawlee believes in and practices participative management. All his employees are responsible. No one can justify a failure with that age-old buck-passing excuse, "I wasn't told to do it." At Northern Airborne Technology, the buck stops with you. And that applies even when you notice something wrong in another area. You had better point it out—but remember to do so co-operatively and without criticizing that person publicly. Shawlee believes this concept of interdependency has been responsible for the company's continued dramatic growth. ▼

- ▼ Different styles of leadership can be used effectively, ranging from autocratic to employee controlled; which style is most effective depends on the people and the situation.
- ▼ A truly successful leader has the ability to change leadership styles to suit the situation and the employee involved.

Leadership depends on followership, and followership depends on the traits and circumstances of the follower. In general, though, one could say that good leaders tend to be flexible, have confidence and trust in their subordinates (and show it), and identify with the goals and values of followers. They are also good communicators, sensitive to the needs of others, and decisive when the situation demands it.

THINKING IT THROUGH

Do you see any problems with the new, more participative managerial style? Do you think it will be adopted by football teams? It is already practiced by some baseball teams. What is the difference between football and baseball players in what they do and how they are managed? How does that relate to the business world?

Can you see a manager getting frustrated when he or she cannot be bossy? Can someone who is trained to give orders (for example, a military sergeant) be retrained to be a participative manager? What problems may emerge? What kind of boss would you be? Do you have evidence to show that?

PROGRESS CHECK

- ▼ Can you explain the differences between autocratic and democratic leadership styles?
- ▼ Why is the participative style of leadership so important now?

SPOTLIGHT ON BIG BUSINESS

Old-Style Leadership Is No Longer Good Enough

Paul Stern, former head of Northern Telecom Ltd.—replaced. Wilbert (Bill) Hopper, former head of Petro-Canada—"relieved of his duties." Ross Dainty, former executive vice-president and chief operating officer of Unitel Communications Inc.—gone. And that's only within the past two weeks. Just what is going on here? Aren't we Canadians supposed to be a patient and forgiving lot? Apparently, not any more.

Corporate Canada, struggling with low morale created by the recession, is facing increasing competition, breakneck change, and overwhelming complexity. The result: increased pressure for results and decreased patience when they are not achieved.

It's not enough any more to make the strategic decisions from Olympian heights and then point the way ahead. Executives today must understand and respect their employees, create shared values and goals, and march forward right alongside them.

Sure, handling the technical and administrative aspects of a company is as important as ever. But more companies are looking for executives with the rare ability to co-ordinate and manage all the human variables in their plan to ensure their efforts produce results.

It's a welcome move for Canadian business, which isn't known for its ability to infuse its work force with any sense of mission. And it's an essential shift, because the world is changing fast. Capable, concerned and consistent leadership is becoming more important than ever.

Few would deny, for instance, that corporate loyalty has declined during the past decade. With layoffs, early retirement, and restructuring becoming standard in good times and in bad, people no longer tie their personal star to a particular company. Motivating an alienated (or even a neutral) work force requires real leadership.

Business has become so complex that strong leadership is essential to bring diverse groups together—getting sales to work with finance, for instance, or building "partnership" relationships with suppliers.

How do you assess your own leadership? In his book *Lead, Follow or Get Out of the Way,* California management consultant Jim Lundy offers a deceptively simple test. He asks: "Are you managing subordinates? Or are you leading followers?" Managers who don't listen to their subordinates, who shout out orders or forget to offer praise or thanks, he says, are likely to find themselves alone when they go blazing trails through the corporate woods.

Don't think it's just the rank and file that's put off by negative leadership. One vice-president I interviewed recently said he was considering a job change because he was tired of being "barked at" by his boss. "Steve didn't want us to think we were doing a good job. He believes that inside every silver lining there's a dark cloud, and he always pointed it out."

Real leaders communicate with subordinates strategically, discussing and listening and deriving the feedback they need to help the subordinates set appropriate goals for themselves. They share their goals but don't stuff them down anyone's throat. By encouraging associates to assist each other, they build stronger teams. And by providing regular forums to review progress, they keep the group on track and moving.

For management, the themes of the '90s are customer service, productivity, and employee empowerment. Succeeding in these areas requires motivated and enthusiastic employees. Managers who can't inspire their subordinates to excellence are vulnerable to the kind of surprises that last month confronted Messrs. Stern, Hopper, and Dainty.

Source: Michael Stern, *Globe and Mail,* February 3, 1993, p. B2. [Michael Stern is president of Michael Stern Associates Inc., an executive search firm headquartered in Toronto and Canadian partner in the Euram Consultants Group Ltd., which has offices in 10 countries.]

TASKS AND SKILLS AT DIFFERENT LEVELS OF MANAGEMENT

Anyone who has ever played a sport such as hockey, football, or soccer knows there is a tremendous difference between being an excellent player and an excellent coach (manager). Often a good player will volunteer to coach the neighbourhood team and will be a disaster as a manager. The same thing happens in business. Few people are trained to be managers. Usually, a person learns how to be a skilled accountant or salesperson or production line worker, and because of his or her skill is selected to be a manager. The tendency is for such managers to become deeply involved in

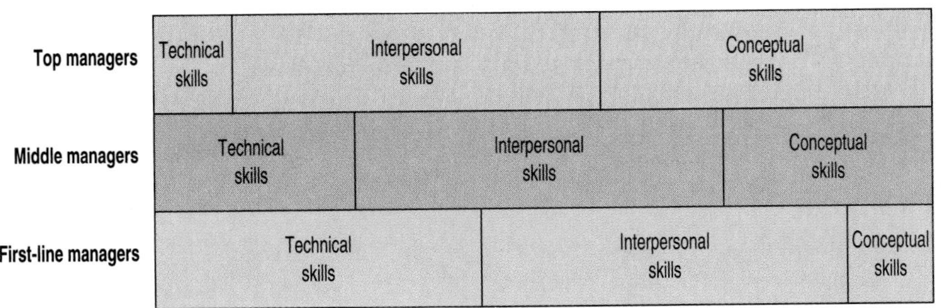

Figure 7–7 Skills needed at various levels of management. All managers need interpersonal skills. At the top, managers need strong conceptual skills. First-line managers need strong technical skills. Middle managers need to have a balance between technical and conceptual

showing others how to do things, helping them, supervising them, and generally being very active in the operating task.

The further up the managerial ladder a person moves, the less such skills are required. Instead, the need is for people who are good planners, organizers, coordinators, communicators, morale builders, and motivators. Figure 7–7 shows that a manager must have three categories of skills: technical, conceptual, and human relations or interpersonal skills.

Let's pause here to clarify the terms:

- **Technical skills** involve the ability to perform tasks of a specific department such as selling (marketing) or bookkeeping (accounting).
- **Conceptual skills** refer to a manager's ability to picture the organization as a whole and the relationship of various parts as well as the ability to perform tasks such as planning, organizing, controlling, systems development, problem analysis, decision making, coordinating, and delegating.
- **Interpersonal skills** include leadership, motivation, coaching, communication, morale building, training and development, help and supportiveness, and delegating.

technical skills
Ability to perform tasks of a specific department (such as selling or bookkeeping).

conceptual skills
Ability to picture the organization as a whole and the relationship of various parts.

interpersonal skills
Ability to lead, communicate, motivate, coach, build morale, train, support, and delegate.

As you look at Figure 7–7, you will notice that first-level managers need to be skilled in all three areas. Most of their time is spent on technical and human relations tasks (assisting operating personnel, giving direction, and so forth). First-level managers spend little time on conceptual tasks. Top managers, on the other hand, need few technical skills. Instead, almost all their time is devoted to interpersonal and conceptual tasks. Someone who is competent at one level of management may not be competent at higher levels, and vice versa. The skills needed are different at different levels.

Spend some time reviewing the definitions of conceptual and interpersonal skills that are so important to top management. Note that delegating is in both conceptual and interpersonal definitions. Another key managerial task is decision making. Because of their importance, we shall explore both delegating and decision making in more detail.

Delegating

One of the most difficult tasks for most managers to learn is **delegating** (assigning authority and accountability to others and letting them do the job while retaining responsibility for results). Remember, many managers are often selected from those who are most skilled at doing what the people they manage are doing. Their

delegating
Assigning authority and accountability to others and letting them do the job, while retaining responsibility for results.

inclination is to pitch in and help or do it themselves. But this keeps workers from learning and having the satisfaction of doing it themselves.

More important, inability to delegate gets managers so bogged down in details that they forget to keep their eye on the managerial ball!

Decision Making

Decision making is choosing among two or more alternatives. It sounds easier than it is in practice. In fact, decision making is the heart of all the management functions: planning, organizing, directing and controlling. The **rational decision-making model** is a series of steps managers should follow to make logical, intelligent, and well-founded decisions. These six steps are shown in Figure 7–8.

rational decision-making model
Consists of six steps: (1) define the problem, (2) define and collect needed information, (3) develop alternatives, (4) decide which alternative is best and also ethically acceptable, (5) do what is indicated to implement the decision, and (6) determine whether the decision was a good one by follow-up.

1. **Define the problem.** The sales manager notes that sales of Product A have been slipping for several months. How to reverse the trend?
2. **Define and collect needed information.** Obtain sales data for each salesperson for the last six months and similar data for the previous two years. Note that John and Maria are responsible for most of the decline. Maria has not been well for some time. John has not kept up with the changes in his territory. Maria has been with the company only three years, but John is a 20-year man.
3. **Develop alternatives.** For Maria, consider two options. (a) Offer her extended sick leave partially covered by company group insurance plan. Have other sales staff fill in. (b) Give her reasonable severance pay and give her notice. Hire replacement. For John, (a) remind him that you have warned him twice about his performance, fire him, and replace him. (b) Ask how he intends to improve performance after previous promises. Evaluate whether he should be given a final chance.
4. **Decide which alternative is best and ethically acceptable.** Alternative (a) is best in both cases. Ethically, Maria is given humane treatment. So is John because he has already had two warnings.
5. **Do what is indicated to implement the decision.**
6. **Determine whether the decision was a good one by follow-up.** Note whether sales improve in the next three months in the two territories.

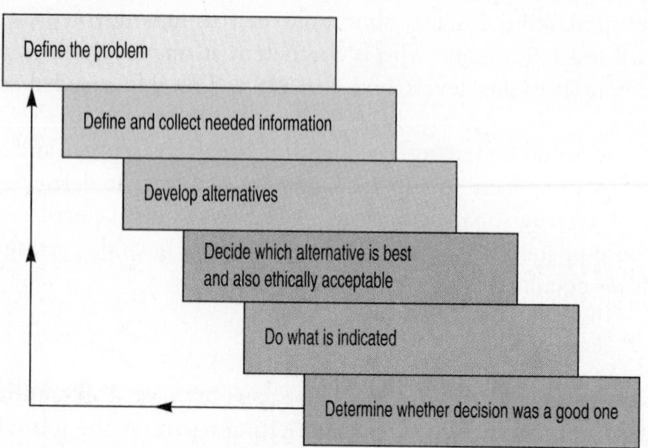

Figure 7–8 The six Ds of decision making: An important step in the decision-making process is to choose the best *ethical* alternative. Other alternatives might generate more money but would be immoral or improper in some way. After the decision is evaluated, the whole process begins again.

The best decisions are based on sound information. That is why this is known as the information age. Managers often have computer terminals at their desks so they can get internal records and external data of all kinds. But all the data in the world cannot replace a manager who is creative and makes brilliant decisions. The facts never speak for themselves. Data must be interpreted and judgments made. Decision making is more an art than a science. It is the one skill most needed by managers because all the other functions depend on it.

Managers Are Needed Everywhere

One of the exciting things about studying management is that it prepares you for a career in any organization. Managers are needed in schools, churches, charities, government, unions, associations, clubs, and all other organizations. Naturally, an important need for managers is in business.

When selecting a career in management, a student has several decisions to make:

- What kind of organization is most attractive? Would you like to work for government, business, or some nonprofit organization?
- What type of managerial position seems most interesting? A person may become a production manager, a sales manager, a human resource manager, an accounting manager, a traffic (distribution) manager, a credit manager, and so on. There are dozens of managerial positions from which to choose.
- What type of industry appeals to you—computer, auto, steel, railroad, or what? Would you prefer to work for a relatively new firm or an established one?
- What courses and training do you need to prepare for various managerial careers? Only careful research will answer this question.

THINKING IT THROUGH

What kind of management are you best suited for: human resources, marketing, finance, accounting, production, credit, or what? Why do you feel this area is most appropriate?

Would you like to work for a large or small firm? Private or government? In an office or out in the field? Would you like being a manager? If you are not sure, read on and see what is involved.

LEARNING MANAGERIAL SKILLS

Now that you have examined what managers do and some of the new managerial styles demanded by tomorrow's organizations, we can look at the skills you will need to be a good manager. In general, it's a good idea to take as many courses as you can in speech, writing, computers, and human relations. In all managerial jobs, these are the skills that are in greatest demand. Naturally, you will also have to develop technical skills in your chosen area. Figure 7–9 lists the six skills you will need to develop your managerial potential: verbal, writing, computer, interpersonal, time management, and technical skills.

Figure 7–9 Evaluating your managerial potential. If you need improvement in any of these areas, it is a good idea to take courses or read books to improve yourself. The best time to do this is *before* you go to work so you are fully prepared when you go job hunting.

Evaluating your managerial potential

Skill needed	Personal evaluation			
	Excellent	Good	Fair	Need work
Verbal skills				
Writing skills				
Computer skills				
Interpersonal skills				
Time management skills				
Technical skills				

Verbal skills are a critical part of a manager's job. Being effective at public speaking, conducting meetings, and communicating ideas to others is extremely important. You can improve your skills by making classroom presentations and working with others on group projects.

Verbal Skills

The bulk of your duties as a manager will involve communicating with others. You will have to explain to subordinates and report to senior managers, give talks, conduct meetings, make presentations, and generally communicate your ideas to others. To prepare for such tasks, you should take speech courses and become active in various student groups. Become an officer so that you are responsible for conducting meetings and giving speeches. You may want to join a choir or other group to become comfortable performing in front of others.

At least half of communication is skilled listening. A good manager mingles with other managers, workers, and clients. He or she listens to recommendations and complaints and acts on them. Active listening requires asking questions and feeding back what you have heard to let others know you are truly interested in what they say.

Writing Skills

Managers must also be able to write clearly and precisely. Much of what you want others to do must be communicated through memos, reports, policies, and letters you write. Organizations everywhere are complaining about the inability of many graduates to write clearly. If you develop good writing skills, you will be miles ahead of your competition. That means you should take courses in grammar and composition. Reading books and magazines helps to improve your vocabulary, grammar, and style. Volunteer to write term papers, even if they are not assigned. To learn to write, you must practice writing. It helps to write anything: a diary, letters, notes, and so on. With practice, you will develop the ability to write as easily as you speak. This skill will make you more ready for a career in management.

Computer Skills

The office of today is full of computers. Memos, charts, letters, and most of your other communication efforts will involve the computer. When you are practicing writing, practice on a computer keyboard. Managers have to do word processing and send messages electronically throughout the world. To prepare for such an environment, begin by taking a course or two in keyboarding. You will not need many advanced computer courses. The new software makes computer use relatively easy, but you will have to know what software is available and how to use it. Practice by writing term papers and other assignments on the computer.

Interpersonal Skills

A manager works with people. Good managers know how to get along with people, motivate them, and inspire them. You learn people skills by working with people. Join student groups. Volunteer to help in a charity, senior citizens group, athletic organization, or a group that helps the needy. Get involved in political organizations. Try to assume leadership positions where you have the responsibility for contacting others, assigning them work, and motivating them. Good leaders begin early by assuming leadership positions in sports, community groups, and so on.

Be aware of how others react to you; if you cause negative feelings or reactions, learn why. Don't be afraid to make mistakes and upset others. That is how you learn. But do learn how to work with people. Ask your friends what you could do to be a more effective and appealing leader.

Managers have to learn how to deal effectively with people from many different cultures. Many workers are East Indian, West Indian, Aboriginal, Asian, or from some other culture. Managers will also be asked to work overseas. The more skilled you can become in other languages now and in working with diverse cultural groups, the better off you will be when you become a manager.

Time Management Skills

One of the most important skills for new (and not so new) managers to learn is how to budget their time effectively. There are so many demands on managers' time that unless they learn how to manage their time properly they will be propelled by events rather than controlling them. Telephone interruptions, drop-in colleagues, questions from subordinates, mail, meetings, customers, superiors—all conspire to make a manager's day total confusion unless he or she learns how to organize time effectively.

See if your school offers courses in time management. Such courses or workshops will help you to develop specific skills: setting priorities, delegating work, choosing activities that produce the most results, doing complex work when you are at peak performance, and dealing with interruptions. These useful skills will help you be more productive at school and at home as well as at work.

Computer skills are important for management positions. You can learn such skills by taking computer courses and by using application packages in your other courses.

Technical Skills

To rise up through the ranks of accounting, marketing, finance, production, or any other functional area, you will have to be proficient in that area. Begin now to choose some area of specialization. You may start with a liberal arts education to practice your oral, written, and interpersonal skills. But to rise to top management, you might supplement that knowledge with an M.B.A. (masters in business administration) or similar degree in government, economics, or hospital administration. More and more students are going on to earn advanced degrees. About 60 percent of top managers have taken courses beyond the bachelor's degree. Many continue to take specialized courses throughout their career in order to keep up to date. The most common areas of technical expertise among top managers are marketing, finance, production, law, and engineering, in that order.

A GLOBAL VIEW OF MANAGEMENT

Business schools are seeing a major mood change these days. As students read about the former communist countries moving rapidly and with great confusion towards a market economy, they want to know more about international business. Many young people know that they will be involved with international business even if they never leave Canada. They also know that companies are looking to business schools for managers who know how to work in the new global context.

What skills and knowledge do the new global managers require? They need to be multilingual despite the fact that English is the major international language. They need knowledge of other cultures so that they can understand different markets and deal with people who have different values. In Part IV, you will see examples of the serious mistakes you can make if you are not aware of how foreign cultures differ from your own.

How are business schools responding to this student demand? Many are revamping their existing curriculum and integrating international examples into basic courses. This reduces the need for specific international courses and brings the international dimension into the mainstream.

Still, some students demand more. They want business courses that are entirely international. Major business schools now offer semester exchange programs with business schools in other countries. Professors are encouraged to participate in international research and to gain teaching experience overseas. Students are encouraged, and in some cases required, to study foreign languages. Students have caught the international fever and have passed their sense of urgency on to the colleges and universities.

Management will be discussed in more detail in the next few chapters. Let's pause now, review, and do some exercises. Management is doing, not just reading.

PROGRESS CHECK

- ▼ What skills do supervisors need more of than do top managers, and vice versa?
- ▼ What are the six Ds of decision making?
- ▼ What are the six skills you should be working on now to become a good manager later?

SUMMARY

1. Many managers are changing their approach to corporate management.

▼ *What reasons can you give to account for these changes in management?*

The four major reasons for management changes are (1) global competition, (2) deregulation, (3) accelerating technological change, and (4) the deep recession.

▼ *Can you describe the changing role of managers?*

Managers are now being trained to lead, guide, and coach employees rather than boss them. The trend is toward working with employees as a team to meet organizational goals.

1. Explain how and why the role of managers is changing in the 1990s.

2. Management has been described as the art of getting things done through people.

▼ *What are the four functions of management?*

Management is the process used to pursue organizational goals through (1) planning, (2) organizing, (3) directing, and (4) controlling.

2. Identify the four functions of management.

3. The planning function involves the process of setting objectives to meet the organizational goals.

▼ *What is the difference between goals and objectives?*

Goals are broad, long-term achievements that organizations aim to accomplish. Objectives are specific, short-term tasks that must be completed to reach the goals.

▼ *What are the three types of planning and how are they related to the organization's goals and objectives?*

Strategic planning is broad, long-range planning that outlines the *goals* of the organization. *Tactical planning,* on the other hand, is specific, short-term planning that lists organizational *objectives*. *Contingency planning* involves developing an alternative set of plans in case the first set doesn't work out.

3. Distinguish between goals and objectives and among strategic, tactical, and contingency planning, and explain the relationships of goals and objectives to the various types of planning.

4. Managers develop a framework that illustrates the relationship of workers, tasks, and resources.

4. Describe the significance of an organization chart and explain the role of each management level in the corporate hierarchy.

▼ *What is this framework called and what are the three major levels of management illustrated on the chart?*

The organization chart pictures who reports to whom and who is responsible for what task. It illustrates the top, middle, and first-line management levels.

5. The directing function of management involves giving assignments, explaining routines, clarifying policies, and providing feedback on performance.

5. Describe the directing function of management and illustrate how it differs at the various management levels.

▼ *How does the directing function vary at different levels of management?*

The farther down the corporate ladder, the more specific the managers' directions become. First-line managers spend a great deal of their time giving very specific, detailed instructions to their subordinates. In contrast, top managers direct middle managers who require only broad, general directions.

6. The control function of management involves measuring employee performance against objectives and standards and taking corrective action if necessary.

6. Summarize the five steps of the control function of management.

▼ *What are the five steps of the control function?*

Controlling incorporates the following: (1) setting clear standards, (2) monitoring and recording performance, (3) comparing performance with plans and standards, (4) communicating results and deviations to employees, and (5) taking corrective action when needed.

▼ *What qualities must standards possess in order to be used to measure performance results?*

Standards must be specific, attainable, and measurable.

7. Executives today must be more than just managers; they must be leaders as well.

7. Explain the differences between managers and leaders and compare the characteristics and use of various leadership styles.

▼ *What is the difference between a manager and a leader?*

A manager sees that the organization runs smoothly and that order is maintained. A leader does this and more. A leader has vision and inspires others to grasp that vision, establishes corporate values, emphasizes corporate ethics, and does not fear change.

▼ *What are the various leadership styles?*

See Figure 7–6 for a continuum of leadership styles ranging from manager-controlled to employee-controlled decision making.

▼ *Which leadership style is best?*

The best (most effective) leadership style depends on the people being led and the situation.

8. Managers must be good planners, organizers, co-ordinators, communicators, morale builders, and motivators.

8. Describe the skills needed by top, middle, and first-line managers.

▼ *What skills must a manager have in order to be all these things?*

Managers must have three categories of skills: (1) *technical skills* (ability to perform tasks such as bookkeeping or selling), (2) *conceptual skills* (ability to see the organization as a whole and how all the parts fit together), and (3) *interpersonal skills* (ability to communicate and motivate).

▼ *Are these skills equally important at all management levels?*

The skills needed are different at different levels. Top managers rely heavily on interpersonal and conceptual skills and rarely use technical skills, while first-line supervisors need strong technical and interpersonal skills and use conceptual skills less often. (See Figure 7–7.)

9. Now that you have examined what managers do, you may be considering a career in management.

9. Illustrate the six skills you will need to develop your managerial potential and outline activities you could use to develop these skills.

▼ *What skills should you be developing now to help you become a better manager in the future?*

You will need to develop six skills to sharpen your managerial potential: (1) verbal skills, (2) writing skills, (3) computer skills, (4) interpersonal skills, (5) time management skills, (6) technical skills.

GETTING INVOLVED

1. Discuss the different requirements for working as a manager in government, business, and non-business organizations. To learn about each, talk to managers from each area and share what you learn with the class.
2. Talk with local managers and find out what they spend the most time doing. Is it planning, organizing, controlling, or directing? Or some entirely different, other task, like paperwork? Which tasks are most interesting to do? Which are hardest? Which would you most enjoy? If possible, observe a manager for a day and see what he or she actually does. Share your findings with the class.
3. Discuss the advantages of not becoming a manager. Do managers or workers seem to enjoy better lifestyles? Discuss.
4. Go through business journals and read about managers. How much do they make? How many hours do they work? Do they earn their pay? Discuss.
5. Review Figure 7–6 and discuss managers you have known or read about who have practiced each style. Which did you like best? Why? Which were most effective? Why? Which would *you* most like to be? Why?
6. Recall all of the situations where you have worked under a manager. How well did he or she delegate? Did the manager assign tasks and give you freedom to work or not? How did you feel about that? Discuss those feelings and the importance of learning to delegate.

PRACTICING MANAGEMENT DECISIONS

Case One In Search of Excellence

In the 1980s, the most popular book on management was called *In Search of Excellence*. It was on the best-seller list for over a year. Clearly, managers saw in it some advice worth taking. The authors visited many of the top firms in the United States to find out what made them better than the other firms. They were searching for excellence. Their findings support what you have read in this book thus far. Basically, excellent organizations insisted on top quality. They cared for their customers. They listened to their employees and treated them like adults. They emphasized human creativity over analysis and high-tech tools. The following are the eight attributes of successful firms.

1. *A bias for action.* "Do it, fix it, try it" was one slogan. The idea is to get on with it and not try to analyze decisions to death. If someone has a new idea, try it and see what happens. Remain flexible. "Ready. Aim. Fire. Learn from your tries. That's enough."
2. *Closeness to the customer.* Excellent companies listen to their customers intently and regularly. They then provide unparalleled quality, service, and reliability. "Probably the most important management function . . . is staying close to the customer to satisfy his needs and anticipate his wants." In this text, we say, "Find a need and fill it."
3. *Autonomy and entrepreneurship.* Excellent companies encourage risk taking and support good tries. "Make sure you generate a reasonable number of mistakes." The key to remaining competitive is innovation, and the way to assure innovation is to support the creative thinkers in the firm. "No support systems, no champions. No champions, no innovations."
4. *Productivity through people.* Basically, this was support for participative management. Treat employees like adults. Seek their input. Treat them as the primary source of productivity gains. "Many of the best companies really do view themselves as an extended family."

5. *Hands on, value driven.* The best companies believe in doing the best, in the importance of details, in superior quality and service, in the importance of informality to enhance communication, and in economic growth and profits.
6. *Stick to your knitting.* Do what you are good at. That is, don't acquire businesses that you don't know how to run. Do one thing well rather than many things in a mediocre way.
7. *Simple form, lean staff.* Keep the organization form simple. Keep staff positions to a minimum. This is the KISS formula: Keep it simple, Sam!
8. *Simultaneous loose–tight properties.* Establish a strong corporate culture emphasizing quality, service, and excellence and then delegate authority to let people achieve.

Soon after his first book came out, Tom Peters wrote *Thriving on Chaos.* It emphasized that there is no such thing as an excellent company—there are only companies that maintain their excellence by adapting quickly to market changes. The secrets to *staying* excellent are to:

1. *Become a niche-oriented market creator,* finding new, small markets and meeting their needs with short production runs. This comes very close to making custom-designed products for individual buyers.
2. *Change the structure of the organization* to have fewer layers of management. This allows the firm to adapt to consumer needs more quickly.
3. *Be responsive, adaptive, and fast* in making such changes.
4. *Be internationalist,* even if you are a small firm. The big markets are in other countries.
5. *Keep the organization small* so it can be flexible. If the organization is large, keep individual units small and semi-autonomous so they can be flexible and adapt quickly.
6. *Involve employees in managerial decision making* and let them share in the profits.

Decision Questions

1. The book *In Search of Excellence* was based on excellent companies, but some began losing market share in the 1980s, so Tom Peters wrote a new book. Given the changes he recommended, what were the problems companies were having that made them lose their excellence?
2. Almost all the changes recommended in *Thriving on Chaos* have to do with making firms faster in responding to changes in the market and more aware of international markets. What happened in the late 1980s that called for such responsiveness?
3. What managerial style or styles are advocated in these books? Why are such styles more advantageous today?
4. Most of the changes recommended in *In Search of Excellence* were managerial changes. Most of the changes recommended in *Thriving on Chaos* were organizational changes. What does that tell you about managerial needs for the 1990s?

Sources: Thomas J. Peters and Robert H. Waterman, Jr., *In Search of Excellence* (New York: Harper & Row, 1982); and Thomas J. Peters, *Thriving on Chaos* (New York: Alfred A. Knopf, 1988).

Case Two One-Minute Managing

Many managers have not mastered the art of praising their employees so that workers feel their accomplishments are recognized. Because of this, a very popular book in the 1980s was *The One Minute Manager,* by Kenneth Blanchard. It was a how-to book on creating feelings of achievement, responsibility, growth, and recognition among employees. The book was short and easy to read, but the message was strong and useful.

The way to praise employees so they feel recognized is to:

- Tell them ahead of time that you are going to let them know how they are doing (good or bad).

- Praise them immediately (look for a good thing to say). This takes only a minute.
- Tell them specifically what they did right.
- Tell them how good you feel about what they did and how it helps the organization.
- Encourage them to do more of the same.
- Shake hands or touch employees on the shoulder to show your support.
- Remember that the personal touch is important.

Instill feelings of achievement, responsibility, and growth by encouraging employees to:

- Agree on some specific goals.
- Write out the goals in less than 250 words.
- Read the goals carefully.
- Take a minute periodically to compare results to goals.

Clear goals give employees a feeling of responsibility, and meeting those goals creates a feeling of achievement and growth. If employees get off track, a one-minute reprimand is in order. Reprimand immediately; be specific about what they did wrong; tell them how you feel; touch them for reassurance; remind them of their value; tell them you know they are good workers, but not in this instance; and drop the matter (no further consequences).

Decision Questions

1. How would you feel if at least once a day you were given one minute of praise for something you were doing well? Does that help explain the popularity of *The One Minute Manager?* Would it motivate you?
2. All of this book is really common sense. Why would managers pay to read what they already know intuitively? Is it one thing to know, another to do?
3. What is your reaction to the one-minute reprimand?
4. What is your reaction to the idea of touching employees whenever you praise or reprimand them to show support?

Source: Kenneth Blanchard, *The One Minute Manager,* (New York: Berkley Books, 1982).

LET'S TALK BUSINESS

1. Have you seen any evidence of managers shifting their emphasis from being bossy to being a coach and team player?
2. The four functions of management are planning, organizing, directing, and controlling. Can you think of ways you have already performed any of these functions? Have you done more than one? Discuss.
3. Why is long-range planning less effective as a managerial tool today than it was in the past?
4. Business leaders must have a vision and establish corporate values and ethics. What is the need for such leaders in the government, schools, and other non-profit organizations?

LOOKING AHEAD

"One of these days we're going to have to get organized," the saying goes. True enough. Businesses today are not just getting organized, they are going through major reorganizations. Why? Companies got so big during the 1960s, 1970s, and 1980s that management became very difficult, slow, and costly. The idea today is to reduce the layers of management and shift more responsibility to lower levels. This process of decentralization and other important concepts will be discussed in Chapter 8.

ORGANIZING FOR EFFICIENT MANAGEMENT

LEARNING GOALS

After you have read and studied this chapter, you should be able to:

1. Define organizational design and explain its importance.
2. Describe the current trends in organizational design.
3. Explain the contributions of Henri Fayol and Max Weber to organizational theory.
4. Compare the advantages and disadvantages of tall and flat organization structures.
5. Explain the concept of span of control.
6. Describe the various ways organizations can be departmentalized.
7. Discriminate between centralized and decentralized organizations.
8. Compare the advantages and disadvantages of line, line and staff, cluster, and matrix organizations.
9. Explain the various ways organizations can co-ordinate activities among departments.
10. Define organizational culture and describe the role of the informal organization in that culture.

KEY TERMS

accountability, p. 234
authority, p. 233
bureaucratic organization, p. 238
centralized authority, p. 245
cluster organization, p. 254
decentralized authority, p. 245
delegation of authority, p. 245
departmentalization, p. 244
flat organization structures, p. 242
formal organization, p. 257
functional structure, p. 244
informal organization, p. 257
information system, p. 254
line organization structure, p. 248
line personnel, p. 249
manageability, p. 233
matrix organization, p. 251
organization chart, p. 241
organizational culture, p. 255
organizational design, p. 233
responsibility, p. 233
span of control, p. 243
staff personnel, p. 249
tall organization structures, p. 242

Lee Iacocca

PROFILE LEE IACOCCA OF CHRYSLER

Lee Iacocca, the former president of Chrysler, was one of the best-known CEOs in the world. In 1978 he left the top position at Ford to undertake the mammoth task of saving Chrysler from almost certain bankruptcy. His first achievement was to get the U.S. government to guarantee $1 billion of bank loans and the Canadian government to guarantee a smaller amount for Chrysler of Canada. These guarantees enabled him to start on the long hill up from disaster. In a few years, he had achieved the miraculous turnaround of Chrysler and paid off those loans.

How did he do it? A major contributing element was the vast restructuring of the company's organization. When he took over, Chrysler had 32 vice-presidents, and communication among them was poor. He cut this number, reduced his own salary to $1 per year, and cut other executive salaries. Instead of salary he gambled on performance-based remuneration. The United Auto Workers union also agreed to wage cuts for workers. Quality was stressed, car sales began to rise, and eventually Chrysler had record profits of $2.4 billion.

In his cost-cutting and quality modes, Iacocca let new-product development slip. Pressure from Japanese cars and GM and Ford forced Chrysler to restructure once more. The auto group was given two presidents: one to focus on marketing and new-car design, the other on production. Managers of individual car lines (Plymouth, Dodge, and Chrysler) were given more responsibility for developing new models. In other words, restructuring is now a continual process at Chrysler, as it is at all modern adaptive organizations.

Iacocca retired, and Chrysler is now being led by Robert J. Eaton, who ran the very successful European Chrysler operation. In 1993, after three very difficult years for the automobile business, Chrysler seems to be well launched into a good year.

Lee Iacocca's story shows us the nature of business today. Yesterday's accomplishments mean nothing in today's fiercely competitive atmosphere. Every organization must continually restructure and search for ways to be more efficient. In this chapter, we will discuss the structure of companies and organizations.

Sources: Peter Finch, ed., "Twenty-Five Executives to Watch," *The Business Week 1000,* 1991 Special Issue, p. 56; Alex Taylor III, "Can Iacocca Fix Chrysler—Again?" *Fortune,* April 8, 1991, pp. 49–54; S. C. Gwynne, "Can Iacocca Do It Again?" *Time,* March 5, 1990, p. 40; Robert M. Bleiberg, "The Iacocca Story—Part 2," *Barron's,* October 8, 1990, p. 12; and Bradley A. Stertz and Paul Ingrassea, "Motown Stunner," *The Wall Street Journal,* March 17, 1992, pp. A1 & A8.

THE IMPORTANCE OF ORGANIZATIONAL DESIGN

Lee Iacocca's experience at Chrysler is being repeated in corporate offices throughout Canada and the United States. Top executives are looking at how their firms are organized and are changing their organizations to make them more efficient. A key question of the 1990s is whether or not business organizations in Canada will be able to adapt to new international competition and become more responsive to new consumer demands. The importance of organizational design, therefore, is that the survival of many firms depends on creating more responsive organizations. Particular attention must be given to communication, employee morale, and manageability.

The trend today is for smaller people-oriented plants. Even in large firms, smaller units are more responsive and are able to create more cohesiveness among employees.

Manageability means that the organization is set up so that everyone knows who is responsible for everything that must be done, who reports to whom, what to do when problems arise, and so forth. You should be getting a feel for what organization design is, now that you know what manageability means. **Organizational design** is the establishment of manageable groups of people who have clear responsibilities and who know how to accomplish the objectives of the organization and the group.

manageability
A system where everyone in the organization knows who is responsible for what, who reports to whom, and what to do when problems arise.

organizational design
The establishment of manageable groups of people who have clear responsibilities and who know how to accomplish the objectives of the organization and the group.

Actually, learning about organizational design should come rather easily to you. You have been following its principles all of your life. Take, for example, a game of baseball. Someone has to pitch, someone else catches, others play the bases, outfield, and so on. Each person knows what his or her function is (after some coaching), and the team works together to accomplish some goal (winning the game). As the game gets more sophisticated, you may add a first-base coach, a third-base coach, and others who advise the players on what to do. A coach and manager give overall guidance and leadership.

Sometimes the organization becomes so formal, so structured, that the game is not as much fun. All the decisions are left to managers. The team may work efficiently, but it may lose the enthusiasm, the creativity, and the esprit de corps that make winners out of even mediocre players. The questions then become, "How much structure should there be? How much decision making should be centralized with the managers? How much freedom should the players have to bat, to steal bases, and to try different positions?" What you know from experience about organizations is this:

- An organization is a group of people working together to accomplish a goal.
- The structure and formality of an organization affect the morale and enthusiasm of its people.

You may not be as familiar with the following terms, but understanding them is essential to understanding the role of managers in organizations:

- **Authority** is the right and power to make decisions and take action.
- **Responsibility** means that when a person is given a task to do, he or she has an obligation to do it.

authority
The right and power to make decisions and take actions.

responsibility
The obligation of a person to complete a given task.

SPOTLIGHT ON BIG BUSINESS

Becoming Lean and Mean

The problem with large organizations is that communication among managers and units is too slow and complex. In today's highly competitive environment, businesses must be able to respond quickly to constant technological and market changes. Consistent failure to detect and react to such developments has created serious difficulties for many hitherto profitable companies. In addition, Canadian companies face the special competitive challenge created by the Free Trade Agreement with the U.S. and the upcoming North American Free Trade Agreement (discussed in previous chapters).

A typical example involves salespeople in the field who have an important special order. By the time they have conferred with their regional sales managers, who have conferred with their divisional sales managers, who in turn have spoken to manufacturing about scheduling the special order, a smaller company could have the product made and delivered to the customer.

These challenges have led to a rash of major restructuring of many companies. Downsizing (eliminating layers of management and many employees) swept through the 1980s and is continuing in the 1990s. This whole process was accelerated by the two recessions of the early 1980s and the early 1990s. It became a matter of survival. Hundreds of thousands of jobs disappeared as companies became leaner and meaner and those that couldn't compete simply folded.

While companies simply cut costs in the earlier recession, they are restructuring in this one. It's the difference between a scalpel and a meat-axe. Alcan Aluminium and Imperial Oil restructured early. Continental Can saw the FTA as a serious threat and changed the nature of its business. Other companies waited until the knife was at their throat before acting. Canada Malting Company didn't wait that long and did a major overhaul of its operations. Canada Packers, our largest food processing firm, separated each of its divisions to force them to act as completely independent units.

Sources: Randall Litchfield, The '90s Way To Tackle the Recession, *Canadian Business* 63, no. 11, November 30, 1990, p. 80; personal interviews.

accountability
Requirement that managers accept the consequences of their actions and report those actions to their immediate supervisor.

Accountability is the requirement that individuals in an organization, when using their authority to carry out their responsibilities, must accept the consequences of their actions (good or bad) and report those actions to their immediate supervisor.

Figure 8–1 shows the relationship of authority, responsibility, and accountability in the organizational hierarchy. Now that you understand the importance of organizational design, let's look briefly at a few recent organization trends.

Understanding Organizational Trends

It is easier to understand what is happening in organizations if you can relate those changes to your own life. For example, to understand why organizations are getting smaller, remember some of your experiences with large organizations. One of the decisions high school students must make if they are going on to college or university is the choice between a large or a smaller, more intimate school.

Many students prefer the smaller school, where they can get to know the other students and where they are more than just another number. They feel they would get "lost" in a big, impersonal university. On the other hand, some students choose to go to a big school. Once there, they find there are many small social groups they can join to get that feeling of being part of a small, meaningful group: fraternities, sororities, professional clubs, political groups, religious groups, or whatever. The point is that often people do not feel comfortable in large, impersonal groups. They want to feel that they *belong,* and that someone knows they are there and *cares.* They get that feeling by joining small, intimate groups. Have you experienced that?

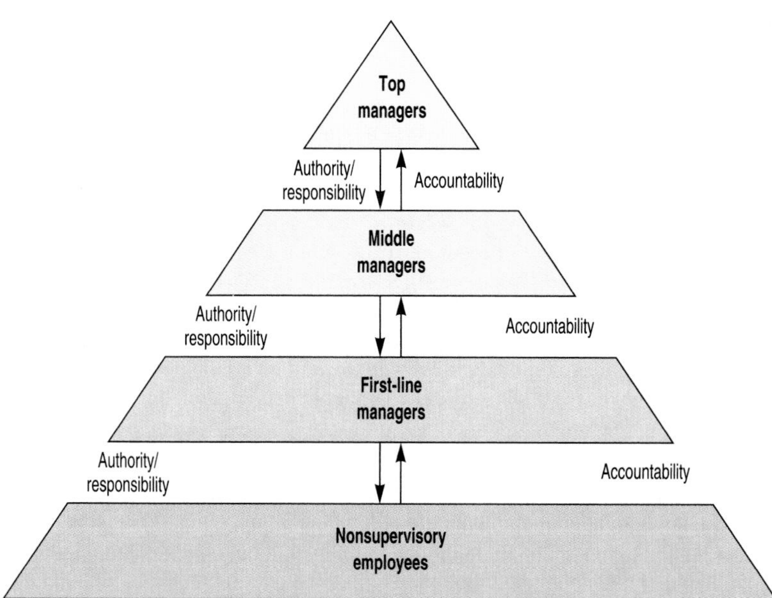

Figure 8–1 The delegation process. Along with *authority* and *responsibility* comes *accountability.* Top managers can delegate authority and responsibility to lower-level managers, but they are still accountable for results. So not all responsibility can be delegated. Similarly, non-supervisory employees are accountable to their supervisors, who are accountable to their managers, and so on up the line. Problems occur when a manager tries to delegate responsibility without delegating the needed authority.

The same feelings carry over to the business world. Employees usually prefer small, cohesive units where people work together, know each other, and co-operate in a common cause. The trend towards small business in many ways reflects the advantages of small units: camaraderie, involvement, flexibility, intimacy, and a feeling of oneness.[1]

Like big universities, big businesses often suffer from too much bureaucracy, too many people to manage and keep track of, and too little clear responsibility for decision making. The idea that "big is better" has shifted to "small is beautiful" in the 1990s. The idea has been to reduce the size of units to make them more responsive to the market and more motivated because of group co-operation and commitment. In other words, many businesses have created the equivalent of fraternities and sororities (that is, small homogeneous units) where employees work together on projects.

The concept that teamwork of smaller units is more productive and yields more human satisfaction and fulfillment is not new. A book by E. F. Schumacher, *Small Is Beautiful,* made a great impact in the 1970s. A European who taught on both sides of the Atlantic and was an important business consultant in Europe, he warned of worshipping unlimited economic growth blindly.

The mania for giantism that gripped the U.S. and Canada in the 1980s—diversification by leveraged buyouts, mergers, and takeovers—has proven unsuccessful in most cases. Many companies are in the process of shedding those units in the attempt to get back to what they know best.

A good example of the movement towards cutting back to a smaller but more efficient and profitable size is the case of General Electric Co. This industrial giant of the U.S. has been led through a revolution by its chairman, Jack Welch. He has reshaped GE into 13 major businesses and slashed the number of employees from 400,000 to 300,000.

> The revolution lies in Welch's desire to see GE, one of the world's largest enterprises, run like a small business. Welch's slogan "Speed, simplicity, and self-confidence" has become the touchstone for judging GE management practice.[2]

MAKING ETHICAL DECISIONS

One of the consequences of restructuring organizations in Canada is that many people are being laid off. CNR, CPR, the banks, the auto companies, and the airlines have let go hundreds of thousands of employees and managers.

Top management has a commitment to make the restructure as non-threatening to employees as possible. Such companies minimize layoffs by reassignment, normal attrition through retirement, early retirement, and retraining.

It is necessary to restructure Canadian firms to make them more competitive with foreign producers, but it is not necessary to fire workers and managers whenever they do not live up to your expectations and then bring in new ones. That can lower morale and create stress and fear in the organization.

What is the moral and ethical thing for a top executive to do when faced with the prospect of firing workers? Do top managers have a greater responsibility to shareholders or to employees? What if the two interests conflict? Should a firm not restructure if it causes massive layoffs? What would be the long-run consequences if all firms did that? Is there a role for government here? ▼

THINKING IT THROUGH

Business is finding that small is beautiful. How might this idea apply to government? Could some national government programs be handled better on a provincial or local basis? Is there any evidence of that happening?

Have you joined any smaller groups in your college or university, such as a fraternity, sorority, or professional society? What has that taught you about the benefits of having small groups within large organizations?

Big Is Not Necessarily Bad

One should not conclude from what is happening in the business world today that big is necessarily bad. There are important advantages to bigness. Large firms usually have access to funds, which they can allocate to the most profitable units. Large companies possess size, scope, and management. These three qualities were essential to the success of industry in the past, and they remain essential to corporate success today.

Most of the large firms in Canada are not successful just because they are large. Rather, they have reorganized into several smaller, more efficient units that are responsive to the market but have the support of a large firm behind them. It is not whether a firm is large that counts but how well it is managed. And how well a firm is managed depends greatly on the organization structure. The successful firms of the future will combine the best features of large companies (access to large amounts of capital and the ability to attract and keep the most talented managers) with the best features of small businesses (focus, flexibility, and speed).

The main purpose of this chapter is to discuss principles of organization such as the notion that companies function better when the operating units are small and manageable. Other organizational decisions are just as important. For example: How many people should report to one manager? How much authority and responsibility should be delegated to lower-level managers and workers? Organizational structure is critical to the creation of morale, commitment, and overall employee/manager satisfaction. To help you understand the principles managers use to design organizations, we will begin with a brief review of the history of organizational development. This will give you a better feel for the reorganization that is going on today.

No company better illustrates the need for good organization than Bombardier. You can see from the picture how large the production area is. Many projects are being worked on at once, and management needs to create the right organizational design to get the projects completed on time.

ORGANIZATION THEORY

Until very recently in history, most organizations were rather small, the processes for producing goods were rather simple, and organization of workers was fairly easy to do. Not until the 20th century and the introduction of mass production did business organizations grow complex and difficult to manage. The bigger the plants, the more efficient production became, or so it seemed. The concept was called economies of scale. This means that the larger the plant, the more efficient it could be because all the employees could specialize in particular aspects of production, marketing, or finance, which would result in more productivity per employee and therefore lower costs. The problem is that managers began to think that bigger was better without limit and in all cases. That's how some companies got too large to be efficient.

It was in this period that organization theorists emerged. In France, Henri Fayol published his book *Administration Industrielle et Générale* in 1919. It was popularized on this side of the Atlantic in the late 1940s under the title *General and Industrial Management.* Max Weber (pronounced *Vayber*) was writing organization theories in Germany a little before Fayol. So it was only about half a century ago that organization theory became popular.

Fayol's Principles of Organization

Fayol introduced principles such as:

Unity of command. Each worker was to report to one, and only one, boss. The benefits of this principle are obvious. What happens if two different bosses give you two different assignments? Which one should you follow? To prevent such confusion, each person reports to only one manager.

Hierarchy of authority. Fayol suggested that each person should know to whom they should report and managers should have the right to give orders and expect others to follow.

Division of labour. Functions were to be divided into areas of specialization such as production, marketing, finance, and so on.

Subordination of individual interests to the general interest. Workers were to think of themselves as a co-ordinated team, and the goals of the team were more important than the goals of individual workers.

Authority. Managers should have the right to give orders and the power to exact obedience. Authority and responsibility are related: Whenever authority is exercised, responsibility and accountability arises. (See Figure 8–1, p. 235).

Degree of centralization. The amount of decision-making power vested in top management should vary by circumstances. In a small organization, it is possible to centralize all decision-making power in the top manager. In a larger organization, however, decision-making power should be delegated to lower-level managers and employees on both major and minor issues. (See participative management, discussed in Chapter 7.)

Clear definition of communication channels. Everyone should understand how to obtain and send information throughout the organization.

Order. Materials and people should be placed and maintained in the proper location.

Equity. A manager should treat employees and peers with respect and justice.

Esprit de corps. A spirit of pride and loyalty should be created among people in the firm.

Management courses in colleges and universities throughout the world taught these principles, and they became synonymous with the concept of management. Organizations were designed so that no person had more than one boss, lines of authority were clear, and everyone knew to whom they were to report. Naturally, these principles tended to become rules and policies as organizations got larger. That led to more rigid organizations and a feeling among workers that they belonged to a *system* rather than a group of friendly, co-operative workers joined together in a common effort.

Max Weber and Organizational Theory

Weber used the term *bureaucrats* to describe middle managers whose function was to implement top management's orders. His book *The Theory of Social and Economic Organizations* was introduced here in the late 1940s. Weber's concept of a **bureaucratic organization** basically consisted of three layers of authority: (1) top managers who were the decision makers, (2) middle managers (the bureaucracy) who developed rules and procedures for implementing the decisions, and (3) workers and supervisors who do the work.

bureaucratic organization
Organization with three layers of authority: (1) top managers who make decisions, (2) middle managers who develop procedures for implementing decisions, and (3) workers and supervisors who do the work.

It was Weber, then, who promoted the pyramid-shaped organization structure that became so popular in large firms (see Figure 8–2). Weber put great trust in managers and felt that the firm would do well if employees simply did what they were told. The less decision making employees had to do, the better. Clearly, this is a reasonable way to operate if you are dealing with uneducated, untrained workers—often the only workers available around 1900. Today, however, most firms feel that workers are the *best* source of ideas and that managers are there to support workers rather than boss them around.

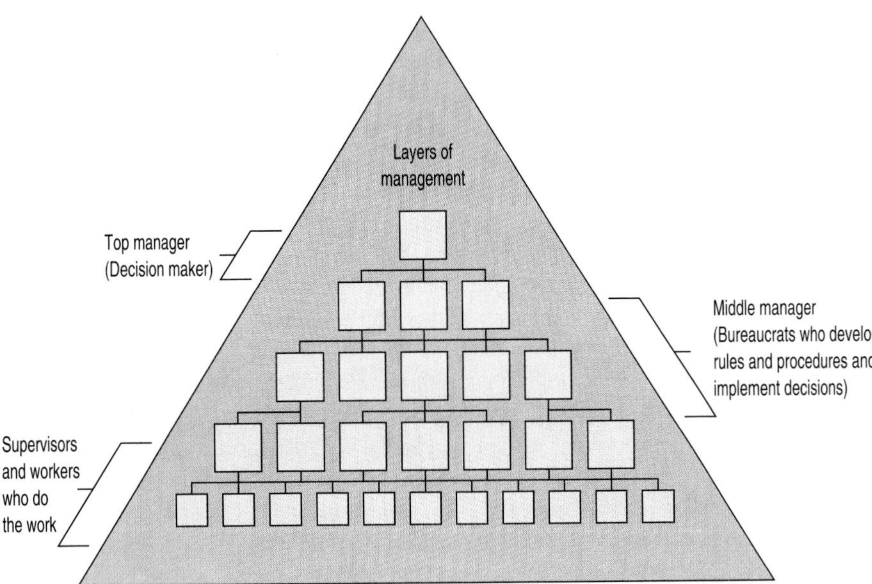

Figure 8–2 Bureaucratic organization structure. This chart shows Weber's concept of a bureaucratic organization, one with clear lines of authority and several layers of management.

Today's more educated work force has made much of what Weber and Fayol said obsolete. Let's see whether these concepts of Weber's still apply:

- Job descriptions. Every job was to be outlined in detail in writing.
- Written rules, decision guidelines, and detailed records.
- Consistent procedures, regulations, and policies.
- Staffing and promotions based on qualifications.

You can thank Weber when you go to a store or government agency and have trouble getting things done because the clerk says, "That's not company policy," or "I can't do that; it's against the rules." Weber felt large organizations demanded clearly established rules and guidelines that were to be followed precisely. This would ensure the consistent application of policies, regulations, and rules, as well as the equal treatment of all people affected by the organization.

The benefits of such concepts and practices are obvious, but zealous enforcement led to inflexibility and insensitivity to customers' needs. Although the word *bureaucrat* did not have negative connotations as used by Weber, the practice of establishing and enforcing rules and procedures became so rigid that *bureaucracy* has become a nasty word for organizations with too many managers who seem to do nothing but make and enforce rules. What is needed today is a way to implement these concepts in a creative and flexible fashion to establish an atmosphere of freedom and incentives that enables employees to work more productively, alone and in teams.

The Contributions of Joan Woodward

Joan Woodward and her associates studied 100 English industrial firms between 1953 and 1971 to see if there was any relationship among how an organization was structured, the technologies it used, and its success. Success was measured by the net income of the corporation (profit) and by increases in market domination. What

Woodward found was that there was no one best way to organize a corporation. Rather, the structure depends greatly on the technical complexity of the company's production process. Today, even the most technically complex companies find that reducing bureaucracy results in better performance.

The trend today is for companies to shed layers of management (bureaucracy) in order to speed up their response to customer needs and demands and to cut costs. Technological developments such as automation and computers have hastened the reduction of the work force and therefore the numbers and levels of management. The advent of computers has reduced the layers of middle management, as senior managers can now access information and exercise control directly from their own terminals.

Businesses are also adopting other radical ideas, such as doing away with job descriptions and masses of rules to permit more flexible deployment of the work force. In other words, they are seeking ways to become more efficient and therefore more competitive. All of these innovations have become possible because the educated work force can, and wants to, take on more responsibility and decision making. Flexibility and adaptability are features of many successful companies that are managing in this new mode.

That is not to say that there is no room at all for the classical method of bureaucratic operation as Fayol and Weber advocated. (McDonald's functions well under their strict procedures.) What must be understood is that the trend today is away from such structures and management styles. International competitive pressures are forcing all companies to react and adapt much more quickly than they used to and to use all their human resources more effectively. Both of these goals are best achieved by opening up company structures and procedures and breaking down rigid bureaucracies. Here are some Canadian examples of this trend:

- David Killins, president of Legacy Storage Systems says, "The giant, centrally-managed monolith is basically obsolete as a corporate model."[3]
- Shell Canada has opened a new lubricants plant in Brockville, Ontario, where "hierarchical structures and the control-and-command mentality have been swept aside by a dynamic organization driven by commitment rather than reward and punishment. 'I feel more independent. I'm given more responsibility,' says Theresa Hetherington."[4]
- The Department of National Defence has started a project in its support services whose "aim is to demonstrate that local level managers can maintain

This UPS sorting centre shows the need for rules and regulations. For example, safety and cleanliness rules must be followed or the sheer volume of business would create chaos.

current levels of service more efficiently and economically if given greater authority over assigned resources."[5]

- PanCanadian Petroleum plans to "push decision making down the ranks. It means, for example, giving field operators signing authority for up to $1,000 of purchases; previously, they needed a foreman's approval to buy a broom."[6]

PROGRESS CHECK

- What were some of the reasons organizations became large. What are some of the drawbacks to large firms?
- Can you name four of Fayol's principles and show how they link with Weber's principles?
- Why are many large organizations moving away from these principles? Are any still valid?

DESIGNING THE STRUCTURE OF ORGANIZATIONS

One of the most common ways to organize a company is by the different functions or departments, such as marketing, finance, production, and so on. The relationship between the different departments and their personnel is traditionally shown in an **organization chart,** a visual diagram of an organization that shows who reports to whom. The top segment of such a chart is shown in Figure 8–3. The entire organization chart tended to look like a pyramid (as was seen in Figure 8–2).

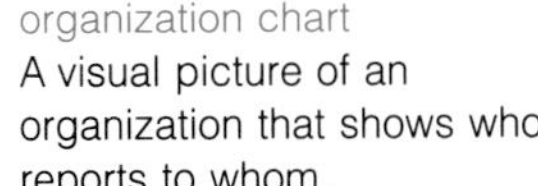

organization chart
A visual picture of an organization that shows who reports to whom.

In large companies, workers, clerks, or salespeople reported to supervisors, who reported to plant, office, or sales managers, who reported to regional managers, who reported to national managers, who reported to vice-presidents, who reported to the president, who reported to the chairman of the board of directors. Such complex organizations required many rules, guidelines, and procedures. (They were bureaucracies.)

By their nature, such organizational structures are slow and unwieldy. One Canadian management consultant reports:

> Research shows that 85–95 per cent of service, quality, or productivity problems stem from the organization's structure and processes. . . . Ask the question: "For whose convenience are systems designed?" Too often they serve accountants, technocrats, or management. Get the cart behind the horse. Your

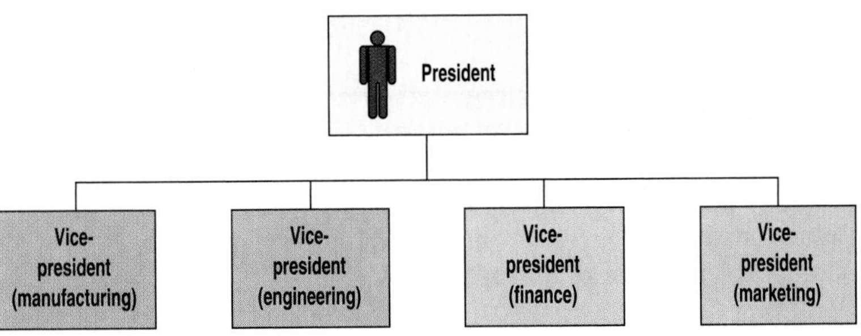

Figure 8–3 Functional organization. The top of a functionally oriented organization chart. Large organizations prospered in the past because of a division of labour. That division is reflected in departmentalization—the assigning of different functions to different departments. This chart shows a typical breakdown of functions.

> systems should serve your customers or those producing, delivering, or supporting your products or services.[7]

That is why current trends are towards smaller, more flexible structures that let companies react more quickly to today's fast-changing, technologically competitive business climate. They also unleash employees' initiative and enable them to participate in decision making. We next examine some of the issues that arise from these changing organizational structures. These issues (some of which are not new) include:

1. Tall versus flat structures.
2. Span of control.
3. Departmentalization.
4. Centralization versus decentralization.

Tall versus Flat Organization Structures

tall organization structures
Organizations with many levels of management.

As organizations got bigger, some began adding layer after layer of management, sometimes resulting in a dozen or more managerial steps in firms such as Bell Canada. Such organizations had what are called **tall organization structures.** This simply means that the organization chart was quite tall because of the various levels of management. The army is an example of how tall an organization can get. There are many layers of management between a private and a general (e.g., sergeant, lieutenant, captain, major, colonel). You can imagine how a message may be distorted as it moves up through so many layers of management.

Business organizations tended to take on the same style of organization as the military. The organizations were divided into regions, divisions, centres, and plants. Each plant might have several layers of management. The net effect was a huge complex of managers, management assistants, secretaries, assistant secretaries, supervisors, trainers, and so on. Office workers were known as *white-collar workers,* as opposed to the *blue-collar workers* who worked on the assembly line. As you can imagine, the cost of keeping all these managers and support people was quite high. The paperwork they generated was unbelievable, and the inefficiencies in communication and decision making became intolerable.

The development of small computers is helping to bring more efficiency to white-collar operations. The trend is to eliminate white-collar positions, including several layers of middle management. One reason corporations were cutting staff was to meet the competition of foreign firms. To give you a feel for the problem, there are five levels of management between the chairman and first-line supervisor at Toyota, a Japanese firm. Ford had over 22 levels. Foreign firms were simply more efficient.

flat organization structures
Organizations with relatively few layers of management.

The trend is toward more **flat organization structures.** That is, organizations are cutting out layers of management and expanding sideways instead. The idea is to have many small semi-autonomous units that report to vice-presidents, who report to the president. Johnson & Johnson, for example, is a $5 billion company made up of 150 independent divisions that sell over $30 million each.

One benefit of having many managers reporting to a higher-level manager is that the higher-level manager simply does not have time to get involved in the day-to-day work of the managers below. This gives lower-level managers more freedom to make changes as they see fit. This makes organizations more responsive and raises the morale of lower-level managers. How many people should report to one manager? We discuss that issue next.

SPOTLIGHT ON SMALL BUSINESS

Growing a Small Business

In 1985, Julio and a few of his cousins started selling landscaping plants that Julio grew in his backyard. A trade magazine gave the business a rave review, and the business started growing fast. Soon Julio hired more workers. Everybody pitched in to do what was needed—pruning, potting, purchasing, and shipping.

The number of workers increased as the orders increased. Julio found he spent more time selecting new employees and explaining benefits than selling. So he made his first staff hire—a secretary to handle personnel and the office. Soon he hired a clerk to assist the secretary and cover shipping. By the time Julio had hired another person to do the bookkeeping and purchasing in 1990, it occurred to him that his company was like some of his tropical vines growing wild. It was time to give it some structure if the business was going to make it.

His new organizational structure clarifies what each employee is supposed to do, to whom each employee reports, and how their work relates to the business's objectives. By shaping his company with the right organization structure before it grew too wild, Julio was saved from having to prune it drastically later.

Source: Jane Elizabeth Allen, "Organizational Structure Is Key to Running a Growing Business," *Washington Business*, February 5, 1990, p. 6.

Span of Control

Span of control refers to the optimum number of subordinates a manager supervises or should supervise. There are many factors to consider when determining span of control. At the lower levels, where the work is standardized, it is possible to implement a wide span of control (15 to 40 workers). However, the number should gradually narrow at higher levels of the organization because work is less standardized and there is more need for face-to-face communication. Variables in span of control include the following:

span of control
The optimum number of subordinates a manager should supervise.

1. *Complexity of the job.*
   a. *Functional complexity.* The more complex the functions are, the narrower the span of control (fewer workers report to one supervisor).
   b. *Functional similarity.* The more similar the functions, the broader the span of control.
   c. *Need for co-ordination.* The greater the need for co-ordination, the narrower the span of control.
   d. *Planning demands.* The more involved the plan, the narrower the span of control.
   e. *Geographic closeness.* The more concentrated the work area, the broader the span of control. (This has become somewhat redundant because of the excellent information linkages that exist now).
2. *Capabilities of the manager.* The more experienced and capable the manager, the broader the span of control.
3. *Capabilities of the subordinates.* The more subordinates and supervisors need supervision, the narrower the span of control.

Other factors to consider include the professionalism of superiors and subordinates and the number of new problems that occur in a day. In business, the span of control varies widely. The number of people reporting to the president may range from one to 80 or more.

Figure 8–4 ties together span of control and tall and flat organization structures. The tall organization with a narrow span of control might describe a lawn care

Figure 8–4 Narrow versus wide span of control. Two ways to structure an organization with the same number of employees. The tall structure with a narrow span of control has two managers who supervise four employees each. Changing to a flat structure with a wide span of control, the company could eliminate two managers and perhaps replace them with one or two employees, but the top manager would have to supervise 10 people instead of two.

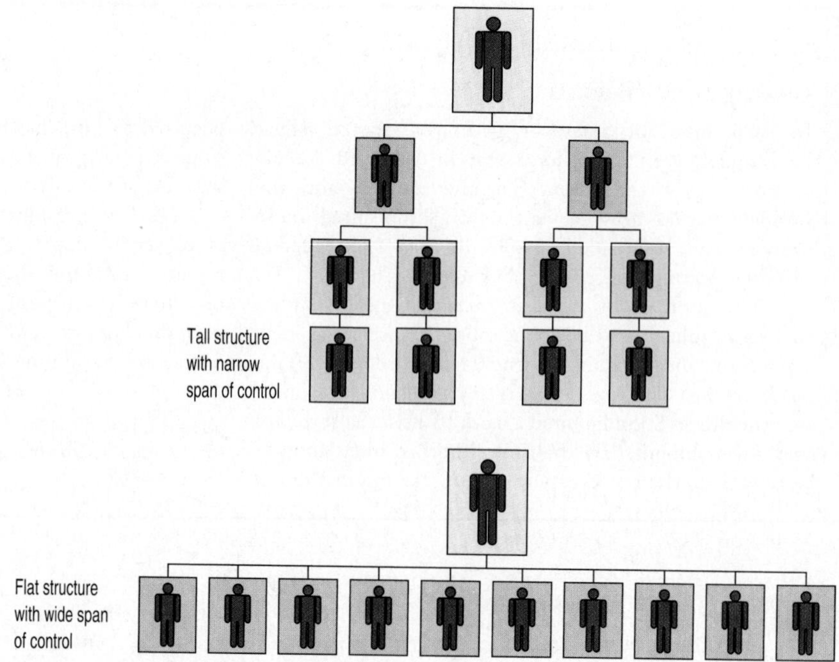

service with two supervisors who manage four employees each (two of whom are more experienced). The flat structure with a wide span of control may work in a plant where all 10 workers are picking crabmeat. The wider the span of control, the greater the decision-making power of each employee. That is the trend today. We shall be looking at this decentralization of power shortly.

Departmentalization

departmentalization
Dividing an organization's structure into homogeneous departments such as manufacturing and marketing.

functional structure
Grouping of workers into departments based on similar skills, expertise, or resource use.

The dividing of an organization's structure into separate homogeneous units is called **departmentalization.** The most widely used technique for departmentalizing an organization is by function. **Functional structure** is the grouping of workers into departments based on similar skills, expertise, or resource use. There might be, for example, a production department, a transportation department, a finance department, an accounting department, a marketing department, a data processing department, and so on. Such units enable employees to specialize and work together more efficiently. The advantages of such a structure include the following:

1. Skills can be developed in depth, and employees can progress within a department as their skills develop.
2. It allows for economies of scale in that all the resources needed can be centralized and various experts can be located in that area.
3. There is good co-ordination within the function, and top management can easily direct and control the activities of the various departments.

The disadvantages include the following:

1. There is a lack of communication among the different departments. For example, production may be isolated from marketing so that the people making the product do not get the proper feedback from customers.

2. Individual employees begin to identify with their department and its goals rather than the goals of the organization as a whole.
3. Response to external changes is slow.
4. People are not trained to take different managerial responsibilities; rather, they tend to become narrow specialists.

Businesses have tried various versions to overcome the limitations of this type of structure. Next we shall discuss some variations on the functional form of structure.

Different Ways to Departmentalize

Figure 8–5 shows five ways a firm can departmentalize. One is by *product*. A book publisher might have a trade book department, a textbook department, and a technical book department. The development and marketing processes vary greatly among such books, so each department specializes in those functions.

The most common way to departmentalize, as discussed above, is by *function*. This text is divided by business function because such groupings are common. Production, marketing, finance, human resources, and accounting are all distinct functions calling for separate skills.

It makes more sense in some organizations to departmentalize by *customer group*. A pharmaceutical company, for example, might have one department that focuses on the consumer market, another on hospitals (institutional market), and another that targets doctors.

Some firms group their units by *geographic locations*. Canada is usually considered one market area. Japan, Europe, and Korea may involve separate departments. The decision about which way to departmentalize depends greatly on the nature of the product and the customers served. A few firms departmentalize by *process* because it is more efficient to separate the activities that way. For example, a firm that makes leather coats may have one department cut the leather, another dye it, and a third sew the coat together.

Often firms use combinations of these methods.

Centralization versus Decentralization of Authority

Imagine for a minute that you are a top manager for a large retail chain such as Reitman's. Your temptation may be to maintain control over all your stores to maintain a uniformity of image and merchandise. You have noticed such control works well for McDonald's; why not Reitman's? The degree to which an organization allows managers at the lower levels of the managerial hierarchy to make decisions determines the degree of decentralization that organization practices.

- **Centralized authority** means that decision-making authority is maintained at the top level of management at headquarters, or central management.
- **Decentralized authority** means that decision-making authority is delegated to lower-level managers who are more familiar with local conditions.

At Reitman's, for example, the customers in Vancouver are likely to demand clothing styles different from those in Montreal or Toronto. It makes sense, therefore, to give store managers in various cities the authority to buy, price, and promote merchandise appropriate for each area. Such an assignment of part of a manager's duties to subordinates is called a **delegation of authority** and is an example of decentralized management.

centralized authority
Maintaining decision-making authority at the top level of management.

decentralized authority
Delegating decision-making authority to lower-level managers who are more familiar with local conditions.

delegation of authority
Assigning part of a manager's duties to subordinates.

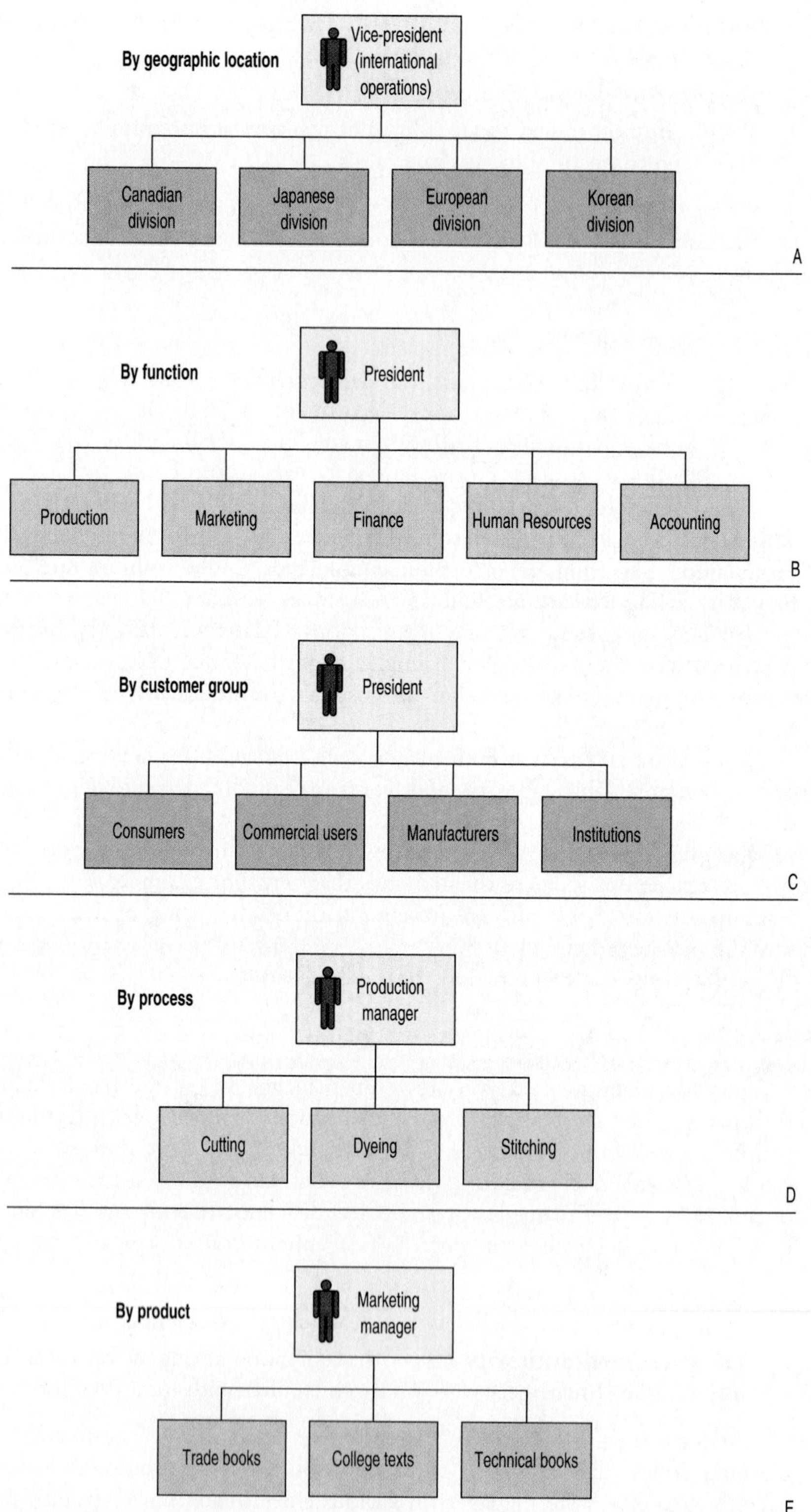

Figure 8–5 Various ways to departmentalize.
A publisher may want to departmentalize by product, a manufacturer by function, a pharmaceutical company by customer group, and a computer company by geography (countries). A leather manufacturer may prefer departmentalization by process. In each case, the structure must fit the goals of the firm.
Often a company will departmentalize by function, process, and product at different levels. While B is by function, E may be the same company one level lower, departmentalized by product.

REACHING BEYOND OUR BORDERS

Campbell Soup in Canada Reorganizes to Compete in U.S. Market

Campbell Canada is a subsidiary of the Campbell Soup Co. in the U.S. In the 1980s, the parent company undertook a drastic restructuring of the entire organization. It merged Canada and the U.S. into one division under the FTA to improve its profitability, which had slipped badly. As part of that process seven Canadian plants have been sold or closed, leaving only four plants here, including one at Listowel, Ontario.

David Clark, president of Campbell Canada, knows its future is at stake. As part of Campbell's restructuring, Clark told the head office he'll produce fewer, more specialized products at his three main plants, do it cost effectively, and export at least half the volume to the U.S.

To attain these difficult targets, Clark is taking a radically different tack from the traditional strategies. He's trying to restructure employees' minds—to transform the way workers relate to their job and their company. He has hired Toronto-based motivational guru Bix Bickson. They set aside Vision Day to get this wildly ambitious plan rolling.

Bickson's main message is: "People who create extraordinary results don't look at their circumstances. They look at possibilities and create their own paths to get there." Clark remembers how difficult it was to get his management team on board. They had difficulty comprehending, much less embracing, the radical notion of the breakthrough required if they were to survive as a Canadian company. Their reaction to the very difficult job ahead? Within six months, three vice-presidents had quit.

Clark had brought in a group of consultants, including Bickson, to work with his top managers. They were divided into nine power teams spanning middle and senior levels of management. They had to come up with "unreasonable, irrational" targets. Each power team had as its first "impossible" assignment the generation of $100,000 of profits in three months. The nine teams came up with plans that would yield profits of $700,000.

When Clark saw some of the plans, he thought the teams were out of their minds. For instance, the Toronto plant had 120,000 defective cases of soup sitting in a warehouse—cans with crooked labels, dents, and so on. The Toronto team committed itself to cutting the number in half in three months by repairing the defects without extra costs. Fifty managers and workers, working unpaid on Saturdays, reduced the number of defective cases to 20,000 by the target date. This was typical of the unusual and difficult tasks the teams set for themselves.

Clark now boasts that his managers are "turned on and juiced up." He has given them another challenge: generate $1 million in profits for the year. Partway through the year, they are way ahead of targets. To help achieve these goals, Clark has eliminated three out of five layers of plant management, converting the redundants into co-ordinators of the new team approach. Some middle managers resisted. Some left. But those who stuck it out claim they get more of a kick out of helping than being disciplinarians.

The Toronto team had started on a breakthrough regime a year earlier, when it cost $3.87 more to produce one case of soup in Toronto than at Campbell's best plant in Maxton, North Carolina. The gap is now only 32 cents. For the future, instead of closing plants, Clark plans to increase employment in three to five years to between 500 and 600 at the Toronto plant because Campbell Canada will be serving the much larger U.S. market.

Source: Wendy Trueman, "Alternate Visions," *Canadian Business* 64, no. 3, March 1991, p. 29.

On the other hand, McDonald's feels that purchasing, promotion, and other such decisions are best handled centrally. There is little need for each McDonald's store to carry different food products. McDonald's, therefore, leans toward centralized authority.

Most organizations have some degree of centralized authority and some decentralized authority. Today's rapidly changing markets, added to geographic differences in consumer tastes, tend to favor decentralization and thus delegation of authority. The box concerning the Campbell Soup Co. illustrates this point.

THINKING IT THROUGH

Can you see the connection among flat and tall structures, span of control, and centralization and decentralization? Does a flatter structure mean a wider span of control and thus more decentralization? Does a taller structure mean a narrower span of control and thus more centralized decision making?

Campbell makes a variety of products, as this picture shows. Since the firm restructured, it has narrowed its product lines and revitalized its management and work force. As a result, costs are down and profits are up.

PROGRESS CHECK

- Can you define authority, responsibility, and accountability?
- Are businesses moving towards taller or flatter organization structures? Centralized or decentralized decision making? Why?
- What are some reasons for having a narrow span of control? Is there any advantage to a wide span of control?
- What are the five ways to departmentalize a company?

ORGANIZATION TYPES

Now that we have explored the basic principles of organizational design, learned the benefits of flat versus tall organizations, and seen how it all comes together in the Campbell Soup example, we can explore in more depth the various ways to structure an organization to accomplish our goals. We shall look at (1) line organizations, (2) line and staff organizations, (3) matrix organizations, and (4) cross-functional, self-managed teams. Figure 8–6 compares the advantages and disadvantages of each form of organization.

Line Organizations

line organization structure Organization in which there are direct, two-way lines of responsibility, authority, and communication running from the top to the bottom of the organization, with every employee reporting to only one specific supervisor.

A **line organization structure** is one in which there are direct two-way lines of responsibility, authority, and communication running from the top to the bottom of the organization, with every employee reporting to only one specific supervisor. A line organization has the advantages of having clearly defined responsibility and authority, being easy to understand, and providing one supervisor for each person. It meets the principles of good organization design. See Figure 8–7.

However, a line organization has the disadvantages of being too inflexible, having few specialists or experts to advise people along the line, having lines of communication that are too long, and being unable to handle the complex decisions involved in an organization with thousands of sometimes unrelated products and literally tons of paperwork.

	Advantages	Disadvantages
Line	▼ Clearly defined responsibility and authority ▼ Easy to understand ▼ One supervisor for each person	▼ Too inflexible ▼ Few specialists to advise ▼ Long lines of communication ▼ Unable to handle complex questions quickly ▼ Tons of paperwork
Line and staff	▼ Expert advice from staff to line personnel ▼ Establishes lines of authority ▼ Encourages co-operation and better communication at all levels	▼ Potential overstaffing ▼ Potential overanalyzing ▼ Lines of communication can get blurred ▼ Staff frustrations because of lack of authority ▼ Tons of paperwork
Matrix	▼ Flexible ▼ Encourages co-operation among departments ▼ Can produce creative solutions to problems ▼ Allows organization to take on new projects without adding to the organization structure	▼ Costly and complex ▼ Can confuse employees ▼ Requires good interpersonal skills and co-operative managers and employees ▼ Time consuming to implement properly
Cross-functional, self-managed teams	▼ Greatly increases interdepartmental co-ordination and co-operation. ▼ Quicker response to customers and market conditions. ▼ Increased employee motivation and morale	▼ Some confusion over responsibility and authority ▼ Perceived loss of control by management ▼ Difficult to evaluate employees and set up reward systems ▼ Requires self-motivated and highly trained workers

Figure 8–6 Types of organizations. Each form of organization has its advantages and disadvantages.

Line and Staff Systems

To minimize the disadvantages of simple line organizations, most organizations today have both line and staff personnel.

- **Line personnel** perform functions that contribute directly to the primary goals of the organization (e.g., making the product, distributing it, and selling it).
- **Staff personnel** perform functions that *advise* and *assist* line personnel in achieving their goals (e.g., marketing research, legal advising, and human resources). (See Figure 8–7.)

line personnel
Employees who perform functions that contribute directly to the primary goals of the organization.

staff personnel
Employees who perform functions that assist line personnel in achieving their goals.

Most organizations have benefitted from the expert advice of staff assistants in areas such as safety, quality control, computer technology, human resources, and investing. Such positions strengthen the line positions and are by no means inferior or low-paying. It is like having well-paid consultants on the organization's payroll.

Staff usually serve an advisory function; that is, they usually cannot tell line managers *or their workers* what to do. Naturally, this can cause conflicts, in that staff experts often know more about correct procedures to follow than line managers.

Figure 8–7 Line versus line and staff organizations

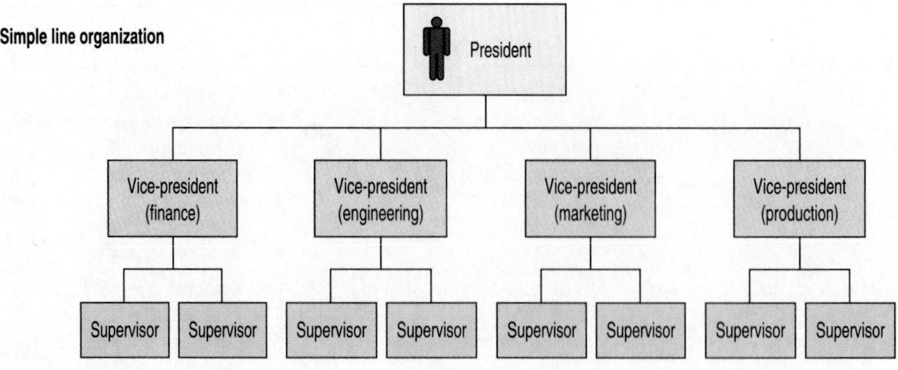

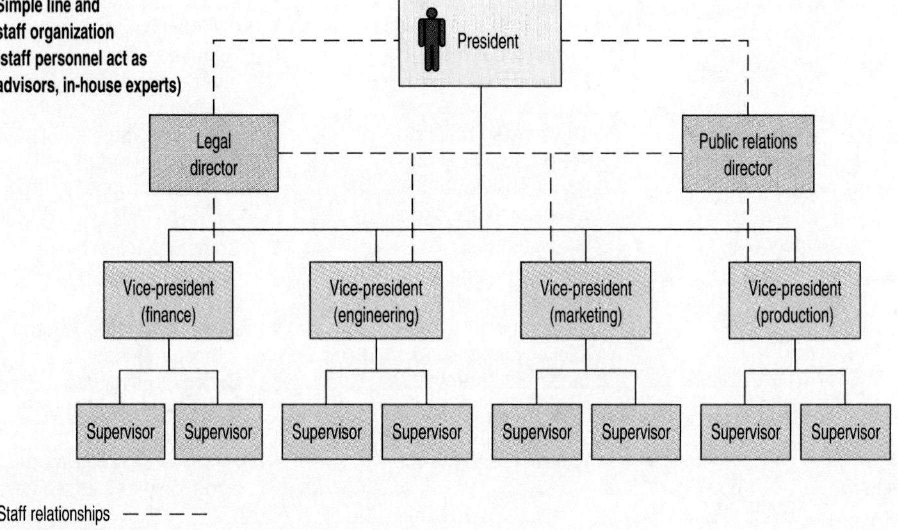

This can be very frustrating for staff people. In fact, different organizations handle line–staff relationships in different ways. In some organizations, line managers must *consult* with staff managers on some issues; on others, they must get staff *approval* for certain actions; and in others, staff people may actually *give orders*.

The benefits of the line and staff organization structure are rather clear. The disadvantages are not so obvious at first. Today, however, some organizations are suffering from too many staff personnel (overstaffing). To justify their existence, staff people may conduct research and generate reports that no one asks for or needs (overanalyzing). The resulting paperwork can be astounding. Lines of authority and communication can become blurred when staff people get involved in decision making (overmanaging). For example, by the time a line manager clears a decision with the legal department, the safety department, and human resources, the initial problem may become much more serious.

The trend today is to cut staff positions or assign staff to smaller, functional units where they truly assist, rather than work independently from, line managers. Much of the attention of top managers today is focused on designing systems that enable

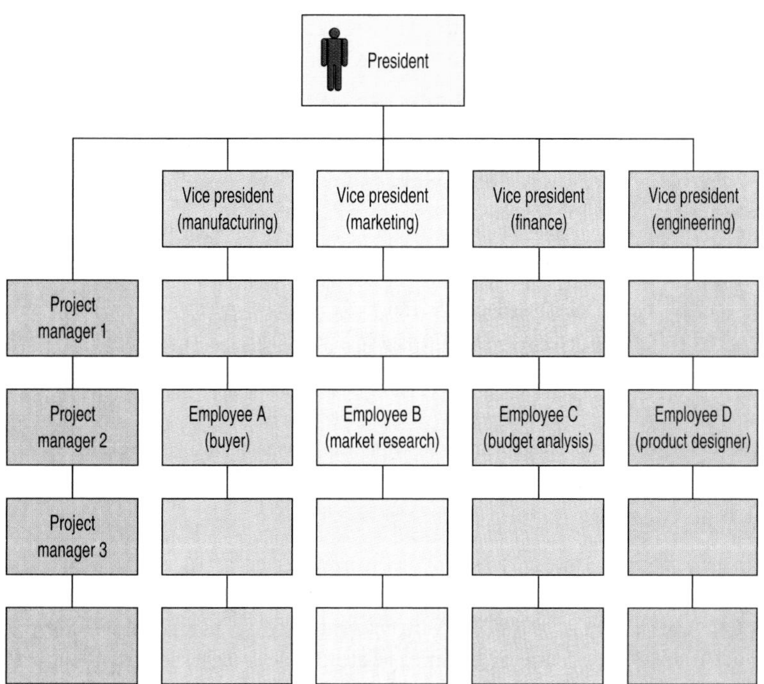

Figure 8–8 A matrix organization. In a matrix organization, project managers are in charge of teams made up of members of several departments. In this case, project manager 2 supervises employees A, B, C, and D. These employees are accountable not only to project manager 2, but also to the heads of their individual departments. For example, employee B, a market researcher, reports to project manager 2 and to the vice-president of marketing.

line and staff managers to co-operate more fully and move more quickly to respond to market changes.

Matrix Organizations

Both line and line and staff structures suffer from a certain inflexibility. Both have established lines of authority and communication and both work well in organizations with a relatively stable environment and evolutionary development (such as firms manufacturing consumer products like toasters and refrigerators). In such firms, clear lines of authority and relatively fixed organization structures are assets that assure efficient operations.

Today's economic scene is dominated by new kinds of organizations in high-growth industries unlike anything seen in the past. These include industries such as telecommunications, robotics, biotechnology, and aerospace. They also include service firms providing consulting advice in finance systems, high-tech, and other highly specialized services. In these industries, new projects are developed quickly, competition with similar projects elsewhere is stiff, and the life cycle of new ideas is very short. The economic, technological, and competitive environments are changing rapidly. In such organizations, emphasis is on new-product development, creativity, special projects, rapid communication, and interdepartmental teamwork. From that environment grew the popularity of the **matrix organization,** where specialists from different parts of the organization are brought together to work on specific projects but still remain part of a line and staff structure (see Figure 8–8). In other words, a project manager can borrow people from different departments to help design and market new product ideas or complete complex projects.

matrix organization
Organization in which specialists from different parts of the organization are brought together to work on specific projects but still remain part of a traditional line and staff structure.

Matrix structures were developed in the aerospace industry at firms such as Boeing, Lockheed, and McDonnell Douglas. The structure is now used in banking, management consulting firms, accounting firms, ad agencies, and school systems.

Although it works well in some organizations, it does not work in others. The advantages of a matrix structure are:

- It gives flexibility to managers in assigning people to projects.
- It encourages interorganizational co-operation and teamwork.
- It is flexible and can result in creative solutions to problems such as new-product development.

The disadvantages are:

- It is complex and costly to implement.
- It can cause confusion among employees as to where their loyalty belongs—to the project manager or their functional unit. (There is a perception of two bosses.)
- It requires good interpersonal skills and co-operative employees and managers.
- It is time consuming to implement properly.

If it seems to you that matrix organizations violate some traditional managerial principles, you are right. Normally a person cannot work effectively for two bosses. (Who has the *real* authority? Which directive has the first priority—the one from the project manager or from one's immediate supervisor?) Figure 8–9 shows how decisions regarding a matrix organization fit in with other organizational decisions.

In reality, the system functions more effectively than one may imagine. Here is how it works best:

- Underlying the matrix system is traditional line and staff organization with clear and recognized lines of authority.

Figure 8–9 Questions for various stages of organization design

Departmentalization	How should departments be established—by product, function, customer, geographic location, process, or some combination of these?
Span of control	How many employees should report to each manager? (A narrow span means few people reporting; a wide span means many people reporting to one manager.)
Lines of authority	What will be the lines of authority and responsibility in the firm? Which positions will be staff (support positions) and which will be line (directly in the chain of command)?
Delegation of authority	Should all key decisions be made by top management? What decisions should be delegated to managers and supervisors, if any?
Matrix organization formation	Who should be assigned to various committees? What authority should be given line managers to borrow employees from other areas for special committee assignments (see matrix organization discussion).
Job design	Who is responsible for doing what? How much job rotation will there be? How much specialization?
Work procedures	What are the rules and procedures of operation? What are the lines of communication?
Follow-through	Delegation without follow-through is abdication. You can never wash your hands of a task. Even if you delegate it, you are still responsible for its accomplishment.

- To develop a new product idea, a project manager may be given *temporary* authority to "borrow" line personnel from engineering, production, marketing, and other line functions. Together, they work to complete the project and then return to their regular positions. In fact, then, they really do not report to more than one manager at a time.
- Such a system evolves easily in an organization where the informal communication system is more important than the formal organization. That is, the corporate culture encourages interaction among departments and ad hoc committees to solve problems. (See the next section.)
- The unit of operation is small enough for such flexibility and yet everyone remains informed and clear as to relationships, goals, and procedures.

Cross-Functional, Self-Managed Teams

To eliminate the problems inherent with the matrix style of organization, some companies are moving towards implementing the self-managed teams mentioned earlier. Such teams eliminate the problems of who is the real manager, because they manage themselves. Furthermore, self-managed teams are a permanent part of the organization structure and have the advantages of matrix-style organizations without most of the disadvantages (see Figure 8–6).

PROGRESS CHECK

- What are the advantages of a line and staff organization versus a pure line organization?
- Why would a firm use a matrix organization? What are the advantages of a self-managed team over a matrix organization?

CO-ORDINATING WITHIN THE ORGANIZATION

One of the major goals of the matrix style of organization is to increase the communication and co-ordination among diverse departments. Listen to what Lee Iacocca says about the situation at Chrysler when he took over:[8]

> I couldn't believe . . . that the guy running engineering departments wasn't in constant contact with his counterpart in manufacturing. But that's how it was. Everybody worked independently.
>
> . . . I'd call in a guy from engineering, and he'd stand there dumbfounded when I'd explain to him that we had a design problem or some other hitch in the engineering–manufacturing relationship. He might have the ability to invent a brilliant piece of engineering that would save us a lot of money. He might come up with a terrific new design. There was only one problem: he didn't know that the manufacturing people couldn't build it. Nobody at Chrysler seemed to understand that interaction among the different functions in a company is absolutely critical. People in engineering and manufacturing almost have to sleep together. These guys weren't even flirting!

As a consequence of all this, Chrysler built a new billion-dollar facility in 1991 that brought together people from design, engineering, production, and marketing in one area. If interdepartmental relationships are not created as Chrysler and others have done, how can you be sure that communication and co-ordination take place? One way is to set up a matrix-style organization where such interrelationships are spelled out in detail. Other ways of creating such co-ordination include committees, information systems, liaison people, and permanent teams, including self-managed teams.

Co-ordinating by Committee or Task Force

One purpose of reorganization is to increase internal co-operation and co-ordination. To learn what people in other areas are doing and to communicate with them, a company may form a task force or committee to discuss the issues. A *task force* is the technical name given a temporary team or committee formed to solve a specific short-run problem involving several departments. The benefit of such a committee is that it can be formed relatively quickly and issues can be resolved quickly. For example, if a company experienced a problem with product tampering, a task force made up of representatives from distribution, public relations, marketing, and production could be gathered to evaluate new forms of packaging. A task force is a way of handling special projects with a wide variety of people from various areas and of making an organization flexible and responsive to changes.

Cluster-Style Self-Managed Teams

A new type of matrix-like organization is emerging in the 1990s. It may prove popular among professional service firms and other organizations seeking to become more responsive to the customer or to give more responsibility to highly skilled workers. It is called a **cluster organization,** a group of people drawn from different functional units who work together on a semipermanent basis.

cluster organization
A group of people from different functional units who work together on a semipermanent basis.

Although this may sound like a matrix organization, it is more permanent. There is no project boss, nor are there permanent leaders. A cluster may consist of top managers who create the vision or overall goals for the company. Or it may be made up of various people and groups from staff or line. It is a kind of troubleshooting or brainstorming centre.

Shell Canada has organized its entire work force in the brand-new plant at Brockville, Ontario, on the basis of self-managing teams. This $75 million lubricants factory employs only 75 people, of whom 15 are senior managers (called co-ordinators) or purely administrative staff. There are 60 team operators (of whom one-third are women). All of these employees are expected to manage everything themselves as individuals or team members. "The teams are responsible for discipline, cost control (including absenteeism), and arranging their own vacation and training schedules."[9]

PanCanadian Petroleum has a new spirit in its production division. "For the past two years, its employees have been immersed in *continuous improvement* (CI), a management program that focusses on employee input, teamwork, and flattened bureaucracy."[10]

There are many examples of Canadian companies that have embraced the new management and organization styles to become more efficient and thus more competitive.

Co-ordinating by Information Systems

One of the newest strategies for communicating within and among departments is to set up a computer network that links all managers. Such an **information system** consists of written and electronically based systems for sending reports, memos, bulletins, and the like. Such systems include electronic mail (letters sent by computer), electronic bulletin boards (notes sent by computer), and teleconferences (meetings held over two-way video networks). One problem is designing software that will let different computer systems talk with one another. Developing such

information system
Network consisting of written and electronically based systems for sending reports, memos, bulletins, and the like.

systems is now a major effort of many computer and software companies. There is intense competition to see who can come up with the best systems.

Other Means of Co-ordination

Some firms have a person responsible for co-ordinating what goes on between or among departments. This person is called a *liaison* (pronounced lee-ay-zon). Very large companies have several liaison positions at corporate headquarters to keep information flowing between headquarters and their industry groups.

Other firms set up a permanent team made up of people from different departments who get together to solve ongoing problems. Such a team is similar to a task force or committee, but it deals with ongoing problems rather than temporary issues. Many firms use such teams to develop new products.

The most sophisticated of such teams are cross-functional, self-managed teams. The co-operation and co-ordination created by self-managed teams have never been duplicated in the past. When such teams are working effectively, communication barriers in organizations are minimized and the whole organization becomes less formal and more integrated.

Remember what we are trying to accomplish with these various ways of co-ordinating. We want to get communication and co-operation among departments so that the whole organization can work as a unified team. If you have ever worked in a large organization, you know that often the marketing people never see, much less talk with, the people in engineering. (The Chrysler case noted earlier is a good example of such confusion.) Similarly, the people in distribution may never meet the people in marketing who are promising that they will deliver tomorrow. It doesn't take long in a large company to see how messages can get lost and that being responsive to customers can be quite a challenge.

It is important for an organization to *want* to be responsive to customers and to operate as a unit. That feeling of oneness has to be established by top management. A few organizations such as Four Seasons Hotels and Blackcomb Skiing Enterprises, are known for their responsiveness to customers and the teamwork among employees. That teamwork (or corporate culture) is created by the top executives and may last long after they die or leave the firm. We shall discuss the creation of such a corporate culture next.

ORGANIZATIONAL CULTURE

One of the most important elements of success in any organization is the overall organizational culture (also called *organizational climate* or *corporate culture*). **Organizational culture** may be defined as widely shared values within an organization that provide coherence and co-operation to achieve common goals. Usually the culture of an organization is reflected in stories, traditions, and myths. Anyone who has been to Disneyland or Disney World cannot fail to be impressed by the values instilled by Walt Disney that permeate the organization. One may have heard about the focus on cleanliness, helpfulness, and friendliness, but such stories cannot prepare you for the near-perfect implementation of those values at the parks. The workers seem to have absorbed the ideals into their very being so that they give total attention to the customer.

organizational culture
Widely shared values within an organization, reflected in stories, traditions, and myths, that provide coherence and co-operation to achieve common goals.

It is also obvious from visiting any McDonald's restaurant that every effort has been made to maintain a culture that emphasizes "quality, service, cleanliness, and

The organizational culture at various Disney projects, such as Epcot Center, reflects an orientation toward friendliness, cleanliness, and helpfulness. Employees seem to truly enjoy their jobs and the public enjoys the atmosphere of responsiveness. In contrast, the organizational culture at the motor vehicle branch often seems to lack a consumer orientation.

value." Each restaurant has the same feel, the same look, and the same atmosphere. In short, each reflects the organizational culture.

The very best organizations have cultures that emphasize service. The atmosphere is one of friendly, concerned, caring people who enjoy working together to provide a good product at a reasonable price. Those companies that have such cultures have less need for close supervision of employees, policy manuals, organization charts, and formal rules, procedures, and controls. This is how they do it:

- Good organizational cultures are built by organizational leaders who create an atmosphere of shared values that have a positive effect on the relationships within the organization and with the various publics of the organization.
- Good organizational leaders create a culture that emphasizes cooperation and friendliness in serving customers, and that culture results in self-motivated employees who need minimal supervision. The key is mutual trust.
- The very best companies stress high moral and ethical values such as honesty, reliability, fairness, environmental protection, and social involvement.

Sometimes the general level of organizational culture is undermined by what is called *political* behaviour. This refers to people being hired, promoted, or fired because somebody makes decisions based on personal reasons rather than performance. Or decisions involving expansion, products, or investments are not based on an impartial judgment of what is best for the company but on who might get a promotion, more power or influence, or an increased salary. Sometimes a good suggestion is shot down because of personal animosity. Obviously, such developments weaken organizational culture, lessen employee co-operation and morale, undermine the basis for decision making, and ultimately result in lower profits for the company.

Thus far, we have been talking as if organizational matters were mostly controllable by management. The fact is that the formal organization structure is just one element of the total organizational system. To create organizational culture, the *informal organization* is at least as important. Let's explore this notion next.

THINKING IT THROUGH

What is the organizational culture at your university or college? Is it known for its excellence, quality, and student orientation? If not, what is it known for? How is that reflected in student attitudes, community support, and faculty attitudes? How could the culture be improved?

The Informal Organization

All organizations have two organizational systems. One is the formal organization, the official system that details the responsibility, authority, and position of each person. But there is also an informal organization. It consists of the various cliques, relationships, and lines of authority that develop outside the formal organization.

- A **formal organization** is the structure that details lines of responsibility, authority, and position. It is the structure shown on organization charts.
- The **informal organization** is the system of relationships that develop spontaneously as employees meet and form power centres. It is the human side of the organization that does not show on any organization chart.

formal organization
The structure that details lines of responsibility, authority, and position. It is the structure shown on organization charts.

informal organization
The system of relationships and lines of authority that develop spontaneously as employees meet and form power centres; it is the human side of the organization and does not show on any formal charts.

Only very small companies can operate effectively without both types of organization. The formal system is often too slow and bureaucratic to enable the organization to adapt quickly. However, the formal organization does provide helpful guidelines and lines of authority to follow in routine situations.

The informal organization is often too unstructured and emotional to allow careful, reasoned decision making on critical matters. It is extremely effective, however, in generating creative solutions to short-term problems, providing a feeling of camaraderie and teamwork among employees, and overcoming bottlenecks created by the formal system.

In any organization, it is wise to learn quickly who the important people are in the *informal* organization. There are rules and procedures to follow for using certain equipment, but those procedures often take days. Who in the organization knows how to get you the equipment immediately without following the normal procedures? Which secretaries should you see if you want your work given first priority?

Key figures are usually older, respected employees who have earned that position of influence. It is interesting to speculate on whether the importance of the informal organization will be diminished in the future because of the radical reorganizations we have discussed. This change often involves drastic reductions in staff, including the early retirement of employees with many years' seniority—precisely those people who are likely to be key to the informal organization. This might be an interesting topic for a research paper.

The informal organization's nerve centre is the *grapevine,* the system through which unofficial information flows between and among managers and employees. It consists of rumours, facts, suspicions, accusations, and all kinds of accurate and inaccurate information. The key people in the information system usually have the most influence in the organization.

In the old "we versus they" system of organizations, where managers and employees were often at odds, the informal system often hindered effective management. In the new, more open organizations, where managers and employees work together to set objectives and design procedures, the informal organization can be an invaluable managerial asset that promotes harmony among workers and establishes the corporate culture. That is a major advantage, for example, of self-managed teams. Some of the more important aspects of the informal organization are the following:

1. *Group norms.* Group norms are the informal rules and procedures that guide the behaviour of group members. They include often unspoken but very clear guidelines regarding things like proper dress; language; work habits (e.g., how fast one works, how many breaks one takes, where one turns for assistance, and so on); and social behaviour (where one goes for recreation, with whom, how often). Deviants from the norm are often verbally abused, isolated, or harassed.
2. *Group cohesiveness.* Often a work group will develop alliances and commitments over time that tie them together strongly. The term used to describe such feelings of group loyalty is *cohesiveness.* Historically, unions have been a strong cohesive force as workers united to fight management. The goal today is to generate such cohesiveness among all corporate employees to create excellence in all phases of operation. For such cohesiveness to develop, employees must feel that they are part of a total corporate team. Often, the informal network created by corporate athletic teams, unions, and other such affiliations can assist in the creation of teamwork and co-operation.

In summary, the informal organization of a firm can strongly reinforce a feeling of teamwork and co-operation or can effectively prevent any such unity. Managers who maintain open, honest communication with employees can create an informal atmosphere that promotes willing commitment and group cohesiveness. As effective as the informal organization may be in creating group co-operation, it can be equally powerful in resisting management directives. Learning to create the right corporate culture and to work with the informal organization is a key to managerial success.

PROGRESS CHECK

- What are five ways an organization can improve communication and co-ordination?
- What is organizational culture? Can you cite an example?
- What role does the informal organization play within an organization?

SUMMARY

1. Organizational design is the establishment of manageable groups of people who have clear responsibilities and who know how to accomplish the objectives of the organization and the group.

1. Define organizaitonal design and explain its importance.

- *Why is organizational design important?*

The survival of a company depends on its becoming a responsive organization. To be responsive, it must be organized so that everyone knows who is responsible for everything that must be done, who reports to whom, what to do when problems arise, and so forth.

▼ *What is the relationship of authority, responsibility, and accountability to the role of a manager?*

Upper-level managers pass authority (the right to make decisions and take action) and responsibility (the obligation to perform a given task) to subordinates. In turn, the subordinates are accountable to those managers. This means that they must accept the consequences of their actions and report those actions to their immediate supervisors.

2. One of the major movements in today's organizations, business and non-business, is towards increasing efficiency and productivity. At one time, the goal was to increase organization *size*. With size came *economies of scale* and greater productivity. Over time, however, organizations tended to become too big. Communication was slow to move up and down through level after level of management. Smaller or more flexible domestic and foreign firms began to steal markets. The result was the major restructuring of organizations now occurring.

▼ *What are some of the trends in restructuring?*

2. Describe the current trends in organizational design.

The most obvious trend is toward smallness. Large firms are breaking up into smaller, more self-sufficient (autonomous) units. Layers of middle-management positions are being eliminated. So are many staff positions (e.g., safety inspectors, advisers, analysts). This is making organization structures flatter and wider; that is, there are fewer layers of management, but more units.

3. Organization theory is the foundation for organization design. Many organizational concepts go back to the early years of this century to theorists like Fayol and Weber.

▼ *What concepts did Fayol introduce?*

3. Explain the contributions of Henri Fayol and Max Weber to organizational theory.

Fayol's principles included unity of command, division of labour, centralization of authority, and clear lines of communication.

▼ *What was the contribution of Weber?*

Weber emphasized job descriptions, written rules, procedures, and regulations, and consistent policies. He was the father of *bureaucratic* organizations.

▼ *What was the contribution of Joan Woodward?*

Woodward studied organizations to determine what structure was most successful. She found that the kind of structure that was most effective varied by the complexity of the technology used. There was no one best way of organizing.

4. Flat organizations have certain advantages over taller organizations.

▼ *What are flat organizations and what are their advantages compared to taller organizations?*

4. Compare the advantages and disadvantages of tall and flat organization structures.

Flat organizations have a minimal number of management levels; they are called flat since the organization chart is flat compared to those of organizations with many layers between the president and workers. Information flows are slower and strained as is flexibility in tall organizations. The trend is to break up firms into smaller, more autonomous, flatter units.

5. There is much discussion about the proper span of control managers should have.

▼ *What does span of control mean?*

5. Explain the concept of span of control.

Span of control refers to the number of subordinates who report to a manager. The best number depends on the complexity of the task, their level in the organization, and other factors. The span may be narrow (i.e., a small number of subordinates report to each manager) or wide (i.e., a large number of subordinates report to each manager).

6. Departmentalization is the division of organizational functions into separate units.

▼ *How can organizations departmentalize?*

6. Describe the various ways organizations can be departmentalized.

Companies can departmentalize by function (production, marketing, etc.), by product, by customer group, by geographic location, or by process.

7. Decision making in an organization may be centralized or decentralized.

▼ *What do these terms mean?*

7. Discriminate between centralized and decentralized organizations.

A centralized organization is one where most decision-making power rests at the top levels of management. A decentralized organization distributes power more widely by delegating authority down to lower levels of management. It not only breaks up larger corporations into smaller units, but gives those units more authority and responsibility for results.

8. There are several types of organization: line, line and staff, cluster, and matrix.

8. Compare the advantages and disadvantages of line, line and staff, cluster, and matrix organizations.

▼ *What's the difference among systems?*

Line organizations have clear lines of authority, with each person having one boss; there are no internal staff advisers. A *line and staff organization* brings in staff personnel (advisers) in areas such as human resources, legal advising, and quality control. In a *matrix organization,* different specialists are brought together to work on a project while maintaining positions in the line or staff. A faculty member working with a program director is an example. A more permanent matrix-style organization is a cross-functional team called a *cluster.*

▼ *What are the advantages and disadvantages of each of these forms of organizations?*

See Figure 8–6 on page 249.

9. One of the major goals of organizations is to improve communication and co-ordination among diverse departments.

9. Explain the various ways organizations can co-ordinate activities among departments.

▼ *What methods can organizations use to improve communication and co-ordination?*

A complex way to improve communication and co-ordination is to set up a matrix-style organization. Simpler ways include committees, information systems, liaison people, and permanent teams.

10. The key to organizational success is not just organizing, but creating an organizational culture that emphasizes excellence in customer service and quality.

10. Define organizational culture and describe the role of the informal organization in that culture.

▼ *What is organizational culture?*

Organizational culture is widely shared values that help provide the coherence and co-operation needed to achieve common goals.

▼ *How does a leader create such a culture?*

The leader of an organization sets the tone by example. Organizational culture is then fostered through stories, traditions, and myths surrounding the leader and other top managers.

▼ *What is the difference between the formal organization and the informal organization?*

The *formal organization* is the structure that details lines of authority, responsibility, and position. It is what is drawn on the organization chart. The *informal organization* is the system of relationships and lines of informal authority that form spontaneously as employees meet and form power centres.

▼ *What is the role of the informal organization?*

The informal organization can create a feeling of teamwork and co-operation across departmental lines. It can also be powerful in resisting management directives. Managerial success depends on learning to create the right corporate culture and to work with the informal organization.

GETTING INVOLVED

1. There is no way to better understand the effects of having 15 layers of management on communication accuracy than to play the children's game of "Message Relay." Take 15 members of the class and have them line up. Have the first person read the following story and whisper it to number 2, who whispers it to number 3, and so on through all 15. Have number 15 tell the story out loud and compare it to the original. The distortions and mistakes are often quite humorous, but are not so funny in organizations that have 15 layers of management. Here's the story:
   Dealers in the western region have received over 130 complaints about steering on the new Commander and Roadhandler models of our mini-vans. Apparently, the front suspension system is weak and the ball joints are wearing too fast. This causes

slippage in the linkage and results in oversteering. Mr. Berenstein has been notified, but so far only 213 out of 4,300 dealers have received repair kits.

2. Write a short description of a situation where you were frustrated because a clerk in a bank, or some other business, government agency, school, or hospital followed "the rules" or "policy" to the letter and caused you much grief and lost time. Share your story with others in the class. Compare stories and then discuss strategies for minimizing such bureaucratic hassles in organizations.
3. Discuss situations in your experience—either at home, at work, or in sports—when you had more than one person telling you what to do and the orders conflicted. Share several such situations and discuss the principle of one employee, one boss. How many people can one person manage? Does it depend on the circumstances? Discuss.
4. No doubt you are familiar with the informal network of communication in schools, communities, and various organizations. Discuss the power of such informal groups. How can business use that power to become more productive *and* meet the needs of workers at the same time?

Case One Reading an Organization Chart

PRACTICING MANAGEMENT DECISIONS

This is the organization chart for Donahue Manufacturing Company.

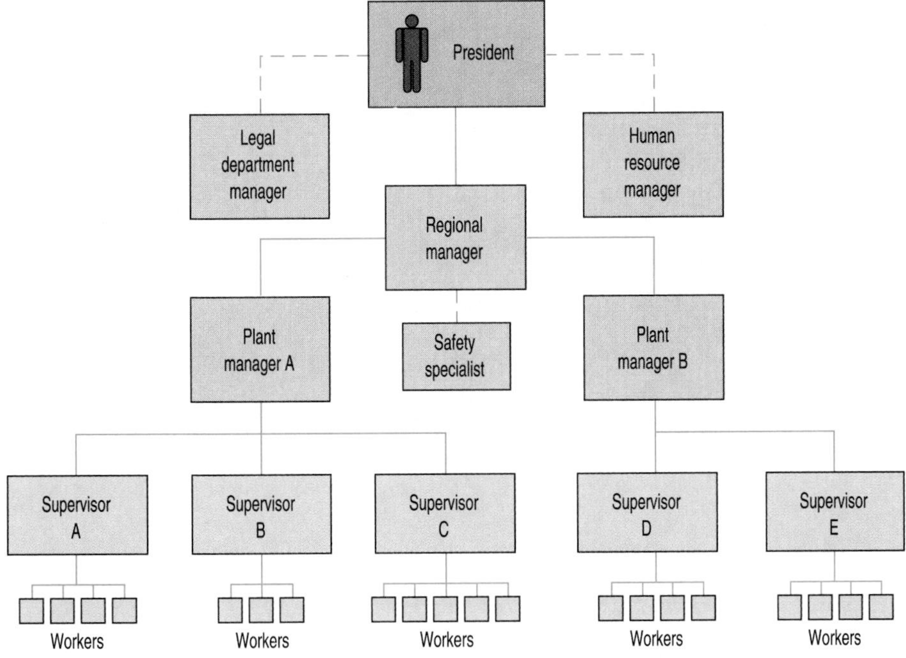

Decision Questions

1. Which people are line managers and which are staff?
2. Which supervisor has the largest span of control? Which plant manager?
3. Would this be considered a tall or flat organization structure?
4. How many line managers are under the direct control of the human resource manager?

Case Two Restructuring Hits Management Positions

Tom Peters, co-author of *In Search of Excellence,* believes the staffs of the Fortune 500 companies are still hopelessly bloated. Peters feels that many of those managers with M.B.A. degrees got to top positions without ever getting real-world experience in designing, making, selling, and servicing products. They tend to rely on technology rather than people for their answers—and ignore the retraining and redeployment of the work force.

Peters recommends that managers get out of their offices and ask their workers how to make the firm more productive. Then they should visit customers and ask what they would like to see changed. Management is no longer viewed as simply an intellectual position involving planning, organizing, leading, and controlling. It is now a hands-on job where managers and employees work as a team to make the firm more productive. Those who used to sit and ponder are out of there, and more cuts will be coming.

Since Peters's comments about U.S. business in 1991, Canadian businesses have made drastic reductions in managerial staff. Many smaller companies have let people go. Even top-flight managers with good work records are not immune to the budget axe. Various studies have indicated that typical 40-year-old white-collar workers will change jobs two or three times during the rest of their careers, at least once voluntarily. This includes a vast group of real estate managers, central purchasing agents, human resource specialists, futurologists, economists, planners, and analysts of all kinds.

Decision Questions

1. What does the reduction in middle-management jobs mean for tomorrow's undergraduate and graduate business students?
2. How would you, as the president of a firm, decide which managers to let go?
3. What are the advantages and disadvantages of cutting staff in areas like human resources, quality control, planning, and auditing? Could there be serious consequences of rapid cutbacks in management?
4. What alternative does a company have when it seems top-heavy with staff other than firing them all and becoming leaner and meaner in one swift action?

LET'S TALK BUSINESS

1. Form groups in class and discuss jobs you have had from the point of view of what organizational structure was in place. Do you know what span of control your boss had? Discuss whether it seemed to be the right span of control. What is your evidence?
2. Go to a local financial institution and find out from the manager how many levels of management there are between him or her and the president. Ask if there have been any recent changes in the number of levels. Inquire if the current structure seems to work well. If the answer is no, find out what the problems are.
3. The lean and mean approach has been criticized by some business commentators as very short-sighted. They argue that when the recession ends and business picks up, those companies who have let go many experienced employees are going to be at a great competitive disadvantage. How should a company balance the need to hold onto its valuable employees with financial pressures to cut costs?
4. Ten years from today, you are operating a successful small business with 35 employees. What kind of organizational structure will you favour, centralized or decentralized? What factors will help you decide? Explain.

LOOKING AHEAD

So far, we have learned something about basic management, including how to structure organizations to accomplish our objectives. It is time, then, to begin producing products.

The problem is that Canada's industrial base is declining. Many factories are old and obsolete. Many foreign competitors are producing high-quality goods for less. Canadian corporations have to learn how to compete.

Chapter 9 discusses production and operations management. To regain a competitive position in manufacturing, Canadian industry will have to improve everything from order processing to manufacturing, quality control, and shipping. We shall discuss how to do all that in Chapter 9. We shall discuss basic production issues and show how Canadian business is improving its competitive position.

PRODUCTION AND OPERATIONS MANAGEMENT

LEARNING GOALS

After you have read and studied this chapter, you should be able to:

1. Describe the role of Canada's manufacturing base in the national economy.
2. Illustrate the production process and explain the importance of productivity.
3. Identify the various methods manufacturers can use to keep costs at a minimum.
4. Classify the various production processes and identify the five indicators manufacturers can use to determine the likelihood of meeting their production goals.
5. Describe the importance of materials requirement planning and discuss the benefits and problems of just-in-time inventory control.
6. Describe the changes in manufacturing processes, including the use of CAD, CAM, CALS, CAE, FMS, DFMA, CIM, and enterprise networking.
7. Illustrate the use of PERT and Gantt charts in production planning.
8. Identify the steps that must occur before people and machines will be combined to revolutionize manufacturing.
9. Describe the changes in production and operations management that are taking place in this decade.
10. Suggest how the service sector might increase productivity through automation.

KEY TERMS

analytic system p. 273
assembly process, p. 273
computer-aided acquisition and logistics support (CALS), p. 282
computer-aided design (CAD), p. 280
computer-aided engineering (CAE), p. 283
computer-aided industrial design (CAID), p. 281
computer-aided manufacturing (CAM), p. 280
computer-integrated manufacturing (CIM), p. 285
continuous improvement, p. 293
continuous process, p. 273
critical path, p. 286
design for manufacturability and assembly (DFMA), p. 284
flexible manufacturing system (FMS), p. 284
form utility, p. 267
Gantt chart, p. 287
industrial park, p. 270
intermittent process, p. 273
just-in-time (JIT) inventory control, p. 276
manufacturing, p. 267
materials requirement planning (MRP), p. 275
networking, p. 285
process manufacturing, p. 273
production, p. 267
production and operations management, p. 267
program evaluation and review technique (PERT), p. 286
quality circle, p. 293
quality control, p. 290
robot, p. 279
synthetic systems, p. 273
total productive maintenance (TPM), p. 286
total quality management (TQM), p. 290

Blaine Hoshizaki

PROFILE BLAINE HOSHIZAKI, CANSTAR'S R&D WHIZ

The new owners of Montreal-based Canstar Sports Inc. had a very simple ambition: they wanted to manufacture the best hockey equipment in the world. That's why one of their first decisions on acquiring the company in 1988 was to lure Blaine Hoshizaki away from McGill University to head their industrial design. "Hoshizaki is the best guy in the world in this field," says CEO Gerald Wasserman, a turnaround specialist who, with partners Icaro Olivieri and Toronto-based Dundee Capital Inc., bought the money-losing company from Peter and Edward Bronfman. "He knows more than anyone else in the business about manufacturing the ideal skate."

For almost three years, Hoshizaki worked closely with designers Rene Bourque, who had designed Lange skates, and Gerry Black, a veteran designer of Bauer skates. Hoshizaki studied the movement of the human foot and the dynamics of ice hockey skating stride to determine the configuration of every part of the skate, from the laces to the structure of the boot to the position of the blade. It was the most comprehensive study ever attempted to manufacture the ideal skate, and it resulted in the introduction in 1987 of a truly awesome product: the Micron Mega skate, the first with a unique anatomical ankle support. By 1991, 70 percent of National Hockey League (NHL) players were wearing either the Micron Mega skate or Canstar's Bauer skates.

These days, as Canstar's vice-president of R&D, Hoshizaki, 39, oversees one of the most remarkable design operations in Canadian industry, supervising the research and design of all the company's skates and hockey equipment. That's no small task. Canstar sells more hockey skates than any other company in the world—about 1 million pairs a year. More than 90 percent of NHL players use Canstar's Tuuk or ICM blades. "When professionals who earn their living playing hockey choose our skates, that says something about their quality," says Wasserman. With its acquisition, in January 1990, of the hockey division of Cooper Canada Ltd., Canstar also became a major-league manufacturer of protective hockey equipment. It carries 1,700 variations of products ranging from hockey gloves, helmets, and goalie pads to garter belts, suspenders, sticks, and visors.

With 1,200 employees, Canstar is a unique example of a mid-sized Canadian company whose entire modus operandi is driven by its commitment to industrial design. This year Wasserman expects to spend 2 to 3 percent of Canstar's $140 million projected revenues designing and testing new products and improving old ones. Says Wasserman: "We recognize the importance of R&D in our goal to remain the leader in the hockey industry. And that's why we commit a great deal of time and money to examining new ideas." Says Hoshizaki: "As a Canadian who has played hockey all my life, I'd hate to think of my equipment being made somewhere else."

Source: Bruce McDougall, "Driven by Design," *Canadian Business* 64, no. 1, January 1991, p. 49.

CANADA'S MANUFACTURING BASE

The Canstar story in the profile illustrates what is happening in Canadian industry. The changes are coming fast and furious. Some of the ideas are new and complex. Even the terminology is confusing at first. Nonetheless, this chapter is one of the more important ones in the text, because it represents the future of Canada and therefore your future as well. Take some time to learn the terms and concepts. If you do not learn this base, catching up will be even harder as companies introduce new variations on the technology already here. Worldwide competition has made these changes necessary. Competition in the workplace means you have to keep up.

Production and operations management have become challenging and vital elements of Canadian business. There are debates about the merits of moving production facilities to the U.S. and Mexico. Serious questions are being raised about the replacement of workers with robots and other machinery. As unemployment remains high, major political decisions will be made regarding protection of Canadian manufacturers through quotas and other free trade restrictions. Regardless of how these issues are decided, however, tomorrow's university and college graduates will face tremendous challenges (and opportunities) in redesigning and rebuilding Canada's manufacturing base.

In Chapter 1, we saw why manufacturing is so important for a modern economy. All the countries that have a high standard of living—Japan, Sweden, Germany, Switzerland, the U.S., Canada—rest on a strong industrial base. We also saw how the emergence of a strong service sector complements the manufacturing base. Managing the production of goods and services in today's high-technology world, where competition has become global and fierce, is the major challenge facing Canadian companies.

The purpose of this chapter, therefore, is to introduce the concepts and issues in production and operations management. **Production and operations management** is just a long name for all the activities of managers to create goods and services. The shorter version, production management, was used before managers realized that these activities were just as relevant to service-producing businesses as they were to goods-producing companies.

production and operations management
Activities of managers to create goods and services.

New production techniques make it possible to virtually custom-make products for individual industrial buyers. The job then becomes one of getting closer to those customers to find out what their product needs are. What the future is coming down to, in other words, is effective marketing combined with effective production and management to make Canadian producers globally effective competitors.

FUNDAMENTALS OF PRODUCTION

Common sense and some experience have already taught you much of what you need to know about production and operations management. You know what it takes to build a model of an airplane or make a dress. You need a place to work, you need some skills, you need money to buy the materials, and you need to be organized to get the task done. The same is true of production. It uses basic inputs to produce outputs (see Figure 9–1). **Production,** then, is the creation of goods and services using the factors of production: land, labour, capital, entrepreneurship, and information. Production creates what is known as form utility. Utility means "value added." **Form utility** is the value added by the creation of goods and services using raw materials, components, and other inputs. (See pp. 325, 326 for a more comprehensive discussion of utility.)

production
The creation of goods and services using the factors of production: land, labour, capital, entrepreneurship, and information.

form utility
The value added by the creation of goods and services using raw materials, components, and other inputs.

Production is a broad term that describes the creative process in all industries that produce goods and services, including mining, lumbering, manufacturing, education, and health care. **Manufacturing** is one part of production. It means making goods by hand or with machinery as opposed to extracting things from the earth (mining and fishing) or producing services.

manufacturing
The process of making goods by hand or with machinery as opposed to extracting things from the earth (mining or fishing) or producing services.

Figure 9–1 The production process. The production process consists of taking the factors of production (land, labour, etc.) and using those inputs to produce goods, services, and ideas. Planning, routing, scheduling, and the other activities are the means to accomplish the objective—output.

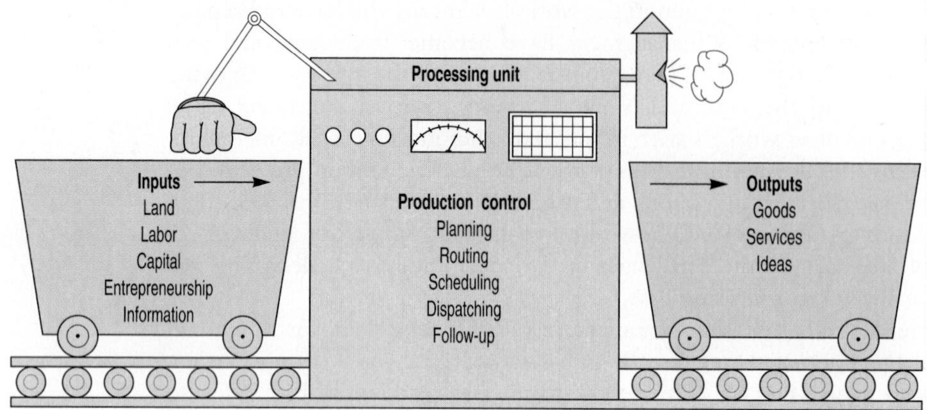

To be competitive, manufacturers must keep the costs of inputs down. That is, the costs of workers, machinery, and so on must be kept as low as possible. Similarly, the amount of output must be relatively high. Remember, the term for output per worker is *productivity*. How does a producer keep costs low and still produce more–that is, increase productivity? This question will dominate thinking in the production sector for years to come.

Challenges to Canada

Canada is a large industrial country with many major industries. We are one of the largest producers in the world of forest products, with plants in nearly all provinces turning out a vast array of wood, furniture, and paper products. Giant aluminum mills in Quebec and B.C.; auto and automotive plants in Ontario and Quebec; aircraft in Ontario, Quebec, and Manitoba; oil, natural gas, and coal produced in Alberta, Saskatchewan, Nova Scotia, and B.C. and processed there or in other provinces; a vast array of metals and minerals from all parts of Canada—these are only some of the thousands of components, products, and natural resources produced or processed in Canada.

Canada is now facing some serious challenges to its ability to remain a modern, competitive, industrial country. Many factors account for our falling behind in the world competitive race. Among them are the severe economic recession, the previously high exchange rate for the Canadian dollar, inadequate education and retraining programs for our work force, our "branch plant economy" subservient to U.S. parent companies, our constant brain drain to the U.S., too little money for research and development, and problems created by the Free Trade Agreement with the U.S. (as discussed in Part I).

This chapter will concentrate on what constitutes efficient and effective production and operations management. This area is probably unfamiliar to many students. There is a growing shortage of engineers, computer specialists, and other highly trained production workers and managers for our manufacturing industries. Think seriously about this field; it may have excellent career potential.

Steel manufacturers create form utility by producing steel in these huge oxygen furnaces and then pouring it out into moulds to form steel products. Manufacturing is one part of production (creating goods).

STAYING COMPETITIVE BY REDUCING COSTS

One of the factors that gives manufacturers an edge over their competitors is lower prices. If you can keep your costs down, you can afford to sell at lower prices. There are three ways to do this (see Figure 9–1).

1. Reduce the cost of inputs (for a given amount of output or production).
2. Increase the volume or value of outputs (for a given cost of inputs).
3. Decrease inputs *and* increase outputs.

Any of these achievements results in greater productivity, which reduces cost per unit. Output refers to the number of units produced and the value of those units. Let's look at inputs first to see how they can be kept down. Throughout this chapter, you will see many examples of Canadian companies that have been successful in reducing costs.

Reducing the Cost of Inputs

Input costs include such items as wages and salaries, raw materials and parts, energy, interest, and costs of operating the factory (overhead) like rent, taxes, insurance, maintenance, and depreciation of equipment. The question of labour costs generally gets a lot of publicity.

It is a common misconception that to reduce costs, companies should look at wages first. Labour costs as a percentage of total manufacturing costs have been dropping steadily for a long time. StatsCan figures show that in the 30 years from 1960 to 1990, the number of people employed in the Canadian manufacturing industry remained constant at about 2 million. Due to automation and other efficiencies, manufacturing output rose enormously, so labour as a percentage of manufacturing cost dropped dramatically (see Chapter 1).

While exact figures of direct labour cost are not available in Canada, they correspond to American figures. By 1988 U.S. direct labour costs in manufacturing were between 8 and 12 percent of total production costs. The prestigious *Harvard Business Review* reported that many companies were no longer recording direct labour as a separate cost because it had become such a small component of total cost.[1]

Site Selection

It makes common sense to select a site, domestic or foreign, for your operations that will give you the most advantages. Factors to consider include wages, markets, raw materials, access to energy, government inducements, work force, cost of living, and quality of life.

Lower wages. Despite the decreasing importance of labour as a component of production costs, the fact remains that where operations are labour intensive or assembly work is relatively unskilled, many Canadian companies have moved these operations to the southern U.S. or Mexico. Wages there are considerably lower (as was discussed in Part I).

Markets. If a particular plant will serve a certain geographic segment of the market, it is a competitive advantage to be close to that market. It speeds up delivery and reduces transportation costs for your customers.

Raw materials and parts. Locating near your principal suppliers eases supply problems and reduces transportation costs.

Access to energy. Some industries consume vast amounts of energy. Quebec, Ontario, Alberta, and B.C. have been successful in attracting such major industries because of their plentiful, low-cost hydro-electric power or oil and gas.

Government inducements. Most provinces and cities try to tempt businesses to locate in their area by offering such benefits as cash grants, lower taxes, interest-free loans, and free land.

industrial park
A planned area in a city where businesses can find land, shipping facilities, and waste disposal outlets so they can build a manufacturing plant or storage facility.

Some cities attract business by designing industrial parks. An **industrial park** is a planned area where businesses can find land, shipping facilities, and waste disposal outlets so they can build a manufacturing plant or storage facility.

Availability of work force. A good source of well-educated, skilled, and semiskilled workers has become a major consideration for companies, given the increasing importance of technology and information in production and operations generally.

Cost of living. Plants are often located away from expensive urban areas because the cost of land, labour, and other services is lower.

Quality of life. It is becoming increasingly important to meet the requirements of all employees for a decent quality of life as they define it. Executives, managers, and the work force in general want access to good schools and child care facilities and want to avoid noisy, dirty, polluted or unsafe neighbourhoods. They also want good public transportation and fairly short commuting distances.

Other Aspects of Reducing Input Costs

The following are discussed at some length in the next section of this chapter, so they are mentioned only briefly here.

Materials handling. This is a major area of cost for business; inefficiencies here can add substantially to input costs.

Inventory. Most companies producing or selling goods invest large amounts of money in inventory. Reducing the amount you have on hand at any one time results in lower input costs. Just-in-time inventory procedures will be discussed shortly.

Equipment. This may be the most important aspect of cost management in manufacturing. An efficient, motivated worker using outdated machinery at Company A will obviously produce less than an equivalent worker with the latest equipment at Company B. This lower productivity results in higher labour costs per unit even if wage rates are equal. This may be true even if the worker in Company B has a higher wage rate than the worker in Company A. This leads us directly into the second theme, increasing outputs.

Increasing the Volume or Value of Outputs

The factors discussed below are dealt with in detail in the next sections on production.

Engineering and design. Just as proper equipment is important for increasing output, so is engineering and design input. The goal is to speed up production by improving the product's design and reducing its number of parts; ensuring the best layout of plant and equipment; and using the most efficient production processes.

Marketing. One responsibility of the marketing department is to find products in demand that are well suited to the company's manufacturing capabilities. This simplifies production and employee training, leading to greater output.

Employee motivation. It is well known that a motivated work force produces more than one that is not motivated. It is the task of management to find ways to motivate employees. This important issue is discussed in great detail in Chapter 14.

Decreasing Inputs and Increasing Outputs

Research and development. R&D can reduce inputs by developing, adopting, or improving technology to reduce the costs of manufacturing. In conjunction with marketing, R&D improves existing products or develops new ones, leading to greater sales and thus to economies of scale—greater outputs for a given cost.

Restructuring for Greater Productivity

In earlier chapters, we referred to the unusual *restructuring* process that has dominated the Canadian business scene since the beginning of the 1990s. Most large service and manufacturing companies have dismissed thousands of employees. Air Canada, CNR, IBM, GM, and many other large and smaller companies, badly squeezed by the recession and by globally competing products and services, have drastically shrunk their work forces. The computer, telecommunication, and robot revolution have also displaced many employees and managers.

The ultimate goal of these developments is an increase in productivity per employee so that costs come down, making companies more competitive. If all goes as expected, the Canadian work force will be more skilled and better paid. But the adjustment period is likely to be long and painful.

An article in the *Montreal Gazette* is typical. The writer comments on an announcement from Chrysler that it was making its largest investment in Canada—a $600 million expansion of an Ontario plant—but it would not create a single new job.

> The experience of Canada and other industrial nations has been that manufacturing maintains its size and importance in the economy, but manages to produce more with fewer workers, just as Chrysler is doing. While this may seem dismaying, you don't have to look very far to find another sector that has gone through a similar adjustment without disaster. In 1931, agriculture occupied 31 percent of Canada's population. Today, it occupies about 4 percent.
>
> We take pride in the fact that our farmers are so productive that such a small number can feed the whole population of Canada and still produce a surplus to export. But behind this achievement lie decades of adjustment in which farm families had to send their children off to work in factories and offices. The improvement in the labour productivity of manufacturers means the same kind of adjustment, which will be hard on those who don't have the skills to excel at office jobs. It can also come as a sharp kick in the head for today's factory workers who are laid off as their companies increase productivity.
>
> But the alternative is worse: a manufacturing sector whose lack of competitiveness would cost it customers and lead to lower wages, fewer jobs, or both.

The article quotes labour analyst Cecile Dumas of StatsCan saying that Canadian manufacturers have "permanently changed their habits." Her evidence is greatly improved exports, a sign of greater competitiveness. She notes that during a recession productivity usually slumps, but in 1990–91 "the productivity of Canadian manufacturers actually rose." Incomplete data for 1992, she says, indicates a continuing improvement.[2]

So we see that the road to better jobs and higher wages is through higher productivity and that Canada is well launched in that direction. Unfortunately, as part of this process we will also have to cope with high unemployment during the next few years as we go through the period of adjustment.

PROGRESS CHECK

- What is production and operations management?
- Explain how the terms *production* and *manufacturing* are related.
- What are the major factors that determine where a plant locates?
- What are inputs and outputs of production? How are they related to competitiveness?

MAKING ETHICAL DECISIONS

Depresso Industries has long been the economic mainstay of its birthplace, Hometown, Canada. Most of Hometown's small businesses and schools support Depresso Industries, either by supplying the materials needed for production or by training Depresso employees. Depresso has found that it can increase profits 50 percent by moving its production facilities overseas. Closing Depresso operations in Hometown will cause many of the town's businesses to fail and schools to close, leaving a great percentage of the town unemployed with no options for re-employment. As a Depresso top manager, you must help decide if the plant should be moved and, if so, when to tell the employees about closing the Hometown plant. The law says, that you must tell them at least six months before closing. What alternatives do you have? What are the consequences of each alternative? Which alternative will you choose? ▼

PRODUCTION PROCESSES

After a site is selected and a factory has been built, manufacturers actually begin making products. There are several different processes manufacturers use. Andrew S. Grove, chief executive officer of Intel, uses a great analogy to explain the production process:[3]

> To understand the principles of production, imagine that you're a waiter . . . and that your task is to serve a breakfast consisting of a three-minute soft-boiled egg, buttered toast, and coffee. Your job is to prepare and deliver the three items simultaneously, each of them fresh and hot.
>
> The task here encompasses the three basic requirements of production. They are to build and deliver products in response to the demands of the customer at a *scheduled* delivery time, at an *acceptable quality* level, and at the lowest possible cost. . . .
>
> Other production principles underlie the preparation of our breakfast. In the making of it, we find present the three fundamental types of production operations: *process manufacturing,* an activity that physically or chemically changes material just as boiling changes an egg; *assembly,* in which components are put together to constitute a new entity just as the egg, the toast, and the coffee together make a breakfast; and *test,* which subjects the components or the total [product] to an examination of its characteristics [by the customer]. . . .

From the breakfast example, it is easy to understand two manufacturing processes: process and assembly. In **process manufacturing,** you physically or chemically change materials. For example, boiling physically changes the egg. In **assembly process,** you put together components such as the egg, the toast, and the coffee to make a breakfast. These two processes are called synthetic systems. **Synthetic systems** either change raw materials into other products (process manufacturing) or combine raw materials or parts into a finished product (assembly process).

The reverse of a synthetic system is called an analytic system. In an **analytic system,** a raw material is broken down into components to extract other products. For example, crude oil can be reduced to gasoline, wax, and jet fuel. So the production process will be either synthetic or analytic. In addition, production processes are either continuous or intermittent.

A **continuous process** is one in which long production runs turn out finished goods over time. In our breakfast shop, for example, you could have eggs on a conveyor belt that lowered them into boiling water for three minutes and then lifted them out on a continuous basis. A three-minute egg would be available whenever you wanted one. An automobile factory is run on a continuous process.

It usually makes more sense when responding to specific customer orders (job-order production) to use an **intermittent process.** This is an operation where the production run is short (one or two eggs) and the machines are shut down frequently or changed to produce different products (like the oven in a bakery or the toaster in the breakfast shop). Manufacturers of custom-designed furniture or metal railings use an intermittent process.

Today, most new manufacturers use intermittent processes. Their computers, robots, and flexible manufacturing processes make it possible to make custom-made goods almost as fast as mass-produced goods were once made (see Figure 9–2). We shall discuss how they do that in more detail later.

process manufacturing
Production process that physically or chemically changes materials.

assembly process
Production process that puts together components.

synthetic system
Production process that either changes raw materials into other products or combines raw materials or parts into finished products.

analytic system
Manufacturing system that breaks down raw materials into components to extract other products.

continuous process
Production process in which long production runs turn out finished goods over time.

intermittent process
Production process in which the production run is short and the machines are shut down frequently or changed to produce different products.

Oil refineries use analytic systems to create gasoline and other products from crude oil. Analytic systems break raw materials down into component parts.

This photo is an example of a continuous process in action. Newspapers are streaming off a Rockwell Colorliner press at 75,000 copies per hour.

THINKING IT THROUGH

Reread the story about making breakfast and imagine instead a factory producing glass that it then puts into frames for pictures. Think through how the same concepts apply. Can you see how the picture frame plant uses both process and assembly manufacturing?

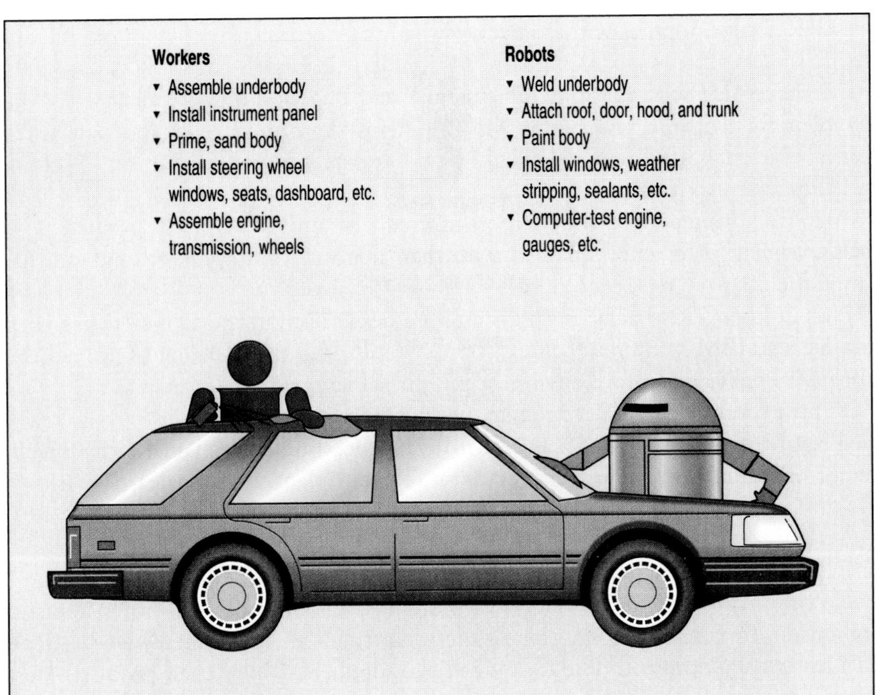

Figure 9–2 Workers and robots assemble a car. Using intermittent processes, manufacturers can produce custom-made cars almost as fast as mass-produced cars.

Managers use five indicators of whether or not they can meet their production goals on any given day:

1. *Sales forecast.* How many breakfasts should you plan to deliver?
2. *Raw material inventory.* Do you have enough eggs, bread, butter, and coffee on hand?
3. *Equipment.* Is everything ready to produce the breakfast?
4. *Manpower.* Are there enough people available to make the sales forecast number of breakfasts?
5. *Quality.* Are customers satisfied?

The production of breakfasts begins with installation of the needed equipment and purchase of the needed food. The food and supplies must be stored in refrigerators and other storage equipment. One place we can look for production efficiency and savings, therefore, is in purchasing and storage.

Materials Requirement Planning (MRP)

The technological changes now taking place in manufacturing have resulted in a whole new terminology for production and operations management. Today's students need to be familiar with this terminology before they can discuss such advances in any depth.

One of the more important terms is **materials requirement planning (MRP).** Materials requirement planning is a computer-based production and operations management system that uses sales forecasts to make sure needed parts and materials are available at the right place and the right time. In our breakfast shop, for example, we could feed the sales forecast into the computer, which would specify how much of each ingredient to order and print out the proper scheduling and routing sequence.

materials requirement planning (MRP)
A computer-based production and operations management system that uses sales forecasts to make sure needed parts and materials are available at the right place and time.

MRP is most popular with companies that make products with a lot of different parts. IBM Canada is such a company. "I couldn't deal with the 30,000 to 40,000 parts we have here without an MRP system," said Eugene Polistuk, manager of the IBM plant in Toronto. As better MRP systems developed over the past three decades, efficiency increased. "We had 30 to 40 people in process control," Polistuk said. "There are six today."[4]

A more advanced but much more difficult system is MRP II, *manufacturing resource planning*. This encompasses more than materials requirements and still has many difficulties to overcome.

Despite their drawbacks, both systems are being used in modern factories with some success. IBM's computer integration systems have dramatically improved the company's quality and productivity, helping it achieve large sales increases.

"Those companies that struggle with MRPs struggle because they really haven't got their arms around the information processing part," said Keith Powell, director of manufacturing at the Northern Telecom plant in Bramalea, Ontario.[5]

Just-in-Time Inventory Control

just-in-time (JIT) inventory control
Arrangements for delivery of the smallest possible quantities at the latest possible time to keep inventory as low as possible.

One of the major costs of production is holding parts, motors, and other items in warehouses. To cut such costs, the Japanese perfected an idea called **just-in-time (JIT) inventory control.** The idea is to have suppliers deliver their products "just in time" to go on the assembly line. A minimum of inventory is kept on the premises. Some Canadian manufacturers have adopted the practice and are quite happy with the results, although it is much more difficult to implement because of the greater distances involved in Canada.

Here is how it works: A manufacturer sets a production schedule using materials requirement planning as described above, and determines what parts and supplies will be needed. It then tells its suppliers what will be needed and when. Each supplier must deliver the goods just in time to go on the assembly line. Naturally, this calls for more effort by the suppliers, who resist what seems at first like a major change of operations. They soon learn, however, that they too can end up with greater savings. Efficiency is maintained by linking the supplier by computer to the producer so the supplier becomes more like another department in the firm than a separate business. The supplier delivers its materials just in time to be used in the production process, so a bare minimum must be kept in storage just in case the delivery is held up for some reason.

You can imagine how the system would work at Andrew Grove's breakfast shop. Rather than ordering enough eggs, butter, bread, and coffee for the week and storing it, he would have his suppliers deliver every morning.

At an auto parts factory, a truck pulls up to the shipping dock and loads wheels right off the production line. Twenty minutes later, the wheels arrive at the auto plant, where they are unloaded and moved a few metres. They reach the assembly line just in time to be bolted on to the next batch of cars coming down the line.

JIT eliminates the need for warehousing and saves hours of materials handling time. Quality improves dramatically; less handling means less damage. The cost savings can be enormous.

But implementation is far from simple: it requires spending months—or years—preparing and reorganizing your production. Your suppliers also have to be geared into it. Suppliers and customers must be in constant communication. After two years, Ford's Oakville, Ontario, assembly line has only 130 of 1,456 parts on the just-in-time system. At General Motors' massive Oshawa, Ontario, complex, almost all parts are on the system. That means that about 1,200 trucks unload each day.[6]

The parts this worker is assembling arrived just in time to go on the assembly line. This shot was taken at a Harley-Davidson assembly plant.

A moment's reflection will tell you some of the problems with JIT systems. What happens if the supplier doesn't deliver on time because of weather conditions or an accident? Are suppliers willing to assume the added costs of more frequent, smaller deliveries? Such questions have to be answered through planning and negotiation. The results are usually worth the effort.

Just-in-Time Supplier Relationships

For many companies, implementation of JIT methods has been rather difficult. Problems develop when producers use JIT as a way of getting suppliers to hold inventories instead of doing it themselves. This means the producers have no back-up inventory if the suppliers deliver the wrong parts or faulty parts or do not deliver any parts by the time they are needed.

For the system to work well, producers have to work closely with suppliers and carefully work out details of the system, making sure that the suppliers are happy with it too. Xerox failed to do that when it first established its JIT system, which caused much supplier discontent. Xerox then developed an elaborate program to develop better supplier relationships and now teaches others how to do that.

Xerox learned how to implement a JIT system from Harley-Davidson. Harley is one of the best practitioners of just-in-time inventory. The U.S. motorcycle company was about to fail because of Japanese competition. Operating costs for motorcycle manufacturers in Japan were 30 percent lower, largely due to a JIT system and quality control procedures such as those discussed later in this chapter. Using Japanese-style techniques, Harley cut its costs for warranty repairs, scrap, and reworking of parts by 60 percent. Meanwhile, the Japanese are experiencing some trouble with their system. It seems so many companies have implemented JIT that the streets of Tokyo are jammed with trucks.[7]

MRP and JIT systems make sure the right materials are at the right place at the right time at the cheapest cost to meet customer needs and production needs. That is the first step in modern production innovation. The next step is to change the production process itself. We shall discuss that in the next section, but first we will look at inventory control systems developed in Canada.

Other Material and Inventory Control Systems

Several large organizations have adopted systems all aimed at reducing the cost of handling inventory. The Halifax plant of Pratt & Whitney, which manufactures gear casings for its line of aircraft engines, has been hailed as a showcase of modern technology in this regard. It uses an integrated materials handling (IMH) system in conjunction with a flexible manufacturing system (FMS) to produce a state-of-the-art facility.[8]

In British Columbia, the B.C. Purchasing Commission had a tough problem. The public sector spends in excess of $5 billion annually. Controlling such vast expenditures was a mammoth task. After scouring North America and finding nothing suitable, the commission developed its own system. Working with two Canadian companies, Cognos Inc. of Ottawa and OGMA Consulting Ltd. of Victoria, it integrated an HP 3000 minicomputer into a very sophisticated system.

After two years, the system was expanded to include complete tracking of all materials and equipment. This computer-assisted materials management system (CAMMS) identifies all materials in stock and their purchase costs. The CAMMS program tracks the total lifetime of all consequential goods, from the time they are first ordered to the time the commission disposes of them.[9]

PROGRESS CHECK

- Can you explain the differences among the following production methods: process, assembly, analytic, continuous, and intermittent?
- What are five indicators of whether or not you will reach your production goals?
- What is materials requirement planning and how does it make production more efficient?
- What is just-in-time inventory control and what are the potential problems with implementing such a system?

MAKING CHANGES IN THE PRODUCTION PROCESS

Another major area for cost saving involves the design of the process used to make final products. You are no doubt familiar with the idea of a production line or assembly line. Usually, the workers are lined up on both sides of a long assembly line and perform one or more simple processes as the product goes by. For example, in making an automobile, one person puts in the seats, another installs the windows, and still others put on tires, bumpers, headlights, and so on. The process involves many, many workers doing a few not-too-complex tasks. (There are about 10,000 parts in a car.)

Investing eight years and $3.5 billion, GM redesigned its production process, abandoning the assembly line. The name given the changeover was Project Saturn. The fundamental purpose of the restructuring was to cut dramatically the number of worker-hours needed to build a car.

GM made many changes, but the most dramatic was to switch to modular construction. This means most parts are preassembled into a few large components called *modules*. Workers are no longer strung out along miles of assembly line. Instead, they are grouped at various work stations where they put the modules together. Rather than do a few tasks, workers perform a whole cluster of tasks. Trolleys carry the partly completed car from station to station. This process takes up less space and calls for fewer workers—both money-saving steps. Suppliers were asked to provide a wider variety of parts and to subassemble certain parts before shipping them.

In addition to these changes, GM designed a casting process for building the engine block that uses 40 percent less machinery. This, too, saves time and money. And finally, GM greatly expanded its use of robots in the manufacturing process. A **robot** is a computer-controlled machine capable of performing many tasks requiring the use of materials and tools (see the photo on p. 284). For example, robots spray paint cars and do welding. They are usually fast, efficient, and accurate. GM had troubles implementing the whole process. Other companies have also had trouble implementing new technologies. That doesn't mean the idea isn't good—the problem is in learning how to manage change.

robot
A computer-controlled machine capable of performing many tasks.

Because of its problems with implementing the new technology, GM switched its emphasis from robots and machinery to people management. It is hiring and training workers who can make the most of the new technology. The company devotes 70,000 square feet to its training and development centre. The Saturn car was so successful that the Saturn workers agreed to a five-day, 50-hour work week to meet production demands.[10]

GM is just one example of how innovations are now occurring in manufacturing. In general, firms are using more robots, more computers, and less labour. Nabisco makes Oreos in a North Carolina plant. The cookies are "untouched by human hands" until you take them apart to eat them. You do take them apart, don't you?

The Japanese auto industry pioneered the systematic use of robots on a large scale in dirty or health-threatening jobs like painting and welding. Most of the robots in Canada are in Ontario in the auto industry. GM Canada uses more than 600 robots in its main centre in Oshawa, Ontario. The plant also employs 9,500 people.

Arnold Norris, a vice-president of Honda Canada, says the fear that robots would replace workers has proven to be unfounded. Workers end up being more highly trained, to operate the robots for example. David Robertson of the Canadian Auto Workers (CAW) union agrees that the new jobs created are more highly skilled and better paying and the jobs that disappear are the ones no one wants to do. However, he says, wherever robotics have been introduced, there are fewer people working than before.

CAW and the robot manufacturer, Ocam, agree that earlier predictions that robots would "take over the world" (of production) were greatly exaggerated. They also say that, while robots have made tremendous changes, they are only one aspect of the larger process of computer automation.[11]

This whole process of automation is quite complex. It is designed to make manufacturers more efficient, increasing their productivity, reducing costs, and making them more competitive in the fiercely contested global market. But many leading Canadian companies—Ford, GM, Northern Telecom, Allen Bradley, to name a few—have discovered that the process requires very careful planning and

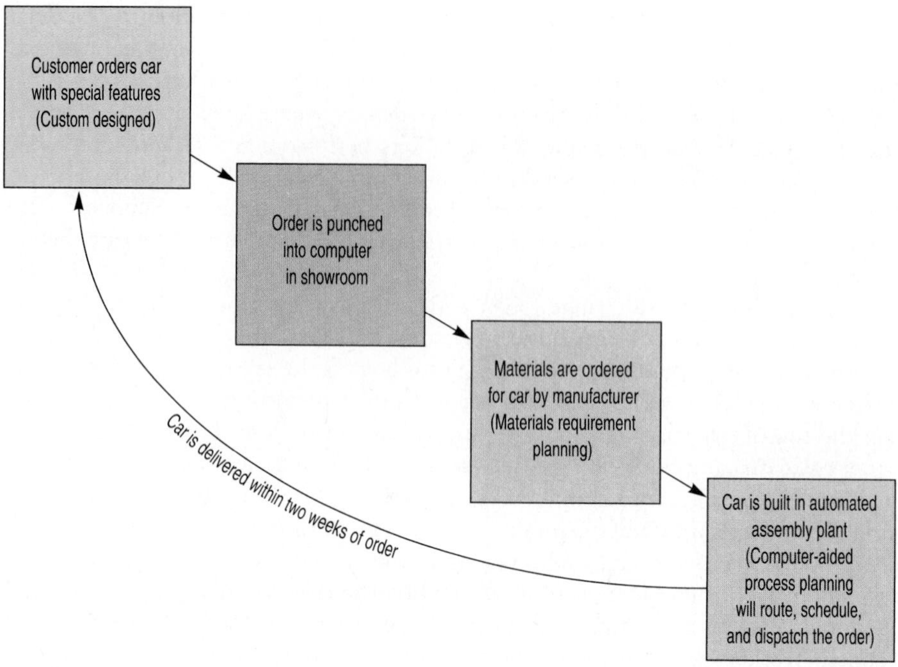

Figure 9–3
Custom-built cars using the latest in automation. Buying a car in the future. Note the custom features ordered by the client. Note too that the car is not produced until an order is received. That allows for custom design in just two weeks.

control. People, they have found, must be fully integrated into the changeover. Being dazzled by the new "toys" has led to many costly errors.[12]

See Figure 9–3 for a look at the future of automation for the auto industry. Again, the goal is to cut costs and increase productivity to keep Canadian business competitive. Next we shall explore the dramatic changes computers are bringing to design and manufacturing.

Computer-Aided Design and Manufacturing (CAD/CAM)

If one development in the 1980s changed production techniques and strategies more than any other, it was the integration of computers into the design and manufacturing of products. The first thing computers did was help in the design of products. The idea is called **computer-aided design (CAD).** The next step was to involve computers directly in the production process. That was called **computer-aided manufacturing (CAM).**

computer-aided design (CAD)
The use of computers in the design of products.

computer-aided manufacturing (CAM)
The use of computers in the manufacturing of products.

CAD/CAM has made it possible to design products to meet the tastes of small markets with very little increase in costs. A producer programs the computer to make a simple design change, and that change can be incorporated right into the production line. Custom products can thus be designed for narrow markets.

An example reveals how helpful the computer can be. A Viennese architect named Josef Hoffman designed a beautiful silver-plated bowl as a gift for Albert Einstein. The original bowl has disappeared; only a photograph remained. To duplicate the bowl by hand through trial and error would have been costly and difficult. Instead, two men used the CAD process to program the dimensions of the bowl. They made 100,000 copies and sold them for $120 each. They could now make a slight change in the design on the computer and produce a new, unique design of their own.

This picture shows running shoes being designed on a computer-aided design (CAD) system. Some day you will be able to buy custom-made shoes for the same price (or nearly so) as mass-produced shoes because of CAD/CAM and flexible manufacturing systems.

Computer-aided manufacturing is used to make cookies in those new fresh-baked cookie shops. On-site, small-scale, semi-automated, sensor-controlled baking makes consistent quality easy.

CAD/CAM is also invading the clothing industry. A computer program establishes a pattern and cuts the cloth automatically. Soon, a person's dimensions will be programmed into the machines to create custom-cut clothing at very little additional cost.

The same flexibility is possible in large plants that produce automobiles, appliances, construction equipment, and other large, expensive items. In the past, any model change resulted in large increases in inventory and set-up costs. (All plant operations—machining, welding, assembling, and so forth—require *set-up time* to prepare for the new process.) Today, many such changes are computerized, and the costs have been lowered dramatically. Over a five-year period, one manufacturer roughly tripled its number of models while reducing inventory by half and doubling the output per worker. How? Computer-aided manufacturing.

In summary, CAD/CAM has revolutionized the production process. Now, everything from cookies to automobiles can be designed and manufactured much more cheaply. Furthermore, customized changes can be made with very little increase in cost. Think what that will mean for the clothing industry, the shoe industry, and other fashion-conscious industries. The age of custom-designed consumer and industrial goods has arrived.

Computer-Aided Industrial Design (CAID)

Even more sophisticated than CAD is **computer-aided industrial design (CAID).** CAID is the creation and modification of models with a three-dimensional perspective. CAID can easily produce free-form designs, a time-consuming task for CAD. Artists can easily work with CAID, but they would have difficulty using CAD.

computer-aided industrial design (CAID)
The creation and modification of models with a 3-D perspective.

SPOTLIGHT ON BIG BUSINESS

How to Make a Small, Smart Factory

Step inside Shell Canada's new lubricants plant, and the first thing that comes to mind is: Where are all the people? There's plenty of activity, to be sure. Black plastic bottles are swept off pallets and shuffle smartly along the bottling lines to be labelled, filled with oil, and put into boxes.

Yet only the occasional worker crosses the floor. Once in a while, a forklift truck whizzes down an aisle. Otherwise, the mixing of oils and various additives into lubricants for autos, airplanes, ships, and industrial machines seems guided by some unseen hand. In fact, 75 people ramble around this ultramodern plant.

This nine-month-old facility is the prototype of a new breed of small, flexible factories, fine-tuned for high productivity and short-run production. The additives that make Shell Brockville hum are highly skilled people plugged into advanced computer technology and workplace ideas. It's the folks on the factory floor—grouped into three teams with access to rich stores of information—who know what needs to be done and who fix problems as they arise.

If plant manager Brian Avis shows up on the floor, jokes operator Terry Seed, he might just be asked: "Are you lost?" Bill Thomas, Shell's Calgary-based director of lubricants and industrial markets, hears jibes about flower-power management and love-ins. But the approach is strictly business. "This is a strategy built around people—to create an environment and the tools where people can better contribute to the business," he says. "These people are better connected to the business than any other operating group I've ever seen, and we're still at an early stage of development."

Shell's decision to build the plant emerged from a strategic review of the lubricants market in 1989. If the company wanted to keep producing quality products at highly competitive prices, it had to replace the 1930s-style plants. One key to that redesign is information technology. It penetrates every corner of the shop, putting a computer at the fingertips of every worker. The plant runs on a powerful network of five integrated computer systems that knits together every operation including marketing. Very little moves or happens without computer involvement.

The new equipment is easy to see: what's less visible is the way it has transformed relationships. Missing are the traditional foremen and supervisors who tell people what to do and how to do it. Every worker, or "team operator," is a supervisor of sorts. He or she (almost one-third are women) can tap into all information relevant to plant operations. That allows employees to manage themselves.

If a problem arises, operators solve it on their own, even if it means calling a supplier to complain and working out a solution. The teams are responsible for discipline and cost control (including absenteeism) and arrange their own vacation and training schedules. The plant's three teams, called "job families," manage the basic processes: bulk handling and blending of the lubricants, packaging, and warehousing. Each operator must master all the jobs within his or her team, plus at least one

The Boeing 777, a twin-engine plane, is scheduled to go into service in 1995. It is the company's first plane to be designed entirely on computers. Boeing's 3-D digital design system has its own computer-generated human model who can crawl into the images on the screen to see how difficult it will be for real people to reach problem areas.[13]

Computer-Aided Acquisition and Logistics Support (CALS)

computer-aided acquisition and logistics support (CALS) A communications system that allows manufacturers to send design specifications to suppliers over a phone line directly to the machine that will do the work.

Computer-aided acquisition and logistics support (CALS) is a communications system that allows manufacturers to send design specifications to suppliers over a phone line directly to the machine that will do the work. This system makes it possible to reduce inventories even further because new parts can be ordered and processed at once and sent almost immediately. CALS reduces the need for design changes and speeds product development.[14]

SPOTLIGHT ON BIG BUSINESS (*concluded*)

skill in each of the other two groups. Jobs change roughly every 18 months.

Production coordinator Joan Bush calls the approach "holistic," a word rarely heard in manufacturing plants, but it comes easily to managers here. They expect every operator to understand all aspects of the business, including where materials come from and where final products go. Shell figures anyone who talks to suppliers and customers brings enthusiasm and imagination to even mundane tasks.

In their 1992 book *Paradigm Shift,* Don Tapscott and Art Caston of DMR Group Inc. of Montreal cited the Brockville plant as a far-reaching implementation of an "open networked operation." As they define it, that's one where hierarchical structures and the old command-and-control mentality have been swept aside by a dynamic organization driven by commitment rather than reward and punishment. In this setting, work is done by self-managed teams of people with a range of skills, treated as professionals and paid according to their accomplishments, not by seniority or position.

The system seems to work in Brockville. Having started up last April, the plant won't reach capacity for another few months. It is hard to measure productivity, but a work force half the size it was before produces the same output. One measure of competitiveness is that the lubricant plant has found customers in 44 countries. Three years ago an export order was a rarity. And staff absenteeism is running about one-third the normal rate in manufacturing.

Seed, who moved from an office job in Montreal to a forklift in Brockville, likes the ambience. He rankles a bit over his diminished responsibilities, "so I try to get my nose into as many things as I can here." His technique: "You open up your mouth. We're all a lot of talkers here. We're not afraid to question."

Shell Brockville is cutting edge in another important way. It can adapt products to fit almost any customer need. In this plant, the product range is 240 lubricants for a wide variety of uses. At the heart of the blending process is an operations control centre, where a bank of computers stores the recipes for the 240 blends and tells the operators, step by step, how to mix them. Meanwhile, computers track every litre of raw material and product wherever it may be in the production process. This data feeds into the rest of the information needed to make the plant work.

This same attention to detail is reflected in how Shell selected people to work in Brockville. Of the 46 Toronto and Montreal employees who applied to move, only 20 passed the screening exercise. Shell tested not only technical skills but the ability to function in teams. For the other 40 positions, more than 1,200 local applications poured in. Applicants went through a battery of written tests, problem-solving exercises, and role-playing sessions.

Even so, says Avis, some new employees are nervous about making mistakes and want to be told what to do. He calls them "victims" of traditional work environments. "We say, 'No, you have to make the step, you have to take the risk. By God, we will learn from any errors you make and we're not here to hammer you into the ground.' "

Source: Bruce Little, "How To Make a Small Smart Factory," *Globe and Mail,* February 2, 1993, p. B24. ▼

The Computerized Factory

Thanks to ideas like CAD/CAM, CAID, and CALS, Canada is now on the brink of a whole new era in production and operations management. The force behind the change is new technology, especially computers and robots. You will be seeing the following terms over the next decade.

computer-aided engineering (CAE)
The computer-generated design and analysis of products, programming of robots and machine tools, designing of moulds and tools, and planning of the production process and quality control.

1. **Computer-aided engineering (CAE).** CAE includes the designing and analysis of products, the programming of robots and machine tools, the designing of molds and tools, and the planning of the production process and quality control. In the past, engineering involved a lot of paperwork—blueprints, drawings, and so forth. Many inefficiencies resulted from the shuffling of such papers from desk to desk to shop floor and so on. Changes were time consuming and costly. Today, the whole engineering process from conception to production is being done by computer in some firms.

These robots are busy helping to build the Ford Taurus and the Mercury Sable. Robots help make Ford more productive.

flexible manufacturing systems (FMS)
Totally automated production centres that include robots, automatic materials handling equipment, and computer-controlled machine tools that can perform a variety of functions to produce different products.

design for manufacturability and assembly (DFMA)
A process used to design products with the least number of parts, thus reducing the cost of assembly.

2. A **flexible manufacturing system (FMS)** is a totally automated production centre that includes robots, automatic materials handling equipment, and computer-controlled machine tools that can perform a variety of functions to produce different products. Shell's new plant uses a flexible manufacturing system with similar cost-saving results.

3. **Design for manufacturability and assembly (DFMA)** is based on the premise that the best-engineered part may be no part at all. Reducing the number of parts needed to build a product reduces the cost of the product. Savings come from lower material cost, less time to assemble, ease in installation and maintenance, and less field service. NCR's newest electronic cash register has only 15 parts, 85 percent fewer parts from 65 percent fewer suppliers than its previous model. The terminal takes only one-quarter of the time previously required to assemble. In fact, an engineer can assemble the new NCR cash register in less than two minutes—blindfolded. Robert Williams, manufacturability engineer at Hewlett-Packard, believes that DFMA is important for products in three areas: (1) where the technology has changed, (2) where parts could be reduced by consolidation or by a more clever design, and (3) where there are known reliability problems.[15]

What you should learn from all this is that factories are being fully automated. That is, almost all personnel are being eliminated. Everything from customer order processing to inventory control planning to forecasting through production, quality control, and shipping is being made more productive through the use of computers and robots.

Today, computerizing a factory is a rather uncoordinated process. Factories have computer-controlled centres performing various functions, but these centres often are not linked. The goal is to integrate the whole production process. As you can guess, this is easier said than done. A few firms, however, have managed it. They call the total system computer-integrated manufacturing. Let's look at how it works.

Computer-Integrated Manufacturing (CIM)

Computer-integrated manufacturing (CIM) combines computer-aided design with computer-aided manufacturing. It then integrates CAD/CAM with other corporate functions such as purchasing, inventory control, cost accounting, materials handling, and shipping.

computer-integrated manufacturing (CIM)
CAD/CAM integrated with other corporate functions such as purchasing, inventory control, cost accounting, materials handling, and shipping.

The Ingersoll Milling Machine Co. was an early user of CIM. This machine tool firm makes products in small lots—one or two at a time—and needed a huge amount of information processing to schedule products through design and production. Its computer-integrated manufacturing system includes scheduling, CAE, inventory control, CAD/CAM, purchasing, cost accounting, and assembly. The system saves Ingersoll over $1 million a year, mostly in machinery design.

New computer breakthroughs will make CIM a reality in thousands of manufacturing firms in the next decade. Leading firms that are developing such systems for others include IBM, GE, Schlumberger, Control Data, Xerox, and Sperry Univac.

Several companies have developed computer software for "factory management systems." One that is sold by IBM is called a Process Operations Management System (POMS). The new factory management systems can help you follow products through the entire production process. They can also tell you whether equipment is available and whether there are people available to operate that equipment. Finally, they can tell you whether or not parts are available in inventory and what the customer requirements are for quality and delivery. Given this information, a plant manager can route materials and allocate resources more efficiently. If a rush order comes in, the manager can immediately determine whether the production process can be altered to handle the new order and how best to do that.

Just-in-time inventory supply systems will link suppliers with producers by computer to form networks of computer-linked firms. One problem with such integration is that different manufacturers producing computers, robots, computer software, and data transmission systems have not standardized their equipment. Thus, it has been difficult in the past to integrate systems within a firm, much less among firms. This problem introduces the concept of enterprise networking.

Enterprise Networking

For real system integration to take place, the computers of one company will have to talk to the computers of another company. This is called **networking.** In the 1990s, it will revolutionize the way marketing and production are handled. Imagine a salesperson talking with a customer and learning that a slight modification in the product is needed. The salesperson could sit down with his or her laptop computer and send the modifications to the company via electronic mail (messages that are sent from computer to computer). The information is fed into a CAD system that, in turn, feeds it to a CAM system. The system automatically adjusts the inventory model and tells suppliers what is needed and when. The supplier's just-in-time system gets the information immediately. That is how the system of the 1990s will work.

networking
Linking firms together by making it possible for their computers to talk to one another.

One problem with implementing such a system is defining common standards among computer and communications industry manufacturers so interfirm systems communication can take place. Such standards are now being developed. There is fierce competition among Canadian, American, European, and Japanese companies to be the first to develop and market such systems. For now, you should know that great changes are occurring in manufacturing that will link suppliers, manufacturers, and business customers in one common computer system that will make the flows of goods and services much more efficient.

Implementing the New Systems

A survey of 250 manufacturing companies was conducted recently to determine the acceptance of new concepts such as computer-integrated manufacturing.[16] The survey found that 52 percent used just-in-time inventory methods, 32 percent used manufacturing resource planning (MRP 2—the more comprehensive form of materials requirement planning), and 41 percent used a flexible manufacturing system. When it came to the manufacturing process itself, 52 percent of the companies used CAD, 38 percent used CAM, and 21 percent used CIM.

As we noted earlier, slowness in getting products to markets cripples competition. Compressing manufacturing and delivery time is essential. Therefore, companies are applying the JIT concept to all crucial business functions. For example, **total productive maintenance (TPM)** is preventive maintenance with total participation of the personnel operating the equipment. Maintenance experts may make periodic inspections and major repairs, but operators are trained to do routine maintenance to keep the machines operating efficiently most of the time. Ford is using TPM to keep its Fordstown (Ohio) plant running round the clock.[17]

total productive maintenance (TPM)
Preventive maintenance with total participation of the personnel operating the equipment.

CONTROL PROCEDURES: PERT AND GANTT CHARTS

Obviously, one of the important functions of a production manager is to be sure that products are manufactured and delivered *on time*. How can one be sure all the assembly processes will go smoothly and be completed by the required time? One of the more popular strategies for monitoring the progress of the production process is called program evaluation and review technique, developed in the 1950s for constructing nuclear submarines. The **program evaluation and review technique (PERT)** is a method for analyzing the tasks involved in completing a given project, estimating the time needed to complete each task, and identifying the minimum time needed to complete the total project.

program evaluation and review technique (PERT)
A method for analyzing the tasks involved in completing a given project, estimating the time needed to complete each task, and identifying the minimum time needed to complete the total project.

critical path
The longest path a product takes from the beginning of the production process until the end.

The steps involved in using PERT are (1) analyzing and sequencing tasks that need to be done, (2) estimating the time needed to complete each task, (3) drawing a PERT network illustrating the information from steps 1 and 2, and (4) identifying the critical path. The **critical path** is the phase of production that takes the longest time to complete. Therefore, the critical path represents the earliest time a project can be completed if all tasks along that path are completed as predicted. The critical path answers the question: "When will the project be finished?" In order for the total project to be completed on time, however, it is "critical" that tasks along the critical path be completed on schedule.[18]

Figure 9–4 illustrates a PERT chart for producing a music video. Note that the triangles on the chart indicate completed tasks and the arrows leading to the triangles indicate the time needed to complete each task. The path from one completed task to the next illustrates the relationships between tasks. For example, the arrow from "set designed" to "set materials purchased" shows that designing the set must be completed before the materials can be purchased. The critical path (indicated by the blue arrows) reflects that producing the set takes more time than

Figure 9–4 PERT chart for producing a music video. The minimum amount of time it will take to produce this video is 15 weeks. To get that number, you add the week it takes to pick a star and a song to the four weeks to design a set, the two weeks to purchase set materials, the six weeks to construct the set, the week before rehearsals, and the final week when the video is made. That is the critical path. Any delay in that process will delay the final video. Delays in the other processes (selecting and choreographing dancers and designing costumes) would not necessarily delay the video because each of these paths takes less than the 15 weeks in the critical path.

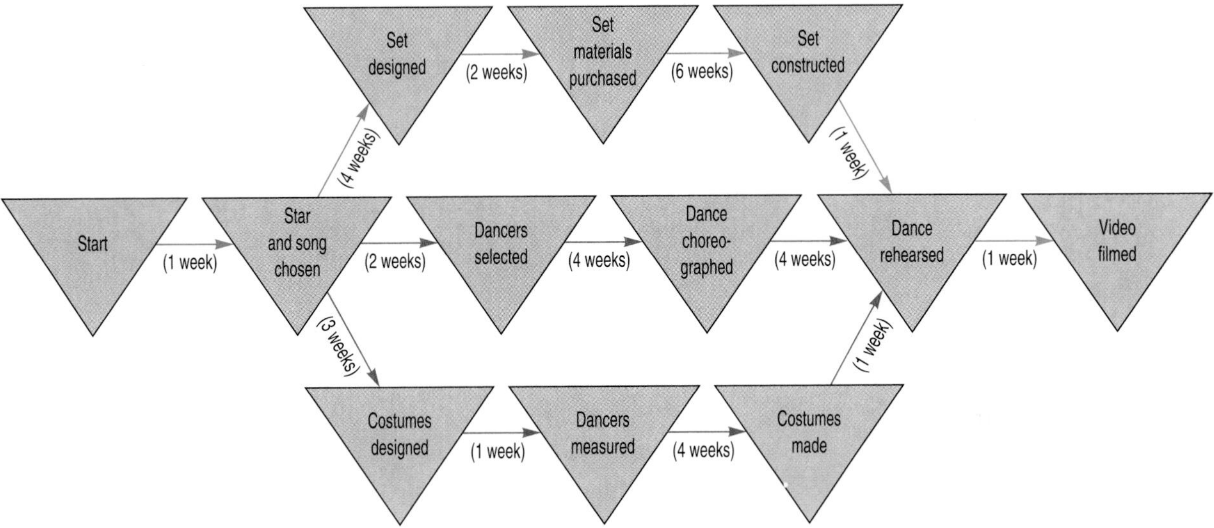

auditioning dancers and choreographing dances or designing and making costumes. The project manager now knows that it is critical that set construction remain on schedule if the project is to be completed on time, but short delays in the dance and costume preparation should not affect the total project.

A PERT network can be made up of thousands of events over many months. Today, this complex procedure is done by computer.

Another basic strategy used by manufacturers for measuring production progress is a Gantt chart (named after its developer, Henry L. Gantt). The **Gantt chart** is a bar graph that clearly shows what projects are being worked on and how much has been completed (on a daily basis). Figure 9–5 shows a Gantt chart for a doll manufacturer. The chart shows that the dolls' heads and bodies should be completed before the clothing is sewn. It also shows that at the end of week 3, the dolls' bodies are ready, but the heads are about half a week behind. All of this was once done by hand. Now the computer has taken over.

Gantt chart
Bar graph showing production managers what projects are being worked on and what stage they are in on a daily basis.

PROGRESS CHECK

- What is the difference between using a production line and producing products using modular units? Which is more flexible? Which offers more challenge to workers?
- What is the difference between CAD/CAM and computer-integrated manufacturing (CIM)?
- Could you draw a PERT chart for making a breakfast of three-minute eggs, buttered toast, and coffee? Which process would be the critical path, the longest process? How could you use a Gantt chart to keep track of production?

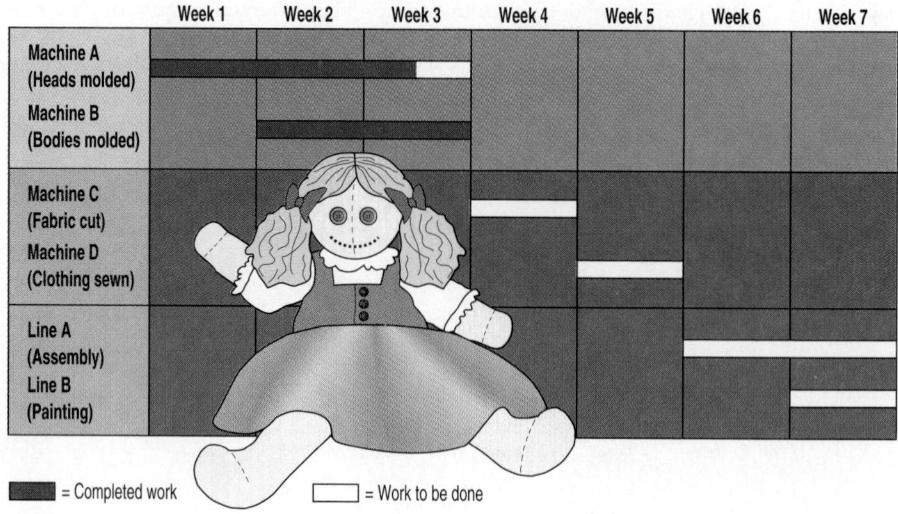

Figure 9–5 Gantt chart for a doll manufacturer. A Gantt chart enables a production manager to see at a glance when projects are scheduled to be completed and what their status now is. For example, the dolls' heads and bodies should be completed before the clothing is sewn, but could be a little late, as long as everything is ready for assembly in week 6. This chart shows that at the end of week 3, the dolls' bodies are ready, but the heads are about half a week behind.

PEOPLE PROBLEMS ON THE PLANT FLOOR

With all of this talk of automation and computers, it is easy to get the idea that using machine-centered production like CIM is the only remedy for improving ailing productivity levels. Recent studies by Ernst & Young indicate that the manufacturing companies that did the best job were those that had a heavy people orientation as well. They call it human-integration manufacturing (HIM).[19]

It is important to remember that production is still dependent on people, and it will be people who will determine the success or failure of future systems. Several steps must occur before people and machines will be combined to revolutionize manufacturing:

- There is an obvious need to train future production workers in the use and repair of computers, robots, and automatic machinery.
- Today's production workers must be retrained or relocated to adapt to the new high-tech systems.
- Major adjustments must be made in the relationships between suppliers and producers to implement concepts such as just-in-time inventory programs and enterprise networking.
- Production managers must be retrained to deal with more highly skilled workers who require a much more participative managerial style.
- Employees must be trained to work in teams and to understand the concepts of competing in time, total quality, and continuous improvement.

THINKING IT THROUGH

Try to imagine working in a factory where all the "dirty" jobs are being done by robots and other machines and employees work behind computer terminals. Is this your idea of what a factory looks like? Can you imagine how the people feel who are working in factories as these changes are introduced?

What are some of the ways technology could affect higher education? What will be the role of videotape recorders, computers, and interactive TV? How will this affect the cost of college tuition? Can you imagine your teacher being replaced by a VCR and an interactive computer? Can your teacher imagine that?

PRODUCTION AND OPERATIONS MANAGEMENT IN THE 1990s

Regardless of whether you are managing a plant that manufactures automobiles, a service facility such as a Purolator unit, or a city government, there are certain concepts that the best organizations are now in the process of implementing. You were introduced to some of the changes in previous chapters. Now we can explore in more depth the following crucial changes in production and operations management:

1. Organizations are adopting a customer (client) orientation, both internally and externally, to a degree never before contemplated.
2. One of the primary battlegrounds in the 1990s is the concept of competing in time. Tardy competitors will be put out of business.
3. Total quality management is emphasized.
4. Focus is also on constant improvement. Everything that is done in the organization is subject to constant change and improvement to better meet the organizational goals.
5. Productivity has become a major issue.

All of these are vital and interdependent components of a well-managed, competitive company. Focusing on the customer is becoming an obsession. Why? Because the customer's requirements drive the whole machine. You must produce the highest-quality products and services that the customer wants and continually improve them. The customer expects the lowest possible price (thus the drive for ever-greater productivity) and on-time delivery. If any of these components is weak, the company's competitive position is endangered.

Governments and non-profit organizations are moving in the same direction. Tight budgetary conditions in Canada are forcing all such organizations to become more efficient, while people are demanding better service—more *bang for their buck.*

We will now examine each of these components of competitiveness and look at some Canadian and other examples of how they are being implemented.

External and Internal Customer Orientation

An external customer orientation means finding customer wants and needs and meeting them better than anyone else does. An *internal* customer orientation means that each department that serves another department in a firm will treat the department being served as a valued customer. The needs of the department being served will be determined and everything that can be done to promote service will be done. Each department must constantly improve its service to the other departments in the company until the "customer" (the department being served) is happy.

Competing in Time

Competing in time is essential to competing at all in a global marketplace. Getting your product to market before your competitors is essential today, particularly in the electronic sector. McKinsey & Co. estimates that going over budget by 50 percent to get the product out on time reduces profit 4 percent. However, staying on budget and getting the product out six months late reduces profit 33 percent. Speed is of the essence. Ford estimates that it must be 25 percent faster in creating new products to match the best.[20]

SPOTLIGHT ON SMALL BUSINESS

The Rolls-Royce of Auto Parts Scrapyards

The customer is in a rush. Quebec's legendary potholes have claimed a wheel on his 1989 Honda Civic, and he is desperate for a replacement. The request is no big deal for the uniformed saleswoman behind the counter in the neon-lit showroom of Pintendre Auto Inc. She calmly punches the make, model year, and coded part number into a computer terminal.

Within seconds, she confirms that, yes, Pintendre has a dozen such wheels in its vast stock of used parts. The screen flashes the range of prices and conditions—as well as the location of each wheel on Pintendre's rambling premises. It's another small coup for Quebec's largest used auto parts dealer, whose stock in trade is as much information and inventory control as crankshafts and oil pans.

In layperson's language, Pintendre Auto is a scrapyard. But Francis Carrier, founder and president of this $16-million-a-year business, bristles at any suggestion that he is a mere scrap dealer. For the past 20 years, this distributor of used auto, truck, and motorcycle components has pioneered notions of service, technology, and strategic alliance in an industry with a seedy, backward image.

"Our aim from the start was to change the image of recycling," says Carrier, 52, a former insurance adjuster who founded Pintendre in 1972 with his brother Bruno and friend Emilie Couture. The trio took over a collection of horse stables in Pintendre, across the St. Lawrence River from Quebec City.

Back then, scrap dealers knew what they had in stock only by scouring unsightly fields full of rusted cars behind their shops. Today, Pintendre's converted stables contain a flexible information system that tracks and manages an inventory of more than 200,000 parts.

Employees—160 in all—handle up to 2,500 telephone requests a day. They know at the touch of a button what's in stock, what they can sell and for how much, and what they need to stock up on. Carrier figures he has spent about $1 million in computer hardware and software since 1978. "Without the computers, it would be hell," he confesses during a tour of his 51-hectare "recycling centre." He adds that "people often ask what I would buy first if I were just starting out. It would be a computer—not a building, not a tow truck."

Bolstered by such technology, Pintendre can offer fast and reliable service: 24-hour delivery anywhere in the province. And it guarantees everything it sells. Customers such as Pierre Mayrand, purchasing manager at a major Quebec City auto body shop, say the quality of Pintendre's parts and service keeps them coming back. "We order a side panel or a door in the morning and we get it in the afternoon," says Mayrand, who works for Michel Potvin Carossier.

In their book *Competing against Time,* Tom Hout and George Stalk, Jr., describe that 0.05 to 5 rule: "Most products and many services are actually receiving value [something is actually happening to them] for only 0.05 to 5 percent of the time they are in the systems of their companies."[21] For example, a manufacturer may take 45 days to get a special-order car to a buyer, but it takes only 16 hours to assemble the car. Hout and Stalk say we routinely waste 95 percent of our time, and 99.5 percent is not unusual. That gives us lots of opportunity for improvement!

Total Quality Management

quality control
The measurement of products and services against set standards.

total quality management (TQM)
Satisfying customers by building in and ensuring quality from all departments in an organization.

Quality control is the measurement of products and services against set standards. Previously, quality control was often done at the end of the production line by a quality control department. Today, things have changed.

Total quality management (TQM) means satisfying customers by building in and ensuring quality from product planning to production, purchasing, sales, and service. Emphasis is placed on customer satisfaction and the fact that quality is the concern of everyone, not just the quality control people at the end of the assembly line. In TQM, the structure is so organized that everybody contributes to quality improvement as part of their job.

Remember that the purpose of quality goods and services is to make the consumer happy. So a TQM program begins by analyzing the consumer to see what

SPOTLIGHT ON SMALL BUSINESS (*concluded*)

Such attention to detail is impressive, considering the volumes. The company buys up to 6,500 cars a year, nearly a fifth of the total destroyed on Quebec roads. Those that can be repaired are sold at the company's used-car lot down the street.

Every morning, an inspector drives a pickup truck through the huge lot to inspect the previous day's arrivals. He gives the cars a cursory inspection, checks the condition of major parts, and applies a separate eight-digit code to as many as 16 large parts on each car. He punches the information into a laptop computer so the sales staff has a quick snapshot of what's in the lot.

On a weekly basis, the eight-employee computer department calls up a software program that sets the work schedule for the body shop. Based on recent sales and a review of its inventory, it will designate 75 to 100 cars for dismantling. At this point, the company's mechanics do a more thorough inspection to identify salvageable parts, estimate the work required to refurbish them, and grade them for quality. That information is immediately logged in one of the company's 70 computer terminals to let salespeople know what's in stock.

The company's 134,000-square-foot warehouse is impressive, but Carrier says the key is to keep it stocked with parts that turn over quickly. Some low-demand cars are not dismantled until a customer comes looking for one of their parts.

An auto contains as many as 450 identifiable parts—everything from complete front ends to ashtrays. Those that Pintendre feels it can use are cleaned, repaired (when necessary), catalogued, and carefully stored in one of its several buildings. The inventory does not hold parts from cars more than 10 years old. Those are immediately resold as scrap metal or sometimes sent as far away as Mexico and the Netherlands, where older cars are still on the road.

Carrier won't divulge the company's profits, but he said its margins are well above the industry average. Pintendre sells its used parts for a quarter to half the price of new parts.

Last year, its thousands of customers—car owners, dealers, garages and body shops—bought 69,200 car parts, including 6,200 wheels, 1,979 doors, 1,800 gas tanks, 1,240 engines and 1,400 radiators. The volumes suggest customers are more likely to find what they need here than just about anywhere else.

Some may also be drawn by the business's outlandish appearance. To drive home his service message, Carrier has styled the front facade of his two-storey warehouse and showroom in the shape of a Rolls-Royce car, complete with headlights, silver grille, and hood ornament. Kitschy perhaps, but it leaves visitors with the clear—and entirely accurate—impression that this is no ordinary scrapyard.

Source: Barrie McKenna, "More Than the Sum of Its Parts," *Globe and Mail,* February 23, 1993, p. B24. ▼

quality standards need to be established. Quality is then designed into products, and every product must meet those standards every step of the production process.[22]

Total quality management in an organization means:[23]

1. Quality is a companywide process involving everyone from the president to the lowest-level employees.
2. Quality does not mean higher cost; doing things right the first time results in *less* cost.
3. Quality involves both individual workers and teams of workers; it has to be part of the corporate culture.
4. Quality improvement is continuous improvement, and that means empowering employees to implement quality changes on a constant or regular basis. Quality and innovation are mutually dependent. The best-quality obsolete product will not sell.
5. Quality must be a part of the total system, involving suppliers, distributors, repair facilities, and all other organizations that affect consumer satisfaction.

Quality and quality control have been hot topics in Canadian manufacturing management since the mid-1980s. The pressure on Canadian and American companies to pay more attention to quality arose primarily from the superiority of Japanese automobiles, electronics, and other products. What happens if we accept 99.9 percent quality instead of 100 percent quality is illustrated in Fig. 9–6.

Figure 9–6 Why zero defects?
One aspect of TQM is making the product or service with zero defects. What happens when you have only 99.9 percent quality rather than 100 percent?

99.9 percent quality would yield:

In Medicine

50 newborn babies would die daily.
500 faulty surgical procedures would be performed weekly.
20,000 drug prescriptions would be improperly filled annually.

In the Postal Service

16,000 pieces of mail would be lost hourly.

Source: M. E. Mengelsdorf, "Why 99.9 Percent Won't Do," *Inc.*, April 1989, p. 26.

As more consumers turned away from the Big Three auto makers and started buying Toyotas, Hondas, Nissans, and other Japanese products they found to be more reliable and less costly, North American producers were forced to sit up and take notice. It is ironic that it was Edwards Deming, an American ignored by U.S. companies, who went to Japan in 1950 to sell his ideas there. The Japanese became very enthusiastic about his emphasis on the importance of quality and how to achieve quality control. Today, the most prestigious prize in Japan, awarded annually to the company judged to have produced the highest-quality products, is called the Deming Award. This elder statesman of production, born in 1900, now lectures tirelessly in North America, stressing that our quality is just not good enough.

Traditionally, our manufacturing system had a quality inspector at the end of the production process who was supposed to reject all the units that did not meet quality standards. Deming taught that quality had to be built right into the production process so that there would be no rejects at the end. We have finally begun to listen him, but the transition to this new philosophy is difficult. Let's have a look at what Deming's system consists of.

> Deming aims his sharpest barbs at top management for not paying attention to quality, especially statistical methods for quality assurance. His recipe for quality control is deceptively simple: tally defects, examine them to find their source, correct the cause, and then keep a record of what happens afterward. He preaches that statistical analysis, not investments in equipment and automation, is the way for America to garner the gains the Japanese have enjoyed, offering the following advice to do so:
>
> - Rely on statistical evidence of quality *during* the process, not at the end of the process. The earlier an error is caught, the less it costs to correct it.
> - Rely on suppliers that have historically provided quality, not on sampling inspections to determine the quality of each delivery. Instead of a number of vendors, select and stick with a few sources that furnish consistently satisfactory quality.
> - Rely on training and retraining to give employees the skills to use statistical methods in their jobs, not on slogans to improve quality. Employees should feel free to report any conditions that detract from quality.
> - Rely on supervision guided by statistical methods to help people do their work better, not on production work standards. Statistical techniques detect the sources of waste and teams of designers, supervisors, and workers eliminate the sources.

- Rely on the doctrine that poor quality is unacceptable. Defective materials, workmanship, products, and service will not be tolerated.

> According to the Deming philosophy, there is little use in exhorting hourly workers to improve quality, because they do not control the resources needed to do it, such as tools, materials, scheduling, and facilities. Management controls the resources, and 85 percent of all quality problems originate in the system itself, not from the workers. The other 15 percent result from special causes, such as defective tools and negligent acts. Deming placed the responsibility for improvement squarely on management, believing that when managers remove the barriers that stand between hourly workers and their right to pride of workmanship, quality soon surfaces.[24]

Today, TQM has become a major concentration in service and manufacturing companies. Case 2 at the end of this chapter presents some examples of Canadian companies that are not enthused about TQM or see it as just a new name for existing practices. Like every new idea, TQM must be carefully studied and applied if it is to have a chance of succeeding. As you can see from Deming's list, it is not easy to institute his system without total, long-term commitment by the entire management team from the president down. TQM will not work if a company is looking for a quick fix with some new fad.

Quality Circles

A technique that was first developed in Sweden to relieve the boredom of assembly-line work is quality circles. They have become quite popular in Japan. According to a Japanese magazine, in a **quality circle,** "a small group voluntarily perform[s] quality control activities within the workshop to which they belong. This small group, with every member [fully] participating, carries on continuously, within the workshop, utilizing quality control techniques, self-development, and mutual-development work, as part of companywide control activities."

quality circle
A small group whose members voluntarily perform quality control activities within the workshop to which they belong.

The number of Japanese workers engaged in quality control circles in 1982 was estimated to be over 5 million in some 56,000 circles. Observers of Japanese productivity growth attribute much of this well-known success story to the "morale-, skill-, and quality-building benefits of QC circles."[25]

Quality circles have so far met mixed results in North America. Nevertheless, companies continue to establish them. Hydro-Quebec, inspired by the enthusiasm for them at Florida Light & Power, a utility of comparable size, has been pushing ahead with its quality circles. In the meantime, its model in Florida has decided to cut back on this program after several years of apparently successful results.

Continuous Improvement

In the 1990s, it will not be enough to institute quality programs and advanced production techniques and then sit back and admire what the organization has done. To stay competitive an organization must train its employees in continuous improvement. **Continuous improvement (CI)** works just like it sounds—the company is set up to ensure and inspire constant creative interaction. No matter what your job, finding better ways to do things must become a daily requirement. Fresh ideas are now one of the most valued raw materials, and the continued success of any endeavour will depend on a high level of creative alertness and innovative problem solving.[26]

continuous improvement (CI)
Procedures designed to inspire constant creative interaction and problem solving.

REACHING BEYOND OUR BORDERS

How a Quebec Bathtub Company Competes in the U.S. and Overseas

Dagmar Egerer has marketed condos in Spain, peddled Maple Leaf gold coins in Belgium, and worked for a hotel chain in Lebanon and Iran. But Egerer, now U.S. sales manager for Maax Inc., a Quebec bathtub and shower manufacturer, has rarely faced as persnickety a customer as Home Depot Inc., a U.S. building supplies retailer.

One of her jobs is to make sure Maax's bathtubs and showers show up on time at Home Depot's New England outlets. When the giant chain says the period from order to delivery is 18 days, it means 18, not 17 or 19.

The bathtubs aren't shipped to some convenient central warehouse, but to widely scattered stores as far as 900 kilometres from Maax's factory. Egerer and her colleagues perform somersaults to arrange trucking schedules. What's more, Home Depot's obsession with defect-free products means Maax must package each fibreglass shower in a box to avoid mishaps in transit. Maax doesn't mind the aggravation, Egerer insists. "They (Home Depot) don't want to lose a sale so they push us."

The wooing, winning, and servicing of Home Depot is a big coup for little Maax, which has annual sales of $21 million and is located 30 minutes south of Quebec City. It has secured a toehold with the largest U.S. warehouse retailer of building materials, whose 194 monster outlets gross $5.4 billion (U.S.) annually.

After filling in two years ago as an emergency supplier of fibreglass showers for two stores, Maax is now shipping to 34 Home Depot outlets in the U.S. Northeast, as far away as Maryland. Home Depot is its third largest customer, accounting for 15 percent of sales. Maax's U.S. sales grew 58 percent in the six months to August 31, [1992], compared with a year ago.

By plugging into Home Depot, Maax joins the ranks of masochistic suppliers who thrive on being abused by tough customers. In the United States, companies that sell to Wal-Mart Stores have to be bent on self-improvement.

Soft-hearted clients are no good for succeeding in the global competitive game, argues Michael Porter, the Harvard University professor and authority on competitive advantage. "A demanding market, rather than a welcoming or easy-to-serve one, is what underpins success," he wrote in a 1991 report for the federal government. (See Chapter 2).

With today's emphasis on just-in-time delivery and customer service, suppliers are increasingly judged by their logistical capability. That means delivering long distances in the right time, quantity, and quality.

To complicate matters, Maax fills every truck before it's sent out to minimize transport costs. A typical order might include shipments to two Long Island, N.Y., outlets and to one in Connecticut. One Long Island store may set a delivery time for midnight while the other, only 20 kilometres away, may insist on 10 hours later. The traffic manager has to juggle to minimize truckers' down time.

It is one thing to *talk* about continuous improvement; it is quite another to truly implement such procedures in an organization. One consulting firm created all kinds of disruption by asking people after every consulting job whether or not any aspect could be improved. Everyone could think of *something* that could have been done better, and morale dropped as the focus shifted from the success of the job to the problems. You can see the problem of constantly being critical of what you're doing.

It is better, in a CI program, to focus on less personal things such as waste. Some sources of waste are unnecessary motion, excessive transportation to and from stockrooms, searching for misplaced items, time-consuming set-up procedures, excessive inspection of incoming materials and finished goods, and high levels of inventory. Obvious forms of waste are scrap and rework.

Continuous improvement demands a great deal of employee training. One-shot training sessions aren't enough. They're like escaping into a cool swimming pool when the temperature outside is 105 and the humidity is 90 percent. You feel great. Then you step out, dry off, and an hour later you feel just as miserable as you did before. To have a lasting effect, training has to be long term.

The major Japanese companies have made a fetish of continuous (or incremental) improvement. Using the procedures outlined earlier, they have gained enor-

REACHING BEYOND OUR BORDERS (*concluded*)

Adaptability is also the rule on the factory floor, a beehive of activity where the lung-searing smell of resin is pervasive. The sheer bulk of the products and frequent changes in models have so far discouraged much automation (Maax has only one robot). But Placide Poulin, president and major shareholder, says the just-in-time demands of customers force more flexible production.

Take thermoforming, the process whereby a sheet of acrylic is heated and then drawn by a vacuum to form the shape of the tub or shower. The existing thermoformers require two to seven hours for a mould change. With 18 models of tubs and showers available, the loss of precious time is immense. So employees have ordered a new thermoformer of their own design that will be able to handle two different models at the same time and can continue operating while the moulds are being changed.

This eagerness to please is paying dividends. Home Depot recently agreed to stock Maax's higher-end acrylic tubs and showers, as well as its lower-value fibreglass lines. It wasn't an easy sell, because acrylic is luxury for practical do-it-yourselfers. The stores already carried acrylic products from another supplier. But last May, a Home Depot buyer requested a "real good price" on a five-foot acrylic whirlpool tub. Egerer came up with a number and the chain ordered a thousand.

With this big order, Maax could bargain harder with its own suppliers for inputs such as whirlpool pumps. The first tubs carried a retail price of $391, a few hundred dollars cheaper than the competition. Home Depot has since made a repeat order.

In time, Maax would like to manufacture in the United States to overcome high transportation costs and to expand markets beyond the Northeast. Poulin is on the acquisition trail. Meanwhile, Egerer is looking ahead to next year, when she will service three Home Depots about 1,000 kilometres away. "I'll find a way of going there. You don't say no to Home Depot," she says.

But there is a risk of becoming too dependent on one big account that could suddenly be snatched away. Egerer is comfortable with Home Depot's 15 percent of sales, but at 20 percent, she'd start to feel vulnerable. Maax's answer is to expand the business elsewhere at the same time. Already strong in Quebec, Maax is working to increase market share in Ontario and abroad. It sells to Hong Kong and Saudi Arabia and is close to a deal in France.

But after dancing to Home Depot's tune, these forays may not seem all that intimidating. "They've got to be learning," says George Dellon, Maax's agent to Home Depot in metropolitan New York. "They're interfacing with the premier building material business in the world. They're getting an education."

Source: Alan Freeman, "Company Enjoys a 'Shower' of Business," Classroom Edition, *Globe and Mail,* January 1993, p. 16.

▼

mous competitive advantage. The movement is catching on in Canada too. The three companies spotlighted in this chapter all practise it. Meat-packer Schneider Corp. of Kitchener, Ontario, attributes its success in overcoming difficult adjustments to market changes to CI.[27] Another Canadian enthusiast for CI is PanCanadian Petroleum Ltd., which has been applying it in engineering and production.

> Two years into CI, PanCanadian smells a winner. The program has moved in-house, with a squad of company coaches taking over from the TeamPro consultants. Plans are afoot to introduce it into the finance department and to create work teams from different departments.
>
> The early experiments uncapped a vast reserve of creativity. The next step is to give this force some direction without slipping back into the old autocratic style.[28]

PRODUCTIVITY IN THE SERVICE SECTOR

The greatest productivity problem in Canada may not be the goods-producing sector of the economy but in the service sector. Seven of 10 jobs in Canada are already in the service sector, with more to come. A truly strong economy, therefore, has to be as progressive in introducing the latest technology to services as it is in manufacturing.

Automated bank machines make banking services more efficient. It is difficult to measure the productivity increases they cause. Therefore, service productivity lags behind manufacturing productivity even through services are improving dramatically. We may need a different measure of service productivity to account for convenience or happiness.

One reason service productivity lags behind manufacturing is that services are more labour intensive, or "people dependent." That is, factories can more readily substitute machines for people and thus get more output from the remaining people. A myth has persisted that no machine can replace people in services such as banking, insurance, education, medicine, and consulting. Many people still think that it takes a mechanic to figure out what is wrong with a car and that offices need people.

Well, a job in the service sector is no longer a safe haven from automation. Some say there will always be jobs for good secretaries. Maybe. However, there won't be many such jobs. As you know, easy-to-use desktop publishing software, low-cost laser printers, optical scanners, and facsimile machines are flooding offices. As these machines become more common, more secretarial jobs will go.[29]

Technology is not always the best answer to increasing productivity in the service sector. Don't fall into the trap of thinking technology will make all things perfect. Left to their own devices, computers can be "dangerously productive." They can produce reams of information. A lot of that information may be unnecessary and may actually create *more* work. (See Appendix B, at end of chapter.)

Clever companies like IBM, Motorola, and Corning have made great progress in increasing white-collar productivity. These companies didn't blindly computerize office work; they re-engineered it. As Carla Paonessa, a partner at Andersen Consulting, puts it: "Just automating something that shouldn't have been done manually won't get you to be more productive. What will work is eliminating bottlenecks, reducing mistakes, focusing on customer service, and then, and only then, introducing new technology."[30]

Computers are only the beginning of improving service-sector productivity. Think about labour-intensive businesses like McDonald's and Burger King. Automation plays a big role in controlling costs and improving service. Today you go to Burger King, order your meal, get your food, and fill your own drink cup. Because the people working at the drive-up window now wear headsets instead of using stationary mikes, they aren't glued to one spot anymore and can do four or five tasks while taking an order.

Today, salespeople can carry their offices with them wherever they go. New laptop computers link them with the home office. Cellular phones keep them in touch with customers. All of this adds to their productivity and effectiveness.

Most of us have been exposed to similar productivity gains in banking. For example, people in many towns no longer have to wait in long lines for harassed tellers to help them deposit and withdraw money. Instead, they use automated bank machines that take a few seconds and are available 24 hours a day.

Another service that was once annoyingly slow was the checkout counter at the grocery. The new system of marking goods with universal product codes enables computerized checkout and allows cashiers to be much more productive.

Airlines represent another service industry that is experiencing tremendous productivity increases through the use of computers for everything from processing reservations to the heavy use of prepackaged meals on board to more standardization of all movements of luggage, passengers, and so on.[31]

There is some evidence that productivity in the service sector is rising, but there is simply no means to measure it. The *quality* of service is greatly improving, but quality is difficult to measure. The traditional way to measure productivity involves tracking inputs (worker-hours) compared to outputs (units-dollars). Assessing service work in that way can lead to some absurd results. For example, before Motorola changed its policy, the goal of the employee recruiting department was to spend less per person it hired each year. Productivity went up without regard to the quality of the people who joined the company. "If you hired an idiot for 39 cents you would meet your goal," says Motorola quality manager Bill Smith. Now Motorola measures the recruiters by how well recruits do on the job. Were they qualified or did they need a lot of retraining? Were they hired at the right salary level or did another company lure them away with a higher salary six months later?[32]

THINKING IT THROUGH

What other service organizations might be changed dramatically by the new technological revolution? Think of the effects on insurance companies, government services, stockbrokers, educational institutions, and hospitals.

PREPARING FOR THE FUTURE

What does all this mean to you? It means that university and college graduates of the future will have marvellous new technological advances available to them. It means new opportunities and a higher standard of living and quality of life. But it also means preparing for these opportunities.

Clearly, the workplace is already dominated by an impressive array of computer hardware that is getting progressively smaller, cheaper, and more powerful. A bewildering variety of software to make use of this growing capability is opening up an incredible world of high technology. Cellular phones, faxes, and modems are advancing in similar fashion.

If all of this sounds terribly cold and impersonal, you recognize one of the needs of the future. People will need much more human contact outside the work environment. There will be new demands for recreation, social clubs, travel, and other diversions. The Canada of the next century will be radically different from the Canada of today. It will take both technically trained people and people skilled in human relationships to guide us through the transition.

Many universities offer courses in manufacturing management and robotics. Some require such courses for an M.B.A. degree. Many have research programs in robotics and intelligent machines. McGill University and the University of Toronto, for example, have substantial research centres. These centres often maintain close relations with industry and do contract work for companies. McGill's clients include such major companies as CAE, Hydro-Quebec and SPAR Aerospace. SPAR developed the robotic arm for U.S. space vehicles, the Canadarm.

The trend is towards making production and operations management courses a requisite for graduate degrees in management. Such courses, in combination with those on organizational behaviour, train students to manage the high-tech workers and managers of the new era. Emphasis is on participative management and the design of a work environment suitable to the new conditions of the 1990s and into the next century. A new era is opening up for both manufacturing and the service sector. There will be many exciting, challenging careers in this field.

PROGRESS CHECK

- The text lists five things that total quality management means. Can you remember all five?
- What are the advantages and potential problems with implementing a continuous improvement program in an organization?
- Why does service productivity seem to lag behind industrial productivity, and what can be done about it?

SUMMARY

1. Describe the role of Canada's manufacturing base in the national economy.

1. Manufacturing has always been the heart of modern economies. After a period of decline, manufacturing is coming back into the forefront in competitiveness. Production and operations managers will play a major role in helping Canada remain a major industrial country.

- *What is production and operations management?*

  Production and operations management is all the activities managers do to create goods and services.

2. Production uses inputs to produce outputs.

▼ *What are these inputs and outputs?*

The inputs of the production process include land, labour, capital, entrepreneurship, and information. The outputs are the products and services that the manipulation of these inputs produces.

▼ *What does form utility have to do with production?*

Production adds form utility—the value added by the creation of finished goods and services from raw materials, components, and other inputs.

2. Illustrate the production process and explain the importance of productivity.

3. Productivity requires keeping costs low and output high.

▼ *How can producers keep costs low?*

The first step in cutting costs is to *select a site:* near inexpensive, trained, or trainable labour; with cheap basic resources (water, electricity, etc.); close to customers; with low taxes and local government support; where land and transportation are available and inexpensive; and where the quality of life and education is high.

3. Identify the various methods manufacturers can use to keep costs at a minimum.

4. Manufacturers can use several different processes to make products.

▼ *What are these processes?*

These processes include synthetic systems (process manufacturing and assembly process) and analytic systems. The systems can be continuous or intermittent.

▼ *What indicators can manufacturers use to see whether or not they can meet their goals?*

The five indicators are (1) sales forecast, (2) raw material inventory, (3) equipment, (4) manpower, and (5) quality.

4. Classify the various production processes and identify the five indicators manufacturers can use to determine the likelihood of meeting their production goals.

5. Materials requirement planning (MRP) uses sales forecasts to make sure that needed parts and materials are available at the right time and place.

▼ *What is just-in-time (JIT) inventory?*

JIT is arrangement for delivery of the smallest possible quantities at the latest possible time to keep inventory as low as possible.

▼ *What problems can develop with JIT?*

The major problem for users of JIT is that they have no back-up inventory in case the suppliers can't or don't deliver the required parts on time. Good relationships with reliable suppliers are essential for an efficient JIT inventory system.

5. Describe the importance of materials requirement planning and discuss the benefits and problems of just-in-time inventory control.

6. Many new techniques are being used to make production more efficient (less expensive).

▼ *What are some of these techniques?*

New production techniques include computer-aided design (CAD), computer-aided manufacturing (CAM), computer-aided acquisition and logistics support (CALS), computer-aided engineering (CAE), computer-integrated manufacturing (CIM), flexible manufacturing systems (FMS), design for manufacturability and assembly (DFMA), and networking with suppliers and customers.

6. Describe the changes in manufacturing processes, including the use of CAD, CAM, CALS, CAE, CIM, FMS, DFMA, and enterprise networking.

7. It is important that project managers be sure their products are produced on time.

▼ *What procedures can managers use to plan the timing of their projects?*

Two procedures include PERT and Gantt charts. PERT is a method of analyzing what tasks need to be done, determining how long each task will take, and identifying the earliest date a project can be finished. The critical path indicates the longest series of steps in the process. A Gantt chart is simply a bar graph that shows what projects are being worked on and how much has been completed on a daily basis. Both procedures are rarely done by hand today, thanks to computers.

7. Illustrate the use of PERT and Gantt charts in production planning.

8. In spite of technological advances, production still depends on people.

▼ *What must happen before the combination of people and machines can revolutionize manufacturing?*

Workers need to be trained to use and repair computers; suppliers and producers must develop strong relationships to implement such concepts as JIT and enterprise

8. Identify the steps that must occur before people and machines will be combined to revolutionize manufacturing.

networking; and production managers need to develop more participative managerial styles in order to work with highly skilled workers.

9. Major changes are occurring in the 1990s in production and operations management.

9. Describe the changes in production and operations management that are taking place in this decade.

▼ *What are five of these changes in production and operations management?*

In the 1990s, production and operations management will focus on (1) competing in time, (2) satisfying both internal and external customers, (3) emphasizing total quality management, (4) training employees in continuous improvement, and (5) increasing productivity.

10. Because Canada is a service society now, automation of the service sector is extremely important.

10. Suggest how the service sector might increase productivity through automation.

▼ *Why is service productivity not increasing as rapidly as manufacturing productivity?*

One important reason is that the service sector is labour intensive. Keep in mind that productivity and quality *are* rising in the service sector, but they are more difficult to measure than outputs of the industrial sector.

GETTING INVOLVED

1. Find the latest articles on computer-integrated manufacturing and enterprise networking. Which companies are making the greatest advances towards having integrated networks? What companies have installed the systems? Share your articles with the class. If everyone brings in one article, you should have quite a collection for your file on the industrial sector.
2. Review all the terms in this chapter: CAD, CAM, CIM, MRP, JIT, FMS, and so on. These are the business terms of the 1990s. Try to use them in class so that they become familiar in different settings. Soon you will be thinking of new ways to advance business yourself, based on your understanding of these terms.
3. Have the class brainstorm all of the applications of high technology in the service sector that have already occurred. Using this information, brainstorm further uses of technology in areas such as recreation, travel, retailing, wholesaling, insurance, banking, finance, and the government.
4. Debate the following proposition: "The federal government should become more involved in the future of Canadian industry through a national industrial policy." Take whichever side of the issue you did not previously agree with, to broaden your thinking on this issue.
5. Debate the following proposition: "Canadian manufacturers should halt the spread of computers and robots used in manufacturing to save jobs for Canadian workers." Again, take the other side of this issue from your normal position.

PRACTICING MANAGEMENT DECISIONS

Case One The Automation of General Motors

No firm is more committed to computerizing production than General Motors. GM invested $8 billion in its Saturn plant in Tennessee. Saturn provides 6,000 jobs in the plant and 10,000 more in nearby facilities. Here are some of the impacts of plants such as Saturn.

In the near future you will be able to go into a GM dealer and order a car, including colours, optional equipment, financing arrangements, and delivery date—all at a computer terminal. The computer will translate your order into parts orders. Radios, air conditioners, tires, and thousands of other parts will be ordered from suppliers all over the world. Computer-designed inventory control will allow just-in-time delivery to the production floor. From order to delivery could take less than two weeks.

Meanwhile, at the factory the car is designed and built using computer-aided design and manufacturing. Robots do much of the assembling and moving of parts. Workers are not on assembly lines; rather, they work in small groups (modules) to build subassemblies. Parts are tested in the modules as part of quality control. The robots and computers are able to "talk" to each other, and control systems catch flaws almost immediately. Productivity in some areas has increased by 800 percent.

Workers are paid a salary, not an hourly wage. There are no more than six job categories, and each worker does a wider variety of work. Workers have a much larger say in how jobs are performed and at what pace. They don't punch a time clock. Employees choose their co-workers. If they get tired of doing one job, they can ask their boss for a transfer. As part of frequent morale-boosting programs, employees have an outdoor obstacle course for off hours.

The whole plant is virtually paperless. Everything from order forms to engineering drawings is on computers. Computer specialists linked the system into computer-integrated manufacturing. When a car is ordered, computers begin designing an inventory of spark plugs, air filters, and other parts to send to automobile dealerships to service the cars for the foreseeable future.

General Motors of Canada, the largest company in Canada by revenues, invested $8 billion in the 1980s modernizing its Canadian manufacturing facilities. Its ultramodern Oshawa Autoplex factory has become one of the largest car-assembly plants in the world. No car factory in the U.S. can compare to its combination of technological advancement and size.

The plant can turn out 730,000 cars and trucks a year from production lines where whirring automatic vehicles carry cars from one robot's work station to the next.

Decision Questions

1. The plants in Tennessee and Oshawa, Ontario, are GM's way of fighting back from some disastrous years. Do you think these are models of production and operations that Canadian companies will have to follow to be world-class competitors? Explain.
2. How will such automated, employee-centred manufacturing operations affect the job market in Canada in the 1990s? What about the number of jobs? The skills and education required?
3. What is the impact of such plants on suppliers and dealers? What is the impact on unions in Canada?
4. Can you think of some other ramifications of such close computer linkage among customers, dealers, sales reps, suppliers, and plants? What effect might it have on quality control? Do you see other advantages or disadvantages of these developments?

Sources: Todd Smith, "Saturn Rings In with Local Dealer," *Washington Times,* April 3, 1991; "GM's Saturn Blends People with Technology Systems," *Tooling & Production,* October 1, 1990; Arthur Johnson, "The World's Biggest Comeback," *Report on Business Magazine, Globe and Mail* June 1989, p. 36.

Case Two Total Quality Management: Is It a Cure-All?

"The current rage for total quality management as a miracle cure-all has a lot of executives tearing their hair in exasperation." So says the *Globe and Mail* in a summary of its article on TQM. It then attempts to sort "through the facts and fiction of business's favourite fad." What is the problem?

In 1984, long before most Canadian companies had even heard of TQM, Culinar Inc. became the Canadian pioneer of TQM. Then CEO Roger Neron hired consultants and sent a key executive to "see what foreign companies were doing." They were hoping to "grab a larger piece of the North American snack food industry."

Today, the $587-million-a-year junk food giant has no formal TQM program at all. Jean-Rene Halde, appointed CEO in 1987, scratched it because it was "billed as the solution to all our problems but it was only one solution to *some* of them." Nobody will talk about it now at Culinar and "TQM has become a dirty acronym." They still use some TQM tools, such as statistical process control and business process redesign, but the "politically correct term for these activities is 'continuous improvement.' "

Apparently Culinar's story is not unusual. Florida Power & Light Co., winner of Japan's coveted Deming prize, has cut back on its quality program. After a scrutiny of companies in North America and Europe, McKinsey & Co. Inc., the giant international consulting firm, says "lack of results kills as many as two-thirds of TQM programs that are more than two years old." Similar results are reported from other large surveys in England and the U.S., which show that only one-third to one-fifth of companies report "tangible benefits" or "significant impact on their competitive positions" as a result of their TQM programs. Nevertheless, most claimed that they reaped some benefits.

Professor Henry Mintzberg of McGill's management faculty has done considerable research and writes often on management theory and practices. He says that any company that goes through the TQM exercise asking itself "Who are we? What is there in here for us? How can we adapt this to our needs?" will probably get some useful results. But any company that thinks that "all we've got to do is to plug this in" will "do worse than fail—it will make everyone cynical."

These sentiments are echoed by Yvan Allaire, a professor at the Universite du Quebec's school of management and chairman of strategy consultants Secor Groupe Inc. of Montreal. He says, "I'm critical of the sloganeering, the faddishness, the overblown expectations and the inevitable disappointments." He warns that TQM should not be seen as a cure-all that solves everything while producing better financial results.

Now that we have heard all the bad news, what do the proponents of TQM have to say? Plenty.

Supporters say that problems arise "from a lack of commitment, understanding, and patience on the part of CEOs." The article looks at three Canadian companies that have benefitted from TQM. Toronto-based Cadet Uniform Services Ltd. is a modest-sized organization with few management layers and sales of $30 million. Winnipeg's Reimer Express Lines Ltd. has sales of more than $250 million, 1,400 vehicles and 1,000 employees. It has a complex operation with facilities across the country. General Electric Canada Inc. has an aircraft-engine component plant in Bromont, Quebec, with 600 employees. Like Cadet, it has few layers of management.

Did these companies have anything in common that enabled them to adopt TQM successfully? All three had:

- Top executives who were highly committed to the program.
- Cultures that were inherently TQM-friendly. They possessed many TQM values and some of its practices.

Cadet and GE also had few layers of management and were of modest size. Reimer reorganized itself to act as if it were a group of smaller companies.

It seems all of these characteristics are necessary for a TQM program to succeed. President Quentin Wahl of Cadet, whose management style is democratic, encountered difficulties until he realized that TQM is not a management program but a "people" program that must involve all employees.

At GE, engineer Diane Buck, who is in charge of quality, says that TQM reminded employees when "people started to forget they were part of a larger entity whose interests superseded their own." At GE, quality and teamwork had always been stressed. This made adoption of TQM much easier.

At Reimer, quality manager John Perry says TQM is tough for service companies. "Management in the service sector tends to be people-driven, [but] it's a big change to go from looking for someone to blame to improving your systems." The company has benefitted enormously over a wide range of activities and Perry is now introducing TQM "to other companies in the Reimer transportation group."

All these companies persevered and their CEOs were strong supporters of TQM. They all favoured participative management. None of them was looking for a quick fix. Perhaps these are critical conditions for TQM to have a chance to succeed.

Decision Questions

1. The surveys of companies showed a low rate of success with TQM. Do you think that may be due to executives looking for results that will show up in their bottom line quickly? Is this part of a general problem of North American management's orientation towards too short a time frame? If so, what could be done about that?
2. Should TQM be applied very selectively? Should only companies with the "right" climate, as noted in the case, attempt to obtain its benefits?
3. Some managers claim that TQM is just a fancy name for practices they have always employed—concern with quality, participative style, teamwork, and so on. Does TQM heighten everyone's consciousness about these issues? Does it bring together under one umbrella various practices and thus help an organization to function better?
4. In the high-tech world of production and operations that now prevails, is there less need for TQM because fewer people are employed? Or is TQM even more important precisely because of this?

Source: Sandy Fife, "The Total Quality Muddle," *Report on Business Magazine, Globe and Mail* November 1992, p. 64ff.

LET'S TALK BUSINESS

1. What are the advantages and disadvantages of locating a manufacturing plant in Mexico? Which of the criteria for site selection does Mexico meet and not meet?
2. Imagine that Bombardier intends to go into the manufacturing of small, light planes. Discuss, using the following terms, how the company could develop a 21st-century plant: materials requirement planning, computer-integrated manufacturing, just-in-time inventory control, and flexible manufacturing systems.
3. Think of how you pictured a manufacturing plant before you read this chapter. Discuss how the plants described in this chapter differ from your picture.
4. Imagine that you are a production plant manager. You are interested in total quality. Go through a typical day and see how much time you waste getting ready for activities, waiting for activities to start, etc. How could you make that time more productive? How could you use continuous improvement to better the situation?
5. Discuss how you might improve the functioning of your municipal government. Think of the various services it provides: sidewalk and road maintenance, water supply, snow removal, welfare payments, garbage collection, tree planting, traffic control, police and fire protection services. How would you improve the quality of these services or increase productivity without any increase in costs? Could you even reduce costs while improving services?

LOOKING AHEAD

It is no accident that books like *In Search of Excellence* and *A Passion for Excellence* have been best-sellers in recent years. What these books emphasized was the need for businesses to work more closely with their customers, to listen, to be more responsive, and more innovative.

The key words are "responsive to the market." Business depends on customer relationships, and as with all relationships, customer relationships rely on open, two-way communication. The function responsible for market responsiveness and communication is marketing.

The next four chapters will explore all phases of marketing: product design, packaging, branding, pricing, distribution, promotion, retailing, and more. Marketing finds out what people want, and then communicates those wants to production so that the firm produces what people want. Marketing (listening) comes first in Chapter 10.

MANAGEMENT INFORMATION SYSTEMS

WHAT IS A MANAGEMENT INFORMATION SYSTEM?

Efficient operation of any organization—business, hospital, government department or college—requires a system of information that provides management with the basis for making decisions. Every organization, large or small, has developed some systematic way of collecting information about its activities.

A good Management Information System (MIS) provides *reliable, relevant* and *complete information* to the *right people* on a *timely* basis. For example, a sales manager who has responsibility for the province of Alberta must get accurate sales reports, say every Monday by 10 A.M., of sales and orders of the previous week from all areas of Alberta. To enable the manager to make useful decisions

1. *complete* information must be received from Alberta.
2. it must be *reliable, true* and *accurate.*
3. to be *relevant* the information must be sales and orders reports, for the previous week, from Alberta.
4. sales information must go to the *right person,* the sales manager.
5. reports must be received *on time*—Tuesday or Wednesday or even Monday afternoon would be much too late to address any weaknesses revealed by the reports.

The same holds true for the manager of any function in any kind of organization. Managerial decision making rests on interpreting information received regularly about past activities—daily, weekly, monthly, quarterly, or annually.

COMPUTERS AND MIS FOR LARGE ORGANIZATIONS

The advent of the computer age has completely altered the nature of MIS. The widespread use of personal computers (PCs), modems, and faxes has revolutionized the method and speed of information gathering and distribution. Before the 1980s, clerks had to examine books, records, and documents, prepare typed reports from these sources, and then have them delivered to the proper managers. If a special report was required, the manager would ask his or her secretary to get it. The secretary would contact the individual who was supposed to prepare the report, who would then proceed as the clerks would. This system was obviously slow and prone to many errors.

With a computer at every manager's desk linked to a company network, every manager now has direct access to all information and reports that are needed. The MIS is so set up that by pressing a few keys the manager can immediately get whatever report is required, in useful format.

As soon as a transaction is recorded—a sale, a purchase order, merchandise received, a cheque received or sent out—summaries and analyses of such transactions are immediately available to the appropriate manager. The information can be viewed on the monitor or printed out as hard copy. As long as all transactions are properly recorded, all reports based on them will automatically be accurate. Information can be summarized in many different ways and charts and graphs produced in seconds. The advantages of a computerized MIS are so enormous that companies quickly took advantage of this technology.

The development of laptop computers, faxes, and cellular phones has pushed the revolution in MIS even further. Airports, homes, cars, and planes are now portable offices. Communication has become so easy and inexpensive that there are almost no limits to receiving reports and giving instructions, no matter where the sender or receiver may be.

Setting up an MIS today for a large organization is a difficult, expensive, and time-consuming task. Planning must be done carefully to keep disruption to a minimum during the installation period. Even more important is the need to make sure the new MIS will function as expected. This is much more difficult than one might imagine. Normally, professional systems consultants are hired to work closely with company personnel and the vendors who supply the hardware. While selecting the right equipment is important, an even more difficult task is deciding on software, the specific programs that tell the computer what to do. There is a wide array of commercial software available, but software may also be customized for specific needs.

COMPUTERS AND MIS FOR SMALL COMPANIES

It is hard to find a company today, no matter how small, that is not using computers. One reason is that computer prices continue to decrease. As new models are introduced, prices of previous models drop sharply. There is also strong competition among hardware manufacturers and among software producers.

An MIS for a small company is usually a lot less complicated and expensive to plan, install, and operate than for a large organization. Large companies require an expensive and powerful *mainframe,* or central computer, to which individual terminals are connected to form a network. In small companies only a few PCs are required and the software is quite inexpensive. Of course, the same care must be taken in planning and implementing an MIS as in large organizations.

THE INFORMATION AGE AND GLOBALIZATION

The rapid explosion in communication technology (which is expected to accelerate even further) has given birth to the *information age*. Just as the production era gave way to the marketing era, which in turn was superseded by the financial era, information is now the magic resource for competitiveness.

In a time of the globalization of business, when national borders have less and less importance, business looks to the whole world to expand. Rapid, reliable transmission of information adds a competitive edge. It enables managers to get up-to-date, worldwide information about their own and competitors' activities and to react quickly. The information age lets managers translate appropriate responses into action in as little time as possible.

THE AGE OF TECHNOLOGICAL MIRACLES

Fibre optics and other technological achievements are truly staggering. One CD-ROM disc as small as the palm of your hand contains the entire 20-volume text of the *Oxford English Dictionary*—60 million words! A combination of lasers and fibre-optic cable can transmit 25,000 times as many signals as the usual copper cable. Computers working in parallel and using tiny chips will soon be able to perform billions of operations per second. Battery-operated, palm-sized units can perform many functions and record data, which can later be transferred to the main computer system via a PC. These advances all gradually work their way into MIS hardware, software, and systems and result in continual increases in effectiveness.

The trend is to make this vast array of technological wonders more user friendly. What this means is that you do not have to know how your hardware or software works in order to make good use of it. You just have to know *what* it can do and *how* to use it. When you start your car or turn on the lights you don't know exactly what is happening, but you know what results your action will have. It is the same with computers and software.

PROBLEMS OF A HIGH-TECH MIS

Unfortunately, all this technology does not come without a price. There are two broad areas of problems with an MIS: the initial installation period and ongoing operations.

Getting Started

Developing and installing a specific MIS is a long, difficult and expensive process. This is so whether it is your company's first computerized MIS or a major expansion or revision of an existing system. Most companies go through a very bad period while the system is being set up because there are usually many *bugs,* which take time to locate and remove. During this period, it is difficult for the organization to get useful information. Installations usually take longer and cost more than estimated and disrupt normal operations. There are some well-known cases of companies that have suffered horrendous losses during this period of MIS installation. It takes careful planning to avoid such disasters.

Operations

Many kinds of problems can arise with MIS during operations. Some of the more common ones are down time, overkill, security risks, viruses, theft, and falsification.

Down time. From time to time the system just conks out; computers are said to be *down.* Sometimes when you are dealing with your bank or your stockbroker, they'll tell you the computers are down and no information is available. This situation may last a few minutes, a few hours, or even several days. The *Globe and Mail* quoted a

U.S. survey that showed "computer systems failed an average of nine times a year for an average of four hours each time." The cost to American business was estimated at many billions of dollars *annually*. There are no comparable figures for Canada, but the Royal Bank of Canada speaks of 2 percent down time.

Overkill. Computers can produce lots of reports quite easily. This becomes a problem because, when the MIS is being planned, this facility to produce reports may lead to an overly ambitious system. When managers are asked if they would like to have a certain report that is not now being produced, they usually say yes. Consultants and hardware and software people all jump on this bandwagon to show what marvels can be produced. This tends to multiply the number of new reports to an unrealistic number.

This has two undesirable effects. First, it produces a blizzard of paper that is more than can be studied, so it piles up in corners gathering dust. Second, it is easy to lose direction. Managers who are overwhelmed by so many reports tend to have difficulty distinguishing the important from the unimportant. This may actually weaken the ability of the manager to function effectively.

Security. As more computers are linked in various ways, often around the world, maintaining control over data becomes more and more difficult. The easier usage and transmission become, the easier it is for unauthorized persons to gain access to confidential information. Computer hackers often see protective walls as challenges to be overcome. Information from hospitals, businesses, and the military has been stolen, leaked, or altered by hackers thousands of miles away, even on other continents. Some of these schemes have been so ingenious it took several years of investigation in Europe and North America to track them down.

Viruses. Computer viruses spread uncontrolled from computer to computer, causing damage to software and hardware and destroying or altering data. A new breed of computer criminals have "fun" devising cunning viruses that give them no benefit but cause much damage. There are hundreds of known viruses, with exotic names such as *stoned, Jerusalem, and Friday the 13th.* There are software programs that scan computers for known viruses and erase them. Sometimes, though, permanent damage has already been done.

Theft. Some old-fashioned thieves have learned how to use computers to steal a company's goods or money. There are numerous cases of merchandise shipped to fictitious customers. The goods disappear and are never paid for. Cheques have been issued for non-existent debts. Often these thefts are organized from the inside by a dishonest employee or by a former employee who is familiar with the system.

Falsification. Owners or managers of businesses in financial trouble may use MIS to record fictitious transactions in order to show inflated profits or a stronger financial position. This enables them to obtain bank loans, services, or merchandise that would otherwise not be available to them. Sometimes this is done to deceive a board of directors and/or shareholders.

Of course, there are procedures to prevent security leaks, viruses, theft, and fictitious entries, but often these safeguards are modified or bypassed to achieve the desired results. Cunning minds who know how the systems work can devise ways around them, and sometimes they get away with it for years. An astute bank employee in the U.S. stole from her employer for 20 years before she was discovered. With complex systems, it becomes more difficult to detect such crimes. Police departments have set up sophisticated divisions to investigate computer crimes.

SOFTWARE AND SYSTEMS—THE DOMAIN OF YOUNG KNOWLEDGE WORKERS

Software is the key to establishing an MIS that will do the required job. There is an explosion in the development of software packages for MIS. In many parts of the world, including Canada, many people (mostly *young* people) are busy designing new and more complex and powerful software to exploit the ever-increasing capacities of computer hardware. In addition, new and improved versions of old war horses continue to be churned out.

There is virtually no limit to the development of hardware and software, which makes it a very exciting field to be in. You can choose a career developing new technology or programming (designing or improving software) if your interests run in that direction. Or you can help design more efficient systems of MIS. You can also learn how to take advantage of all the capabilities that modern software makes available. This would make you a valuable employee for many companies.

There is a steady stream of new or improved versions of hardware and software and fierce competition between the companies that produce them. In Canada today, many people—computer scientists, engineers, designers, programmers, marketing experts, installers, systems experts, maintenance and repair people—most of them young, work in some aspect of information age technology. Add the large number of people who use these products on a regular basis in business and other organizations, sometimes referred to as *knowledge workers,* and we have an industry that employs hundreds of thousands of persons. It is believed to be the largest employer in Canada. Twenty-five years ago none of these jobs existed.

In sum, there are many excellent, exciting career opportunities in various aspects of the computer world. They continue to expand without any end in sight.

PART
IV
FUNDAMENTALS OF MARKETING

Miss Saigon
Miss Saigon
The Princess of Wales Theatre

MARKETING PRINCIPLES

LEARNING GOALS

After you have read and studied this chapter, you should be able to:

1. Describe marketing's role in society and its importance.
2. Explain the evolution of the marketing concept and describe its three parts.
3. Illustrate the steps in the marketing process.
4. Identify the four Ps of the marketing mix.
5. Explain the role of an environmental scan in marketing.
6. List the eight traditional functions of marketing.
7. Explain how marketing adds utility to goods and services.
8. Differentiate between consumer and industrial markets.
9. Compare the various forms of market segmentation and describe how target markets are selected.
10. Discuss the process of using market research to understand consumer behaviour.
11. Define industrial (business-to-business) marketing and explain how industrial markets differ from consumer markets.

KEY TERMS

Jerry Goodis

PROFILE JERRY GOODIS: CANADA'S MARKETING GENIUS

Have you ever seen any of these advertising slogans?
We Care About The Shape You're In (Wonderbra).
Harvey's Makes a Hamburger a Beautiful Thing.
For Barefoot Comfort Put Yourself in Our Shoes (Hush Puppies).
At Speedy You're a Somebody (Speedy Muffler).
Buy Canadian. The Rest of the World Does (Canadian Club Whiskey).
Salada Tea Picks You Up and Never Lets You Down.

The man behind these and hundreds of other successful slogans is Canada's *wunderkind,* marketing and advertising guru Jerry Goodis. For almost four decades he has operated his own advertising agencies, alone or in partnership with others. His success has been phenomenal in bringing concepts of quality to market, in the process endowing everyday products and services with a kind of animistic power. He is a copywriter of genius, the finest that Canada has produced, certainly one of the best in the world. He has written two books and the CBC and the National Film Board have produced a one-hour documentary on Goodis.

His client and former client list reads like the who's who of Canadian business: banks, insurance companies, governments, hotel and fast-food chains, manufacturing giants, and many other categories. He is in constant demand as a speaker and lecturer at universities and other organizations across the country. What can turn advertising from hucksterism into an art form is the fact that a few of its practitioners are willing to lavish passion on its evolution. Jerry Goodis is such a man.

In the mid-1950s, he founded the first successful Canadian folksong group, the Travellers. They performed widely in concerts, on radio and TV, and on many best-selling record albums. Jerry Goodis is a maverick, an *enfant terrible,* who does not conform to the stereotype of the ad man. He has not hesitated to criticize the advertising industry for its excesses and weaknesses. He is an unabashed Canadian nationalist, a man with a social conscience, and an innovator.

Sources: Peter C. Newman, foreword, *Have I Ever Lied To You Before?* McClelland and Stewart, Toronto, 1972; John Robert Colombo, foreword, *Goodis,* Jerry Goodis with Gene O'Keefe, Fitzhenry & Whiteside, 1991; Randy Scotland, "Goodis Gets Back," *Marketing,* April 22, 1991, p. 1.

THE ROLE OF MARKETING IN SOCIETY

Jerry Goodis is successful in business because he knows what marketing is. He understands that a business succeeds or fails on its ability to *satisfy customers.* The key to success in any enterprise was summarized in the best-selling book *A Passion for Excellence.* The whole of the book is summed up in this passage:[1]

> In the private or public sector, in big business or small, we observe that there are only two ways to create and sustain superior performance over the long haul. First, take exceptional care of your customers . . . via superior service and superior quality. Second, constantly innovate. That's it.

Too many people think that marketing is little more than a combination of good selling and effective advertising. Ask people what comes to mind when they hear the word marketing and most will say selling or advertising or some other word having to do with manipulating or persuading consumers. Executives like Jerry Goodis realize that marketing means much more. It means paying careful attention to consumer wants and needs and then satisfying them. Effective marketing means that a business *listens* to consumers and responds to them. A popular slogan to describe marketing is this: Find a need and fill it.

A more precise definition—the one we will be using throughout this text—is that **marketing** is the process of studying the wants and needs of others and then satisfying those wants and needs with appropriate goods and services.

marketing
The process of studying the wants and needs of others and then satisfying those wants and needs with appropriate goods and services.

Marketers satisfy consumer wants and needs by assisting in the exchange of items of value. Certain conditions must be met before an exchange can take place:

1. There must be at least two participants.
2. Each participant must have something that is of value to the other participant(s).
3. Each participant can communicate with others.
4. Each participant is free to accept or reject the offer of others.
5. Participants feel that it is appropriate or desirable to exchange with others.

THE IMPORTANCE OF MARKETING

A recent survey of executives from the fastest-growing 500 *small* businesses in the United States found that *marketing* was the greatest source of strength for these firms. Some 55 percent of respondents indicated that marketing strategy was their strong point.

The real competitive edge, according to these leading small-business executives, is gained by providing good *customer service* and quality.

A recent poll of executives from *large* corporations found similar results. The executives selected "foreign competition" as public enemy number one. As a consequence, 54 percent said they were spending more time on marketing.[2]

Whether small or large, Canadian businesses feel their future success is greatly dependent on marketing. To them, that means better customer service, high-quality products, and innovation in product design.

Marketing is not limited to business firms. Non-profit organizations such as public schools and hospitals, charities, churches, and social causes like the Western Canada Wilderness Foundation all do marketing as well. Marketing is also done by individuals. For example, athletes use marketing to win higher salaries. Job applicants use marketing to obtain a satisfying job. Marketing is the way all individuals and organizations meet some of their wants and needs by exchanging goods and services with others. We are focusing on business marketing in this text because business is the subject of the course. But if you decide to major in marketing in college or university, you will learn strategies for marketing in all kinds of organizations.

THE CHANGING BUSINESS ORIENTATION

What marketers do at any particular time depends on what needs to be done to satisfy consumer wants, which change continually. In the 1800s and early 1900s, consumers primarily needed the basic necessities of life—food, clothing, and shelter. The marketing problem was producing enough goods and getting them from the producer to the consumer. Since the most basic need was for food, marketers concentrated on the distribution and storage of food products. Manufacturers also needed raw materials to produce various products, so the distribution of industrial goods (coal, steel, wood) was important too.

Since most of today's consumers have the basic necessities, marketers no longer consider distribution and storage their most important functions, although they are still important. Today, marketers are most concerned with learning what consumers want and need and then providing the desired products and services. Let's look briefly at how this change of emphasis from production to marketing took place.

From Production to Marketing

From the time the first settlers began their struggle to survive in Canada until the start of this century, the general philosophy of business was, "Produce as much as you can because there is a limitless market." Given the limited production capability and the vast demand for products in those days, such a philosophy was both logical and profitable. Business owners were mostly farmers, carpenters, and trade workers who were catering to the public's basic needs for housing, food, and clothing. There was a need for greater and greater productive capacity, and businesses naturally had a **production orientation.** That is, the goals of business centered on production rather than marketing. This was satisfactory at that time, because most goods were bought as soon as they became available. As we noted earlier, the marketing need was for distribution and storage.

production orientation
Businesses focus on producing goods rather than marketing them.

In the early 20th century, businesses developed mass-production techniques. Automobile assembly lines are a prime example of this development. Production capacity often exceeded the immediate market demand. The business philosophy turned in the 1920s from a production orientation to a **sales orientation.** Businesses turned their attention to promoting their products and mobilized much of the firm's resources in the sales effort.

sales orientation
Firms focus on promoting their products.

After World War II (1945), there was a tremendous demand for goods and services among the returning soldiers who were starting a new life with new families. These post-war years launched the baby boom (the large increase in the birth rate after the war), which continued for two decades, and a boom in consumer spending. Competition for the consumer's dollar was fierce. Business owners recognized the need to be more responsive to consumers, and a new orientation

Marketers have changed their orientation from producing as much as possible because commodities were scarce, to meeting the specific needs of selected markets. Today, for example, marketers provide all kinds of cereals to meet specific consumer wants. There are bran and other health cereals for adults, sugared cereals for children, and so on. Learning what consumers want and providing for those wants has replaced production and selling as the key marketing function.

emerged called the marketing concept. The **marketing concept** is a relatively new philosophy of marketing that emphasizes a consumer orientation, the training of employees, and a profit orientation. This trend has intensified in the 1980s and 1990s as competition has become international and fierce.

marketing concept
Refers to a three-part business philosophy: (1) a consumer orientation, (2) training of all employees in customer service, and (3) a profit orientation.

THE MARKETING CONCEPT

The marketing concept that emerged in the 1950s and has dominated marketing thought for nearly 40 years has three parts:

1. A *consumer orientation.* That is, find out what consumers want and give it to them.
2. The *training of employees from all departments in customer service.* Everyone in the organization has the same objective—consumer satisfaction.
3. A *profit orientation.* That is, market those goods and services that will earn the firm a profit and enable it to survive and expand to serve more consumer wants and needs, in order to earn more profits.

Marketing is the window through which business most often communicates with the customer.

Consumer Orientation

Henry Ford is reported to have said, "You can have any colour car as long as it's black." He seemed more interested in production than in adapting to consumer wants and needs. He felt that the best car was a good, reliable, inexpensive one. In fact, up until 1926, Ford sold half the new cars made in this country. But when the people at General Motors talked with consumers, they found a basic desire for individuality and status. They began making cars in all colours and shapes and eventually took away much of Ford's market. This is an example of a **consumer orientation** at work. Today, all the car companies are working harder than ever to

consumer orientation
Finding out what consumers want and giving it to them.

Once you acquire marketing skills, you can use them in any organization. Non-profit charities, causes, and government agencies need marketers with promotion skills.

be more responsive to consumer wants and needs. Foreign competition has become fierce, and only those firms that give consumers what they want will survive.

Training All Employees in Customer Service

To provide optimum consumer satisfaction, all elements of marketing (product, price, place, and promotion) must be co-ordinated and integrated with other departments. For example, salespeople often promise delivery on a certain date, and then the delivery people fail to show up. Such lack of performance annoys the consumer and prevents consumer satisfaction. Similarly, a salesperson may write up a sale and promise credit terms, only to find that the credit department turns down the customer's application. Again, this may cause resentment. A consumer orientation must be taught to *all* employees in all departments.

Profit Orientation

The purpose of adopting a new business philosophy was to improve consumer relations, because better relationships would also benefit the firm and increase profits. The major goal of all business firms is to optimize long-term profits. This is called a **profit orientation.** Profit enables a firm to grow and hire more people, to provide even more satisfaction to consumers, to generate more profits, and to strengthen the economy as a whole.

profit orientation
Marketing those goods and services that will earn the firm a profit.

A More Societal Marketing Concept for the 1990s

Is it enough to give individuals what they want? Don't firms have some obligation to society as well? There is some evidence today that organizations are adopting a broader **societal orientation** that includes a consumer orientation. There is much pressure on large business firms and non-profit organizations to become involved in programs designed to train the disadvantaged, improve the community, reduce the use of energy, cut back pollution, provide consumer information and consumer education, involve employees in community projects, and generally respond to the broader needs of society. A consumer orientation thus has become only one of the many social goals of today's progressive organizations and marketing managers.

societal orientation
Includes a consumer orientation, but adds programs designed to improve the community, protect the environment, and satisfy other social goals.

Andora Freeman and Joy Ernst started a toy-recycling centre to teach children the importance of conservation and to make a profit for themselves. Used toys are sold at bargain prices, and the original owners keep 50 percent of the take. The store, Toy Go Round, could earn higher profits if it carried toy guns and G.I. Joe dolls, but the owners refuse because they do not like the social effects on children of playing with war toys.

People are now demanding satisfaction of wants and needs that businesses often cannot and do not provide. For example, people are demanding a cleaner environment, a greater involvement with the arts, and better education programs. This has led to a whole new dimension of marketing—non-profit organization marketing.

No longer is the objective simply to "Find individual needs and fill them." Rather, the goal is to meet the broader needs of society as well. Standard marketing practices were applied to tasks such as promoting public hospitals and universities, colleges, museums, associations, government programs, and more. But more sophisticated tools were needed to create new social attitudes and behaviours for such programs as stopping smoking, avoiding drinking and driving, wearing seat belts, picking up litter, and so on. Much future growth in marketing will be in this area.

Molson's "Take Care" program has been in place for a number of years to promote drinking responsibly or not drinking at all.

PROGRESS CHECK

- What orientations did businesses have *before* the marketing concept was adopted?
- What are the three major elements of the marketing concept?
- How does the societal marketing concept differ from the traditional marketing concept?

LEARNING ABOUT MARKETING

To help you learn about marketing, we shall first give you an overview of the marketing process by taking one product and quickly following it through the process. Remember, the basis of marketing is finding a need and filling it. So our first step is to find a need. Imagine that you and your friends do not eat big breakfasts. You want something for breakfast that is fast, nutritional, and good tasting. Some of your friends eat Quaker's 100% Natural cereal but are not happy with its sugar content. You ask around among your friends and acquaintances and find that there is a huge demand for a breakfast cereal that is good tasting, nutritious, high in fibre, and low in sugar. "Aha," you say to yourself, "I have found a need."

You have now completed one of the first steps in marketing. You have researched consumer wants and needs and found a need for a product that people want that is not yet available.

The next step is to develop a product to fill that need. A **product** is any physical good, service, or idea that satisfies a want or need. In this case, your proposed product is a multigrain cereal made with NutraSweet, an artificial sweetner.

product
Any physical good, service, or idea that satisfies a want or need.

It is a good idea at this point to do *concept testing*. That is, you develop an accurate description of your product and ask people whether or not the concept (the idea of the cereal) appeals to them. If it does, you must go to a manufacturer

Müeslix is a popular cereal in Europe. Kellogg decided to try to market it here. The best way to convince people that the cereal tastes good is to get them to try some. A 75-cents-off coupon provides the incentive to buy and try the product.

that has the equipment and skills to design such a cereal and begin making prototypes. Prototypes are samples of the product that you take to consumers to test their reactions. The process of testing products among potential users is called **test marketing.**

test marketing
The process of testing products among potential users.

If consumers like the product, you may turn the production process over to an existing manufacturer or you may produce the cereal yourself. Production is *not* part of the marketing process. Marketing helps determine what products should be made, but it does not make them.

Once the product is made, you have to design a package, think up a brand name, and set a price. A **brand name** is a logo, word, letter, or group of words or letters that differentiate the goods and services of a seller from those of competitors. Cereal brand names, for example, include Cheerios, Red River, and Raisin Bran. You name your cereal Fiberrific to emphasize the high fibre content and terrific taste. We shall discuss the product development process, including packaging, branding, and pricing, in detail in the next chapter. Now we are simply picturing the whole process to get an overall view of what marketing is all about.

brand name
A logo, word, letter, or groups of words or letters that differentiate the goods and services of a seller from those of competitors.

Once the product is manufactured, you have to choose how to get it to the consumer. You may want to sell it directly to supermarkets or health food stores or you may want to sell it through organizations that specialize in distributing food products. Such organizations are called **marketing middlemen** because they are in the middle of a series of organizations that distribute goods from producers to consumers. We shall discuss middlemen and distribution in detail in Chapter 12.

marketing middlemen
Individuals or organizations that help distribute goods and services from the producer to the consumers.

The last step in the marketing process is to promote the product to consumers. Promotion consists of all the techniques sellers use to capture markets. They include advertising, personal selling, publicity, and various sales promotion efforts such as coupons, rebates, samples, and cents-off deals. Promotion will be discussed in detail in Chapter 13.

THINKING IT THROUGH

Fiberrific is the brand name selected for testing. Can you think of a better brand name? What kind of people would you select to test this new cereal? Can you think of other breakfast foods people might want that you could sell along with this cereal?

The Marketing Mix

If you think through this process, you will see that managing the marketing process involves four factors after a need is discovered: (1) Design a want-satisfying *product,* (2) set a *price* for the product, (3) get the product to a *place* where people will buy it, and (4) *promote* the product. These four factors have become known as the **four Ps of marketing.** These are marketers' tools to make the greatest impact possible on potential customers. Customer perception is what determines consumer behaviour.

four Ps of marketing
Product, price, place, and promotion.

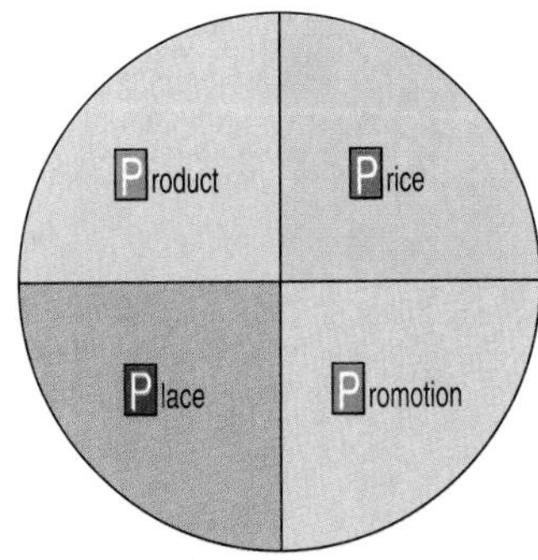

These four factors are also known as the **marketing mix** because they are the ingredients that go into a marketing program. Each of the factors of the marketing mix will be discussed in more detail in the next three chapters.

A **marketing manager** (or a product manager) designs a marketing program that effectively combines these ingredients of the marketing mix (see Figure 10–1). The American Marketing Association recently redefined the role of marketing managers as follows:[3] *Marketing (management)* is the process of planning and executing the conception, pricing, promotion, and distribution (place) of ideas, goods, and services (products) to create exchanges that satisfy individual and organizational goals. Such a program is called a marketing strategy.

marketing mix
The strategic combination of product decisions with decisions regarding packaging, pricing, distribution, credit, branding, service, complaint handling, and other marketing activities.

marketing manager
Person who plans and executes the conception, pricing, promotion, and distribution of ideas, goods, and services to create exchanges that satisfy individual and organizational goals.

A Marketing Strategy

Every product or service, whether industrial or consumer, that a company is planning to sell requires a specific marketing strategy. That strategy has two main components:

1. Selecting the specific target market (or markets) at which the product or service is aimed.
2. Determining the proper marketing mix that will enable the organization to reach that target market satisfactorily.

Later in the chapter we look at the various ways that a market is segmented to narrow the search to the actual potential users of a particular product or service.

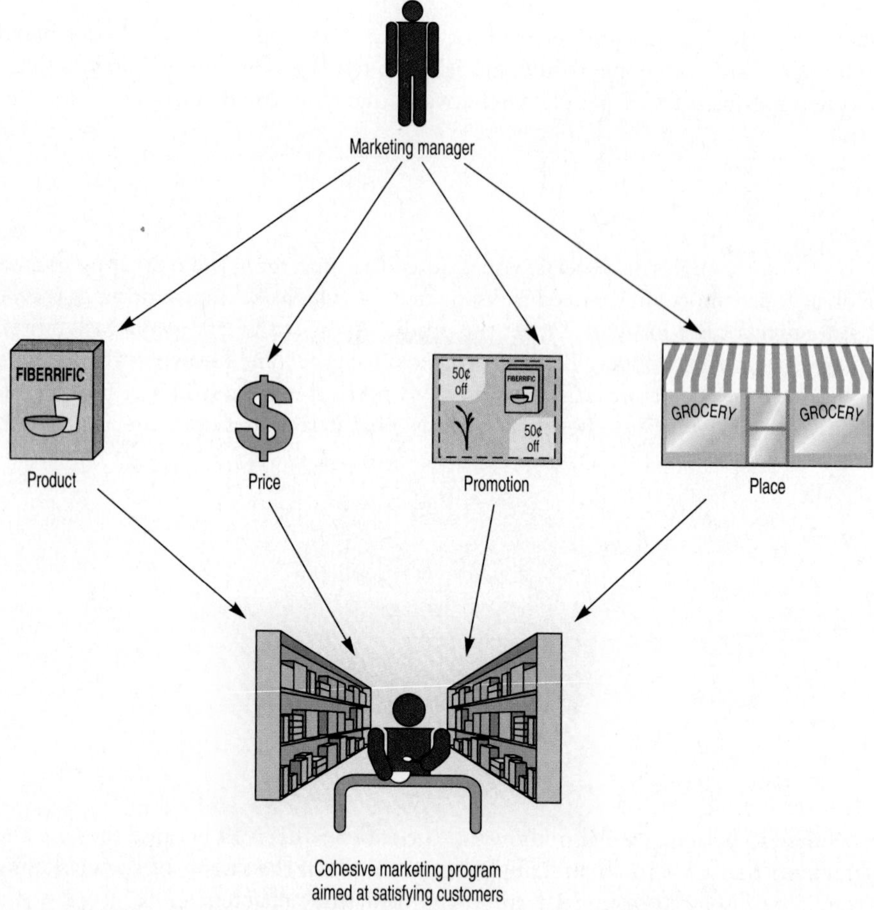

Figure 10–1 The four Ps and the marketing manager's role. The marketing manager chooses the proper price, promotion, and place to develop a comprehensive marketing program. This figure shows the mix for Fiberrific cereal. It would include decisions about packaging, couponing, and more.

Then we examine the four components that make up the marketing mix. An effective marketing strategy combines these two elements to achieve the organization's objectives.

For example, when Canadian Aviation Electronics (CAE) wants to sell flight simulators used to train pilots, it must

1. Determine which airplane it wishes to simulate and then adapt its simulator to that specific model.
2. Then develop a marketing mix that will enable it to best go after those companies that use that particular plane.

In this particular case, distribution (place) is not a major problem; these multimillion dollar products are sold directly to the airlines. But the remaining elements of the marketing mix, price and promotion, must be carefully considered.

Before a marketing strategy can be adopted, the company must be aware of a wide variety of developments in its environment. We look at this next.

SCANNING ENVIRONMENTAL FACTORS OF MARKETS

Successful marketing managers realize that business survival depends on predicting potential opportunities and future competition in their markets. Losing sight of what is going on in the market—in the environment of the business—can be

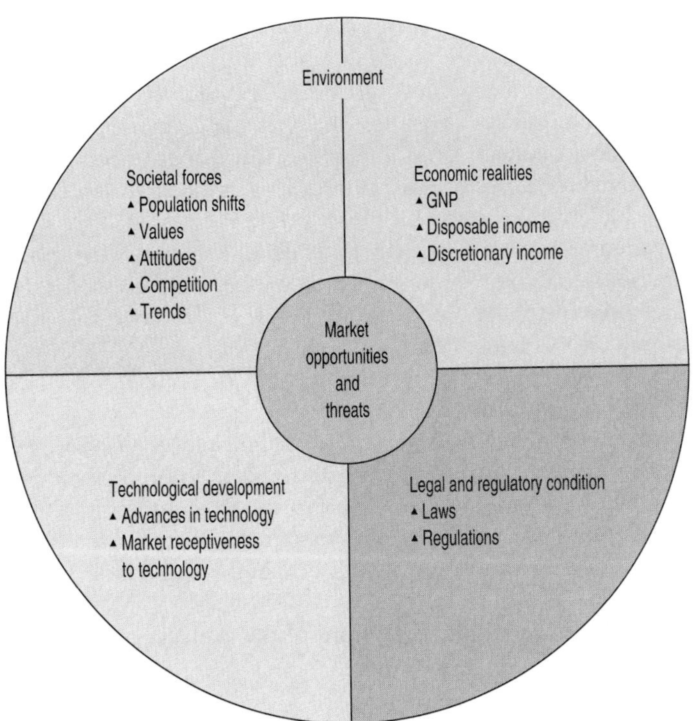

Figure 10–2 Environmental forces affecting marketing decisions. A marketing manager must constantly adjust to changes in the environment. For example, people may decide that they want more rice bran in cereal rather than oat bran. The laws may change regarding what you can or must say on cereal boxes. The economy may slow, making people more conscious of price. This figure shows that the environment creates both opportunities and threats to marketing managers.

disastrous. (See for example, the story on Procter & Gamble in Japan in the market research section of this chapter.) Therefore, marketing managers today often use a practice called **environmental scanning** to help identify trends in markets and decide if the trends present opportunities or threats to the company. Today, shifting global markets and intensified competition make continuous monitoring of a firm's market environment, or surroundings, more necessary than ever before.

environmental scanning
Analysis of societal forces, economic realities, technological development, and legal and regulatory conditions.

An environmental scan includes a thorough analysis of four environmental factors: (1) societal forces, (2) economic realities, (3) technological developments, and (4) legal and regulatory conditions (see Figure 10–2). The ability to serve a market depends on a marketer's understanding of changes in the market environment.

Societal Forces

Marketers must constantly be aware of changes in society. Often, societal shifts signal important trends that affect a company's operations by creating opportunities in a market. Kmart introduced its Jaclyn Smith line of maternity clothes to meet the increasing demand of pregnant women who continued to work throughout pregnancy. Caffeine-free colas, low-salt food, and your own Fiberrific were developed in response to the increasing demands of health-conscious consumers. These same developments led to declines in sales of eggs and beef.

Similarly, the AIDS crisis has created problems for companies selling blood products but helped those selling syringes, medical gloves, and condoms. Concerns for the physical environment have put pressures on "dirty" producers and created opportunities for waste management and recycling.

The progressive, forward-thinking marketer never loses touch with important societal forces in a market.

Economic Realities

Canadian consumers probably find it hard to envision a market where buyers purchase items such as aspirin, cigarettes, and chewing gum one piece at a time. Yet, in such low-income markets as the Philippines, this is not uncommon. Therefore, marketers must include a careful economic analysis in the environmental scan. What do marketers look for in a market's economy? Factors such as disposable and discretionary income often indicate the potential of a market. **Disposable income** is money available after taxes for consumers to use for essentials such as food, shelter, and clothing. **Discretionary income** is money a consumer has after taxes and essentials to buy non-essential items.

disposable income
Money available after taxes for purchase of essentials.

discretionary income
Money available after taxes and essentials for purchase of non-essential items.

Other factors to consider: Are imports a major competitive challenge? Is a recession just starting or ending?

The People's Republic of China, with its billion-plus population, might appear to be an attractive market for products such as suntan lotion and wine coolers. But the economic realities of this market show that most consumers in China could not purchase these items because they have extremely limited discretionary income available. However, even a market of 10% of China's population would consist of 100 million people.

Do you think the economic conditions of the Canadian market can support a product like Fiberrific?

Technological Developments

Advances in technology and the market's acceptance of these advances are two important factors that help us understand the opportunities in a market. Companies such as Apple Computer, Microsoft, and Sony have experienced great success in world markets by introducing technologically superior products.

We now live in a technological society and a technological era. We see a constant stream of new gadgets, products, and inventions in the consumer market. The industrial market is undergoing the same process, though sometimes less visibly. The result is that raw materials, manufacturing processes, equipment, and products are undergoing constant change. Marketers have to be very alert to avoid letting new technology make products or whole lines obsolete. Examples are when plastics began to replace glass for containers and when compact disks made LPs and record players obsolete.

These same innovations can offer new opportunities to marketers. Can you think of some recent news stories that highlight this whole process?

As prospective producers of Fiberrific, you may be tempted to develop a product that provides daily nutritional needs in a single, time-saving capsule. Just pop one in and you don't have to worry about eating the rest of the day! Keeping in mind what you know about Canadian culture, how do you think such a product might be accepted here?

Legal and Regulatory Conditions

The conduct and direction of business is firmly tied to the legal and regulatory environment. Marketers must possess a clear understanding of major legislation enacted to protect the interests of consumers, competition, and society in general.

For example, zoning restrictions in some cities limit the choice of locations for new business. But limited zoning laws in others allow businesses to build in residential as well as industrial areas.

In Canada, business operations are heavily affected by various federal, provincial, and local laws. Chapter 3 reviewed many of the important laws and regulations at all levels of government as they affect business. You will be seeing more about this in later chapters. Before you begin developing Fiberrific, it would be wise to review the laws that might affect you, such as restrictions on use of certain ingredients, requirements for packaging, and regulations affecting advertising. You should also be aware of environmental regulations that might affect your production processes and waste disposal.

SWOT Analysis

After scanning their environment, marketing managers analyze their company and its relation to its surroundings at that particular moment. This analysis determines the Strengths and Weaknesses of the company and the Opportunities and Threats (SWOT) in the environment. The idea is to develop a marketing strategy that builds on the company's strengths, avoids its weaknesses, and cashes in on the opportunities that are deemed to exist, while at the same time avoiding the threats that pose a potential danger.

For example, let us imagine a scenario where Northern Telecom, (Nortel) Canada's telecommunications giant, is considering bidding on some major contracts to install a new telephone system and equipment in Belgrazia, an imaginary developing country. The contracts total almost $1 billion over five years. Nortel's major competitors, Thompson of France, Siemens of Germany, and Matsushita of Japan are preparing to bid as well. Nortel's SWOT analysis, in very brief outline, reveals:

Strengths

- Valuable experience from a similar job in China.
- Well-trained, highly skilled, and dedicated crews.
- Large inventory of many of the required parts.
- High-quality equipment and material.
- Very good international reputation.

Weaknesses

- It is in the midst of several other major contracts that will not be completed before the start date of the Belgrazia job. That means its experienced crews will not be available, so new, unproven employees will have to be hired.
- Three of its key bidding managers are seriously ill from food poisoning at a project and cannot participate in this bid.
- There are some bugs in a new high-tech product that will be required for this project.

Opportunities

- Successful conclusion of this contract may lead to several similar ones in the area.
- Several aspects of the contract require use of a new process that Nortel developed, thus allowing it to jump into world leadership in this field.
- Landing this contract will enable Nortel to hire two senior engineers it has been after for some time, because they are very interested in certain technology involved in it.
- Because interest rates are low now, financing can be obtained at a very favourable rate.

Threats

- Belgrazia is known to be quite unstable politically, which could threaten the actual working conditions. In fact the contract itself might be subject to review or cancellation if new rulers seized power.
- Belgrazia has a poor reputation when it comes to paying its bills.
- The climate is very humid with regular torrential downpours that make outside work very difficult.
- The country's infrastructure—roads, power, food distribution, etc.—is quite poor, further complicating carrying out the contract.
- The president of Siemens has been a good friend of the president of Belgrazia since their university days.

Nortel will now evaluate the situation and make a decision based on its judgment of the significance of these factors.

WHAT MARKETERS DO: ASSISTING EXCHANGE THROUGH MARKETING FUNCTIONS

After the company does an environmental scan and a SWOT analysis, the marketing task begins. Keep in mind that marketing helps buyers and sellers exchange items of value. By the 1920s, marketers had expanded their efforts beyond storage and distribution of products. They were described as performing eight basic functions (see Figure 10–3):

1. Buying
2. Selling
3. Transporting
4. Storing
5. Financing
6. Standardizing (grading)
7. Risk taking
8. Research

Let's see how these eight functions apply to Fiberrific. First of all, *research* was needed to find an unmet need. Research was also needed to test the product in the market and determine the most effective way to price, promote, and distribute the cereal. Marketing research is thus important throughout the design of the marketing mix.

To produce the cereal, one has to buy raw materials such as wheat, oats, and corn from farmers. Retail stores will buy the cereal from us and consumers will buy from the retail store. Thus, *buying* and *selling* are important marketing functions.

Financing (credit) was once a very important marketing function because marketers provided the credit. Today, credit is often a separate department with

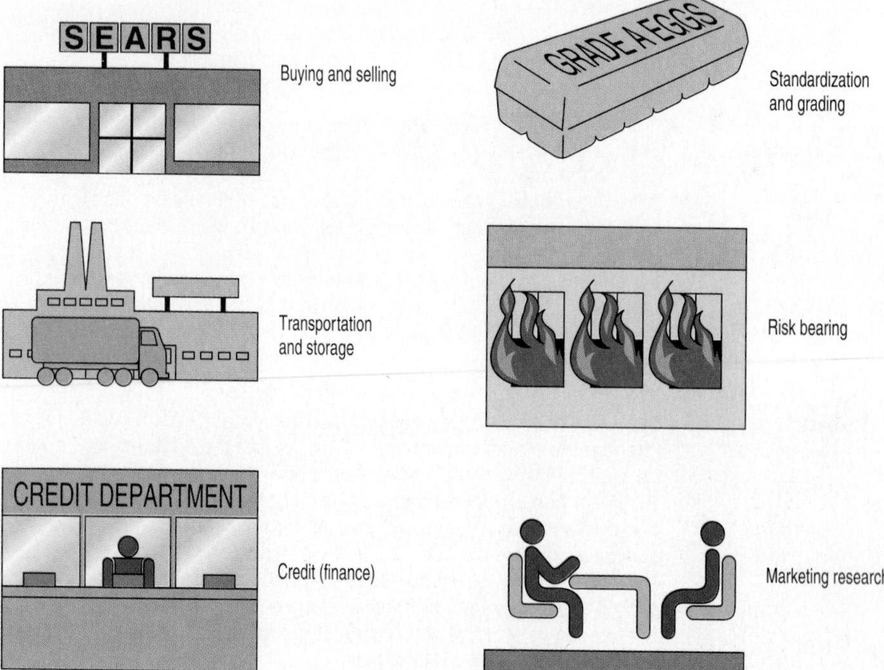

Figure 10–3 The traditional eight functions of marketing. Buying and selling are the heart of marketing. But buying and selling (trading) do not take place unless goods are transported to where they are wanted and stored until buyers are ready to buy (distribution). Without financing, who can afford to buy a house? Marketing of farm products demanded standardization and grading of goods. Marketers assumed the risks that something would happen to the stored goods. The whole process begins and ends with research (knowing what the market wants).

separate managers, but it is still an important function to marketing managers. Supermarkets, for example, buy cereal and other foods on credit from their suppliers.

Transportation involves moving grain from the farm to the producer and moving boxes of cereal from the producer to the retailer and other middlemen.

The word *store* comes from the fact that retailers store items on their shelves so that consumers can buy goods whenever they want. Producers and middlemen also have *storage* facilities. Consumers may also perform the storage function by buying several boxes of cereal on sale and storing them in their homes. Whenever you buy products for resale and store them, you assume the *risk* that they will be stolen or damaged or become obsolete. Assuming the risks of storage and distribution has traditionally been considered a marketing function, but risk management has now become a separate function.

The last traditional marketing function is *standardization* and *grading*. No doubt you have seen "Grade A eggs" and various classifications of beef (e.g., prime). These are forms of grading. Although cereal such as Fiberrific is not graded, its packaging does list how the product compares to certain standards—the recommended daily allowance (RDA) of vitamins and minerals.

How Marketing Adds Utility

All of marketing's functions are performed to move goods from producers to consumers. The functions allow marketing to create *utility,* the value that marketing adds to goods and services. There are five types of utility: (1) form, (2) time, (3) place, (4) possession, and (5) information. We will look briefly at each type of utility now, but you will learn more about them in Chapter 12.

Form utility refers to the changing of raw materials to a finished product. Taking grains and turning them into our Fiberrific cereal is an example of form utility in action. Form utility is usually considered mainly a production function rather than a marketing function.

Transportation is one of the most expensive and thus most important marketing functions. For example, grain has to be transported from the fields to the producers of Fiberrific. After the cereal is produced, it has to be shipped to wholesalers, stored, and shipped again to retailers.

Mac's convenience stores provide both time and place utility. Such stores stay open 24 hours a day (time utility) and are in convenient locations close to customers (place utility).

time utility
Making products available during convenient hours.

place utility
Making products and services available in convenient locations.

possession utility
Making the exchange of goods between buyers and sellers easier.

information utility
Letting buyers know that the product exists, how to use it, the price, and other information.

Time utility helps consumers by making products available when the consumer wishes. Supermarkets that are open 24 hours a day provide time utility for Fiberrific.

Place utility makes sure that goods and services are conveniently located to meet consumer needs. Convenience stores help provide place utility for Fiberrific.

Possession utility helps make the exchange of goods between buyers and sellers easy. For example, supermarket cheque-cashing services make it easier for Fiberrific customers to complete their shopping. Anything that helps complete the sale—delivery, installation, warranties, credit—is considered part of possession utility.

Information utility informs buyers that the product exists, how to use it, its price, and other information. Such information is provided through advertising, salespeople, and packaging.

The word marketing comes from the root word market. A *market,* remember, is defined as people with unsatisfied wants and needs who have both the resources and the willingness to buy. Thus, if there are people who want a high-fibre, low-sugar cereal like Fiberrific and have the resources and willingness to buy it, then we say that there is a market for Fiberrific. We learn whether there is a market for our cereal by studying consumer markets.

PROGRESS CHECK

- What are the four Ps of marketing and what else are they called?
- Can you name five of the eight traditional functions of marketing and give examples for each of them?

RECOGNIZING DIFFERENT MARKETS: CONSUMER AND INDUSTRIAL

consumer market
All the individuals or households who want goods and services for personal consumption.

There are two major markets in marketing, the consumer market and the industrial market. The **consumer market** consists of all the individuals or households who want goods and services for personal consumption or use. Fruit, lawnmowers, and insurance policies are examples of items commonly considered consumer products and services.

The **industrial market** consists of all the individuals and organizations that need goods and services in order to produce other goods and services or to sell, rent, or supply the goods to others. Oil drilling bits, cash registers, display cases, office desks, public accounting audits, and corporate legal advice are examples of industrial goods and services. This might be called the business-to-business market.

industrial market
Individuals and organizations that purchase goods and services to produce other goods and services or to rent, sell, or supply the goods to others.

The important thing to remember is that the buyer's reason for buying and the end use of the product determine whether a product is considered a consumer product or an industrial product. For example, a box of Fiberrific bought for a family's breakfast is considered a consumer product. However, if the same box of Fiberrific were purchased by Dinnie's Diner to sell to its breakfast customers, it would be considered an industrial product.

MARKETING TO CONSUMERS

The consumer market consists of the approximately 27 million people in Canada and the over 5 billion people in world markets. We learned in Chapter 1 that consumer markets are changing. The international market is growing in importance and the domestic market keeps changing as technology, the economy, and social trends change.

Obviously, consumers vary greatly in age, educational level, income, and taste. Because consumers differ so greatly, marketers must learn to develop products and services specially tailored to the needs of particular groups or segments of the population. If a consumer group is large enough, a company may design a marketing program to serve that market.

Campbell Soup noticed that one-quarter of all households consisted of single people living alone. Most of these people are busy at work. They have little time to cook, but they do have money for convenience foods. Therefore, Campbell introduced many new products to appeal to singles and married young, urban professionals (yuppies). Included are Le Menu frozen dinners, French Chef frozen soups, Great Starts frozen breakfasts, and Souper Combo, a frozen, microwavable soup and sandwich combination.[4] Campbell is just one company that has had great success studying the consumer market, breaking it down into categories, and then developing products for those separate groups.

SPOTLIGHT ON BIG BUSINESS

McLobsters and McLean Deluxe: Market Segmentation Works

A story in the *Globe and Mail,* from Halifax, bore this headline: "McLobsters roll onto market." McDonald's Canada had decided to sell traditional East Coast lobster rolls—lobster meat in an oversized hot-dog bun with lettuce and mayonnaise—in its 50 franchises in the Atlantic provinces. McLobsters are being marketed as a regional item that will probably not be sold in other parts of Canada.

An item in the *Financial Post,* indicated that McDonald's Canada was interested in reaching another segment of the market. It was going to join its U.S. parent in the introduction of a leaner hamburger. The McLean Deluxe would be a 91 percent fat-free burger with reduced calories and lower cholesterol. This was the latest in a series of new products designed to appeal to the growing health-conscious segment of the market. These products now include fresh salads, low-fat milk, low-fat frozen yogurt, and cholesterol-free apple bran muffins.

Sources: Deborah Jones, "McLobsters Roll Onto Market," *Globe and Mail,* June 18, 1991, p. B1; Susan Smith, "Leaner, Healthier Big Mac Attack," *Financial Post,* March 14, 1991, p. 5.

Campbell Soup has had great success targeting profitable markets such as breakfast eaters (Great Starts) and busy professionals (Le Menu). When evaluating a market segment, it is important to look at its size and growth potential, the reachability of the market, and the potential of your company to develop a product for that segment.

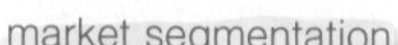

market segmentation
The process of dividing the total market into several submarkets (segments) that have similar characteristics.

market targeting
The process by which an organization decides which markets to serve.

The process of dividing the total market into several groups (segments) that have similar characteristics is called **market segmentation.** Usually a business cannot serve all of these markets, so it must decide which markets to serve. **Market targeting** is the process by which an organization decides which market segments to serve.

Segmenting the Consumer Market

geographic segmentation
The process of dividing the market into separate geographic areas.

demographic segmentation
Dividing the market into groups by age, sex, income, and similar categories.

psychographic segmentation
Dividing the market by values, attitudes, and interests.

benefit segmentation
Dividing the market by benefits desired.

volume segmentation
Dividing the market into user categories: heavy, medium, light, and non-users.

There are several ways a firm can segment (divide) the market for marketing purposes. Remember, the idea is to break the market down into smaller submarkets (segments) with similar characteristics (for example, all men, teenagers), and then aim the product at one or more of these groups. Let's say, for example, in trying to sell Fiberrific we begin our marketing campaign by focusing on a certain region such as British Columbia, where fitness is a major issue. Dividing the market by geographic area is called **geographic segmentation** (see Figure 10–4).

Or, we could aim our promotions towards people aged 25 to 45 who had some university training and high incomes—yuppies, like those Campbell Soup targeted with its Le Menu line. Segmentation by age, income, and education level is part of **demographic segmentation** (see Figure 10–5).

We may want our ads to portray the lifestyle of this group. To do that, we could study the group's values, attitudes, and interests. This segmentation strategy is called **psychographic segmentation** (see Figure 10–6).

What benefits should we talk about? Should we emphasize high fibre, low sugar, price, health in general, or what? Determining which benefits are preferred is called **benefit segmentation** (see Figure 10–7).

Who are the big eaters of cereal? Children eat cereal, but so do adults. Separating the market by usage (volume of use) is called **volume segmentation.** Most cereal companies seem to aim at children. Why not go for the adults, a less competitive market? (see Figure 10–8).

Selecting a Target Market

The best segmentation strategy is to use all the variables to come up with a consumer profile (a target market) that is clear, reachable, and sizeable. Let's look more closely at procedures for selecting a target market.

Size and growth potential of segment. The proper size for a market segment depends on the size of the seller and the objectives of the firm. A small business might select a

Variable	Typical Segments
Region	British Columbia, Prairies, southwest Ontario, metropolitan Toronto, northwest Ontario, metropolitan Montreal, the rest of Quebec, Atlantic Provinces.
City or county size	Under 5,000; 5,000–19,999; 20,000–49,999; 50,000–99,999; and so on
Population density	Urban, suburban, rural

Figure 10–4 Geographic segmentation variables. This figure shows one way marketers use to divide the market. The aim of segmentation is to break the market into smaller units of homogeneous composition.

Variable	Typical Segments
Age	Under 5; 5–10; 11–18; 19–34; 35–49; 50–64; over 64
Education	Elementary school or less; some high school; high school graduate; college graduate; some university; university graduate; graduate degree
Family size	1; 2–3; 4–5; over 5
Family life cycle	Young, single; young, married, no children; young, married, oldest child under 6; young, married, youngest child 6 or over; older, married with children; older, married, no children; older, single; other
Income	Under $10,000; $10,000–14,999; $15,000–19,999; $20,000–40,000; over $40,000
Area of origin	Britain, Western Europe, Eastern Europe, Southern Europe, Caribbean, Latin America, North Africa, Mid-Africa, South Africa, China, India, Pakistan, Vietnam, Hong Kong, other East Asia, Mideast, Russia
Occupation	Professional, managerial; technical, official or proprietor; clerical, sales; supervisor; factory worker; farmer; student; home manager; retired; unemployed
Sex	Male, female
Social class	Lower lower; upper lower; lower middle; upper middle; lower upper; upper upper

Figure 10–5 Demographic segmentation variables

Variable	Typical Segments
Attitudes	LOV (list of values)
Behaviour patterns	Self-respect
Interests	Security
Lifestyles	Warm relationship with others
Opinions	Sense of accomplishment
Personality	Self-fulfillment
Self-image	Being well-respected
Values	Sense of belonging
	Fun and enjoyment in life

Figure 10–6 Psychographic segmentation variables. Using the variables in this figure would identify the lifestyles of a group of people. Can you think of an ad related to attitudes?

Figure 10–7 Benefit segmentation variables. Which of these benefits are most important to you? Marketing managers need to know which variables people value.

Variable	Typical Segments
Comfort Convenience Durability Economy Health Luxury Safety Status	Benefit segmentation divides an already established market into smaller, more homogeneous segments. Those people who desire economy in a car would be an example. The benefit desired varies by product.

Figure 10–8 Volume market segmentation. Knowing who uses a product the most is an important consideration in marketing.

Variable	Typical Segments
Usage	Heavy users, light users, non-users
Loyalty status	None; medium; strong absolute (repeat purchases)

small market segment that has been ignored by larger firms but is large enough to be profitable for the small firm. The segment may be too small to attract larger competitors, leaving that market to the smaller firm. You may have noticed the many small, ethnic grocery stores that have emerged in ethnic neighbourhoods. The owners could not compete against the giant food retailers in national markets, but in those neighbourhoods, they can be quite competitive if the size of the ethnic population is large enough and shows growth potential.

How reachable the segment is. The marketer must be able to reach the target group and still make a profit. One may see the potential of selling a product in China because there are over a billion consumers there, but the cost of trying to reach those consumers may be too high.

The nature of the market. A marketer must look at how many competitors are already going after that market, potential new competitors, and the buying power of customers. If there are too many existing competitors or potential competitors, one may hesitate to enter certain markets. The same is true if the buying power of the target market is too low. The government has held hearings to determine if the cereal industry is so powerful that it is preventing competition from new businesses. We might want to get a copy of those hearings before we consider making and selling Fiberrific.

The nature of the company. Just because a market need exists and could be profitable does not mean a company should enter that market. Management must consider its present product mix, company strengths and competence. For example, it might be a mistake for an automobile company to enter the food business. Bell Canada Enterprises was unsuccessful in running BCED because its executives simply did not have the expertise to run a real estate development business even if market potential existed.

MAKING ETHICAL DECISIONS

Marketers have long recognized that children can be an important influence in the buying decisions of parents. In fact, many direct appeals for products are focussed directly at children. At Fiberrific, we have experienced a great response to our new high-fibre, high-protein cereal among health-conscious consumers. The one important group we haven't been able to attract is children. The product management team is considering the introduction of Fiberrific Jr to help solve this problem.

Fiberrific Jr may have strong market potential if we follow two recommendations of our research department. First, we coat the flakes generously with sugar (significantly changing its nutritional benefits). Second, we promote the product extensively for children. Such a promotion strategy should create a strong demand for the product, especially if we offer a premium in each box. The consensus in the research department is that "kids will love the new taste," plus parents will agree to buy Fiberrific Jr because of the positive impression they have of our best-selling brand. The research director commented, "The chance of a parent actually reading our label and noting the addition of sugar is nil!"

Would you introduce Fiberrific Jr according to the recommendations of research? What are the benefits of doing this? What are the risks involved? What would you do if you were the marketing manager?

Regardless of the consumer segment a company chooses, it is important to know as much as possible about the target market. Marketers use market research to tell them what they need to know about their markets.

MARKETING RESEARCH

Take a moment to think about this situation. You have this terrific idea for crunching the cereal market. When friends ask you why you think you should dive into the cereal business you say you have "a gut feeling the health-conscious yuppies will love Fiberrific." Do you immediately prepare for production and marketing of a new line of cereal to milk the market? Not unless you're flaky!

It is possible that you could be right about Fiberrific being the cream of the cereal market. However, the risk in acting on just a gut feeling is too great. It would be worthwhile to conduct some **marketing research.**

marketing research
A major function used to find needs and determine the most effective and efficient ways to satisfy those needs.

If the goal of marketing is to find a need and fill it, then a major function must be to do research to find needs and determine the most effective and efficient ways to satisfy those needs. Marketing research performs those tasks. You will learn about marketing research in Chapter 13. For now, we want you to understand that market research helps businesspeople understand how consumers are likely to act. It is important to understand consumer behaviour in general. In the late 1960s, marketing scholars began to take an active interest in learning how consumers think and act. Eventually, they developed textbooks in the area, and *consumer behaviour* has become one of the major courses in marketing.

Using Market Research to Understand Consumer Behaviour

Review the box about the diaper market. Japanese producers of diapers captured the market from Procter & Gamble by doing better research. They talked to hundreds of consumers to learn what they wanted in a diaper. They then designed a superior diaper and won a huge market share.

North American manufacturers have long used marketing research, but the research process has become too sophisticated. The secret to understanding consumers is simply to listen to them.[6] There are techniques for doing that, such

REACHING BEYOND OUR BORDERS

How Complacency Destroyed Market Dominance

Procter & Gamble, a company that prides itself on leading the way in product improvement, got beaten at its own game in the Japanese disposable-diaper market. P&G lost out to Japanese competitors that designed better products and got them on the shelves faster.

Complacency was P&G's biggest problem. P&G was making diapers with old-fashioned paper pulp, when Japan's Uni-Charm Corp. introduced a highly absorbent, granulated polymer to soak up wetness and hold it in the form of a gel, keeping babies drier longer. P&G didn't introduce its polymer-packed Pampers in Japan until January 1985—three years after Uni-Charm's "super-slurper" polymer product. The result: P&G's share of the market dropped to 7 percent in early 1985 from 90 percent several years before. Since the company began marketing its improved superabsorbent product, its market share has rebounded to about 15 percent.

Loss of the technological lead may have been P&G's biggest blunder, but it also fell behind the Japanese in market research. Uni-Charm spent two years studying buying habits in Europe and the United States before it came out with its superabsorbent diaper. It polled 300 Japanese mothers three times each on their opinions of foreign diapers. Using these opinions, Uni-Charm added leg gatherings and reusable adhesive closures and re-shaped them for better fit long before P&G did. "P&G's product wasn't adapted for Japanese consumers," says Takasi Nomoto, an analyst with Nikko Research Center Ltd. in Toyko.[5] ▼

as focus groups, that we shall discuss in Chapter 13. At this point, it is important to note that effective marketing research calls for getting out of the office and getting close to customers to find out what they want and need. Laboratory research and consumer panels can never replace going into people's homes, watching them use products, and asking what improvements they seek. Many companies now do that, but many do not.

In international markets, the need is the same. One must learn the culture of the people and talk with them directly. What is attractive in one country may be an inconvenience in another. Marketing often is easier than some people make it. The goal, remember, is to find a need and fill it. That means listening to people constantly and adapting to what they say. It does not mean trying to sell them what they do not want.

The Consumer Decision-Making Process

Figure 10–9 illustrates the kinds of subjects that are studied in a consumer behaviour course. The core involves studying the consumer purchase decision process. "Problem recognition" may result from the fact that your washing machine broke down. This leads to an information search. That is, you look for ads about washing machines and begin reading brochures about them. You may even consult *Consumer Reports* and other information sources. Then you evaluate alternatives and make a purchase decision. After the purchase, you may ask others how much they paid for their machines and do other comparisons, including the performance of your new machine. Marketing researchers investigate consumer thought processes and behaviour at each stage to determine the best way to facilitate marketing exchanges.

Consumer behaviour researchers also study the various influences on consumer behaviour. Figure 10–9 shows that such influences include the marketing mix variables, psychological influences such as perception and attitudes, situational influences such as the type of purchase and the physical surroundings, and

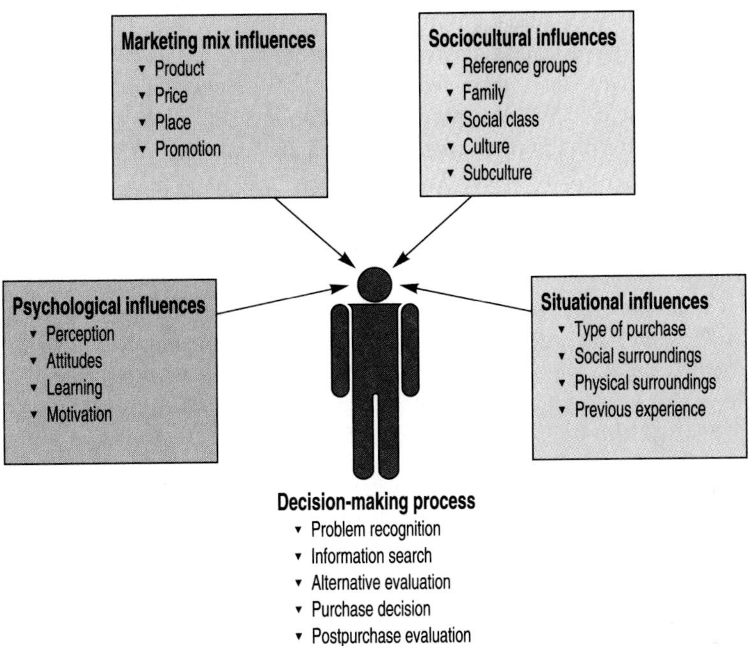

Figure 10–9 The consumer decision-making process and outside influences. There are many influences on consumers as they decide which goods and services to buy. Marketers have some influence, but it is not usually as strong as sociocultural influences. Helping consumers in their information search and their evaluation of alternatives is a major function of marketing.

sociocultural influences such as reference groups and culture. Some terms that may be unfamiliar to you include:

Learning involves changes in an individual's behaviour resulting from previous experiences and information.

Reference group is the group that an individual uses as a reference point in the formation of his or her beliefs, attitudes, values, or behaviour.

Culture is the set of values, attitudes, and ways of doing things transmitted from one generation to another in a given society.

Subculture is the set of values, attitudes, and ways of doing things that result from belonging to a certain nationality group, religious group, racial group, or other group with which one closely identifies (for example, teenagers).

Cognitive dissonance means that consumers may have doubts after the purchase about whether they got the best product at the best price. That means marketers may have to reassure consumers *after* the sale if they want to establish a long-term relationship. Auto manufacturers do this by sending new-car owners a questionnaire.

MARKETING TO INDUSTRY

As consumers, we have a tendency to think of marketing as a system designed to satisfy our needs. There is another side of marketing that we know must exist but do not encounter as often. That market consists of all the exchanges that go on among major organizations in society. For example, somebody has to sell coal to the electric utilities that use coal. Someone else sells electricity to the major manufacturers of cars, trucks, machinery, and computers. Then someone sells these manufactured goods to farmers, government agencies, and other large organizations.

Using all the resources provided by these exchanges, producers, farmers, and government agencies begin the process of satisfying the needs of consumers. But there are still many middlemen who must be contacted before goods and services reach the final consumer. There are wholesalers who provide transportation and storage services; communications firms who keep the information flowing among the organizations (for example, ad agencies); and retailers who store the merchandise until we are ready to buy.

The marketing of goods and services to manufacturers, institutions (for example, hospitals or schools), commercial operations (retail stores), and the government is called *industrial* marketing or *business-to-business* marketing. The basic principle of this kind of marketing is still find a need and fill it, but the strategies are different because the buyers are different. Some of the things that make industrial marketing different are the following:

1. The market for industrial goods is a *derived* demand. That is, the demand for consumer products such as automobiles creates the demand for industrial goods and services including tires, batteries, glass, metal, plastics, and engines.
2. The demand for industrial goods is relatively *inelastic.* That is, the quantity demanded does not always change significantly with minor changes in price. The reason for this is that industrial products are made up of so many parts that a price increase for one part is not usually a significant problem.
3. The *number of customers* in the industrial market is relatively *few.* That is, there are just a few construction firms or mining operations compared to a consumer market segment of hundreds of thousands or millions.
4. The *size* of industrial customers is relatively *large.* That is, a few large organizations may account for most of the employment and production of various goods and services.
5. Industrial *markets* tend to be *concentrated.* For example, oil fields tend to be concentrated in Alberta. Consequently, marketing efforts often may be concentrated on a particular geographic area, and manufacturers may reduce distribution problems by locating warehouses near industrial "centres."

The demand for industrial goods is a derived demand. For example, the demand for tires depends partially on the sale of new cars. The same is true of batteries, spark plugs, and other auto parts. Of course, repair parts make up a whole different market.

Sales and Advertising Management Jobs		
Year	Annual Growth Rate	All Jobs
1981–89	4.6%	1.5%
1989–95 (estimated)	3.9%	1.5%

Figure 10–10 Employment growth in sales and advertising management is well ahead of rate for all jobs.

Source: *Job Futures: An Occupational Outlook to 1995* 1, 1990, Canadian Occupational Projection System (COPS), Department of Employment and Immigration, cat. no. MP43-181/1990-1-1E.

6. Industrial *buyers* generally are *more rational* and experienced in their selection of goods and services. They use specifications and carefully weigh the "total product offer," including quality, price, and service.
7. Industrial *sales* tend to be *direct*. Manufacturers sell products such as tires directly to automobile manufacturers but tend to use wholesalers and retailers to sell to consumers.

Industrial markets are often more complex than consumer markets because the products are sold many times before they reach the ultimate consumer. Many universities now have courses in industrial or business-to-business marketing. In such courses, you would learn how to segment industrial markets using government data. You would also learn about the various kinds of industrial goods and how they are marketed. In general, industrial goods are sold through a sales force as opposed to using advertising like consumer goods. That is because the customers tend to be large and concentrated, so it is more efficient and effective to call on them in person.

Let's pause now and review marketing careers in general. You will see that few areas in business offer more variety in careers than marketing.

CAREER PROSPECTS IN MARKETING

A recent survey indicates that the rate of job growth in sales and advertising management occupations was three times the rate for all occupations in the 1980s. In the first half of the 1990s, the rate of job growth in this field is expected to continue to outstrip the growth rate for all jobs by two and a half times. (See Figure 10–10.)

PROGRESS CHECK

- What are the three methods of targeting consumer markets?
- Can you describe the technique and give examples of how a company would use the following segmentation strategies: geographic, demographic, psychographic, benefit, and volume?

SUMMARY

1. Describe marketing's role in society and its importance.

1. Marketing is the process of studying the wants and needs of others and then satisfying those wants and needs with appropriate products or services.

- *Why is marketing more important now?*

Overseas competition and domestic competition have made marketing the major difference among firms.

2. The marketing philosophy has changed over time. At first, emphasis was on production, then on sales. In the 1950s, the philosophy that emerged was called the *marketing concept.*

2. Explain the evolution of the marketing concept and describe its three parts.

▼ *What is the marketing concept?*

It is (1) a consumer orientation, (2) the training of employees from all departments in customer service, and (3) a profit orientation.

▼ *What is the future direction of marketing?*

The aim is to satisfy all needs, including needs not met by businesses. Businesses are adopting a *societal orientation* that broadens the consumer orientation.

3. The basis of marketing is finding a need and filling it.

3. Illustrate the steps in the marketing process.

▼ *What are the basic steps in the marketing process?*

After finding a need, the next step in the marketing process is finding a product or service to fill the need. Marketers test their ideas before developing a prototype of the proposed product and testing it in the marketplace. The product development process includes packaging, branding, and pricing. Marketing middlemen distribute the product to consumers. The final step in the marketing process is promoting the product to consumers.

4. The ingredients that go into a marketing program are called the four Ps of marketing.

4. Identify the four Ps of the marketing mix.

▼ *What are the four Ps of marketing?*

The four Ps of marketing are product, price, place, and promotion.

5. Business survival depends on predicting potential opportunities and future competition. Environmental scanning helps companies identify trends and decide if the trends present opportunities or threats.

5. Explain the role of an environmental scan in marketing.

▼ *What factors are included in an environmental scan?*

An environmental scan includes a thorough analysis of four factors: (1) societal forces, (2) economic realities, (3) technological developments, and (4) legal and regulatory conditions.

6. Marketing helps buyers and sellers exchange items of value.

6. List the eight traditional functions of marketing.

▼ *What do marketers do?*

The eight traditional marketing functions are buying, selling, transportation, storage, finance (credit), risk bearing, standardization, and research.

7. Utility refers to the value that marketing adds to goods and services.

7. Explain how marketing adds utility to goods and services.

▼ *What are the five types of utility?*

The types of utility are (1) form, (2) time, (3) place, (4) possession, and (5) information.

8. There are two major markets, the consumer market and the industrial market.

8. Differentiate between consumer and industrial markets.

▼ *How do industrial markets differ from consumer markets?*

Consumer markets consist of those who buy products for their personal consumption. Industrial markets consist of those who purchase products to produce other products or to sell, rent, or supply products to others.

9. Because consumers differ greatly, marketers must learn to select different consumer groups for which to develop products and services.

9. Compare the various forms of market segmentation and describe how target markets are selected.

▼ *What is a target market?*

It is that group or groups selected for special marketing effort.

▼ *How are those groups chosen?*

Market segmentation breaks the total population down into segments with similar characteristics. Segmentation might be:

Geographic: Various areas of the country are targeted.
Demographic: Age, sex, income, religion, race, and other variables are used.
Psychographic: Values, attitudes, and interests are some of the variables.
Benefit: Comfort, convenience, and other benefit categories are chosen.
Volume: Heavy, light, medium, and non-users are identified.

10. Companies use market research to understand consumers.

10. Discuss the process of using market research to understand consumer behaviour.

▼ *What is the secret to understanding consumers?*

The secret to understanding consumers is *listening*—getting close to customers and finding out what they want and need.

▼ *What factors influence buyer behaviour?*

The various influences on consumer behaviour include marketing mix influences, psychological influences, sociocultural influences, and situational influences.

11. The marketing of goods and services to organizations is called industrial or business-to-business marketing.

11. Define industrial (business-to-business) marketing and explain how industrial markets differ from consumer markets.

▼ *How does industrial (business-to-business) marketing differ from consumer marketing?*

Industrial marketing is more complex than consumer marketing. Industrial goods are more frequently sold through salespeople than through advertising as are consumer goods.

GETTING INVOLVED

1. It is easy to document the social ills for which marketing is partially responsible. Discuss the social benefits and social costs imposed by marketing. Take the position you have not held previously and defend it (that is, defend marketers if you have opposed them and vice versa). Discuss whether less developed countries would or would not benefit from more marketing.
2. Businesses began with a *production orientation,* producing what they wanted and selling it later. Discuss how some artists and colleges continue that orientation. What would happen if artists and colleges switched to the marketing concept? Would that be appropriate?
3. Talk to several people who work in marketing (for example, retailers, salespeople, marketing researchers, advertising people) and see how they enjoy their jobs. Which careers look best? Discuss your findings with the class.
4. Take a product and show how you would segment the market for it using the five variables listed in this chapter.
5. Go to the library and find information about SIC codes. Look through the information, take notes, and put them in a file under industrial marketing.
6. Think of a product other than cereal that your friends want but cannot get near campus. Think of a product to fill that need, do a concept test, evaluate the total market, think of a brand name and a package, develop a promotional scheme, and consider how you would distribute it to students. Begin thinking about a marketing plan for the overall business plan so you can get funding for the project later.

PRACTICING MANAGEMENT DECISIONS

Case One Seagram Hires Nabisco Fixer

Seagram Co. Ltd. has chosen a tough cookie to pick up the pieces at its struggling beverage group.

In an impressive hiring coup, Montreal-based Seagram lured Ellen Marram, 47, away from the president's job at Nabisco Biscuit Co. to become president of its beverage division, which includes Tropicana juices and low-alcohol coolers.

Marram is one of the highest-ranking female executives in the United States. At Nabisco Biscuit, which is based in Parsippany, N.J., she earned widespread recognition as a tough and creative manager who boosted sales of such products as cookies and margarine with a stream of product and marketing innovations.

Although half the size of Nabisco, Seagram was able to entice Marram with a sweeping mandate to build a global consumer business.

"The attraction of the job is an opportunity to build existing franchises and new franchises on a worldwide basis," Marram said. She will start her new job at Seagram's New York headquarters in May.

Seagram has two compelling reasons for diversifying into global markets.

First, its core alcohol business, which accounts for about 70 percent of sales, has dim growth prospects in an era when consumers are demanding healthier drinks. Second, brand labels such as Tropicana are under siege from private label products sold directly by retailers because the product is so easily duplicated.

Marram has lots of practice protecting brand labels from discounters. One of her biggest marketing triumphs during her 17-year career at Nabisco and its subsidiary Standard Brands Inc. was to transform Fleischmann's margarine into a high-profile health food from an ordinary bread spread.

"Some people say all margarines are alike, but Fleischmann's built a unique and strong image," she said.

Marram's first challenge will be to defend Tropicana from private label goods.

According to Information Resources Inc., a Chicago data company, private labels accounted for 18.4 percent of all goods sold in supermarkets last year. A decade ago, private labels were barely a blip on consumer databases.

Nowhere is their popularity more apparent than in the refrigerated and frozen juice market. Private label juice sales grew 18 percent last year to $868 million or 29 percent of the $3-billion U.S. market. Tropicana came in second, with 27.4 percent of the market. Atlanta-based Coca-Cola Co.'s Minute Maid had 24.4 percent.

Cookies and crackers are easier to diversify than juices, so it is widely expected that Seagram will diversify into new beverages and food products through acquisitions.

The biggest expansion opportunities for Seagram, however, lie outside the United States. Tropicana has been sold in France for years and in the past two years the company has expanded sales into Canada, Sweden, Britain, and Japan.

Progress has been slow. Less than 10 percent of the company's $6.1-billion sales are generated globally.

Decision Questions

1. International business was discussed in Chapter 2 and franchising was examined in Chapter 6. Marram sees opportunity for expansion into franchising on a global basis. Can you see how a such an opportunity exists with fruit juices or coolers? Might it involve acquiring suitable franchisers?
2. The case refers to brand labels being under heavy attack by private labels that undercut them in pricing. Is it possible that the recession has made consumers very price conscious? What marketing tactics might you try to make your name-brand juice more popular despite its higher price?
3. Can you think of a marketing strategy you might use to introduce Tropicana into countries where fruit juice is not yet popular? Would you favour educating young people to drink fruit juice by introducing it into the schools free? Would you combine this with advertising and various promotions? Who would be your target markets?
4. How about low-alcohol coolers? Is the situation different from that confronting Tropicana fruit juices? What differences are there?

Source: Jacquie McNish, "Seagram Hires Nabisco Fixer," *Globe and Mail,* April 19, 1993, pp. B1, B9.

Case Two Kellogg: Marketing Breakfast Cereal

It all started back in the 1800s with Dr. John H. Kellogg. He was a strict vegetarian and a leader in the Seventh Day Adventist community. Dr. Kellogg noticed that the typical American breakfast consisted of salt pork, biscuits, and ham gravy or pancakes and molasses. As director of a health spa, Dr. Kellogg fed those who attended corn, wheat, and oatmeal—ground and baked. No salt and no sugar.

C. W. Post was one of his patients. He decided to go into business to market what was to become Post Grape-Nuts. Post added sugar to make his cereal tastier. Dr. Kellogg and his brother, Will K. Kellogg, countered by offering a sweetened cereal of their own. The breakfast battle was on.

The big Kellogg cereal in the 1800s was Corn Flakes. Guess what a big seller is today? You guessed it: Corn Flakes. Also popular is sugar-covered corn flakes (Frosted Flakes). Kellogg has about 36 percent of the consumer market, down a little in the last couple of years. It is now in a head-to-head battle with General Mills' Total. Kellogg feels that its Just Right cereal is as nutritious as Total and has a better taste.

Let's see how Kellogg has attacked certain market segments. For adults, it has developed high-fibre cereals like Nutri-Grain, Bran Products, and Cracklin' Oat Bran plus the vitamin-pill-in-a-cereal Special K. For children, it's Froot Loops, Sugar Pops, Sugar Smacks, and Apple Jacks. For traditionalists, there are Corn Flakes, Rice Krispies, and Raisin Bran.

Post Raisin Bran is now part of General Foods. It, too, has targeted certain markets. There is Grape-Nuts for the old-timers. Kids can feast on sugary cereals such as SmurfBerry Crunch, Super Sugar Crisp, and Honey-Nut Crunch Raisin Bran. Joggers might go for C. W. Post Hearty Granola or just plain Bran Flakes. Altogether, General Foods has between 10 and 11 percent of the market.

The old Cheerios is still popular for General Mills. Honey Nut Cheerios is also a good seller, along with Apple Cinnamon Cheerios. Together, the Cheerio brands are the number one cereal in America. Anyone over 40 may remember eating graham crackers with milk. Now, General Mills makes it easy for you with Golden Grahams. Kids can sugar up on Trix and Lucky Charms. The General Mills market share is 24 percent or so.

General Mills is going after more share with two new products: Basic 4, an adult cereal that, together with milk, provides four basic food groups, and Triples, an all-family cereal combining corn, rice, and wheat. It's positioned to go up against Rice Krispies. General Mills already took a big bite out of Kellogg's Raisin Bran with its Big G's Raisin Nut Bran, Oatmeal Raisin Crisp, and Total Raisin Bran.

A popular cereal in the Quaker Oats line is 100% Natural. It also makes Life and Cap'n Crunch and Halfsies. Market share is about 9 percent.

We can't forget Ralston Purina, with its 6 percent plus market share. It has given us Donkey Kong, Cookie Crisp, Waffelos, and Dinky Donuts. Its big seller is Chex. One of the latest cereals is Barbie so young girls can have "breakfast with Barbie."

Nabisco's number one seller is Shredded Wheat. It has only about a 4 percent market share.

Most of the best-sellers in the cereal industry are relatively nutritious. For a while, oat bran cereals were popular, but they faded with the reports that they were not as healthy as they were promoted to be.

How far have we come from the original intent of Dr. Kellogg to give us a healthy, nutritious, sugar-free, salt-free breakfast food? Cookie Crisp is 47 percent sugar. A one-ounce serving of Mr. T's Cereal has 230 milligrams of sodium. That's 30 more milligrams than Lay's packs into an equal amount of potato chips. Sugar Golden Crisp is 51 percent sugar, and Honey Smacks has 57 percent refined sweetener (including honey). In fact, there is little fibre in most children-oriented cereals.

The cereal industry is now doing about $6.9 billion a year in sales. Some $50 million was spent on advertising just to introduce Basic 4 and Triples.

Decision Questions

1. Cereal makers have followed the marketing slogan of "Find a need and fill it" by giving us any kind of cereal we want, including cereals that are mostly sugar or very high in salt content. This is definitely an example of a consumer orientation. Would the same mix of cereals be available if cereal companies adopted a more societal orientation?
2. Dropping those cereals with high sugar content would cut profits dramatically at cereal companies. Under what circumstances would a company make such cuts?
3. Cereal companies have provided us with high-fibre, high-vitamin cereals. Adults eat them, but children often choose the cereals that are half sugar. What reaction do you have to this trend?
4. Kellogg has introduced two new cereals from Europe called Müeslix. Five-grain Müeslix contains oats, wheat, corn, rice, and barley. Bran Müeslix contains bran, chopped dates, figs, and almonds. These cereals have 20 percent of the total European market. How would you market them here compared to how Kellogg did it? Give brand names, markets, price, and promotional ideas. Does it sound as if Kellogg has destroyed the market for Fiberrific?
5. Rainforest Products has introduced two new cereals called Rainforest Crisp and Rainforest Granola. Profits from these cereals will be shared with environmental groups, and the cereal is packaged in recycled paper. Do you think consumers will respond favorably to these new socially aware cereals?

Sources: Julie Liesse, "New Cereals Power Big G's Market Push," *Advertising Age,* November 19, 1990, pp. 1 and 56; Jesus Sanchez, "Watch Out Corn Flakes—Barbie Takes On Breakfast," *Los Angeles Times,* August 23, 1989, p. 1 of Part IV; Thomas V. Di Bacco, "Upset Stomachs, Cereal Wars," *Washington Post Health,* May 19, 1992, p. 17.

LET'S TALK BUSINESS

1. Imagine you are the president of a small liberal arts college. Enrollment has declined dramatically and the college is in danger of closing. Show how you might revive the college by applying the marketing concept. How would you implement the three phases: 1) a consumer orientation, 2) the training of employees in all departments in customer service, and 3) a profit orientation? Would you recommend a more societal orientation as well? How so?
2. If the fundamental concept in marketing is "Find a need and fill it," what are some of the marketing opportunities near your school?
3. There are many careers available in industrial marketing, especially jobs in selling, yet many students are unaware of companies that are involved in industrial sales. What are some of the products that are sold to manufacturing companies? What companies produce these products? Think of steel, tires, boxes, computer software, machinery, oil, chemicals, office and factory supplies, and other industrial goods.
4. How many segmentation strategies could you use to segment the market for a new, nutritious soft drink that contains no sugar but provides the daily vitamin requirement. Combine the strategies to describe the target market you think would be the most profitable.

LOOKING AHEAD

In Chapter 6 you learned that a business plan calls for a marketing plan. That plan includes a review of the industry size, trends, and the target market segment. We have discussed how to do these things in Chapter 10. You may want to review segmentation strategies when writing your business plan. Chapter 11 helps you look at your product and discuss its strengths and weaknesses relative to competition. Chapter 11 also discusses the pricing information you will have to include in a business plan, such as the number of products you will have to sell to break even.

XP
FL 4784 GK

PRODUCT DEVELOPMENT AND PRICING

LEARNING GOALS

After you have read and studied this chapter, you should be able to:

1. Explain the difference between a product and a product offer.
2. Define and give an example of a product mix and a product line.
3. Describe how businesses create product differentiation for their goods and services.
4. Identify the three classes of consumer products and how they are marketed.
5. Identify the two major classes of industrial goods and how they are marketed.
6. List the four functions of packaging.
7. Give examples of a brand, a brand name, and a trademark.
8. Explain the role of a product manager.
9. Outline the five steps of the new product development process.
10. Identify and describe the stages of the product life cycle and describe marketing strategies at each stage.
11. Give examples of various pricing objectives.
12. Discuss the use of break-even analysis and calculate the break-even point.
13. Describe various pricing strategies.

KEY TERMS

brand, p. 354
break-even analysis, p. 367
break-even point, p. 367
competition-oriented pricing, p. 370
convenience goods and services, p. 350
demand-oriented pricing, p. 370
generic goods, p. 356
generic names, p. 356
industrial goods, p. 351
knockoff brand, p. 355
market modification, p. 364
national brand names, p. 355
penetration price strategy, p. 369
price leadership, p. 370
private brands, p. 356
product differentiation, p. 349
product life cycle, p. 361
product line, p. 347
product manager, p. 357
product mix, p. 348
product modification, p. 365
product offer, p. 346
production goods, p. 351
shopping goods and services, p. 350
skimming price strategy, p. 369
specialty goods and services, p. 351
support goods, p. 351
trademark, p. 355
value pricing, p. 370

Dave Nichol

PROFILE DAVE NICHOL, KING OF PRIVATE-LABEL PRODUCTS

Shoppers in a Loblaw's supermarket in Toronto are surprised to see a man they recognize charging about with two men in tow. Millions of Canadians regularly see Dave Nichol on TV advertising his President's Choice (PC) products. He is selling his ideas and products to executives of a large Australian supermarket chain. He has already sold his PC products to many American chains, including the largest retailer in the U.S.—Wal-Mart, with over 1,900 stores.

Dave Nichol grew up in many small Ontario towns as his father, a railway station agent, was transferred from one place to another. His roommate at the University of Western Ontario was Galen Weston, whose grandfather had founded giant conglomerate George Weston Ltd. Weston is the parent company of Loblaw's, the largest supermarket chain in Canada. After earning an M.B.A., Nichol went on to collect law degrees at the University of British Columbia and Harvard and ended up in management consulting, while Weston went to work in the family business. A decade later Weston called on his old roommate to save the failing Loblaw's chain.

In 1972 the chain was in terrible shape, but Nichol defied all predictions and succeeded in turning Loblaw's around by coming up with generic, or No Name, products. These grocery products were packaged in bright yellow boxes with bold, black names. In both product and promotion he was not an innovator but followed a French and American idea, respectively.

In 1983 Nichol launched the President's Choice line. It started with the Classic, a rich chocolate-chip cookie, and the President's Blend, a special blend of coffee beans from seven countries. This time he was copying an English company. He then made an important discovery: he

> recognized a generational shift in Canadian shoppers. With two-income families the norm by the '80s, most shoppers valued convenience and a little bit of pleasure above almost everything else. . . . No longer is grocery shopping simply about satisfying hunger. Now it's a way to show superior knowledge and taste.

He soon developed a whole line of PC products with exotic names such as Zipper Back shrimp, Memories of Ancient Damascus Tangy Pomegranate, and Memories of Hong Kong Spicy Black Bean and Garlic Sauce.

PC Cola has seriously hurt Coca-Cola sales in Canada. In total, PC and No Name products now bring in $1.5 billion, or 32 percent of Loblaw's retail business annually, and generate higher profit margins than the national brands. Now, as head of Loblaw International Merchants, Nichol is busily promoting PC all over the world.

There is a twofold appeal to retailers: higher profit margins and more control of what products they put on their shelves. This is forcing the big name national brands like Nabisco, Coke, and Pepsi to fight back as they see their market shares dropping. They are lowering prices, thus reducing their hitherto large profit margins. They are losing their ability to control shelf space as supermarkets flex their private-label muscles and increase their profits in the process.

Dave Nichol believes that supermarkets are going to win this battle because the big brands spend so much on advertising and other marketing methods that they are locked in to high costs the private labels do not have. A major battle is shaping up. So far Nichol has been right. The question is, are we witnessing a permanent shift in consumer buying habits or is it a temporary trend?

Source: Mark Stevenson, "Global Gourmet," *Canadian Business*, July 1993, pp. 22–33.

PRODUCT DEVELOPMENT OVER TIME

International competition today is so strong that Canadian businesses are losing markets to foreign producers. One way to regain those markets is to design better products. That means products of high quality at a competitive price. As we shall see in this chapter, whether or not a consumer perceives a product as better depends on many factors. To satisfy consumers, marketers must learn to listen better and adapt constantly to changing market demands. A critical part of the impression consumers get about products is the price. This chapter, therefore, will explore two critical parts of the market mix: product development and price.

Dave Nichol has learned that the problem of adapting products to markets is a continuous one. An organization cannot do a one-time survey of consumer wants and needs, design a line of products to meet those needs, put them in the stores, and relax. There must be a *constant* monitoring of customer wants and needs, because consumer and business needs change over time.

Nowhere is the problem of consumer choice more keenly felt than in the fast-food business. Firms such as McDonald's and Burger King are constantly monitoring consumers to detect trends, preferences, and lifestyle changes that call for new offerings. The more sophisticated firms become in marketing, the more important it becomes for others to follow. A few years ago Wendy's didn't even have a research and development staff. Today it has 42 people in that area.

The number of products in the development stage ranges from 20 or so at McDonald's to more than 50 at Wendy's. Burger King uses a computer to predict how much labour a new product will require, what effect it might have on sales of other menu items, and how much total profit it will generate.

Fast-food organizations must constantly monitor all sources of information for new product ideas. McDonald's got the idea for the Big Mac, the Filet-O-Fish sandwich, and the Egg McMuffin from franchisees. Chicken McNuggets were developed when the head chef was experimenting with Onion McNuggets. McDonald's chairman suggested that the chef try chicken and after much market testing, a new product was born. Researchers also monitor grocery store shelves and

Wendy's is constantly looking at ways to satisfy the consumer. Their research and development staff now has 42 people working on new products. As many as 50 new products can be under development at a given time.

cookbooks for new ideas. A whole new range of environmentally friendly products has been developed. Product development, then, is a key activity in any modern business.

One place you may not expect to see new product development is in the produce section of the supermarket. Yet Frieda Caplan has a specialty foods company that is regularly introducing new products into produce areas. For example, many grocery stores still carry only a few varieties of apples. Now growers are working on 35 types, including Northern Spys, Golden Russets, and Opalescent. The trend toward Caribbean meals has led supermarkets to sell fruits and vegetables such as yucca, malanga, boniato, and calabaza. Exotic vegetables such as osone, frisee, and tsoisin are catching on. Organically grown produce is making significant headway. You get the idea.

There is a lot more to new product development than merely introducing new products, however. What marketers do to create excitement for those products is as important as the products themselves.

Developing a Total Product Offer

Let's review the role of products in marketing before we get too far into product concepts. We have said that marketing is the process of finding wants and needs and satisfying those wants and needs with appropriate goods and services (products). We defined a *product* in Chapter 10 as any physical good, service, or idea that satisfies a want or need.

product offer
Consists of all the tangibles and intangibles that consumers evaluate when deciding whether or not to buy something.

From a marketing management viewpoint, a product offer is more than just the physical good or service. A **product offer** consists of all the tangibles and intangibles that consumers evaluate when deciding whether or not to buy something. Thus, a product offer may be a washing machine, car, or can of beer, but the product offer also consists of the:

- Price.
- Package.
- Store surroundings.
- Image created by advertising.
- Guarantee.
- Reputation of the producer.
- Brand name.
- Service.
- Buyers' past experience.

When people buy a product, they evaluate some or all these things and compare product offers on these dimensions.

Obviously, consumers will do a more comprehensive evaluation for a car than for a can of beer. Also, different segments of the market evaluate differently for the same product. Younger beer drinkers may drink anything at a party, while mature consumers may have developed specific preferences. A successful marketer must begin to think like a consumer and evaluate the product offer as a total collection of impressions created by all the factors listed.

Let's go back and look at our highly nutritious, high-fibre, low-sugar breakfast cereal, Fiberrific, for example. The product offer as perceived by the consumer is much more than the cereal itself. Anything that affects consumer perceptions about the benefits and value of the cereal may determine whether or not it is purchased.

Bombadier Inc. now has a wide variety of product lines. From its original product the Ski-Doo, Bombardier is now recognized as a world-class designer and manufacturer of transportation equipment, aerospace, defense and motorized consumer products. UTDC, a division of Bombardier Inc., built Vancouver's SkyTrain: the world's longest fully automated rapid transit system.

The price certainly is an important part of the perception of product value. Often a high price indicates high quality. The store surroundings are also important. If the cereal is being sold in an exclusive health food store, it takes on many of the characteristics of the store (e.g., healthful and upscale). A guarantee of satisfaction can increase the product's value in the mind of consumers, as can a well-known brand name. Advertising can create an attractive image, and word of mouth can enhance the reputation. If a buyer has tried the product before, he or she has certain predispositions to buy or not. Thus, Fiberrific is more than a cereal as a product offer; it is a whole bundle of impressions in the minds of consumers.

THINKING IT THROUGH

When Armand Bombardier started his small company more than half a century ago, it manufactured his new invention, a Ski-Doo snowmobile. Three decades later, Bombardier Inc. was producing railway and subway cars for Canadian and American needs. Fifteen years later the company was making aircraft on an international scale with companies in Canada, the U.S., and Ireland. What do you think prompted such major changes in its product lines? Why was Bombardier looking for other lines? Why was it expanding in these directions?

The Product Mix

Companies usually do not sell just one product. Rather, they sell several different but complementary products. Figure 11–1 shows the product lines of Procter & Gamble. A **product line** is a group of products that are physically similar or are intended for a similar market. The product lines for Procter & Gamble include bar soaps, detergents, and dishwashing detergents. In one product line, there may be several competing brands. Thus, Procter & Gamble has many brands of detergent in its product line, including Bold, Cheer, Tide, and Ivory Snow. All of P&G's product lines make up its product mix.

product line
A group of products that are physically similar or are intended for a similar market.

McCain, Canada Packers, Schneider, and Highliner have all introduced product lines of microwavable snack foods that are capturing the market. These include frozen microwavable milkshakes, hamburgers, french fries, and other products. The companies hope to add to their product line—microwavable snack foods—in coming years.[1]

Figure 11–1 Procter & Gamble's product mix and product lines. Most large companies make more than one product. Here you can see the various products and brands Procter & Gamble makes. Note how physically similar the products are in each product line.

Product Lines	Brands
Bar soaps	Camay, Coast, Ivory, Kirk's, Lava, Monchel, Safeguard, Zest
Detergents	Bold, Cheer, Dash, Dreft, Era, Gain, Ivory Snow, Liquid Bold-3, Liquid Cheer, Liquid Tide, Oxydol, Solo, Tide
Dishwashing detergents	Cascade, Dawn, Ivory Liquid, Joy, Liquid Cascade
Cleaners and cleansers	Comet, Comet Liquid, Mr. Clean, Spic & Span, Spic & Span Pine Liquid, Top Job
Shampoos	Head & Shoulders, Ivory, Lilt, Pert Plus, Prell
Toothpastes	Crest, Denquel, Gleem
Paper tissue products	Banner, Charmin, Puffs, White Cloud
Disposable diapers	Luvs, Pampers
Shortening and cooking oils	Crisco, Crisco Oil, Crisco Corn Oil, Puritan

The Oldsmobile product mix consists of passenger cars, vans, and more. Automobile companies may also include trucks, tanks, and other vehicles in their product mix. The product line for automobiles is likely to include small, mid-size, and large cars.

product mix
The combination of product lines offered by a manufacturer.

Product mix is the term used to describe the *combination* of product lines offered by a manufacturer. As you can see in Figure 11–1, P&G's product mix consists of product lines of soaps, detergents, toothpastes, shampoos, and so on.

In the case of automobile manufacturers, the product mix consists of everything from passenger cars to small trucks, large tractor trailers, and tanks. One auto manufacturer's product line for passenger cars may include large luxury cars, mid-size cars, compact cars, mini-vans, and station wagons.

Manufacturers must decide what product mix is best. The mix may include both goods and services to spread the risk among several industries. Companies must be careful not to diversify so widely that they lose their focus and their competitive advantage.

REACHING BEYOND OUR BORDERS

Costly Attempts to Broaden Product Mix

During the merger and conglomerate wave that swept through Canada and the U.S. in the 1980s, many companies sought to broaden their product mix by acquiring companies unrelated to their core businesses. In many cases this has not worked out well, and a hasty retreat often turned into a rout.

For example, Lavalin, the huge international engineering group based in Quebec, went broke because of its acquisition of a petrochemical complex. BCE Inc., parent company of Bell Canada, was badly burned with its BCED venture into real estate development in the U.S. Robert Campeau's attempt to become the kingpin of U.S. retailing resulted in disaster and the loss of his large real estate development company.

Sources: Various articles, Report on Business, *Globe and Mail,* Dec. 29, 1990; David Hatter, "BCE Phones Home," *Canadian Business* 63, no. 8, Aug. 1990, p. 28; Barrie McKenna, "SNC Buys Lavalin's Prized Engineering Firm," Report on Business, *Globe and Mail,* Aug. 13, 1991, pp. B1, B5. ▼

PRODUCT DIFFERENTIATION

Product differentiation is the attempt to create in the minds of consumers perceptions that make one product seem superior to others. Often the *actual* product differences may be quite small, so marketers use a clever mix of pricing, advertising, and packaging to create a unique and attractive image. One of the more successful attempts at product differentiation was accomplished by Perrier. Perrier made its sparkling water so attractive through pricing and promotion that often people order it by brand name instead of a Coke or Pepsi.

product differentiation
The attempt to create perceptions in the minds of consumers that one product is superior to others.

There is no reason why a company could not create a similar image for Fiberrific. With a high price and creative advertising, it could become the Perrier of cereals. The ultimate example of product differentiation would be to package and sell air. Well, guess what? The Japanese have been rather successful selling canned oxygen for $5. Michael Jackson triggered the boom by bringing his own air on his Japanese tour.[2] Would you believe that they now sell air in different "flavours" or odours? Different products call for different marketing strategies, as we'll see. What kind of strategy would you use to sell canned air?

Product Development in the Service Sector

Much has been written about improving product quality in the goods sector. Relatively little is being said about improving quality in the service sector. One of the biggest complaints consumers have is waiting in line. This occurs at banks, auto licence bureaus, car rental desks, and more. The product of service firms would be much better if the waiting time could be reduced or eliminated. Other improvements could greatly increase consumer satisfaction. That is what product development in the service sector is all about.

Car rental firms and hotels are adopting fast check-in and check-out procedures that do away with waiting in lines. Automated self-service machines at banks eliminate long lines and provide 24-hour service. Supermarkets have attached calculators to shopping trolleys so customers can compare unit prices as well as calculating their total shopping bill to make sure they have enough cash.

The key to success in the 1990s is good service at reasonable prices. Those service organizations that improve their products will prosper by capturing a larger share of the market.

Marketing Different Classes of Consumer Goods and Services

Several attempts have been made to classify consumer goods and services. One traditional classification has three general categories: convenience goods and services, shopping goods and services, and specialty goods and services. These classifications are based on consumer shopping habits and preferences.

convenience goods and services
Products the consumer wants to purchase frequently and with a minimum of effort.

Convenience goods and services. Products the consumer wants to purchase frequently and with a minimum of effort (for example, milk, beer, banking) are **convenience goods and services.** Location is very important for marketers of convenience goods and services. Brand awareness and image also are important.

shopping goods and services
Products the consumer buys only after comparing quality and price from a variety of sellers.

Shopping goods and services. Products the consumer buys only after comparing value, quality, and price from a variety of sellers are **shopping goods and services.** Shopping goods and services are sold largely through shopping centres where consumers can "shop around." Because consumers carefully compare such products,

Expensive specialty items are often sold through specialty magazines. For example, these Rossignol skis were sold through *Ski* Magazine. People will go out of their way to buy specialty ski products that have a popular brand name.

marketers can emphasize price differences, quality differences, or some combination of the two. Examples include clothes, shoes, appliances, and auto repair.

Specialty goods and services. Products that have a special attraction to consumers, who are willing to go out of their way to obtain them, are **specialty goods and services.** Examples include expensive fur coats, jewellery, cars, and services provided by medical specialists or business consultants. These products are often marketed through specialty magazines. For example, specialty skis may be sold through ski magazines and specialty foods through gourmet magazines.

specialty goods and services
Products that have such a special attraction to consumers they are willing to go out of their way to obtain them.

The marketing task varies depending on the kind of product; that is, convenience goods are marketed differently from specialty goods, and so forth. The best way to promote convenience goods is to make them readily available and create the proper image. Price and quality are the best appeals for shopping goods, and specialty goods rely on reaching special market segments through advertising.

Whether or not a good or service falls into a particular class depends on the individual consumer. What is a shopping good for one consumer (for example, coffee) could be a specialty good for another consumer (for example, imported coffee). Some people shop around comparing different dry cleaners, so dry cleaning is a shopping service for them. Others go to the closest store, making it a convenience service. Perrier took what was basically a shopping good in the mind of the consumer (sparkling water) and tried to make it a specialty good by making it look very different and special. One could do the same for canned oxygen with the right combination of packaging, branding, pricing, and promotion.

Marketing Industrial Goods and Services

Industrial goods are products used to produce other products. Some products can be classified as both consumer and industrial goods. For example, a Macintosh computer could be sold to consumer or industrial markets. As a consumer good, the computer might be sold through computer stores like Computerland or through computer magazines. Most of the promotional task would go to advertising. As an industrial good, the Mac is more likely to be sold by a salesperson. Advertising would be less of a factor in the promotion strategy. You can see that classifying goods by user category helps determine the proper marketing mix strategy.

industrial goods
Products used in the production of other products.

Industrial goods are often divided into two major categories: production goods and support goods (see Figure 11–2). **Production goods** include raw materials like grain and steel that enter into the final product. Component parts such as electric motors and springs are also categorized as production goods. Producers of such goods usually sell directly to other manufacturers, using salespeople as the major promotional technique. **Support goods** are purchased to assist in the production of other products. Some of the major categories and how they are promoted include:[3]

production goods
Industrial goods such as grain and steel that enter into the final product.

support goods
Industrial goods such as accessory equipment and supplies that are used to assist in the production of other products.

- *Installations* include buildings and equipment. These are usually expensive items and are sold through sales representatives. Pricing is often by competitive bid.
- *Accessory equipment* such as tools and office equipment is often purchased in small quantities. As a consequence, these goods are usually sold through distributors who have many outlets and can contact many buyers.
- *Supplies* include items like paper clips, stationery, and cleaning items. These may be purchased through distributors or ordered directly from the producer, with little negotiating taking place over time.

- *Services* include maintenance and repair services, sold through salespeople and through a bidding process, and legal and accounting services, usually sold through personal contacts, referrals, and advertising.

In general, industrial producers rely on salespeople much more heavily than do producers of consumer goods. This means more job opportunities in sales for you in the industrial sector. The average industrial sales call costs a producer over $250 and it takes several calls to close a sale, so you can see why industrial salespeople get excellent training and receive outstanding wages.

PROGRESS CHECK

- What is the difference between a product and a product offer as viewed by a marketing manager?
- What is the difference between a product line and a product mix?
- Name the three classes of consumer goods and services. Give examples of each.
- What are the two different classes of industrial goods and how are they marketed?

Figure 11–2 Types of Consumer and Industrial Goods and Services.
Marketers have developed categories of goods and services to help in designing marketing strategies. A different strategy is needed for convenience goods (location) than for shopping goods (price/quality). Similarly, industrial goods and services are categorized because the marketing task for each category is different and the process of categorizing makes it clearer which strategies to use.

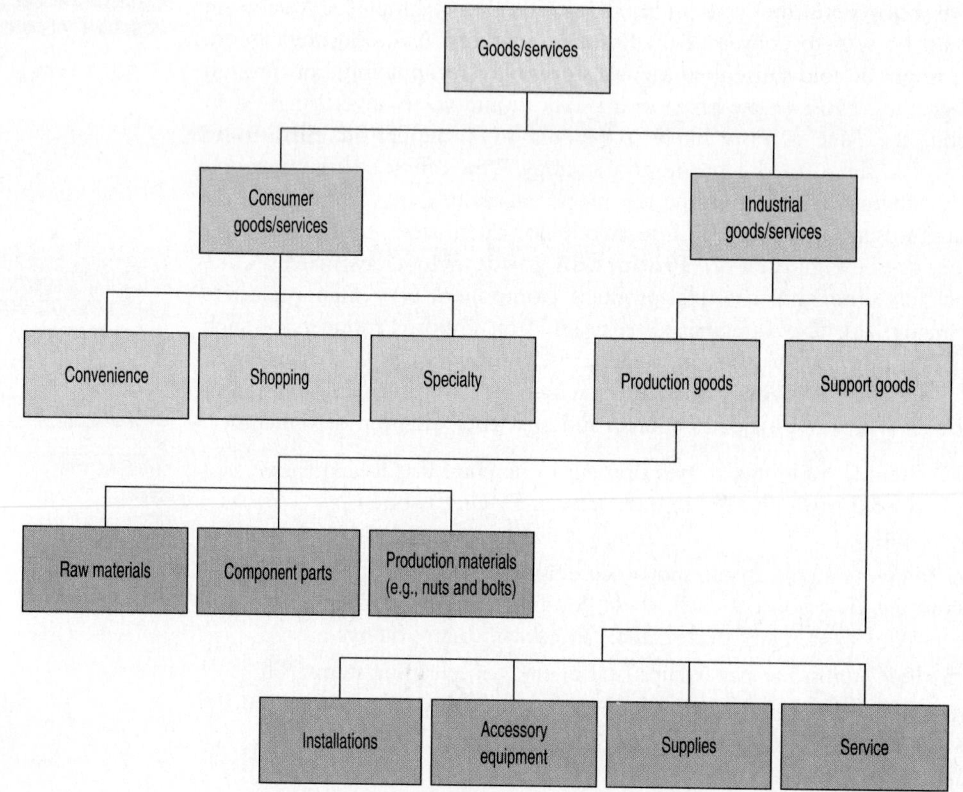

PACKAGING CHANGES THE PRODUCT

We have said that consumers evaluate many aspects of the product offer, including the package and the brand. It is surprising how important packaging can be. Many years ago people had problems with table salt because it would stick together and form lumps whenever the weather was humid or damp. The Morton Salt Co. solved that problem by designing a package that kept the salt dry in all kinds of weather. Thus the slogan, "When it rains, it pours." Packaging made Morton's salt more desirable than competing products, and it is one of the best-known salts in Canada and the United States.

The Morton Salt Co. knew how to use packaging to improve its basic product. Other companies have used similar techniques. Thus, we have had squeezable catsup bottles, plastic bottles for oil that eliminate the need for funnels, stackable potato chips in a can, toothpaste pumps, plastic cans for tennis balls, microwavable snack packages, dinners than can be boiled in a pouch and served immediately, whipped cream in dispenser cans, vegetables in climate-controlled packages, and so forth. In each case, the package changed the product in the minds of consumers and opened large markets. Packaging can also make a product more attractive to retailers. For example, the Universal Product Codes on many packages make it easier to control inventory. In short, packaging changes the product by changing its visibility, usefulness, or attractiveness.

The Growing Importance of Packaging

Packaging has always been an important aspect of the product offer, but today it is carrying more of the promotional burden. Many goods that were once sold by salespersons are now being sold in self-service outlets, and the package has been given more sales responsibility. The package must (1) attract the buyer's attention; (2) describe the contents and give information about them; (3) explain the benefits of the good inside; (4) provide information on warranties, warnings, and other consumer matters; (5) give some indication of price, value, and uses; and (6) protect the good, stand up under handling and storage, be tamperproof, and yet be easy to

Packaging changes products by changing their visibility, usefulness, or attractiveness. Breweries often change the appearance of their cans or the labels on their bottles to make them more eye-catching.

The Coca-Cola Co. introduced the first-ever plastic soft drink bottles made with a blend of recycled and non-recycled plastic. While plastic soft drink bottles have been recycled for some time to make products such as carpeting, fiberfill stuffing, and plastic lumber, this marks the first time that polyethylene terephthalate (PET) plastic soft drink bottles can be used to make the same product from which they came.

open and use. Clearly, packaging has become a critical part of product design. A critical part of the package is the label.

Labelling. What are the qualities that make for a successful label? Some of the photos in this chapter show some examples of well-known consumer products. Can you see how these labels do their job? They must be attractive and informative. They must also meet Canadian legal requirements regarding ingredients, bilingualism, grading, and expiration date (if applicable). From the marketing point of view, a good label helps to identify the product and differentiate it from competing products. We are swamped by many competing brands of everything from chocolate bars to toothpaste to soaps, so you can see why making the consumer aware of a particular product by differentiation is a major concern of marketers.

BRANDING

brand
A name, symbol, or design (or combination of these) that identifies the goods or services of one seller or group of sellers and distinguishes them from those of competitors.

Closely related to packaging is branding. A **brand** is a name, symbol, or design (or a combination of them) that identifies the goods or services of one seller or group of sellers and distinguishes them from those of competitors. The term *brand* is sufficiently comprehensive to include practically all means of identification of a product except perhaps the package and its shape. As we saw in Chapter 10, a brand name is that part of the brand consisting of a logo, word, letter, or group of words or letters comprising a name that differentiates the goods or services of a seller from those of competitors. Brand names you may be familiar with include Chevrolet,

MAKING ETHICAL DECISIONS

Manufacturers today are torn between making packages that are good for the environment and packaging that is good for marketing. Compact disks, for example, were packaged in 6-inch by 12-inch cardboard or plastic boxes a half-inch thick. This was to hold a wafer-thin, 4¾-inch disc. The excess packaging material on such products created an environmental problem throughout the United States. In 1992, the recording industry responded to environmental concern by introducing a smaller package.

In Canada also, record producers have voluntarily agreed to eliminate the "long box" for CDs, and Europe has done the same. U.S. producers saw the large box as an excellent marketing tool. They used large, eye-catching graphics on them, which will not be as noticeable on the new, smaller boxes. Also, large boxes discouraged shoplifting. Nonetheless, manufacturers responded to pressure and changed the package. The cost to retailers will be quite high because they have to put in new display units.

Environmentalists have put great pressure on all firms to be more environmentally concerned in their packaging. McDonalds, for example, trashed its foam containers made of polystyrene. Both Coke and Pepsi have announced that they plan to use recycled bottles (see the photo on p. 354).

There is scientific evidence that polystyrene may actually be more environmentally sound than paperboard. For example, paperboard weighs more and consumes three times its weight in raw wood. The atmospheric emissions involved in producing paper are two to three times those for producing polystyrene, and the waterborne wastes are 70 percent higher for paper. Other research has shown that insulated polystyrene bowls are better for the environment than coated paper. Nonetheless there is much pressure being exerted by various environmental groups to turn to coated paper.

When forced to choose between a package that makes a product more marketable and one that is recyclable or less damaging to the environment (e.g., less litter), which package should a marketer choose? What if you knew that polystyrene was better for the environment than coated paper, but you could get a lot of publicity by shifting from polystyrene to paper. Would you shift to paper to get the publicity? What would be the consequences of your actions?

Would you have voted for new laws to require producers to make smaller packages for CDs, even if that resulted in fewer sales? What are the ethical issues?

Source: Warren Brookes, "The Big Flack Attack on Polystyrene," *Washington Times,* November 19, 1990, p. G3; Martha M. Hamilton, "Wrapped Up in Waste," *Washington Post,* April 1, 1990, pp. H1 and H5; and Sheila Rule, "Smaller CD Boxes Promised Amid Clamor about Waste," *New York Times,* February 28, 1992, p. A1. ▼

Sony, Del Monte, Campbell, President's Choice, Jordache, Esso, Michelin, Molson, and Colgate. Such brand names give products a distinction that tends to make them attractive to consumers. Those images last a long time.

A **trademark** is a brand that has been given exclusive legal protection for both the brand name and the pictorial design. People are often impressed by certain brand names, even though they say they know there is no difference between brands in a given product category. For example, when someone who says that all aspirin is alike, asks for an aspirin, put out two bottles—one with the Excedrin label and one labeled with an unknown brand. See which one he or she chooses. Most people choose the brand name even when they say there is no difference. What does this indicate?

trademark
A brand that has been given exclusive legal protection for both the brand name and the pictorial design.

Brand Categories

Several categories of brands are familiar to you. **National brand names** are the brand names of manufacturers that distribute the product nationally. They include well-known names such as Xerox, Polaroid, Kodak, Sony, and Chevrolet. **Knockoff brands** are illegal copies of national brand name goods such as Lacoste shirts or Rolex watches. If you see an expensive brand name item for sale at ridiculously

national brand names
Brand names of manufacturers that distribute their products nationally.

knockoff brands
Illegal copies of national brand name items.

low prices, you can be pretty sure it's a knockoff. Counterfeiters in many countries who copy brand names steal billions of dollars annually.

private brands
Products that carry the name of a distributor or retailer instead of the manufacturer.

Private brands are products that do not carry the manufacturer's name and carry the name of a distributor or retailer instead. Well-known names include Viking (Eaton's) and Kenmore (Sears). These are also known as "house" brands or "distributor" brands. Today, some distributor brands are as well known as national brand names such as President's Choice. Major supermarket chains carry their own house brands of products, which are usually manufactured by the major brand name companies.

generic names
Names of product categories.

What many manufacturers fear is having their brand names become generic names. **Generic names** are the names for product *categories*. Did you know that *aspirin* and *linoleum,* which are now generic names for products, were once brand names? So were *nylon, escalator, kerosene,* and *zipper.* All of those names became so popular, so identified with the product, that they lost their brand status and became *generic* (the name of the product category). The producers then had to come up with new names. The original *Aspirin,* for example, became *Bayer* aspirin. Companies that are working hard to protect their brand names today include Xerox (one ad reads, "Don't say 'Xerox it'; say 'Copy it' ") and Styrofoam.

generic goods
Nonbranded products that usually sell at a sizeable discount from national or private brands, have very basic packaging, and are backed with little or no advertising.

Generic goods are non-branded products that usually sell at a sizeable discount from national or private brands, have very basic packaging, and are backed with little or no advertising. The quality varies considerably among generic goods. Some are copies of national brand names and may be close to the same quality, but others may be of minimum quality. There are generic tissues, generic cigarettes, generic peaches, and so forth. All it says on the label of the can is "Peaches," with no brand name. Consumers tend to buy generic goods when quality is not important to them or when they cannot afford brand name goods.

Brand Images

You might try an experiment for yourself. Buy an attractive but inexpensive tie and put in a very attractive box from an exclusive store. Then buy a similar tie from the

President's Choice is a private brand of products manufactured by the Loblaw supermarket chain. The President's Choice products have been extremely successful in Canada and are now being sold in other countries. In many cases, President's Choice products are as well known and received as national brand names. For example, for the year ending February 1993, the Decadent Chocolate Chip Cookie rang up more sales in Canada than RJR Nabisco's Chips Ahoy.

exclusive store and put it in a box from an inexpensive discount store. Tell your friends that you can't decide which tie is better and ask them to choose. If experience is any guide, most will choose the inexpensive tie in the more expensive box. Laboratory experiments support these suggestions. The concept that explains such behaviour is that people often cannot determine the value of products by physical inspection; they therefore turn to other indicators of quality such as labels, packaging, brand names, and price. A higher-priced, expensively packaged item is usually perceived as better regardless of its actual physical qualities.

Knowing that products are perceived as better with a brand name, some companies are putting brand names where you have never seen them before. For example, the Natural Pak company has created the brand name TomAHto for its tomatoes. Packaged in an airtight package, these tomatoes stay fresh-looking red for four weeks. As a result, they can sell for 30 cents a pound more than unbranded tomatoes.

PROGRESS CHECK

- What are the five functions that packaging must perform now that retail help is declining?
- What is the difference between a brand name and a trademark?
- Can you explain the differences among a national brand, a private brand, and a generic brand?

PRODUCT MANAGEMENT

A **product manager** coordinates all marketing efforts for a particular product (or product line) or brand, including the selection of a package and a brand name. The concept of product management originated over 50 years ago with Procter &

product manager
Person who coordinates all the marketing efforts for a particular product (or product line) or brand.

SPOTLIGHT ON SMALL BUSINESS

Product Design for Entrepreneurs and Small Businesses

One major advantage small businesses have over large businesses is that small businesses can get closer to the customer and provide more personal and friendly service. One cannot assume, however, that a small business does provide better service. Small-business managers must constantly improve their products and services. They should poll their customers and employees to see what they think, using this feedback as the catalyst for change.

Small businesses cannot blame their customers for the demands the customers put on them. Rather, they must encourage employees to give customers friendly and responsive service. Fail to do so, and competitors that emphasize service will take away your business.

A good idea for small businesses is to analyze two major competitors to find weaknesses in their products or services. Then exploit those weak links, using them as a competitive edge. Small businesses must constantly review their product mix and eliminate those products that no longer appeal to the market niche being served. That means constantly monitoring consumer trends and adapting the product/service mix quickly to meet current demands.

Source: Mark Stevens, "Resolve To Do Better in New Year," *Washington Times,* January 3, 1991, p. C2; and P. Ranganath Nayak, "New-Product Development Must Be Better, Must Be Much Faster," *Boardroom Reports,* April 1, 1992, pp. 8–9. ▼

Gamble, and over the last 25 years product managers have come to occupy important positions in many firms. Product management may offer a truly challenging career if you are interested.

Product managers have direct responsibility for one brand or one product line, including all the elements of the marketing mix: product, price, place, and promotion. It's like being the president of a one-product business. Imagine being the product manager for Fiberrific if it were purchased by a large cereal producer such as Kellogg. You would be responsible for everything having to do with that one brand. One reason companies have created this position is to have greater control over new product development and product promotion. The following material explores the success rate for new product introductions. It then outlines steps to follow in product development, including pricing strategies.

New Product Success

For many years it was commonly believed that about 90 percent of new products failed. Consequently, many firms hesitated to bring out new products. Instead, they tended to copy proven products from other companies. More recently, a study of medium-sized and large firms showed that failure rates were closer to 33 percent. One reason for the improved success rate is that firms are doing more careful consumer research and are not launching products until research shows a probable demand. (A "successful" product was one that was "sent to the market and met management's original expectations in all important respects.")[4] Some key findings from the study were:

- Firms selling mainly to industrial markets launched an average of eight major new products during the preceding five years, compared with six for consumer-oriented firms.
- Insufficient and poor market research is the leading cause of new product failure. Cited next as reasons for failure are technical problems in design or production and errors in timing the product's introduction.

Smaller firms may experience a lower success rate, but not if they do proper product planning. We shall discuss such planning in the next section.

The New Product Development Process

Product development consists of several stages:

1. Idea generation.
2. Screening and analysis.
3. Development.
4. Testing.
5. Commercialization (bringing the product to the market).

New products continue to pour into the market every year, and the profit potential looks tremendous. Think, for example, of the potential of two-way cable TV, high-definition TV sets (HDTV), cellular phones, compact video disks, hand-held video recorders and computers, and other innovations. Where do these ideas come from? How are they tested? What is the life span for an innovation? That is what the following material is all about.

Generating New Product Ideas

Figure 11–3 gives you a good idea of where new product ideas come from. Note that 38 percent of the new product ideas for consumer goods come from analyzing competitors. This was true of 27 percent of new industrial products. Such copying of competitors in favour of discovering new products slows the introduction of new ideas.

A strong point can be made for listening to employee suggestions for new product ideas. The number one source of ideas for new industrial products was company sources other than research and development. It was also a major source for new consumer goods. That is partly due to successful marketing communication systems that monitor suggestions from all sources.

Look through Figure 11–3 carefully and think about the implications. Notice that more than a third of all new product ideas for industrial products came from users, user research, or supplier suggestions. This emphasizes the notion that a firm should listen to its suppliers and customers and give them what they want.

Product Screening and Analysis

Product screening is designed to reduce the number of ideas being worked on at any one time. Criteria needed for screening include the product's fit with present products, profit potential, marketability, and personnel requirements (see Figure 11–4). Each of these factors may be assigned a weight and total scores computed.

Product analysis is done after product screening. It is largely a matter of making cost estimates and sales forecasts to get a feeling for profitability. Products that do not meet the established criteria are weeded from further consideration.

Consumer Products (Based on a survey of 79 new products)	**Percent***
Analysis of the competition	38.0
Company sources other than R&D	31.6
Consumer research	17.7
Research and development	13.9
Consumer suggestions	12.7
Published information	11.4
Supplier suggestions	3.8
Industrial Products (Based on a survey of 152 new products)	**Percent***
Company sources other than R&D	36.2
Analysis of the competition	27.0
Research and development	24.3
Product users	15.8
Supplier suggestions	12.5
Product user research	10.5
Published information	7.9

Figure 11–3 This survey shows where the ideas for new products come from. As you know, research plays an important role in the development of new products.

*Percentages add up to more than 100 because more than one source was named for some products.
Reprinted by permission of the A. C. Nielsen Company.

Figure 11–4 Some marketing considerations for new brands. Ideas for new products are carefully screened. This screening helps the company identify the areas where new products are needed and reduces the chance of a company working on too many ideas at a time.

- Areas of company strengths and weaknesses
- Tie-ins with, or potential impact on, other company brands
- Production capabilities
- Consumer attitudes toward category awareness
- Satisfaction with existing brands
- Regional consumer differences
- Advertising and merchandising norms, timing, and directions
- Consumer promotional considerations
- Nature of competition
- Market segments
- Distribution channels
- Trade perceptions of category
- Turnover rates/optimum inventory allocations
- Seasonal characteristics
- Profit margins

Reprinted by permission of the A. C. Nielsen Company.

Figure 11–5 Three basic elements before test marketing. Product development, communication development, and strategy development all are used as a company develops a new product. Extensive testing is used to guarantee the success of the new product.

Product Development

- Identify unfilled need in particular market segment
- Preliminary profit/payout plan for each concept
- Concept test
- Determine whether product can be made
- Test concept and product (and revise as indicated)
- Develop product
- Run extended product use tests

Communication Development

- Select name
- Design package and test
- Create copy theme and test
- Develop complete ads and test

Strategy Development

- Set marketing goals
- Establish marketing strategy
- Develop marketing mix (after communication development)
- Estimate cost of marketing plan and payout (after product development)

Reprinted by permission of the A. C. Nielsen Company.

Product Development and Testing

If a product passes the screening and analysis phase, the firm begins to develop it further. A product idea can be developed into many different product concepts (alternative product offerings based on the same product idea that have different meanings and values to consumers). For example, a firm might want to test the concept of a chicken dog—a hot dog made of chicken that tastes like an all-beef hot dog.

We noted earlier that concept testing involves taking a product idea to consumers to test their reactions (see Figure 11–5). Do they see the benefits of this new product? How frequently would they buy it? At what price? What features do they like and dislike? What changes would they make? Different samples are tested

SPOTLIGHT ON BIG BUSINESS

Commercialization Is Not Always Predictable

Even if a product tests well, it may take quite a while before it achieves success in the market. Take the introduction of the zipper, for example. It is hard to imagine a world without this ubiquitous little product, yet it had one of the longest development efforts on record for a consumer product. Whitcomb Judson received his first patents in the U.S. in the early 1890s. It took more than 15 years to perfect the product, but even then consumers weren't interested. The company suffered numerous financial setbacks, name changes, and relocations before settling in Meadville, Pennsylvania. Finally, the U.S. Navy started using Judson's zippers during World War I. Today, Talon Inc. is the leading U.S. zipper maker, producing some 500 million of them annually.

Most Hollywood producers preview their films in a few carefully chosen cities and towns. They attend the screenings and observe audience reaction personally. Then they pore over audience response cards. Finally, they re-edit and sometimes reshoot some scenes. Then they are ready to launch their multimillion-dollar products, accompanied by a sea of advertising and promotional efforts whose cost may exceed the actual cost of production.

Despite this careful preparation by experienced, tough producers and their cohorts, many a film does not achieve commercial success. The history of this business has shown that there is no sure-fire formula for success. The same may be said for any product or service. ▼

using different packaging, branding, ingredients, and so forth, until a product emerges that is desirable from both a production and a marketing perspective. Can you see the importance of concept testing for Fiberrific?

The International Challenge

Dave Nichol learned **through** experience that the secret to success in today's rapidly changing technological environment is to bring out new products and bring them out quickly. This is especially true in light of the rapid development process occurring in other countries.

Xerox executives were surprised by Japanese competitors who were developing new copier models twice as fast as Xerox, at half the cost. Xerox had to lose market share or slash its traditional four- to five-year product development cycle. After millions of dollars of investment, Xerox can now produce a new copier in two years (still not as fast as the Japanese).

The big three auto makers all formed task forces to cut product development cycles that had swollen to nearly five years. The Japanese were taking about three and a half years.

Lee Iacocca was quoted in *Fortune* magazine as saying, "If I made one mistake, it was delegating all the product development and not going to one single meeting." New product development is now high on Chrysler's priority list. It should be interesting to see the new cars in the coming years—to find out if Chrysler was able to implement its new strategy.

PRODUCT STRATEGY AND THE PRODUCT LIFE CYCLE

product life cycle
The four-stage theoretical depiction of the process from birth to death of a product class: introduction, growth, maturity, and decline.

Once a product has been developed, tested, and placed on the market, it goes through a life cycle consisting of four stages: introduction, growth, maturity, and decline. This is called the product life cycle (see Figure 11–6). The **product life**

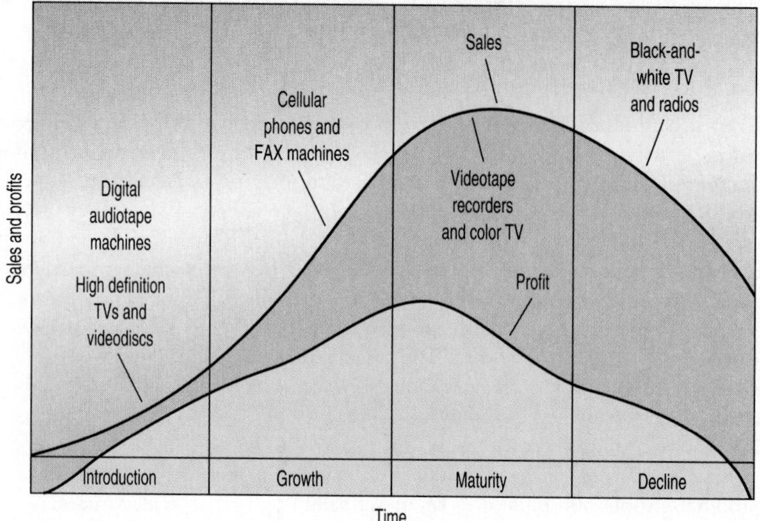

Figure 11–6 Sales and profit curves of typical product class. Note that profit levels start to fall *before* sales reach their peak. When profits and sales start to decline, it is time to come out with a new product or remodel the old to maintain sales and profits.

cycle is a theoretical model of what happens to a product *class* (for example, all freeze-dried coffee) over time. Not all products follow the life cycle, and particular brands may act differently. For example, while frozen foods as a generic class may go through the entire cycle, one brand may never get beyond the introduction stage. Nonetheless, the product life cycle provides a basis for anticipating future market developments and for planning marketing strategies accordingly. Some products, such as microwave ovens, stay in the introductory stage for years. Other products, such as fad clothing, may go through the entire cycle in a couple of months.

As a theoretical model, Figure 11–6 is useful for analyzing product life cycles, but it is far from being a universal rule that applies to all products. This limits its use as a predictive tool for the longevity of any particular product.

Many brands seem to go on forever. Ivory soap, Kellogg's Corn Flakes, and Coke go back to the last century. Life Savers, Chiclets, and Wrigley's chewing gum also go way back. All of these have hardly changed over the years and are still leaders in their fields. Games like Monopoly—and Snakes and Ladders, which is much older—also never seem to change or die. Can you think of other products that defy the product life cycle model?

Figure 11–7 shows what happens to sales volume, competition, and profit/loss during the product life cycle. Such figures are revealing. For instance, they show that a product at the mature stage may reach the top in sales growth while profit is decreasing. At that stage, a marketing manager may decide to create a new image for the product to start a new growth cycle. Note, for example, how Arm & Hammer baking soda gets a new image every few years to generate new sales. One year it is positioned as a deodorant for refrigerators and the next as a substitute for harsh chemicals in swimming pools. Knowing what stage in the cycle a product is in helps marketing managers to decide when such strategic changes are needed.

Figure 11–8 outlines the marketing mix decisions that might be made. As you go through the table, you will see that each stage calls for multiple marketing mix changes. Next, we shall walk through the product life cycle and discuss what happens at each stage.

Life Cycle Stage	Sales	Profits	Competitors
Introduction	Low sales	Losses may occur	Few
Growth	Rapidly rising	Very high profits	Growing number
Maturity	Peak sales	Declining profits	Stable number, then declining
Decline	Falling sales	Profits may fall to losses	Declining number

Figure 11–7 Sales, profit, and competition at various stages in the product life cycle. Many products go through these stages at various times in their life cycle. What happens to sales as a product matures?

Figure 11–8 Strategies through the product life cycle

		Marketing Mix Elements		
Life Cycle Stage	**Product Policy**	**Pricing**	**Distribution**	**Advertising**
Introduction	Offer market-tested product; keep product mix small	Go after innovators with high introductory price (skimming strategy) or use penetration pricing	Use wholesalers, selective distribution	Dealer promotion and heavy investment in primary demand advertising and sales promotion to get stores to carry the product and consumers to try it
Growth	Improve product; keep product mix limited	Adjust price to meet competition	Increase distribution	Heavy competitive advertising
Maturity	Differentiate your product to satisfy different market segments	Further reduce price	Take over wholesaling function and intensify distribution	Emphasize brand name; product benefits and differences
Decline	Cut product mix; develop new product ideas	Consider price increase	Consolidate distribution; drop some outlets	Reduce advertising to only loyal customers

THINKING IT THROUGH

In what stage of product life cycle are personal computers? What does Figure 11–8 indicate firms should do at that stage? What will the next stage be? What might you do at that stage to optimize profits?

Most soft drinks are in the mature or decline stage of the product life cycle. Does that explain why Coke introduced new Coke? What other new soft drinks have been introduced in the last few years? Have any reached rapid growth?

The Product Life Cycle

We can see how the product life cycle works by looking at the introduction of instant coffee. When it was introduced, most people did not like it as well as "regular" coffee, and it took several years to gain general acceptance (introduction stage). At one point, though, instant coffee grew rapidly in popularity, and many brands were introduced (stage of rapid growth). After a while, people became attached to one brand and sales leveled off (stage of maturity). Sales went into a slight decline when freeze-dried coffees were introduced (stage of decline). At present, freeze-dried coffee is at the maturity stage. Think through the product life cycle of products such as hot cereals, frozen orange juice, analogue watches, and mechanical calculators.

The importance of the product life cycle to marketers is this: Different stages in the product life cycle call for different strategies. Figure 11–8 summarizes the entire concept. It shows how a product manager changes his or her objectives and strategies over the life of a product. It is important to recognize what stage a product is in, because such an analysis leads to more intelligent marketing decisions.

Extending the Life Cycle

Most products are in the maturity stage of the product life cycle at any particular time; therefore, marketing managers deal often with mature products. The goal is to extend product life so that sales and profits do not decline. One strategy, called **market modification,** means that marketing managers look for new users and market segments. Did you know, for example, that the backpacks that so many students carry were originally designed for the military? The search for new users led to the present-day backpack.

market modification
Technique used to extend the life cycle of mature products by finding new users and market segments.

Market modification also means searching for increased usage among present customers. That is what Arm & Hammer does by finding new uses for baking soda over time. Many industrial firms develop products along with customers to be sure the product meets the buyers' needs.[5] Finally, a marketer may reposition the product to appeal to new market segments. Once 7-Up was considered a mix for drinks using whiskey or bourbon. It was repositioned as an alternative to colas (the UnCola) and captured whole new markets. What do you suppose we could do to

A company can extend the product life cycle by finding new uses for its products. Arm & Hammer, for example, has found 38 uses for its products. It is one of the more successful firms that use this strategy.

extend the product life cycle if Fiberrific reaches the decline stage? Alternatives include going for a different market, such as senior citizens, or positioning it as a snack instead of a cereal. Many people already eat cereal as a snack instead of just for breakfast. Cereal companies have introduced cereal bars for breakfast (like a candy bar but more nutritious).

Another product extension strategy is called **product modification.** It involves changing product quality, features, or style to attract new users or more usage from present users. American auto manufacturers are using quality improvement as one way to recapture world markets. New features are keeping the sales of videotape recorders going. One can now edit tapes, receive stereo broadcasts, watch one show and have another show in the corner of the screen, and more. Style changes can also extend the life of a product. Note, for example, how auto manufacturers once changed styles dramatically from year to year to keep demand from falling. That strategy was called *planned obsolescence* because it made cars obsolete in *style* long before they were obsolete in engineering.

product modification
Technique used to extend the life cycle of mature products by changing the product quality, features, or style to attract new users or more usage by present users.

Now, however, American auto manufacturers are using quality improvement (example, "At Ford, Quality is Job 1") as their main method of trying to recapture the domestic and international market share they lost to Japanese auto companies. They realized late in the day that the market had changed; consumers had become more concerned with quality, pollution, and gas consumption than with annual style changes.

Different stages in the product life cycle call for different pricing strategies. We shall discuss pricing—a key management decision in product design—next.

PROGRESS CHECK

- What are the five steps in the new product development process?
- Draw a product life cycle and label its parts. Can you give one marketing strategy in product, price, place, or promotion for each stage? (See Figure 11–8.)
- Explain the difference between market modification and product modification and give examples of each.

PRICING

Pricing is so important to marketing that it has been singled out as one of the four Ps in the marketing mix, along with product, place, and promotion. Price is also a critical ingredient in consumer evaluations of the product. In this section, we shall explore price as both an ingredient of the product and a strategic marketing tool.

Typically, pricing strategies are designed to achieve one or more of the following objectives:

Build traffic. Supermarkets have high fixed expenses, so they are always looking for ways to attract more people. The additional traffic produces very profitable sales. (See the next section, on breaking even.) One popular method of building traffic is to advertise "loss leaders," items sold below cost to lead customers into the store. This has two results: once in the store, people will buy other regularly priced items, and they will also become loyal customers over the long term.

Increase market share. Growth in market share has many benefits. It gives greater assurance of long-term profits, weakens competitors, ultimately reduces costs, and has other major and minor beneficial effects. Japanese auto and electronics companies have used market share gain as a major competitive strategy to establish themselves in North America, Europe, and elsewhere. U.S. auto companies have been battling strenuously (*desperately* may not be too strong a word) for almost a decade to recapture lost market share. This accounts for all the rebates, discounts, and freebies they have been offering in very intensive advertising campaigns. At the very least, companies will fight hard to maintain their market share.

Create an image. Certain perfumes and watches are deliberately priced high to give an image of exclusivity and status. Perrier used this strategy successfully for its bottled mineral water from France. Can you think of other examples?

Pricing Objectives

The ultimate objective of all marketing activities of a company is the long-term growth in profits. Pricing strategies are aimed at achieving that goal. There are various strategies and tactics that can be adopted in the pursuit of this objective. Short-term tactics might involve lower prices to attract a larger market, after which prices might be raised.

Each product usually requires its own pricing strategy because it has to compete in a particular market segment and at a particular stage in its life cycle. Pricing decisions are part of a strategic marketing plan, so they are affected by such other marketing components as product design and quality, packaging, branding, and promotion.

Often pricing can add prestige to a product. The high price of a Jaguar, for example, gives the customer a feeling of exclusivity and pride. Ads like this one contribute to the image with terms such as "classic luxury" and "mirror-matched burl walnut."

Usually a target profit is set for a particular period of time. For example, for Fiberrific we might shoot for a $3-million profit over 18 months. This might be broken down into three-month (quarterly) goals:

1st quarter	$ −400,000 (loss)
2nd quarter	−100,000 (loss)
3rd quarter	200,000
4th quarter	500,000
5th quarter	1,000,000
6th quarter	1,800,000
	$ 3,000,000 profit

Price Determination

Normally, every product is sold into a market that has many competing products. This means that, in the long run, prices are determined by the interaction between many buyers and many sellers. But other considerations influence price determination.

Cost-Based Pricing

Of course, cost does establish a floor below which you cannot continue to sell your products for very long if you hope to stay alive. You normally set prices above cost. What exactly is cost? This is a much more complex question than you might imagine, especially for large companies in manufacturing and other complex activities like searching for oil and gas. How should the cost of a barrel of oil be determined when 25 wells are dry and only one is a producer in a particular area? How should a bottle of vitamins be costed when the actual material and production cost are minimal but the cost of research and development is enormous and often produces no results? Many books and articles address this topic.

Large firms, whose products may dominate the market, sometimes adopt a below-cost strategy to drive out weaker competitors who cannot stand a long period of losses. They must be sure they are not abrogating fair competition laws and regulations that are designed to outlaw such *predatory pricing*. There have been allegations of this practice in regard to the price wars between Air Canada and Canadian Airlines International.

Producers often use cost as a primary basis for setting price. They develop elaborate cost accounting systems to measure production costs (including materials, labour, and overhead), marketing costs, add in some margin of profit, and come up with a satisfactory price. The question is whether the price will be satisfactory to the market as well. In the long run, the *market,* not the producer, determines what the price will be.

Break-Even Analysis

Before we go into the business of producing Fiberrific cereal, it may be wise to determine how many boxes of cereal we would have to sell before we began making a profit. We would then determine whether or not we could reach such a sales goal. **Break-even analysis** is the process used to determine profitability at various levels of sales. It tells managers whether the firm will make money (or break even) at a particular price, given a certain sales volume. The **break-even point** is the point beyond which a certain quantity of sales results in profits. The *profit equation* is as follows:

break-even analysis
Process used to determine the profitability at various levels of sales.

break-even point
The point beyond which a certain quantity of sales results in profits.

Gross profit = Sales − Cost of goods sold

Before we do such an analysis for our cereal company, certain terms need to be explained.

- *Gross profit (P)* is the profit after the cost of goods sold is deducted but before expenses are deducted.
- *Fixed cost (FC)* is the sum of the expenses of the firm that are stable and do not change with the quantity of the product that is produced and sold. Examples include rent, executive salaries, and insurance.
- *Variable cost (VC)* is the sum of the costs that vary directly with the quantity of products produced and sold. Examples include raw materials such as wheat, oats, and rice and the direct actual labour used in producing the product—cereal in our case.

Using these terms and the figures that go with them, we can calculate the break-even point for our cereal. Remember, that is the point where we start making a profit! The formula is:

$$\begin{array}{l}\text{Break-even point (BEP)}\\ \text{(number of units)}\end{array} = \frac{\text{Fixed cost (FC)}}{\text{Price of one unit} - \text{Variable cost of one unit}}$$

Let's put some figures in the formula to see how it works. Suppose our company has a total fixed cost of $2,000 per month. (That is the total cost of rent, insurance, executive salaries, etc.) We price our cereal at $2.00 a box. The variable cost per box is $1.00 (for the ingredients, package, and labour). Then the break-even point (the quantity we would have to sell to just break even) would be 2,000 boxes per month. Here is how we reach that figure:

$$\text{BEP} = \frac{\text{FC}}{\text{Price} - \text{Unit variable cost}} = \frac{\$2{,}000}{\$2.00 - \$1.00} = 2{,}000 \text{ boxes}$$

Figure 11–9 shows how the results of the calculations look when placed on a chart.

Figure 11–10 shows the same information in graph form. They both show that the break-even point is where the quantity is 2,000 boxes and the price is $2.00 a box. At less than 2,000 boxes, we would lose money. For example, if we sold only 1,000 boxes, we would lose $1,000. However, if we could increase sales to 5,000 boxes, we would make $3,000 profit. Figure 11–10 shows the results in an easy-to-read format.

Figure 11–9 Break-even analysis for Fiberrific for one month.

Quantity Sold (Q)	Price Per Box	(Sales) Total Revenue (TR)	Unit Variable Cost (UVC)	Total Variable Cost (TVC) (Q × UVC)	Fixed Cost (FC)	Total Cost (TC) (TVC + FC)	Net Profit TR – TC
0	$2	0	$1	$ 0	$2,000	$2,000	–$2,000
1,000	2	$ 2,000	1	1,000	2,000	3,000	–1,000
2,000	**2**	**4,000**	**1**	**2,000**	**2,000**	**4,000**	**0**
3,000	2	6,000	1	3,000	2,000	5,000	1,000
4,000	2	8,000	1	4,000	2,000	6,000	2,000
5,000	2	10,000	1	5,000	2,000	7,000	3,000

THINKING IT THROUGH

What would the break-even point be if we increased the price to $3.00 a box? How would increasing the price affect the rest of the marketing effort?

Pricing Strategies

Let's say a firm has just developed a new product such as video recorders. The firm has to decide how to price these recorders at the introductory stage of the product life cycle. One strategy would be to price the recorders high to recover the costs of developing the product and take advantage of the fact that there are few competitors. A **skimming price strategy** is one in which the product is priced high to make optimum profit while there is little competition. Of course, those large profits will attract others to produce recorders. That is what happened with high-priced camcorders when they were first introduced.

skimming price strategy
Pricing the product high to make optimum profit while there is little competition.

A second strategy, therefore, is to price the recorders low. This would attract more buyers and discourage others from making recorders because the profit is so low. This strategy enables the firm to penetrate or capture a large share of the market quickly. A **penetration price strategy,** therefore, is one in which a product is priced low to attract more customers and discourage competitors. The Japanese successfully used a penetration strategy with videotape recorders. No domestic firm could compete with the low prices the Japanese offered.

penetration price strategy
Pricing the product low to attract more customers and discourage competitors.

Ultimately, price is determined by supply and demand in the marketplace, as described in Chapter 4. For example, if we charge $2.00 for our cereal and nobody buys it at that price, we will have to lower the price until we reach a price that is acceptable to customers and to us. The price that results from the interaction of buyers and sellers in the marketplace is called the market price.

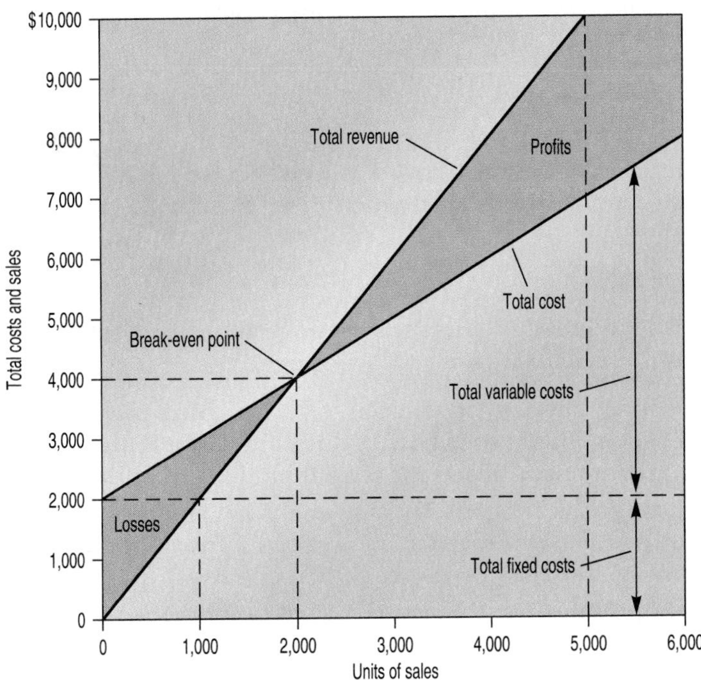

Figure 11–10 The break-even point for Fiberrific for one month. Below the break-even point, a company experiences losses. Above the break-even point, profits increase rapidly.

demand-oriented pricing
Pricing strategy based on consumer demand.

price leadership
Procedure by which all the competitors in an industry follow the pricing practices of one or more dominant firms.

competition-oriented pricing
Pricing strategy based on all the other competitors' prices.

Recognizing the fact that different consumers may be willing to pay different prices, marketers sometimes price on the basis of consumer demand rather than cost or some other calculation. Such **demand-oriented pricing** is reflected by movie theaters when they charge less for children and by drugstores that have discount rates for senior citizens.

Another factor in the marketplace besides supply and demand forces is competition. **Price leadership** is the procedure by which all the competitors in an industry follow the pricing practices of *one or more* dominant firms. You may have noticed that practice among oil and cigarette companies. **Competition-oriented pricing** is a strategy based on what *all* the other competitors are doing. The price can be at, above, or below competitors' prices. Pricing depends on customer loyalty, perceived product differences, and the competitive climate.

The Pricing Revolution

value pricing
Offering consumers brand name goods and services at discount prices.

Discounters and warehouse merchandisers price on the basis of high volume, low cost, and low profit margins. They hope to make a satisfactory total profit by **value pricing,** offering consumers brand name goods and services at discount prices. In addition, they market their own house or private labels aggressively to increase their profits and cut into the market shares of well-known brands. Price Club and Costco now operate in a number of Canadian cities.

A good example of this development was reported in the *Globe and Mail.*[6] Seagram's Ltd., the giant Canadian TNC, is having trouble with its brand label Tropicana juices.

> . . . brand labels such as Tropicana are under siege from private label products sold directly by retailers. Analysts predict few consumer goods will be safe from the price wars. Retailers from Wal-Mart Stores Inc., [the largest retailer in the U.S.] to Loblaw's Cos. Ltd., of Toronto, are increasingly winning over traditional brand label customers with their cheaper Sam's Choice or President's Choice brands. The specialty labels can offer premium goods at lower prices because they spend so little on marketing.
>
> . . . In recent weeks, prices on products from Marlboro cigarettes to Luvs diapers have been slashed to the bone to recover market share lost to discount brands.

Many reports indicate that price has become perhaps the most important competitive tool in the ever-fiercer battle for the consumer dollar.

Additional Pricing Tactics

It is impossible to cover all pricing tactics in detail in this book. However, you should at least be familiar with the following terms:

1. *Adaptive pricing* allows an organization to vary its prices based on factors such as competition, market conditions, and resource costs. Rather than relying on one set price, the firm adjusts the price to fit different situations.
2. *Cost-oriented pricing* is the strategy of setting prices primarily on the basis of cost. For example, retailers often use cost plus a certain markup, and producers use a system of cost-plus pricing.
3. *Customary pricing* means that most sellers will adapt the product to some established, universally accepted price such as the price for gum or candy

bars. When the customary price goes up, almost all producers raise their prices.

4. *Product-line pricing* is the procedure used to set prices for a group of products that are similar but aimed at different market segments. For example, a beer producer might have a low-priced beer, a popular-priced beer, and a premium-priced beer.
5. *Target pricing* means that an organization will set some goal such as a certain share of the market or a certain return on investment as a basis for setting a price. Usually, market conditions prevent a firm from establishing prices this way, but such goals do give some direction to pricing policies.
6. *Uniform pricing,* also known as a *single-price policy,* means that all customers buying the product (given similar circumstances) will pay the same price. Although the most common policy in Canada and the United States, uniform pricing is unusual in many foreign markets, especially among private sellers.
7. *Odd pricing,* or psychological pricing, means pricing an item a few cents under a round price ($9.98 instead of $10) to make it appear less expensive.
8. *Price lining* is the practice of offering goods at a few set prices such as $30, $40, and $50. Such a tactic makes pricing easier, makes check-out easier, and appeals to a market segment interested in that level of pricing.

Non-Price Competition

In spite of the emphasis placed on price in microeconomic theory, marketers often compete on product attributes other than price. You may have noted that price differences between products such as gasoline, cigarettes, candy bars, and even major products such as compact cars are often small or non-existent. Very rarely will you see price used as a major promotional appeal on television. Instead, marketers tend to stress product images and consumer benefits such as comfort, style, convenience, and durability.

Many organizations promote the services that accompany basic products rather than price. The idea is to make a relatively homogeneous product "better." For example, airlines stress friendliness, promptness, more flights, better meals, and other such services. Motels stress "no surprises" or cable TV, swimming pools, and other extras. IBM often counters the price advantages of clones by stressing better service.

Quite often the reason marketers emphasize non-price differences is because prices are so easy to match. Few competitors can match the image of a friendly, responsive, consumer-oriented company.

PROGRESS CHECK

- List two short-term and two long-term pricing strategies. Are the two compatible?
- What is wrong with using a cost-based pricing strategy?
- What is the purpose of break-even analysis?
- Can you calculate the break-even point of a product where the fixed monthly cost of producing it is $10,000, the price of one unit is $20, and the unit variable cost is $10?

SUMMARY

1. If the goal of marketing is to find a need and fill it, the heart of marketing is finding what products people want and seeing that they get them. Product is one of the four Ps of the marketing mix.

1. Explain the difference between a product and a product offer.

▼ *What is the difference between a product and a product offer?*

A product is any physical good, service, or idea that satisfies a want or need. A product offer is much more than a physical object. A product offer involves all the tangibles and intangibles that consumers evaluate when deciding to buy. These include things like price, brand name, quality, satisfaction in use, and more.

2. Manufacturers usually produce more than one product.

2. Define and give an example of a product mix and a product line.

▼ *What is the difference between a product line and a product mix?*

A product line is a group of products that are physically similar (a product line of gum may include chewing gum, sugarless gum, bubble gum, etc.). A product mix is a company's combination of product lines (a manufacturer may offer lines of gum, candy bars, chewing tobacco, etc.).

3. Marketers must make their product appear to be better than the competitors'.

3. Describe how businesses create product differentiation for their goods and services.

▼ *How do marketers create product differentiation for their goods and services?*

Marketers use a mix of pricing, advertising, and packaging to make their products seem unique and attractive.

4. Consumer goods and services are classified according to consumer shopping habits and preferences.

4. Identify the three classes of consumer products and how they are marketed.

▼ *What are the three classifications of consumer goods and services?*

There are convenience goods and services (minimum shopping effort), shopping goods and services (where people compare price and quality), and specialty goods and services (where consumers will go out of their way to get them).

▼ *Are the different classifications of consumer goods and services marketed differently?*

Yes. Convenience goods and services are best promoted by location, shopping goods and services by some price/quality appeal, and specialty goods and services by word of mouth.

5. Industrial goods are products used in the production of other products. There are two major categories of industrial goods: production goods and support goods.

5. Identify the two major classes of industrial goods and how they are marketed.

▼ *What is the difference between production goods and support goods?*

Production goods consist of raw materials (like steel or cement) that make up the final product. Support goods are the types of products that help make other products (such as supplies and equipment).

▼ *How are industrial goods marketed?*

Industrial goods are usually sold by salespeople in the field.

6. Packaging changes the product and is becoming more important, taking over much of the sales function for consumer goods.

6. List the four functions of packaging.

▼ *What are the functions of packaging?*

Packaging adds visibility and convenience, minimizes damage, and keeps the goods in manageable sizes.

7. Branding also changes a product.

7. Give examples of a brand, a brand name, and a trademark.

▼ *Can you give an example of a brand, a brand name, and a trademark?*

There are endless examples you could give. One example of a brand and brand name of salmon is Cloverleaf. The brand consists of the name as well as the symbol (a gold four-leaf clover). The brand name and the symbol are also trademarks, since Cloverleaf has been given legal protection for this brand.

8. Product managers are like presidents of one-product firms.

▼ *What are the functions of a product manager?*

Product managers co-ordinate product, price, place, and promotion decisions for a particular product.

8. Explain the role of a product manager.

9. There are many sources of new product ideas (see Figure 11–3).

▼ *What are the five steps of the product development process?*

It consists of generating new product ideas, screening and analysis, development, testing, and commercialization.

9. Outline the five steps of the new product development process.

10. Once a product is placed on the market, marketing strategy varies as the product goes through various stages of acceptance—called the product life cycle.

▼ *What are the stages of the product life cycle?*

They are introduction, growth, maturity, and decline.

▼ *How do marketing strategies change at the various stages?*

See Figure 11–8.

10. Identify and describe the stages of the product life cycle and describe marketing strategies at each stage.

11. Pricing is one of the four Ps of marketing. It can also be viewed as part of the product concept.

▼ *What are pricing objectives?*

Objectives include achieving a target profit, building traffic, increasing market share, increasing sales, creating an image, and meeting social objectives.

11. Give examples of various pricing objectives.

12. Break-even analysis tells a firm whether or not it would be profitable to produce a product at all.

▼ *What is the break-even point?*

At the break-even point, total cost equals total revenue. Sales beyond that point are profitable. See Figure 11–10.

12. Discuss the use of break-even analysis and calculate the break-even point.

13. Marketers use a variety of strategies to determine a product's price.

▼ *How are prices determined?*

Some firms use cost as a basis, but ultimately prices are set by the market; that is, supply, demand, and competition.

▼ *What strategies can marketers use to determine a product's price?*

A skimming price strategy is one in which the product is priced high to make optimum profit while there is little competition; a penetration strategy is one in which a product is priced low to attract more customers and discourage competitors. Demand-oriented pricing is based on consumer demand rather than cost. Competition-oriented pricing is based on the prices of all other competitors. Price leadership occurs when all competitors follow the pricing practice of one or more dominant companies. Please review pp. 369–71 to be sure you understand all the terms used for other pricing tactics.

13. Describe various pricing strategies.

GETTING INVOLVED

1. Look around at the different shoes that students are wearing. What product qualities were they looking for when they chose those shoes? What was the importance of price, style, brand name, manufacturer reputation, and color? Do different students buy shoes for different reasons?
2. Discuss how packaging has changed the attractiveness of the following products:
   a. Beer.
   b. Mustard.
   c. Salt.
   d. Soda (pop).
3. Determine where in the product life cycle you would place each of the following products and then prepare a marketing plan for each product based on the recommendations in this chapter:
   a. Alka-Seltzer.
   b. Cellular phones.

c. Electric automobiles.
d. Campbell's chicken noodle soup.

4. List at least seven sources of new product ideas in order of most importance. Explain why you chose that order.
5. Discuss how the faculty at your college or university could increase student satisfaction by working more closely with students in developing new products (courses) and changing existing products (courses). Would it be a good idea for all marketers to work with their customers that way? Discuss.
6. Go to a shopping mall and go through several stores such as department stores, shoe stores, and clothing stores. Then go to a supermarket. Look at the prices of items that are comparable. That is, compare the prices of various brands of peas and so on. What pricing strategy is being followed by the various producers? Do any patterns emerge? Which producers make several different products in the same category so that they can use multiple pricing strategies? You can do the same analysis using prices in the newspaper and bring the paper to class to discuss strategies.

PRACTICING MANAGEMENT DECISIONS

Case One Packaging to Reach New Markets

Ways to extend the product life cycle of products include increasing consumption among present users and attracting new buyers. Often this can be accomplished through packaging innovation. Take products like beef stew and macaroni and beef. These products have been available for years in cans, but sales were slow. Dial Company changed the whole market around by introducing the Lunch Bucket, a shelf-stable, single-serve, microwavable product line of entrees and soups. Shelf-stable means the products can be stored on the shelf for long periods of time without losing taste or freshness.

Chef Boyardee Microwave Pasta from Canadian Home Products comes in an innovative container. One opens the container, peels off the protective lid, replaces the plastic cover, and microwaves the container for 90 seconds. The special material on the container prevents it from getting hot.

The Stouffer's division of Nestlé Enterprises of Toronto has come up with Handwich, a bread bun available with six different fillings. Microwavable in two minutes, the Handwich is closed at one end, making it less messy to hold.

Decision Questions

1. What are the social and technological changes that led to the development of these new lines of products? What other products or services may become more popular as a result of these social and technological changes?
2. Would you have chosen Lunch Bucket as the brand name for a new line of foods? What are the advantages and disadvantages of that name? What name do you feel might be better?
3. What other foods could be made into shelf-stable microwavable products to extend their product life cycle?
4. Can you think of other ways to increase the product life cycle of products such as soup and canned beef?

Sources: "Lunch Buckets Appeal to Chord of Familiarity," *Marketing Communications,* February 1988, p. 54; *Canadian Grocer,* July 1990, p. 12; "Stouffer's Sandwich Stopper," *Marketing* 94, no. 14, April 3, 1989, p. 2.

Case Two Cola Wars Enter a New Era

Nothing touched off more discussion and debate in marketing in the 1980s than the introduction of New Coke. The new Coke was made sweeter to taste more like Pepsi, and a marketing campaign was launched to sell this new taste. At first, sales were up as consumers rushed to try the new Coke. But reaction was negative and people began hoarding the old Coke. Minor campaigns to bring back the old Coke were started by fans.

Faced with hostile consumers from coast to coast, Coca-Cola relented and brought back old Coke under the name Coca-Cola Classic. For the 1990s, Coke is bringing back the new Coke under the name Coke II. It is said to have "real cola taste" and to be as sweet as Pepsi. Coca-Cola also introduced a new sports-market drink called PowerAde to compete with Pepsi's All Sport.

Furthermore, both companies are competing head to head to capture the new Eastern European market. Coke is king in Europe now and has a bottling plant in Dunkirk, France. Pepsi is not conceding the market, however, and will be launching major competitive promotional campaigns. It has already captured the former Soviet Union.

Coke hopes that Coke II will be able to recapture the 15 percent market share that New Coke once had (it fell to just 1.4 percent). Coke also hopes to capture some of the market from Quaker Oats' Gatorade. Unlike Gatorade and All Sport, PowerAde will be sold only as a fountain product. Gatorade was encroaching on Coke's fountain sales, and this move is meant to keep that segment.

Because of a slowdown in diet drink sales, Coke and Pepsi are trying to reach new markets. For example, Pepsi is trying a new flavoured water drink to reach the "natural" market. It is called H2Oh. Going after the same market, Coca-Cola is considering packaging Fresca, its diet grapefruit drink, in a green glass bottle. Both companies are also exploring the market for iced tea and iced coffee.

Decision Questions

1. Do you think it is a good strategy for Coke to say that its new Coke II is as sweet as Pepsi? Doesn't that indicate that people may prefer Pepsi to Coke? Could the same message be made in a better way?
2. What is your impression of the name Coke II? Could you think of a better brand name for a sweeter Coke?
3. The market for sports drinks is now about $600 million a year. Do you think it is wise for both Pepsi and Coke to bring out a sports drink? What is your impression of selling PowerAde only from fountains? Does that influence its image as a sports drink?
4. Both Coke and Pepsi spend megabucks to advertise during football's Super Bowl. Are you and your friends sometimes confused by which commercial is for which product? Some ads are for Coke, some for Diet Coke, some for Pepsi, and so on. Is there a better way to differentiate the competitors? What about packaging? What about pricing?
5. What stage of the product life cycle are Coca-Cola and Pepsi in? Can you see why they would be bringing out new offerings at this time? How successful do you think they will be with sports drinks, "natural" drinks, and iced coffee and tea drinks?

Sources: Annetta Miller and Vern E. Smith, "The Soda War Fizzes Up," *Newsweek,* March 19, 1990, p. 38; Laurie M. Grossman, "Slimmer Diet-Cola Sales Growth Prompts Beverage Firms To Seek New Smash Drink," *The Wall Street Journal,* November 19, 1991, pp. B1, B4; and Andrea Rothman, "Can Wayne Calloway Handle the Pepsi Challenge?," *Business Week,* January 27, 1992, pp. 90–98.

LET'S TALK BUSINESS

1. A few years back, Loblaw's, the giant supermarket chain based in Ontario, introduced No-Name products to its customers. These were goods packaged in bold yellow boxes with black labels. Soon many other chains followed suit. Everything from beer to pasta to canned fruit and soap flakes was available on retail shelves across Canada. These products are enjoying success everywhere except Quebec. Can you explain why No-Name brands became popular? Doesn't it fly in the face of traditional

marketing concepts like advertising and branding? Or was this part of new product development?

2. Canadian software companies have been very successful in developing a steady stream of products for an ever-expanding domestic and foreign market. Why is product development so important for this industry? Do you think pricing is as important?
3. You are planning to establish a retail gift and entertainment store in your neighbourhood. After examining the figures with your accountant, you are somewhat discouraged. They show that the gross margin on forecast sales will not cover your expenses, so you will be operating at a loss. What can you do to improve the situation? Which of the three items mentioned (gross margin, sales, expenses) will be easier to modify and which will be harder? Why?
4. Think about all the products and services that you or other students use fairly regularly. Can you suggest any improvements or new products that will give better satisfaction? What is lacking now—quality, long life, or any other unfulfilled need?

LOOKING AHEAD

A product cannot fully meet the wants and needs of consumers unless it is at the right place at the right time. Several marketing organizations have emerged to perform the functions needed to move goods from producers to consumers. Your neighbourhood stores are one example. Chapter 12 looks at the distribution of products and the organizations that move and store goods on their way to your home.

Laura Secord

DISTRIBUTION: WHOLESALING AND RETAILING

LEARNING GOALS

After you have read and studied this chapter, you should be able to:

1. Explain why we need marketing middlemen.
2. Describe how middlemen create exchange efficiency.
3. Give examples of how middlemen perform the five utilities mentioned in economics literature.
4. Discuss how a manufacturer can get wholesalers and retailers in a channel system to co-operate by forming systems.
5. Explain the role of a channel captain.
6. Describe the role of a physical distribution manager.
7. Make a chart listing the various distribution modes and their advantages.
8. Identify the criteria used to select distribution systems.
9. Explain the purposes of the two types of warehouses.
10. Contrast the different types of wholesale middlemen and the kinds of functions they perform.
11. Name the major categories of retailers and the major trends in retailing.
12. Differentiate among intensive, selective, and exclusive distribution systems.
13. Describe the ways producers can distribute their products overseas.

KEY TERMS

administered distribution system, p. 381
brokers, p. 381
cash-and-carry wholesaler, p. 397
channel captain, p. 388
channel of distribution, p. 381
containerization, p. 393
contractual distribution system, p. 387
corporate distribution system, p. 387
drop shipper, p. 397
electronic data interchange (EDI), p. 388
exclusive distribution, p. 404
full-service wholesaler, p. 396
general merchandise wholesaler, p. 397
intensive distribution, p. 404
limited-function wholesaler, p. 397
materials handling, p. 394
merchant wholesaler, p. 396
network marketing, p. 402
physical distribution, p. 380
physical distribution manager, p. 391
piggybacking, p. 391
rack jobber, p. 397
retailer, p. 396
selective distribution, p. 404
scrambled merchandising, p. 403
supply chain management (SCM), p. 388
telemarketing, p. 402
truck jobber, p. 398
utility, p. 385
wholesaler, p. 396

Jean-Pierre Louis

PROFILE JEAN-PIERRE LOUIS

The sales of JPL International Inc. rocketed from $138,000 in 1985 to $6.4 million in 1990—a 4,500 percent increase. Such success has earned the company many awards, including a Canada Award for Business Excellence and *Profit* magazine's No. 1 spot as the fastest-growing company in 1991.

The key to JPL's success, says company founder Jean-Pierre Louis, is nothing more than an aggressive marketing strategy that puts the customer first. Born in Germany and brought up in Egypt, Louis learned the realities of the professional hair-care world from the "roots up." A four-year stint as a sales rep for a Montreal distributor taught him the rules of the game—and convinced him it was time for a change. "I saw that manufacturers through distributors were ripping off salons," he says.

With $20 cash to his name, Louis launched JPL in 1984. A credit card financed his first shipment of professional irons, scissors, and combs imported from the U.S. The basement of an abandoned school housed his first inventory. The breakthrough came in the second year, when JPL landed the Canadian rights to the California-based Paul Mitchell line.

By 1986 Louis was formulating a complete line of shampoos, sculpting sprays, lotions, and conditioners. Two prestigious lines, TIGI Linea and Brocato, soon established JPL as one of the country's market leaders. He estimates his market share at 41 percent, making JPL number one in Canada.

Unlike the competition, Louis concentrates on hairdressing salons. That's where he spends his marketing dollars—15 percent of annual sales. Louis says he tops his multinational competitors such as Clairol, Revlon, and L'Oreal when it comes to promoting professional care products.

Source: *Profit* 10, no. 4, June 1991, pp. 18–24.

WHAT DISTRIBUTION IS

physical distribution
The movement of goods and services from producer to industrial and consumer users.

We have looked at two of the four Ps of the marketing mix—product and price. In this chapter, we shall look at the third of the four Ps—*place*. Products have to be physically moved from where they are produced to a convenient place where consumer and industrial buyers can see them and purchase them. **Physical distribution** is the movement of goods from producers to industrial and consumer users. It involves functions such as transportation and storage.

How efficiently this task is performed often makes the difference between failure and success of the whole system. The system is made up of a whole series of marketing organizations called *middlemen*.

One of the major problems facing the former Soviet Union in its transition from a communist to a capitalist economy is the lack of such middlemen. In 1992 it was reported that potatoes were rotting in the fields because there was no system of distribution to get them to hungry urban consumers. City people were picking potatoes on farms.

A marketing middleman is an organization that assists in the movement of goods and services from producer to industrial and consumer users. They are called middlemen because they are in the middle of a whole series of organizations that join together to help distribute goods from producer to consumers. It is easy to understand, therefore, why these organizations as a group are known as a channel of distribution.

A **channel of distribution** consists of marketing middlemen such as wholesalers and retailers who join together to transport and store goods in their path (or channel) from producers to consumers. Figure 12–1 pictures channels of distribution for both consumer and industrial goods.

channel of distribution
Marketing middlemen such as wholesalers and retailers who join together to transport and store goods in their path (channel) from producers to consumers.

As you study the various institutions in the channel of distribution, think of them as potential employers and you will find the material more interesting. Not too many people know about all the different wholesale and retail institutions and the careers available in them. The competition for jobs in the lesser-known institutions is not as stiff.

Distribution is also paramount to manufacturing companies as markets in general become more international in scope. Since this makes distribution more complex, specialists in this field are of growing importance.

WHY DO WE NEED MIDDLEMEN?

Manufacturers do not need marketing middlemen to sell their goods to consumer and industrial markets. Figure 12–1 shows manufacturers that sell directly to buyers. So why have marketing middlemen at all? The answer is that middlemen perform certain marketing functions such as transportation, storage, selling, and advertising more effectively and efficiently than could be done by most manufacturers. A simple analogy is this: You could deliver your own packages to people anywhere in the world, but usually you do not. Why not? Because it is usually cheaper and faster to have them delivered by the post office or some private agency such as Purolator, Loomis, or Air Canada.

Similarly, you could sell your own home or buy stock directly from other people, but most people do not. Why? Again, because there are specialists called brokers who make the process more efficient and easier. **Brokers** are marketing middlemen who bring buyers and sellers together and assist in negotiating an exchange but do not take title to the goods. Usually they do not carry inventory, provide credit, or assume risk. The examples with which you are probably most familiar include insurance brokers, real estate brokers, and stockbrokers. Figure 12–1 shows that brokers act as intermediaries in other situations as well. Food brokers, for example, sell commodities such as wheat, corn, and potatoes.

brokers
Marketing middlemen who bring buyers and sellers together and assist in negotiating an exchange.

Middlemen and Exchange Efficiency

The benefits of marketing middlemen can be illustrated rather easily. Suppose that five manufacturers of various food products tried to sell directly to five retailers. The number of exchange relationships that would have to be established is 5 times 5, or 25. But picture what happens when a wholesaler enters the system. The five manufacturers would contact one wholesaler to establish five exchange relationships. The wholesaler would have to establish contact with the five retailers. That would mean another five exchange relationships. Note that the addition of a wholesaler reduces the number of exchanges from 25 to only 10. This process can be visualized as shown in Figure 12–2.

Middlemen create exchange efficiency by lessening the number of contacts needed to establish marketing exchanges. Not only are middlemen an efficient way to conduct exchanges, but they are often more effective as well. That is, they are often better at performing their functions than a manufacturer or consumer would be.

Figure 12–1 Channels of distribution for industrial and consumer goods and services

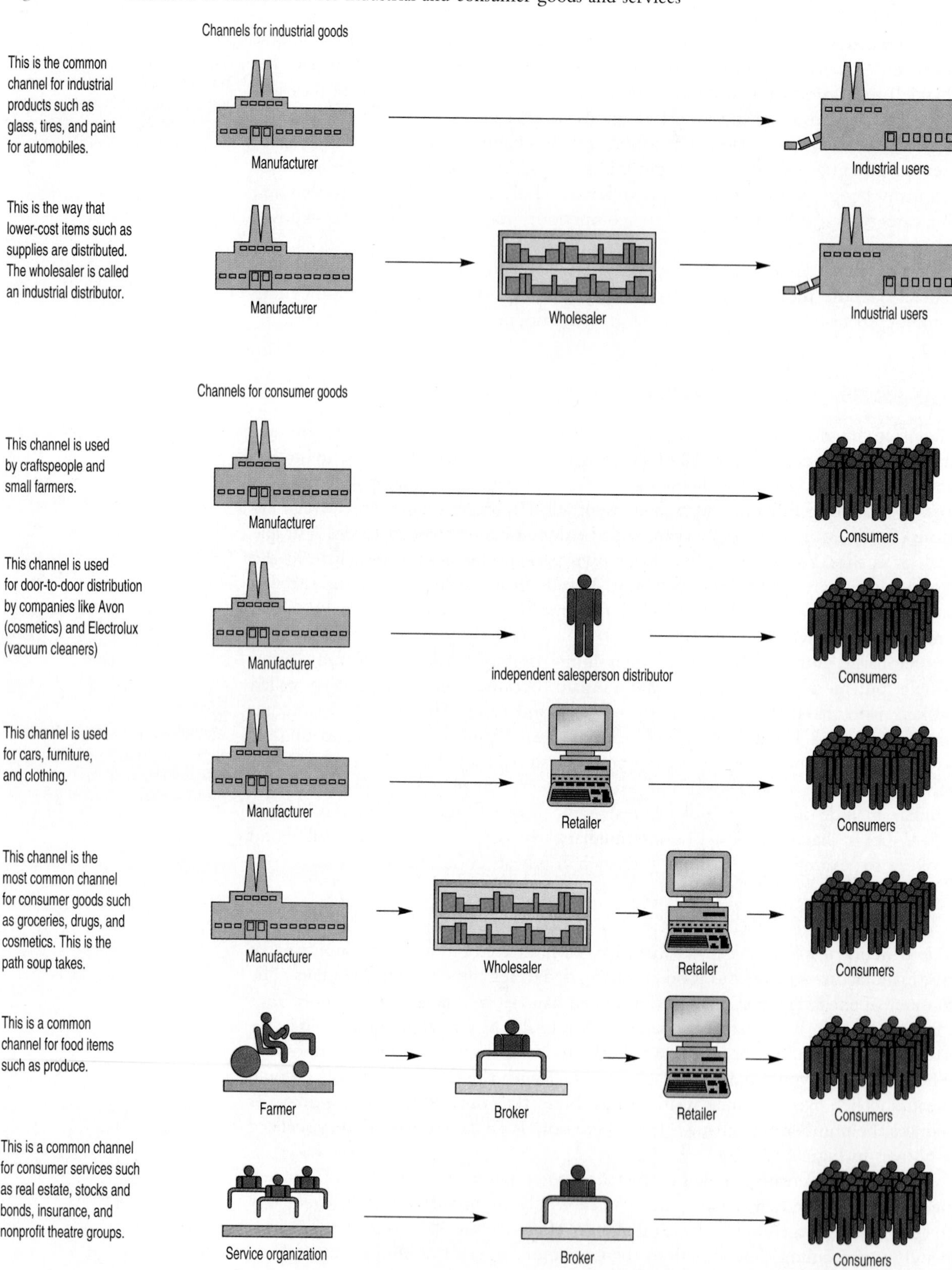

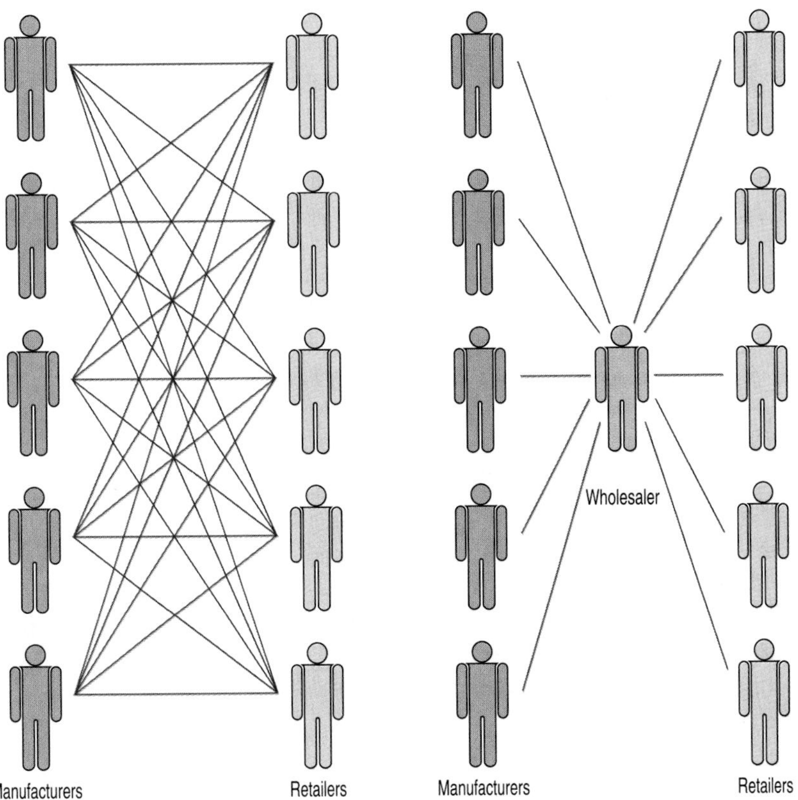

Figure 12–2 How middlemen create exchange efficiency. This figure shows that adding a wholesaler to the channel of distribution cuts the number of contacts from 25 to 10. This makes distribution more efficient.[1]

The Value Created by Middlemen

The public has always viewed marketing middlemen with some suspicion. Surveys have shown that about half the costs of the things we buy are marketing costs that go largely to pay for the work of middlemen. People reason that if we could only get rid of middlemen, we could greatly reduce the cost of everything we buy. Sounds good, but is the solution really that simple?

Let's take as an example a box of cereal such as Fiberrific. How could we, as consumers, get the cereal for less? Well, we could all drive to Saskatchewan, where some of the cereal is produced, and save some shipping costs. But would that be practical? Can you imagine millions of people getting in their cars and driving to Saskatchewan just to get some cereal? No, it doesn't make sense. It is much cheaper to have some middlemen bring the cereal to the major cities. That might involve transportation and warehousing by wholesalers. But these steps add cost, don't they? Yes, but they add value as well, the value of not having to drive to Saskatchewan.

The cereal is now somewhere on the outskirts of the city. We could all drive down to the wholesaler's outlet store and pick up the cereal; in fact, some people do just that. But that is not really the most economical way to buy cereal. If we figure in the cost of gas and time, the cereal would be rather expensive. Instead, we prefer to have someone move the cereal from the warehouse to another truck, drive it to the corner supermarket, unload it, unpack it, stamp it with a price, put it on the shelf, and wait for us to come in to buy it. To make it even more convenient, the supermarket may stay open 24 hours a day, seven days a week. Think of the *costs*. Think also of the *value*. For less than $3, we can get a box of cereal when we want, where we want, and with little effort on our part.

If we got rid of the retailer, we could buy a box of cereal for a little less, but we would have to drive miles more and spend time in the warehouse looking through rows of cereals. If we got rid of the wholesaler, we could save a little more, but then we would have to drive to Saskatchewan. But this value and convenience must be paid for—to the point where marketing may total 75 cents for every 25 cents in manufacturing costs. Figure 12–3 shows where food money goes in the distribution process. Notice that the largest percentage of your food dollar goes to people who drive trucks and work in the wholesale and retail organizations that have emerged to serve your needs. Only 3.5 cents goes to profit.

Three basic points about middlemen are the following:

- Marketing middlemen can be eliminated, but their activities cannot be eliminated. That is, you can get rid of retailers, but then consumers or someone else would have to perform the retailer's tasks, including transportation, storage, finding suppliers, and establishing communication with suppliers.
- Middleman organizations survive because they perform marketing functions more effectively and efficiently than others can.
- Middlemen add costs to products, but these costs are usually more than offset by the values they create.

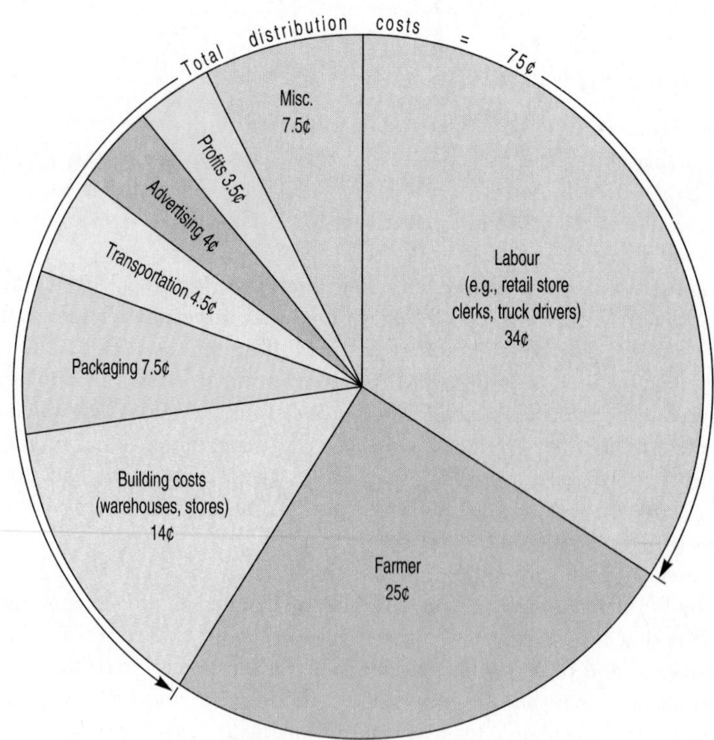

Figure 12–3 How distribution affects your food dollar. Note that the farmer gets only 25 cents of your food dollar. The bulk of your money goes to middlemen to pay distribution costs. Their biggest cost is labour (truck drivers, clerks). The next biggest costs are for warehouses and storage.[2]

THINKING IT THROUGH

Imagine that we got rid of middlemen and you had to go shopping for groceries and shoes. How would you find out where the shoes and groceries were? How far would you have to travel to get them? How much money do you think you would save for your time and effort? Which middleman do you think is most important and why?

How Middlemen Add Utility to Goods

Utility is an economic term that refers to the value or want-satisfying ability that is added to goods or services by organizations because the products are made more useful or accessible to consumers. Five utilities are mentioned in the economics literature: form, time, place, possession, and information.

utility
Value or want-satisfying ability that organizations add to products by making them more useful or accessible to consumers.

Form Utility

The first of the five, form utility, is performed mostly by producers. It consists of taking raw materials and changing their form so that they become useful products. Thus, a farmer who separates the wheat from the chaff and the processor who turns that wheat into flour are creating form utility. Marketers sometimes perform form utility as well. For example, a retail butcher may cut pork chops off of a larger roast and trim off the fat. Normally, however, marketers perform the other four utilities: time, place, possession, and information. Following are some examples of how they do that.

Time Utility

Jacques LaRue was watching TV with his brother when he suddenly got the urge to have a hot dog and a Coke. The problem was that there were no hot dogs or Cokes in the house. Jacques ran down to the corner store and bought some hot dogs, buns, Cokes, and potato chips. Jacques was able to get these groceries at 10 P.M. because the store was open from 7 A.M. to 11 P.M.

Middlemen, such as retailers, add time utility to products by making them available *when* they are needed.

Convenient food stores give you time utility. They stay open long hours so you can get what you want when you want it.

Place Utility

Li Weining was traveling through the Prairies and was getting hungry and thirsty. She saw a sign saying that Wall Drug with fountain service was up ahead. She stopped at the store for some refreshments. She also bought sunglasses and souvenir items while she was there.

Middlemen add place utility to products by having them *where* people want them.

Possession Utility

Tracy Chow wanted to buy a nice home in the suburbs. She found just what she wanted but did not have the money she needed. So she went with the real estate agent to a financial institution and borrowed the money to buy the home. Both the real estate broker and the institution are marketing middlemen.

Middlemen add possession utility by doing whatever is necessary to transfer ownership from one party to another, including providing *credit*.

Information Utility

Radislaw Melchek could not decide what kind of TV set to buy. He looked at various ads in the newspaper, talked to the salespeople at several stores, and read product data at the library. He also got some material from the government about radiation hazards and consumer buying tips. The newspaper, salespeople, library, and government publications were all information sources made available by middlemen.

Middlemen add information utility by opening two-way flows of *information* between marketing participants. For consumers to receive the maximum benefit from marketing middlemen, the various organizations must work together to assure a smooth flow of goods and services to the consumer. Historically, there has not always been total harmony in the channel of distribution. As a result, channel members have created channel systems that make the flows more efficient. We shall discuss those systems in the next section of this chapter.

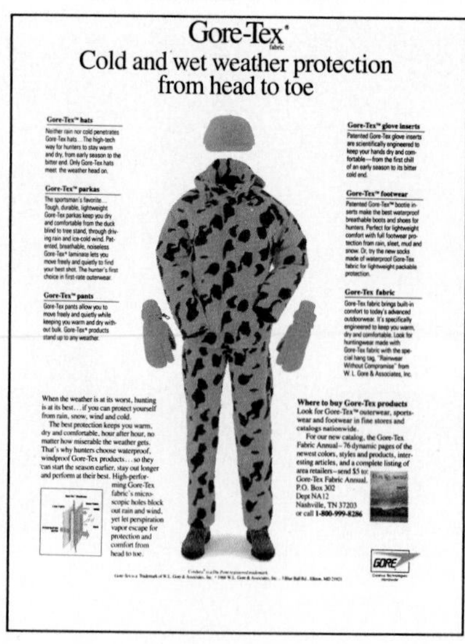

This ad for Gore-Tex products provides much information to consumers. Gore-Tex is a relatively expensive product, so consumers need to be convinced that the benefits far outweigh the cost. Advertisements and salespeople are two sources of information utility.

CO-OPERATION IN CHANNEL SYSTEMS

At one time, channel relationships were rather informal. Manufacturers, wholesalers, brokers, retailers, and other channel members were tied together only loosely by short-term agreements. Each organization remained rather independent of the other organizations in the channel, and conflict was as typical as co-operation. Many retailers were especially proud of their independence and often co-operated with manufacturers or wholesalers only when they felt that it was to their advantage. Similarly, manufacturers and wholesalers often had different philosophies of business.

How could manufacturers get wholesalers and retailers to co-operate to form an efficient distribution system? One answer was to link the firms together somehow in a formal relationship. Three systems emerged to tie firms together: corporate systems, contractual systems, and administered systems.

Corporate Distribution Systems

A **corporate distribution system** is one in which all the organizations in the channel are owned by one firm. If the manufacturer owns the retail firm, clearly it can exert much greater control over its operations. Au Coton, for example, owns its own retail stores and thus co-ordinates everything: display, pricing, promotion, inventory control, and so on. Other companies that have tried corporate systems include Goodyear and Firestone—manufacturers who had their own retail outlets. Paramount Pictures in the U.S. owns Canadian Famous Players' chain of cinemas across Canada.

corporate distribution system
Distribution system in which all the organizations in the channel are owned by one firm.

Contractual Distribution Systems

If a manufacturer cannot buy retail stores, it can try to get the retailers to sign a contract to co-operate. A **contractual distribution system** is one in which members are bound to co-operate through contractual agreements. There are three forms of contractual systems: First, there are franchise systems such as McDonald's, Kentucky Fried Chicken, Baskin-Robbins, and Speedy Muffler. The franchisee agrees to all of the rules, regulations, and procedures established by the franchisor. This results in the consistent quality and level of service you find in most franchised organizations.

contractual distribution system
Distribution system in which members are bound to co-operate through contractual agreements.

Second, there are wholesaler-sponsored chains such as IGA food stores. Each store signs an agreement to use the same name, participate in chain promotions, and co-operate as a unified system of stores, even though each store is independently owned and managed.

A third form of contractual system is a retail co-operative. This arrangement is much like a wholesaler-sponsored chain except it is initiated by smaller retailers. They form a central buying organization to gain substantial clout. The same co-operation is agreed to, and the stores remain independent.

Administered Distribution Systems

What does a producer do if it cannot buy retailers or get them to sign an agreement to co-operate? The best thing to do is to manage all the marketing functions yourself, including display, inventory, control, pricing, and promotion. The management by producers of all the marketing functions at the retail level is called an **administered distribution system.** Kraft does that for its cheeses. Retailers cooperate with producers in such systems because they get so much help for free. In fact, large retail companies exert powerful pressure on manufacturers to build, staff, and maintain their own selling space in stores and keep the shelves stocked, if they

administered distribution system
Distribution system in which all the marketing functions at the retail level are managed by producers.

want to distribute their products there. All the retailer has to do is ring up the sale and make money.

The Channel Captain

The greatest problems in traditional independent systems arise from the fact that we live in a democracy. People just do not easily give up their freedom of action. Thus, retailers do not always like to do what wholesalers want, wholesalers do not always want to do what manufacturers want, and manufacturers do not always respond to the needs of their suppliers, distributors, and dealers. The channel becomes a source of conflict, antagonism, and inefficiency.

But in the wings stands a powerful link in the system—the channel captain. The channel captain's role is to somehow gain control over the channel members and get them to work together. The captain may be the manufacturer, the wholesaler, or the retailer. For example, in the automobile distribution system the manufacturer has much control over what the dealers do and when and how they do it. Retailers such as Eaton's have the power to control manufacturers that supply them. In other cases, it is the wholesaler who takes charge.

channel captain
The dominant organization in the marketing channel that gets the other members to work together in a co-operative effort.

In each case, a channel captain usually has the power to get the other channel members to co-operate. A **channel captain,** therefore, is the dominant organization in the channel of distribution; it gets all the channel members to work together in a co-operative effort so that the whole channel is more efficient and more competitive with other channels in the same industry. The captain may have more buying power, financial resources, better marketing intelligence, or more managerial know-how. Regardless of the source of power, this organization maintains control. You can see how channel captains benefit themselves and often all the members of the channel by motivating them to co-operate.

Supply Chain Management

supply chain management (SCM)
The overall process of minimizing inventory and moving goods through the channel faster by using computers to improve communications among the channel members.

electronic data interchange (EDI)
Software that enables the computers of producers, wholesalers, and retailers to talk with each other.

Most firms in a channel of distribution are forced to carry higher levels of inventory than absolutely necessary to assure that goods will be available when needed. Much lower levels of inventory could be carried if those firms had better communication links with and faster response times from their suppliers. That is exactly what is happening today. **Supply chain management (SCM)** is the overall process of minimizing inventory and moving goods through the channel faster by using computers to improve communications among the channel members.[3]

Electronic Data Interchange (EDI) enables the computers of producers, wholesalers, and retailers to "talk" with each other.[4] EDI makes it possible for a retailer to be directly linked with a supplier electronically. As a result, the supplier can ship new goods as soon as the retail sale is made. EDI thus becomes a critical part of an effective supply chain management system.

Total cost reductions using supply chain management have been 30 percent or more. Similar reductions in inventory have also been achieved. Bergin Brunswig, a major distributor of pharmaceuticals and health care products, has cut the amount of time from when an order is placed until it is delivered to just 12 hours.[5] You can see how the retailer can carry much less inventory and still never be out of a product with such quick response time.

Companies such as Procter & Gamble, Xerox, 3M, Nabisco, and Black & Decker have experienced inventory reductions and service improvements using supply chain management. Such companies implement the system by working together on functions such as forecasting, distribution, and marketing. Data are shared among the firms so the whole system can be operated as a unit and

SPOTLIGHT ON BIG BUSINESS

"We Don't Sell Products, We Sell Relationships"

As general manager of the polyethylene division of Atlantic Packaging Products Ltd. of Toronto, Roger Keeley sells plastic bags, shrink-wrap, and industrial and commercial packaging to large retailers such as Canadian Tire Corp. Ltd. and Loblaw Cos. Ltd. His aim is to be part of his customers' strategic teams.

How does a plastic bag or a roll of shrink-wrap fit into retail strategy? Keeley says it's a matter of finding out how Atlantic's resources can give the client an edge. "It's consultative selling," he says. "You've got to prove to them there's an advantage to doing business with you. You sell the relationship, not the product."

As an integrated manufacturer that also makes corrugated boxes, Atlantic provides such services as a creative design team that conjures up logos and colorful graphics for product packaging; a fleet of more than 100 trucks and trailers that guarantees prompt delivery, as well as pickup of old boxes for recycling; and training videos to show retailers how to pack groceries so the bags don't break.

The search for a fit with customers arises out of the relentless quest in the '90s for value. "Customers are smarter and busier," says Keeley. "They look for good value in all their purchases." For instance, Atlantic and Kodak Canada Inc., one of its customers, formed a troubleshooting team with members from both companies that meets regularly. In one case, the team noticed that Kodak was ordering cartons by the thousand. When the pallets of cartons were stored in Kodak's warehouse upon delivery from Atlantic, they left a lot of wasted unused space—which was not very cost effective. The team recommended that Kodak order cartons by the skid load, which would fill up each storage space completely. "Kodak got better space utilization [in its warehouse] and, in fact, reduced the total cost of inventory," says Keeley. "It's a win-win situation all the way down."

Keeley, a sales, marketing and general manager with Atlantic for 22 years and a past president of the Canadian Professional Sales Association, still goes on sales calls in his managerial role—along with salespeople from the newsprint, paper bag and paper tissue divisions. The team also includes appropriate sales and divisional managers and designers—and sometimes even the company president, Irving Granovsky.

Group selling involving senior executives, plant managers, and engineers is only to be expected. The close relationships that sales teams seek with their customers have to be forged at senior levels. Co-ordinated schedules, changes to packaging or even modifications to the product demand nothing less. And that means a different kind of sales force. It should be hired on the basis of business and political acumen, not on knowledge of a product or smoothness of delivery. It's called "senior executive bonding ability," where the sales force uses its business knowledge to build a trusting relationship with clients, to shift the focus of sales from selling on price to selling on value, and from selling on product features to selling on benefits to the customer.

Sources: John Southerst, "Secrets of Sales Superstars," *Canadian Business,* December 1992, p. 59.

world-class products can be sent through the system in world-class time. New EDI computer software makes all of this possible. Such high-quality service and management is demanded in the highly competitive 1990s.

Managing the flows of goods from producer to consumer has become a major career area in marketing. Many universities now have a major in transportation and logistics. We shall discuss that function next.

PROGRESS CHECK

- What is the relationship among middlemen, channels of distribution, and physical distribution? Why do we need middlemen?
- Can you illustrate how middlemen create exchange efficiency? How would you defend middlemen to someone who said that if we got rid of them we would save millions of dollars?
- Give examples of the five utilities and how middlemen perform them.
- Can you illustrate how computers make distribution and retailing more efficient and less costly?

PHYSICAL DISTRIBUTION

Historically, the reason for middlemen was to help perform the physical distribution function; that is, help move goods from the farm to consumer markets or move raw materials to factories and so forth. It involved the movement of goods by truck, train, and other modes, and the storage of goods in warehouses along the way. (*Modes,* in the language of distribution, are the various means used to transport goods such as trucks, trains, planes, ships, and pipeline.) The first courses in marketing had titles such as "The Distribution of Products." Physical distribution is still the most costly marketing function.

This section will introduce you to the principles of physical distribution and give you some insights into physical distribution management. If you are attracted to careers in this area, you can find courses covering transportation, distribution management, and related topics such as carrier management. Sometimes these courses have the word *logistics* in the title. Although logistics is sometimes viewed as a slightly different concept, the course content is largely physical distribution, storage management and all factors relating to movement of goods.

One cannot overemphasize the importance of physical distribution, even in an era when the service sector is dominant. Physical distribution begins with raw materials (for example, at the mine) that have to be shipped to manufacturers, who change them into useful products. Physical distribution also includes those activities involved in purchasing goods, receiving them, moving them through the plant, inventorying them, storing them, and shipping finished goods all the way to final users (including all the warehousing, reshipping, and physical movements of all kinds involved). Have you ever thought about how easy it is to get products from almost anywhere in the world in Canada? This does not happen in less developed countries because they lack the efficient distribution system we have.

The Physical Distribution Manager

A smart physical distribution manager can do wonders for a firm's profitability. For example, one firm was shipping finished cabinets in carload lots to four warehouses. The traffic manager found that the company could save 40 percent by shipping the shelving separately from the bolts and nuts. This was possible because the shipping rates for components were much less than for finished parts. The increase in cost for

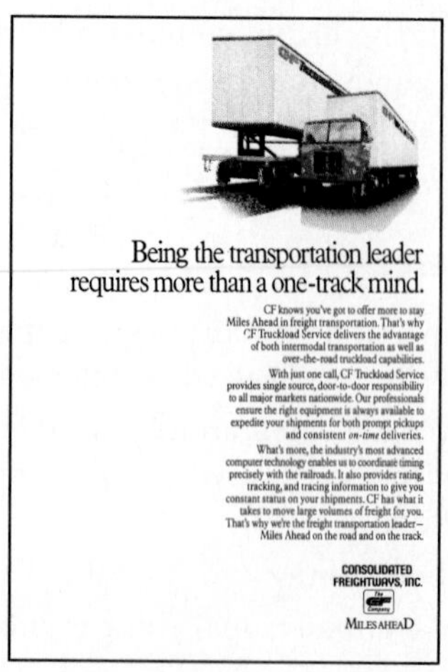

This ad promotes door-to-door service using trains and trucks. Emphasis is placed on consistent on-time delivery and customer service. Advanced computer technology and industry co-operation are revolutionizing the distribution industry and reducing costs enormously.

handling and packaging the component parts was $40,000, but the savings in shipping costs was $320,000, for a net saving of $280,000. Such are the savings possible when physical distribution is carefully managed.

Physical distribution costs have been a concern of marketers for many years, but there has been more talk and theory development than action. Recently, however, the development of computers, marketing information systems, and integrated channel networks have led to a new position called **physical distribution manager.** This person is responsible for co-ordinating and integrating all movement of materials including transportation, internal movement (materials handling), and warehousing. Few organizations actually have such a position, but many have accepted the concept, and a "total systems approach" is slowly being implemented. Only recently have firms begun to recognize the need for physical distribution management throughout the channel system rather than just within the firm itself. That is, a department in one firm can co-ordinate and integrate as much of the movement of goods through the entire channel as possible. The idea is to keep distribution costs low for the whole system as well as for each individual organization in the channel.

physical distribution manager
The person responsible for co-ordinating and integrating all movement of materials including transportation, internal movement, and warehousing.

Transportation Modes

In Canada we have always had a particular economic problem regarding the transportation component of operating costs. We are a very large country with a very low population density. None of our main business competitors face this problem. Our main competitor, the U.S., as well as Japan and European countries, have high population densities and relatively short distances to their main domestic markets. The transportation factor makes unit costs in Canada higher, which makes us less competitive.

This Canadian situation makes the job of distribution managers particularly important. They select transportation modes that minimize cost while maintaining the required level of service—speed and reliability. Since the inception of substantial railroad service in the middle of the last century, this mode has carried the overwhelming bulk of goods in Canada where water transport was not available. With the establishment of a wide network of paved highways in the middle of this century, trucking became an important mode of transportation.

In the early 1980s, freight tonnage carried by trucks surpassed rail tonnage for the first time. By the end of the decade, truck tonnage exceeded rail tonnage by some 30 percent.[6] Of course, the progress of modern technology in transportation is making it increasingly difficult to make clear distinctions between these and other modes.

We are all familiar with the huge trailer trucks that dominate our highways with their detachable trailers and containers. These usually complete their journey in a different mode, so the process is called **piggybacking,** shipping the cargo-carrying part of a truck on a railroad car or ship over long distances. This makes the total trip as efficient as possible and blurs the lines between the different modes of transport. Sealed container transport has become a major form of transportation all over the world. (See the section on containerization.)

piggybacking
Shipping the cargo-carrying part of a truck on a railroad car or ship over long distances for greater efficiency.

In Canada we have a unique waterway that stretches from the Atlantic Ocean through the St. Lawrence River and the Great Lakes to the heart of the continent—Thunder Bay in western Ontario and Detroit and Chicago in the U.S. This major transportation artery carries a huge volume of tonnage through the St. Lawrence Seaway channel (which is closed for the three winter months). The locks at Sault Ste. Marie and the Welland Canal are among the busiest in the world. This

This picture shows the piggyback process in action. A truck chassis is positioned to receive a container from a double-stack train. The truck can move the cargo directly to a retail store or other user.

system has made Quebec City, Montreal, and Toronto into significant ports. Our ports on the Atlantic and Pacific oceans are busy all year long receiving and shipping vast amounts of cargo all over the world.

While trucks and railway cars carry similar products, ships are most useful for very large bulky objects. Airplanes, which have the obvious advantage of speed, have the disadvantage of high cost and size limitations. They are an economic mode for high-cost, small items like jewellery or replacement parts for downed equipment that is delaying huge projects or important manufacturing processes. They are also ideal for the daily transport of parcels and envelopes that form the bulk of the rapid delivery required by business. Thus we have companies like Canada Post, Purolator, Federal Express, and Air Canada guaranteeing overnight delivery to any part of Canada or the U.S.

Pipelines are a form of transportation used mostly for oil and natural gas. They criss-cross the North American continent carrying these natural resources long distances, 24 hours a day, 365 days a year, immune from weather and other hazards. They also carry coal and other products along in small pieces in water, or *slurry*. The water is removed at the end of the journey.

The job of the distribution manager is to find the most efficient combination of these forms of transportation. Figure 12–4 shows the advantages and disadvantages of each.

Criteria for Choosing Physical Distribution Systems

Two criteria dominate thinking in physical distribution planning. One is *customer service*. Customer wants and needs come first. In Japan, the goal is to serve all a firm's customers' needs with 100 percent reliability. Such a goal would be prohibitively expensive. But most distribution managers do strive for an 85 to 95 percent level of customer satisfaction.

Figure 12–4 Comparing transportation modes

Mode	Cost	Speed	On-Time Dependability	Flexibility Handling Products	Frequency of Shipments	Reach
Railroad	Medium	Slow	Medium	High	Low	High
Trucks	High	Fast	High	Medium	High	Most
Pipeline	Low	Medium	Highest	Lowest	Highest	Lowest
Ships (water)	Lowest	Slowest	Lowest	Highest	Lowest	Low
Airplane	Highest	Fastest	Low	Low	Medium	Medium

Combining trucks with railroads lowers cost and increases locations reached. The same is true when combining trucks with ships. Combining trucks with airlines speeds goods long distances and gets them to almost any location.

The other criterion is *cost.* Marketing systems are designed to accomplish mutually satisfying exchanges. This means that the buyer *and* the seller must be satisfied. The objective of distribution is to provide a certain standard of customer service at the lowest cost that will result in a profit for the seller.

- Transportation modes vary from relatively slow carriers, such as barges, to high-speed jet airplanes. Generally speaking, the faster the mode, the higher the cost.
- Marketers must select those transportation modes that deliver goods at a reasonable price and maintain an acceptable level of customer service.

Some marketers have found huge savings by switching transportation modes. For example, one firm eliminated most of its warehouses and flew goods to customers when speed was demanded. Otherwise, deliveries were made by truck. As noted above, many firms are combining distribution modes to get the advantages of several modes and minimize the disadvantages. You can see in Figure 12–4 the value of combining railroading with trucking to get less expensive transportation by railroad and more flexible distribution with trucks.

Containerization

You can imagine the problem of moving many small items from place to place in large trucks, railroad cars, or other forms of transportation. There is the danger of damage, theft, and loss, especially of small items. An effective answer is to pack and seal groups of items in one large container that can be easily moved and stored. The process of packing and sealing a number of items into one unit that is easily moved and shipped is called **containerization.** More and more companies are using this technique so that shipping has become more efficient and goods flow more smoothly. It is the most common method of international shipments.

containerization
The process of packing and sealing a number of items into one unit that is easily moved and shipped.

The Storage Function

About 25 to 30 percent of the total cost of physical distribution is for storage. This includes the cost of buying and operating warehouses plus movement of goods within the warehouses. There are two kinds of warehouses: storage and distribution.

There is tremendous competition today among delivery services. Competition involves price, speed, and customer service. More competition means better service for us.

A *storage warehouse* stores products for a relatively long time. Seasonal goods such as lawnmowers would be stored in such a warehouse.

Distribution warehouses are facilities used to gather and redistribute products. You can picture a distribution warehouse for Canada Post, Federal Express or United Parcel Service handling vast numbers of packages for a very short time. Many students work part-time in such facilities while in school and go on to be traffic managers who control the shipment of goods.

GE built a combination storage and distribution facility in San Gabriel Valley, California, that will give you a feel for how large such buildings can be. This distribution center is 475 feet short of a half-mile in length and is 465 feet wide. It is big enough to hold three Statues of Liberty, two Queen Marys, *and* one Empire State Building.

Materials Handling

materials handling
The movement of goods within a warehouse, factory, or store.

Materials handling is the movement of goods within a warehouse, factory, or store. It is instructive to go to a warehouse and watch the operations for a while. You may see forklift trucks picking up stacks of merchandise and moving them around. In more modern warehouses, computerized vehicles and robots move the materials. Warehouse management could be an interesting career possibility for business students. Why not go to a local warehouse and see for yourself?

PROGRESS CHECK

- What are some of the activities involved in physical distribution?
- Which of the transportation modes is fastest? Cheapest? Most flexible? Which modes can be combined to improve the distribution process?
- What are the two criteria for selecting a distribution system?

REACHING BEYOND OUR BORDERS

A Supersalesman Goes After Megaprojects

If you want to observe Ian McKay making a sale, set aside a little time. Five years should just about do it—if he's dealing with a customer who's in hurry-up mode. But be patient. Some of McKay's deals simmer for the better part of a generation. McKay spends four to six months of the year fighting jet lag as he spans the globe in search of business. In one period of 12 months, he made five trips to China.

Should this sound nightmarish to you, forget about pursuing a sales career in the decade ahead. Travel aside, McKay's way will be much closer to the norm than the exception for successful selling in the '90s. From the time McKay, manager of international sales of hydraulic turbines for General Electric Canada Inc. in Montreal, hears about a pending hydro development to the time the contract to supply turbines and generators is awarded, he can spend more than 15 years trying to land the business.

McKay is among the vanguard of salespeople of the '90s. They're still out to move product in a big way, but they're selling benefits to customers rather than just product features, building customer relationships rather than accounts, and thinking strategy rather than tactics. That means they're developing fewer but much tighter, more extensive, and more profitable bonds with their clients.

"It's Got To Be a Team Effort"

GE's McKay says that hearing promptly about hydro projects depends on developing worldwide networks of multinational sales representatives, consultants, embassy liaisons, World Bank envoys, and officials responsible for developing their countries' energy policies. Because of the massive scale of major projects, bidding means working in teams and consortia, and co-operating with other suppliers—including competitors—of many nationalities. McKay may find himself working with several representatives from other companies, another 15 to 20 engineers, plus consultants and officials representing the user, at meetings that can last from a few hours to five days with breaks only for meals and sleep. Says McKay, "It's a team effort by everyone in the organization over several years, spearheaded by the salesman."

McKay is working on a proposal worth $500 million to GE for China's Three Gorges project, one of the world's largest hydro-electric power developments. While still at the preliminary stage—the turbines and generators won't be needed until about 1997—McKay is concentrating on what he calls "strategic positioning," keeping GE's name at the forefront of potential bidders.

His best completed deal was a contract worth more than $100 million for the 1,200-megawatt Geheyan power project in central China, awarded in 1988. GE won the contract as a member of a consortium that included five Canadian competitors, among them subsidiaries of GCE-Alsthom BV of France and Switzerland-based Sulzer-Escher Wyss Ltd.

GE has teamed up with a U.S. company to supply turbines to Argentina and is bidding on separate projects in Chile and Venezuela with Norwegian and Japanese partners. "A fundamental is that you have to be globally competitive to begin with," says Paul Scholfield, vice-president and general manager of GE's power systems division. "And then, having achieved that, [you must] negotiate the best partnership to [gain] technology benefits and access to the best blend of financing."

Scholfield emphasizes the changing role of sales in his business: "Our future growth will be in the export market, and that drives our sales and marketing people toward becoming junior diplomats, world travellers and, above all, consummate deal makers."

Source: John Southerst, "Secrets of Sales Superstars," *Canadian Business,* Dec. 1992, p. 58.

WHOLESALE MIDDLEMEN

Now that we have talked about channels of distribution and physical distribution management, it is time to talk about the organizations that make up the channel. We begin with wholesalers. Remember that one goal of this discussion is to introduce you to the variety of career possibilities available in this area. Most students know little or nothing about wholesaling, yet the rapid growth of warehouse clubs is providing many career possibilities. Have you ever visited one? The prices are amazingly low. If there are none in your area now, there may be soon. They are spreading rapidly across the country.

Warehouse Clubs such as Price Club now operate in many Canadian cities. They provide a special type of cash-and-carry service to their members only.

wholesaler
A marketing middleman that sells to organizations and individuals but not to final consumers.

retailer
A marketing middleman that sells to consumers.

A **wholesaler** is a marketing middleman that sells to organizations and individuals but not to final consumers. A **retailer** is an organization that sells to ultimate consumers. There is much confusion as to the difference between wholesalers and retailers. For example, many retail outlets have signs that say "wholesale distributors" or something similar.

What difference does it make whether an organization is called a wholesaler or a retailer? One difference is that all provinces, except Alberta, impose a sales tax on retail sales. To charge such a tax, the province must know which sales are retail sales and which are not. Retailers are sometimes subject to other rules and regulations that do not apply to wholesalers.

For practical marketing purposes, it is helpful to distinguish wholesaling from retailing and to clearly define the functions performed so that more effective systems of distribution can be designed. Some producers will not sell directly to retailers but will deal only with wholesalers. Some producers will give wholesalers a bigger discount than retailers. What confuses the issue is that some organizations sell much of their merchandise to other middlemen (a wholesale sale) but also sell to ultimate consumers (a retail sale). Warehouse clubs are a good example.

The issue is really rather simple: A retail sale is a sale of goods and services to consumers for their own use. A wholesale sale is the sale of goods and services to businesses and institutions (e.g., hospitals) for use in the business or to wholesalers, retailers, and individuals *for resale*. Wholesalers cannot legally sell goods to consumers for their own use. That is why you must "qualify" to become a customer at a warehouse club. If a wholesaler sells something to you for your use, that is called a retail sale, and the wholesaler will have to pay a retail tax on that sale. One organization can be both a retailer and a wholesaler, but that gets confusing when it comes time to collect (or not collect) the retail sales tax.

Merchant Wholesalers

merchant wholesaler
Independently owned wholesalers that take title to goods that they handle.

full-service wholesaler
A merchant wholesaler that performs all eight distribution functions.

Merchant wholesalers are independently owned firms that take title to goods they handle. About 80 percent of wholesalers fall into this category. There are two types of merchant wholesalers: full-service wholesalers and limited-function wholesalers. **Full-service wholesalers** perform all eight distribution functions: transportation, storage, risk bearing, credit, market information, funding, buying, and selling (see Figure 12–5). Risk bearing includes buying merchandise that you may not be able to sell or may have to sell at a loss. It also includes selling on credit to retailers and

1. *Provide a sales force* to sell the goods to retailers and other buyers.
2. *Communicate* manufacturers' advertising deals and plans.
3. *Maintain inventory,* thus reducing the level of the inventory suppliers have to carry.
4. Arrange or undertake *transportation.*
5. *Provide capital* by paying cash or quick payments for goods.
6. Provide suppliers with *market information* they cannot afford or are unable to obtain themselves.
7. Undertake *credit risk* by granting credit to customers and absorbing any bad debts, thus relieving the supplier of this burden.
8. *Assume the risk* for the product by taking title.

The wholesaler may perform the services listed below for its customers:

1. *Buy* goods the end market will desire and make them available to customers.
2. Maintain *inventory,* thus reducing customers' costs.
3. *Transport* goods to customers quickly.
4. Provide *market information* and business consulting services.
5. Provide *financing* through granting credit (critical to small retailers especially).
6. *Order* goods in the types and quantities customers desire.

Figure 12–5 **Functions of a full-function wholesaler.**

Source: Thomas C. Kinnear and Kenneth L. Bernhardt, *Principles of Marketing,* 2nd ed., Glenview, IL: Scott, Foresman, 1986, p. 369.

risking that the retailer may not be able to pay for the goods. **Limited-function wholesalers** perform only selected functions but do them especially well.

limited-function wholesaler
A merchant wholesaler that performs only selected distribution functions.

Full-Service Wholesalers

General merchandise wholesalers (full-service wholesalers) carry a broad assortment of merchandise. They are found in industries such as pharmaceuticals, hardware, and clothing.

general merchandise wholesaler
A merchant wholesaler that carries a broad assortment of merchandise.

Rack jobbers furnish racks or shelves full of merchandise to retailers, display products, and sell on consignment. This means that they keep title to the goods until they are sold and then share the profits with the retailer. Merchandise such as toys, hosiery, and health and beauty aids are sold by rack jobbers. (If a rack jobber does not supply credit to customers, he or she is classified as a limited-function wholesaler.)

rack jobber
A full-service wholesaler that furnishes racks or shelves full of merchandise to retailers, displays products, and sells on consignment.

Limited-Function Wholesalers

Cash-and-carry wholesalers serve mostly smaller retailers with a limited assortment of products. Retailers go to them, pay cash, and carry the goods home; thus the term *cash-and-carry.* Cash-and-carry wholesalers have begun selling to the general public in what are called *warehouse clubs,* which are open to members only and sell merchandise at 20 to 40 percent below supermarkets and discount stores. The primary function of such clubs is to provide small businesses (that are too small to have wholesalers service them) with merchandise and supplies at low prices. What makes these new stores different is that you and I can join these clubs for an annual fee and buy goods at a 5 percent markup (above cost) if we belong to a credit union, are government employees, or otherwise meet the qualifications. Costco operates in western Canada and Price Club in various parts of the country.

cash-and-carry wholesaler
A limited-function wholesaler that serves mostly smaller retailers with a limited assortment of products.

Drop shippers solicit orders from retailers and other wholesalers and have the merchandise shipped directly from a producer to a buyer. They own the merchandise but do not handle, stock, or deliver it. That is done by the producer. Drop shippers tend to handle bulky products such as coal, lumber, and chemicals.

drop shipper
A limited-function wholesaler that solicits orders from retailers and other wholesalers and has the merchandise shipped directly from a producer to a buyer.

truck jobber
A small, limited-function wholesaler that delivers goods by truck to retailers.

Truck jobbers are small wholesalers who deliver goods by truck to retailers. They are like cash-and-carry wholesalers on wheels. They provide no credit. They handle items like bakery goods, dairy products, and tobacco products.

Perhaps the most useful marketing middlemen as far as you are concerned are retailers. They are the ones who bring goods and services to your neighbourhood and make them available day and night.

RETAIL MIDDLEMEN

Next time you go to the supermarket to buy groceries, stop for a minute and look at the tremendous variety of products in the store. Think of how many marketing exchanges were involved to bring you the 10,000 or so items that you see. Some products (spices, for example) may have been imported from halfway around the world. Other products have been processed and frozen so you can eat them out of season (for example, strawberries).

A supermarket is a retailer—a marketing middleman who sells to consumers. In Canada there are approximately 230,000 retail stores, selling everything from soup to automobiles. Retail organizations employ more than a million people. They are a major employer of marketing graduates. There are many careers available in retailing in all kinds of firms.

Retail Store Categories

There are so many new retail establishments opening today that it is difficult to keep up. Some of the more important categories are the following.

Department Stores

A department store sells a wide variety of products and services in a large multi-storey building. Most large malls or shopping centres have one or two such stores, usually at either end of the mall, which serve as *anchors*. That is, they are large and popular enough to attract business to the centre. Names that come to mind are Eaton's, The Bay, and Sears.

Department stores like The Bay offer a wide variety of products and services under one roof. The Hudson's Bay Company played a significant role in the history of our country.

Canadian Tire is an example of a retailer that started as a specialty store but now sells a variety of different product lines.

Discount Stores

Discount stores are self-serve outlets that sell general merchandise below department store prices. This retail category has made tremendous gains at the expense of department and other types of stores. (See Case One, Practicing Management Decisions, at end of chapter.)

Specialty Stores

A specialty store sells a single category of merchandise such as toys, clothing, shoes, flowers, or books. Some large chains in this category are Toys "R" Us, Sam the Record Man, Coles bookstores, and Reitman's. However, many of these stores have become less "special" as they broaden their product lines. Service stations sell snacks, ice, and charcoal; drugstores sell food, and so on.

Supermarkets

These are usually large self-serve stores that started as grocery stores but now have a bakery, fresh fish, salad bar, and deli and a wide variety of non-food items. We are all familiar with the large chains, which may be regional or national in scope. Sobey's, Safeway, Metro, and Loblaw's are some examples. The supermarket concept was pioneered in Canada by Sam Steinberg. He opened the first Steinberg store in Montreal in the 1930s and then went on to develop a hugely successful retail and real estate empire.

Hypermarkets

A hypermarket is a giant supermarket. Such stores have spread from France to North America. They are about four times the size of normal supermarkets. Real Canadian Superstore and Save-on-Food in B.C. and Hypermarché in Montreal are some examples.

Convenience Stores

These "corner" stores carry a limited, often expensive selection, but they are near the customer and are open late, often all night. Consumers are willing to pay more for these conveniences.

Catalogue Stores

As the name suggests, these stores provide consumers with catalogues as well as some merchandise displays. Items selected are then provided from attached warehouses in larger centres, or sent to the customer from warehouses located elsewhere. Sears and Consumers Distributing are good examples.

General Stores

General stores are the forerunners of today's retail stores. They carry a wide variety of goods and are still to be found in small communities, where they continue to be the place to meet friends and neighbours.

Chain Stores

A retail company that operates more than one store is a chain. They are often specialized, like the Florsheim or Aldo Shoe chain and Reitman's clothing chain. Others are Pharmaprix or Jean Coutu drugstores. Canadian Tire, Woolco, and Zellers chains carry a wide variety of merchandise.

New Retailing Megamalls

Recent trends of retailing show up best in the new megamalls in the U.S. They are being patterned after the West Edmonton Mall in Edmonton. The mall has 800 stores and shops, including *three* McDonald's. There are 19 movie and stage theaters, a miniature golf course, an indoor water park with 20 water slides, an indoor amusement park with 28 rides, a saltwater lake, and a skating rink where the Edmonton Oilers sometimes practice. Case Two of Practicing Management Decisions examines this phenomenon.

The Wheel of Retailing

The wheel of retailing describes a situation that has occurred in retailing over the years. What happens is that new retailers tend to enter a market by emphasizing low price, limited service, and out-of-the-way locations. The new warehouse clubs are a good example. As business improves, they add services such as credit and get better locations. Soon prices must be raised to cover the added services, and the store must now compete with traditional department stores and specialty stores. Once a store has added services, it is difficult to go back. Because the store is now competing

MAKING ETHICAL DECISIONS

Marketers of new grocery products are finding it difficult to get shelf space. Supermarket chains are demanding incentive money to place new goods on already crowded shelves. The practice is known as *slotting allowances*. Stores claim that these funds are needed to add the product to the computer system, to warehouse the goods, and to promote the new products. This fee is getting higher and higher as new products enter the market. Smaller producers may eventually be forced to drop new product introductions because of these fees for shelf space.

Imagine you are a large producer of grocery products and can easily afford such fees. Would you pay them with no protest knowing that, in the long run, they will benefit you by restricting competition? Since this is a common practice, do you feel that such payments are ethical? Should anything be done about it? If so, what?

Source: "Industry Voices," *Advertising Age*, May 9, 1988, p. 54.

with department stores that are more attractive, it often fails (for example, Miracle Mart). However, new stores then enter the market at low prices and repeat the cycle. The wheel of retailing, therefore, looks like Figure 12–6.

Non-Store Retailing

While non-store retailing is on the rise, its share of the total retail market remains small. By the end of the 1980s, all the non-store modes of retailing amounted to less than 3 percent of the $185 billion retail sales market. Continuing technological innovations in telecommunications and other fields may see an increase in home shopping and direct selling. This trend is heightened by the declining amount of time available for shopping. With both spouses working and hours at work

One of the many attractions of the West Edmonton Mall is the regulation NHL-sized ice rink. The Mall has become a vacation destination for shoppers and thrill-seekers from across North America.

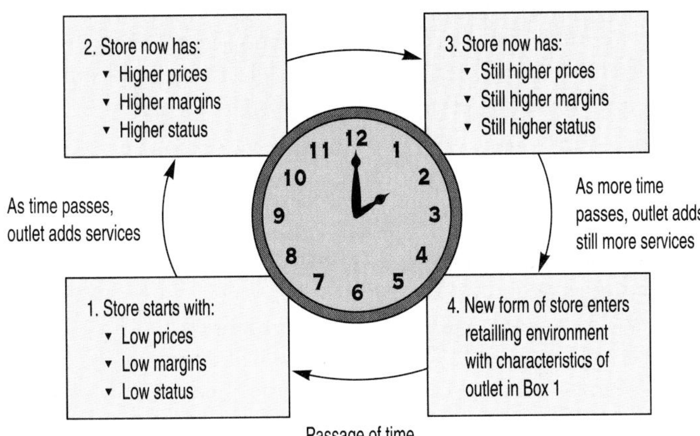

Figure 12–6 An example of this wheel of retailing is provided by discount department stores. They began by offering low prices and few services. They added services such as credit and delivery to meet the competition. The new services forced them to raise prices, making their products less competitive. Catalogue stores and warehouse clubs entered the market with low prices. Watch for many of them to add services and get more expensive too.

growing, non-store retailing may be given a big boost.[7] Types of non-store retailing include the following.

Telemarketing

telemarketing
The sales of goods and services by telephone.

Telemarketing is the sale of goods and services by telephone. Thousands of companies use telemarketing today to supplement or replace in-store selling. Many send a catalogue to consumers and let them order by calling an 800 toll-free number. This is a fast-growing area in marketing.

Vending Machines

A vending machine dispenses convenience goods when consumers deposit enough money. The benefit of vending machines is their convenient location in airports, office buildings, schools, service stations, and other areas where people want convenience items.

Japan is far ahead of us in vending, and thus can show us the future. Vending machines in Japan sell everything from bandages and face cloths to salads and spicy seafoods. Distribution and retailing will be exciting areas to watch throughout the 1990s as such innovations are introduced in Canada.

Door-to-Door Sales

Door-to-door sales involves selling to consumers in their homes. Major users of this category include encyclopedia publishers (Britannica), cosmetics producers (Avon), and vacuum cleaner manufacturers (Electrolux). The newest trend is to sell lingerie, art work, plants, and other goods at house "parties" sponsored by sellers. No doubt you have heard of Tupperware parties. Because so many women are working and not at home during the day, such companies are sponsoring parties at workplaces or on weekends or in the evening.

Mail-Order Retailers

A mail-order retailer sends catalogues to consumers who then order goods by mail or phone. Two popular ones are L. L. Bean and Land's End from the U.S. and Sears in Canada. Some of this business is now being shifted to telemarketing.

Even though we have covered most of the major categories of retailers, many more could be mentioned. Think of all the gasoline stations, restaurants, video stores, bakeries, butcher shops, rental stores, dry cleaning establishments, and more that you see in your travels. Certainly, retailing offers a variety of careers in many different settings.

Network Marketing

network marketing
People are recruited to recruit other people until a huge network of salespeople and users is created.

A number of companies have had great success using **network marketing.** Network marketing creates customers by direct sales. They then become salespeople, recruit others as users, who then recruit others until a huge network of salespeople and users is created. The best-known example is Amway, which has been successful around the world in selling a wide variety of products.

If you can get in on the beginning of such a venture, the rewards can be tremendous. Your job is to recruit several people who will recruit others to sell and use the product. If you recruit 10 people and they each recruit another 10 who in turn each recruit another 10, and so on, you soon have thousands of people under you who use and sell the product. You receive a commission from all of those sales.

One such company experiencing phenomenal growth during the early 1990s is Nu Skin, a company selling skin and hair care products.

This method has caused a lot of controversy because of its resemblance to *pyramiding,* which is illegal in many areas. Like pyramiding, network marketing starts with one person and the base and height of the pyramid get bigger and bigger as more people are recruited. The steps in the chain look like this:

			Total at each step
Step 1	1 person recruits 10	=	11
2	10 persons each recruit 10	=	111
3	100 persons each recruit 10	=	1,111
4	1,000 persons each recruit 10	=	11,111
5	10,000 persons each recruit 10	=	111,111
6	100,000 persons each recruit 10	=	1,111,111

Even if not everyone recruits 10 people, you can see how lots of people get stuck with lots of merchandise they will not be able to sell.

Home Shopping Networks

One of the more popular ways of shopping at home is home shopping TV shows. They have spawned whole new shows that sell homes and automobiles on TV. For example, the new home shows feature homes in various parts of the city and give you a number to call for more information and directions. To learn more about home shopping networks, tune to a channel that has such a show and watch how they work. You will see mostly close-out items at bargain prices and lots of jewellery and household goods. No doubt you will see more of these shows as people get more comfortable with shopping at home.

Other New-Tech Retailing

Many restaurants in business districts have installed fax machines. Customers regularly fax in their lunch orders before noon, usually with a pickup time indicated. This results in substantial time saving for customers and restaurants and much better service for the customer. The restaurant can prepare orders in advance and the customer doesn't have to wait at the restaurant. Because the order is in writing, there is no chance for error as there would be with a telephone order.

New, low-cost computer programs are introducing thousands of customers to buying groceries by computer. Your computer transmits your order via telephone/ modem directly to the computers of participating supermarkets. You tell them whether you want delivery or will pick up your order. If this proves popular, the potential is great for selling virtually any consumer or industrial good by computer.

THINKING IT THROUGH

How important are middlemen such as wholesalers, retailers, trucking firms, and warehouse operators to the progress of less developed countries? What products should be distributed first? How do middlemen contribute to the development of a less developed country?

Scrambled Merchandising

scrambled merchandising
The strategy of adding product lines to a retail store that are not normally carried there.

One long-running trend that makes categorizing retailers difficult is the trend toward scrambled merchandising. **Scrambled merchandising** is the adding of product lines to a retail store that are not normally carried (such as auto supplies in a supermarket). A moment's reflection will remind you of how often you have seen this occur. You can buy lawn furniture and fertilizer in a drugstore and drug sundries in a supermarket. Discount stores are selling food, and food stores are selling merchandise normally found in discount stores. No wonder it is called scrambled merchandising.

Retail Distribution Strategy

A major decision marketers must make is selecting retailers to sell their products. Different products call for different retail distribution strategies. There are three categories of retail distribution: intensive distribution, selective distribution, and exclusive distribution.

intensive distribution
The distribution strategy that puts products into as many retail outlets as possible.

selective distribution
The distribution strategy that uses only a preferred group of the available retailers in an area.

exclusive distribution
The distribution strategy that uses only one retail outlet in a given geographic area.

Intensive distribution puts products into as many retail outlets as possible, including vending machines. Products that need intensive distribution include candy, cigarettes, gum, and popular magazines (convenience goods).

Selective distribution is the use of only a preferred group of the available retailers in an area. Such selection helps assure the producers of quality sales and service. Manufacturers of appliances, TV sets, furniture, and clothing (shopping goods) usually use selective distribution.

Exclusive distribution is the use of only one retail outlet in a given geographic area. Because the retailer has exclusive rights to sell the product, he or she is likely to carry more inventory, give better service, and pay more attention to this brand than to others. Automobile manufacturers usually use exclusive distribution, as do producers of specialty goods.

DISTRIBUTION IN OVERSEAS MARKETS

It is one thing to decide to sell a product overseas; it is something else again to implement such a program. How are you going to reach the consumer? You could, of course, send people overseas to contact people directly, but that would be costly and risky. How can you get your product overseas at a minimum cost and still have wide distribution?[8]

Use brokers. A broker is a middleman who keeps no inventory and takes no risk. A broker can find distributors for you. Brokers sell for you and make a commission on the sale. This is the least expensive way to enter foreign markets, but you still assume the risks of transportation.

Use importers. Importers import the product into a foreign country, take all the risks of business, and sell your product there. They will find distributors or wholesalers or may do the selling to retailers or to ultimate consumers themselves.

Call on distributors directly. You can bypass importers and brokers and export to distributors yourself. In that case, you deliver directly to distributors, but again you assume many risks.

Sell direct. The most costly and risky way to sell overseas is to set up your own distribution system of wholesalers and retailers. On the other hand, this is the way to maximize profits in the long run. Many firms start out selling through importers and end up setting up their own distribution system as sales increase.

Physical distribution often means sending goods overseas or bringing them in from other countries. Volume shipments often go by ship. Smaller, more expensive items like jewellery are usually shipped by air. Working for international distributors can be exciting and rewarding.

PROGRESS CHECK

- Can you name six categories of retailers and describe the stores?
- What are the advantages and disadvantages, as you see them, of having an intensive distribution strategy versus an exclusive one?
- Explain the wheel of retailing and scrambled merchandising?

SUMMARY

1. Physical distribution is the movement of goods from producers to industrial and consumer users.

- *What is the role of marketing middlemen in the distribution process?*
  Marketing middlemen assist in the movement of goods from producers to consumers.
- *Why do we need middlemen?*
  Middlemen perform certain marketing functions (such as transportation, storage, selling, and advertising) more effectively and efficiently than most manufacturers.

1. Explain why we need marketing middlemen.

2. Middlemen help make the exchange between producers and consumers more efficient.

- *How do middlemen create exchange efficiency?*
  Middlemen create exchange efficiency by lessening the number of contacts needed to make a marketing exchange.

2. Describe how middlemen create exchange efficiency.

3. Middlemen add utility to goods.

- *What do we mean by utility?*
  Utility refers to the value or want-satisfying ability added to products by middlemen. The products have value added in that they are made more useful or accessible to consumers.

3. Give examples of how middlemen perform the five utilities mentioned in economics literature.

▼ *What are the different types of utilities added by middlemen?*

Normally, marketing middlemen perform the following utilities: (1) time, (2) place, (3) possession, and (4) information. Sometimes middlemen also perform form utility, but that is usually done by manufacturers.

4. One way of getting manufacturers, wholesalers, and retailers to co-operate in distributing products is to form efficient distribution systems.

4. Discuss how a manufacturer can get wholesalers and retailers in a channel system to co-operate by forming systems.

▼ *What are the three types of distribution systems?*

The three distribution systems that tie firms together are (1) corporate systems, in which all organizations in the channel are owned by one firm; (2) contractual systems, in which members are bound to co-operate through contractual agreements; and (3) administered systems, in which all marketing functions at the retail level are managed by manufacturers.

5. One of the biggest problems of independent distribution systems is getting people to work together. That's where the channel captain comes in.

5. Explain the role of a channel captain.

▼ *What is a channel captain and what is its role in the distribution system?*

A channel captain can be a manufacturer, wholesaler, or retailer, whichever has power to get the other channel members to co-operate. The channel captain's role is to get the channel members to work together.

6. Physical distribution can be a very complex process. That is why some firms are creating a new position called physical distribution manager.

6. Describe the role of a physical distribution manager.

▼ *What is the role of a physical distribution manager?*

This person is responsible for co-ordinating and integrating all movement of materials including transportation, internal movement, and warehousing.

7. Selecting transportation modes with minimum costs and assuring a certain level of service is a concern of the distribution manager.

7. Make a chart listing the various distribution modes and their advantages.

▼ *What are the advantages and disadvantages of the various modes of transportation?*

See Figure 12–4.

8. There are two major criteria for choosing distribution systems.

8. Identify the criteria used to select distribution systems.

▼ *What are these two criteria?*

When selecting distribution systems, both customer service and profit are important.

9. There are two kinds of warehouses: storage and distribution.

9. Explain the purposes of the two types of warehouses.

▼ *How are storage and distribution warehouses different?*

Storage warehouses store products for a long time; distribution warehouses store products for only a short time until they are redistributed.

▼ *What is materials handling?*

Materials handling is the movement of goods within a warehouse, factory, or store.

10. Wholesalers are marketing middlemen who sell to businesses but not to consumers. Wholesalers may specialize in just one or two marketing tasks.

10. Contrast the different types of wholesale middlemen and the kinds of functions they perform.

▼ *What are some categories of wholesalers?*

Merchant wholesalers own the goods they handle and include both *full-service wholesalers* (general merchandise wholesalers and rack jobbers) and *limited-function wholesalers* (cash-and-carry wholesalers, drop shippers, and truck jobbers). See pages 397 and 398.

11. A retailer is a marketing middleman that sells to consumers.

11. Name the major categories of retailers and the major trends in retailing.

▼ *What are some categories of retailers?*

Retailers include retail stores and non-store shopping. There are many new non-store retailing trends. See pp. 398–400.

12. Different products call for different distribution strategies.

12. Differentiate among intensive, selective, and exclusive distribution systems.

▼ *What are the three categories of retail distribution strategies?*

The categories of retail distribution include (1) *intensive distribution,* which puts products in as many retail outlets as possible; (2) *selective distribution,* which uses only a preferred group of retailers; and (3) *exclusive distribution,* which uses only one retail outlet in a given geographic area.

13. Many Canadian companies are distributing their products overseas.

▼ *How can you get your product overseas at a minimum cost and still have wide distribution?*

You can distribute your product overseas by (1) using brokers, (2) using importers (lowest cost), (3) calling on distributors directly, or (4) selling directly.

13. Describe the ways producers can distribute their products overseas.

GETTING INVOLVED

1. Go to the school library and look up books on physical distribution and/or logistics. What do they cover? Does it look interesting as a career?
2. Look around your community to find where the different wholesalers are located. Go visit those wholesalers and learn what they do. Look around the facilities. Are there interesting careers available?
3. When you are visiting retailers in your area, walk around the store for a while. Which stores would be the most fun to work for? Check on salaries, chances for promotion, and hours. Draw a map of a local shopping mall and show the traffic patterns to get a feel for how such malls are planned to get shoppers to buy more.
4. Visit the newest stores in your province, such as warehouse clubs, hypermarkets, or giant supermarkets. Compare their prices with those of older stores. What trends in retailing seem most significant to you? Be sure to watch the home shopping networks to see what they are doing.
5. Take some time to observe railroad cars as they go by. Do you see truck trailers? Have you noticed the new double-trailer trucks on the road? What seems to be the future of distribution modes? How can you take advantage of that in career preparation?
6. Go to a telemarketing centre in your area and watch the operation. Ask some questions and learn all you can. This is a growing part of marketing, so you should become familiar with it.

PRACTICING MANAGEMENT DECISIONS

Case One Department Store Blues

Free trade, the recession, the onset of the goods and services tax, the resultant boom in cross-border shopping, and fresh competition from such innovative U.S. chains as The Gap and Price Club have left Canadian retailers in the worst shape since the 1930s. Sears and The Bay both lost money in 1990 and 1991, and they were among the luckier ones. Other retailers, including such household names as Simpson's, Henry Birks & Sons Ltd., Peoples Jewellers Ltd. and Woodward's Ltd., either disappeared or stumbled into insolvency or receivership. Bargain Harold's Discount Ltd., supposedly recessionproof, declared bankruptcy.

This year, for the first time in Canada, the sales of discount and warehouse outlets will exceed those of conventional department stores—$9.3 billion versus $9.1 billion, according to retail consultant John Williams. He speaks of the "instant dominance" of chains such as Price Club, which will have 20 superstores in Canada by the end of [1993].

Scarier still for retailers, customers aren't behaving the way they used to. It's debatable whether that large, yuppified market for $1,000 Armani blouses, $4,000 Rolexes and $250 jeans ever really existed. But too many retailers acted as if it did. Today, after hundreds of store closures, "upscale" is practically a dirty word and shoppers are more value- and price-conscious than ever before.

This shift in consumer attitudes may be hurting Canadian department stores worse than those south of the border because, according to a growing body of statistical evidence, they are much less competitive than their U.S. counterparts. A recent study compares the performance of similar retailing units in Canada and the U.S. By almost every measure,

Canadian retailers have it easier. Canada has fewer stores earning more money per square foot than their U.S. counterparts. In almost every merchandise category, there are fewer suppliers here than in the U.S. Although retail vacancy rates have soared in the U.S. during the current recession, Canadian shopping malls have suffered surprisingly little.

That competitive cushion helps explain why Eaton's, and other large retailers, have been able to flourish for so long, despite what retail analyst George Hartman of BBN James Capel Inc. calls the "inherently poor management" of Canadian retailers. Historically, Eaton's has been less obsessed with profits and growth than a public company could afford to be. During the Depression, the family earned a reputation for hanging onto its employees while everyone else was laying off theirs. John David Eaton is said to have discouraged his executives from trying to make the firm too profitable. He considered a return of 3 percent on sales to be perfectly adequate, and saw no point in squeezing larger margins out of the operation.

That sort of insouciance, if it ever existed, is no longer affordable. That could mean layoffs and store closures this year. The chain includes some troublesome locations, such as the Woodgrove shopping centre in Nanaimo, B.C., the downtown store in Kitchener, Ont., and Bower Place in Red Deer, Alta., which is such a consistent money-loser that it's known as "Bowser Place"—a real dog.

Decision Questions

1. Scrambled merchandising, discounters, and especially warehouse clubs have been steadily taking market share away from department stores. Are we truly in a new marketing era where price is the single dominant consumer value? What should department stores do to meet this decade-long decline in their fortunes?
2. Some majors like Sears are restructuring to meet the challenge by cutting back on staffing, closing stores, and other drastic cost-cutting measures. Some analysts see this as reacting to problems without a thorough analysis of long-term solutions. Should these retailers be considering major policy changes in purchasing, location, and pricing? Do they need new blood to move in new, bold directions?
3. Department stores like Eaton's are sitting on valuable downtown real estate. Is it time to consider cashing in these chips and using the substantial profits to enter new ventures? Department stores were new ventures a century ago. Can new directions be taken now, in the face of today's challenges?
4. Suppose the current problems are a temporary phenomenon, a passing fad. Is it possible that a new generation will go back to department store shopping and abandon price as the sole concern? If you had to make decisions at Eaton's, would you bet on this happening? What would you do?

Source: Alexander Ross, "The Eaton's Nobody Knows," *Canadian Business,* May 1993, p. 47.

Case Two The Megamalls Are Coming

It all started in Canada at the West Edmonton Mall, a 5.2 million square foot extravaganza that must be seen to be believed. Who can picture a mall with a Ferris wheel, a huge aquarium, and a church? There are 825 stores, two auto dealerships, and 32 movie theatres! There are also an ice-skating rink, an underground lake, an 18-hole miniature golf course, and 132 restaurants. Imagine Disneyland combined with the largest mall you have ever seen and you have some idea of what the West Edmonton Mall looks like. The mall has been a tourist attraction for years.

Now a similar mall is coming to the Toronto area. Imagine a mall the size of 80 football fields! A new mall to be built in Bloomington, Minnesota, will be 4.2 million square feet in size.

It is no mistake that malls are called "shopping centres" by many people. The key to malls was developed by a man named Victor Gruen about 30 years ago. His goal was to change "destination shoppers" into "impulse shoppers." Here's how it works. You run to the mall to buy a pair of shoes. You go into a shoe store to get what you want, but cannot find it. You then proceed to walk through the mall to another shoe store. During that walk, you may stop for an ice cream cone, drop in to a bookstore for a paperback novel, and window shop at several clothing stores. You went to the mall for shoes (a destination shopper) and ended up buying ice cream, books, and maybe a sweater (an impulse shopper).

Malls are ingeniously designed to foster impulse shopping. Shoe stores are usually widely separated so you have to travel the length of the mall to shop for shoes. Most malls are anchored by a couple of major department stores (e.g., Sears) that are at opposite ends, like anchors holding the mall together. Notice how the malls have spread the distance between clothing stores and other places to shop.

Decision Questions

1. Most new malls have no supermarkets. Why?
2. Imagine a megamall coming to your area. Would you enjoy going to the mall every time you wanted to go to a movie or to a restaurant? Compare such a mall to the shopping centres you now have. Which do you prefer? Why?
3. Do you see megamalls as the future for retailing? Are malls to become the entertainment centres of Canada? What would be the advantages and disadvantages?
4. Shopping malls were meant to be places where you could window shop and buy impulse items. Megamalls are now so large that such shopping would take all day. Do you think this will cut back on the frequency of mall visits and result in less business per store?

Source: Information provided by West Edmonton Mall; "Quotables," *Marketing Communication*, September 1988, p. 7.

LET'S TALK BUSINESS

1. The trend in business is toward global marketing. The problem is that distribution systems are not designed to go from country to country. Discuss in class what you think may be the most critical global distribution problem during the 1990s.
2. The five utilities of marketing are form, time, place, possession, and information. Can you give examples of organizations specifically designed to perform each of these functions?
3. Many students want to go into retailing when they graduate, but few have wholesaling as their goal. Why is that? Which job do you think may have greater career potential? Which may be more challenging?
4. What is the latest in the battle between trucks and railroads over market share? The railways claim that the truckers have an unfair advantage because roads are maintained by governments but rail lines are the responsibility of the two national railways. What do you think?

LOOKING AHEAD

The last of the four Ps of marketing is promotion. We shall discuss this important function in depth in Chapter 13. All of the four Ps of marketing—product, price, place, and promotion—rely on information about markets, consumer behaviour, and more. Companies obtain that information by conducting marketing research. We conclude Chapter 13 with an analysis of marketing communication systems and the role of research in providing marketing managers with the information they need to make decisions in today's dynamic market environment.

Bank of Montreal and the AIR MILES™ Reward Program

Together, we'll take you there.

Turn your banking into a great vacation. Or into a family visit. Or give a loved one a holiday trip. Whatever your pleasure, Bank of Montreal and AIR MILES Travel Miles can take you there.

Collect travel miles through your everyday banking needs, and without sacrificing competitive rates and features. There's a Bank of Montreal AIR MILES MasterCard®* card, AIR MILES Chequing and AIR MILES Savings Accounts, plus AIR MILES Travel Miles loan and mortgage offers.*

You can shop at a growing network of AIR MILES Sponsors, but no other bank offers AIR MILES Travel Miles. It's another way that we take our customers to new heights.

ADVERTISING, PROMOTION, AND MARKETING RESEARCH

CHAPTER 13

LEARNING GOALS

After you have read and studied this chapter, you should be able to:

1. Define promotion and list the various elements of the promotional mix.
2. Explain how advertising differs from the other promotional tools and discuss the advantages and disadvantages of different advertising media.
3. Explain the differences among different forms of advertising such as retail and trade advertising and industrial and institutional advertising.
4. Debate the advantages of regionalism versus globalism in advertising.
5. Illustrate the seven steps of the selling process.
6. Explain the importance of word of mouth as a promotional tool.
7. Describe the functions of the public relations department and the role of publicity in that function.
8. List sales promotion tools and explain how they are used both internally with employees and externally to customers.
9. Describe the major steps in the process used to conduct marketing research.
10. Differentiate between secondary and primary data and discuss the role of each in market research.
11. Explain the three parts of a marketing communication system.

KEY TERMS

Jean-Pierre Grenier

PROFILE HOW TO TURN IDEAS INTO GOLD

Many people have great ideas. Few know how to develop them into profitable businesses. Forty-three-year-old Jean-Pierre Grenier is not one of them. A dropout from industrial design school, he has a knack for spotting potentially winning designs and knows how to improve and then promote these products into the world market. He has done his market research so well that he knows what can sell.

In 1978 Grenier started Diffusion Jean-Pierre Grenier Inc., and by 1984 he had built it into a $6 million business by representing designers, artists, and small manufacturers. He then sold his company to concentrate on small-scale exporting. His first success came with a moulded plastic attache case. It is still a "hot retail item" and more than 2 million have been sold "in most parts of the world."

"It's a design classic and is even available at the Museum of Modern Art in New York," says Grenier. So is a CD holder called Compakt which has won five international design awards and is selling well in Germany and the U.S. Another winner is Travel Shave, a pen-size shaver that includes razor and shaving cream and is good for 10 shaves.

These three products, manufactured by different Quebec Firms, were produced by three different designers whom Grenier took under his wing. The Travel Shave, invented by Quebec City designer Raymond Savard, is a good example of how Grenier operates. Grenier immediately saw its marketing potential but "its appearance could render it a dud." He took it to Michel Dallaire, designer of the very successful moulded plastic case, who gave it "a refined Italian look." Then designer Danielle Perry "joined the team and created different packages for retail sales and promotional giveaways."

Travel Shave was introduced at the International Luggage and Leather Goods Show in Las Vegas in April 1992 and four months later at the New York Gift Show. "Our strategy was to go forward step-by-step. First we hit the trade shows, then we called on men's accessory buyers for retailers and airline catalogues," said Grenier. At the same time he kept up a barrage of editorial press coverage and advertising.

These well-planned efforts paid off with 600,000 units exported in 1992 to European countries and the U.S. At a trade show in Paris in the fall of 1993 he "hooked into a distribution network with 1,300 accounts."

His talent for spotting potential winners, knowing what is marketable, getting the product improved to meet that market demand, and then knowing how to promote the product have made Jean-Pierre Grenier a success story. In Chapter 13 we explore marketing research and promotion.

Source: Annabelle King, "Designer Guru Turns Ideas into Gold," Montreal Gazette, October 12, 1993, pp. C8, 9.

THE IMPORTANCE OF PROMOTION AND RESEARCH

No matter how much time and effort a marketer may put into product, pricing, and distribution (place) decisions, the whole process is likely to fail without good promotion. Promotion is the last, but not the least, of the four Ps of marketing. Marketers now spend over $12 billion yearly on advertising trying to convince industrial and consumer buyers to choose their products. They spend even more on sales promotion efforts such as conventions and trade shows, where producers and customers meet to discuss and arrange marketing exchanges. Marketers spend the most money sending salespeople out into the field to talk personally with customers. Jean-Pierre Grenier works very hard, and so do many thousands of other skilled men and women in promotional jobs such as advertising, publicity, sales promotion, and selling.

Marketing research is a managerial tool that marketers use to improve the effectiveness of all the other marketing efforts. The marketing process begins, as we now know, by researching consumer wants and needs. Then product development calls for marketing research to test products. Research is needed to make pricing decisions and distribution decisions as well. Perhaps most important, research is used to make promotional efforts more effective. Research is the tool managers use to choose the best mix of all the marketing elements. We shall discuss research at the end of the chapter. Before we look at this important tool, though, let's explore promotion in detail.

WHAT IS PROMOTION?

What do you think of when you hear the word promotion? Most people think of advertising. But promotion is much more than just advertising. **Promotion** is an attempt by marketers to persuade others to buy their products or services. Marketers use many different tools—advertising, personal selling, word of mouth, public relations, publicity, and sales promotion—to inform potential consumers about their organization and its goods and services. This combination of promotional tools is called the company's **promotional mix** (see Figure 13–1).

promotion
An attempt by marketers to persuade others to buy their products or services.

promotional mix
The combination of tools marketers use to promote their products or services.

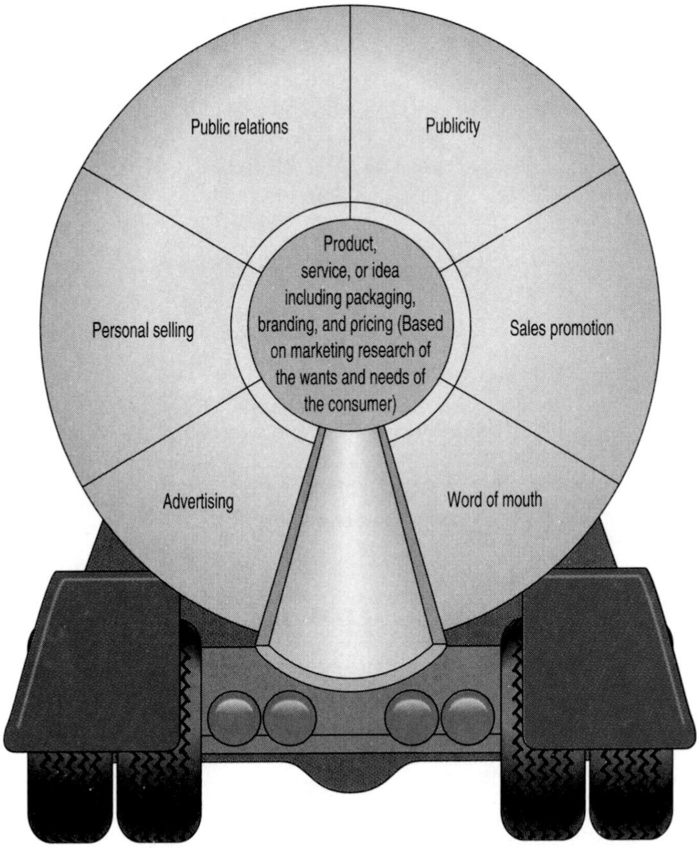

Figure 13–1 The promotion mix. This figure shows that the product offer is the central focus of the promotion mix. The offer is based on marketing research. All of the communication elements are designed to promote the sale of the product.

Advertising

advertising
Paid, non-personal communication through various media by organizations and individuals who are in some way identified in the advertising message.

One reason most people mistake promotion for advertising is that they do not understand the differences among promotional tools such as advertising, personal selling, publicity, and word of mouth. **Advertising** is limited to *paid, nonpersonal* communication through various *media* by organizations and individuals who are in some way *identified* in the advertising message. As you will see more clearly later in the chapter, word of mouth is not a form of advertising because it does not go through a medium (newspaper, TV, etc.), it is not paid for, and it is personal. Publicity is different from advertising in that media space for publicity is not paid for. Personal selling is face-to-face communication and does not go through a medium; thus, it is not advertising. The advertisement for advertising (This Ad Is Full of Lies) debunks some myths about ads.

Now that you understand what advertising is not, let's look at what advertising *is*. Anyone who watches television, listens to the radio, or reads magazines cannot help but notice the importance of advertising in our lives.

Push Strategies versus Pull Strategies

push strategy
Use of promotional tools to convince wholesalers and retailers to stock and sell merchandise.

pull strategy
Use of promotional tools to motivate consumers to request products from stores.

There are two ways to promote the movement of products from producers to consumers. The first is called a **push strategy.** In push strategy, the producer uses advertising, personal selling, sales promotion, and all other promotional tools to convince *wholesalers* and *retailers* to stock and sell merchandise. If it works, consumers will then walk into the store, see the product, and buy it. The idea is to push the product down the distribution system to the stores. One example of a push strategy is to offer dealers one free case of soda for every dozen cases they purchase.

A second strategy is a **pull strategy,** in which heavy advertising and sales promotion efforts are directed towards *consumers* so they will request the products from retailers. If it works, consumers will go to the store and order the products. Seeing the demand for the products, the store owner will then order them from the wholesaler. The wholesaler, in turn, will order them from the producer. Products are thus pulled down through the distribution system. Most television advertising is

People have certain perceptions about advertising. Many think it helps sell bad products and is a waste of money. This ad for advertising addresses these issues and more. What do you think?

a pull strategy to increase demand. Of course, a company could use both a push and a pull strategy at the same time in a major promotional effort.

The Importance of Advertising

When people refer to advertising, they are usually talking about TV advertising. For example, the debate about the effect of advertising on children is really about TV and children. Similarly, when people talk about advertising being offensive, intrusive, manipulative, and so on, they are thinking primarily of TV advertising. But since only about 18 percent of total advertising budgets is spent on TV advertising, there is much more to advertising than most people normally imagine. (See Figure 13–2.)

The public benefits from advertising expenditures. First, advertising is informative. The number one medium, newspapers, is full of information about products, prices, features, and more. Does it surprise you to find that businesses spend more on direct mail than on radio and magazines? Direct mail (using mailing lists to reach an organization's most likely customers) is an informative shopping aid for consumers. Each day consumers receive mini-catalogues in their newspapers, in the mail, or by door-to-door delivery that tell them what is on sale, where, at what price, for how long, and so on.

Advertising not only informs us about products but also provides us with TV and radio programs, because advertisers in effect pay for these programs. Advertising also covers the major costs of producing newspapers and magazines. When we buy a magazine, the purchase price usually covers only the mailing or promotional costs.

Later in the chapter, Figure 13–6 discusses the advantages and disadvantages of various advertising media to the advertiser. Newspapers and radio are especially attractive to local advertisers. Television has many advantages to national advertisers, but it is expensive. Figure 13–3 shows that the cost of one minute of advertising in the U.S. during the telecast of the Super Bowl is up to \$1.5 million. The cost of a 30-second prime-time commercial during the Grey Cup Game in 1990 was \$45,000. How many bottles of beer or bags of dog food must a company sell to pay for such a commercial? Is it any wonder that companies are now buying 15-second commercials to save money?

	1991	
Medium	**\$000**	**Percentage**
Daily newspapers	\$2,002	23.0
Direct mail and catalogues	1,680	19.0
Television	1,633	18.0
Phone and city directories	837	9.5
Outdoor billboards, etc.	828	9.5
Radio	741	8.0
Weekly newspapers	654	7.0
General magazines	260	3.0
Business magazines	156	2.0
All other	93	1.0
	\$8,884	100.0

Figure 13–2 Advertising expenditures by medium. This includes advertising by governments and commercial companies. These figures are based on direct costs only—amounts paid to the various media. They do not include production costs and costs of maintaining in-house advertising departments.

Source: *Marketing* 97, no. 32, Aug. 17, 1992, p. 1.

Figure 13–3 Super Bowl marketing. The growth of America's premier sporting event is reflected in the rising cost of a 60-second TV commercial over the years. One minute of advertising during the Super Bowl now costs over $1.5 million.*

Super Bowl	Year	Cost of "60 Spot"
I	1967	$ 80,000
V	1971	200,000
X	1976	250,000
XV	1981	550,000
XX	1986	1,100,000
XXV	1991	1,500,000

*Now commercials are sold in 30-second spots; the first six Super Bowls had only 60-second spots.
Source: *Washington Post,* January 20, 1989, p. G.1 and other sources.

These costs are for time only. To this must be added the very substantial fees and costs of the advertising agencies that produce these ads. Most companies selling consumer goods use ad agencies to plan, organize, and produce all their advertising, publicity, and promotional campaigns and material.

Major Categories of Advertising

Different kinds of advertising are used by various organizations to reach different market targets. The following are some major categories.

retail advertising
Advertising to consumers by retailers.

trade advertising
Advertising to wholesalers and retailers by manufacturers.

industrial advertising
Advertising from manufacturers to other manufacturers.

institutional advertising
Advertising designed to create an attractive image for an organization rather than for a product.

product advertising
Advertising for a good or service to create interest among consumer, commercial, and industrial buyers.

advocacy advertising
Advertising that supports a particular view of an issue.

comparison advertising
Advertising that compares competitive products.

- **Retail advertising**—advertising to consumers by various retail stores such as supermarkets and shoe stores.
- **Trade advertising**—advertising to wholesalers and retailers by manufacturers to encourage them to carry their products.
- **Industrial advertising**—advertising from manufacturers to other manufacturers. A firm selling motors to automobile companies would use industrial advertising.
- **Institutional advertising**—advertising designed to create an attractive image for an organization rather than for a product. "A Whole Lot More for a Whole Lot Less" at Canadian Tire and "Where the Lowest Price Is the Law" at Zellers are examples. "Virginia Is for Lovers" and "I ♥ New York" are two institutional campaigns by government agencies.
- **Product advertising**—advertising for a good or service to create interest among consumer, commercial, and industrial buyers.
- **Advocacy advertising**—advertising that supports a particular view of an issue. For example, an ad in support of gun control or against nuclear power plants. Such advertising is also known as *cause advertising.*
- **Comparison advertising**—advertising that compares competitive products. For example, an ad that compares cold-care products on speed and benefits would be a comparative ad.

The Global Marketing and Advertising Debate

Professor Theodore Levitt of Harvard is a big proponent of global marketing and advertising. His idea is to develop a product and promotional strategy that can be implemented worldwide. Certainly that would save money in research costs and in

This billboard helps encourage people to drink milk rather than advertising a specific brand of milk. Which category of advertising best describes this advertisement?

advertising design. However, other experts think that promotion targeted at specific countries may be much more successful since each country has its own culture, language, and buying habits.

The evidence supports the theory that promotional efforts specifically designed for individual countries work best. For example, commercials for Camay soap that showed men complimenting women on their appearance were jarring in cultures where men don't express themselves that way. A different campaign is needed in such countries. People in Brazil rarely eat breakfast and treat Kellogg's Corn Flakes as a dry snack like potato chips. Kellogg is trying a promotional strategy of convincing people in Brazil to eat cereal with cold milk in the morning.[1]

Many more examples could be cited to show that international advertising calls for doing research into the wants, needs, and culture of each specific country and then designing appropriate ads and testing them.

Even in Canada we have regional differences that are important enough to constitute separate market segments. Each province has its own history and culture and different populations and Quebec has a different language. The large metropolitan areas like Toronto, Montreal, Vancouver, Edmonton, Calgary, Winnipeg, Ottawa, and Quebec City are different from the rest of the provinces in which they are located. All require their own promotions and advertising.

PROGRESS CHECK

- What are the six elements of the promotion mix?
- Could you describe how to implement a push strategy for Fiberrific cereal? A pull strategy?
- Give examples of retail, trade, industrial, institutional, and product advertising.
- Can you list the advertising media in order based on the total dollar amount spent by advertisers?

Personal Selling

personal selling Face-to-face presentation and promotion of products and services plus searching out prospects and providing follow-up service.

Personal selling is the face-to-face presentation and promotion of products and services plus searching out prospects and providing follow-up service. Effective selling is not simply a matter of persuading others to buy (see Figure 13–4). In fact, it is more accurately described as helping others to satisfy their wants and needs. Selling can be an exciting, rewarding, and challenging professional career.

To illustrate the importance of personal selling in our economy and the career opportunities it provides, let us look at a few figures. Canadian census data show that nearly 10 percent of the total labour force is employed in personal selling.

The cost of a single sales call to a potential industrial buyer is over $250. Surely no firm would pay that much to send out anyone but a highly skilled, professional marketer and consultant. But how does one get to be that kind of sales representative? What are the steps along the way for men and women who want to enter industrial sales? Let's take a closer look at the process of selling.

Steps in the Selling Process

The best way to get a feel for personal selling is to go through the selling process with a product and see what is involved. One product that you are probably familiar

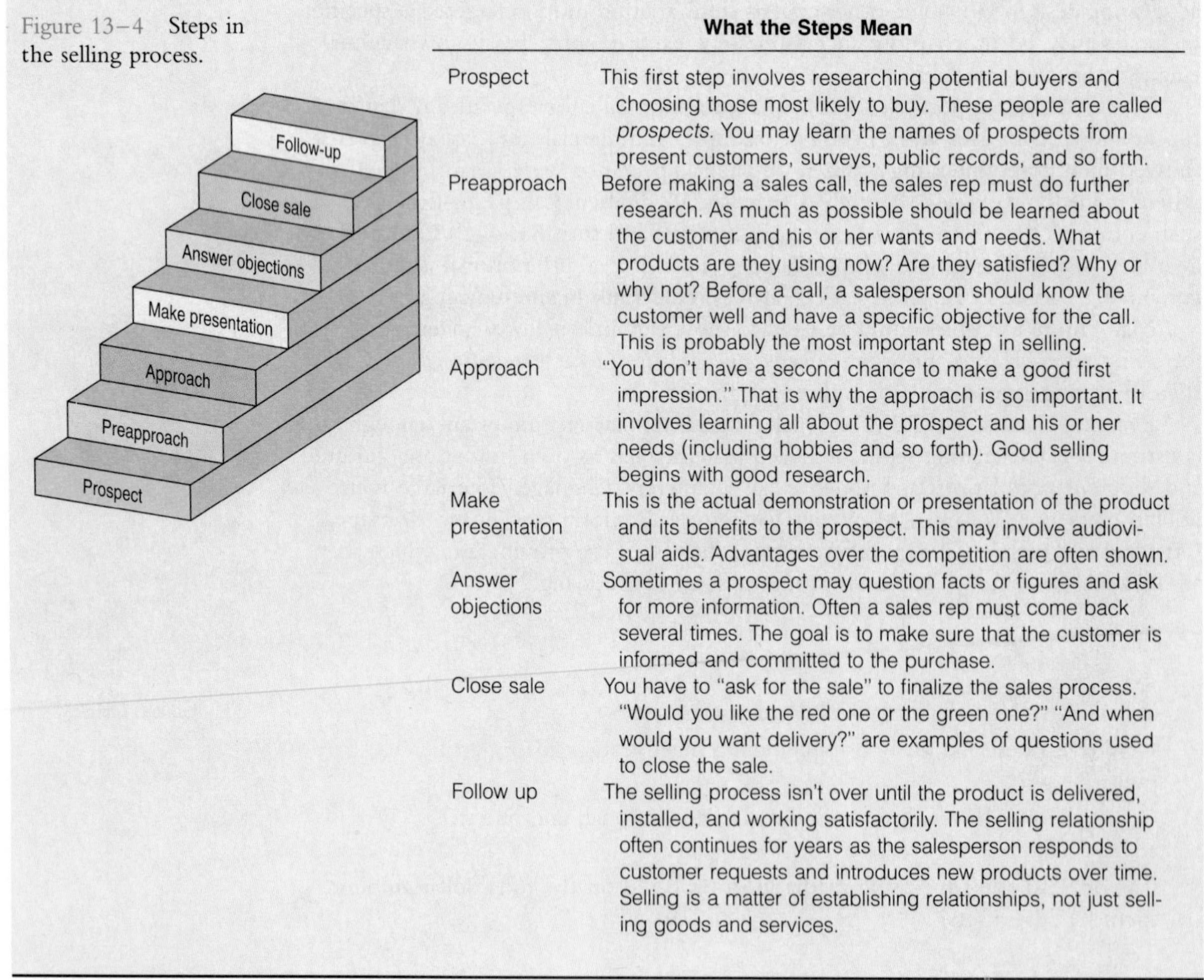

Figure 13–4 Steps in the selling process.

What the Steps Mean

Prospect	This first step involves researching potential buyers and choosing those most likely to buy. These people are called *prospects*. You may learn the names of prospects from present customers, surveys, public records, and so forth.
Preapproach	Before making a sales call, the sales rep must do further research. As much as possible should be learned about the customer and his or her wants and needs. What products are they using now? Are they satisfied? Why or why not? Before a call, a salesperson should know the customer well and have a specific objective for the call. This is probably the most important step in selling.
Approach	"You don't have a second chance to make a good first impression." That is why the approach is so important. It involves learning all about the prospect and his or her needs (including hobbies and so forth). Good selling begins with good research.
Make presentation	This is the actual demonstration or presentation of the product and its benefits to the prospect. This may involve audiovisual aids. Advantages over the competition are often shown.
Answer objections	Sometimes a prospect may question facts or figures and ask for more information. Often a sales rep must come back several times. The goal is to make sure that the customer is informed and committed to the purchase.
Close sale	You have to "ask for the sale" to finalize the sales process. "Would you like the red one or the green one?" "And when would you want delivery?" are examples of questions used to close the sale.
Follow up	The selling process isn't over until the product is delivered, installed, and working satisfactorily. The selling relationship often continues for years as the salesperson responds to customer requests and introduces new products over time. Selling is a matter of establishing relationships, not just selling goods and services.

with is life insurance. An insurance salesperson has a difficult job persuading people to buy life insurance and an even more difficult job persuading them to buy one company's policy versus another. Let's go through the selling process with a salesperson to see what can be done to make the sale.

Prospect and qualify. The first step in the selling process is *prospecting*. It involves researching potential buyers and choosing those most likely to buy. The choosing process is called *qualifying*. It is the market segmentation process brought down to the sales level. To qualify people means to make sure they have the ability to pay and are willing to listen to a sales message. People who have enough funds and are willing to discuss a potential purchase are called **prospects.** You may find prospects by asking present customers for names, calling on people randomly (this is a *cold call*), and checking public records. One source of prospects for life insurance, for example, is public records of people who recently married or had children.

prospects
People who can afford and are willing to discuss a potential purchase.

Preapproach. Before making a sales call, the sales representative must do further research. As much as possible should be learned about customers and their wants and needs. Before you try to sell someone insurance, for example, you want to know their names, whether or not they have children, and some idea of family income. Such information can be obtained when a customer refers you to another client. You can also observe the neighbourhood to get an idea of family income.

Approach. "You don't have a second chance to make a good first impression." When you call on a customer for the first time, your appearance is very important, as are your opening comments. The idea is to create an impression of friendly professionalism. The objective of the initial sales call will probably not be to make a sale that day. Rather, the goal may be to listen to the client, learn his or her insurance needs, and get some feel for the amount desired and what kind of insurance is appropriate. Of course, if the client seems ready to buy, an order can be taken that day.

Make the presentation. This is the actual presentation of the policy and its benefits to the prospect. It may involve audiovisual aids and flip charts. Showing the advantages of your product over the competition is often included. Since you have done your homework and know the wants and needs of the prospect, the policy will be tailored to the family's needs and be relatively easy to present.

Insurance is one of the more difficult services to sell because so few people understand the differences among insurance policies. Insurance salespeople have to use all the steps to satisfy the wants and needs of consumers.

Answer objections. A salesperson should view questions as opportunities for creating better relationships, not as a challenge to what he or she is saying. Customers have legitimate doubts and salespeople are there to resolve them. If a dialogue were not necessary, salespeople could easily be replaced by advertising. A salesperson must be prepared to come back several times if necessary to answer any questions or bring more data. A salesperson must also be aware of when a customer is stalling or merely hesitant about making a decision. That is the time when closing is important.

Close the sale. You have to "ask for the sale" to finalize the sales process. A salesperson has limited time and cannot spend forever with one client answering questions and objections. There is a time when the salesperson should say something like this: "This policy is designed to meet your present and future insurance needs. It was designed specifically to protect *your* family. Sign here and you'll be covered immediately." Remember your ABCs—always be closing.[2]

Follow up. The selling process isn't over until the policy is written and signed and the customer is happy. The selling relationship often continues for years as the salesperson responds to new customer needs and requests for information. Each time a new child is born, a client may want to get an insurance policy on the child or to increase the insurance coverage on the parents. Selling is a matter of establishing relationships, not just selling goods or services.

THINKING IT THROUGH

What kind of products would you enjoy selling? Think of the customers for those products. Can you imagine yourself going through the seven-step selling process with them? Which steps would be most difficult? Which easiest? Which step could you avoid by selling in a retail store?

Word of Mouth

word-of-mouth promotion
Consumers talking about products they have liked or disliked.

Word-of-mouth promotion encourages people to tell other people about products they have enjoyed. Word of mouth is one of the most effective promotional tools, but many marketers do not use it to full effectiveness.

SPOTLIGHT ON SMALL BUSINESS

Small Business Reaches Global Markets with Telemarketing

New technology is making it easier for small businesses to reach consumers without sending expensive salespeople into the field to talk to customers personally. London's Muddy Fox Mountain Bikes, for example, wanted to reach consumers in the United States. There are some 5,000 bicycle dealers in the U.S. and the market was already crowded with various brands of mountain bikes. Muddy Fox needed distribution but could not afford to send a salesperson to all the dealers.

The answer was telemarketing. Muddy Fox called various retailers on the phone. The list of customers came from a database developed from a mailing list the company bought. Telemarketing software made it possible, at a push of a button, to get the entire call history of a customer on a computer screen. That information included what other mountain bikes the store already carried.

Using telemarketing, Muddy Fox earned revenues from the United States of about $4 million in 1990. Many small companies are learning that telemarketing is an inexpensive way to reach markets with a personal sales message at a low cost.

Source: "Pedaling Toward Rising Sales," *Success,* Jan./Feb. 1991, p. 12.

Anything that encourages people to talk favourably about an organization is effective word of mouth. Notice, for example, how stores use clowns, banners, music, fairs, and other attention-getting devices to create word of mouth. Clever commercials can generate much word of mouth. You can ask people to tell others about your product or even pay them to do so. Samples are another way to generate word of mouth.

But the best way to generate word of mouth is to have a good product, provide good services, and keep customers happy. We consumers are happy to tell others where to get good services and reliable products. However, we are also quick to tell others when we are unhappy with products and services. Negative word of mouth hurts a firm badly. Taking care of consumer complaints quickly and effectively is one of the best ways to lessen negative word of mouth.

Basil and Annette Greenberg opened Annette's Pottery, a tiny shop, in the giant West Edmonton Mall. They are thriving because of their lively activities that lead to word-of-mouth promotion. This has proven so successful that they hope to exceed sales of $1,000 per square foot—an achievement matched by few retailers. Says University of Alberta marketing analyst H. Clifton Young, "It's not just the first-time buyer you want, it's the ones that keep coming back." Word-of-mouth promotion is an excellent way to assure this.[3]

To promote positive word of mouth, advertise to people who already use your product. They have a commitment to that product and are more likely to read the ad. They will then go out and tell others how smart they were to buy the product. This results in positive word of mouth for you. For example, sending brochures about a beautiful vacation resort to people who have already been there gives them something to use to tell others how exciting the place was. This word-of-mouth promotion is very effective in getting others to come.

Public Relations

Public relations (PR) is defined by the *Public Relations News* as the management function that evaluates public attitudes, identifies the policies and procedures of an individual or an organization with the public interest, and executes a program of action to earn public understanding and acceptance.

public relations
The management function that evaluates public attitudes, identifies policies and procedures consistent with the public interest, and takes steps to earn public acceptance.

PR departments aim to give their company or organization the best public image possible. When there is good news, like a plant expansion, a major contract, or removal of an environmental hazard, the job of the PR department is to give that news the widest possible distribution. On the other hand, when there is bad news—pollution or other violations of laws or regulations—the PR people do their best to limit the damage to the company's reputation.

They keep an eye on the media for any reports that could be detrimental to their company and try to counter such reports (perform damage control) by issuing their own press releases and being interviewed on TV and radio. They also alert senior managers to the existence of such reports so they may consider changes in company policy.

Publicity

Publicity is one of the major functions of the public relations department. Here is how it works. Suppose that when we want to introduce our new Fiberrific cereal to consumers, we have very little money to promote it. We want to get some initial sales to generate funds. One effective way to reach the public is through publicity.

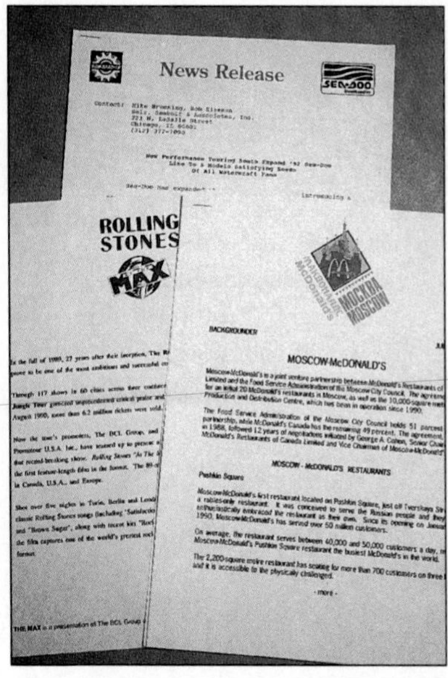

Public relations personnel send press releases to the various media. If the stories are well prepared and interesting, the media publish them free and generate many favourable impressions for the organization or its products.

publicity
Any information about an individual, a product, or an organization that is distributed to the public through the media and is not paid for or controlled by the sponsor.

Publicity is any information about an individual, a product, or an organization that is distributed to the public through the media and is not paid for or controlled by the sponsor. We might prepare a publicity release describing Fiberrific and research findings supporting its benefits and send it to the various media. (We shall not go into detail on how this is done, but there is much skill involved in writing the story so that the media will want to publish it.) Release of the news about Fiberrific will reach many potential buyers (and investors, distributors, and dealers), and we may be on our way to becoming wealthy marketers.

The best thing about publicity is that the various media will publish publicity stories free if the material is interesting or newsworthy. The idea, then, is to write publicity that meets these criteria.

In addition to being free, publicity has several advantages over other promotional tools such as advertising. It may reach people who would not read an advertising message. It may be placed on the front page of a newspaper or in some other very prominent position. Perhaps the greatest advantage of publicity is its believability. When a newspaper or magazine publishes a story as news, the reader treats that story as news, and news is more likely to be believed than advertising, which we know is paid for by the advertiser.

There are several disadvantages to publicity as well. The media do not have to publish a publicity release, and most are thrown away. Furthermore, the story may be altered so that it is not so positive.

Publicity may also be generated by news stories published or broadcast by the media. This may be favourable ("Air Canada reduces fares") or unfavourable ("CPR conductor ejects handicapped passenger"). Once a story has appeared, it is not likely to be run again unless it is a major news item that is followed up.

Advertising, on the other hand, can be repeated as often as needed. One way to see that the media handle publicity well is to establish a friendly relationship with media representatives, co-operating with them when they seek information. Then, when you want their support, they will co-operate with you.

Activities of the PR Department

You may get a better idea of what public relations involves if we list some of the activities of PR departments:

- Establishing contact with civic groups, consumer organizations, and other concerned citizens to learn their views of the organization, to answer their questions, and to provide information (or education).
- Opening lines of communication with customers, suppliers, distributors, retailers, shareholders, government agencies, educators, and community leaders.
- Conducting studies to find the economic, environmental, and social consequences of organizational practices and to learn how to make a more positive contribution to customers, shareholders, and society.
- Alerting the company to the need to adjust its goals, policies, practices, personnel policies, products, and programs to meet the needs of changing markets.
- Assisting all members of the firm in developing effective programs of consumer information and education.
- Sending speakers to schools, clubs, and other such groups to maintain an open dialogue with students and other socially active members of society.
- Creating incentives for employees to participate in public-affairs activities such as raising funds for charitable groups, advising young people in Boy Scouts, Girl Scouts, or Junior Achievement groups, and being active in community associations.
- Answering consumer and other complaints promptly and correcting the problem.
- Training employees or volunteers to provide prompt, friendly, courteous, and helpful service to anyone who contacts the organization in person, by phone, or by written correspondence.
- Demonstrating to society that the organization is listening, reacting, adjusting, and progressing in its attempt to satisfy its diverse publics.
- Opening two-way communications with employees to generate favourable opinion and to motivate employees to speak well of the organization to others.

This list is not a complete description of all the activities and responsibilities of the PR staff, but it should give you some feeling for what they do. The talking arm of the public relations function is publicity.

Sales Promotion

Sales promotion is the promotional tool that stimulates consumer purchasing and dealer interest by means of such *short-term* activities as displays, shows and exhibitions, and contests (see Figure 13–5).

Those free samples of products that people get in the mail; the cents-off coupons they clip out of the newspapers; the contests that various retail stores sponsor; the catalogues you look through; and those rebates that have been so popular in recent years all are examples of sales promotion activities. Sales promotion programs supplement personal selling, advertising, and public relations

sales promotion
The promotional tool that stimulates consumer purchasing and dealer interest by means of *short-term* activities (displays, shows and exhibitions, contests, etc.).

REACHING BEYOND OUR BORDERS

A Quartet of Quebec Companies Go Global

In 1976 Groupe Equipements Denis Inc. was a family-owned repair garage in Abitibi. By 1990 it had grown to an international company with annual sales of $46.5 million. It has evolved into an integrated forest-harvesting equipment firm. Its star asset? A machine that strips the limbs from felled trees and chops them up to desired lengths. It competes with giants like Komatsu, Hitachi, Caterpillar, and John Deere but Laurent Denis has successfully promoted his equipment into the U.S., the Russian Republic and other countries.

Montreal's Enerquin Air Inc., an upstart entry in heat recovery and drying systems for the pulp and paper industry, is competing against the two giant Swedish and Finnish companies that dominate this industry. The brainchild of five engineers—Robert Scullion, Peter Hartley, Remi Turcotte, Bill Boyd and David Young—who were dissatisfied with management changes at their previous employment, Enerquin has found a profitable niche. They have successfully marketed their products in the U.S., Australia, Japan, and Indonesia, for nearly $25 million in sales in 1990.

Francesco Bellini founded his biotechnology firm, IAF Biochem, in 1986. As a medicinal chemist, he had garnered some 20 patents at his previous employers. Working in three major fields—vaccines, diagnostic kits, and new drugs for cancer and AIDS—IAF is now teamed up with international pharmaceutical giants Glaxo, Behringwerke, and others in complex joint venture and licensing deals to finance research and market its products worldwide.

Tri-Steel Industries Inc. has two plants in the Montreal area, employs some 300 people, and does business in 30 countries. Steve Legler acquired technology and assets from another Quebec company and developed and patented a new device. This is a tri-anchor that anchors utility and transmission poles on top of a rock rather than in the rock. To his knowledge there is no similar product anywhere else in the world.

Sources: Robert Bryant, "Montreal's Enerquin Is Hot Stuff in Heat Recovery, Quebec Technology Taking On the World," *Montreal Gazette,* This Week in Business, March 24, 1990, pp. 2, 3; Francois Shalom, "Fast-growing Equipements Denis Now a Global Player," *Montreal Gazette,* July 2, 1990, p. 3. ▼

Figure 13–5 Sales promotion techniques. Spend some time with this list. Most students are not familiar with all the activities involved in sales promotion, and this is the time to learn them.

- Displays (store displays)
- Contests ("You may have won $1 million!")
- Samples (toothpaste, soap)
- Coupons (10¢ off)
- Premiums (free glass when you buy a meal)
- Shows (fashion shows)
- Deals (price reductions)
- Trade shows
- Bonuses (buy one, get one free)
- Incentives (the gift in a Cracker Jack box)
- Rebates (refunds from producers)
- Lotteries
- Audiovisual aids
- Catalogues
- Demonstrations
- Special events
- Exhibits
- Portfolios for salespeople
- Trading stamps
- Conventions
- Sweepstakes

efforts by creating enthusiasm for the overall promotional program. Canadian marketers send out billions of catalogues and coupons, so you can see how important sales promotion is.

Sales promotion can be both internal (within the company) and external (outside the company). It is just as important to get employees enthusiastic about a sale as potential customers. Often, the most important internal sales promotion efforts are directed at salespeople and other customer-contact employees like complaint handlers and clerks. Sales promotion tries to keep the salespeople enthusiastic about the company through sales training; the development of sales aids

The makers of Cheerios recognized the desire for oat bran and promoted that benefit (benefit segmentation). They also recognized that children love marshmallows, so they included them in a cereal. The use of coupons to promote these cereals is part of sales promotion.

such as flip charts, portable audiovisual displays, and movies; and participation in trade shows where they can get leads. Other employees who deal with the public may also be given special training to make them more aware of company programs and a more integral part of the total promotional effort.

After enthusiasm is generated internally, it is important to get distributors and dealers involved so that they, too, are enthusiastic and will co-operate by putting up signs and helping to promote the product.

After the company's employees and salespeople have been motivated with sales promotion efforts, and middlemen are involved, the next step is to promote to final consumers using samples, coupons, cents-off deals, displays, store demonstrators, premiums, and other incentives such as contests, trading stamps, and rebates. Sales promotion is an ongoing effort to maintain enthusiasm, so different strategies are used over time to keep the ideas fresh.

When thinking about a sales promotion scheme for Fiberrific, we might learn from General Food's promotion in the U.S. of Super Golden Crisp, Honeycomb, Fruity Pebbles, and other children's cereal. They sent a "fun book" to children featuring the character Sugar Bear. Cents-off coupons were placed in the book for the parents. Sales went up 80 percent, and 90 percent of the households replying wanted more mailings.[4]

PROGRESS CHECK

- What are the seven steps in the selling process?
- The text mentions 11 activities of a public relations department. How many can you remember?
- Promoters spend more money on sales promotion than on advertising. The text lists 21 different sales promotion techniques. How many can you recall?

Measuring the Effectiveness of Advertising or Promotion

How does a marketing department know how successful a particular ad or promotion has been? Often it is possible to get direct feedback. After advertising or promoting a specific product, you can track the results: Did sales go up? Asking consumers to bring in a coupon or an ad is a direct way to see results. Conversely,

Figure 13–6 Advantages and disadvantages of different advertising media. The most effective media are often very expensive. The inexpensive media may not reach your market. The goal is to use the most efficient medium that can reach your desired market.

Medium	Advantages	Disadvantages
Newspapers	Good coverage of local markets; ads can be placed quickly; high consumer acceptance; ads can be clipped and saved	Ads compete with other features in paper; poor colour; ads get thrown away with paper (short life span)
Television	Uses sight, sound, and motion; reaches all audiences; high attention with no competition from other material	High cost; short exposure time; takes time to prepare ads
Radio	Low cost; can target specific audiences; very flexible; good for local marketing	People may not listen to ad; depends on one sense (listening); short exposure time; can't keep ad
Magazines	Can target specific audiences; good use of colour; long life of ad; ads can be clipped and saved	Inflexible; ads often must be placed weeks before publication; cost is relatively high
Outdoor	High visibility and repeat exposures; low cost; local market focus	Limited message; low selectivity of audience
Direct mail	Best for targeting specific markets; very flexible; ad can be saved	High cost; consumers reject "junk mail"

if you stop a regular ad and sales remain constant, you may infer that the ad had no effect.

Preparing the Promotional Mix

Each target group calls for a separate promotional mix. For example, large numbers of consumers are usually most efficiently reached through advertising. Large organizations are best reached through personal selling.

To reach specific market segments, the mix must be aimed at the target. Figure 13–6 shows the ability of various media in this regard. Promotional efforts must be co-ordinated to complement each other. So we often see a specific advertising campaign supplemented by publicity and promotions to provide a promotional mix designed for maximum effectiveness. You can see this clearly when new automobile models are introduced. There will be an intense campaign including ads, auto shows, interviews in the media, articles and pictures in magazines and newspapers, direct mailings by dealers to their customer list, and so on.

To motivate people to buy now rather than later, companies may use sales promotion efforts such as coupons, discounts, special displays, and premiums. Publicity adds support to the other efforts and can create a good impression among all publics. Word of mouth is often the most powerful promotional tool and is generated effectively by listening, being responsive, and creating an impression worth passing on to others. How do marketers decide the best promotional mix to use? They turn to marketing research for guidance.

MARKETING RESEARCH

We end our discussion of marketing by looking at one of the most important parts of marketing today—marketing research. Marketers use research to help make

Advertising Research

1. Motivation research
2. Copy research
3. Media research
4. Studies of ad effectiveness
5. Studies of competitive advertising

Business Economics and Corporate Research

1. Short-range forecasting (up to one year)
2. Long-range forecasting (over one year)
3. Studies of business trends
4. Pricing studies
5. Plant and warehouse location studies
6. Acquisition studies
7. Export and international studies
8. MIS (Management Information System)
9. Operations research
10. Internal company employees

Corporate Responsibility Research

1. Consumers' "right to know" studies
2. Ecological impact studies
3. Studies of legal constraints on advertising and promotion
4. Social values and policies studies

Product Research

1. New product acceptance and potential
2. Competitive product studies
3. Testing of existing products
4. Packaging research

Sales and Market Research

1. Measurement of market potentials
2. Market share analysis
3. Determination of market characteristics
4. Sales analysis
5. Establishment of sales quotas and territories
6. Distribution channel studies
7. Test markets, store audits
8. Consumer panel operations
9. Sales compensation studies
10. Promotional studies

Figure 13–7 Marketing research topics. Many organizations do research to determine market potential, evaluate market share, and learn more about the people in various markets. Most also do short- and long-range sales forecasting and competitor analysis.

Source: D. W. Twedt, *Survey of Marketing Research,* Chicago: American Marketing Association.

decisions in all four areas of marketing: product, price, place, and promotion. They also research business trends, the ecological impact of their decisions, international trends, and more (see Figure 13–7). Businesses need information to function, and marketing research is the activity that gathers that information. All the money spent on computers and information specialists is wasted, however, if the information is not used correctly.

Finding out what people want means more than sending out questionnaires regularly. It means getting out of the office and sitting down with people to listen to what they have to say. It also means paying attention to what shareholders, dealers, consumer advocates, and employees have to say. Managing all that information calls for a marketing communication system. We shall end this chapter by discussing such a system. First, let's look at the process we call marketing research.

The Marketing Research Process

Marketing research is the process used both to determine what consumer and industrial clients want and need and to select the most effective way to satisfy those wants and needs. In short, marketing research provides the information needed to make intelligent marketing decisions. Although marketing research can take many forms, the key steps are to (1) define the problem and determine the present situation, (2) collect data, (3) analyze the research data, and (4) make recommendations. The following sections take a closer look at each of these steps.

Define the Problem and Determine the Present Situation

It is as important to know what an organization does well as what it does not do well, and marketing research should report both sides. Marketing researchers should be given the freedom to help discover what the problems are, what the alternatives are, what information is needed, and how to go about gathering and analyzing it.

Problem solving is the basis of the marketing research process. It is critical that the organization accurately defines its problem to determine the scope of the research needed. The problem may not be what it appears to be on the surface, and investigation is needed to find what the real problems are. For example, we may think that the problem is how to price Fiberrific when we introduce it, but the real question may be whether or not we should produce Fiberrific at all.

How does the public perceive the company and its products? What products are profitable? These are the kinds of questions that determine the present situation.

Collect Data

Obtaining usable information is vital to the marketing research process. Nevertheless, it is important to first determine the scope and estimated costs of doing research. Research can become quite expensive, so some trade-off must be made between information needs and cost.

secondary data
Already published research reports from journals, trade associations, the government, information services, libraries, etc.

To minimize costs, it is best to gather all relevant secondary data first. **Secondary data** are already published research reports from journals, trade associations, the government, information services, libraries, and so forth. Secondary data also include previously published internal research reports. There is no sense reinventing the wheel, so find out what other research has been done first. Figure 13–8 lists some of the more popular secondary sources of marketing information.

The amount of secondary data available is mind-boggling. Internal sources include accounting and sales records, cost figures, inventory practices, and management experience. There is a constant stream of information from many sources, much of it *unplanned.* It includes compliments and complaints from customers, letters, comments by employees, conversations overheard in airports, and millions of other bits and pieces of information picked up by corporate executives, employees, and friends. Such information is simply there, to be used or ignored as the company wishes. If it is used, it is a powerful source of information.

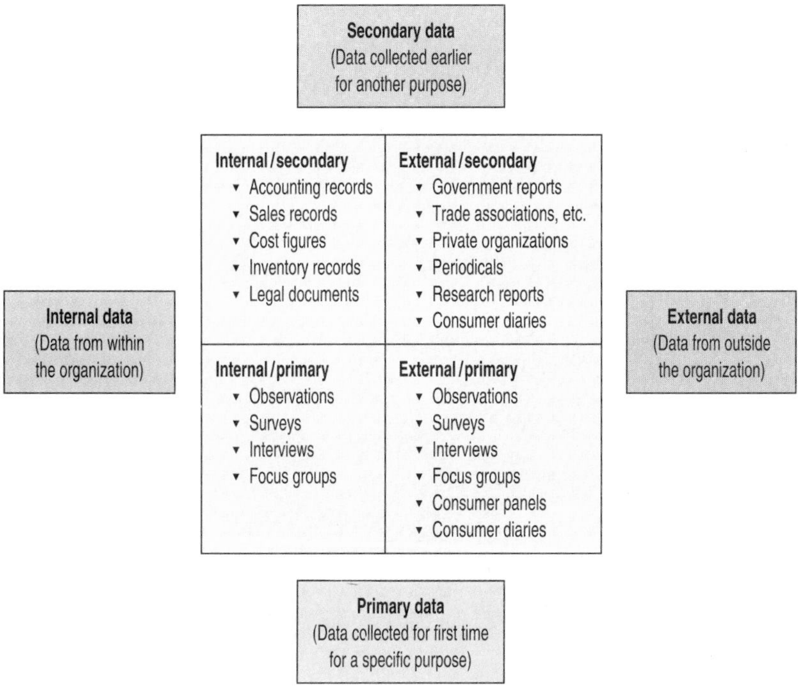

	Secondary data (Data collected earlier for another purpose)		
	Internal/secondary ▾ Accounting records ▾ Sales records ▾ Cost figures ▾ Inventory records ▾ Legal documents	**External/secondary** ▾ Government reports ▾ Trade associations, etc. ▾ Private organizations ▾ Periodicals ▾ Research reports ▾ Consumer diaries	
Internal data (Data from within the organization)			**External data** (Data from outside the organization)
	Internal/primary ▾ Observations ▾ Surveys ▾ Interviews ▾ Focus groups	**External/primary** ▾ Observations ▾ Surveys ▾ Interviews ▾ Focus groups ▾ Consumer panels ▾ Consumer diaries	
	Primary data (Data collected for first time for a specific purpose)		

Figure 13–8 Marketing research data sources. In marketing, it is best to gather as many secondary data as possible because they are relatively inexpensive to obtain. That includes internal records. Don't underestimate the value of observing people's shopping behaviour too for inexpensive external data.

For example, as you prepare to market Fiberrific, it will be important to look at both internal and external secondary data. Internal secondary data can tell you whether you have the resources to produce and market a new line of cereal. An external source such as StatsCan census data can tell you the current trends in the birth rate, marriages, and shifts in population—information vital to an organization considering moving into a specialized product category. Figure 13–8 lists all the marketing research data you might consider.

Usually, secondary data do not provide all the information necessary for important business decisions. When additional, more in-depth information is needed, marketers turn to **primary data,** results from doing your own research. Some sources are listed in Figure 13–8. Primary data are generally collected using the observation method, the survey method, or focus groups.

primary data
Results from doing your own research.

In the **observation method,** researchers collect data by observing the actions of potential buyers. One classic example of the observation technique involved Charles Parlin, often acknowledged as the founder of marketing research. He wanted to prove to Campbell Soup Co. that the wives of blue-collar workers bought soup in a can rather than making their own. He did this by collecting garbage! He collected a scientific sample of garbage from various parts of the city, dumped the contents on an armory floor, and counted the number of soup cans. He was able to convince Campbell that it should advertise in the *Saturday Evening Post* because that publication reached the working-class people who were prime customers for canned soup. The garbage count was the convincing argument. Can you think of a way we could use the observation method to gather information we need to promote Fiberrific?

observation method
Method of collecting data by observing the actions of potential buyers.

The **survey method** involves direct questioning of people to gather facts, opinions, or other information. The survey method is the most widely used

survey method
Direct questioning of people to gather facts, opinions, or other information.

Companies often use market research to gather valuable and useful data from consumers. One way a firm may collect information is the survey method. This popular method includes interviewing potential consumers about the product.

technique for collecting primary data. Telephone surveys, mail surveys, and personal interviews are the most common methods of gathering survey information. In the 1980s, focus groups became a popular method of surveying individuals. A **focus group** consists of a small group of people (8 to 14 individuals) who meet under the direction of a discussion leader to communicate their opinions about an organization, its products, or other important issues.

focus group
A small group of people who meet under the direction of a discussion leader to communicate their feelings concerning an organization, its products, or other important issues.

Realistically, it's impossible for an organization to survey all potential buyers of a product. Therefore, marketers select a sample of the target market. A **sample** is a representative group of a market population. In a **random sample,** all people have an equal chance of being selected to be part of the representative group.

sample
A representative group of a market population.

random sample
A sample in which all people have an equal chance of being selected to be part of the representative group.

Analyze Research Data

Until the collected data are systematically organized and analyzed, they are of little use to an organization. A dictionary is a collection of words, but until a selection of those words is organized into meaningful sentences and paragraphs, the words do not communicate much to a reader. Likewise, the collected data communicate little until they are organized. Statistics is the tool used to reduce the collected data into useful information. If you decide to take more business courses, you will learn what statistics mean and how they are used.

Careful and honest interpretation of data collected can provide useful alternatives to specific marketing problems. The same data can mean different things to different people. Sometimes people become so intent on a project that they are tempted to ignore or misinterpret data. For example, if our data indicate the market will not support another brand of cereal, we would do well to accept the information and drop Fiberrific rather than to slant the results as we would like to see them and go ahead with the project.

SPOTLIGHT ON BIG BUSINESS

Not All Research Leads to Success

Marketing research has become a major requirement before a new product or service is launched. Unfortunately, not all such efforts end in a successful new product. There are many such cases in recent marketing history but one of the most famous occurred in the 1950s. The Ford Motor Co., after long and careful research, came to the conclusion that there was a gap in the automobile market where a consumer need was not being met. Their research showed that there was a need for a mid-priced car.

The result was the Edsel, named after Henry Ford's grandson. Unfortunately, it was doomed to become the most spectacular failure in modern times. The car-buying public rejected it completely. After vainly trying all sorts of promotion and advertising, Ford was forced to withdraw the car and it was quietly forgotten. This error cost the company, in current dollars, something like $1.5 billion. Companies try to learn valuable lessons from their own mistakes as well as those of their competitors in order to avoid a repetition of that experience.

Today marketers are very cautious before they introduce a new product or service. Whether it is a new film, soap, or university program, many preliminary market tests will have been made to ensure favourable acceptance. If the researchers discover any resistance or flaws, they will adjust the product to make it more acceptable.

Make Recommendations

Researchers are not supposed to implement strategy based on their findings. Rather, they present alternatives to management and recommend which strategy may be best and why. It is important to include ethical and moral considerations at this point. That is, we must consider what is the *right* thing to do as well as the profitable thing to do. This step could add greatly to the social benefits of management decisions. The last steps in a research effort involve following up on the actions taken to see if the results were as expected. If not, corrective action can be taken and new research studies done in the ongoing attempt to provide consumer satisfaction at the lowest cost.

One problem with marketing research projects is that they are conducted periodically and take much time to complete. Meanwhile, the market is changing rapidly and research data may become obsolete before they are analyzed. How can a company keep close watch on the market and be responsive to market changes as soon as they occur? The answer is to institute a formal mechanism for constantly monitoring the market and using that information to make management decisions. Such a mechanism would make it possible to collect marketing research periodically and have other information coming in daily to supplement it. That mechanism is called a marketing communication system. We shall discuss the concepts in detail after you pause and apply what you have learned so far.

THINKING IT THROUGH

If you conducted a focus group about your college or university, who would you invite to participate? How would you choose them? Would the school benefit from conducting such groups periodically? What would you say about this class and this text if you were in a focus group? Feel free to write the authors and say what you think. How would the focus group help you to design a marketing research study to supplement the information from the focus groups? Can you see the benefit of *constantly* monitoring student opinions? (That is, the benefit of a marketing communication system.)

MAKING ETHICAL DECISIONS

Suppose you are the chief executive officer of an international public relations firm. You are approached by the dictator of a foreign country who has been linked to international drug trafficking. You feel these charges against him are well founded and have little doubt he is guilty. This person wants your firm to advise him on how to change his image. He offers to pay over $1 million for your expertise. He agrees to keep your relationship confidential and to pay you from an account unrelated to him. What are your alternatives? What are the consequences of each alternative? Which alternative is the most ethical? Which do you choose? ▼

MARKETING COMMUNICATION SYSTEMS

marketing communication system
Listening to the market, responding to that information, and promoting the organization and its products.

A **marketing communication system** is a formal mechanism for making an organization responsive to its environment. It consists of three steps:

1. *Listen* constantly to the groups that are affected by the organization, including customers and potential customers.
2. *Respond* quickly to that information by adjusting company policies and practices and by designing wanted products and services for target markets.
3. *Promote* the organization and its products to let concerned groups, including customers, know that the firm is listening and responding to their needs.

Listen to Groups Affected by the Organization

You may have noticed how often we stress listening as part of the marketing process. We do that because most people still think of marketing as talking—that is, promoting things to the public. Listening involves collecting information from consumer letters, sales data about your competitors, reports, rumours, overheard conversations, and dozens of other sources that indicate what customers, competitors, and potential customers are thinking. It is also important to know what other groups affected by or associated with the firm are thinking, including suppliers, shareholders, media people, dealers, and employees.[5]

One of the leading firms in the United States, when it comes to listening and responding, is Procter & Gamble. Every year P&G spends more than $1 billion on advertising, making it one of the top advertisers in the United States and Canada. Therefore, most people think of P&G as a firm that promotes heavily and believe that is how P&G became so successful. But the truth is that P&G is at least as proficient at listening to and working with customers as it is at promoting to them.

In one year, P&G will visit some 1.5 million people as part of about 1,000 research projects designed to discover what people like and dislike about P&G's products compared to competitive products. Researchers at Procter & Gamble study how people go about basic household chores such as washing clothes, doing dishes, and so on. Any problems present an opportunity for P&G to invent new products or create new solutions to people's needs. P&G truly operates on the principle of "Find a need and fill it and your needs will be met as well."

Do Internal Marketing

You may think that a marketing communication system is only for listening to customers and potential customers. But successful marketers have learned that organizations have many target groups that must be satisfied in a total marketing program. An important group is the firm's employees.[6] The marketing concept calls for co-ordination and co-operation from all members of the firm to provide consumer satisfaction. An **internal marketing program** is one designed to commit employees to the objectives of the firm. Like all marketing efforts, internal marketing begins with listening and being responsive to employees.

internal marketing program
Marketing program designed to commit employees to the objectives of the firm.

The secret of success of many marketing consultants, including marketing researchers, is this: "If you want to know what is going right and wrong in a business, don't ask the managers, ask the employees. Rewrite their recommendations and insights and turn them in as your consulting report." Including employees in research shows them that they are part of a team and that their input is considered important. The psychological effect is amazing. Not only can employees teach you much about how the business is being run, but they can also give you many helpful ideas for improvements. Naturally, employees will more easily and swiftly implement improvements they've recommended. Can you see the benefits of listening and responding to shareholders, suppliers, dealers, community leaders, and other people who come into contact with your organization?

Respond Quickly to Wants and Needs

The second part of an effective marketing communication system calls for responding to the wants and needs of various target markets. One of the most difficult marketing tasks in a firm is to convince managers that they must adapt to what various groups want and need. Most marketing organizations are so busy trying to think of ways to get consumers to buy their products that they neglect trying to get their firm to make what consumers want.

To be responsive to groups outside the firm, management must get constant reports from those in contact with outside groups. Managers must then respond promptly.[7] Most of the time, that does not happen. Salespeople often fail to report suggestions (or complaints) by customers. When employees do report information to managers, the information is often ignored or dismissed as being foolish or irrelevant. When managers refuse to listen, employees soon learn not to pass on information. Nobody knows what's going on because everybody is afraid to speak up. You've probably noticed that happening in many organizations.

A responsive firm adapts to changing wants and needs quickly and captures the market from other, less responsive firms. That is why information is so vital to organizations today and why so much money is spent on computers to analyze data. One reason why small firms are capturing markets from large firms is that small firms tend to be better listeners, to have fewer layers of management in which information gets lost, and to be more responsive to changes in the market.

When a firm is responsive, it must make that fact known to the public. That takes a variety of promotional efforts, including public relations and publicity (see Figure 13–9). All employees should be encouraged to join community organizations and volunteer for charitable causes. This makes the organization more visible and gives employees a chance to gather information from the public and to tell people about the programs and products of the firm. When an organization is responsive to the public and promotes that fact, it will inevitably profit and grow, creating more jobs and more benefits for society. Ultimately, marketing is the way society meets its needs by exchanging goods and services. Marketing communication systems create the information flows that make such exchanges possible.

PROGRESS CHECK

- What are the four major steps in the marketing research process?
- What are the three steps in a marketing communication system?

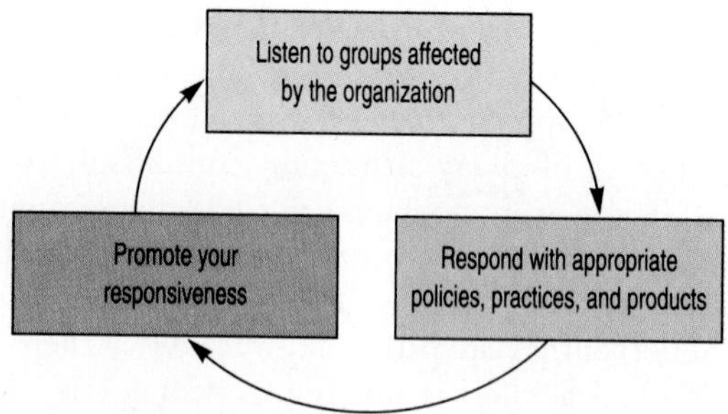

Figure 13–9 The marketing communication system. All organizations would be more effective if they listened more, were more responsive, and promoted that responsiveness.

Note that a marketing communication system is a closed loop. That is, information is constantly flowing into and out of the firm as it adjusts to changing markets. Marketing research is part of the information flow, but only a part.

SUMMARY

1. Promotion is an attempt by marketers to persuade others to participate in exchanges with them. Marketers use many different tools to promote their products and services.

1. Define promotion and list the various elements of the promotional mix.

▼ *What tools make up the promotional mix?*

Promotional tools include advertising, personal selling, word of mouth, public relations, publicity, and sales promotion.

2. Many people mistake promotion for advertising.

2. Explain how advertising differs from the other promotional tools and discuss the advantages and, disadvantages of different advertising media.

▼ *How does advertising differ from the other promotional tools?*

Advertising is limited to *paid, nonpersonal* communication through various *media* by organizations and individuals who are in some way *identified* in the advertising message.

▼ *In terms of total dollars, what is the number one advertising medium?*

Many people think TV is the top medium, but it is newspapers. Review the advantages and disadvantages of the various advertising media in Figure 10–6.

3. Different target markets are reached by different kinds of advertising.

3. Explain the differences among different forms of advertising such as retail and trade advertising and industrial and institutional advertising.

▼ *What are the major classes of advertising?*

The major classes include (1) retail advertising (from retail stores to consumers), (2) trade advertising (from wholesalers and retailers to manufacturers), (3) industrial advertising (from manufacturers to other manufacturers), and (4) institutional advertising (to create a favourable image for an organization).

4. Advertising is moving away from globalism to regionalism.

4. Debate the advantages of regionalism versus globalism in advertising.

▼ *What are the advantages of regionalism versus globalism in advertising?*

Although developing a product and promotional strategy that can be implemented worldwide (globalism) can save money in research costs and in advertising design, promotion targeted at specific countries (regionalism) may be much more successful since each country has its own culture, language, and buying habits.

5. Personal selling is the face-to-face presentation and promotion of products and services plus the searching out of prospects and follow-up service.

5. Illustrate the seven steps of the selling process.

▼ *What are the seven steps of the selling process?*

The steps of the selling process are (1) prospect and qualify, (2) preapproach, (3) approach, (4) make the presentation, (5) answer objections, (6) close the sale, and (7) follow up.

6. Word-of-mouth promotion encourages people to talk about an organization.

▼ *What is the best way to generate positive word of mouth?*

The best way to generate positive word of mouth is to have a good product, provide good services, and keep customers happy.

6. Explain the importance of word of mouth as a promotional tool.

7. Public relations is the management function that evaluates public attitudes, identifies the policies and procedures of an organization with the public interest, and executes a program of action to earn public understanding and acceptance.

▼ *What are the three major steps in a good public relations program?*

The three major steps in a good public relations program are: (1) listening, (2) developing policies and procedures in the public interest, and (3) earning public understanding and acceptance. One effective way to reach the public is through publicity (information distributed by the media that is not paid for or controlled by the sponsor). Publicity's greatest advantage is its believability.

7. Describe the functions of the public relations department and the role of publicity in that function.

8. Sales promotion is the promotional tool that stimulates consumer purchasing and dealer interest by means of *short-term* activities.

▼ *How are sales promotion activities used both within and outside of the organization?*

Internal sales promotion efforts are directed at salespeople and other customer-contact employees to keep them enthusiastic about the company. Internal sales promotion activities include sales training, sales aids, audiovisual displays, and trade shows. External sales promotion (to consumers) involves samples, coupons, cents-off deals, displays, store demonstrators, premiums, and other incentives.

8. List sales promotion tools and explain how they are used both internally with employees and externally to customers.

9. Marketing research is the systematic gathering, recording, and analyzing of data about problems relating to the marketing of goods and service.

▼ *What are the major steps of the marketing research process?*

There are many steps in the marketing research process. They can be condensed into four major steps: (1) defining the problem, (2) collecting data, (3) analyzing the data, and (4) making recommendations.

9. Describe the major steps in the process used to conduct marketing research.

10. Collecting useful information is essential to marketing research.

▼ *What kinds of data are collected in the marketing research process?*

Research data are classified by two characteristics: (1) where they were collected (either *internally* from within the organization or *externally* from outside the organization), and (2) when and for what purpose they were collected. *Secondary data* consist of information already published and available; *primary data* consist of information collected for the first time for a specific project (see Figure 13–8).

10. Differentiate between secondary and primary data and discuss the role of each in market research.

11. A marketing communication system is a formal mechanism for making an organization responsive to its environment.

▼ *What are the three steps in a marketing communication system?*

The marketing communication system consists of (1) listening, (2) responding, and (3) promoting.

11. Explain the three parts of a marketing communication system.

GETTING INVOLVED

1. Explain the importance of internal marketing to a total marketing program. Give examples (from your experience or knowledge) of good and bad internal marketing.
2. Bring in samples of advertising to show how informative consumer advertising can be. Bring in other ads that are not so informative. Discuss both sets of ads with the class to see which are more effective in attracting consumer interest.
3. Go through your newspaper and cut out examples of publicity (stories about new products you see in the paper) and sales promotion (coupons, contests, sweepstakes). Discuss the effectiveness of such promotional efforts with the class.

4. How would you go about generating word-of-mouth promotion for the following?
   a. A dance coming up at school.
   b. A new restaurant in the area.
   c. A great vacation spot.
   d. A microwave oven.
5. Go to the library and look up *Advertising Age* and *Marketing* magazines. They cover current advertising, promotion, and sales promotion topics, including direct marketing. Copy and save articles you find particularly interesting and share them with the class before filing them.

PRACTICING MANAGEMENT DECISIONS

Case One Impact of Baby Boomers on Marketing Research

University of Toronto economist David Foot, "the nation's most outspoken demographer," believes that the baby boomer bulge, as it moves through the population, is the most significant factor in understanding business trends. In 1992, the nine million boomers aged between 26 and 45 were the largest segment of the Canadian adult market. In 2002 they will be ages 36 to 55. The needs and lifestyles of this large segment have ruled the marketplace for many years and will continue to do so for many more years.

Foot gives examples of the economic impact of the boomers' changing demands as they move through their life cycle. When they were children, toys, schools, housing, and baby clothes were in great demand. When they became adults and had their children, that cycle was repeated. Their lifestyle led to a boom in recreational-related products and services—sportswear and athletic equipment, health clubs, moving from cities to suburban areas.

In 1994 the baby boom peak will reach [age] 34. "That's the average age at which Canadians buy homes," says Foot. So he predicts that demand for housing will begin to fall off after 1995. Other changes he foresees are:

> The beer and beef industries are in trouble; young people drink beer and eat beef and that market's getting older. . . . Per capita, chicken has been rising as the baby boomers are getting older. Madonna, hockey, football, and skiing will all see declining markets for the same reason.
>
> But coming on strong [are] walking and picnicking; hard liquor for insomnia, which starts to hit in the late 40s. Optically perfect binoculars will be a good niche market because bird-watching will be . . . fast-growing. The fastest-growing sports in the 1990s will be darts, curling, walking, golfing, bowling—things you can do in your 40s and 50s without too much trouble.

David Foot ends by urging businesses to look at the demographic profile, by age, of the consumers who buy their products or services. By relating this information to the baby boom bulge, they should have a good picture of what is likely to happen to their market.

Decision Questions

1. Can you think of what marketing research you should do to test the validity of Foot's predictions? Would you try to set up some focus groups of baby boomers? What else would you do?
2. Assume that Foot is correct in his predictions. What business opportunities do you see that you might take advantage of? What additional market research would you undertake to support that business idea?
3. Suppose you own a small supermarket. Do you think that you will have to make any changes in the type of products you carry, if you accept Foot's analysis? If so, what changes should you make? Would you do some market research before deciding? What exactly would you do?

4. If Foot is correct, will businesses have to continually shift the nature of their products and services to adapt to the market changes as the boomers age? Would that involve continuous market research? Some products, like corn flakes, never seem to lose their popularity. How is this explained?

Source: David K. Foot, "Let Us Now Appraise Famous Trends," *Canadian Business,* Nov. 1992, p. 63.

Case Two Canadian Companies Successfully Promote Themselves Abroad

Montreal-based SNC-Lavalin International has signed a $350 million (U.S.) contract with the Volgograd Refinery to modernize its plant on the Volga River in south Russia. The project involves feasibility studies, engineering, procurement, and construction supervision. It is not their first venture into the former Soviet Union.

Edmonton-based Canadian Utilities Ltd. (CU) "has struck it big" in its first international foray. Through its 50 percent stake in British-based Thames Power Ltd., CU is building a $1.5 billion gas turbine power station. It will be one of the first of a new generation of power stations in the U.K. designed to minimize environmental impact and maximize efficiency. CU beat out 20 other international competitors in the bid for this project. CEO John Wood sees it as a "stepping stone into Europe."

Ottawa-based SHL Systemhouse Inc. is involved with a Mexican computer systems management and maintenance firm "in the largest-ever computer services contract, a 10-year deal worth $500 million, half of which goes to Systemhouse. The two companies will build and manage the computer systems for the revenue, taxation, and customs functions performed by Mexico's finance ministry."

There are many such stories about Canadian companies becoming known overseas and getting important business.

Decision Questions

1. How would you promote your company overseas? What market research would you do to find out where to do promotional work? Would you take advantage of government services discussed in Chapters 2 and 3?
2. Is there any advantage to seeking overseas markets? Why do companies do this when it is obviously more complicated? Aren't promotional efforts more costly too?
3. Given that foreign countries have different cultures, would you consult with local advertising companies about how to promote your company and its products? As this might be costly, would you be tempted to use Canadian promotional methods and material? Would that be a good idea?
4. In the examples cited above, the companies are dealing with governmental bodies. How do you promote yourself to these organizations? Are international trade shows a good medium?

Source: Randall Litchfield, "Trillion Dollar Tune-Up," *Canadian Business,* Dec. 1992, p. 3.

LET'S TALK BUSINESS

1. Many firms ignore their employees when designing a marketing communication system. What steps should they take to avoid the resulting decline in employee morale and therefore in the effectiveness of the system? Should they consult employees and customers and act on the suggestions they receive? Should they publicize the fact that employees' and customers' needs have been taken into account?
2. What products have you been influenced to buy by word of mouth? Do you think this is an effective method? How can companies encourage more word-of-mouth promotion?

3. Some people believe that marketing research is the most important activity of a company. Do you agree or disagree? Why?
4. Make a list of 20 goods and services that most students acquire. Discuss which promotional techniques prompt you and other students to buy these products: advertising, personal selling, publicity, sales promotions, or word of mouth.
5. Give examples from your experience with businesses to prove that "the more communication with customers that occurs, the less promotion to customers is necessary." Are there successful firms in your area that do little promotion? Why are they successful?

LOOKING AHEAD

In Part V, we will look at the broad topic of human resource management, which covers all aspects of managing the work force. In Chapter 14, we will examine the theory and practice of motivating employees.

PART V

MANAGEMENT OF HUMAN RESOURCES

MOTIVATING EMPLOYEES

LEARNING GOALS

After you have read and studied this chapter, you should be able to:

1. Explain Taylor's scientific management.
2. Describe the Hawthorne studies and relate their significance to human-based management.
3. Identify the levels of Maslow's needs hierarchy and relate its importance to employee motivation.
4. Differentiate between Theory X and Theory Y.
5. Describe Theory Z and its application in North America.
6. Distinguish between motivators and hygiene factors identified by Herzberg.
7. Explain how job enrichment affects employee motivation and performance.
8. Identify the steps involved in implementing a management-by-objectives program.
9. Describe the implementation of motivation theory in the 1990s.

KEY TERMS

extrinsic rewards, p. 442
goal-setting theory, p. 457
Hawthorne effect, p. 446
hygiene factor, p. 453
intrinsic rewards, p. 442
job enlargement, p. 457
job enrichment, p. 456
job rotation, p. 457
job simplification, p. 457
management by objectives (MBO), p. 457
motion economy, p. 444
motivators, p. 453
physiological needs, p. 447
safety needs, p. 447
scientific management, p. 444
self-actualization needs, p. 447
self-esteem needs, p. 447
social needs, p. 447
time–motion studies, p. 444

Don Brommet

PROFILE CHOICE OF MOTIVATIONAL TOOLS: THE CARROT OR THE STICK

Don Brommet is president of Partners in Performance Inc., a Toronto area company specializing in setting up "reward and recognition" programs. They are designed to improve companies' productivity, and therefore profits, by revving up their employees' motivation. He points out that firms are quick to ask their workers to share the hard times, but they are much slower to ask them to share the good times.

Brommet notes that this is particularly bad for Canada because, as our manufacturing base has been eroding to be replaced by the service sector (see Chapter 1), the human resource factor has become very important. That is because "in a service company, the most valuable asset [is] the staff." He argues that the drive for quality and excellence has put the human component "at the wrong end of the scale." You can only achieve these goals if you have motivated your employees by a proper reward system. They will then "beget" customer satisfaction.

But, according to Tanja Parsley, vice-president of the consulting firm Outcomes, you cannot use the carrot method (reward system) if your employees work in an atmosphere where the stick has created fear and victimization attitudes. Change the attitudes, she maintains, realign the company, and then the carrot will work. Rewards will then lead to attitudinal shifts which will lead to changes in behaviour. That results in a better-motivated work force.

The precise opposite is argued by Stephen Frey of the United States. He says that if you change the behaviour, you will get a change in attitudes. He is the joint owner of Cin-Made Corporation, a small Cincinnati manufacturer of mailing tubes. After a couple of years of hard struggle with his employees and their union, he finally won them over to a full participatory style management and a generous profit-sharing scheme. Now they are highly motivated and play a very active role in running the company. Frey says that the employees' attitude did not change until they tried the new system. That is why he maintains that changed behaviour leads to changes in attitudes and not the other way around.

Regardless of who is right, and it may not be a simple black-and-white proposition, everyone agrees that motivation of the work force is a major key to a company's ability to grow, be profitable, and compete.

Sources: Laura Ramsay, "Why Carrot Beats Stick as Motivational Tool," *Financial Post,* September 18, 1993, p. S30; Robert Frey, "Empowerment or Else," *Harvard Business Review,* September–October 1993, pp. 80–94.

THE IMPORTANCE OF MOTIVATION

intrinsic rewards
Reinforcement from within oneself; a feeling one has done a good job.

extrinsic rewards
Reinforcement from someone else as recognition for good work, including pay increases, praise, and promotions.

No matter where you end up being a leader—in school, business, sports, the military—the key to your success will be whether or not you can motivate others to do the best they can. That is no easy job today when so many people feel bored and uninterested in their work. Yet the fact is that people are willing to work hard *if* they feel that their work is appreciated and makes a difference. People are motivated by a variety of things, such as bonuses, recognition, accomplishment, and status. **Intrinsic rewards** come from the feeling that one has done a good job and come from within a person. **Extrinsic rewards** come from someone else as recognition for good work and include pay increases, praise, and promotions.

Even the best athletes, like Montreal's Larry Walker, sometimes need help in getting motivated. Baseball managers will try a variety of techniques to keep their players at top form over the gruelling 162-game schedule.

Ultimately, motivation comes from within, and there are ways to stimulate people that bring out that natural drive to do a good job.

Why is motivation so important that we devote a whole chapter to this topic? All organizations know that a motivated work force is much more productive than an unmotivated one. You can easily see this when a baseball, hockey, or football team loses its will to win. The coach will give the players a pep talk to motivate them to win and the manager will try various other strategies to remotivate them. Same team, same strategies, same salaries: motivated, they produce; unmotivated, their performance slides.

Earlier we saw how all companies are striving to increase productivity to be competitive in the tough global environment. Motivation is the key to releasing employee power. You have already seen such key words as employee empowerment, teamwork, participative management, quality circles, wide span of control, and decentralized decision making. All of these aim to motivate employees to do much more than they have ever done before.

This style of management and leadership is growing rapidly. It is illustrated in this book in many of the profiles, spotlight boxes and cases about successful companies. You will see such companies in this chapter as well.

Motivation has become even more important as companies have reduced the size of their work forces during the massive restructuring process of the last few years. Fewer employees means more responsibility for each. Every one of them must become a self-starter and use lots of initiative.

This chapter will begin with a look at some of the traditional theories of motivation. We shall discuss the Hawthorne studies because they created a whole new interest in worker satisfaction and motivation. Then we'll look at some assumptions about employees: Are they basically lazy, or willing to work if given the proper incentives? We shall also explore the traditional theorists. You will see their names over and over in business literature: Mayo, Herzberg, Maslow, and McGregor.

Finally, we shall look at the modern applications of these theories and the managerial procedures for implementing them.

Early Management Studies (Taylor)

Several books on management in the 19th century presented management principles. For example, Charles Babbage (1792–1871) designed a mechanical computer and wrote a book on how to manage a manufacturing firm.[1] However, Frederick Taylor earned the title "father of scientific management." His *Principles of Scientific Management* was published in 1911. Taylor's goal was to increase worker productivity so that both the firm and the worker could benefit from higher earnings. The way to improve productivity, Taylor thought, was to study scientifically the most efficient ways to do things and then teach people those methods. Three elements were basic to his approach: time, methods, and rules of work. His most important tools were observation and the stopwatch.

A classic Taylor story involves his study of men shoveling rice, coal, and iron ore with the same shovel. Taylor felt that different materials called for different shovels. He proceeded to invent a wide variety of sizes and shapes of shovels and, with stopwatch in hand, measured output over time in what were called **time–motion studies**—studies of the tasks performed to complete a job and the time needed to do each task. Sure enough, an average person could shovel more (from 25 tons to 35 tons per day) with the proper shovel using the most efficient motions. This led to time–motion studies of virtually every factory job. The most efficient way of doing things was determined and became the standard for setting goals.

time–motion study
Study of the tasks performed to complete a job and the time needed to do each task.

Taylor's scientific management became the dominant strategy for improving productivity in the early 1900s. There were hundreds of time–motion specialists in plants throughout the country. One follower of Taylor was H. L. Gantt. He developed charts by which managers plotted the work of employees down to the smallest detail a day in advance. Frank and Lillian Gilbreth used Taylor's ideas in a three-year study of bricklaying. They developed the principle of **motion economy,** which showed that every job could be broken down into a series of elementary motions called a *therblig*—an anagram for Gilbreth. They then analyzed each motion to make it more efficient.

motion economy
Theory that every job can be broken down into a series of elementary motions.

You can imagine how workers felt having time and motion people studying their every move. **Scientific management** viewed people largely as machines that needed to be properly programmed. There was little concern for the psychological or human aspects of work. Taylor felt that workers would perform at a high level of effectiveness (that is, be motivated) if they received high enough pay because money would allow them to meet their basic needs.

scientific management
The study of workers to find the most efficient way of doing things and then teaching people those techniques.

Some of Taylor's ideas are still being implemented today. The difference is that machinery is being used to standardize how work is done. Nonetheless, much emphasis in some plants is still placed on conformity to work rules rather than creativity, flexibility, and responsiveness.[2] But the benefits of relying on workers to come up with creative solutions to productivity problems have long been recognized as we shall discover next.

The Hawthorne Studies (Mayo)

One of the studies that grew out of Taylor's research was conducted at the Western Electric Co.'s Hawthorne plant in Cicero, Illinois. The study began in 1927 and ended six years later as one of the major studies in management literature.

This shot of the inside of the Hawthorne plant is a classic. This is where human-based motivational theory was born. Before then, people were programmed to work like robots.

Elton Mayo and colleagues from Harvard University set out to test the degree of lighting associated with optimum productivity. In this respect, it was a traditional scientific management study: keep records of productivity performed under different levels of illumination.

The problem with the initial experiments was that the productivity of the experimental group compared to other workers doing the same job went up regardless of whether the lighting was increased or decreased. Productivity went up even when the lighting was reduced to about the level of moonlight. These results confused and frustrated the researchers.

A second series of experiments was conducted. A separate test room was set up where temperature, humidity, and other environmental factors could be manipulated. A series of 13 experimental periods were recorded and productivity went up each time, by a total of 50 percent. When the experimenters repeated the original condition (expecting productivity to fall to original levels), productivity kept increasing. The experiments were a total failure at this point. No matter what the experimenters did, productivity went up. What was causing the increase?

Mayo guessed that some human or psychological factor was involved. Thus, workers were interviewed about their feelings and attitudes toward the experiment. What the researchers found was to have a profound change in management thinking that continues today. Here is what they concluded:

- The women in the test room thought of themselves as a social group. The atmosphere was informal, they could talk freely, and they interacted regularly with their supervisors and the experimenters. They felt special and worked hard to stay in the group. This motivated them.

- The women were involved in planning the experiments. For example, they rejected one kind of pay schedule and recommended another, which was used. The women felt that their ideas were respected and that they were involved in managerial decision making. This, too, motivated them.
- The women enjoyed the atmosphere of their special room and the additional pay they got from more productivity. Job satisfaction increased dramatically.

Hawthorne effect
The tendency for a group of people to be more motivated when they are being studied and take a more active part in the experiment.

Researchers now use the term the **Hawthorne effect** to refer to the tendency for a group of people to be more motivated when they are being studied and to take a more active part in the experiment. The results of the Hawthorne studies encouraged researchers to begin to study human motivation and the managerial styles that lead to more productivity. The emphasis of research shifted away from Taylor's scientific management to Mayo's new, human-based management.

Mayo's findings led to completely new assumptions about employees. One of those assumptions, of course, was that pay was not the only motivator. In fact, money was found to be a relatively low motivator. That change in assumptions led

SPOTLIGHT ON SMALL BUSINESS

The Winning Way

Don Dangelmaier was trying to recall some of his failings as a manager—the character traits that work against an efficient, motivated workplace. He turned to office manager and financial officer Dave Jantzi for help. "What are some of the things I do wrong?" he asked, after explaining the request. Jantzi thought carefully for a few seconds, then ventured that Dangelmaier should be more considerate of the concentration Jantzi needs to complete a project. Jantzi quickly went on to list other shortcomings—bringing off new ideas too quickly, expecting results too soon—and Dangelmaier's head seemed to droop lower.

But the point was well made. Best bosses are not superhumans without faults; they share the flaws we all carry. They do create an atmosphere where problems can be aired openly and solved without recrimination, even when it hurts a little. And Dangelmaier, president of compressed-air component distributor Coast Industrial Supply Ltd. of Surrey, B.C., runs a company that crackles with the honest give-and-take of a family gathering.

Coast does, in fact, employ family. Dangelmaier's wife Pat acts as receptionist and bookkeeper; son-in-law Niall Ross is sales manager; and daughter Pam is sales rep. But the closeness extends to Coast's other seven employees, too. Dangelmaier lunches with an employee every week and often invites staff to his house when entertaining, "so that it's social," he says, "and not business."

Sales and purchasing agent Lorraine Unruh says togetherness makes hard work easier to bear. "It's the only reason they can work me to death," she says, laughing. But, she adds, close staff relations also mean "they listen to you when you make a suggestion."

Dangelmaier started Coast in his basement in 1981 after recessionary cutbacks cost him his job as manager of Hawker Siddeley Canada Inc.'s fluid-power division. For three years he operated hand-to-mouth, without even a line of credit, building his customer list and working alongside his former partner, his wife, and two employees. In 1983, Coast moved into its Surrey offices: five years later, Dangelmaier bought the building. In 1989, when sales hit $3 million, he constructed a warehouse on the back of the existing office. The new digs house a shower for employees to clean up after lunch-hour baseball games, and half-complete offices on the second floor with skylights for every room without a window.

With such detailed concern for staff, it's not surprising that Dangelmaier puts most operational matters on the table for discussion. Sales staff decide in open meetings whether to take on new lines, how to price them, how they will be discounted, and how to improve overall profitability. "Our people play a key role in selecting what they sell and what they sell it for," says Dangelmaier. And when they exceed monthly, quarterly, and year-end sales targets, they receive generous bonuses.

Source: John Southerst, "The Winning Way," *Profit,* November 1990, p. 31.

to many theories about the human side of motivation. One of the best-known motivation theorists was Abraham Maslow.

MOTIVATION AND MASLOW'S NEED HIERARCHY

Abraham Maslow believed that to understand motivation at work, one must understand human motivation in general. It seemed to him that motivation arises from need. People are motivated to satisfy *unmet needs;* needs that have been satisfied no longer provide motivation. He thought that needs could be placed on a pyramid of importance.

Figure 14–1 shows Maslow's hierarchy of needs. The basic needs from lowest to highest are:

Physiological needs—the need to be physically comfortable, including the needs to drink, eat, and be sheltered from heat and cold.

Safety needs—the need to feel secure at work and at home.

Social needs—the need to feel loved, accepted, and part of the group.

Self-esteem needs—the need for recognition, acknowledgment, and status.

Self-actualization needs—the need to accomplish established goals and develop to your fullest potential.

physiological needs
The need for basic, life-giving elements such as food, water, and shelter.

safety needs
The need for peace and security.

social needs
The need to feel loved, accepted, and part of the group.

self-esteem needs
The need for self-confidence and status.

self-actualization needs
The need for achievement and to be all you can be.

When one need is satisfied, another, higher-level need emerges and motivates the person to do something to satisfy it.[3] In fact, lower-level needs (for example, hunger, thirst) may emerge at any time they are not met and take our attention away from higher-level needs such as the need for recognition or status.

Most of the world's workers struggle all day simply to meet the basic needs for food, shelter, and safety. In developed countries, such needs no longer dominate, and workers seek to satisfy growth needs (social, self-esteem, and self-actualization needs).

To compete successfully, firms must create a corporate environment that motivates the best and the brightest workers. That means establishing a corporate culture that includes goals such as social contribution, honesty, reliability, service,

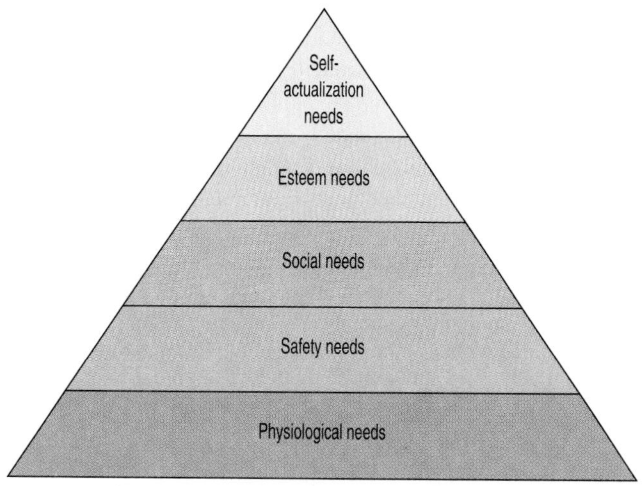

Figure 14–1 Maslow's need hierarchy is based on the idea that motivation comes from unmet needs. If a need is met, it no longer motivates and a higher-level need becomes the motivator. This chart shows the various levels of needs.

Activities such as picnics and sports events such as this baseball game create an atmosphere where employees can feel part of the group. This meets their social needs and they can move on to accomplish things at work to satisfy their self-esteem and self-actualization needs.

quality, dependability, and unity. Participative management is an important element in motivating employees.

THINKING IT THROUGH

When in your life have you felt strongly motivated to do something? Try to think of several different incidents. Now look at Maslow's need hierarchy to see what need was motivating you. Can you see how helpful Maslow's theory is in understanding motivation by applying it to your own life?

Applying Maslow's Theory

Andrew Grove, president of Intel, observed Maslow's concepts in action in his firm. One woman, for example, took a low-paying job that did little for her family's standard of living. Why? Because she needed the companionship her work offered (social/affiliation need). One of Grove's friends had a mid-life crisis when he was made a vice-president. This position had been a lifelong goal, and when the man reached it he had to find another way to motivate himself. People at a research and development lab were knowledge centred. They were self-actualized by the desire to know more, but they had little desire to produce results, so little was achieved.[4] Grove had to find new people who were results oriented.

Once a manager understands the need level of employees, it is easier to design programs that will trigger self-motivation. Grove believes that all motivation comes from within and that self-actualized people are achievement oriented. He thus designed a managerial program that emphasized achievement. Now managers are highly motivated to achieve their objectives because they feel rewarded for doing so.

PROGRESS CHECK

- What are the similarities and differences between Taylor's scientific management and Mayo's Hawthorne studies? How did Mayo's findings influence scientific management?
- Can you draw Maslow's need hierarchy and label the parts?
- According to Andrew Grove, what is the ultimate source of all motivation?

McGREGOR'S THEORY X AND THEORY Y

The way managers go about motivating people at work depends greatly on their attitudes toward workers. Douglas McGregor observed that managers had two different attitudes that led to entirely different managerial styles. He called the two systems *Theory X* and *Theory Y.*

Theory X

The assumptions of Theory X management are:

- The average person dislikes work and will avoid it if possible.
- Because of this dislike, the average person must be forced, controlled, directed, or threatened with punishment to motivate him or her to put forth the effort to achieve the organization's goals.
- The average worker prefers to be directed, wishes to avoid responsibility, has relatively little ambition, and wants security.

The natural consequence of such attitudes, beliefs, and assumptions is a manager who is very "busy" and who hangs over people telling them what to do and how to do it. Motivation is likely to take the form of punishment for bad work rather than reward for good work. Workers are given little responsibility, authority, or flexibility. Those were the assumptions behind Taylor's scientific management and all the theorists who preceded him. No doubt you have seen such managers in action. How did this make you feel? Is that how you prefer to be managed? Are these assumptions accurate regarding your work attitudes?

For years, the typical manager operated from such assumptions. That is why management literature focused on time and motion studies that calculated the "one best" way to perform a task and the "optimum" time to be devoted to a task. It was assumed that workers needed to be trained and carefully watched to see that they conformed to the standards. Would you like to be told exactly how to do something in a given amount of time with no room for creativity, flexibility, or time to relax and take a breather?

Theory Y

Theory Y makes entirely different assumptions about people:

- The average person likes work; it is as natural as play or rest.
- The average person naturally works towards goals to which he or she is committed.
- The depth of a person's commitment to goals depends on the perceived rewards for achieving them.
- Under certain conditions, the average person not only accepts but seeks responsibility.
- People are capable of using a relatively high degree of imagination, creativity, and cleverness to solve problems.
- In industry, the average person's intellectual potential is only partially realized.

Rather than emphasize authority, direction, and close supervision, Theory Y emphasizes a managerial atmosphere in which workers are free to set objectives, be creative, be flexible, and go beyond the goals set by management.[5] Have you ever worked in such an atmosphere? How did that make you feel? Would you prefer to work under a Theory X or Theory Y manager? How willing would you be to be a Theory Y manager with your children or your workers?

Traditional managerial styles were based on one of two major assumptions:

- Workers are basically lazy and must be given direction, threatened, and negatively motivated (Theory X); *or*
- Workers are basically goal oriented and self-motivated, and the best managerial style is to offer them incentives and freedom (Theory Y).

Applying Theory X and Theory Y

The trouble with these neat theories is that no company is run in strict accordance with either Theory Y or Theory X, not even the Army. We have known managers who prefer to be told what to do, who do not want responsibility for making crucial decisions, but who, when given precise instructions, perform their assigned tasks with care and diligence. We have also known managers who are self-starters and perform best only when they share in the decision-making process; in fact, they resent being given orders. Both these types of managers were working for the same company. If you were the chief executive, how would you run that company—by Theory X or Theory Y? Or would you use your common sense and act according to the circumstances at hand? Theory G: You cannot run a business, or anything else, on a theory.[6]

It is wise for managers to be flexible in applying Theory X or Y to those they supervise. Some people do better with direction; others do better with more freedom. Your natural inclination may be to choose a Theory Y-type manager as your supervisor, while your friend may prefer a Theory X-type supervisor.

The trend in most businesses is toward Theory Y management. One reason for a more flexible, permissive managerial style is to meet competition from foreign

Scientists are usually managed using Theory Y. These men and women are goal oriented and motivated, and they like their work. A manager needs to give them support and encouragement, not directions and punishment for failed experiments.

firms. William Ouchi, a professor of business at UCLA, wrote a best-selling book on management called *Theory Z: How American Business Can Meet the Japanese Challenge.*

THEORY Z (OUCHI)

Many organizations in Japan are run quite differently from those in Canada or the United States. Out of the Japanese system has come a concept called Theory Z, which has several major elements:[7]

- Long-term employment, virtually guaranteed, for all employees of large companies.
- Emphasis on collective decision making.
- Relatively slow evaluation and promotion.
- Creation of a sense of involvement, closeness, and co-operation in the organization (family atmosphere).
- Expectation of individual responsibility (like Theory Y).
- Trust among all managers and workers.
- Few levels of management.

Several U.S. firms are attempting to adopt elements of this managerial style. Ouchi cites Hewlett-Packard as one such American firm. He quotes from a preamble to corporate objectives written by David Packard and William Hewlett: "The achievements of an organization are the results of the combined efforts of each individual in the organization working toward common objectives." The preamble goes on to list several requirements, including (1) the most capable people should be selected for each assignment, (2) enthusiasm should exist at all levels, and (3) all levels should work in unison toward common objectives.

The corporate philosophy at Hewlett-Packard is to have overall objectives that are clearly stated and agreed to and to give people the freedom to work towards those goals in ways they determine best for their own areas of responsibility. When Harold Geneen was chief executive officer of ITT, he reviewed Theory Z. He noted that U.S. corporate life is just the opposite from the basics of Theory Z: relatively short-term employment, rapid promotions and dismissals, individual decision making and responsibilities, and a sense of personal rather than corporate loyalty.

Geneen questioned whether Americans would want to trade their heritage of personal freedoms and individual opportunity for the ingrown paternalism, humility, and selflessness of the Japanese system. He doubted whether we could instill such feelings, even if we wanted to.[8] A job for life in a firm may sound good until you think of the implications: no chance to change jobs and no opportunity to move up quickly through the ranks. There are fewer layers of management in Japan, thus fewer management positions. Geneen concluded that Theory Z would not work as well in the U.S. as in Japan because of cultural differences. This emphasizes the fact that the appropriate managerial style is one that matches the culture, the situation, and the specific needs of individual employees. Ouchi recognized that fact in his book and did not expect Theory Z to catch on in many U.S. firms. See Figure 14–2 for a summary of Theories X, Y, and Z.

What *are* the factors that motivate workers in Canada? That is the question we address next.

Figure 14–2 A comparison of theories X, Y, and Z.

Theory X	Theory Y	Theory Z
1. Employees dislike work and will try to avoid it	1. Employees view work as a natural part of life	1. Employee involvement is the key to increased productivity
2. Employees prefer to be controlled and directed	2. Employees prefer limited control and direction	2. Employee control is implied and informal
3. Employees seek security, not responsibility	3. Employees will seek responsibility under proper work conditions	3. Employees prefer to share responsibility and decision making
4. Employees must be intimidated by managers to perform	4. Employees perform better in work environments that are not intimidating	4. Employees perform better in environments that foster trust and co-operation
5. Employees are motivated by financial rewards	5. Employees are motivated by many different needs	5. Employees need guaranteed employment and will accept slow evaluations and promotions

MOTIVATING FACTORS: HERZBERG

Theories X, Y, and Z are concerned with styles of management. Another direction in managerial theory is to explore what managers can do with the job itself to motivate employees (a modern-day look at Taylor's research). Of all the factors controllable by managers, which are most effective in generating an enthusiastic work effort? In other words, this section is more concerned with the *content of work* than the style of management.

The most discussed study in this area was conducted by Frederick Herzberg.[9] He asked workers to rank the following job-related factors in order of importance as motivation. That is, what creates enthusiasm for them and makes them work to full potential? The results were:

1. Sense of achievement.
2. Earned recognition.
3. Interest in the work itself.
4. Opportunity for growth.
5. Opportunity for advancement.
6. Importance of responsibility.
7. Peer and group relationships.
8. Pay.
9. Supervisor's fairness.
10. Company policies and rules.
11. Status.
12. Job security.
13. Supervisor's friendliness.
14. Working conditions.

Herzberg noted that the factors receiving the most votes were all clustered around job content. Workers like to feel that they contribute (sense of achievement was number one). They want to earn recognition (number two) and feel their jobs are important (number six). They want responsibility (which is why learning is so important), but they want that responsibility to be recognized with a chance for growth and advancement. Of course, workers also want the job to be interesting.

Herzberg noted further that factors having to do with the job environment were not considered motivators by workers. It was interesting to find that one of those factors was pay. Workers felt that the absence of good pay, job security, friendly supervisors, and the like could cause dissatisfaction, but the presence of those factors did not motivate them; they just provided satisfaction. John McConnell of steelmaker Worthington Industries gives employees bonuses of $10,000 or more. He realizes money is not a motivator; instead he calls it part of an overall recognition process. It is the recognition, not the money, that motivates.[10]

The best motivators in business are achievement, recognition, and a chance for advancement. Reward ceremonies like this, where employees are given plaques and are praised by their bosses, are real motivators. It is not enough to reward employees at such once-a-year gatherings, however. They need recognition every day.

Motivators	Hygiene Factors
(These factors can be used to motivate workers.)	(These factors can cause dissatisfaction, but changing them will have little motivational effect.)
Work itself	Company policy and administration
Achievement	Supervision
Recognition	Working conditions
Responsibility	Interpersonal relations (co-workers)
Growth and advancement	Salary, status, and job security

Figure 14–3 Herzberg's motivators and hygiene factors. There is some controversy over Herzberg's results. For example, sales managers often use money as a motivator. Recent studies have shown that money can be a motivator if used as part of a recognition program.

The conclusions of Herzberg's study were that certain factors of management did motivate employees (were **motivators**) and gave them a great deal of satisfaction (see Figure 14–3). These factors mostly had to do with job content and were grouped as follows:

motivators
Factors that provide satisfaction and motivate people to work.

- Work itself.
- Achievement.
- Recognition.
- Responsibility.
- Growth and advancement.

Other factors of management were merely what Herzberg called **hygiene factors.** These had to do mostly with job environment and could cause dissatisfaction if missing but would not necessarily motivate if increased. They were:

hygiene factors
Factors that cause dissatisfaction if they are missing but do not motivate if they are increased.

- Company policy and administration.
- Supervision.
- Working conditions.
- Interpersonal relations.
- Salary.

SPOTLIGHT ON BIG BUSINESS

A Motivation Success Story in the Oil Patch

Clocks, prominent in the lobby at Canadian Hunter's office, hint at attitudes within. One (set normally) is labelled "Calgary Time." Alongside it, another (five minutes fast) is identified as "Canadian Hunter Time." A sign tells employees: "Stay Ahead."

Canadian Hunter thinks of itself as being smarter than the competition. It hires the best people and rewards them handsomely. Pay is outstanding even by the historically generous standards of the oil patch, and some of the benefits have a surreal quality to them.

President John Masters boasts so proudly about the excellence of his work force that he provokes a question about encouraging elitism. His response is quick: Certainly he encourages elitism—he even preaches it. And if outsiders sometimes think he hypes the capabilities of his people too much, he is not apologetic. He quotes the Roman poet Virgil, who wrote 2,000 years ago: "They can because they think they can."

The employee handbook sets a rather self-satisfied tone:

> You have been hired to find and produce oil and gas fields. Nothing is more essential to our lives. We welcome you into an exciting company which has a different style than you may be accustomed to.
>
> We have chosen you because, from the many who apply to us, we think you are outstanding. We hire only the best. We want you to work with us and we want you to join our family. At Canadian Hunter you will feel an atmosphere of accomplishment. We are doing a big job developing energy, and we are serious about it.
>
> Every day, all of us are trying to make real progress. We help each other and we'll help you. We are friends. Many of us are highly skilled and we have great respect for each others' talents and experience. . . . When someone asks you where you work, you may be forgiven a little inner smile when you say "Canadian Hunter."

Hunter is decidedly different. Masters and executive Vice-President Jim Gray, both geologists, founded the company and have put their personal stamp on it to a degree rarely encountered in Canadian business. Their free-wheeling, entrepreneurial style isn't what one would expect to find in a wholly owned subsidiary of a multinational resource giant.

The two men are given great freedom to run their own show and they thank Noranda (the parent company) for it. The names of the two senior executives crop up endlessly in conversations with employees: "John and Jim like to do this, John and Jim believe . . ." Employees said they find it hard to imagine what Canadian Hunter would be like without these two very strong personalities at the helm. Some even worry about it a bit.

Hunter is remarkably free of bureaucracy, and individual initiative is encouraged. Says one junior employee, "We are expected to think." For many who have spent time in regimented, hierarchical companies, being expected to think and offer suggestions is refreshing. Even better is that their ideas are actually listened to and acted upon.

Many employees said they were performing duties that would be reserved for people much higher up the command ladder in other oil companies. There's a small staff turnover, resulting in limited opportunities for promotion. This doesn't seem to trouble employees, however, who find a flat management structure to their liking.

Managers said their job satisfaction and rewards came in the opportunity to work closely in teams with other professional disciplines and to champion projects. The chance to seek professional excellence was in itself a major reward.

If we combined McGregor's Theory Y with Herzberg's motivating factors, we would come up with these conclusions:

- Employees work best when management assumes that they are competent and self-motivated. Theory Y calls for a participative style of management.
- The best way to motivate employees is to make the job interesting, help them to achieve their objectives, and recognize that achievement through advancement and added responsibility.

Applying Herzberg's Theories to Modern Workers

Inc. magazine polled some 2,800 workers from the 500 fastest-growing small firms in the U.S. to see what motivates them. In terms of pay and benefits, these

SPOTLIGHT ON BIG BUSINESS (*concluded*)

There are more tangible rewards, too, in the high pay scales. Clerical/secretarial staff are being paid at about the 80th or 85th percentile for the industry, which Masters feels comfortable with. Some professional salaries are [among the highest in Canada]. A "soft landing" is currently in progress to bring them down a little.

Exceptional effort is recognized in several ways. Department managers can provide small dinner parties or time off for their workers. Senior officials may authorize trips for an employee and spouse, or up to a month's bonus pay. High achievers among the lower-salaried employees sometimes get a leather pouch with 50 gold dollars. More significant achievements—such as the discovery of a new oil field—are rewarded by a net profit interest in the field, which could reach a value exceeding $1 million.

Masters and Gray have a personal arrangement with Noranda under which they share 12.5 percent of the net profit from Hunter's oil and gas fields once exploration and development costs have been repaid. This share of earnings ranges from $10 million to $15 million a year.

The two top executives give away half of this to about 75 people in the company to reward them for the part they have played in hydrocarbon discoveries. These rewards are structured to keep top talent at Hunter. To ensure this, there is a delay before entitlements are vested, and anyone leaving Hunter forfeits half the award.

Masters says the scheme has been very effective in sharing the wealth of the company with a lot of people. "I'd say we probably have more millionaires in Canadian Hunter than any other company in town."

Masters believes Hunter employees perform at perhaps 95 percent of their potential, compared with 40 to 50 percent of potential achieved by workers in big oil companies around Calgary. His staff also feels this is an accurate statement.

New employees, no matter how junior, are taken around and introduced to everybody. They have half a dozen interviews and meet Masters before they are hired. He occasionally exercises the right of veto on new hires.

The atmosphere at Canadian Hunter is open and friendly. Employees feel free to walk up to Masters and Gray and chat casually about business and social activities, and everyone is expected to know the names of all co-workers. This was easy a few years ago when Hunter was smaller, but today it requires effort. New employees are advised to learn the names of 50 fellow workers a week until they have them all down pat.

Hunter places great emphasis on teamwork, and it reinforces team building with a range of outside social and sporting activities, fully paid or generously subsidized by the company. Not surprisingly for a company in the high-risk oil and gas exploration business, these include such hazardous activities as kayaking, ice climbing, rock climbing, and mountain biking.

Vacations are generous. Most professionals get six weeks off after five years. Employees get six Fridays off each year, and the company closes down between Christmas and New Year. There's also a sports day and the annual skiing trip.

The benefits seem endless: subsidized YMCA membership, an annual $100 allowance for meals and accommodation in nearby national parks, education assistance, a $38-a-month transportation allowance, and kitchens stocked with tea, coffee, bread, jam, and muffins. Hunter also offers a stock savings plan, to which it adds 30 cents for every $1 invested by employees in Noranda shares.

Source: Eva Innes, Jim Lyon, and Jim Harris, *The Financial Post 100 Best Companies to Work for in Canada* (Toronto: HarperCollins, 1990). ▼

employees lagged behind the employees of larger corporations. But they felt satisfied and highly motivated nonetheless because of job-related factors, just as Herzberg predicted. Employees especially enjoyed the challenge and sense of accomplishment they felt working for smaller firms. They also enjoyed the small-business culture that values initiative and ideas.[11]

One revealing finding from the study was that about half the employees intended to leave their companies in the next few years. Why? Because they saw little chance for advancement. Remember that opportunity for advancement was high on Herzberg's list of motivators.

One conclusion of the *Inc.* study was that "large companies try to 'Taylorize' their professionals (Frederick Taylor, that is)—they worry about their productivity and try to manage them as they would manage a welder."[12] By contrast, the new,

SPOTLIGHT ON BIG BUSINESS

Empowering Employees is the Key

Today, managers are beginning to support a belief that workers have embraced for years. Workers don't just need jobs, they need a reason for working. Often it's the actions of workers that make an ultimate difference in an organization, not the actions of managers. Empowerment is a key to motivating workers and managers to achieve their personal goals as well as the objectives of the organization. Let's see how this works by looking at the example of John Allegretti of Hyatt Hotels Corp.

John felt discouraged with the slow promotional track required to become a hotel manager. He figured eight years was too long to wait, especially since his job was repetitive and boring. So John quit Hyatt to look for an interesting job that would also help the environment. After an extensive search he landed the job of his dreams—at Hyatt. To keep John with the company, vice-president Don DePorter asked him to take charge of a project to reduce waste at his 2,000-room hotel. John performed so well Hyatt empowered him to develop and manage a new waste-consulting company called International ReCycleCo Inc. Keeping employees hyped is considered good business at Hyatt. The company now helps employees with novel ideas that are outside the core company business set up free-standing companies. Hyatt Corp. would be the first to agree that you can't expect employees to treat the company or its customers any better than they are treated themselves.[13] ▼

young managers at smaller firms enjoyed the informality of beer blasts and tennis courts, the company condo in Vail, challenging work, up-to-date equipment, and the opportunity to see their ideas implemented.

How can companies make their jobs as interesting for blue-collar workers as they do for managers? We discuss that next.

JOB ENRICHMENT

job enrichment
A motivational strategy that emphasizes motivating the worker through the job itself.

Both Maslow's and Herzberg's theories were extended by job enrichment theory. **Job enrichment** is a motivational strategy that emphasizes motivating the worker through the job itself. Work is assigned to individuals so that they have the opportunity to complete an identifiable task from beginning to end. They are held responsible for successful completion of the task. The motivational effect of job enrichment can come from the opportunity for personal achievement, challenge, and recognition. Review Maslow's and Herzberg's work to see how job enrichment grew out of those theories. Five characteristics of work are believed to be important in affecting individual motivation and performance.

1. *Skill variety.* The extent to which a job demands different skills of the person.
2. *Task identity.* The degree to which the job requires working with a visible outcome from beginning to end.
3. *Task significance.* The degree to which the job has a substantial impact on the lives or work of others in the company.
4. *Autonomy.* The degree of freedom, independence, and discretion in scheduling work and determining procedures.
5. *Feedback.* The amount of direct and clear information that is received about job performance.

Variety, identity, and significance contribute to the meaningfulness of the job. Autonomy gives employees a feeling of responsibility, and feedback contributes to feelings of achievement and recognition.

Sherwin-Williams began a job enrichment program in its Richmond, Kentucky, plant in the 1980s. Employees were grouped into teams and each member was trained to do all the jobs assigned the team. The teams have autonomy to decide where members work, what they do, and how they train others. The group is responsible for results. Raises are based on performance as evaluated by team leaders and peers. Employees are encouraged to feel responsible for the entire production process.

The program was quite successful. Absenteeism is much lower than at other Sherwin-Williams plants. Turnover is low and productivity is higher than at other plants. Cost per gallon of paint is also much lower. Similar results were obtained at Harley-Davidson. Tom Peters uses the term *limitless* when discussing the potential of job enrichment in work teams.[14] (Does this remind you of the quality circles discussed in Chapter 9?)

Job enrichment is based on Herzberg's higher motivators such as responsibility, achievement, and recognition. This is in contrast to **job simplification,** which produces task efficiency by breaking down the job into simple steps and assigning people to each of those steps. There is not much motivation in doing boring, repetitive work, but some managers still operate on the Taylor level of motivation and use job simplification.

job simplification
Producing task efficiency by breaking down the job into simple steps and assigning people to each of those steps.

One way to increase motivation is **job enlargement,** which combines a series of tasks into one assignment that is more challenging, interesting, and motivating. For example, Maytag redesigned its work so that employees worked on an entire water pump instead of separate parts. **Job rotation** also makes work more interesting and motivating by moving employees from one job to another. You can see the problem of having to train employees to do several different operations, but usually the resulting morale building and motivation more than offset the additional costs.

job enlargement
Job enrichment strategy involving combining a series of tasks into one assignment that is more challenging and interesting.

job rotation
Job enrichment strategy involving moving employees from one job to another.

Job design is a good way to rethink jobs so that people feel responsibility and a sense of accomplishment. Another way to increase motivation is to get everyone to agree on specific corporate objectives.

GOAL-SETTING THEORY AND MANAGEMENT BY OBJECTIVES

Goal-setting theory is based on the notion that the setting of specific ambitious but attainable goals is related to high levels of motivation and performance if the goals are accepted, accompanied by feedback, and facilitated by organizational conditions.[15] Nothing makes more sense intuitively than the idea that all members of an organization should have some basic agreement about the overall goals of the organization and the specific objectives to be met by each department and individual in it. It follows, then, that someone would develop a system to involve everyone in the organization in goal setting and implementation. Such a system is called **management by objectives (MBO).** MBO was very popular in the 1960s.

goal-setting theory
Theory that setting specific, attainable goals can motivate workers and improve performance if the goals are accepted, accompanied by feedback, and facilitated by organizational conditions.

Management by objectives is a system of goal setting and implementation that involves a cycle of discussion, review, and evaluation of objectives among top- and middle-level managers, supervisors, and employees. It meets the criteria of goal-setting theory when implemented properly and can be quite effective. There are six steps in the motivational MBO process (see Figure 14–4).

management by objectives (MBO)
A system of goal setting and implementation that involves a cycle of discussion, review, and evaluation of objectives among top- and middle-level managers, supervisors, and employees.

Ford executives taught the method to the U.S. Defense Department and from there it spread to other large corporations and government agencies in Canada and the U.S. MBO is much less common now, but many of its features can still be found in some currently popular concepts and practices. Management practices at giant

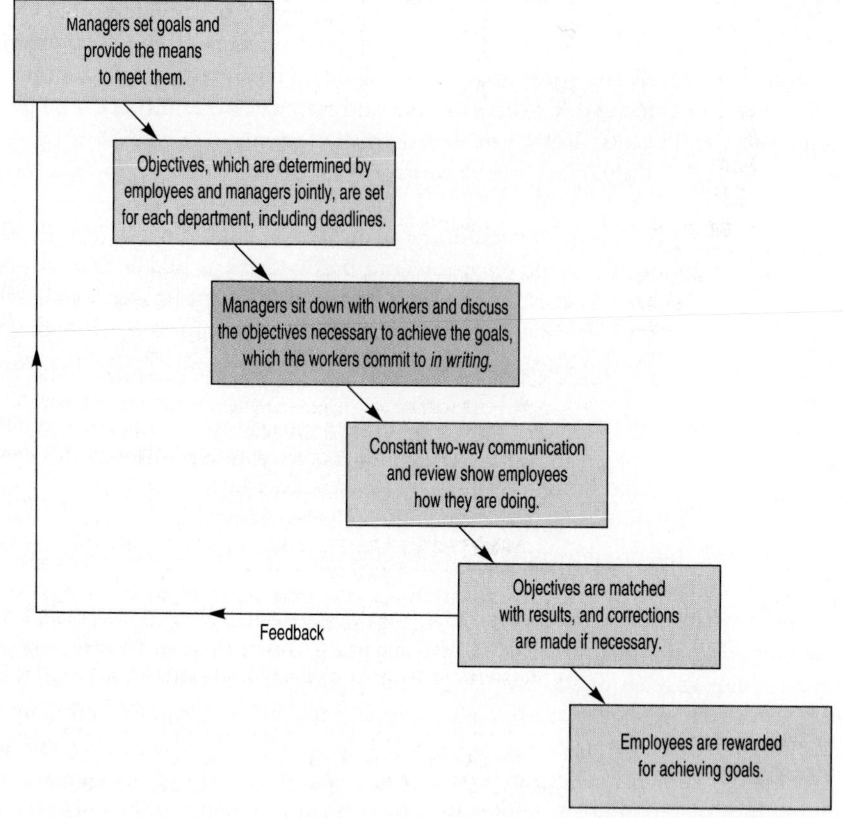

Figure 14–4 Management by objectives. The critical step in the MBO process is the one where managers sit down with workers, discuss the objectives, and get the workers to commit to those objectives in writing. Commitment is the key.

retailer Wal-Mart, discussed later in the chapter, are an excellent example of the practical application of MBO derivatives.

Problems arise when management uses MBO as a strategy for forcing managers and workers to commit to goals that are not really mutually agreed upon. Every MBO program should be assessed to see that it promotes co-operation and motivation rather than forced compliance with top management's goals. Motivation is often enhanced when objectives and appraisals are done by groups. MBO used to be largely a program for motivating individuals, but today emphasis in many firms is on team-building group interaction. In such cases, group objectives replace individual employee objectives.[16]

It is also important for managers to understand the difference between helping and coaching subordinates. *Helping* means working with the subordinate, doing part of the work if necessary. *Coaching* means acting as a resource—teaching, guiding, recommending—but not helping (that is, not participating actively in the task).

Helping subordinates tends to make them weak, dependent, and irresponsible. Coaching subordinates tends to make them feel part of a team and capable of doing it on their own once they learn the system. It is highly motivating. Bill Eaton, a member of Levi Strauss's executive management committee, probably illustrates this best. He says that on a day-to-day basis, his "passion and satisfaction come from backing the efforts of employees, getting them what they need for the job, educating them, and working with them as members of the team."[17]

PROGRESS CHECK

- Briefly describe the managerial attitudes behind Theories X, Y, and Z.
- Employees at smaller firms seem relatively happy with their jobs, yet about half plan to leave in a few years. What is lacking in small firms that causes employees to leave?
- Relate job enrichment to Herzberg's motivating factors.
- What are the six steps in management by objectives?
- What is the difference between helping and coaching? Which motivates workers more?

IMPLEMENTING THE NEW CONCEPTS: MOTIVATION THROUGH COMMUNICATION

Management by objectives teaches us that one key to successful management and motivation, in any organization, is the establishment and maintenance of open, two-way communication between and among managers and workers so that everyone understands the objectives and works together effectively and efficiently to achieve them. Communication must flow two ways among all members of an organization. The problem today is that most communication flows only one way, from top management down. This communication takes the form of directives, policies, announcements, memos, rules, procedures, and the like.

The flow upward, from workers to managers, is usually severely clogged. Rarely do organizations have any formal means of upward communication (from employees to management) equivalent to directives and announcements. Instead, the burden falls on workers to initiate contact with supervisors and present their ideas and suggestions. As you know, few people in any organization tell the boss when things are not going well. Children don't tell parents when they've broken something, students don't tell teachers when someone has goofed, and employees don't tell bosses. Such a system creates an "us against them" attitude, where workers feel united in their distrust and avoidance of managers. To create an atmosphere of "us working together," managers have to become active listeners and valued assistants to workers. Such a change demands radical retraining of managers and careful creation of new attitudes and beliefs among workers.

Teamwork between and among managers and employees does not just happen. The whole organization must be structured to facilitate dialogues. Some procedures for encouraging open communication follow.

- Top management must first create an organizational culture that rewards listening by being listeners themselves; by creating facilities (for example, conference rooms) for having dialogues; and by showing others that talking with superiors counts—by providing feedback, adopting employee suggestions, and rewarding upward communication, even if it is negative. Employees must feel free to say anything.
- Supervisors and managers must be trained in listening skills. Most people receive no such training in school or anywhere else, so organizations must do the training themselves or hire someone to do it.
- Barriers to open communication must be removed and facilitating mechanisms installed. Barriers include separate offices, parking spaces, bathrooms, dining rooms, and other such facilities for various levels of management and workers. Such facilities foster an "us versus them" attitude.

REACHING BEYOND OUR BORDERS

Tapping the Power of Workers' Minds

By any yardstick, GSW Water Heating Co. should be struggling just to survive. The hourly labour costs of its unionized work force are the highest of any water heater manufacturer in North America and as much as double those of U.S. rivals with which it competes head to head. The company claims no competitive advantage from unique technology or state-of-the-art plant. Its factory is a concrete dinosaur, having been on its present site since 1911 with only modest updating.

Yet at a time when hardly a day goes by without grim news of manufacturing layoffs, GSW Water Heating is expanding its work force, doubling the capacity of its assembly lines, and beginning to compete aggressively and successfully in the United States. All this springs from a collaboration of management, employees, and the union, aimed at improving the plant's products and processes and cutting waste and costs. By passing on cost savings to customers, this unit of Toronto-based GSW Inc. has been able to strengthen its competitive position.

"The company said we had to become a world-class manufacturer to survive, and I want to survive," said Robb Rosso, a three-year assembly-line worker who embodies the spirit in the 296-worker plant. Rosso is part of an employee team that has been sifting through worker suggestions to design a bigger production line. The new line will double the plant's annual capacity to 700,000 heaters by next spring and add 20 jobs to the work force, already up 30 from last February.

GSW Water Heating's survival strategy is one response to the often-heard argument that high labour costs prevent Canadian manufacturers from competing. Rather than dwell on the wage gap, management has worked to reduce other costs and increase productivity by tapping the brain power of plant workers, whose wage and benefit packages average $24 an hour.

This approach is combined with an unusually trusting relationship between the company and the local of the United Steel Workers of America. An open-door, no-secrets policy gives the local access to all operating and financial information.

Only two years ago, GSW Water Heating seemed an unlikely change candidate. It did not have a rich history of employee involvement. "Our attitude used to be that employees parked their brains at the door when they reported for work and picked them up when they left," said Roger Lippert, director of human resources and a key player in the new approach.

But with the arrival of Canada–U.S. free trade, management, led by president Terry Parsons, was determined to cut costs. It seized on the idea of world-class manufacturing, a generic term for teamwork, training, and continuous improvement. The inspiration came from the ideas of W. Edwards Deming, the American consultant who taught total quality management to the Japanese.

In launching the program 18 months ago, Parsons assured workers this was not a recipe for downsizing. Specific jobs would be lost, he told them, but employment would not be reduced.

Sensitive to competitive pressures, the workers accepted the need for change, volunteering in large numbers for training sessions. "Our biggest problem was explaining to employees why they couldn't all participate at the same time," Lippert said.

There have been mistakes. In the early stages, supervisors were neither instructed in the new processes nor assigned to teams. This was to avoid the perception that they would be put in charge of the teams. "It haunted us," Lippert said, "because first-line supervisors felt they were being stripped of their power. And because they lacked understanding of the process, they became uncooperative." Now supervisors are being trained and assigned as team members, and usually a supervisor serves as a team facilitator.

Teams are continually being formed to tackle assignments; there are now 14 in the plant. The biggest job has fallen to Rosso's five-member group: designing a new assembly line that will cost $1.3 million to install. But even simple suggestions have saved hundreds of thousands of dollars.

One team wondered why water heaters had as many as 14 labels dealing with everything from safety to general instructions. By reducing the number of unnecessary labels, the company saved $1 for each heater, or about $350,000 a year. The apparatus for spraying porcelain enamel on the liners of heater tanks was not leaving a uniform deposit. So the problem was handed to a team, whose proposals saved $250,000 a year.

As costs have fallen, the company has embarked on a sales thrust in the United States, where it holds 2 percent of the water heater market (compared with a 52 percent share in Canada.) The target is the U.S. Northeast within 1,000 kilometres of Fergus, Ontario, where GSW owns a freight cost advantage over major competitors in the U.S. Southeast and Southwest.

Source: Wilfred List, "Tapping the Power of Workers' Minds," *Globe and Mail,* Nov. 10, 1992, p. B26. ▼

> Other barriers include different dress codes, different ways of addressing one another (for example, calling workers by their first names and managers by their last), and so on. Removing such barriers takes imagination and a willingness to give up the special privileges of management. Facilitating efforts include large lunch tables where all organizational members eat, conference rooms, organizational picnics, organizational athletic teams, and other such outings where managers mix and socialize with each other and with workers. Note that managers in small firms called such activities very important to their motivation in the *Inc.* survey mentioned earlier.

Larger firms are taking the hint as we see in the next section. Much of the success of Japanese companies is attributed to their adoption of unifying techniques as a regular practice.

Open Communication and Self-Managed Teams

Companies that have developed highly motivated work forces usually have several things in common. Among the most important are open communication systems and self-managed teams. Whether it is Walter Shawlee of small Northern Airborne Technology in Kelowna, B.C., profiled in Chapter 7, or giant Winnipeg-based Great-West Life, discussed in Chapter 15, open communication is key to motivating employees. This is also a feature at the Rimouski, Quebec, plant of Toronto-based Phillips Cables Ltd., which produces hair-thick fibre-optic cable in a state-of-the-art factory. This is part of a joint venture with Furukawa Electric of Japan called Phillips-Fitel.

Despite the fact that the Furukawa managers speak no French and the plant employees speak almost no English, there is an open communication system that has helped to create a strongly motivated work force. According to union president Marcel Rouleau, "The only boss we have is the plant manager. We don't have incompetents telling us what to do when we know better. Now they consult us. . . . We feel a lot more creative and it's rewarding."

CEO Malcolm Stagg notes that there has been a remarkable change in the attitude of the work force. The whole experiment is being carefully observed to see if it can be duplicated at other Canadian plants.[18]

Open communication and teamwork have helped make Motorola Canada Ltd. very competitive. Teams compete fiercely in devising ways to reduce costs and increase efficiency. There is a formal competition among all 3,700 teams of Motorola's 107,000 employees worldwide.

> Nine months of intense preparation have come down to a 12-minute performance to a jury of Motorola Canada Ltd. executives on a Saturday morning in a Toronto hotel. "At 4 o'clock in the morning we were still fine-tuning the presentation," says a nervous Jim Kiriacou, one of nine men and women in Motorola's Toronto paging operations who make up the team.
>
> Despite the stress, the UltraEagles team performed flawlessly. Garbed in hockey jerseys with team logo, they used charts and statistics to explain how they save close to $50,000 a year by improving the accuracy of customer accounts. . . . They managed to narrowly defeat the Montreal Express, becoming Canadian paging champions for the third year in a row.[19]

For companies to implement such groups or teams, managers must re-invent work groups. We shall discuss that next.

Meetings that are free-wheeling and informal give employees an opportunity to contribute, and that motivates them. Intel calls such meetings "decision making by peers." Such meetings should not be rare events but a normal part of the routine when problems arise.

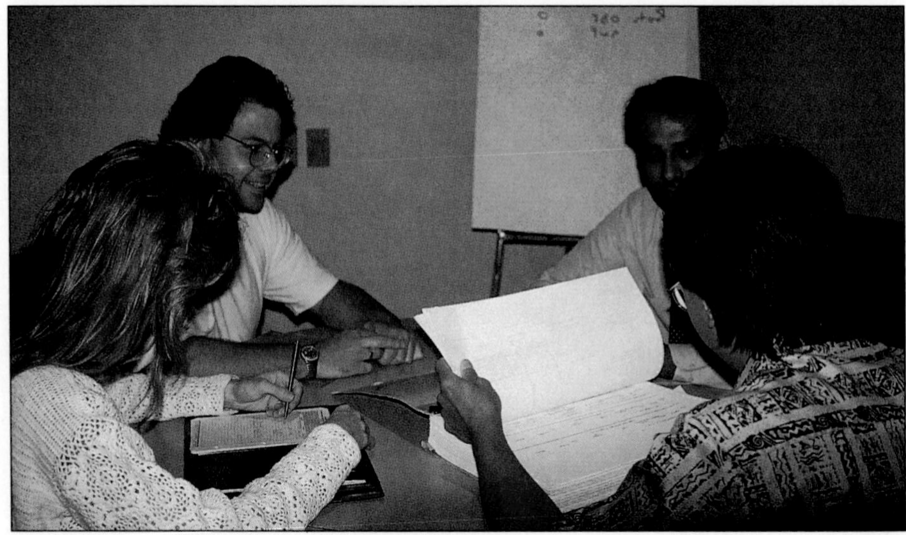

Rethinking the Corporation

In 1985, John Naisbitt and Patricia Aburdene co-authored a book called *Re-Inventing the Corporation* (Warner Books, 1985). The goal of management, according to Naisbitt and Aburdene, is to adopt "new humanistic values." Such new values enable employees to motivate themselves because they feel more a part of a unified corporate team.

They suggested certain steps for creating a better corporate atmosphere. These included calling everyone by his or her first name, eliminating executive parking spots and bathrooms, having everyone answer his or her own phone, eliminating files, doing business only with pleasant people, and throwing out the organization chart.

The authors also suggested that managers re-invent work. This means respecting workers, providing interesting work, rewarding good work, developing workers' skills, allowing some autonomy, and decentralizing authority.

Other points: (1) The manager's role is that of teacher, mentor, and coach; (2) the best people want ownership in the firm; (3) the best managerial style is not top down, but a networking, people style of management; (4) quality is the new key to success; (5) successful large corporations copy the entrepreneurial flavor of small businesses; and (6) the information age enables firms to locate where there is a high quality of life, since they don't have to be concerned exclusively with such industrial considerations as raw materials.

All of these ideas are consistent with management thought in the 1990s. Publications such as *Workplace 2000* reinforce the ideas of Naisbitt and Aburdene. Clearly, there *is* a trend toward different management styles. The point of this chapter is that the new management styles are largely motivational tools to bring out the best in more educated, better-trained workers. Those are the workers of the future, and they include you and me. Look through the points outlined above and see if you don't agree that you would have more fun and be more productive working in such an organization.

MAKING ETHICAL DECISIONS

You work as a manager for a rather prestigious department store. Each year to offset the rush of buyers at Christmas you are required to hire temporary help. You know that *all* the temporaries will be discharged on January 10. However, as you interview prospective temporaries, you give the impression the store will permanently hire at least two full-time retail salespeople for the coming new year. You even instruct your permanent employees to emphasize that good work over Christmas is the way to a permanent position. Is this an ethical way to try to motivate these employees? What is the danger of using this tactic? ▼

Changing Organizations Is Not Easy

We have come a long way from the time–motion studies of Frederick Taylor. Maslow, Mayo, Herzberg, and others have taught us to treat employees as associates and to get them more involved in decision making. This increases motivation and leads to greater productivity.

The problem is that many managers were brought up under a different system. Some were in the military and are used to telling people what to do rather than consulting with them. Others come from the football-coach school of management. They, too, tend to yell and direct rather than consult and discuss.

Furthermore, employees are often not used to participative management. The transition from Theory X to Theory Y management, from Taylor to Herzberg, is still going on. It is important, then, to have examples to follow when trying to implement the new approaches.

Wal-Mart: A Model for the Future

Perhaps the best example of a new company that achieved enormous success in the last 30 years and became the largest retailer in North America is Wal-Mart. Many of this company's management practices were well ahead of its competitors and of most companies in Canada and the U.S. Wal-Mart attributes a good deal of its success to its employee motivation strategies. Because it is such an outstanding example of successful employee motivation, Canadians should pay close attention to the Wal-Mart story.

Wal-Mart was founded in 1962 by Sam Walton. Walton, who preferred to be called Sam, saw the great potential for discount retailing in the United States. However, Wal-Mart sold the same merchandise as its competitors, so how could the company be different and take advantage of this potential boom? Walton felt the key to success in the industry was the development of a family-type relationship with the firm's employees, whom he preferred to call associates. He believed if you did not involve employees in the organization you were making a serious mistake, for employees are the only ones that can make an organization work.

In the 1990s, Wal-Mart became the nation's largest retailer. The firm operates over 1,500 stores, full-line discount stores, wholesale clubs, Super Centres, and hypermarkets. The company was awarded the Retailer of the Decade award by *Discount Stores News,* and Mr. Sam became the richest man in America, with a fortune estimated at over $18 billion in 1991.

How did all of this happen? Wal-Mart's success can be attributed to many factors. For example, the company was on the cutting edge of technology. It was one of the first firms to implement bar-code scanners in all of its stores. It also developed satellite-based transmissions that moved information rapidly from store to store, store to headquarters, and store to suppliers. Wal-Mart demanded a good deal of effort from suppliers but managed to develop positive and long-lasting relationships with them. This efficiency in distribution helped Wal-Mart fulfill its promise of everyday low prices. Many firms, including Sears, have tried to emulate this successful strategy. However, what Wal-Mart did best overall was develop a successful partnership with its associates. Sam Walton firmly believed that only people can make a business grow. He staked his future and that of the company on this basic principle.

Walton laid the foundation of his partnership with employees on three basic principles:

1. Treat employees as partners. Share with them both good news and bad so they will strive to excel. Also, let employees share in the rewards they help achieve.
2. Encourage employees to question and challenge the obvious. Walton believed the path to success included some failures. What was important was to use those failures to advantage by learning from them.
3. Involve associates at all levels in the decision-making process. Managers should be facilitators, sharing ideas with employees and soliciting ideas from them. Employees should not be asked to be involved; they should be required to be involved.

While many companies proclaimed such ambitious partnerships, Wal-Mart actually created one. The company regularly provided the good news and bad news just as it promised. Associates were kept informed on costs, freight charges, profit margins, and any other issues considered critical to the firm. Wal-Mart backed up its promise of sharing the wealth by providing a generous bonus plan to deserving employees. Company executives, including Sam Walton, practiced participative decision making by visiting Wal-Mart stores throughout the country seeking ideas, advice, and opinions from associates. The company even delegated authority to sales clerks, checkers, and stockpeople to order merchandise they thought they could sell. All employees were encouraged to get involved in operations and make the company better.[20]

Learning from the Wal-Mart Experience

Sam Walton developed not just a business but a true American success story. You can prepare for a business career by getting involved in campus activities. Learn to (1) get along with people by listening; (2) be a more concise, clear writer so that you can write short, readable memos and reports; and (3) speak in public by becoming involved in campus clubs and giving talks. Corporate recruiters complain that business graduates lack creativity, people skills, aptitude for teamwork, and the ability to speak and write clearly and concisely.[21] Remember, the best way to lead is by example, and the Wal-Mart management team is a model for employees and for managers in all types of firms. Lessons we can learn from the Wal-Mart example include:

- The future growth of industry and business in general depends on a motivated, productive work force.
- Motivation is largely internally generated by workers themselves. The process that releases that energy includes giving employees more freedom to be creative and rewarding achievement when it occurs.

- The first step in any motivational program is to establish open communication among workers and managers so that a family-type atmosphere of co-operation and teamwork is generated.

THINKING IT THROUGH

What do you think would have happened had top management at Wal-Mart decided not to actually practice the basic principles laid down by Sam Walton? Would a participative managerial style work for a football team as well as it did at Wal-Mart? What are the motivational differences, if any, between retail store employees and professional football players?

Motivation in the 1990s

What can we learn from all the theories and experiences discussed in this chapter? Will they work in the service economy of the 1990s as well as they did in the industrial economies of the past? The answer is "yes, if." Yes, people can be motivated much as they were in the past if managers know which technique to use and when.

Today's customers expect high-quality, customized goods and services. That means employees must provide extensive personal service and pay close attention to details. Employees have to work smart as well as hard. No amount of supervision can force an employee to smile or go the extra mile to help a customer. In fact, no theory of motivation will work with *all* workers.

What is the key to success in the 1990s? Michael Maccoby thinks he has the answer in his new book called *Why Work: Leading the New Generation.* The idea, he says, is to de-emphasize external motivators and instead understand people's inner drives, interests, and values. The company's goals have to be accomplished through people, and people have their own goals. The manager's problem, therefore, is to find a way to meet the company's goals by first meeting the individual employee's goals.[22]

Maccoby identifies different types of workers and shows how each needs a different type of motivational effort. For example, half of the respondents in Maccoby's study considered themselves *experts,* or people who get their satisfaction mainly from the work itself. Experts like their independence and do not want managers to coach or cajole them. A good motivational technique for them, therefore, is to give them their freedom and recognize their achievements with rewards. *Self-developers,* on the other hand, see work as a way to develop their own knowledge and skills. Self-developers want a more collaborative relationship with managers. A good technique for them is to give them opportunities to learn new tasks and give them plenty of information about the company's goals and how each new job helps reach those goals.

Maccoby identifies other groups, which we won't go into here. The point is that employees are not alike; different employees respond to different managerial and motivational styles. Tomorrow's managers will not be able to use any one formula for all employees. Rather, they will have to get to know each worker as an individual and "taylor" (pun intended) the motivational effort to the individual.

In general, motivation will come from the job itself rather than from external punishments or rewards. Managers need to give workers what they need to do a good job: the right tools, the right information, and the right amount of co-operation.

You see, motivation is not so difficult. It begins with acknowledging a job well done and telling those who do it that you appreciate them, especially in front of others. The best motivator is often the words, "Thanks, I appreciate what you have done for me."

PROGRESS CHECK

- What are several steps firms can use to increase internal communications and thus motivation?
- What are the six steps in "re-inventing work" and how are they related to motivation?
- Where does Sam Walton's approach fit into Maslow's theory? Herzberg's theory?
- What problems may emerge when you try to implement participative management?
- Why is it important today to adjust motivational styles to individual employees? Are there any general principles of motivation that today's managers should follow?

SUMMARY

1. Don Brommet (see profile) realizes that people make or break a company. This is true of any business because satisfied customers are a must. Frederick Taylor was one of the first people to study motivation.

1. Explain Taylor's scientific management.

- *Who is Frederick Taylor?*

  Frederick Taylor is the father of scientific management. He did time–motion studies to learn the most efficient way of doing a job and then trained workers in those procedures. He published his book on scientific management in 1911. The Gilbreths and H. L. Gantt were followers of Taylor.

2. Management theory moved away from Taylor's scientific management and towards theories that stress human factors of motivation.

2. Describe the Hawthorne studies and relate their significance to human-based management.

- *What led to the more people-oriented managerial styles that were used to increase motivation?*

  The greatest impact on motivation theory was generated by the Hawthorne studies in the late 1920s and early 1930s. Elton Mayo found that human factors such as feelings of involvement and participation led to productivity gains despite difficult physical conditions.

3. Maslow studied basic human motivation and found it was based on need. An unfilled need motivated people to satisfy it and a satisfied need no longer motivated.

3. Identify the levels of Maslow's needs hierarchy and relate its importance to employee motivation.

- *What were the various levels of need identified by Maslow?*

  From the bottom of Maslow's hierarchy up, the needs are physiological, safety, social, self-esteem, and self-actualization.

- *Can managers use this theory?*

  Yes. They can recognize what needs a person has and organize the work to provide the necessary satisfaction.

4. McGregor held that managers can have one of two attitudes towards employees. They are called Theory X and Theory Y.

4. Differentiate between Theory X and Theory Y.

- *What are these theories and when were they developed?*

  Theory X assumes that the average person dislikes work and will avoid it if possible. Therefore, people must be forced, controlled, and threatened with punishment to accomplish organizational goals. Theory Y assumes that people like working and will accept responsibility for achieving goals if rewarded for doing so. Douglas McGregor published these theories in 1970.

5. In response to McGregor's Theories X and Y, Ouchi introduced Theory Z.

▼ *What is Theory Z?*

Theory Z comes out of Japanese management and stresses long-term employment, co-operative decision making, and other factors. Some aspects are practiced in North America.

5. Describe Theory Z and its application in North America.

6. Herzberg found that some factors are motivators and others are hygiene factors. That is, they cause job dissatisfaction if missing but do not motivate if present.

▼ *What are the factors called motivators?*

The work itself, achievement, recognition, responsibility, growth, and advancement.

▼ *What are the hygiene factors?*

Company policies, supervision, working conditions, interpersonal relations, and salary.

6. Distinguish between motivators and hygiene factors identified by Herzberg.

7. Job enrichment describes efforts to make jobs more interesting.

▼ *What characteristics of work affect motivation and performance?*

The job characteristics that influence motivation are (1) skill variety, (2) task identity, (3) task significance, (4) autonomy, and (5) feedback.

▼ *What are two forms of job enrichment that increase motivation?*

Job enrichment strategies include job enlargement and job rotation.

7. Explain how job enrichment affects employee motivation and performance.

8. One procedure for establishing objectives and gaining employee commitment to those objectives is called MBO (management by objectives).

▼ *What are the steps in an MBO program?*

(1) Managers set goals, (2) objectives are established for each department, (3) workers discuss the objectives and commit themselves in writing to meeting them, (4) progress is reviewed, (5) feedback is provided and adjustments made, and (6) employees are rewarded for achieving goals or assisted in reaching goals in the future.

8. Identify the steps involved in implementing a management-by-objectives program.

9. The transition from old-style management to human-based management is still going on.

▼ *What is the key to successful human-based management?*

In a word, the key to successful management is allowing employees to participate in management by using self-managed teams.

9. Describe the implementation of motivation theory in the 1990s.

GETTING INVOLVED

1. Talk with several of your friends about the subject of motivation. What motivates them to work hard or not work hard in school and on the job? How important is self-motivation to them?
2. Look over Maslow's hierarchy of needs and try to determine where you fit on the hierarchy. What needs of yours are not being met? How could a company go about meeting those needs and thus motivate you to work better and harder?
3. One of the newest managerial ideas is to let employees work in self-managed teams. There is no reason why such teams could not be formed in colleges as well as businesses. Discuss the benefits and drawbacks of dividing your class into self-managed teams for the purpose of studying, doing cases, and so forth.
4. Think of all of the groups with whom you have been associated over the years—sports groups, friends, and so on—and try to recall how the leaders of those groups motivated the group to action. Did the leaders assume a Theory X or Theory Y attitude? How often was money used as a motivator? What other motivational tools were used and to what effect?

PRACTICING MANAGEMENT DECISIONS

Case One Using Compensation to Motivate

Jon Wehrenberg is a businessperson always up to a challenge. Three years ago a friend called and told Jon he knew of a large building-products company that was looking for a domestic supplier of plumbing assemblies. The firm was currently importing products from Korea and was hoping to improve its turnaround time and quality. The deal was worth about $1 million a year to Jon's firm, Jamestown Advanced Products, if he could commit to producing and delivering the specified quantity of custom-ordered metal products every week. There was also one other stipulation. Jon's company would have to do the work at the same price the Korean supplier was currently charging.

The challenge inspired Wehrenberg, and he carefully compiled the important financial information needed. He discovered that a pretax profit margin of 12 percent was possible, but only if he could keep direct labour expenses down to 11 percent of company sales.

The problem he faced was obvious. The estimated production per worker was realistic only if his work force wanted to sustain a high level of quality and productivity. But many workers tend to be cynical about management and lose their motivation if they see productivity increasing without any benefit to them. He decided the solution was logical and simple. In addition to a competitive base wage, he would pay the workers a quarterly bonus if they could get the firm's labour costs under 11 percent.

Wehrenberg also agreed that at the end of each week he would provide information concerning sales totals, gross payroll numbers, or any other information workers needed to verify the efficiency of the system. He believed that it was possible over time to get labour costs down to 9 percent, which would mean a quarterly bonus of $1,500 to each worker.

Workers liked the idea and accepted the challenge. Jamestown Advanced Products agreed to a three-year contract to supply the building-products company.

Decision Questions

1. What does Jamestown Advanced Products do to motivate people using money that other firms do not do? Can you see how money can be a motivator?
2. How effective would implementing self-managed teams be in a situation like this?
3. What kind of workers would enjoy working at Jamestown Advanced Products? What kind would not? Can you see how productivity at Jamestown would increase as certain kinds of employees self-selected themselves out of the company and others came in who fit the system better?
4. Would such a revenue-sharing system work at most companies? For what kinds of companies would it work best?

Source: Jon W. Wehrenberg, "How My Company Learned To Run Itself," *Inc.*, Jan. 1991, pp. 54–60.

Case Two Motivation in an Era of "Disposable Workers"

News reports from Canada and the U.S. indicate a new trend in the job market. A decreasing number of people are being given permanent jobs of the kind we used to expect as normal employment. Security of employment with all the usual fringe benefits is being reserved for a privileged few. U.S. data indicate that up to half of all new jobs are temporary, part-time, or some other unconventional type of employment, and this number is expected to grow. What is behind this trend?

Many Canadian companies have adopted a form of work-force management that they believe will enable them to compete better in the world market. They keep a "core of managers and valued workers whom they favour with good benefits and permanent jobs. They take on and shed other workers as business spurts and slumps." These jobs pay less and have few if any benefits. Many Canadians have lost good jobs and are finding only these unsatisfactory new jobs. Many Canadian students are finding only these poor-quality jobs available upon graduation.

According to Robert Reich, Secretary of Labour in the Clinton administration in the U.S., "The entire system has fragmented." He estimated that about 30 percent of the American work force was composed of contingent workers, but current statistics suggest this estimate is low.

Current Canadian data are not yet available, but various Statistics Canada reports indicate that many new jobs are of a similarly insecure nature. Apparently Canadian companies that let go hundreds of thousands of employees in the deep recession and restructuring of the 1990s are not rushing to rehire permanent employees if they can avoid it.

Decision Questions

1. What is likely to be the impact of this trend on employee motivation? Will temporary workers be as motivated as permanent employees, especially if they continue to look for a "decent" job?
2. How will this, in turn, affect production and service to customers? Given the growing importance of teamwork and co-operation, is quality production likely to suffer?
3. What about the long-term impact on the competitiveness of companies? Are companies being too short-sighted in thinking only of current bottom lines?
4. How can companies develop employees' long-term loyalty in such circumstances? Is this still important? Why?

Sources: Peter T. Kilborn, "New Jobs Lack the Old Security in a Time of 'Disposable Workers,' " *New York Times,* March 15, 1993, p. A1; *Globe and Mail, Financial Post,* various issues in February and March 1993. Peter Hadekel, "Very Soon the Working World Will Be Divided into Two Types of People," *Montreal Gazette,* March 10, 1993, p. B14.

LET'S TALK BUSINESS

1. Think of all the bosses (managers/leaders) you have had over time in sports, clubs, and so forth. Did they assume a Theory X or Y style of leadership? How did you feel about that? Would you have worked harder or less hard if they had followed the other strategy? What does this tell you about motivation? Discuss with the class.
2. Herzberg found that pay was not a motivator. If you were paid to get better grades, would you be able to get them? Have you worked harder as a result of a large raise? Discuss money as a motivator with your friends and class. Do you agree 100 percent with Herzberg?
3. Have you ever volunteered to work on a project where you felt your efforts really made a difference? How did you feel about that? If you haven't, how do you feel about that fact? Do you envy people with an obvious mission in life? How could you find a job that would satisfy your basic needs for food, shelter, safety, and esteem and feel as if you were making a difference in the world? Discuss options with classmates.
4. If you were made a manager, would you be willing to treat your employees as equals? Would you be willing to eat with them, socialize with them, and generally be their friend as well as their boss? Would it make a difference if they were from a different ethnic group, country, or social class? What kind of people, if any, do you feel need Theory X management? Discuss.
5. You have had the most experience in motivation in school. Which teachers got you to work hardest? How did they do it? What was their managerial style? What motivators did they use? Discuss your findings with the class.

LOOKING AHEAD

Organizations succeed or fail on the ability of the people they employ. Therefore, hiring, training, motivating, and developing human resources is a vital element in business success. This task is becoming more difficult with new hiring rules, new employee demands, and new technologies. Certainly human resource management will be an interesting and challenging career in the future. We discuss that function next in Chapter 15.

What's your
paper personality?
It's never to

HUMAN RESOURCE MANAGEMENT

LEARNING GOALS

After you have read and studied this chapter, you should be able to:

1. Explain the importance of human resource management and describe current issues in managing human resources.
2. Summarize the six steps in planning human resources.
3. Describe methods companies use to recruit new employees and explain some of the problems that make recruitment difficult.
4. Outline the six steps in selecting employees.
5. Describe the various types of employee training methods.
6. Trace the six steps in appraising employee performance.
7. Summarize the objectives of employee compensation programs and describe various pay systems and benefits.
8. Explain scheduling plans managers use to adjust to workers' needs.
9. Describe training methods used in management development programs.
10. Illustrate the effects of legislaticn on human resource management.

KEY TERMS

affirmative action, p. 497
apprenticeship, p. 482
cafeteria-style benefits, p. 489
compressed work week, p. 492
core time, p. 491
employee benefits, p. 488
employee orientation, p. 482
flextime plans, p. 491
human resource management, p. 473
job analysis, p. 475
job descriptions, p. 475
job sharing, p. 489
job simulation, p. 483
job specifications, p. 475
journeyman, p. 482
management development, p. 493
mentors, p. 494
networking, p. 494
off-the-job training, p. 483
on-the-job training, p. 482
performance appraisal, p. 484
recruitment, p. 477
reverse discrimination, p. 497
selection, p. 479
training and development, p. 482
vestibule training, p. 483

Herbert Siblin

PROFILE ZITTRER, SIBLIN, STEIN, LEVINE

Zittrer, Siblin, Stein, Levine (ZSSL) is Canada's 16th-largest firm of chartered accountants. A senior human resource consultant describes it as "anything but a traditional accounting firm." There are 377 partners and employees, the majority at the head office in Montreal and the balance in Toronto. Estimated revenues for 1990 were $30 million.

One of the things that make ZSSL different is that professional employees "learn the meaning of the work they're doing that otherwise would be so boring," managing partner Herbert Siblin says. "If we go to a major meeting with a bank, for example, we frequently invite staff to come with us just to see the process and see the work they did."

The firm has a strong people-oriented approach to a profession not known for high job satisfaction and enrichment among junior employees. In contrast to the more common accounting "sweatshops," where low pay, hard work, and long hours are the norm for apprentice accountants, even the students seem to like working at ZSSL. In fact, in the past two years, 90 percent of summer students opted to return for full-time work.

Once they're on the payroll, ZSSL tries to maintain a sense of individuality and create an intimacy with clients by splitting its operations into 14 distinct audit teams, almost firms within the firm. Each team of 10 to 25, headed by one or more partners, handles a small group of diversified clients on an ongoing basis. The client gets continuity and a personal small-firm touch and looks on the members of the team as his or her accountants.

All of this provides enrichment for employees as well as partners. Even junior staff have the unique opportunity to see all sides of a variety of businesses. Employees can identify with a small group of colleagues while enjoying the support and benefits of a large firm. Each team develops its own esprit de corps.

ZSSL is also making strides to improve its male–female ratio. In a profession dominated by men, the firm recently designated four women partners and principals. Four years ago, there weren't any. With a work force that's 46 percent female, 33 percent of supervisors and managers are now women and 50 percent of all new recruits are women. The company also adopted a more flexible maternity leave policy, allowing women to take up to six months' leave without jeopardizing their jobs. And in a profession where working overtime is considered part of the territory, another policy rules out the need for overtime work for women with young children.

The major rewards for professional employees stem from the small-firm environment, the variety, and the opportunity to grow. They're proud of the firm's partners—"some really bright people you can learn a lot from"—who willingly share their knowledge.

Sources: E. Innes, J. Lyons and J. Harris, *The Financial Post 100 Best Companies To Work for in Canada,* Toronto: HarperCollins, 1990, pp. 108–10; interview with senior partner, Boris Levine Sept. 13, 1991.

THE HUMAN RESOURCE FUNCTION

In your career search, you may be in and out of many human resource offices. While you are there, take a few minutes to observe. Talk to some of the employees and managers. Perhaps this is the field in which you would like to work.

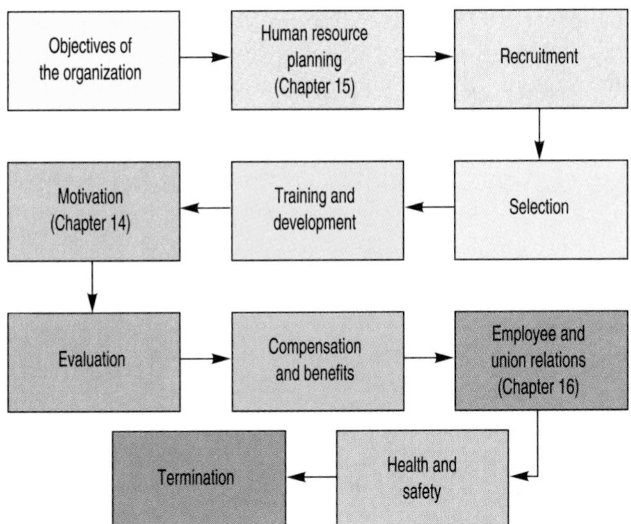

Figure 15–1 Human resource management. Note that human resource management includes motivation (discussed in Chapter 14) and union relations (discussed in Chapter 16). As you can see from the chart, human resource management is more than hiring and firing personnel.

There is an old story about the student who wanted to go into human resources "because I want to work with people." It is true that human resource managers work with people, but they are also deeply involved in planning, record keeping, and other administrative duties. This chapter will discuss the human resource function (formerly called personnel), which involves recruiting, hiring, training, evaluating, compensating, and when necessary firing people. **Human resource management (HRM)** is the process of evaluating human resource needs, finding people to fill those needs, and optimizing this important resource by providing the right incentives and job environment, all with the goal of meeting the organization's objectives (see Figure 15–1). Let's explore some of the trends in the area of HRM.

human resource management (HRM)
The process of evaluating human resource needs, finding people to fill those needs, and optimizing this important resource by providing the right incentives and job enrichment, all with the goal of meeting the organization's objectives.

The Importance of HRM

One reason that human resource management (or personnel management) is receiving increased attention now is because of the major shift from traditional manufacturing industries to service industries and high-tech manufacturing organizations that require more technical job skills. Companies now have fewer employees, but the ones that remain require more education and skills. A major problem today is retraining workers for new, more challenging jobs.

When ZSSL moved into new premises, they built a permanent training centre, underlining their commitment to continuous training and development. Each member of the firm must attend at least 10 days of courses annually. Each employee or partner also receives a personalized program to help monitor his or her progress.

Here are some other examples:

- Canada Mortgage and Housing Corp., a crown corporation, has numerous training programs and job exchanges. Temporary vacancies are often filled by people from other departments wanting to enrich their own experience. Each year CMHC hires 10 university graduates under a two-year training program that exposes them to 10 or 12 departments.
- Allen-Bradley Canada Ltd. manufactures industrial automation equipment. It has over a thousand employees in three plants in Ontario and emphasizes training. At its Cambridge plant it employs seven full-time and three

part-time instructors. The other locations have four full-time instructors. New marketing employees go through a three-month training and orientation program. All new employees attend a two-week business course.

- Du Pont Canada Inc., employing over 4,000 people, has a strategy that heavily emphasizes education, training, and development. Gerry Fox, vice-president of human resources, says that increased productivity is the result of a well-trained staff. The company spent 3.5 percent of its payroll, or about $1,700 per employee, on education in 1990.[1]

Some people have called employees a company's most important resource, and, when you think about it, nothing could be truer. People develop the ideas that eventually become the products that satisfy our wants and needs. Take away their creative minds, and organizations such as Northern Telecom, Bombardier, Canadian Tire, Magna International, and other leading firms would be nothing.

Most firms used to assign the job of recruiting, selecting, training, evaluating, compensating, motivating, and, yes, firing people to the various functional departments. For years, the personnel department was viewed more or less as a clerical function responsible for screening applications, keeping records, processing payroll, and finding people when necessary.

Today, the job of human resource management has taken on an entirely new role in the firm. In the future, it may become *the* most critical function in that it is responsible for the most critical resource—people. In fact, the human resource function has become so important that it is no longer the function of just one department; it is a function of all managers. Most human resource functions are shared between the professional human resource manager and the other managers. In smaller companies where there is no HRM department, one manager or the owner has this responsibility. What are some of the problems in the human resource area that managers face?

The Human Resource Challenge of the 1990s

No changes in the Canadian business system have been more dramatic and had more impact on the future success of the economy than changes in the labour force. Canada's ability to compete in international markets depends on an increase in new ideas, new products, and as we saw in Chapter 14, a higher level of productivity from its workers. All of these factors critically depend on the ultimate resource—people with good ideas. Problems being encountered in the human resource area include:

- Shortages in people trained to work in the growth areas of the future such as telecommunications, computers, biotechnology, robotics, and the sciences.
- A huge population of skilled and unskilled workers (from declining industries such as textile apparel manufacturing and steel and modernizing industries such as automobiles) who are unemployed or underemployed and who need retraining.
- A shift in the age composition in the work force, including many older workers. (See Chapter 1 for a discussion of demographic trends.)
- A complex set of laws and regulations involving hiring, firing, safety, unionization, and equal pay that limits organizations' freedom to create an optimum labour force. For example, it is becoming very difficult to fire an inefficient or ineffective worker.

- A tremendous influx of women into the labour force and the resulting demand for day care, job sharing, maternity leave programs, and special career advancement programs for women.
- A shift in employee attitudes toward work. Leisure time has become a much higher priority, as have concepts such as flextime and a shorter work week.
- A challenge from other labour pools available for lower wages and subject to few laws and regulations. This results in many jobs being shifted to other countries.
- An increased demand for benefits tailored to the individual. (We shall discuss these cafeteria-style benefit plans later in the chapter.)
- A growing concern over such issues as health care, day care facilities, smoking on the job, and equal pay for jobs of equal value. Special attention is also being paid to affirmative-action programs.

Given all these issues, and others that are sure to develop, you can see why human resource management has taken a more central position in management thinking.

THINKING IT THROUGH

Does human resource management seem like a challenging career for the 1990s? Do you see any other issues likely to affect this function? What have your experiences been in dealing with people who work in HRM? Would you enjoy working in such an environment?

PLANNING HUMAN RESOURCES

All management, including HRM, begins with planning. Six steps are involved in the human resource planning process. They include:

1. Preparing forecasts of future human resource needs.
2. Preparing a human resource inventory that includes names, education, capabilities, training, specialized skills, and other information pertinent to the specific organization (for example, languages spoken). Such information reveals the status of the labour force.
3. Preparing a job analysis. A **job analysis** answers the question, "What do employees who fill various job titles do?" Such analyses are necessary in order to recruit and train employees with the right skills to do the job. The results of job analysis are two written statements: job descriptions and job specifications (see Figure 15–2). **Job descriptions** specify the objectives of the job, the type of work to be done, responsibilities and duties, skills needed, working conditions, and the relationship of the job to other functions. **Job specifications** specify the qualifications (education, skills, etc.) required of a worker to fill a specific job. In short, job descriptions are statements about the *job,* whereas job specifications are statements about the *person* who does the job. Job analysis information can be obtained through observation, interviews, and diaries, or some combination of techniques. As you will see later, changes in law have made the preparation of these guidelines extremely important.

job analysis
A study of what is done by employees who fill various job titles.

job descriptions
Summaries of the objectives of a job, the type of work, responsibilities of the job, skills needed, the working conditions, and the relationship of the job to other functions.

job specifications
Summary of the qualifications required of a worker to do a particular job.

Figure 15–2 A job analysis yields two important statements: job descriptions and job specifications. Here you have a job description and job specifications for a Fiberrific cereal sales representative.

Job Analysis

Observe current sales representatives doing the job.
Discuss job with sales managers.
Have current sales reps keep a diary of their daily activities.

Job Description

Primary responsibility is to sell Fiberrific to food stores in Territory Z. Other duties include servicing accounts and maintaining positive relationships with clients. Examples of duties required:

- Introducing the new cereal to store managers in the area.
- Helping the store managers estimate the volume to order.
- Negotiating prime shelf space.
- Explaining sales promotion activities to store managers.
- Stocking and maintaining shelves in stores that wish such service.

Job Specifications

Characteristics of the person qualifying for this job include the following:

- Two years' sales experience.
- Positive attitude.
- Well-groomed appearance.
- Good communication skills.
- High school diploma and two years of college credit.

4. Assessing future demand. Changing technology often means that training programs must be started long before the need is apparent. Human resource managers who are proactive (in this case that means, anticipate what the future of their organization will be) have the trained human resources available when needed.
5. Assessing future supply. The labour force is constantly shifting: getting older, becoming more technically oriented, attracting more women and foreign workers and so forth. There are likely to be increased shortages of some skills in the future (for example, computer and robotic repair) and oversupplies of others (for example, production line workers).
6. Establishing a strategic plan for recruiting, selecting, training and developing, appraising, and scheduling the labour force, given the previous analysis. We will look at each element of the strategic human resource plan in the next sections. See Figure 15–3 for an overview of the planning process.

Some companies have been moving away from the traditional, rigid job description as a basis for organizing their operations management. Tom Peters points out that companies that want to be most productive and react quickly to competitive demands have moved towards flexibility. That means managers and employees do whatever is required and are not bound by job descriptions. This allows for greater employee initiative and participation, leading to more motivated employees. In today's fast-moving world, reacting quickly gives businesses a competitive edge. In small companies, employees have long functioned as generalists, not limited by strict job descriptions. For bigger businesses, this represents a new trend.

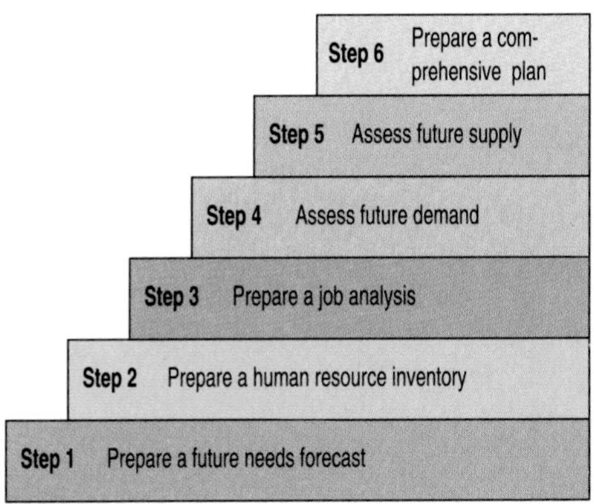

Figure 15–3 Steps in human resource planning. Human resource planning is a complex process involving several crucial steps. A job analysis that involves job descriptions and job specifications is an important step.

The very large companies have been pushing their unions for some time to allow for greater flexibility in moving employees about to do what is required. Unions have usually been suspicious of this demand because they worry that it will be used to reduce pay rates. The Big Three auto companies have begun to get important concessions in this regard from the auto workers' unions in Canada and the U.S. They have drastically reduced the number of job descriptions, allowing for more efficient deployment of their work forces. These companies are waging a tough fight to be more competitive with Japanese auto makers, and this is one way to improve their productivity.

W. Edwards Deming, the American quality expert revered in Japan, goes much further than that. He stresses the importance of co-operation among workers. He says, "Workers in Japan learned how to co-operate because it was the only chance for the country's survival, given its limited resources and land. . . . People must learn to work together, but it will take time. North American industry must change its philosophy of every man for himself."[2]

RECRUITING EMPLOYEES

Recruitment is the set of activities used to obtain a sufficient number of the right people at the right time and to select those that best meet the needs of the organization. One would think that, with a continuous flow of new persons into the work force, recruiting would be easy. But the truth is that recruiting has become very difficult for several reasons:

recruitment
The set of activities used to obtain a sufficient number of the right people at the right time to select those who best meet the needs of the organization.

- Legal restrictions, such as the Charter of Rights and Freedoms, make it necessary to consider the proper mix of women, minorities, people with disabilities, and other qualified individuals. Often people with the necessary skills are not available, so others must be hired and trained internally.
- The emphasis on corporate cultures, teamwork, and participative management makes it important to hire skilled people who also fit in with the culture and leadership style of the organization.
- Firing unsatisfactory employees is getting more difficult to justify legally. This is especially true of discharges involving possible discrimination by age, sex, sexual preference, or race. Therefore, it is important to screen and evaluate employees carefully to be sure they will be effective long-term members of the organization.

▼ Some organizations have unattractive workplaces, have policies that demand promotions from within, operate under union regulations, or have low wages that make recruiting and keeping employees difficult or subject to outside influence and restrictions.

Because recruiting is a difficult chore that involves finding, hiring, and training people who are an appropriate technical and social fit, human resource managers turn to many sources for assistance (see Figure 15–4). These include internal promotions, advertisements, public and private employment agencies, university or

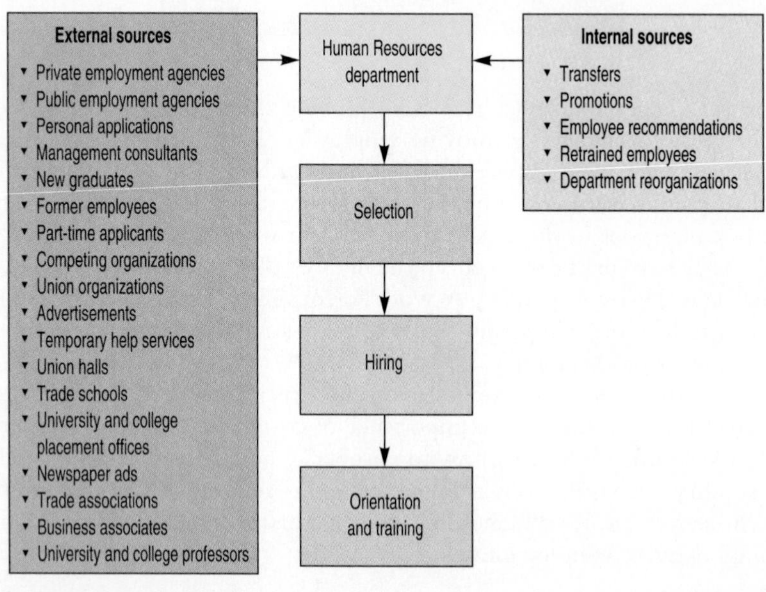

Figure 15–4 Employee sources. Internal sources are often given first consideration. Therefore, it is wise to get a recommendation from a current employee of the firm for which you want to work.

Your university or college placement office is one of the best places to start searching for a job. Be sure to go early to learn where it is, what information is available there, and how the interviewing process is handled. Get a head start now on the competition.

college placement bureaus, management consultants, professional organizations, referrals, and applicants who simply show up at the office. A recent survey by *Fordyce Letter,* a newsletter for professionals in employment, revealed that 99 percent of the employers hire "walk-ins" and 98 percent hire from résumés in their files. The findings also show an increase in employee referrals and use of free public employment agencies.[3] An interesting trend in human resource management has been the increase in the number of temporary workers. Temporary, part-time, and contract workers make up nearly one-third of the work force today.

SELECTING EMPLOYEES

Selection is the process of gathering information to decide who should be hired, under legal guidelines, for the best interests of the organization and the individual. High turnover has made the cost of selecting and training employees prohibitively high in some firms. Think of the costs involved—interview time, medical exams, training costs, unproductive time spent learning the job, moving expenses, and so on. It's easy to see how such expenses can run over $50,000 for a manager. Even entry-level workers can cost thousands of dollars to recruit, process, and train. Thus, the selection process is an important element in any human resource program. A typical selection process involves six steps (see Figure 15–5).

selection
The process of gathering information to decide who should be hired, under legal guidelines, for the best interests of the organization and the individual.

1. *Completion of an application form.* Once this was a simple procedure. Today, legal guidelines limit the kinds of questions one can ask. (Sex, race, religion, age, or nationality are taboo). Nonetheless, such forms help discover educational background, past work experience, career objectives, and other information directly related to the requirements of the job.
2. *Initial and follow-up interviews.* Applicants are often screened in a first interview by a member of the HRM staff. If the interviewer considers the applicant a potential employee, the manager who will supervise the new employee interviews the applicant as well. Many managers and even some human resource managers are not highly skilled in conducting job interviews. However, such interviews are helpful in testing an applicant's ability to communicate clearly, adapt to a stressful situation, and clarify his or her goals, career objective, and background. It's important that managers prepare adequately for the interview process to avoid selection errors they may regret.
3. *Employment tests.* Employment tests have been severely criticized due to charges of discrimination. Nonetheless, organizations continue to use them to measure basic

MAKING ETHICAL DECISIONS

As human resource manager for Technocrat, Inc., you aim to recruit the best employees. You completed a human resource inventory that indicated that Technocrat currently has an abundance of qualified designers and that several lower-level workers will soon be eligible for promotions to designer positions as well. In spite of the surplus of qualified designers, you are considering offering a similar position to a designer who is now with a major competitor. Your thinking is that the new employee will be a source of information about the competition's new products. What are your ethical considerations in this case? Will you lure the employee away from the competition even though you have no need for a designer? What will be the consequences of your decision? ▼

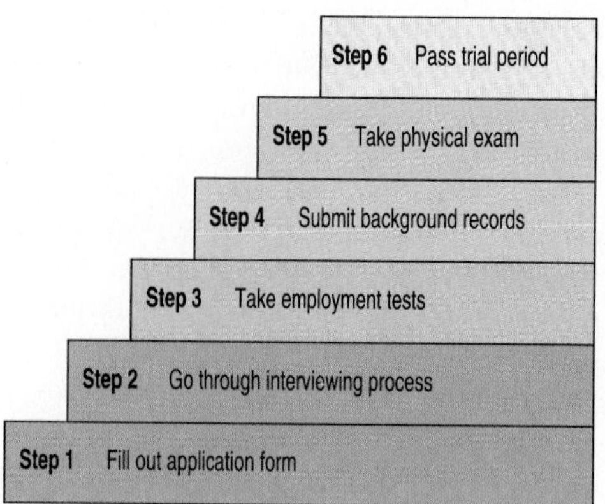

Figure 15–5 Steps in the selection process. There are several steps you must take to obtain a job. First, you fill out an application form. Then you must go through an interviewing process and the other steps shown here. The goal is to find a job that is satisfying to you and that you will do well.

competencies, test specific job skills (for example, welding, typing), and help evaluate applicants' personalities and interests. It's important that the employment test be directly job related. This will make the selection process more efficient and often satisfy legal requirements.

4. *Background investigations.* Most organizations are becoming more careful about investigating a candidate's work record, school record, and recommendations. It is simply too costly to hire, train, motivate, and lose people, and then have to start the process over. Background checks help weed out candidates least likely to succeed and identify those most likely to succeed. It is not always easy to obtain this information, however. Many companies no longer provide references for fear of liability suits if they give negative reports.

5. *Physical exams.* A complete medical background and check-up help screen candidates. There are obvious benefits in hiring physically and mentally healthy people. However, medical tests cannot be given just to screen out specific applicants. If such tests are given, they must be given to everyone at the same point in the selection process. A major controversy erupted in the late 1980s related to pre-employment testing to detect drug or alcohol abuse or AIDS.

Over 70 percent of CEOs endorse drug testing in some instances. The Toronto Dominion Bank asked 250 top executives to undergo drug tests and made testing mandatory for all new employees. The Canadian Civil Liberty Association has asked the Canadian Human Rights Commission to quash this program as discriminating on the basis of disability. David Korn, president of The Donwood Institute, a public hospital in Toronto, said company funds should not be used in the search for a quick technological fix to a very complex issue. Levi Strauss & Co. (Canada) Inc. does not test prospective employees for AIDS but has a thorough educational program for them. By contrast, the Canadian AIDS Society, in a survey of 500 businesses, discovered that only 4 percent are developing policies and programs to deal with AIDS; 22 percent said it was not their job to inform employees about AIDS.[4]

6. *Trial periods.* Often an organization will hire an employee conditionally. This enables the person to prove his or her worth on the job. After a period of perhaps six months or a year, the firm has the right to discharge that employee based on evaluations from supervisors. Such systems make it easier to fire inefficient or problem employees but do not eliminate the high cost of turnover.

SPOTLIGHT ON SMALL BUSINESS

Brother, Can You Spare a Job?

Relatives are often the lifeblood of small businesses. Many small businesses would be dead without dedicated family members giving their all to keeping a business going. But small-business owners need to consider the negative aspects of employing family members. Do this *before* problems come up.

The Pros	The Cons
▼ You have a pool of workers ready. It is often difficult for small companies to find competent help.	▼ Family feuds could transfer to business and sabotage the company.
▼ Relatives are dedicated to making sure the family-owned business succeeds.	▼ No matter how much they are told to "treat her like everyone else," other employees may have trouble supervising family members.
▼ Families provide a stable climate that helps make even unrelated employees feel secure and satisfied.	▼ Employees can't help wondering whether your sister was promoted for who she is or what she's done. (Often, neither can your sister.)

Source: "Pros and Cons of Hiring Relatives to Work in Your Business," *Profit-Building Strategies for Business Owners,* Aug. 1, 1990.

The selection process is often long and difficult, but it's worth the effort because of the high costs of replacing workers. The process helps assure that the people an organization hires are competent in all relevant areas, including communications skills, education, technical skills, experience, social fit, and health.

Most firms recruit people who have the potential to be productive employees. They realize that potential involves effective training programs and proper managerial incentives. Carefully orienting individuals to their new environment can be an important step for the human resource manager.

PROGRESS CHECK

- What is human resource management?
- What are the six steps in human resource planning?
- What factors make it difficult to recruit qualified employees?
- What are the six steps in the selection process?

TRAINING AND DEVELOPING EMPLOYEES

New technologies such as word processors, computers, and robots have made it necessary to do more and more training, much of which is quite sophisticated. Today's forward-thinking organizations are recognizing that people are their most vital resource and are integral to achieving increased productivity. Therefore, many firms are getting much more involved in continuing education and development programs for their employees. Career development is no longer just a haphazard system of promotions, moves, and occasional training programs. Rather, it is a long-term organizational strategy for assisting employees to optimize their skills and

training and development
All attempts to improve employee performance through learning.

advance their education. **Training and development** include all attempts to improve employee performance through learning. The next sections look at various training and development programs: employee orientation, on-the-job training, apprenticeship, off-the-job training, vestibule training, and job simulation.

Employee Orientation

employee orientation
The activity that introduces new employees to the organization, to fellow employees, to their immediate supervisors, and to the policies, practices, and objectives of the firm.

Employee orientation is the activity that initiates new employees to the organization, to fellow employees, to their immediate supervisors, and to the policies, practices, and objectives of the firm. Orientation programs vary from quite informal, primarily verbal, efforts to formal schedules that have employees visit various departments for a day or more and include lengthy handouts. Formal orientation programs may cover:

- History and general policies of the organization.
- Descriptions of products or services provided by the organization to the public.
- The organization's chain of command (organizational chart).
- Company safety measures and regulations.
- Human resources policies and practices.
- Compensation, benefits, and employee services.
- Daily routines and regulations.
- Introduction to the corporate culture—the values and orientation of the organization.
- Organizational objectives and the role of the new recruit in accomplishing those objectives.

On-the-Job Training

on-the-job training
The employee immediately begins his or her tasks and learns by doing, or watches others for a while and then imitates them, right at the workplace.

The most fundamental training programs involve on-the-job training. **On-the-job training** means that the employee immediately begins his or her tasks and learns by doing, or watches others for a while and then imitates them, right at the workplace. Salespeople, for example, are often trained by watching experienced salespeople perform. Naturally, this can be either quite effective or disastrous, depending on the skills and habits of the person being watched. On-the-job training is the easiest kind to implement and can be effective where the job is easily learned, such as clerking in a store, or performing repetitive physical tasks such as collecting refuse, cleaning carpets, and mowing lawns. More intricate jobs require a more intense training effort.

Apprentice Programs

apprenticeship
A time when a new worker works alongside a master technician to learn the appropriate skills and procedures.

journeyman
A worker who has successfully completed an apprenticeship.

Many skilled crafts, such as bricklaying or plumbing, require a new worker to serve several years as an apprentice. An **apprenticeship** is a period of time when a learner works alongside a skilled worker to learn the skills and procedures of a craft. Trade unions often require such periods to assure excellence among their members as well as to limit entry to the union. Workers who successfully complete an apprenticeship earn the classification of **journeyman** and get their card from the appropriate provincial body.

In the future, there are likely to be more but shorter apprenticeship programs to prepare people for skilled jobs in changing industries. For example, auto repair

On-the-job training means that you learn a skill while actually doing a job. You may watch other people doing similar work and ask questions as you go along. But right from the start you are being productive and learning.

requires more intense training now that cars have computers and electronic advances.

Off-the-Job Training

Training is becoming more sophisticated as jobs become more sophisticated. Furthermore, training is expanding to include education (up to the Ph.D. level) and personal development (for example, time management, stress management, health education, wellness training, physical education, nutrition, and even classes in art and languages).

Some firms do such training internally and have elaborate training facilities. Other firms assign such training to outside sources. **Off-the-job training** consists of internal and external programs to develop a variety of skills and to foster personal development that occurs away from the workplace. This includes classes, lectures, conferences, films, as well as workshops, tapes, reading programs, and the like.

off-the-job training
Internal and external programs to develop a variety of skills and foster personal development away from the workplace.

Vestibule Training

Vestibule training is done in schools where employees are taught on equipment similar to that used on the job. Vestibule schools enable employees to learn proper methods and safety procedures before assuming a specific job assignment in an organization. Computer and robotic training is often completed in a vestibule school.

vestibule training
Training conducted away from the workplace where employees are given instructions on equipment similar to that used on the job.

Job Simulation

One of the faster-growing aspects of training is simulation exercises. **Job simulation** is the use of equipment that duplicates job conditions and tasks so that trainees can learn skills before attempting them on the job. This is the kind of training given astronauts, airline pilots, army tank operators, ship captains, and others who must learn highly skilled jobs off the job. Astronauts, for example, must learn to work, eat, sleep, wash, and live in an environment of weightlessness. Simulation training

job simulation
The use of equipment that duplicates job conditions and tasks so that trainees can learn skills before attempting them on the job.

This is the inside of a flight simulator. It simulates the sights, sounds, and feel of actually flying a plane. Naturally, it's a lot safer to learn to fly in a simulator than in a real plane. Modern simulators can create storms and other hazards to give you flight experience in all kinds of situations. They are extremely realistic. Canadian Aviation Electronics is a leading producer of such simulators.

sometimes takes place underwater (to simulate weightlessness) and in a variety of laboratories that can artificially create real-life experiences.

Imagine the benefits of simulating the landing of an airplane in a major storm for the first time or docking a huge ocean liner in a small port facility. Such tasks are better learned in a simulator, where many variables can be programmed to give people practical experience in a laboratory setting.

Computers can simulate the sounds, sights, smells, and emotions of the most trying circumstances (for example, fighting another jet plane in aerial combat). Given such capability, it is easy to simulate other skills, such as managing the operating room of a nuclear power plant or operating new equipment of any kind.

The damage caused by the Exxon *Valdez* oil tanker off Alaska shows how important such training is. A Very Large Crude Carrier (VLCC) like the *Valdez*, takes 6 miles to stop when running at 15 knots. By reversing the engines, you can cut the stopping distance to "only" two miles. At any of the half dozen training institutions in Canada, trainees learn how to pilot such ships on a simulator that resembles a giant video game. You can imagine piloting a ship as long as the C. N. Tower in Toronto is high, through a narrow passage, with boats all around you. Any accident can cause serious environmental damage. You don't want to learn such skills on the job in a trial-and-error fashion!

APPRAISING EMPLOYEE PERFORMANCE

performance appraisal
An evaluation of the performance level of employees against standards to make decisions about promotions, compensation, additional training, or firing.

All managers must supervise employees. (Remember, that is one definition of management—getting work done through others.) They must be able to determine whether or not their workers are doing an effective and efficient job with a minimum of errors and disruptions. Such a determination is called a performance appraisal. A **performance appraisal** is an evaluation of the performance level of employees against established standards to make decisions about promotions, compensation, additional training, or firing. Performance appraisals consist of these six steps:

1. DON'T attack the employee personally. Critically evaluate his or her work.
2. DO allow sufficient time, without distractions (take the phone off the hook or close the office door) for appraisals.
3. DON'T make the employee feel uncomfortable or uneasy. *Never* conduct an appraisal where other employees are present (such as on the shop floor).
4. DO include the employee in the process as much as possible. (Let the employee prepare a self-improvement program.)
5. DON'T wait until the appraisal to raise problems about the employee's work that have been developing for some time.
6. DO end the appraisal with positive suggestions for employee improvement.

Figure 15–6 Making appraisals and reviews more effective

Source: Leon C. Megginson, *Personnel Management,* Homewood, IL: Richard D. Irwin, 1985, p. 434.

1. *Establishing performance standards.* This is a crucial step. Standards must be understandable, measurable, and reasonable.

2. *Communicating those standards.* Often, managers assume that employees know what is expected of them, but such assumptions are dangerous. Employees must be told clearly and precisely what the standards and expectations are and how they are to be met.

3. *Evaluating performance.* If the first two steps are done correctly, performance evaluation is relatively easy. It is a matter of evaluating the employee's performance to see if it matches standards.

4. *Discussing results with employees.* Most people will make mistakes and fail to meet expectations at first. It takes time to learn a new job and do it well. Discussing an employee's successes and areas that need improvement is an opportunity to be understanding and helpful and to guide the employee to better performance. The performance appraisal can also be a good source of employee suggestions on how a particular task could be better performed. Employees often know their jobs better than anyone else. It's important for the manager to remember that employees are not always to blame when standards are not met. An astute supervisor will learn that top management asks four questions when employees don't do well: (1) Who hired them? (2) Who trained them? (3) Who motivates them? (4) Who should be fired if they fail? The answers make it pretty clear that supervisors are responsible for their employees' performance.

5. *Taking corrective action.* The performance appraisal is an appropriate time for a manager to take corrective action or provide corrective feedback to help the employee perform his or her job better. Remember, the key word is *performance.* The primary purpose of conducting a performance appraisal is to increase employee performance, if possible. Sometimes standards are unrealistic and must be revised.

6. *Using the results to make decisions.* Decisions about promotions, compensation, additional training, or firing are all based on performance evaluations. An effective performance appraisal system is a way of satisfying certain legal conditions concerning promotions, compensation, and firing policies.

The measure of any employee's work is results. Were the objectives met or not? Management means getting results, and a key ingredient is top performance by employees. Figure 15–6 illustrates do's and don'ts for the manager in communicating with employees in order to make performance appraisal more useful.

This list must be understood in relation to the trend towards teamwork, quality circles, employee empowerment, and participative management. Managers must see that employees are involved and concerned with objectives from the beginning. The essence of self-managed teamwork is the team's responsibility for its work and results. It engages in self-criticism and review to improve its effectiveness. This requires a Theory Y management style, not Theory X (see Chapter 14).

PROGRESS CHECK

- Can you name and describe four training techniques?
- Why is employee orientation important? Did your university or college do a good job of orientating you to student life?
- What is the primary purpose of a performance appraisal?
- How does performance appraisal fit with self-managed teams?

COMPENSATING EMPLOYEES

Employee compensation is one of the largest operating costs for many organizations. The long-term success of a firm—perhaps even its survival—may depend on how well it can control employee costs and optimize employee efficiency. For example, service organizations such as hospitals, airlines, and banks have recently struggled with managing high employee costs. This is not unusual since these firms are considered *labour intensive;* that is, their primary cost of operations is the cost of labour. Firms in the airline, auto, and steel industry have asked employees to take reductions in wages to make the organizations more competitive. The alternative is to risk going out of business and losing jobs forever. In other words, the competitive environment of the 1990s is such that compensation and benefit packages are being given special attention and are likely to remain of major concern in the near future. (See Figure 15–7.)

A carefully managed compensation and benefit program can accomplish several objectives. They include:

Figure 15–7 Common compensation methods. Talk to someone who gets paid in each of the ways described. You will learn how quickly the money can accumulate when you receive overtime. Ask about the pressure of piecework versus the added potential for earnings. Each compensation plan has its benefits and drawbacks. See if you can learn what they are.

Payment Method	Description
Straight salary	Weekly, monthly, or annual amount
Hourly wages	Number of hours worked times agreed-on hourly wage
Commission system	Sales times some fixed percentage
Salary plus commission	Base salary (weekly, monthly, or annual) plus sales times some fixed percentage
Piecework	Number of items produced times some agreed-on rate per unit
	Added Compensation
Overtime	Number of hours worked beyond standard (for example, 40 hours) times hourly wages, time and a half or double time for weekends, after hours, and holidays
Bonuses	Extra pay for meeting or exceeding objectives
Profit sharing	Additional compensation based on company profits
Cost-of-living allowances (COLAs)	Annual increases in wages based on Consumer Price Index increases

- Attracting the kind of people needed by the organization in sufficient numbers.
- Providing employees with the incentive to work efficiently and productively.
- Keeping valued employees from going to competitors or starting competing firms.
- Maintaining a competitive position in the marketplace by keeping costs low through high productivity.
- Protecting employees from unexpected problems such as layoffs, sickness, and disability.
- Assuring employees of funds to carry them through retirement.

Compensation for Women

For many years statistics have shown that Canadian women earn less than men do. As more women obtain university degrees, the salary differential in professional and executive categories is decreasing. However, for the past decade there has been little progress in the huge gap between the earnings of the average woman and the average man. Women have remained stuck at about 65 percent of men's earnings.

In July 1993 the *Toronto Star* carried a report from an annual United Nations study which showed that "Canadian women make 63 percent of the wages of Canadian men." Reporter Debra Black quotes Ms. Menon, the policy analyst in the human development report office of the UN: "In Japan it's 51 percent. In no industrial country is it 90 percent or above. Sweden has the best record with 89 percent." Menon adds that the report's conclusion is, "Canadian women are still getting short shrift when it comes to politics and wages. Women in Canada just aren't treated the same as men." She notes, "Canada has done a lot in terms of literacy and education, but not enough has been done in terms of employment wages. . . ."[5] There are many historical reasons for this large wage gap. The traditional *women's* jobs—teacher, nurse, secretary—have always paid poorly. But there is much evidence of outright salary discrimination in other types of jobs.

As noted in Chapter 1, there are now laws banning such discrimination. Pay equity legislation is beginning to make its way through the provinces and has passed federal hurdles. This requires equal pay for work of comparable value, which requires defining *comparable*. For example, which job is more important, nurse or trash collector? HRM departments are alert to this problem and for new job hires most firms are practicing equality of pay for women and men.

Pay Systems

Like other aspects of HRM, pay systems have undergone an evolutionary development. When work was done at home or in small factories, individuals were paid by piecework—so much for each unit produced. When production became more complex and large numbers of employees worked in big factories where the processes involved joint efforts, piecework was replaced by hourly or daily wages.

Today piecework is prevalent only in low-wage countries or industries. In Canada and all modern industrial countries, this method of compensation has been replaced by a whole range of methods in conformity with a better understanding of employee motivation (as discussed in Chapter 14), the realities of modern production, competitive standards, and modern social attitudes. With the overwhelming numbers of Canadians employed in the service sector, hourly and salary remuneration has

SPOTLIGHT ON BIG BUSINESS

Why Are These Employees Smiling?

They're smiling because they work for the Great-West Life Assurance Co., a major player in the insurance business in North America. Its life insurance business in force is getting on to $150 billion and its annuity funds are over $12 billion. It has offices in all Canadian provinces and American states. Its Canadian work force is 4,000 people. In June 1989, an outside consultant polled the employees about how they liked working for the company. In every category, the company got an approval rating of 90 percent plus. Why are workers so satisfied?

The company has an unusual array of benefits. Besides the typical ones, it offers such things as insulin supply coverage for diabetics up to $700 annually plus a one-time $350 allowance for equipment. It offers mortgages at 80 percent of current rates and contributes $1 for each $3 a worker saves in an employee savings plan. Workers can also buy life insurance free of commission charges.

Employees take time out to take work-related courses and the company pays the cost of tuition plus up to $500 for successful graduates. There is a 20,000-volume library and a beautiful art collection, as well as large comfortable lounges, a fitness club, a 240-seat theatre, and a bank on the premises. Postage stamps and bus passes are also available.

If you are concerned about your health, a staff nurse will check your blood pressure or give you an eye examination. You can get free financial and personal counselling. In 1987 the Canadian Mental Health Association honoured the company with a Work and Well-Being Award for its impressive integrated programs, services, and policies designed to look after employees' health and other needs as well as providing satisfying work and workplaces.

In addition to all of this, the company has good pay levels, promotion opportunities, and job security. Wouldn't you smile if you worked for such a company?

Source: E. Innes, J. Lyons, and J. Harris, *The Financial Post 100 Best Companies To Work for in Canada,* Toronto: HarperCollins, 1990, pp. 57–60.

become the norm. Commissions are the only payment method that are in effect piecework. (See Figure 15–7.)

Employee Benefits

employee benefits
Sick leave pay, vacation pay, pension plans, health plans, and other benefits that provide additional compensation to employees beyond the basic wage.

Employee benefits include sick leave pay, vacation pay, pension plans, and health plans that provide additional compensation to employees. They may be divided into three categories. One group derives from federal or provincial legislation (which varies somewhat from province to province) and requires compulsory deductions from employees' paychecks and/or employer contributions. These include the Canada/Quebec pension plan, unemployment insurance, Medicare, and workers' compensation. You have probably seen some of these deductions from your pay. The second group consists of legally required benefits, including vacation pay, holiday pay, time and a half or double time for overtime, and unpaid maternity leave with job protection.

All other benefits stem from voluntary employer programs or from employer–union contracts. Some are paid by the employer alone and others are jointly paid by employer and employee. Among the most common are bonuses, company pension plans, group insurance, sick leave, termination pay, and paid rest periods.

The list of fringe benefits is so long and has become so significant—around 35 percent of regular pay—that the term *fringe* is being replaced by *employee* benefits. Nowadays, labour negotiations are more likely to concern employee benefits than wage rates. They are no longer at the fringe of employee income. The example of the Great-West Life Assurance Co. illustrates this well.

For executives and more highly paid managers, the benefits package is more important than additional remuneration. They are already in a high tax bracket and

Employee benefits include vacation time. Cafeteria plans let you choose among benefits. You could choose more vacation time, a better group insurance program, child care, dental care, or other options. You could choose the mix of options that best meets your needs.

any additional direct income would be taxed at 50 percent or higher, so increases in such non-taxable benefits as dental and health insurance, company contributions to pension plans, and stock options are very attractive.

Employee benefits can also include everything from paid vacations to group insurance plans, recreation facilities, company cars, country club memberships, day care services and executive dining rooms. Managing the benefits package is a major HRM issue. Employees want packages to include dental care, legal counselling, maternity leave, and more. (Some types of benefits are recognized as taxable by Revenue Canada.)

To counter these growing demands, many firms are offering **cafeteria-style benefits** from which employees can choose the type of benefits they want up to a certain dollar amount. *Choice* is the key to flexible cafeteria-style benefit plans. Employees' needs are more and more varied. Managers can equitably and cost-effectively meet these individual needs by providing benefit choices. For example, older employees might be more interested in good pension plans and holidays while younger employees might concentrate on child care, maternity or paternity leave, or an education package.

cafeteria-style benefits
Benefit plans that allow employees to choose which benefits they want up to a certain dollar amount.

SCHEDULING EMPLOYEES

By now, you are quite familiar with the trends occurring in the work force. You know, for example, that many more women are working now. You also know that managers and workers are demanding more from jobs in the way of flexibility and responsiveness. From these trends have emerged several new or renewed ideas such as job sharing, flextime, compressed work weeks, and in-home employment. Let's see how these innovations affect managing human resources.

Job-Sharing Plans

Job sharing is an arrangement whereby two part-time employees share one full-time job. The concept received great attention in the 1980s as more and more

job sharing
An arrangement whereby two part-time employees share one full-time job.

women with small children entered the labour force. Job sharing enabled mothers and fathers to work part-time while the children were in school and be home when the children came home. Job sharing has also proved beneficial to students, older people who want to work part-time before fully retiring, and others who can work only part-time.

- Job sharing offers employment opportunities to people who cannot or prefer not to work full-time.
- An employee is more likely to maintain a high level of enthusiasm and productivity for four hours than for eight hours, so two part-time employees are often much more productive than one full-time employee.
- Problems such as absenteeism and tardiness are greatly reduced with part-time employees. Part-time people are usually better able to handle other duties or problems in their off hours.
- Employers are better able to schedule people into peak demand periods (for example, banks on payday) when part-time people are available.

REACHING BEYOND OUR BORDERS

Social Benefits, Motivation, and the Free Trade Agreement

Ever since the Free Trade Agreement between Canada and the United States was signed in 1988, various business leaders have been suggesting that the "high" costs of Canada's social benefits are hindering the ability of our companies to compete with American companies. The Business Council on National Issues (BCNI), which represents the very largest companies in Canada, the Canadian Manufacturers Association (CMA), the Canadian Federation of Independent Businesses (CFIB), and individual businesspeople have made such comments. They point out that such costs are lower in the U.S., which weakens the competitiveness of Canadian companies.

When the FTA was being fiercely debated before the 1988 election, these same organizations and other groups who supported the FTA (including former Prime Minister Brian Mulroney) repeatedly assured Canadians that the agreement would pose no threat to our social safety net and our social programs. Now we see them claiming that Canada cannot afford such programs and still remain competitive.

In early 1992, the federal government announced that it was not going ahead with its oft-promised national child-care scheme. The program has been a major demand of a large number of working parents who cannot afford the high cost of private arrangements. Ottawa also abolished family allowances in 1993 and unemployment insurance benefits were reduced. Our Medicare system is also under considerable attack as being too expensive. So once again the question of social benefits is on the agenda, especially as Mexico is being brought into the North American Free Trade Agreement (NAFTA).

We have seen how important a highly motivated work force is in boosting productivity, thus reducing costs and making businesses more competitive. Successful companies consider expenditures on employee benefits a very good investment. Far-seeing, progressive companies realize that well-motivated employees more than pay for the costs of keeping them motivated. The evidence is very clear on this point. (See Profile and Spotlight on Big Business).

A working parent who has no anxiety about whether his or her children are being well looked after in affordable child-care facilities is a better-functioning employee. Similarly, knowing that the health of your family is looked after by our national Medicare system boosts morale and therefore productivity. It seems very shortsighted to think only about immediate dollar outlay rather than about the long-term benefits to companies of having a less worried work force.

North American executives are often faulted for having a short-term outlook. This is in contrast to companies and governments from the Pacific Rim and Europe who are top international competitors because they have a long-term focus.

We have quoted various commentators who say we have to learn to work smart, not cheap and point out that Germany, one of the most competitive countries in the world, has better social benefits than we have. That also applies to Scandinavian countries. In Japan, large companies provide a very extensive network of benefits to their employees. Which path will we follow? ▼

However, as you might suspect, disadvantages include having to hire, train, motivate, and supervise twice as many people and to prorate some employee benefits. Nonetheless, most firms that were at first reluctant to try job sharing are finding the benefits outweigh the disadvantages.

Flextime Plans

Flextime plans give employees some freedom to adjust when they work, as long as they work the required number of hours. The most popular plans allow employees to come to work at 7, 8, or 9 A.M. and leave between 4 and 6 P.M. (see Fig. 15–8). Usually flextime plans incorporate **core time,** particular hours of the day when all employees are expected to be at their job stations. For example, an organization may designate core time hours between 10:00 A.M. and noon and 2:00 P.M. and 4:00 P.M. During these hours, *all* employees are required to be there. Flextime plans, like job-sharing plans, are designed to allow employees to adjust to the new demands of the times, especially the trend towards two-income families. Flextime has been found to boost employee productivity and morale. Specific advantages of flextime include:

flextime plans
Work schedule that gives employees some freedom to adjust when they work, within limits, as long as they work the required number of hours.

core time
The period when all employees must be present in a flextime system.

- Working parents can schedule their days so that one partner can be home to see the children off to school and the other partner can be home soon after school.
- Employees can schedule doctor's appointments and other personal tasks during working hours by coming in early and leaving early or by coming in late and leaving late.
- Traffic congestion is greatly reduced as employees arrive and leave over several hours instead of all at once.
- Employees can work when they are most productive; some people are most alert early in the morning, while others can't get going until 9 A.M.
- Having some choice about sleeping late once in a while or taking off early on Friday afternoon in the spring gives a person a big psychological boost.

There are some real disadvantages to flextime as well. It does not work in assembly line processes where everyone must be at work at the same time. Nor is it effective for shift work.

Figure 15–8 A flextime chart. Employees can start any time between 6:30 and 9:30. They then take half an hour for lunch and can quit from 3:00 to 6:30. Everyone works an 8-hour day. The red arrows show a typical flextime day.

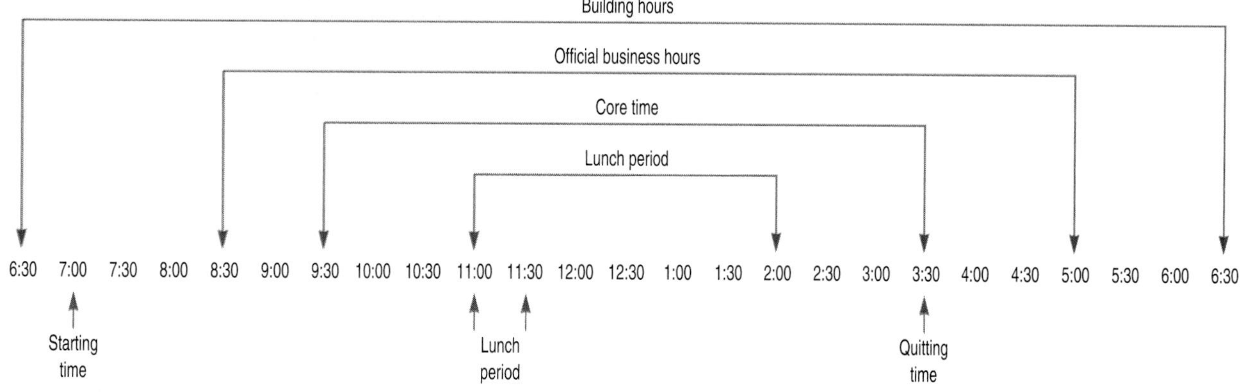

Another disadvantage to flextime is that managers often have to work longer days to be there to assist and supervise employees. Some organizations operate from 6 A.M. to 6 P.M. under flextime, a potentially long day for supervisors. Flextime also makes communication more difficult; certain employees may not be there when others need to talk to them. Furthermore, some employees could abuse the system, if not carefully supervised, and that could cause resentment among others.

In spite of the difficulties, flextime has become quite popular. It has obvious advantages for creative people who are most productive at certain times of the day. But it also is helpful for anyone who likes the flexibility of sleeping late once in a while or working long hours when a proposal is due.

Compressed Work Weeks

compressed work week
Work schedule made up of four 10-hour days.

Another popular option in some organizations is a **compressed work week.** That means that an employee works four 10-hour days and then enjoys a three-day weekend, instead of working five 8-hour days with a traditional weekend. There are the obvious advantages of working only four days and having three days off, but some employees get tired working such long hours, and productivity could decline. Many employees find such a system of great benefit, however, and are quite enthusiastic about it.

The Royal Bank is one large Canadian company that is paying careful attention to the needs of its employees. The work and family program of its human resource planning and development department consists of an elaborate series of services covering a wide range of issues. Each service is explained in an attractive brochure titled "Quality People." Services include eldercare information, child care information, and access to the employee and family assistance program. There are libraries in Montreal and Toronto where employees can access magazines, articles, books, and videotapes.

There are also three detailed brochures concerning flexible work arrangements: part-time/job sharing, flextime and compressed work week, and flexiplace. Manager Norma Tombari says flexible working arrangements are becoming increasingly popular.

Working at Home

Until the late 1700s, there were no factories or plants as we know them today. People who sewed or knitted or wove or did a variety of other jobs did them at home. This still survives in many countries, including Canada. Go into any large city and you will find contractors or subcontractors who farm out work. Usually the workers are women, recent immigrants who have no other skills, who do not speak English or French, or who have small children. They are paid by piecework.

In the last decade a new phenomenon has arisen—a modern homeworker of a totally different type. Typically he or she has a computer and other electronic communication equipment and may be self-employed or employed by a large company. When these workers are employees they are paid like other employees, but they can perform their duties at home, thus reducing many costs as well as travelling time. They save on eating out, extra clothing, commuting costs, and so on. Employers also cut costs by needing less office space and furniture and having more motivated employees.

As mentioned in the first chapter, working at home is expected to become a major aspect of life in the 1990s and beyond. How does this affect the responsibility of HRM? The solutions are now being discussed as HRM strives to cope with this new factor.

THINKING IT THROUGH

What effect have dual-career families had on the human resource function? Have you noticed any changes in nepotism rules with so many marriages involving two professionals? (*Nepotism* means favouring relatives when hiring.) What problems can arise when family members work together in the same firm? What is your reaction to employees who date one another? Are such questions interesting enough to make you think about becoming a human resource manager?

DEVELOPING MANAGERS

In the past, employees were eager to become managers and were quite willing to make sacrifices for that honour. For example, people were willing to relocate often. (There was once a joke that *IBM* meant "I've been moved.") People were also willing to work longer hours, take on additional responsibilities, and "do what it takes" to move up the corporate ladder.

Things are different today. Moving is not only costly but affects the employee's children, friendships, community ties, and more. These disruptions have become less acceptable today. Furthermore, with the growing number of dual-income families, it's difficult to convince husbands or wives to give up their careers to follow the other partner. It's safe to conclude that management responsibilities are stressful and tiring and affect family life. For these reasons and more, it is becoming more difficult to find and keep good managers. Those who are willing to be managers must be trained to assume an entirely different role: counsellor, adviser, trainer, educator, coach, and assistant. As we have noted, managers are no longer mere bosses or rule makers and enforcers.

Managers need different training from most employees. They need to be good communicators and especially need to learn listening skills and empathy. They also need time management, planning, and human relations skills.

Management development is the process of training and educating employees to become good managers and then developing managerial skills over time. Management development programs have sprung up everywhere, especially at colleges, universities, and private management development firms. Managers participate in role-playing exercises, solve various management cases, and are exposed to films, lectures, and all kinds of management development processes.

management development
The process of training and educating employees to become good managers and then developing managerial skills over time.

In some organizations, managers are paid to take university-level courses through the doctoral level. Most management training programs also include several of the following features.

On-the-job coaching. A senior manager assists a lower-level manager by teaching him or her needed skills and generally providing direction, advice, and helpful criticism. On-the-job coaching is effective only when the senior managers are skilled themselves and have the ability to educate others. This is not always the case.

Understudy positions. Job titles such as "undersecretary of" and "assistant to" reveal a relatively successful way of developing managers. They work as assistants to higher-level managers and participate in planning and other managerial functions

Management development classes help managers in all phases of their jobs. They include courses on time management, stress management, employee relations, supervision, and many other subjects. The idea is to keep managers up to date and effective on the job.

until they are ready to assume such positions themselves. Such assistants may take over when higher-level managers are on vacation or on business trips.

Job rotation. To expose managers to different functions of the organization, they are often given assignments in a variety of departments. Top managers, and potential top managers, of course, must have a broad picture of the organization; such rotation gives them that exposure.

Off-the-job courses and training. Managers periodically go to schools or seminars for a week or more to hone their technical and human relations skills. Such courses expose them to the latest concepts and create a sense of camaraderie as the managers live, eat, and work together in a college-type atmosphere. This is often where case studies and simulation exercises of all kinds are employed.

The Importance of Networking

Over time, male managers have developed what has been called an old boy network through which certain senior managers become mentors to certain junior managers. They introduce them to the important managers, enroll them in the "right" clubs, and guide them into the "right" social groups. Young managers are thus socialized regarding proper dress, behaviour, and procedures to follow to rise up the corporate hierarchy.

networking
Establishing and maintaining contacts with key managers in one's own and other organizations and using those contacts to weave strong relationships that serve as informal development systems.

mentors
Experienced employees who supervise, coach, and guide lower-level employees by introducing them to the right people and groups and generally act as their organizational sponsors.

Networking is the process of establishing and maintaining contacts with key managers in one's own organization and in other organizations and using those contacts to weave strong relationships that serve as informal development systems. Of equal or greater importance to potential managers are **mentors,** corporate managers who supervise, coach, and guide selected lower-level employees by introducing them to the right people and groups and generally act as their organizational sponsors. An informal type of mentoring goes on in most organizations on a regular basis as older employees assist younger workers. However, many organizations such as Federal Express use a formal system of assigning mentors to employees considered to have strong potential.

As women moved into management, they also learned the importance and value of networking and having mentors. But since most older managers are male,

Networking can take place anywhere—on the golf course, in restaurants, and at people's homes. Men have long had networks. Women are now developing similar networks where relationships are established, job information is exchanged, and people learn how to move up the corporate ladder.

women often have more difficulty attracting mentors and entering the network. A series of court rulings has made men-only clubs illegal in Canada, so women are now entering these formerly male preserves and making all the usual business contacts. More and more, women are entering the system or, in some instances, creating their own networking systems.[6]

It's important to remember that networking can go beyond the business environment. For example, your university or college experience is a perfect environment to begin your networking. Associations you nurture with professors, local businesspeople, and especially your classmates can provide you with a valuable network through which you can develop for the rest of your career. Ties with university or college classmates have always been widely used in business and government. People also network with fellow members of country clubs, yacht clubs, health clubs, charitable and social organizations, and so on.

PROGRESS CHECK

- Can you name and describe five alternative compensation techniques?
- Can you list five important employee benefits?
- Why is flextime useful?
- Define the terms *networking* and *mentors*.

TERMINATING EMPLOYMENT

Employment is normally terminated in one of three ways: retirement, resignation, or firing (or layoff). HRM is always involved, since it is responsible "from cradle to grave" for all employees. The better companies help employees prepare for retirement in various ways. They range from seminars on how to plan your financial affairs as income drops and how to develop activities to keep you occupied, to a gradual reduction in working hours so you can adjust more easily to being retired.

Voluntary Departure

When an employee leaves as a normal departure, there is no problem. However, if someone leaves because of perceived discrimination—whether because of age, nationality, sex, colour, or race—then it is a different story. Similarly, if a woman leaves because she feels sexually harassed, the situation is quite different from a person quitting to get a better job or to go back to school. HRM must be alert to any signs or complaints of discrimination or sexual harassment. Not only are these undesirable practices, indicating some potentially serious problems, but they are also illegal.

Laying Off Employees

The issue of layoffs has become very important because of the large number of people let go in the early 1990s. Many companies counsel these employees to enable them to better cope with their loss of job and to help them find new jobs. Some set up in-house outplacement facilities so that employees can get counselling on obtaining a new job. For senior managers, the company usually pays for private agency career counselling.

The threat of job loss has introduced a strong feeling of insecurity into the Canadian work force. Insecurity undermines motivation, so HRM must deal with this new issue. Keeping employees fully informed and having a clear policy on termination pay helps to remove some uncertainty.[7]

LAWS AFFECTING HUMAN RESOURCE MANAGEMENT

Canada has many laws affecting nearly all aspects of human resource management. We have referred to these laws earlier in this chapter, but now we'll take a closer look.

Because Canada is a confederation of provinces, jurisdiction over many aspects of our lives is divided between the federal and provincial governments. The federal government legislates on national issues, such as unemployment insurance and pensions, while the provinces have jurisdiction over most matters, including minimum wages, hours of work, workers' compensation, and discrimination in the workplace.

But it's a little more complicated than that. The federal government also has jurisdiction over certain types of businesses that are deemed to be of a national nature. Banks, insurance companies, airlines, railways, shipping companies, telephone, radio, TV, cable companies, and others are subject to federal law, as are all federal employees. The national Charter of Rights and Freedoms, which is part of the Canadian constitution, overrides all other laws. The federal government had to amend the Unemployment Insurance Act because the Supreme Court had ruled that the act went against the charter in denying coverage to employees over age 64.

What all this means is that there are literally hundreds of laws and regulations, federal and provincial, that apply to all aspects of human resource management. Furthermore, they are constantly being revised because of social pressure or rulings by human rights commissions or courts. One of the most regulated areas involves discrimination.

Laws in all jurisdictions in Canada make it illegal to discriminate against employees because of age, sex, nationality, colour, religion, or marital status. Only the Yukon fails to ban discrimination due to physical handicap or disability; Saskatchewan, Alberta, and the Yukon do not ban discrimination in the case of mental handicap or disability. On the other hand, only Quebec and Ontario forbid discrimination against lesbians and homosexuals. There are some other forms of discrimination that are banned in some provinces or under federal law.

When an employer selects, hires, trains, pays, promotes, transfers, retires, or fires an employee, HRM must ensure that what is being done and how it is being done do not infringe any laws. HRM must also make sure health and safety laws are obeyed. So you can see how important the job of HRM is. Managers working in this area must be very sensitive not only to legal requirements but also to union contracts, social standards, and expectations (which may be even more demanding).

Affirmative Action

A well-known 1980s case of discrimination highlights a major problem and how it was solved. A group of women accused the CNR of not hiring them because they were women. The CNR, like many other companies, did not hire women for traditionally men's jobs, where heavy physical labour was required. In this case, the jobs involved maintenance and repairs of the tracks. The Canadian Human Rights Commission ruled in favour of the women. The CNR appealed and the courts ruled against it all the way to the Supreme Court of Canada. There the CNR was told that it had to adopt an **affirmative action** plan to ensure that women would gradually form a significant part of the maintenance crews.

affirmative action
Employment activities designed to "right past wrongs" endured by females and minorities by giving them preference in employment.

Affirmative action refers to employment activities designed to "right past wrongs" endured by females and minorities by giving them preference in employment. This means that CNR had to develop a plan that would result in more women than men being hired for such jobs until the balance would be more even. The result is that where a man and a woman are equally qualified the woman must be given preference for a number of years to allow the balance to be adjusted over time.

Some people argue that affirmative action is really a form of reverse discrimination. **Reverse discrimination** refers to the unfairness unprotected groups (say, white men) may perceive when protected groups receive preference in hiring and promoting. The Canadian Charter of Rights specifically allows for affirmative action as a method to overcome long-standing discrimination against groups. Therefore the courts accept it as being non-discriminatory in the legal sense.

reverse discrimination
The unfairness unprotected groups may perceive when protected groups receive preference in hiring and promoting.

PROGRESS CHECK

- ▼ Can you name five areas of HRM responsibility affected by government legislation?
- ▼ Explain what affirmative action is and give one example.
- ▼ Why should HRM be concerned about legislation or court rulings when terminating employment?

SUMMARY

1. Explain the importance of human resource management and describe current issues in managing human resources.

1. *Human resource management* is the process of evaluating human resource needs, finding people to fill those needs, and optimizing this important resource by providing the right incentives and job environment, all with the goal of meeting organizational objectives.

▼ *What are some of the current problems in the human resource area?*

Many current problems revolve around the changing demographics of workers: more women, minorities, immigrants, and older workers. Other problems concern a shortage of trained workers and an abundance of unskilled ones; skilled workers in declining industries requiring retraining; changing employee work attitudes; and complex laws and regulations.

2. Like all types of management, human resource management begins with planning.

2. Summarize the six steps in planning human resources.

▼ *What are the steps in human resource planning?*

The six steps are (1) forecasting future human resource needs; (2) inventorying human resources; (3) preparing job analyses; (4) assessing future demands; (5) assessing future supply; (6) establishing a plan for recruiting, hiring, educating, and developing employees.

3. *Recruitment* is the set of activities used to legally obtain enough of the right people at the right time and to select those that best meet the needs of the organization.

3. Describe methods companies use to recruit new employees and explain some of the problems that make recruitment difficult.

▼ *Why has recruitment become more difficult?*

Legal restrictions complicate hiring and firing practices. Finding suitable employees can also be difficult if companies are considered unattractive workplaces. Also, it is increasingly difficult to find candidates with the higher educational and technical levels needed now.

4. *Selection* is the process of gathering information to decide who should be hired.

4. Outline the six steps in selecting employees.

▼ *What are the six steps in the selection process?*

The steps are (1) obtaining complete application forms; (2) conducting initial and follow-up interviews; (3) giving employment tests; (4) conducting background investigations; (5) giving physical exams; and (6) conducting a trial period of employment.

5. Employee *training and development* includes all attempts to increase an employee's ability to perform through learning.

5. Describe the various types of employee training methods.

▼ *What are some of the procedures used for training?*

They include employee orientation, on- and off-the-job training, apprentice programs, vestibule training, and job simulation.

6. A *performance appraisal* is an evaluation of the performance level of employees against established standards to make decisions about promotions, compensation, additional training, or firing.

6. Trace the six steps in appraising employee performance.

▼ *How does one evaluate performance?*

(1) Establish performance standards; (2) communicate those standards; (3) evaluate performance; (4) discuss results; (5) take corrective action when needed; and (6) use the results for decisions about promotions, compensation, additional training, or firing.

7. Employee *compensation* is one of the largest operating costs for many organizations.

7. Summarize the objectives of employee compensation programs and describe various pay systems and benefits.

▼ *What compensation systems are used?*

They include salary systems, hourly wages, piecework, commission plans, bonus plans, and profit sharing plans.

▼ *What are employee benefits?*

Benefits include sick leave, vacation pay, pension plans, health plans and other services that provide additional compensation to employees.

8. Workers' increasing need for flexibility has generated innovations in *scheduling* workers.

8. Explain scheduling plans managers use to adjust to workers' needs.

▼ *What scheduling plans can be used to adjust to employees' needs for flexibility?*

Such plans include job sharing, flextime, compressed work weeks, and working at home.

9. *Management development* is the process of developing managerial skills over time.

9. Describe training methods used in management development programs.

▼ *What methods are used to develop managerial skills?*

Management development methods include on-the-job coaching, understudy positions, job rotation, and off-the-job courses and training.

▼ *How does networking fit into this process?*

Networking is establishing contacts with key managers within and outside the organization to get additional development assistance.

▼ *What are mentors?*

Mentors are experienced staff members who coach and guide selected lower-level people and act as their organizational sponsors.

10. There are many *laws* that affect human resource planning.

▼ *What areas do these laws cover?*

All areas are affected because of laws prohibiting discriminatory practices, setting standards such as minimum wages, and regulating health and safety conditions, hours of work, holiday and vacation pay, retirement and firing, pensions, and unemployment insurance.

10. Illustrate the effects of legislation on human resource management.

GETTING INVOLVED

1. Visit the HRM offices of your university or college and of several businesses. Talk with employees and several managers. What do they do all day? Do they enjoy the work? How did it appear to you? Share your impressions with others in the class.
2. Read the current business periodicals to find the latest court rulings on issues such as pay equity, affirmative action, unjustified firing, discrimination, and other HRM issues. What seems to be the trend? What will this mean for tomorrow's graduates?
3. Recall the various training programs you have experienced including both on-the-job and off-the-job training. What is your evaluation of such programs? How would you improve them? Share your ideas with the class.
4. Look up the unemployment figures for individual provinces. Notice there are pockets of very high unemployment. What causes such uneven unemployment? What can be done to retrain workers who are obsolete because of a restructured economy? Is that the role of government or of business? Discuss. Could government and business co-operate in this function?
5. Find several people who work under flextime or part-time systems. Ask them their reactions. Share your findings with the class.

PRACTICING MANAGEMENT DECISIONS

Case One The Dangers of Firing an Employee

If someone is fired, HRM must be certain the employee's legal and union (if there is one) rights are not abrogated and relevant federal and provincial laws are followed. The history of employer–employee relations has been one of movement from the absolute right of the employer to do as it wishes to important protections for employee rights. One area of protection relates to termination of employment.

Claire Bernstein, a Montreal lawyer and syndicated columnist, has written a number of columns about this issue. She cites a case of an Alberta employer who fired an employee for refusing to work on Easter Monday. Mondays were the busiest day in his company and all employees knew they had to work that day. The employee took the owner to court and the case went all the way to the Supreme Court, which ruled in his favour. The court agreed with his contention that his religious rights had been violated since his religion forbade him from working on Easter Monday.

Other cases concern workers fired without notice and without cause. For a longtime employee, even a year's pay has been held insufficient. Courts have awarded increased amounts as well as punitive damages for "brutal and callous firing," meaning without notice or cause.

Decision Questions

1. What are the implications for the HRM department of legal rulings against firing for unjust cause?
2. If you were an employer, would you put more effort into screening and training employees, given these rulings? How would this help? Who might benefit or be hurt by such changes?
3. In some cases, an arbitrator has been brought in to settle wrongful discharge cases. What are the benefits of arbitration rather than legal action? Who benefits?

Source: Claire D. Bernstein, *That's Business, But Is it Legal?*, Toronto: Methuen, 1985.

Case Two Dual-Career Planning

Carey Moler is a 32-year-old account executive for a communications company. She is married to Mitchell Moler, a lawyer. They have one child. Carey and Mitchell had not made any definite plans about how to juggle their careers and family life until Carey reached age 30. Then she decided to have a baby, and career planning took on whole new dimensions. A company named Catalyst talked to 815 dual-career couples and found most of them, like the Molers, had not made any long-range career decisions regarding family lifestyle.

From the business perspective, such dual-career families create real concerns. There are problems with relocations, child care, and other issues that affect recruiting, productivity, morale, and promotion policies.

For a couple like the Molers, having both career and family responsibilities is exhausting. But that is just one problem. If Carey is moving up in the firm, what happens if Mitchell gets a terrific job offer 1,500 miles away? What if Carey gets such an offer? Who is going to care for the baby? What happens if the baby gets ill? How do they plan their vacations when there are three schedules to balance? Who will do the housework?

Dual careers require careful planning and discussion, and those plans need to be reviewed over time. A couple who decide at age 22 to do certain things may change their minds at 30 about whether or not to have children; where to locate; and how to manage the household. All these issues and more can become major problems if not carefully planned.

The same is true for corporations. They, too, must plan for dual-career families. They must give more attention to job sharing, flextime, paternity leave, transfer policies, nepotism rules, and more.

Decision Questions

1. What are some of the issues you can see developing because of dual-career families? How is this affecting children in such families?
2. What corporate policies need changing to adapt to these new realities?
3. What can newlywed couples do to minimize the problems of dual careers? What are the advantages of dual careers? Disadvantages? How can a couple achieve the advantages with a minimum number of problems?

LET'S TALK BUSINESS

1. Do you feel there is less or more unfairness in employment practices today than before? On what do you base your opinion?
2. So many hundreds of thousands of jobs have been lost in the early 1990s in Canada that job security has become many employees' greatest worry. What can management do to raise workers' morale by removing their worries in this regard?
3. You are a senior manager in the HRM department of your company. You face a difficult decision. There are two important programs you want to launch, but you

have sufficient funds for only one. How do you choose between a child care facility and a retraining program? Both are badly needed. What should you do?

4. A husband and wife both work for the same company but in different departments. They approach HRM with a request: they want to work flexible hours so that their children can be better looked after. HRM has been discussing making a flextime program available but it is not yet ready for implementation. The couple is quite insistent as one of their children has a difficult long-term illness. What do you do? What alternatives do you have?
5. What do you think of networking? Have you done any yet? Are you planning to?

LOOKING AHEAD

Human resource management is an area that has been receiving more attention lately because of issues such as pay equity and executive pay. One major issue is the role of unions in business, both now and in the future. Chapter 16 will discuss these issues, with special attention to the history and future of unions. Anyone who gets involved with business today should understand union issues and other employee–management concerns.

Before turning to Chapter 16, we will take some time to focus on a key objective of this course—helping you progress in your career. The appendix that follows will teach you how to write a cover letter and résumé and how to prepare for job interviews.

GETTING THE JOB YOU WANT

Now that we have explored human resource management from the business side, let's look at the process from your perspective. You now know that businesses are actively searching for good employees who can produce. Similarly, you are looking for an organization where your talents will be used to the fullest and where you will enjoy working. How can you find a job that will provide the optimal satisfaction for both you and the organization? That is the goal of this appendix.

If you are older and looking for a new career, your self-assessment has probably revealed that you have handicaps and blessings that younger students do not have. First of all, you may already have a full-time job. Working while going to school is exhausting. Many older students must juggle family responsibilities in addition to the responsibilities of school and work. But take heart; you have also acquired many skills from these experiences. Even if they were acquired in unrelated fields, these skills will be invaluable as you enter your new career.

Whether you are beginning your first career or your latest career, it's time to develop a strategy for finding and obtaining a personally satisfying job.

A FIVE-STEP JOB SEARCH STRATEGY

There are many good books available that provide guidance for finding the right job. This appendix will summarize the important steps.

1. *Complete a self-analysis inventory.* A couple of such programs were discussed earlier. If you want to do an assessment on your own, see Richard Nelson Bolles, *What Color Is Your Parachute?* (Berkeley: Ten Speed Press, latest edition). See Figure 15A–1 for a sample assessment. Career Navigator is a software program that will walk you through five modules of job-seeking strategies from "Know Yourself" to "Land that Job." This program will also help you establish an interviewing strategy.
2. *Search for jobs you would enjoy.* Begin at your university or college placement office, if it has one. Keep interviewing people in various careers, even after you have found a job. Career progress demands continuous research.
3. *Begin the networking process.* Start with your family, relatives, neighbours, friends, professors, and local businesspeople. Be sure to keep a file with the names, addresses,

Figure 15A–1 A personal assessment scale

Interests

1. How do I like to spend my time?
2. Do I enjoy being with people?
3. Do I like working with mechanical things?
4. Do I enjoy working with numbers?
5. Am I a member of many organizations?
6. Do I enjoy physical activities?
7. Do I like to read?

Abilities

1. Am I adept at working with numbers?
2. Am I adept at working with mechanical things?
3. Do I have good oral and written communication skills?
4. What special talents do I have?
5. In which abilities do I wish I were more adept?

Education

1. Have I taken certain courses that have prepared me for a particular job?
2. In which subjects did I perform best? Worst?
3. Which subjects did I enjoy the most? The least?
4. How have my extracurricular activities prepared me for a particular job?
5. Is my GPA an accurate picture of my academic ability? Why or why not?
6. Do I aspire to a graduate degree? Do I want to earn it before beginning my job?
7. Why did I choose my major?

Experience

1. What previous jobs have I held? What were my responsibilities in each?
2. Were any of my jobs relevant to positions I may be seeking? How?
3. What did I like most about my previous jobs? Least?
4. Why did I work in the jobs I did?
5. If I had it to do over again, would I work in these jobs? Why?

Personality

1. What are my good and bad traits?
2. Am I competitive?
3. Do I work well with others?
4. Am I outspoken?
5. Am I a leader or a follower?
6. Do I work well under pressure?
7. Do I work quickly? Am I methodical?
8. Do I get along well with others?
9. Am I ambitious?
10. Do I work well independently of others?

Desired Job Environment

1. Am I willing to relocate? Why or why not?
2. Do I have a geographic preference? Why or why not?
3. Would I mind travelling in my job?
4. Do I have to work for a large, nationally known firm to be satisfied?
5. Must I have a job that initially offers a high salary?
6. Must the job I assume offer rapid promotion opportunities?
7. In what kind of job environment would I feel most comfortable: centralized or decentralized structure?
8. If I could design my own job, what characteristics would it have?

Personal Goals

1. What are my short- and long-term goals?
2. Am I career oriented, or do I have broader interests?
3. What are my career goals?
4. What jobs are likely to help me achieve my goals?
5. What do I hope to be doing in 5 years? In 10 years?
6. What do I want out of life?

Source: Eric N. Berkowitz, Roger A. Kerin, and William Rudelius, *Marketing,* Homewood, IL: Richard D. Irwin, 1989, p. 630.

and phone numbers of contacts, where they work, the person who recommended them to you, and the relationship between the source person and the contact.

4. *Prepare a good cover letter and résumé.* Samples are provided in this appendix.
5. *Develop interviewing skills.* We shall give you some clues as to how to do this.

The Job Search

The placement bureau at your school is a good place to begin reading about potential employers. On-campus interviewing is by far the number one source of jobs (see Figure 15A–2).

Figure 15A–2 Where university and college students find jobs. When looking for a job, be sure to check the sources. Use those sources that will guarantee your success as you begin your job search.

Source of Jobs
On-campus interviewing
Write-ins
Current employee referrals
Job listings with placement office
Responses from want ads
Walk-ins
Co-operative education programs
Summer employment
University/college faculty/staff referrals
Internship programs
High-demand major programs
Minority career programs
Part-time employment
Unsolicited referrals from placement
Women's career programs
Job listings with employment agencies
Referrals from campus organizations

Source: J. Singleton and P. Scheetz, *Recruiting Trends,* Michigan State University.

The second most important source of jobs involves sending companies a good cover letter and résumé. You can find help identifying companies to contact in your university or college library. Your library may also have annual reports that will give you even more information about your selected companies.

The third best source of jobs is networking; that is, finding someone in a firm to recommend you. You find those people by asking friends, neighbours, family, and others if they know anyone who knows someone. Then you track those people down, interview them, and seek their recommendation.

Other good sources of jobs include the placement centre, want ads, summer and internship programs, and walking into firms that appeal to you and asking for an interview.

The *Occupational Outlook Quarterly,* produced by the U.S. Department of Labour, says this about job hunting:

> The skills that make a person employable are not so much the ones needed on the job as the ones needed to *get* the job, skills like the ability to find a job opening, complete an application, prepare the résumé, and survive an interview.

Read the interview rating sheet in Figure 15A–3. Note what the recruiters want. Interviewers will be checking your appearance (clothes, haircut, fingernails, shoes), your attitude (friendliness is desired), your verbal ability, and your motivation (be enthusiastic). Speak loud enough to be heard clearly. Note also that interviewers want you to have been active in clubs and activities and to have set goals. Have someone evaluate you on these scales now to see if you have any weak points. You can then work on those points before you have any actual job interviews.

It is never too early in your career to begin designing a résumé and thinking of cover letters. Preparing such documents reveals your strengths and weaknesses more clearly than most other techniques. Your résumé lists all your education, work experience, and activities. By preparing a résumé now, you may discover that you have not been active enough in outside activities to impress an employer. That information may prompt you to join some student groups, become a volunteer, or

For each characteristic listed below there is a rating scale of 1 through 7; 1 is generally the most unfavorable rating of the characteristic and 7 the most favorable. Rate each characteristic by *circling* just *one* number to represent the impression you got in the interview you just completed.

Name of Candidate ______________________________

1. Appearance
Sloppy 1 2 3 4 5 6 7 Neat

2. Attitude
Unfriendly 1 2 3 4 5 6 7 Friendly

3. Assertiveness/Verbal Ability
a. Responded completely to questions asked
Poor 1 2 3 4 5 6 7 Excellent
b. Clarified personal background and related to job opening and description
Poor 1 2 3 4 5 6 7 Excellent
c. Able to explain and sell job abilities
Poor 1 2 3 4 5 6 7 Excellent
d. Initiated questions regarding position and firm
Poor 1 2 3 4 5 6 7 Excellent
e. Expressed thorough knowledge of personal goals and abilities
Poor 1 2 3 4 5 6 7 Excellent

4. Motivation
Poor 1 2 3 4 5 6 7 High

5. Subject/Academic Knowledge
Poor 1 2 3 4 5 6 7 Good

6. Stability
Poor 1 2 3 4 5 6 7 Good

7. Composure
Ill at Ease 1 2 3 4 5 6 7 Relaxed

8. Personal Involvement/Activities, Clubs, Etc.
Low 1 2 3 4 5 6 7 Very high

9. Mental Impression
Dull 1 2 3 4 5 6 7 Alert

10. Adaptability
Poor 1 2 3 4 5 6 7 Good

11. Speech Pronunciation
Poor 1 2 3 4 5 6 7 Good

12. Overall Impression
Unsatisfactory 1 2 3 4 5 6 7 Highly satisfactory

13. Would you hire this individual if you were permitted to make that decision right now?
Yes No

Figure 15A–3 Interview rating sheet. Some employers use an interview rating sheet like this. When you go for a job interview, put your best foot forward.

otherwise enhance your social skills. You may also discover that you are weak on experience, and seek an internship or part-time job to fill in that gap. In any event, it is not too soon to prepare a résumé. It will certainly be helpful in deciding what you would like to see in the area marked "education" and help you to choose a major and other coursework. Let's discuss how to prepare these materials.

Writing a Résumé

A *résumé* is a document that lists all the information a potential employer needs to evaluate you and your background. It describes your immediate goals and career objectives. This information is followed by an explanation of your educational background, experience, interests, and other relevant data.

If you have exceptional abilities but you do not communicate them to the employer on the résumé, those abilities are not part of the person he or she will evaluate. You must be comprehensive and clear in your résumé in order to communicate all your attributes.

Your résumé is an advertisement for yourself. If your ad is better than the other person's ad, you are more likely to get the interview. In this case, "better" means that your ad highlights your attributes in an attractive way.

In discussing your education, for example, be sure to highlight your extracurricular activities such as part-time jobs, sports, and clubs. If you did well in school, put down your grades. The idea is to make yourself look as good on paper as you are in reality.

The same is true for your job experience. Be sure to describe what you did, any special projects in which you participated, and any responsibilities you had.

If you include a section on "other interests," do not just list your interests, but describe how deeply you were involved. If you organized the club, volunteered your time, or participated more often than usual in an organization, say so in the résumé. Figure 15A–4 shows an unedited version of a résumé, part of a guide to building a résumé prepared by the Chrysler-Plymouth Corp. Look it over and see what you think. Then turn to Figure 15A–5 for an improved version. Can you see how important planning and writing a résumé can be? See Figure 15A–6 for the type of words you should use in your résumé.

Writing a Cover Letter

A cover letter is used to announce your availability and to introduce the résumé. The cover letter is probably one of the most important ads you will write in a lifetime—so it should be done right.

First, the cover letter should show that you have researched the organization in question and are interested in a job there. Mention what sources you used and what you know about the organization in the first paragraph to get the reader's attention and show your interest.

You may have heard that "It is not what you know but whom you know that counts." This is only partly true, but it is important nonetheless. If you do not know someone, you can get to know someone. You do this by calling the organization (or better yet, visiting its offices) and talking to people who already have the kind of job you are hoping to get. Ask about training, salary, and other relevant issues. Then, in your cover letter, mention that you have talked with some of the firm's employees and that this discussion increased your interest. You thereby show the letter reader that you "know someone," if only casually, and that you are interested enough to actively pursue the organization. This is all part of networking.

Second, in the description of yourself, be sure to say how your attributes will benefit the organization. For example, do not just say, "I will be graduating with a degree in marketing." Say, "You will find that my university/college training in marketing and marketing research has prepared me to learn your marketing system quickly and begin making a contribution right away." The sample cover letter in Figure 15A–7 will give you a better feel for this.

Third, be sure to "ask for the order." That is, say in your final paragraph that you are available for an interview at a time and place convenient for the interviewer.

Maria Adzony
18 Nautical Lane
Windsor, Ont.

Age: 21
Height: 5′6″
Weight: 123 lbs.
Hair: Red
Eyes: Hazel
Marital Status: Single
Health: Good

OBJECTIVE

To apply management experience and French language skills in a corporation overseas.

EDUCATION

B.Com., McGill University, Montreal
Also completed a semester of study abroad in London, England (McGill University)

Additional Areas of Academic Competence:

8 Credit Hours in computers using Lotus 1-2-3, Small Business Counselling.

University Courses included Marketing, French, English Literature, Computer Programming, Data Processing, Statistics, Sociology, Economics.

High School Diploma: St. Agatha's High School, Windsor, Ont.: College Preparatory, National Honour Society, Graduated in top 25% of class.

WORK EXPERIENCE

6/89—Present — Les fleurs Johanne, Montreal, Que. Responsibilities included: bookkeeping, inventory, floral design, selling merchandise, both person to person and by use of computer.

5/90—8/90 — Waitress, Citronella's Taverna, London, England. Learned to work effectively with an international clientele.

5/92—9/92 — Hostess, The Clam Shell, Windsor, Ont.

Activities — Canadian Marketing Association, Student Marketing Association, Fencing Club.

Figure 15A–4 Inadequate, poorly organized résumé. Stamp out bad résumés. A good résumé should:

1. Invite you to read it and have a clear layout, top-quality printing, and eliminate extraneous information.
2. Start sentences with action verbs such as organized, managed, and designed, rather than with lead-ins ("I was the person responsible for . . .").
3. Highlight those accomplishments related to future work.
4. Be free of spelling, punctuation, and grammatical errors.
5. Speak the reader's language by using the vocabulary of the industry you are targeting.
6. Make a strong statement. This means using only the most relevant information—nothing less, nothing more.

Source: Special advertising section in *Business Week's Guide to Careers* ("The Chrysler-Plymouth Guide to Building a Resume").

Again, see the sample cover letter in Figure 15A–7 for guidance. Notice how Tom subtly showed that he read business publications and drew attention to his résumé.

Some principles to follow in writing a cover letter and preparing your résumé:

- Be self-confident. List all your good qualities and attributes.
- Do not be apologetic or negative. Write as one professional to another, not as a humble student begging for a job.
- Research every prospective employer thoroughly before writing anything. Use a rifle approach rather than a shotgun approach. That is, write effective marketing-oriented letters to a few select companies rather than to a general list.
- Have your materials typed on a good typewriter or word processor by an experienced typist. For best results, have your résumé printed. (If you have

Figure 15A–5 Well-organized, complete résumé. Building a résumé. Check out the new, upgraded version of Maria's résumé, and compare its impact with the former version.

Things to notice:

1. You would be surprised how many people forget to include their home (permanent) phone number. You can use a second—school—number as well.
2. Eliminate high school data if it doesn't add to the total picture. Employers will get this information on the application form anyway.
3. Use action words (see Figure 15A–6) at beginnings of sentences and paragraphs where you can.
4. Use numbers and quantities where possible.
5. It simplifies matters to eliminate month designations.
6. Rewards and citations help.
7. Note more detail on real results, and the communication of value stressed over simple "duties."
8. It is permissible to claim a piece of the overall successes.
9. If you have any awards or distinctions, they should be listed as a separate category. (Distinction can include being captain of a team.)

Maria Adzony, B. Com.
18 Nautical Lane
Windsor, Ontario HIJ 2K3
(519) 201-0568

EDUCATION

1992	Bachelor of Commerce (Marketing), McGill University Among courses taken: marketing research, sales, management, consumer behaviour
1990	Semester abroad, McGill/London, England
1989	8 credit hours, Lotus 1-2-3, small business training—computer science

CAPABILITIES/SKILLS

- ▼ Perceive motivations in others, allowing them to produce results based on their goals and commitments.
- ▼ Listen to subtle communications and convert them into active resolutions.
- ▼ Provide spirit of trust and enthusiasm so that business transactions can occur harmoniously.
- ▼ Handle administrative details under pressure to allow boss to pursue higher levels of thinking and decision making.
- ▼ Speak and write French fluently.

EXPERIENCE

- ▼ Sold floral arrangements at \$800–\$1,200/month, in person and by telephone and computer.
- ▼ Managed all administrative details of medium-size floral shop for five seasons.
- ▼ Recognized by British restaurant manager for outstanding courtesy and efficiency.
- ▼ Served as restaurant hostess/junior manager when patronage increased over 33% in a three-month period.

1989–present	Les Fleurs Johanne, Montreal, Quebec Sales Assistant
1990 (Summer)	Citronella's Taverna, London, England Waitress
1992 (Summer)	The Clam Shell, Windsor, Ontario Hostess/Junior Manager

PROFESSIONAL ASSOCIATIONS

Member: Canadian Marketing Association
Student Marketing Association

Source: Special advertising section in *Business Week's Guide to Careers* ("The Chrysler-Plymouth Guide to Building a Resume").

Managed	Wrote	Budgeted	Improved
Planned	Produced	Designed	Increased
Organized	Scheduled	Directed	Investigated
Co-ordinated	Operated	Developed	Sold
Supervised	Conducted	Established	Served
Trained	Administered	Implemented	Handled

Figure 15A–6 Sample action words to use in your résumé.

Dear Mr. Franklin,

A recent article in the *Financial Post* mentioned that your company is expanding its operations into the East. I have always had an interest in your firm, so I read more about you in the *Globe and Mail* Business Report. It seems as though you will be needing good salespeople to handle your expanding business. Mr. Lee Yo, your Toronto sales representative, is a neighbour of mine. He confirmed the newspaper report about your expansion.

I will be graduating from McGill University in June with a Bachelor of Commerce degree, having majored in marketing. My employers have commended me for having very good communication skills, for being resourceful, and for learning quickly in new situations. I believe that these would be useful qualities if I were selling for your company.

I would be pleased to provide additional information at a personal interview to be arranged at your convenience.

Respectfully yours,

[signed] Maria Adzony

Figure 15A–7 Model cover letter. Things to notice:

1. The first paragraph of the letter mentions someone in the firm (a networking strategy).
2. The second paragraph mentions specific courses and experience applicable to the job.
3. The third paragraph asks for an interview.

access to a word processing system with a letter-quality laser printer, you can produce individualized letters efficiently.)

- Have someone edit your materials for spelling, grammar, and style. Don't be like the student who sent out a second résumé to correct "some mixtakes." Or another who said "I am acurite with numbers."
- Do not send the names of references until asked.
- Keep both the résumé and the cover letter short to increase their chances of being read.

PREPARING FOR JOB INTERVIEWS

Companies usually do not conduct job interviews unless they think the candidate meets the requirements for the job. The interview, therefore, is pretty much a make-or-break situation. If it goes well, you have a very good chance of being hired. So it is critical that you be prepared for your interviews. Following are five stages of interview preparation.

1. Research prospective employers. Learn what industry the firm is in, its competitors, the products or services it produces and their acceptance in the market, and the title of your desired entry-level position. You can find such information in the firm's annual reports, in Standard & Poor's, Moody's manuals, and various business publications such as the *Financial Post,* the *Globe and Mail, Canadian Business,* and *Les*

Affaires. Ask your librarian for help. Together, you can look in the Canadian Business Index and find the company name to look for articles on it. This is a very important first step. It shows your initiative and interest in the firm.

2. Practice the interview. Figure 15A–8 lists some of the more frequently asked questions in an interview. Practice answering these questions and more at the placement office and with your roommate, parents, or friends. Do not memorize your answers, but be prepared—know what you are going to say. Also, develop a series of questions to ask the interviewer. Figure 15A–9 shows some sample questions you might ask. Be sure you know who to contact, and write down the names of everyone you meet. Review the action words in Figure 15A–6 and try to fit them into your answers.

3. Be professional during the interview. "You don't have a second chance to make a good first impression," the saying goes. That means that you should look and sound professional throughout the interview. Do your homework and find out how the managers dress at the firm. Then dress appropriately.

When you meet the interviewers, greet them by name, smile, and maintain good eye contact. Sit up straight in your chair and be alert and enthusiastic. If you have practiced, you should be able to relax and be confident. Other than that, be yourself, answer questions, and be friendly and responsive.

When you leave, thank the interviewers. If you are still interested in the job, tell them so. If they don't tell you, ask them what the next step is. Maintain a positive attitude. Figure 15A–10 outlines what the interviewers will be evaluating. A few important things *not* to do at an interview in order to maintain a professional image:

- Do not use vulgar or colloquial language.
- Do not knock previous employers or reveal information about their operations, even if pressed to do so.
- Do not go on at length when answering questions. Keep your replies concise and to the point.
- Do not volunteer negative information about yourself. But, if asked directly, reply honestly.
- Do not rush to ask about salary. Wait for an indication that you are being seriously considered for the job.

4. Follow up on the interview. First, write down what you can remember from the interview: names of the interviewers and their titles, any salary figures mentioned,

Figure 15A–8 Be prepared for these frequently asked questions.

- How would you describe yourself?
- What are your greatest strengths and weaknesses?
- How did you choose this company?
- What do you know about the company?
- What are your long-range career goals?
- What courses did you like best? Least?
- What are your hobbies?
- Do you prefer a specific geographic location?
- Are you willing to travel (or move)?
- Which accomplishments have given you the most satisfaction?
- What things are most important to you in a job?
- Why should I hire you?
- What experience have you had in this type of work?
- How much do you expect to earn?

- Who are your major competitors and how would you rate their products and marketing relative to yours?
- How long does the training program last and what is included?
- How soon after school would I be expected to start?
- What are the advantages of working for this firm?
- How much travel is normally expected?
- What managerial style should I expect in my area?
- How would you describe the working environment in my area?
- How would I be evaluated?
- What is the company's promotion policy?
- What is the corporate culture?
- What is the next step in the selection procedures?
- How soon should I expect to hear from you?
- What other information would you like about my background, experience, or education?
- What is your highest priority in the next six months and how could someone like me help?

Figure 15A–9 Sample questions to ask the interviewer.

1. *Ability to communicate.* Do you have the ability to organize your thoughts and ideas effectively? Can you express them clearly when speaking or writing? Can you present your ideas to others in a persuasive way?
2. *Intelligence.* Do you have the ability to understand the job assignment? Learn the details of operation? Contribute original ideas to your work?
3. *Self-confidence.* Do you demonstrate a sense of maturity that enables you to deal positively and effectively with situations and people?
4. *Willingness to accept responsibility.* Are you someone who recognizes what needs to be done and is willing to do it?
5. *Initiative.* Do you have the ability to identify the purpose for work and to take action?
6. *Leadership.* Can you guide and direct others to achieve the recognized objectives?
7. *Energy level.* Do you demonstrate a forcefulness and capacity to make things move ahead? Can you maintain your work effort at an above-average rate?
8. *Imagination.* Can you confront and deal with problems that may not have standard solutions?
9. *Flexibility.* Are you capable of changing and being receptive to new situations and ideas?
10. *Interpersonal skills.* Can you bring out the best efforts of individuals so they become effective, enthusiastic members of a team?
11. *Self-knowledge.* Can you realistically assess your own capabilities? See yourself as others see you? Clearly recognize your strengths and weaknesses?
12. *Ability to handle conflict.* Can you successfully contend with stressful situations and antagonism?
13. *Competitiveness.* Do you have the capacity to compete with others and the willingness to be measured by your performance in relation to that of others?
14. *Goal achievement.* Can you identify and work towards specific goals? Do such goals challenge your abilities?
15. *Vocational skills.* Do you possess the positive combination of education and skills required for the position you are seeking?
16. *Direction.* Have you defined your basic personal needs? Have you determined what type of position will satisfy your knowledge, skills, and goals?

Figure 15A–10 Traits recruiters seek in job prospects

Source: "So You're Looking for a Job?" The College Placement Council.

dates for training, and so on. Put the information in your career file. Send a follow-up letter thanking each interviewer for his or her time. You can also send a letter of recommendation or some other piece of added information to keep their interest. "The squeaky wheel gets the grease" is the operative slogan. Your enthusiasm for the company could be a major factor in hiring you.

5. Be prepared to act. Know what you want to say if you do get a job offer. You may not want the job after hearing all the information. Do not expect to receive a job offer from everyone you meet, but do expect to learn something from every interview. With some practice and persistence, you should find a rewarding and challenging job.

BE PREPARED TO CHANGE JOBS

If you are like most people, you will follow several different career paths over your lifetime. This enables you to try different jobs and stay fresh and enthusiastic. The key to moving forward in your career is a willingness to change jobs, always searching for the career that will bring the most personal satisfaction and growth. This means that you will have to write many cover letters and résumés and go through many interviews during your career. Each time you change jobs, go through the steps in this appendix to be sure you are fully prepared. Good luck.

LABOUR–MANAGEMENT RELATIONS

LEARNING GOALS

After you have read and studied this chapter, you should be able to:

1. Understand that the most difficult issue facing labour and management today is retraining.
2. Understand the history and role of labour unions in Canada.
3. Discuss the major legislation affecting labour and management.
4. Outline the collective bargaining process.
5. List the elements normally included in a collective agreement.
6. Describe union and management pressure tactics during negotiations.
7. Describe the usual grievance procedure.
8. Explain a strike and a lockout and who uses these procedures.
9. Explain the difference between mediation and arbitration.
10. See to what extent the work force is unionized and follow the structure of labour organizations in Canada.

KEY TERMS

Alan Gold

PROFILE CHIEF JUSTICE ALAN GOLD, A STAR LABOUR MEDIATOR

For almost a quarter of a century, some of the toughest and most stubborn characters in Canada have succumbed to the charms of Alan Gold. From grizzled longshoremen to armed Mohawk warriors, he has succeeded in winning their trust and reaching agreements where few people expected any progress.

Gold, former Chief Justice of Quebec Superior Court, gained fame in 1968 when he headed off a strike by longshoremen at the port of Montreal. He mediated a strike by 56,000 rail workers in 1973, ended a bitter postal strike in 1981, and has played a key role in resolving many other labour disputes in construction and airlines as well as at the Royal Mint and the Department of External Affairs.

He was chief arbitrator under the collective agreements between the Quebec government and its employees from 1966 to 1983, when he was appointed Chief Justice of the Superior Court. He is a member of the National Academy of Arbitrators (USA), a founding member of the Society of Professionals in Dispute Resolution (USA) and an honorary member of the Corporation professionelle des conseillers en relations industrielles du Québec.

In the summer of 1990, Gold astonished many observers by negotiating an agreement on human-rights issues in the Oka crisis in Quebec. It was a complex three-way negotiation among the federal government, the Quebec government, and Mohawk warriors at Oka. Before his arrival on the scene, the Oka standoff had seemed virtually impossible to resolve. But his mediation led to the only significant breakthrough in the entire 78-day crisis.

"Whether people are carrying guns or they have economic guns to your head, there are all kinds of pressures . . . in these situations," said Gold's son, Marc Gold, who is a law professor at Osgoode Hall Law School (Toronto). He said his father always enjoys a tough job, even if it is regarded as hopeless. He likes to be challenged.

Stewart Saxe, a labour lawyer who has worked with Chief Justice Gold in labour negotiations, notes that Gold has a history of handling the most intractable disputes "where nobody has the slightest idea of how anyone is ever going to solve the mess."

The key to his father's success, says Marc, is that "He's known to be fair and people trust him to do the fair thing. He's also a very good listener. Most important, he understands that all these issues are human issues. He deals with them on a very human level. He's wonderfully good with people—he likes people." At crucial moments in negotiations, Chief Justice Gold is not afraid to use humour to defuse a tense situation.

The long and distinguished career of Chief Justice Gold as a jurist, conciliator, arbitrator, and mediator has led to many honours and degrees being showered on him. He has sat on or chaired the boards of many major educational and cultural institutions in Quebec.

Sources: Geoffrey York, Peacemaker Has Fine Record, *Globe and Mail,* Sept. 7, 1991, p. A8; *Thursday Report,* Concordia University, Sept. 12, 1991.

RETRAINING: THE MOST DIFFICULT ISSUE

Throughout this book we have highlighted the importance of technological change and its impact on the economies of modern industrial societies. You have also seen how maintaining the ability to compete in a globalized trading system is essential if companies want to survive. Canada is greatly affected by both of these developments, and they have led to many serious issues in management–labour relations.

As Canadian companies try to compete more effectively under the demands of technology and world competitiveness, management seeks to replace human labour with computers, robots, and other automated procedures. Management must do what its strongest competitors everywhere are doing—adopt the most advanced technological methods—or their companies will not be able to survive. More problems arise from competition from U.S. companies because of the Free Trade Agreement. The severe economic recession and the cross-border shopping phenomenon have also hit Canadian companies hard.

Plant Closings and Layoffs

These pressures on companies have led to numerous layoffs of employees, plant closings, and the loss of over 300,000 manufacturing jobs in Canada in the early 1990s.[1] Skilled employees with 15, 20, or 25 years' experience at their company were finding themselves without a job and wondering what had hit them. Hardly a week went by without announcements of companies closing, laying off people, or moving to the U.S. or Mexico. Job security became a major demand of unions in contract negotiations with employers.

So the stage was set for sharp conflicts between unions and management. Unions tried desperately to hold onto jobs for their members, and management fought desperately to stay alive in the fiercely competitive world they found themselves in.

The Impact of Old Attitudes

The problems are greatly complicated by old attitudes that each side brings to the bargaining table. You will recall from Chapter 14 that some managers believe in Theory X for managing people: Work is unpleasant and workers have to be treated by the carrot and stick method. Other managers follow the Herzberg/Maslow/Theory Y approach: Workers must be treated as humans. They need self-fulfillment and like to participate in decision making.

Similarly, many union representatives are suspicious of management's intentions. They believe that management has one goal, to cut wages, reduce the number of jobs, and weaken the union. More far-seeing union leaders realize that there are major, long-term problems that require co-operative efforts to solve.

The result is that specific negotiations succeed or fail depending to a large extent on which of these attitudes the negotiators bring to the table. These issues are not going to disappear. So you can see why there is a continuing need for skilled conciliators like Judge Alan Gold.

Transformation of the Canadian Economy

We are in the midst of a historic transformation of modern industrial society from labour-intensive manufacturing to an automated manufacturing and service economy, where machinery does most of the hard, dirty, dangerous, boring, repetitive jobs and human beings use their brains rather than their muscles to fashion a better life for everyone. This process has been developing slowly over the past 200 years but picked up speed in the early 1950s and is now rolling along in high gear.

As more and more of the traditional labour-intensive jobs are lost, retraining must be given the highest priority to prepare the Canadian labour force for the jobs of the future. Retraining is the most critical issue in management–labour relations today.

How management and labour adapt to this issue will determine our economic and political well-being in the years ahead. It will require substantial funding and close co-operation among government, management, and unions. There are some promising signs of labour–management co-operation that augur well for the future. (See Spotlight on Big Business.)

HISTORY AND ROLE OF TRADE UNIONS IN CANADA

A long, rocky road has been travelled in Canada to arrive at the current stage of relatively civilized relationships between owners/managers of businesses and their employees. A complex and often bitter series of events over the last century and a half has involved workers, owners/managers, and government in a long process of evolution that has transformed the rights and obligations of all the parties. This was occurring not only in Canada but in England, the U.S., and other countries that were experiencing the Industrial Revolution.

The Rise of Industrial Capitalism

The 19th century witnessed the emergence of modern industrial capitalism. The system of producing the necessities of society in small, home-based workplaces gave way to production in large factories driven by steam and later electricity, both new inventions. Large numbers of people left their homes (or homelike workplaces) to work in large, noisy, dark, dangerous, cold or hot, impersonal places. Accidents were frequent and injured workers were just thrown out and replaced by others. Many writers described these depressing conditions in dramatic terms; the phrase "dark, satanic mills" (coined by William Blake) became well known.

SPOTLIGHT ON BIG BUSINESS

Labour, Management, and Government Co-operate in Retraining

When put to the test, labour and management *can* work together. It's happening at Algoma Steel Corporation Ltd., where NDP Premier Bob Rae of Ontario appointed some union heads to a special task force. In fact, the steel industry's co-operation with labour at Algoma and other sites, well before the special Ontario committee was formed, is seen as one of the few bright lights on the horizon. The Canadian Steel Trade and Employment Congress, a union–management initiative with federal funding, has arranged for retraining for 5,000 steelworkers over a three-year period. In some cases, that has meant entirely new careers such as teaching and nursing. In 1993 the Congress is working with 1,300 labourers at Algoma; it may have to deal with 6,000 more workers by the mid-'90s.

The forest sector is organizing similar retraining initiatives, while high-tech electronics manufacturing and communications companies have even more innovative programs. The powerful Canadian Auto Workers (CAW), (formerly led by Bob White, probably the most important union leader in Canada and now leader of the Canadian Congress of Labour) is moving along the same lines. In the 1990 contract with the Big Three auto companies, the union negotiated an income-security clause to assist workers laid off due to technological changes. The CAW also insisted on a three-year program to certify 10,000 workers as having trained on specific types of technical equipment. This retraining program will increase their job mobility.

The recession of the 1990s has seen hundreds of thousands of workers lose their jobs without finding new ones. This has made the question of retraining a pressing economic, social, and political issue. ▼

This almost total disregard of the human needs of workers—especially marked by a dawn-to-dusk work day for miserable wages—was infamous for the brutal exploitation of very young children. Charles Dickens became world-famous in the mid-1800s because of his novels about the maltreatment of these children in England. It was not very different in Canada.

Towards the turn of the century, 8-year-old Canadian children still worked in textile mills on a 12-hour shift for less than $100 a year. Small boys worked long hours in mines, in areas that were inaccessible to adults, for a few cents an hour. A work week of 80 hours was not uncommon.

Beginnings of Trade Unionism

It was these conditions that gave impetus to the fledgling union movement, started earlier in the new railway and printing industries. Unions set out to establish more humane working conditions and provide workers with a living wage. The struggle was not an easy one because before 1872 it was illegal to attempt to form unions in Canada. The pioneers in the early struggles were treated as common criminals—arrested, beaten, and often shot.

Long after it was no longer illegal, the idea of workers forming unions to protect their interests was still regarded with suspicion by employers and governments in Canada. Democratic rights for all was still a weak concept and the idea of people getting together to fight for their rights was not accepted as it is today. The union movement was greatly influenced by immigrants from Britain and Europe, who brought with them the ideas and experiences of a more advanced and often more radical background. As democracy gradually gained strength, the union movement grew with it. Its participation, in turn, helped democracy sink deeper, wider roots in Canada.

Workers' Rights Entrenched in Law

As with other movements for greater fairness and equality in our society—women's vote, equal rights for minorities and women, protection of children, etc.—when

Retraining is the most critical issue facing labour/management relations today. This photo shows a Rockwell training instructor explaining a new inking system.

support for employees' rights became widespread in Canada, laws were passed to enforce them. Today we have laws establishing minimum wages, paid minimum holidays and vacation, maximum hours, overtime pay, health and safety conditions, workers' compensation for accidents, unemployment insurance, the Canada/Quebec Pension Plan, and a host of other rights. It is strange to realize that at one time or another these were all on the agenda of unions and were opposed by employers and governments for many years. They often denounced these demands as radical notions.

The effect of unions goes far beyond their numbers. Companies that want to keep unions out provide compensation, benefits, and working conditions that match those found in union plants or offices. Thus the levels established by unions spill over to non-union companies.

LEGISLATION AFFECTING LABOUR–MANAGEMENT RELATIONS

Because of the nature of confederation in Canada, under the Constitution Act of 1867, power and authority are divided between the provinces and the federal government. The federal government has control over certain key industries that operate in more than one province—for example, banks, railways, airlines, telephone companies, and pipelines. So federal legislation applies to unions and labour–management relations in these businesses, as well as to all federal crown corporations and federal civil servants. All other companies are subject to provincial laws, covering perhaps 90 percent of all employees.

Labour Relations Board
A quasi-judicial body consisting of representatives of government, labour, and business. It functions more informally than a court but has the full force of law. It administers labour codes in each jurisdiction, federal or provincial.

Over the years, the federal government passed various laws affecting labour–management relations for those areas under its jurisdiction. These were all consolidated in 1971 into the Canada Labour Code, which is administered by the Department of Labour of the federal government through the Canada Labour Relations Board. The **Labour Relations Board** is a quasi-judicial body consisting of representatives of government, labour, and business. It functions more informally than a court but has the full force of law. Similar provincial codes and labour relations boards operate in each province for those areas under their jurisdiction. The laws, regulations, and procedures vary from province to province.

PROGRESS CHECK

- What is the major issue facing management–labour relations?
- What is being done to solve this problem?
- Can you name the legal body that regulates these relations?

THE COLLECTIVE BARGAINING PROCESS

collective bargaining
The process by which a union represents employees in relations with their employer.

The Labour Relations Boards (LRBs) oversee **collective bargaining,** the process by which a union represents employees in relations with their employer. It includes how unions are selected, the period prior to a vote, ongoing contract negotiations, and behaviour both while a contract is in force and during a breakdown in negotiations for a renewal of contract. The whole bargaining process is shown in detail in Figure 16–1. It is now illegal for employers to fire employees for union activities.

1. A union signs up enough employees (usually 40 percent) to request the relevant LRB to supervise a secret ballot. In some cases, if enough people sign up, no vote is required.
2. If a majority vote approves that union, it becomes the sole bargaining agent for all the employees at that location. This is called the **certification** process. If the union does not get a majority, it is not certified and usually cannot reapply for anywhere from six months to a year.
3. A union local (of a larger central body) is established and officers are elected to administer its activities. They appoint a negotiating committee to represent the union in negotiations with management to agree on a contract to govern relations between the company and its employees. In the case of large companies with many locations in Canada (say, General Motors), a large, central union body (in this case, the Canadian Auto Workers) to which all the locals belong may bargain for all the employees and negotiate a master contract. This also applies to government employees' local unions.
4. When a contract is hammered out, the members vote on whether to accept or reject it.
5. This contract then governs a whole range of relations between management and workers (see Figure 16–2) during its life (usually one to three years). Strikes or lockouts are illegal during the life of the contract.
6. A grievance committee, consisting of members from both sides, handles complaints from employees who believe any of their rights under the contract have been violated.
7. As the expiry date of the contract draws near, negotiations start on drafting a new contract.
8. If no agreement is reached before the contract expires it automatically remains in force, rendering strikes and lockouts illegal until prescribed LRB conciliation procedures have been followed. If either a strike or a lockout then occurs, the contract lapses.

Figure 16–1 **Steps in collective bargaining**

certification
The process by which a union becomes the sole bargaining agent for a group of employees. This usually requires a majority vote obtained by secret ballot supervised by an LRB.

Hiring Conditions

One of the important clauses in a union contract concerns the conditions attached to hiring employees. There are basically four types of conditions.

1. The one favoured by unions is called a **closed shop,** which means that all new hires must be union members. In effect, hiring is done through the union. Unemployed members of the union register for employment or show up daily at a union hiring hall.

2. One step down is a union shop. In a **union shop,** the employer is free to hire anybody but the recruit must then join the union within a short period, perhaps a month.

3. One of the most common conditions is an **agency shop,** which is based on the **Rand formula.** The new employee is not required to join the union but must pay union dues. This historic formula was devised by Supreme Court Justice Rand in 1946 when he arbitrated a major case involving Ford of Canada Ltd. The argument for this requirement is that all employees who benefit from a contract signed by the union should help to pay for the costs of maintaining that union—its officers, union expenses, negotiating committee, shop stewards, etc.

4. The hiring condition least popular with unions and one favoured by employers is the **open shop,** where employees are free to join or not join the union and to pay or not pay union dues.

Regardless of which hiring condition prevails, the contract usually contains a **check-off** clause requiring the employer to deduct union dues from employees' pay and remit them to the union (except for non-members in case 4). It would obviously be a lot harder to collect union dues individually.

closed shop
Workplace in which all new hires must already be union members.

union shop
Workplace in which the employer is free to hire anybody, but the recruit must then join the union within a short period, perhaps a month.

agency shop (Rand formula)
Workplace in which a new employee is not required to join the union but must pay union dues. This historic formula was devised by Justice Rand.

open shop
Workplace in which employees are free to join or not join the union and to pay or not pay union dues.

check-off
Contract clause requiring the employer to deduct union dues from employees' pay and remit them to the union.

Figure 16–2 What is in a union contract.

In general, the contract defines the rights of each party, union and management. There is a long list of topics included in such contracts. The major points include:

1. Wages, salaries and other forms of compensation, including the important cost-of-living adjustment clause (COLA).
2. Working hours and time off—regular; overtime; mealtimes; paid holidays, vacations, rest periods and sick leave; leaves of absence; flextime.
3. Seniority rights—promotions; transfers; layoffs and recalls.
4. Benefit programs—Group insurance: medical, dental, and life insurance; pensions; child care; supplementary unemployment insurance; terminal pay; maternity leave.
5. Grievances—composition of committee, processing of grievances.
6. Health and safety—provision of special clothes or equipment and safe working conditions.
7. Union activities—collection of union dues by the employer (check-off); shop stewards on the floor; union notices.
8. Hiring conditions—closed shop, union shop, agency shop, or open shop.
9. Discipline—rights of management regarding suspension, fines, and termination; hearing process.

THINKING IT THROUGH

You have seen how the nature of work is changing. Companies are downsizing and modernizing, so fewer workers are to be found in large workplaces. More and more people are working out of their homes. What adjustments do you think unions will have to make to accommodate these developments? What signs are there that they are making such changes? Will the nature of unions change?

Grievance Procedure

No matter how carefully union contracts are drafted, it is impossible to avoid disagreements. There are always differences of opinion on the exact meaning or interpretation of certain words or clauses. Every day management takes action on transfers, promotions, layoffs, disciplining, change in work procedures, and more. Sometimes these actions cause individual workers or the union local to perceive that the contract has been violated. So they file a **grievance,** a formal protest by an individual employee or a union.

grievance
A formal protest by an individual employee or a union when they believe a particular management decision breached the union contract.

Where relations between management and union are poor or deteriorating, there is usually a big backlog of unresolved grievances. Where relations are good, there are few grievances and those that arise are quickly settled.

Figure 16–3 indicates all the steps, specified by the contract, in the processing of a grievance. (Grievances in non-union shops are disposed of in comparable manner). Typically there are five or six levels in this procedure. If the grievance cannot be settled at one level, it moves up to the next level. The final step is an outside arbitrator or arbitration board. Many grievances are settled informally and never put in writing.

Arbitration

arbitration
The process of resolving all disputes, not only grievances, through an outside, impartial third party.

Arbitration is the process of resolving all disputes, not only grievances, through an outside, impartial third party. The arbitrator renders a decision that is binding on

	Management	Union
Stage 1	First-level supervisor	Shop steward
Stage 2	Second-level supervisor	Chief steward
Stage 3	Plant manager	Chief grievance officer
Stage 4	Director of industrial relations	National or international union official
Stage 5	CEO or president	President of union or central labor body
Stage 6	Dispute goes to arbitration (quite rare)	

Figure 16–3 Stages in processing grievances.

both disputing parties. The arbitrator may be a single person or a three-person board that is acceptable to both sides.

Arbitration may be *voluntary:* both sides decide to submit their case to an arbitrator. Or it may be *compulsory:* imposed by the government or by Parliament or provincial legislature. Compulsory arbitration usually occurs in a major or prolonged strike with serious consequences for the public. Usually, non-grievance arbitration (say, for contract disputes) is voluntary and grievance arbitration is compulsory.

Mediation

Sometimes, in bitter disputes between management and labour, arbitration may not be acceptable to both sides. When the differences between the two are extreme or there is much distrust or neither side wants to risk an all-or-nothing decision by an arbitrator, they may opt for mediation. **Mediation** is the use of a third party to attempt to bring the parties to a resolution of their dispute.

mediation
The use of a third party to attempt to bring the parties to a resolution of their dispute.

Mediators must possess certain important qualities to undertake such a difficult task. After all, they are attempting to bring together parties that are far apart or may hardly be talking to each other. They obviously must be well-respected, have excellent negotiating skills, and be patient and determined. It is a high-pressure job involving long sessions and sometimes round-the-clock meetings.

We are fortunate in Canada to have a number of outstanding people who possess such qualities and have resolved some very bitter disputes. One of these is William Kelly, who is now retired after many years of outstanding service. He was a railway man, an officer in one of the rail unions, who was appointed to head up the conciliation branch of the Federal Department of Labour. He settled many notable disputes, thus avoiding strikes in the rail and telephone industries, the postal service, and grain shipping. He was awarded the Order of Canada for his successful mediation efforts.

Former Chief Justice Alan Gold, of the Superior Court of Quebec, is another outstanding individual with a notable record of achievement in mediation. He has also settled many bitter labour–management conflicts involving longshoremen in Quebec, the postal service, and others. He is profiled at the beginning of this chapter.

WHEN UNIONS AND MANAGEMENT DISAGREE

Because the media give a lot of attention to strikes, you might get the impression that this is the usual pattern of negotiations. But in reality, only a small fraction of contract negotiations between unions and management end in such bitter altercations. Let us examine what happens when an agreement is not reached. What tactics and strategies are available to each side?

Usually, the union is demanding some improvement in benefits, working conditions, or pay increases to keep up with inflation. The employer usually offers less or very little or sometimes nothing. It is therefore up to the union to take actions to try to force the employer to meet its demands. These actions may include such tactics as work-to-rule (working to the exact letter of the agreement), slowdowns, refusal to work overtime, and booking off sick. A favourite negotiating tactic of the police is to refuse to hand out tickets, thus reducing the flow of income to provincial or municipal governments that are unwilling to budge from their bargaining position.

Strikes and Lockouts

If union leaders feel there is strong support among the members they will call for a strike vote, which is a secret ballot authorizing the union leadership to call a strike when they see fit. If they get a strong mandate, say over 80 percent in favour, they use this as a lever to convince management to accept their demands without actually going on strike. If management does not give in, the union will have to strike. Of course, if there is a slim majority, say 55 percent, for a strike, union leaders will be very hesitant to call a strike.

Before a strike can be called, all legal requirements must be met. In most jurisdictions in Canada the union must first ask the government to appoint a conciliator, who has a certain time limit to try to bring the parties together. If he or she fails, the union is then legally able to go on strike. The employer is then also free to declare a lockout.

lockout
A drastic negotiating strategy in which the employer locks the premises against the employees.

In a **lockout,** the *employer* locks the premises against the employees. In either a strike or a lockout, employees are no longer paid their wages or salaries. Clearly, a strike is a weapon of last resort, used only when all else fails. Similarly,

In a lockout situation, an employer locks employees out of their place of employment. The employees do not receive wages or salary during a lockout or strike.

management is reluctant to lock out its employees and call a halt to operations. No product, no profits. A lockout that received a great deal of attention was when the owners of the major league baseball teams locked out the players during spring training in 1990.

Battles for Public Support

In major cases where the public is affected—the postal service, nurses, doctors, teachers, transportation, telecommunication, civil servants at all levels—each side plays a propaganda game to win the public to its side. It can be difficult for those not directly involved to really sort out the issues. Sometimes management, if it thinks the public is on its side and the union is perhaps not well organized or lacks strong support, will provoke the union into an unsuccessful strike, weakening the union's bargaining position.

Unions sometimes ask the public and other union members to **boycott,** or not buy the employer's products or services. One of the most famous and lengthy boycotts in recent history was led by Cesar Chavez of the United Farm Workers, centred in California. The workers were low-paid Mexican immigrants who waged a multi-year battle to improve miserable conditions. In the 1970s they asked people to boycott California grapes to force the growers to negotiate with them.

boycott
Urging union members and the public at large not to buy a particular company's products or services.

Their cause was taken up by many organizations in Canada and the United States. At supermarkets in both countries, people picketed and paraded with signs asking shoppers not to buy California grapes. After several years, the growers finally relented and negotiated more reasonable conditions. Most boycotts, in contrast, tend to fizzle out without achieving their goal.

Other Tactics

Union tactics include rotating strikes—on and off or alternating among different plants or cities—rather than a full-fledged strike, where all employees are off the job for the duration. With rotating strikes, employees are always getting some pay, which would not be the case in an all-out strike. Many unions build up a strike fund from union dues and use it to give their members strike pay, but that's usually a small fraction of their normal wages. Sometimes, in important or long-lasting strikes, other unions will give moral or financial aid.

Management may announce layoffs or a shortened work week and blame it on declining business. It may say the company is having trouble competing due to high labour costs. It may even adopt the lockout tactic when it seems less costly to close down and cease paying wages than to put up with slowdowns, rotating strikes, or work-to-rule union tactics, all of which can be very disruptive. This may force the union to reduce its demands if individual members cannot do without an income for very long or if there was a weak strike-vote majority.

It is important to remember that arbitration and mediation are always available to the parties in dispute. They may take advantage of these procedures before, during, or after a strike or lockout.

PROGRESS CHECK

- Can you list the eight steps in the collective bargaining process?
- What are the major areas included in a union contract?
- What is the difference between arbitration and mediation?

STRIKES, LOCKOUTS, AND THE LAW

When a strike is in progress, striking workers usually picket the place (or places) of employment. **Picketing** is the process whereby strikers carrying picket signs walk back and forth across entrances to their places of employment. The aim of these picketers is to publicize the strike and to discourage or prevent people, vehicles, materials, and products from going in or out. They usually allow management personnel through, since they are not union members.

picketing
The process whereby strikers carrying picket signs walk back and forth across entrances to their places of employment to publicize the strike and discourage or prevent people, vehicles, materials, and products from going in or out.

Sometimes, when a company tries to bring in strikebreakers (called **replacement workers** by management and **scabs** by the union) to carry on normal activities, bitter feelings are engendered. This often leads to violence. Picketers mass in large numbers to block buses carrying these strikebreakers. Shouts are uttered, articles are thrown, the vehicles are attacked, and so on.

replacement workers
Management's name for strikebreakers.

scabs
Unions' name for strikebreakers.

If management's tactics are not successful, it may ask for police protection for the vehicles or ask the courts for an injunction to limit the number of picketers. An **injunction** is an order from a judge requiring strikers to limit or cease picketing or some threatening activity. Injunctions are not as commonly granted now as they used to be.

injunction
An order from a judge requiring strikers to limit or cease picketing or some threatening activity.

In Quebec and Ontario, it is illegal for companies to hire replacement workers when a legal strike is in progress. Management employees may continue to work and try to do some of the tasks formerly done by the striking work force.

Restrictions on Right to Strike

There are restrictions on the right to strike of various levels of civil servants and quasi-government employees such as hospital workers and electric and telephone utility workers. The provinces and the federal government forbid some employees under their jurisdiction from striking. In other cases, certain minimum levels of service must be provided. For example, when the federal civil service went out on strike in the fall of 1991, employees of the customs service, prison guards, meat inspectors, airport firefighters, and certain other employees were not allowed to strike. When employees of the public bus system in Montreal went on strike in 1990, the provincial Essential Services Council decided what minimum level of services had to be provided during the strike. In nearly all provinces, firefighters and police officers are not allowed to strike.

Legislating Strikers Back to Work

Governments have the power to end a particular strike by passing specific legislation to that effect. Provincial and federal governments have done this from time to time to end strikes by teachers, nurses, postal workers, bus drivers, and others. Governments pass back-to-work legislation when they believe they have enough support among the population for such action because of serious hardship to businesses or individuals. For example, the government in British Columbia ordered teachers back to work during the spring of 1993.

Back-to-work legislation is a denial of the legal right to strike, so it is to a certain extent a restriction of the democratic rights of individuals. Consequently, there is often much controversy about such legislation. It is rarely used to deal with strikes against private businesses.

Striking union locals often turn to affiliated unions for help. Let us look at the structure of unions in Canada so we can better understand these relationships.

During a strike, employees will set up a picket line to draw attention to their dispute and try to interrupt the normal activities of the business.

STRUCTURE AND SIZE OF TRADE UNIONS IN CANADA

The history and organization structure of unions in Canada is quite complex. The most important central labour body is the Canadian Labour Congress/Congrès du travail du Canada (CLC/CTC). There are provincial divisions (for example, the Ontario Federation of Labour) to which different unions in the province belong. Smaller divisions are local labour councils.

Many of these different unions (e.g., United Steel Workers, Musicians' Guild) are also part of a parent union of the same or similar name in the U.S. They are called international unions. Then there are some unions like the Canadian Auto Workers, which broke away from the United Auto Workers of the U.S. to form an independent union. These are called national unions. The CAW is affiliated with the CLC/CTC.

To make matters more complicated, there are other central labour organizations not affiliated with the CLC. The Confederation of National Trade Unions/Confédération des syndicats nationaux (CNTU/CSN) is essentially a Quebec organization. The Canadian Union of Public Employees (CUPE) and the Public Service Alliance of Canada (PSAC) are two of the largest unions in Canada. Both represent government employees and are affiliated with the CLC.

Figure 16–4 shows union membership by congress affiliation in 1989. Some union locals are affiliated with their provincial council as well as with the international union that they are part of. Other locals are affiliated with a provincial council as well as being part of a national union. All are affiliated to a national body, usually the CLC.

Figure 16–5 indicates that union membership in Canada grew steadily from 1962 to 1989 to almost 4 million members. It also shows that the number of members in national unions surpassed the number in international unions in 1983 and continued to climb thereafter.

Figure 16–6 shows that union members constitute 34 percent of the total work force. It also shows that more men than women are union members and that unionization rates are highest in the public service and the educational sector. On a provincial basis, Newfoundland has the highest rate of unionization. While it is difficult to pin down these figures precisely, it has been estimated that if the agricultural sector were omitted and non-union members in shops with union contracts were included, nearly half the work force would be covered by union contracts.

Figure 16–4 Percentage distribution of union membership by Congress affiliation.

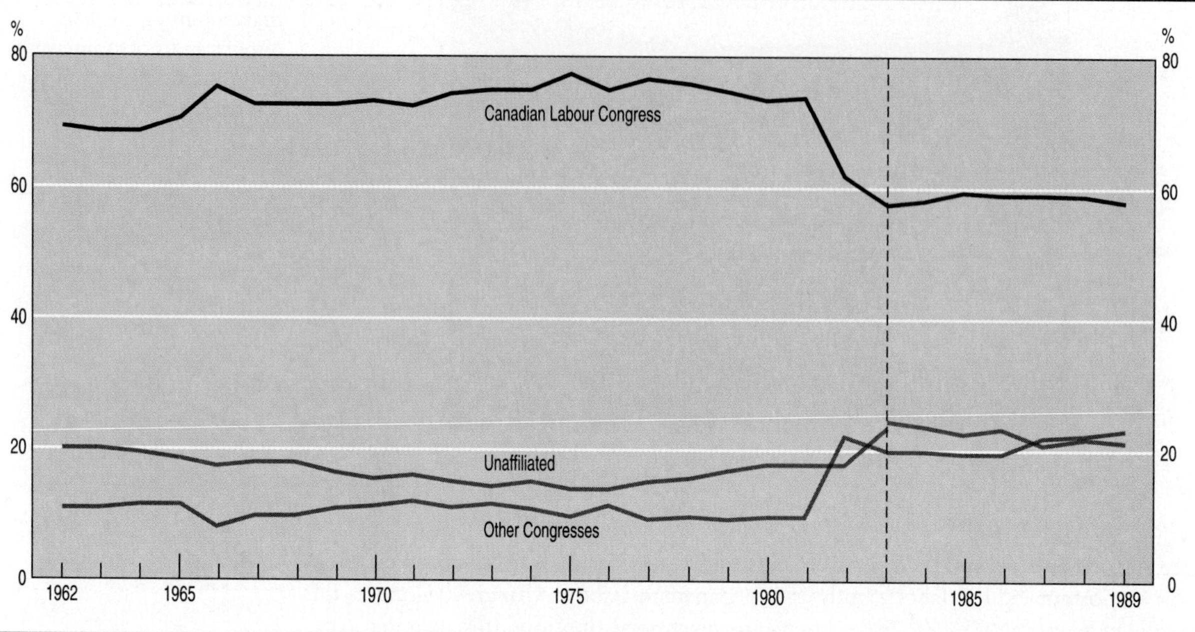

Congress Affiliation of Canadian Membership, 1989

	All unions		International		National		Government	
	Total	Women	Total	Women	Total	Women	Total	Women
	000's							
Canadian Labour Congress – Congrès du travail du Canada	2,222.2	820.3	818.4	280.0	972.4	321.2	431.4	219.1
Confederation of National Trade Unions – Confédération des syndicates nationaux	218.3	105.5	—	—	218.3	105.4	—	—
Canadian Federation of Labour – La fédération canadienne du travail	206.6	16.5	198.9	10.7	6.6	5.4	1.1	0.1
American Federation of Labour and Congress of Industrial Organizations only	231.3	14.3	231.3	14.3	—	—	—	—
Other Congresses	204.2	95.0	—	—	204.2	94.5	—	—
Unaffiliated	798.4	466.9	6.7	4.8	694.6	426.6	97.1	36.4
Total	**3,881.0**	**1,518.5**	**1,255.3**	**309.8**	**2,096.1**	**953.1**	**529.6**	**255.6**

Source: Annual report, 1989, *CALURA,* cat. no. 71-202, Statistics Canada, p. 23.
*The dotted line indicates a change in method of calculation in 1983.

Figure 16–5 Union membership in Canada, 1962–1989.

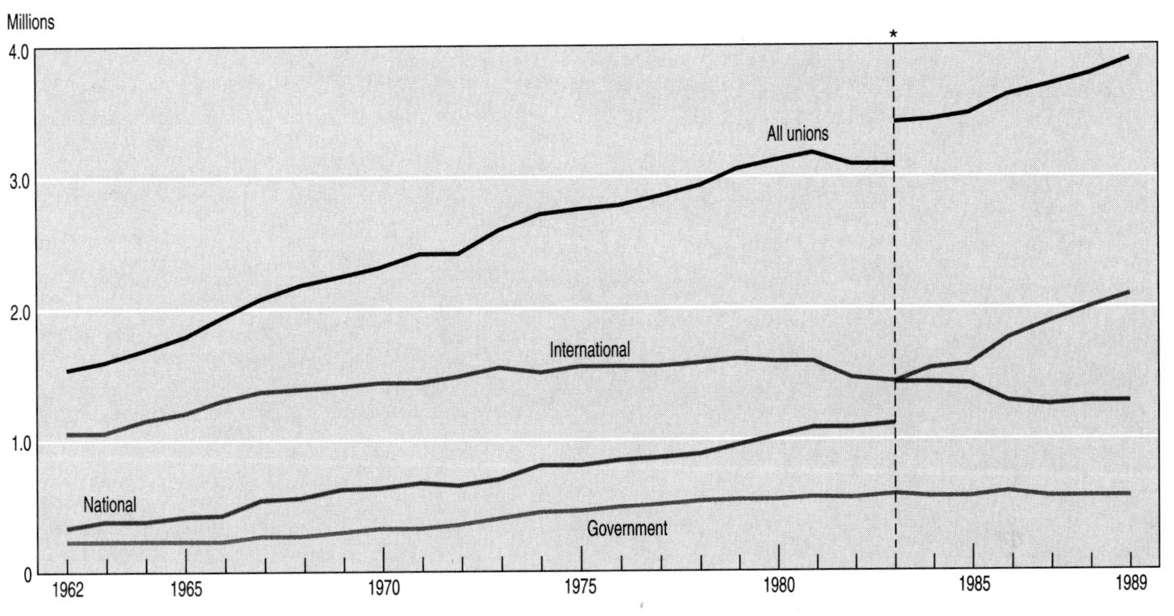

Source: Annual report, 1989, *CALURA,* cat. no. 71-202, Statistics Canada, p. 14.
*The dotted line indicates a change in method of calculation in 1983.

Figure 16–6 Union membership statistics.

Membership

Almost 3.9 million Canadians were members of labour unions in 1989, an increase of 2.7% over 1988.

Women accounted for 39.1% of all union members in Canada in 1989, up from 37.5% in 1988.

Industrial Distribution of Membership

More than 53% of female members were concentrated in health services and educational services. Manufacturing industries accounted for 25% of male members.

Rates of Unionization

The overall rate of unionization of Canadian industry stood at 34.1% in 1989, up marginally from the 1988 rate.

The rate for men increased a full percentage point to 38% in 1989. For women, the rate remained relatively stable at around 29%. The rate of unionization for women employed in health services and educational services was 60% in 1989. For all other industries, the rate was only 18.9%.

Public administration and educational services were the most highly unionized industries in 1989, with rates of 79.1% and 73.2%, respectively.

Rates of Unionization by Province

Newfoundland registered a unionization rate of 52% in 1989 and continued to be the only province with more unionized than non-unionized workers. The least unionized province was Alberta at 25.8%.

Source: Annual report, 1989, *CALURA,* cat. no. 71-202, Statistics Canada, p. 11.

The Canadian Labour Congress (CLC) is the largest and most important labour organization in Canada.

HAVE UNIONS OUTLIVED THEIR USEFULNESS?

What about the 1990s? Obviously we have come a long way in working conditions, hours of work, and wage levels. Many of these gains are now protected by law. Are unions then still necessary? We are fortunate to be living in a democratic country where free and private enterprise is the vital feature of our capitalist economic system. We believe that all citizens have the right to do what they can, within legal and ethical limits, to better themselves. Improving your financial situation is an admired goal, and those who do so are usually seen as good examples.

In this book you have seen many profiles and other examples of such successful men and women. You are probably thinking about what skills and education you need to achieve financial success and security. We have given you many suggestions of paths you might follow as either an employee or an entrepreneur.

If you select the entrepreneurial route, you will try to build a successful company by providing a necessary service or product in a manner that your customers appreciate. If you are successful, you will ultimately accumulate profits and personal wealth. Perhaps you will be very successful and accumulate great wealth and financial security for yourself and your family. One of the costs of doing business you will be keeping an eye on is wages, salaries, and benefits paid to employees. Will you want a well-trained, smart work force capable of keeping up with the rapid pace of technological advances, or will you want your employees to work "cheap"? Will you consider unions nothing but a hindrance?

Suppose you do not see yourself as an entrepreneur and instead go the employee route. Imagine yourself 10 years down the road: You are married with two children and are now a computer software specialist working for a large company in a non-managerial role. Will you seek the best salary you can possibly get? Will you want to be part of a group insurance plan to protect your family? How about working hours? Your spouse also works and you need flexible arrangements to be able to spend time with your children and deliver them to school and various other activities. How about overtime demands on the job that cut into time with your children? Will you have adequate, affordable child care?

Can you and your co-workers arrange these and a host of other issues—bonuses, sick leave, termination pay, pensions, retraining, holidays, and more—on a

REACHING BEYOND OUR BORDERS

The Future of Management–Labour Relations

Canada faces a choice of the road that management–labour relations will travel. We can either stay on the embattled road we have travelled so far or look to other countries like Germany, the Scandinavian countries, Austria, and Japan, where a different ideology is at work. All of these countries are making the transition to modern high-tech, competitive economies where unemployment rates are lower and workers are well-educated and trained for the new skilled jobs so they can enjoy high incomes and social benefits. There they are learning to work smart, not cheap.

This path requires significant changes in the attitude of workers, unions, managements, and governments. All of us have to change our ways. What is required is a massive, long-term co-operative program involving better education, on-the-job training and retraining programs, substantial investments in new equipment, and government-led incentives to help make it all happen. Nothing less than such an all-out effort will make us more competitive, develop new job opportunities, and keep those opportunities expanding. Are we prepared for such a great challenge? Do we have a choice? ▼

personal basis? Or are you better off with an organization—a union—to represent all of you in making proper contractual arrangements with your employer so that your rights and obligations as well as the employer's are clearly spelled out?

What about all the workers who are less skilled than you are? Some are illiterate; many did not graduate from high school. Hundreds of thousands of employees have lost their jobs in the 1990s through no fault of their own. Do they need a strong union to protect their interests? These questions have to be addressed by the people affected.

Can Unions and Management Still Afford Adversarial Roles?

Obviously there are conflicting interests between employers and employees. But every firm seeks to have a highly motivated work force, which requires good labour–management relations. That means that each side has to appreciate the needs of the other. A progressive union with modern attitudes can co-operate with a progressive, modern management to arrive at workable compromises.

In recent years, these relations have been greatly strained because of the massive layoffs and plant closings that have dominated the industrial landscape of Canada. The most important concern of the average worker has become job security. How can he or she be sure that the job will continue to exist next week, next month, or six months from now? This is a period of great stress in the lives of tens of thousands of Canadian families.

At the same time, businesses are desperately trying to hang on in the face of the many problems that are hurting their ability to compete in the marketplace. These issues have been discussed in various chapters of the book. Bankruptcies have been occurring at record levels, so business owners and managers also wonder if they will still be around next month or next year.

These serious economic problems have made management–labour relations very difficult as each side struggles for existence in the highly competitive, globalized business world that now exists. These issues are made more complicated by the lingering suspicions that each party is trying to take advantage of the other. Until these barriers are replaced by co-operation, it will be impossible to move into the new era demanded by the competitive conditions of today and tomorrow. Both sides will have to take a good hard look at themselves if progress is to be made.

Other Issues

Many other issues involve labour–management relations: testing for drugs and AIDS, working with employees who have AIDS, pay equity for women, affirmative action, and so on. These issues are often difficult to address because of differences of opinion among union members as well as among managers.

HOW ETHICAL ARE UNIONS?

An oft-heard opinion is that unions are too powerful in Canada. This opinion is demonstrated by the inconvenience caused by strikes that disrupt public services from time to time. We also hear charges that some union leaders are more interested in building and protecting their little empires than protecting their members' interests. Added to this list of criticisms is the charge of a lack of democracy in union operations and even some cases of corruption. It is important to maintain a proper perspective when considering these and other charges against unions. An overall assessment is difficult in this complex situation.

We should remember that from time to time businesses are accused of illegally trying to fix prices. They are also charged with polluting the environment or breaking environmental laws. Companies that provide food or pharmaceutical products are sometimes accused of playing with people's health. From time to time some of these companies are found guilty of the charges. Obviously this does not mean that *all* managements should be condemned. Similarly, we should exercise caution when evaluating the charges of corruption or careerism in unions.

EXECUTIVES AS EMPLOYEES OF COMPANIES

We normally think of senior and middle managers as people who run companies. While they are not labour and are not eligible to join unions, they are also employees and are subject to company policies.

MAKING ETHICAL DECISIONS

You are the owner of a small manufacturing company in British Columbia. Business has been poor lately and you have been looking for ways to reduce costs and increase productivity. To add to your problems, you discover that one of your employees has AIDS. You know that this will mean very heavy medical claims from the group insurance plan and result in a large increase in premiums. In addition, work will be disrupted due to missed days and concerns of the other employees.

You were already considering installing automated equipment that would eliminate the department where this employee works. It is not certain if this new equipment can really do the job, so you have hesitated. Now you are afraid that you will be accused of adopting a roundabout method of getting rid of this employee to circumvent the law against firing people with AIDS.

You have always had good relations with the union local representing your employees and you would not like to upset this relationship. Yet you are tempted to get around the problems that will be created by having this employee for the next few years. So you are seriously considering automating the department even though there is some uncertainty as to whether it will work. What should you do? Is your decision good for the business? Is your decision ethical? ▼

Executive Compensation

Most senior executives are well paid and have generous benefits such as stock options, pensions, and bonuses. They carry heavy responsibility, and their compensation is proportional to that responsibility. In the U.S. information relating to public companies must be published, but it is not required under Canadian law so exact figures are mostly speculative. Nevertheless, there has been much criticism in Canada about the high levels of such compensation and some generous settlements when CEOs' employment was terminated. These are called *golden parachutes* because they provide a gentle landing. The critics directed their fire at the fact that many companies were being so generous with their top people despite the fact that those companies were incurring substantial losses.

Problems of Middle Managers

The main problem facing middle managers today is the decimation in their ranks. Computers, the recession, employee empowerment, and fiercer global competition have all combined to play havoc with the role of these managers. Levels of management have been reduced and bureaucracies have become flatter as companies become decentralized. This reduces costs while enabling greater participation in decision making by all employees and faster responses to market conditions. Thus a major problem of this group of managers is unemployment.

Women Executives

There are several problems that women executives raise. On the average, their income is below that of male colleagues. Their career path is slower and often blocked by the *glass ceiling*. They can see higher up the ladder but can't pass through to the highest levels. They are also subject to sexual harassment. We have examined issues of illegal discrimination previously. Case Two at the end of this chapter looks at some career problems for women.

Although the number of women in business has increased dramatically in recent years, a recent survey by the *Financial Post Magazine* showed that only 1.6 percent of top management positions (vice-president and above) in Canada's largest companies are held by women.

PROGRESS CHECK

- ▼ What is the relationship between injunctions and picketing?
- ▼ When is back-to-work legislation used?
- ▼ How do labour and management have to co-operate to solve current problems?

SUMMARY

1. Understand that the most difficult issue facing labour and management today is retraining.

1. There are many difficult issues facing labour and management.

▼ *What is the most difficult?*

The tough recession, plus competitive and technological pressures, forces management to pare labour costs to the bone. This results in large job losses at a time when new jobs are hardest to find. Systematic retraining on a large scale has emerged as a key issue. It requires substantial funding and close co-operation among government, management, and unions.

2. Understand the history and role of labour unions in Canada.

2. Unions have a long history in Canada.

▼ *What was their main objective and was it achieved?*

Their main purpose was to improve workers' poor conditions and wages by forming unions that would fight for their rights. All this has been largely achieved and many early demands are now entrenched in law.

3. Discuss the major legislation affecting labour and management.

3. Much labour legislation has been passed by federal and provincial governments.

▼ *What is the major piece of legislation?*

The Canada Labour Code of 1971 consolidated all the federal laws into one. It set up the Canada Labour Relations Board to administer the code.

4. Outline the collective bargaining process.

4. The whole process of employees bargaining with their employers through a union is called collective bargaining.

▼ *What are the steps in this process?*

See Figure 16–1 for the steps in collective bargaining.

5. List the elements normally included in a collective agreement.

5. A contract with a union includes all the important issues in labour–management relations.

▼ *What are these issues?*

The major topics are compensation, working hours and time off, benefit programs, grievance procedures, discipline, seniority rights, and union activities.

6. Describe union and management pressure tactics during negotiations.

6. During negotiations, each side employs various tactics to further its strategy.

▼ *What tactics are commonly used?*

Labour may engage in slowdowns, book off sick, refuse to work overtime, work-to-rule, or take a strike vote. Management may announce layoffs or shorter work weeks, claiming lack of orders because of uncompetitiveness due to high costs.

7. Describe the usual grievance procedure.

7. When employees feel that their rights under the contract have been violated, they may file a formal grievance.

▼ *What is the procedure in settling grievances?*

There is usually a five-step process as shown in Figure 16–3.

8. Explain a strike and a lockout and who uses these procedures.

8. When negotiations break down management and labour can employ their ultimate weapons.

▼ *What are these?*

Employees can go on strike, withdrawing their services. Management can lock out its employees—literally shut the doors and prevent them from coming to work.

9. There are methods of settling differences when the parties are at a stalemate.

▼ *What are these methods?*

Arbitration is one option. This means a third party is asked to settle the points of disagreement by ruling in favour of one side or the other. Mediation is another option. This involves asking a third party to try to reconcile the parties. This means asking both to modify their demands.

9. Explain the difference between mediation and arbitration.

10. Not all employees in Canada are represented by unions. Nor are all unions part of one organization.

▼ *What percentage of employees are in unions and what is the structure of union organizations?*

About 35 percent of the work force is represented by unions. The unions themselves are part of different central labour organizations. The largest central body in Canada is the Canadian Labour Congress (CLC). There are also provincial divisions of the CLC. Many unions are also part of international unions headquartered in the U.S.

10. See to what extent the work force is unionized and follow the structure of labour organizations in Canada.

GETTING INVOLVED

1. Debate the following in class: Unions are necessary because the only way employees can protect their interests is by having their own organization to represent them and fight for their rights.
2. Develop a list of three issues of importance to employees that are not mentioned in this chapter.
3. Your union is divided on the question of employment equity to correct the inferior position of women in your industry. Some men say that it is unfair to them to allow preferential hiring for women. What do you think? Is this reverse discrimination? Is it justifiable?
4. In some unions where a long craft apprenticeship is required and admittance is limited, relatives of union members are often favoured. What do you think of this procedure? Are they entitled to preferential treatment?
5. Child care, parental leave, and flexible working hours are important questions for many fathers and mothers. Do you think that legislation is necessary to meet these requirements? Is there any other way to achieve this?

PRACTICING MANAGEMENT DECISIONS

Case One Plant Closings, Unions and Concessions

The early 1990s were disastrous for hundreds of thousands of Canadian employees, especially in the manufacturing area. Hundreds of plants and offices closed due to bankruptcy, consolidation, or transfer of operations to the U.S. or Mexico. In some cases management advised unions that the only way they could avoid closing would be substantial concessions in wages and other changes in existing contracts.

Union leaders and their members are in a quandary when faced with such decisions. Sometimes they think management is bluffing. Sometimes they are reluctant to give up contract conditions they fought long and hard for. Accepting wage cuts or benefit reductions when the cost of living continues to rise is not easy. Agreeing to staff reductions to save other jobs is also a tough decision. Unions worry about where these concessions will end. Will there be another round in a few months?

Some unionists would like to know exactly what the company's financial position is before making such decisions. They would like access to company records and perhaps get some union people onto the board of directors. Others oppose unions being involved in management decision making. Unions on boards of directors are fairly common in countries like Germany, but this idea has not taken hold in Canada and the U.S. Both labour and management tend to be opposed to it here.

Decision Questions

1. What would you recommend to union workers whose employer is threatening to close down unless they agree to wage and/or other concessions?
2. Is there some alternative to cutting wages or closing down? What is it?
3. Union workers often feel that the company is bluffing when it threatens to close. How can such doubts be settled so that more open negotiations can take place?
4. Closing laws have been passed that require plants with more than a certain number of employees to give up to six months' notice of intention to close. Do you think that such legislation helps businesses to show employees that they are serious about closing a plant and thus get concessions from labour? Are such tactics ethical? Do these laws have any effect on investment decisions?

Case Two Mommy and Daddy Tracks

In 1989 an article by Felice N. Schwartz called "Management Women and the New Facts of Life" appeared in the *Harvard Business Review.* The article dealt with the increase of women in the workplace and the career challenges they would face in the highly competitive work environment of the 1990s. Schwartz said that the problem in the past has been that women had to choose between the fast track at work or staying home to care for their children. What she proposed was called a "mommy track" in business.

Fundamentally, a woman could opt for one of two choices in her work career. She could choose not to have children and to get on the fast track, thus competing equally with men. Then she would have a shot at making partner in the law firm or chief executive officer in her business career. Or she could choose the mommy track, where options for taking extended leave or working part-time would allow balancing work and family. The second choice would pretty much preclude a woman from making partner or becoming the top executive. Many women cheered the article because they felt it brought attention to a major issue in employee relations. The National Association of Female Executives membership endorsed the idea with over a 60 percent majority.

The mommy track controversy was not overlooked by business. Extended parental leaves, flexible work schedules, and job sharing were just a few of the creative ways business sought to deal with the problem of balancing work and home. Today the controversy has taken a new turn. Daddy tracking is a key employee issue emerging in the 1990s. The daddy track appears to be reserved mostly for professionals, such as Mark Janosky of Eastman Kodak, who took off four months from the company (with benefits but no pay) to be a full-time father. Janosky is typical of many men trying to balance the questions of career and family. James A. Levine, director of the New York-based Fatherhood Project, suggests that if legal trends continue, firms that offer maternity leaves for women may have to provide paternity leaves for men.

How far will men go toward pursuing the daddy track? It's hard to tell. Men do earn on the average almost a third more than women, so the family budget could suffer a big setback. Also, many men feel the hint of a daddy track could be detrimental to their career and provoke negative reactions from family and work peers.

Even the thought of such a tracking system causes much controversy. The debate is healthy and productive because it is an important question. Canada can only benefit from getting this issue out into the open and trying to develop practical, ethical solutions.

Decision Questions

1. Divide the class into two groups: those who like the idea of mommy and daddy tracks and those who do not. Each group should defend the position it is normally against so you have a chance to view the controversy from the other side. Debate the issue and see if you can come to some consensus.

2. In some European countries companies pay full salaries for up to 15 months to men and women who take family leave. Is such a benefit possible or acceptable in the Canadian system?
3. Is the issue of family responsibility the same for men and women or do you see some real differences? What specific differences, if any, do you note? Should companies put equal emphasis on both mommy tracks and daddy tracks?
4. Do you think it's possible for a man or woman to be on the mommy or daddy track at one stage in life and then move to the career fast track when the children get older?

Source: "The Mommy Track Debate," *The Wall Street Journal,* May 23, 1989, p. A1: Keith H. Hammonds, "Taking Baby Steps Toward a Daddy Track," *Business Week,* April 15, 1991, pp. 90–92; Interviews with LC Consultants, Montreal, May 1993.

LET'S TALK BUSINESS

1. What is your attitude towards unions? Do you know why you have this attitude? Has this chapter contributed anything towards your understanding of unions?
2. What do you think are the disadvantages and advantages of unions? Who or what benefits from unions?
3. Many executives are reluctant to hire women of child-bearing age because of the disruption if they become pregnant. In Canada a woman cannot be fired due to maternity leave and her job must be kept for her. How would you resolve this conflict between ethical and practical behaviour?
4. Should a librarian make as much as a truck driver? Can you determine what the actual facts are in your area?
5. Do you think it's fair that an employee with lower seniority, usually a younger person, is laid off before someone with higher seniority? If you think this system is not right, what do you suggest? Is your suggestion fairer to all?

LOOKING AHEAD

We have now covered basic management and some of the issues involved. It is time to explore in more depth the inner workings of a firm. We shall begin with accounting in Chapter 17. Then we shall explore finance and other important topics. You may not be as familiar with these topics as you were with management topics, so plan to spend more time learning the concepts. These subjects are not hard, but the terminology is new and you'll need it to understand the discussions.

PART VI

ACCOUNTING AND FINANCE

Some People Are Born Accountants. For The Rest Of Us, There's New ACCPAC Simply Accounting For Windows.

Easy To Learn, Easy To Use And Only $199.

Now there's an accounting program anybody can use—new ACCPAC® Simply Accounting™ For Windows,™ the quickest and easiest way to take care of your books.

You'll have it up and running in minutes. And with the Windows interface, you can do anything with just a few clicks of the mouse. Write a check. Print out an invoice. Do your payroll. Manage your receivables.

What used to take hours now takes just minutes. So you can spend less time counting your money—and more time making it.

And since it costs only $199, you can take care of your books without breaking the bank.

Call us today at 1-800-645-3003 for the location of your nearest dealer.

It's the accounting program anybody can use.

And we mean anybody.

COMPUTER ASSOCIATES
Software superior by design

For Only $199 You'll Get: · General Ledger · Accounts Payable · Accounts Receivable · Payroll · Inventory Control · Job Costing · Prints Checks, Statements, Invoices and Mailing Labels · Produces Standard Accounting Reports · Quick Set-Up

ACCOUNTING FUNDAMENTALS

LEARNING GOALS

After you have read and studied this chapter, you should be able to:

1. Define accounting and explain the differences between managerial accounting and financial accounting.
2. Compare accounting and bookkeeping.
3. Identify and describe the major accounts used to prepare financial statements.
4. Understand simple income statements and balance sheets, and explain their functions.
5. Describe the role of computers in accounting.
6. Explain the concept of cash flow.
7. Explain how a business can be making profits and still be short of cash.
8. Understand the new concerns of accounting.

KEY TERMS

accounting, p. 544
accounting system, p. 544
assets, p. 550
balance sheet, p. 556
bookkeeping, p. 548
cash flow, p. 563
cost of goods sold, p. 558
current assets, p. 550
depreciation, p. 562
financial accounting, p. 546
financial statements, p. 556
fixed assets, p. 550
fundamental accounting equation, p. 559
gross margin (profit), p. 558
income statement, p. 556
independent audit, p. 547
ledger, p. 554
liabilities, p. 552
liquid, p. 550
managerial accounting, p. 545
net income, p. 559
net sales, p. 556
operating expenses, p. 558
other assets, p. 557
owners' equity, p. 553
private accountant, p. 546
public accountant, p. 546
ratio analysis, p. 561
retained earnings, p. 558
revenue, p. 556

Robert A. Leadley

PROFILE ROBERT A. LEADLEY: THE McDONALD'S OF ACCOUNTING

Leadley, Gunning and Culp is the McDonald's of the Canadian accounting world. The St. Catharines, Ont., company has made a splash in the staid accounting industry by using techniques mastered by the fast-food king—franchising and marketing savvy.

In just four years, Leadley has multiplied from a small-town, seven-partner firm into a publicly traded company with 194 franchised offices in Canada and the United States. In April, Leadley penned a $2-million deal to buy General Business Services, a U.S. accounting firm with 400 franchisees.

When the company opened its first branch office in 1988 in Fort Erie, also in southwestern Ontario, its expansion plans called for 25 new locations in seven years, said vice-chairman Robert Jason. "We had not really expected there were that many people out there wanting to run their own businesses in this area," he said.

Leadley's appeal, said franchisee Bruce Pound, is that it allows him to be his own boss while providing a network of colleagues and specialists he can tap into at any time. "I wanted to have a support group because of the horrendous amount of information that is continually changing and coming out," Pound said from his office in Camrose, Alta. "To take it on yourself would just be too formidable." Last year, the 46-year-old Pound quit dairy farming after 18 years because of its uncertain future and back-breaking labour. He decided the franchise was the ideal way to get into business while upgrading his rusty accounting skills.

Franchise holders pay $40,000 up front and give up 10 percent of their annual billings, paid monthly. In return, said Jason, they get extensive help in starting the business, from choosing the office site to training in running a practice and using Leadley's systems. Leadley marketing specialists also teach the franchise holders how to advertise themselves and get clients. In addition, the franchisees can call the head office or each other for specialized advice or the latest developments in accounting and tax law.

Besides allowing franchisees to run their own businesses, the other key to Leadley's growth has been its focus on what Jason said is the neglected area of accounting for small businesses. "They've been traditionally underserved by the large accounting firms," Jason said. "The larger firms have concentrated on the larger markets." That's why many Leadley offices are found in places like Beeton, Ont., and Oliver, B.C.

Jason conceded that many small cities and towns already have competent accountants but said they may lack the ongoing training and up-to-date information Leadley offers. Leadley offices also provide business counselling that helps business owners detect problems in their operation. Jason said most Leadley offices are run by people with an accounting background, but about one-third of them, like Pound, do not have formal accounting degrees. The company's growth has been rapid, but some franchises have failed and others have been cancelled for refusing to adopt the company's systems.

Leadley, the only major Canadian-owned accounting franchiser, plans to combine its operations with General Business Services and move its senior managers to that company's headquarters in Columbia, Maryland. The purchase is part of the company's ambitious plan to become the North American leader in the industry. Leadley will have the most franchises, though California-based Comprehensive Business Services will still have higher total billings.

Source: Murray Oxby, "Franchiser Called McDonald's of Accounting," *Montreal Gazette,* June 23, 1992, p. F3.

THE IMPORTANCE OF ACCOUNTING

Leadley's success is due to small business owners discovering the importance of accounting. Take Sharon and Brian Rowan, for example. They learned the hard way that you'd better keep track of the figures, even if your company seems to be doing well. After receiving a large inheritance, the Rowans opened an electric appliance store and advertised aggressively. Six months later they were doing $75,000 business monthly, so they believed things were going great.

Soon after, Sharon said to Brian that perhaps they ought to engage an accounting firm to deal with income taxes and see if they were handling the GST properly. That's when they found out they were really incurring losses. It was hard to believe because they were always able to pay their bills. Yet, as Brian said, "We were spending $60 to make $50."

Brian and Sharon knew how to sell appliances, but they knew almost nothing about accounting. Neither of them had ever seen an income statement. They couldn't understand how their sales could be increasing and they could pay their bills on time and still have losses instead of profits. We will explain at the end of the chapter what their accountants told them. Where they went wrong was in not getting accounting advice *before* they started.

Accounting Is the Heart of Business Management

Brian and Sharon Rowan's story is repeated often throughout the country. Small businesses often fail because they do not know where they are going or what is really happening. Accounting is different from marketing, production, and human resource management. We have all had some experience with marketing or production. We have observed and understand management concepts, and human resource procedures seem relatively easy to grasp. But we know almost nothing about accounting from experience. What is it? What do accountants do? Is it interesting?

The truth is that many people, including some business majors, are not interested in accounting at all. There are thousands of businesspeople who are highly skilled in most areas of business but relatively ignorant when it comes to accounting. The result? Like the Rowans, they plunge into the world of trade and seem to be doing well for a while. Sales go up. They appear to have enough cash, but in reality they are losing money. Soon their losses catch up with them. The net result is business failure. Others are operating profitably but because they are short of cash and cannot pay their bills, they think they are incurring losses. This chapter will explain how both of these things can happen.

The fact is that you must know something about accounting if you really want to understand business. Furthermore, accounting is not that hard. You will have to learn a few terms; that is mandatory. Then you have to understand bookkeeping and how accounts are kept. That is not too difficult, either. From the figures accountants gather and record, they prepare reports called financial statements. These reports tell a businessperson how healthy the business is. It is almost impossible to run a business effectively without being able to read, understand, and analyze accounting reports and financial statements. These statements are as revealing of the health of a business as pulse rate and blood pressure are in revealing the health of a person. It is up to *you,* however, to make sure your accountants give you the information you need in the form you need it. That means you must know something about accounting too.

The purpose of this chapter is to introduce you to basic accounting principles. By the end of it, you should have a good idea of what accounting is, how it works, and why it is important. Spend some time learning the terms and reviewing the accounting statements. A few hours invested in learning this material will pay off repeatedly as you become more involved in business or investing, or simply in understanding what's going on out there in the world of business and finance.

WHAT IS ACCOUNTING?

accounting
The recording, classifying, summarizing, and interpreting of financial transactions to provide management and other interested parties with the information they need.

Accounting is the recording, classifying, summarizing, and interpreting of financial transactions to provide management and other interested parties with the information they need. Transactions include buying and selling goods and services, acquiring equipment, using supplies, and receiving and paying cash. Transactions may be recorded by hand or in a computer system. Most businesses use computers because the process is repetitive and complex, and computers greatly simplify the task. Computers can handle large amounts of data more quickly and more accurately than manual systems.

accounting system
The methods used to record and summarize accounting data.

After transactions have been recorded, they are usually classified into groups that have common characteristics. For example, all purchases are grouped together, as are all sales transactions. The business is thus able to obtain needed information about purchases, sales, and other transactions that occur over a given period of time. The methods used to record and summarize accounting data are called an **accounting system** (see Figure 17–1). Systems that use computers enable an organization to get financial reports daily if desired. One purpose of accounting is to help managers evaluate the financial condition and the operating performance of the firm. They compare results to those forecast and are better able to make decisions for the future. Another purpose is to report financial information to people outside the firm such as owners, lenders, suppliers, and the government (for tax purposes).

Figure 17–1 The accounting system. The inputs to an accounting system include sales, purchases, and other documents. The data are recorded, classified, and summarized. They are then put into summary financial statements such as the income statement and balance sheet.

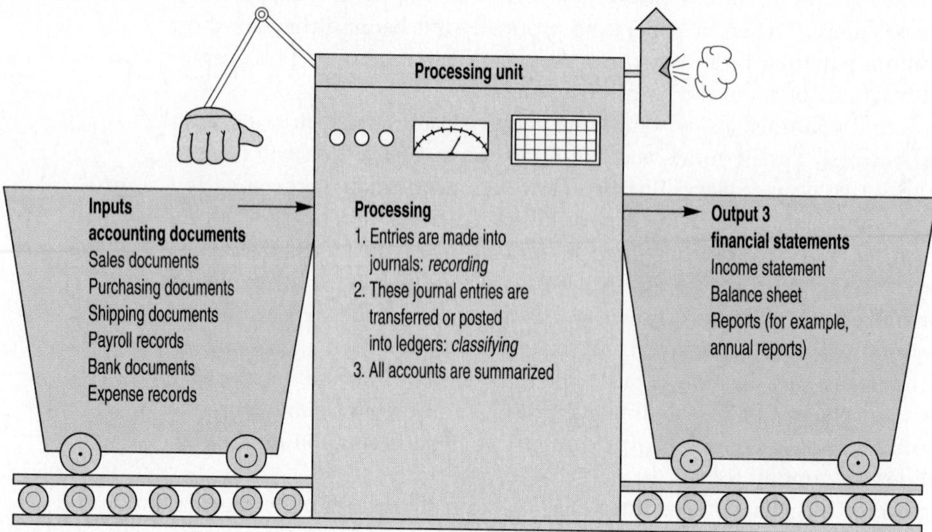

Accounting Is User Oriented

In more basic terms, accounting is the measurement and reporting to various users (inside and outside the organization) of financial information regarding the economic activities of the firm (see Figure 17–2). Accounting has been called the language of business, but it is also the language used to report financial information about non-profit organizations such as churches, schools, hospitals, and governmental units. Accounting can be divided into two major categories: managerial accounting and financial accounting.

Managerial Accounting

Managerial accounting is used to provide information and analyses to managers within the organization to assist them in decision making. Managerial accounting is concerned with measuring and reporting costs of production, marketing, and other functions (cost accounting); preparing budgets (planning); checking whether or not departments are staying within their budgets (controlling); and designing strategies to minimize taxes (tax accounting).

managerial accounting
Providing information and analyses to managers within the organization to assist them in decision making.

Simple analysis of corporate figures can disclose important information. For example, a slight month-to-month increase in payroll costs may not appear significant. But multiply that increase by 12 months and the increase in costs can be disastrous. Monitoring profit margins, unit sales, travel expenses, cash flow, inventory turnover, and other such data is critical to the success of a firm. Management decision making is based on such data.

Some of the questions that managerial accounting reports are designed to answer include:

- What goods and services are selling the most and what promotional tools are working best?
- How quickly are we selling what we buy and how does that compare with other firms in the same industry?
- How much profit is the firm making and does that compare favourably with other firms? If not, why not?
- What are our major expenses and are they in line with what other firms spend?

Users	Type of Report
Government taxing authorities (e.g., Department of National Revenue)	Tax returns
Government regulatory agencies	Required reports
People interested in the income and financial position of the organization: owners, creditors, financial analysts, suppliers, others	Financial statements found in annual reports (e.g., income statement, balance sheet)
Managers of the firm	Financial statements and other financial reports distributed internally

Figure 17–2 Users of accounting information and the required reports. Many different types of organizations use accounting information to make business decisions. The kinds of reports these users need vary according to the information they require. An accountant, then, needs to prepare the appropriate reports.

- How much money do we make on the owners' investment in the firm and does that compare favourably with other firms in the same industry? If not, why not?
- How much tax are we paying and how can we minimize that amount?
- Will we have enough cash to pay our bills and if not, have we made arrangements to borrow that money somehow?
- Are our costs of doing business in line with the costs of other firms in the industry and if not, why not?

In all cases, results are compared with budgets to see if results are achieving targets set for the current year. When they do not, management must figure out how performance can be improved.

You can see how important such information is. That is why accounting is a good subject to learn in school.

Financial Accounting

financial accounting
The preparation of financial statements for people inside and outside of the firm (for example, investors).

Financial accounting mainly differs from managerial accounting because unlike managerial accounting the information and analyses are also needed by people outside of the organization. This information goes to owners and prospective owners (new shareholders), creditors and lenders, employee unions, customers, government units, and the general public. The external users are interested in the organization's profits, its ability to pay its bills, and other financial information. Much of the information is contained in the annual report, a yearly statement of the financial condition and progress of the firm. Various quarterly (every three months) reports keep the users more current. These are required by law for the shareholders of all public companies (those whose shares trade on the stock exchange).

Financial accounting reports answer such questions as:

- Has the company's income been satisfactory? Should we invest in this company?
- Should we lend money to this company? Will it be able to pay it back?
- Can the company afford to raise its salaries?
- Is the company financially strong enough to stay in business to honour product warranties?
- Should we sell to this company? Will it be able to pay its bills?

We hope you are getting the idea that accounting is critical to business and to anyone who wants to understand business. You may want to know more about accounting firms, who the people are who prepare these reports, and how you can be sure that they know what they are doing. Accounting data can be compiled by accountants who work for the firm or by outside accounting firms.

Private and Public Accountants

private accountant
Employee who carries out managerial and financial accounting functions for his or her employer.

public accountant
Independent firm that provides accounting, auditing, and other professional services for clients on a fee basis.

Private accountants are employees who carry out managerial and financial accounting functions for their employer. Many have degrees in accounting and are qualified professionals. Very small companies often cannot afford or do not require accounting employees, so they hire independent public accounting firms.

Public accountants are independent firms that provide accounting and other professional services for different clients on a fee basis. They employ qualified accountants and auditors, apprentices, and other types of personnel. The most

One purpose of accounting is to report financial information to people outside the company. Investors (owners) and potential investors need all kinds of information, such as sales, profits, and debts. The annual report is an excellent vehicle for communicating financial information.

prestigious professional accounting degree in Canada is that of chartered accountant (C.A.). This degree is granted by a provincial Institute of Chartered Accountants that supervises the training, education, and practice of chartered accountants in that province. The final examinations are very rigorous to ensure that only qualified candidates will earn the degree of C.A.

All provincial institutes have together organized the Canadian Institute of Chartered Accountants, which sets accounting and auditing standards across the country. It also prepares the Uniform Final Exams (UFE), which are given on the same day semi-annually in various cities.

There are chartered accountants or their equivalents in all industrialized countries. All the national organizations co-ordinate their work and theories by membership in international accounting associations.

There are other associations of professional accountants in Canada. Certified General Accountants (CGA) and the Society of Management Accountants (CMA) also train accountants. Large companies, governments, and non-profit bodies employ many accountants; some do financial accounting, others managerial accounting. Many financial accountants have a C.A. degree, while managerial accountants generally opt for a CMA degree. Many CGAs are employed by governments.

There are three other important functions of public accounting firms. Their most important activity for business and other organizations—and their largest income producer—is performing independent audits (examinations) of the books and financial statements of companies. **Independent audits** provide the public, governments, and shareholders (owners) with an outside opinion of the fairness of financial statements. This is required by law for all public corporations in Canada.

independent audit
Examination of a company's books by public accountants to give the public, governments, and shareholders an outside opinion of the fairness of financial statements.

Public accounting firms also provide consulting services to management, give tax advice to companies and individuals, and prepare their income tax returns. Large accounting and auditing firms operate internationally to serve large transnational companies.

As you can see, a variety of interesting challenges are part of the daily fare of professional accountants. Many successful executives who are in senior management positions started their careers as public accountants. Think carefully about a career for yourself in this field. It is a continually expanding area with many specialties. Yes, it is difficult, but what worthwhile professional career is not?

ACCOUNTING VERSUS BOOKKEEPING

bookkeeping
The recording of transactions.

Bookkeeping involves the recording of transactions. It is a rather mechanical process that does not demand much creativity. Bookkeeping is part of accounting, but accounting goes far beyond the mere recording of data. Accountants *classify* and *summarize* the data. They *analyze* and *interpret* the data and *report* them to management. They also *suggest strategies* for improving the financial condition and progress of the firm. Accountants are especially valuable for income tax advice and preparation of tax returns.

Now that you understand what accountants do and whom they do it for, we can get down to the fundamental aspects of bookkeeping and accounting.

In the following sections, you will follow the steps accountants take in their day-to-day work. When we are finished, you should have a better idea of what accountants do and how they do it. You should also be able to read and understand financial statements and discuss accounting intelligently with an accountant and others in the world of business. The goal is not to learn how to be an accountant, just to learn the terms and concepts. So let's start at the beginning.

A bookkeeper gathers accounting documents, such as sales slips, bills, cheques, and travel records, and records them in journals and ledgers. These are the first steps in an accounting system that provides managers and interested outside parties with the information they need about the financial progress and condition of the firm.

What Bookkeepers Do

If you were a bookkeeper, your main task would be to record all of the transactions of your department, which might include:

- Sales documents (sales slips, cash register receipts, and invoices).
- Purchasing documents.
- Shipping documents.
- Payroll records.
- Bank documents (cheques, deposit slips).
- Various expense documents.

You record the data from the original transaction documents (sales slips, cheques, etc.) into record books. (Thus the term *bookkeeping*.) The books where accounting data are first entered are called *journals* (from the French word *jour,* or *day*—recording the daily transactions.)

PROGRESS CHECK

- Can you explain the difference between managerial and financial accounting?
- Could you define accounting to a friend so that he or she would clearly understand what is involved?
- What is the difference between a private and a public accountant? What professional degrees do accountants have?
- What is the difference between accounting and bookkeeping?
- Can you name five original transaction documents that bookkeepers use to keep records?

THINKING IT THROUGH

In business, hundreds of documents are received or created every day. So you can appreciate the valuable role a bookkeeper plays. Can you see why most businesses have to hire people to do this work? Would it be worth the owners' time to do all the paperwork? Can you understand why most businesses find it easier to do this work on a computer?

THE "ACCOUNTS" OF ACCOUNTING

After recording the original transactions in appropriate journals (sales, purchase, cash, etc.) the bookkeeper transfers the data to certain accounts. Hence the term *accounting*. Six major categories of accounts are used in an accounting system:

1. *Assets.* Things of value owned by a firm (land, buildings).
2. *Liabilities.* Amounts owed by the firm to others (debts).
3. *Owners' equity.* The book value of the business. This consists of total assets minus total liabilities.
4. *Revenues.* Sales of goods or services rendered.
5. *Cost of goods sold.* The cost of the goods that were sold and recorded as revenues (item 4).
6. *Expenses.* Costs incurred in operating the business (rent, salaries, insurance, etc.).

SPOTLIGHT ON SMALL BUSINESS

Keep Your Banker Happy with a Steady Flow of Information

As you learned in Chapter 6, positive or negative relations with your banker can often predict success or failure for a small business. Entrepreneurs learn fast that keeping their banker happy can pay off, particularly if the company finds itself in a financial crunch. How do you keep your bank happy? That question occupies a good deal of the entrepreneur's time. One answer is accounting information. Few entrepreneurs realize that financial ratios (see Appendix D after Chapter 18) are important numbers to bankers and often form the basis of the decisions bankers make concerning financing requests.

Financial ratios not only can help the entrepreneur manage his or her business more efficiently, but they also can make your banker a more reliable business partner. Bankers see ratios as useful measurements to use when comparing a company's financial position to that of competing companies. Also, they see ratios as an effective guide in evaluating the firm's performance compared to industry standards or trends that are occurring in the market. What are some of the more important ratios at which the banker looks closely?

Banks feel a firm's ability to repay bank loans and make timely interest payments is important in evaluating financing requests. Liquidity ratios such as the current ratio (current assets divided by current liabilities) are important in determining the firm's short-term financial strength. Is it best for a firm to always maintain a high current ratio? Not necessarily! If a company has too high a current ratio, bankers may feel it is making poor use of resources. If your current ratio is falling, you must be prepared to explain why this is happening. Staying on top of the situation may mean receiving continued financial support from your bank. Keeping track of inventory and the debt position of the firm will also impress your banker. Low turnover of inventory could suggest to bankers that trouble is ahead. Excess inventory can boost interest rates and possibly lower profits. Ratios such as inventory turnover can offer valuable insights into preventing these problems and keeping the bank on your side. Debt is a potential source of worry for both the businessperson and the bank. Therefore, debt to equity and total debt to total assets are ratios of major concern.

What should small-business managers do to build a working relationship with their bankers? Working closely with their accountant, they should prepare and regularly update a report binder that contains key financial ratios as well as cash-flow forecasts and projections. The entrepreneurs should discuss with the banker what ratios are most relevant to their businesses and then keep track of them on a regular basis. With such diligence, you not only build a good working relationship with your banker, but you also build a partnership with an informed partner.

Source: Richard J. Maturi, "The Numbers Game," *Inc.,* Oct. 1991, pp. 42–45.

The following material will give you additional information about these categories of accounts.

The Asset Accounts

assets Things of value owned by a business.

Assets are things of value owned by the business. They include the following: cash on hand or in bank, accounts receivable (money owed by customers) inventory, investments, buildings, trucks and cars, patents, and copyrights.

liquid How quickly an asset can be turned into cash.

Assets are listed according to how liquid they are. **Liquid** refers to how quickly an asset can be turned into cash. When inventory is sold and the customer pays, this asset becomes cash. Because this normally happens in a few months, inventory and accounts receivable are said to be liquid assets. Assets are divided into three main categories, listed in order of liquidity. (See Figure 17–3.)

current assets Cash and assets that are normally converted into cash within one year.

fixed assets Items that are acquired to produce a business's services or products. They are not bought to be sold.

1. **Current assets**—items that are normally converted into cash within one year.
2. **Fixed assets**—items that are acquired to produce the business's services or products. They are not bought to be sold. These include equipment, buildings, trucks, and the like.

Figure 17–3 Classifications of assets. Assets are classified by what normally happens to them. Cash and those that usually turn into cash (inventory and accounts receivable) are considered to be liquid. They are called *current assets.* Those that are bought to run the business (equipment, trucks, etc.) are not bought to be sold, so they are called *fixed assets.* Patents and copyrights are listed in a third class called *other assets.*

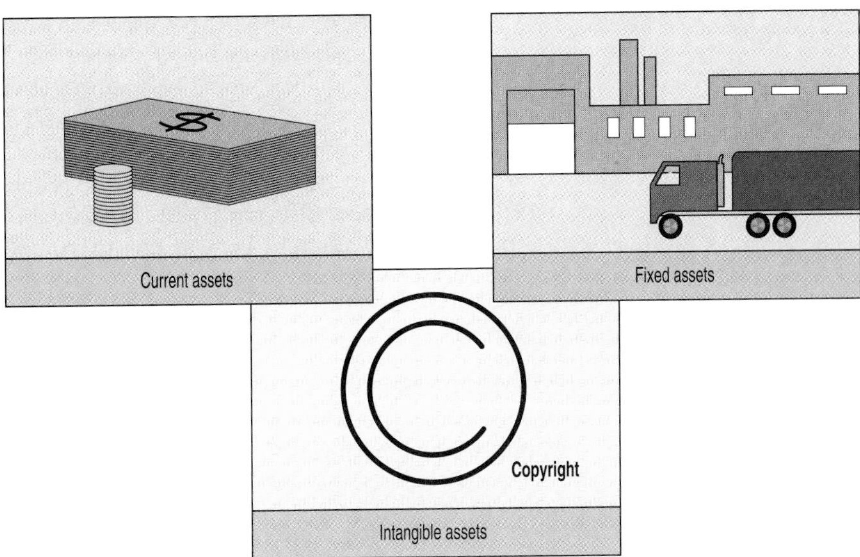

Trucks and buildings are called assets of the firm. Assets are tangibles and intangibles that have monetary value. Your tangible personal assets include the money you have, your clothes, appliances, and other objects you own that could be sold for cash. Your intangible assets include your skills, education, and experience.

3. **Other assets**—items that are not included in the first two categories. This catch-all group includes items such as copyrights and patents.

other assets
Assets that are not current or fixed. This catch-all group includes items such as copyrights and patents.

You can see why one of the key words in accounting is *assets.* Take a few minutes to go through the list, visualizing the assets. Notice that they are things of value.

The valuation of assets can be a complex matter beyond the scope of this book. All assets are normally recorded at the cost of acquisition. When you look at a balance sheet (see Figure 17–7 later in this chapter), you see assets listed at their original cost. The real values are often different from their *book values*. In other words, the market value—what would be realized if the asset were sold—is normally different from the value as shown on the books.

The long, steady period of inflation that we have witnessed since the 1960s has resulted in most book values being substantially below market value. For example, a building purchased in 1960 for $1 million would have a market value of perhaps 20 times that amount in 1993. Nevertheless, it remains on the books at original cost. So this asset, and therefore total assets, are grossly understated.

Obviously this is not a satisfactory state of affairs. The accounting profession and other interested parties have been struggling with alternatives for many years. It's a problem awaiting a creative solution. Perhaps one of you will take up the challenge and come up with the answer.

The Liabilities Accounts

liabilities
Amounts owed by the organization to others.

Another important term in accounting is liabilities. **Liabilities** are what the business *owes* to others. As with assets, you will more easily understand what liabilities are when you review a list of some examples:

SPOTLIGHT ON BIG BUSINESS

Accounting for New Kinds of Assets and Liabilities

Technology is not the only thing that is changing today. A host of new issues in accounting are causing the profession some giant headaches. One area of problems relates to environmental issues.

There are four aspects to this question. One is the production process that harms the environment. Smoke emission containing harmful gases and liquid emission into rivers and lakes into the ground are two common problems. Then there are solid wastes that are accumulated or dumped into rivers and lakes. Third, there is the problem of acquiring a site that a previous user/owner has polluted unbeknown to the new owner. Finally, there is the issue of accidents—nuclear, oil spills, PCB and tire dump fires, and many others. All of these have occurred in Canada and elsewhere in the world.

In all of these cases, liability for past damage and/or cost of future clean-up arises. The difficulties lie in assessing the dollar amount and determining who is liable. The issue is further complicated by the fact that different environmental laws came into force at different times in different provinces and countries. It is a nightmare scenario from the accounting point of view, because the amounts involved can be extremely large.

A different topic relates to the fact that in today's high-tech world, knowledge is a major asset. Indeed some people argue that it may be more important than all the physical assets of companies. Giant IBM is in trouble despite its billions of physical assets perhaps because of decisions affecting the use of knowledge. How does a company evaluate the education, skills, and experience of its work force? These are called *off-balance sheet* assets because they do not show up there and yet they may be the crucial assets for many important companies. In Canada we have hundreds of software companies whose real assets are the brains of their owners and employees.

These problems are obviously not easy to solve, but they must be dealt with if financial statements are to reflect reality. These challenges and many more await the next generation of accountants and auditors. They make this profession a lot more interesting than the image that is commonly portrayed.

Sources: Nelson Luscombe, "A Learning Experience," *CA Magazine*, Feb. 1993, p. 3; "Sustainable Decision Making," ibid., p. 19; Robert Walker, "In Search of Relevance," ibid., p. 26; Michael Stanleigh, "Accounting for Quality," ibid., Oct. 1992, p. 40.

- *Accounts payable*—money owed to others for merchandise and services purchased on credit but not yet paid. If you have such an unpaid bill, you have an account payable.
- *Accrued expenses payable*—expenses the firm owes but has not been billed by the end of the month, when financial statements are prepared (e.g., utilities bills, credit card statements).
- *Bonds payable*—long-term loans to the business.
- *Notes payable*—usually shorter-term loans from banks.

All liabilities that are due within one year from the balance sheet date are classified as *current liabilities*. Those due later are called *long-term liabilities*. You can see this in Figure 17–7.

The Owners' Equity Accounts

The **owners' equity** in a company consists of all that the owners have invested in the company *plus* all the profits that have accumulated since the business commenced but have not yet been paid out to them. This *always* equals the book value of the assets minus the liabilities of the company, as you will see later on. Why this is so will be discussed shortly.

owners' equity
Owners' investments in the company plus all net accumulated profits.

In a partnership, owners' equity is called *partners' equity* or *capital*. In a sole proprietorship, it is called owner's or *proprietor's equity* or capital. In a corporation, it is called *shareholders' equity* and is shown in two separate accounts. What the owners (shareholders) invest is shown in one account, called *common stock,* while the accumulated profit that remains after dividends have been paid to shareholders is shown in an account called *retained earnings*. You can see this in Figure 17–7.

The Revenue Accounts

The revenue accounts are where income from all sources is recorded. That includes sales, rentals, commissions, royalties, and other sources of income. These are shown in the income statement. (See Figure 17–6 for a sample income statement.)

The Cost of Goods Sold Accounts

The cost of goods sold accounts are used when a company sells products. The account shows all the costs of selling the products that were recorded in the sales (revenues) account. These costs include inventory, purchases, transportation, purchase discounts, and packaging. These appear on the income statement. The cost of goods sold will be discussed further in the section on financial statements.

The Expense Accounts

The expense accounts are where the expenses of running a business are recorded. These are the costs incurred in operating the business such as rent, insurance, salaries, utilities, and advertising. They are also shown on the income statement.

Figure 17–4 summarizes all the specific account titles discussed above.

Figure 17–4 Sample of specific account titles.

For the Balance Sheet			For the Income Statement		
Assets	**Liabilities**	**Owners' Equity**	**Revenues**	**Expenses and Costs**	
Accounts receivable	Accounts payable	Capital stock	Sales	Wages	Interest
Inventory	Notes payable	Retained earnings	Rentals	Rent	Donations
Investments	Bonds payable	(Accumulated profits	Commissions	Repairs	Licenses
Equipment	Taxes payable	not paid out)	Royalties	Travel	Professional fees
Land				Insurance	Supplies
Buildings				Utilities	Advertising
Motor vehicles				Entertainment	Taxes
Goodwill				Storage	Purchases
Cash					

ACCOUNTING JOURNALS

The day-to-day accounting task is to record all the transactions involving cash and cheques received or paid out, sales and purchases, and any other transactions. In the pre-computer age, the standard three-step procedure was as follows:

1. Record transactions in appropriate journals.
2. Post to ledger accounts from these journals (see next section).
3. Prepare financial statements from the ledger accounts.

Computers have changed the entire procedure and the use of journals. Once transactions are input into a computer, all the information can be easily produced—journals, ledger accounts, or financial statements. There is no longer any sequencing.

Unless you work for a very small company that does not have a computerized accounting system, you will not see the journal used as the book of original entry on which the rest of the system is based.

Accounting Ledgers

In a non-computerized system, suppose that a businessperson wanted to determine how much was paid for office supplies in the first quarter of the year. That would be difficult even with accounting journals. The businessperson would have to go through every transaction seeking out those involving supplies and then add them up. This is true of other categories such as inventory and accounts receivable.

Clearly, what businesspeople need is another set of books that has pages (accounts) labeled "Office Supplies," "Accounts Receivable," and so on. Entries in the journal can be transferred to these pages, and information about various accounts can be found quickly and easily. A **ledger,** then, is a loose-leaf accounting book in which information from accounting journals is entered (*posted*) into homogeneous groups (accounts) so that managers can find all the information about one type of transaction in the same place. All the journals are totalled and posted into ledgers monthly (see Figure 17–5).

ledger
A loose-leaf book in which information from accounting journals is entered (posted) into homogeneous groups (accounts) so that managers can find all the information about one type of transaction in the same place.

Double-Entry Accounting System

The method of recording transactions that is practised throughout the world is called the *double-entry* accounting system. As the name implies, two entries are made

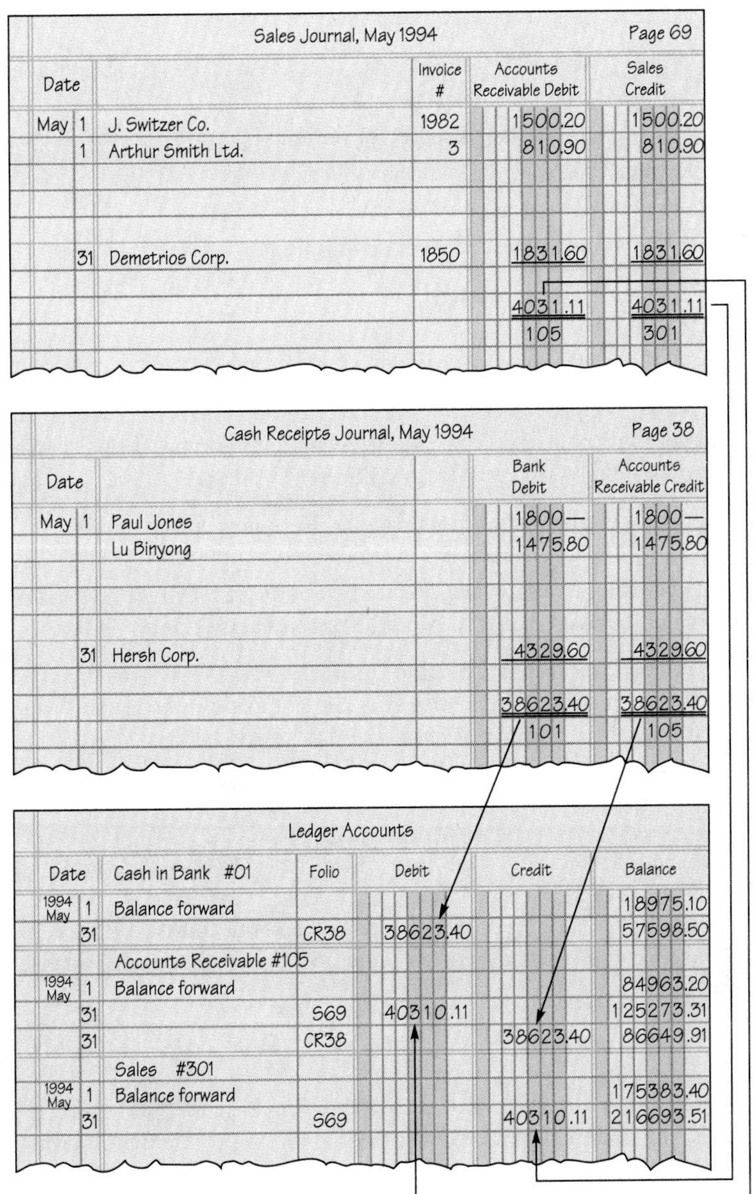

Sales Journal, May 1994 — Page 69

Date			Invoice #	Accounts Receivable Debit	Sales Credit
May	1	J. Switzer Co.	1982	1500.20	1500.20
	1	Arthur Smith Ltd.	3	810.90	810.90
	31	Demetrios Corp.	1850	1831.60	1831.60
				4031.11	4031.11
				105	301

Cash Receipts Journal, May 1994 — Page 38

Date			Bank Debit	Accounts Receivable Credit
May	1	Paul Jones	1800—	1800—
		Lu Binyong	1475.80	1475.80
	31	Hersh Corp.	4329.60	4329.60
			38623.40	38623.40
			101	105

Ledger Accounts

Date		Cash in Bank #01	Folio	Debit	Credit	Balance
1994 May	1	Balance forward				18975.10
	31		CR38	38623.40		57598.50
		Accounts Receivable #105				
1994 May	1	Balance forward				84963.20
	31		S69	40310.11		125273.31
	31		CR38		38623.40	86649.91
		Sales #301				
1994 May	1	Balance forward				175383.40
	31		S69		40310.11	216693.51

Figure 17–5 Journal entries. This figure shows how the information from the journal is posted to various ledger accounts. The idea is to have all similar transactions in one place. That is, all cash transactions are recorded in one ledger account, all sales transactions in another, and so on.

for each transaction—a debit and a credit. For example, when a sale is made on credit for $100, the accounts receivable account is debited for $100 and the sales account is credited with $100. When the customer pays for this sale, the cash account is debited and the accounts receivable account is credited. You can see this in Figure 17–5.

This ingenious method, reputed to have been invented in Northern Italy about 600 years ago, has an important feature. When you make a monthly summary listing of all the ledger accounts (a *trial balance*), the sum of all the debits must equal the sum of all the credits. If it doesn't, you know you have made some errors. You must find them and redo your trial balance to see if the debits now equal the credits. Computers eliminate the need for a trial balance because they do not make the arithmetic errors that humans can and do make.

PROGRESS CHECK

- Name the six classes of "accounts" that are used in accounting and give two examples of items that go into those accounts.
- Can you list various assets by degree of liquidity?
- What goes into the category called liabilities?
- What is the formula for owners' equity?
- What is the difference between an accounting journal and a ledger?

FINANCIAL STATEMENTS

financial statements
Report the success and position (condition) of a firm; they include the income statement and balance sheet.

income statement
Reports revenues, expenses, and profit or loss during a specific period of time.

balance sheet
Reports the financial position of a firm at the end of a specific period of time. Balance sheets consist of assets, liabilities, and owners' equity.

The accounting process consists of two major functions: (1) recording data from transactions, and (2) preparing **financial statements.** Financial statements report the success and condition of a firm. The two most important financial statements are the income statement and the balance sheet.

1. The **income statement** reports revenues, expenses, and profit or loss resulting from operations *during* a specific period of time.
2. The **balance sheet** reports the financial position of a firm at the *end* of that period which consists of assets, liabilities and owners' equity.

Think of a balance sheet as a snapshot or freeze-frame of a company at a certain point of time. The income statement shows the company in action and the results of activities for a period ending on the same date as the balance sheet.

Financial statements are an important indication of the health of a firm. That is why they are of interest to the owners (shareholders), banks, suppliers, and future investors.

To understand accounting, you must be able to read and understand both the income statement and the balance sheet as well as understand cash flow. In the following sections, we shall explore financial statements and cash flow. Once you learn the concepts, you will know more about accounting than many small-business managers today.

The Income Statement

The financial statement that shows "the bottom line," that is, profit after expenses and taxes, is the income statement or profit and loss statement. The income statement summarizes all the resources that come into the firm from operating activities (called *revenue*), resources that are used up (called *cost of goods sold* and *expenses*), and what resources are left after all costs and expenses are incurred (called *net income* or *net loss*). It reports the results of operations over a period of time. The formulas for the income statement are as follows:

Revenue − Cost of goods sold = Gross margin (Profit)

Gross margin − Operating expenses = Net income before taxes

Net income before taxes − Income taxes = Net income

net sales
Sales revenue minus discounts, returns, and other adjustments made for customers.

revenue
The value of what is received for goods sold and/or services rendered.

Gross Sales, Net Sales, and Revenue

The figure that is most important near the top of the income statement is **net sales** (see Figure 17–6). To determine net sales, a firm must add up all of its sales **revenues** and subtract discounts, returns, and other adjustments made for customers.

Note the terms *revenues* and *sales*. Most revenue (money coming in to the firm) comes from sales, but there are other sources of revenue such as rents received,

Classic Cereals, Inc.
Makers of Fiberrific

CLASSIC CEREALS, INC.
Income Statement
For the Year Ended December 31, 1993

Revenues:			
Gross sales		$720,000	
Less: Sales returns and allowances	$ 12,000		
Sales discounts	8,000	20,000	
Net sales			$700,000
Cost of goods sold:			
Beginning inventory, Jan. 1		$200,000	
Merchandise purchases	400,000		
Freight	40,000	440,000	
Cost of goods available for sale		$640,000	
Less: Ending inventory, Dec. 31		230,000	
Cost of goods sold			$410,000
Gross profit (gross margin)			$290,000
Operating expenses:			
Selling expenses:			
Salaries for salespeople	$ 90,000		
Advertising	15,000		
Supplies	2,000		
Other sales expenses	3,000		
Total selling expenses		$110,000	
General expenses:			
Office salaries	67,000		
Depreciation	1,500		
Insurance	1,500		
Rent	28,000		
Light, heat, power	12,000		
Miscellaneous expenses	2,000		
Total general expenses		$112,000	
Total operating expenses			$222,000
Net profit (Income) from operations			68,000
Less: Interest expense			10,000
Net income before taxes			58,000
Less: Income tax expense			13,500
Net income (profit) after taxes			$ 43,500

Figure 17–6 Classic cereals income statement. Note that revenues are at the top of the income statement and income is at the bottom. A simple formula for the income statement is revenue minus costs and expenses equals income.

admissions, fares, fees, payments to the firm for use of its patents or copyrights, (royalties), interest earned, and so forth. The top of the income statement looks only at sales revenues. Thus, revenues and sales are synonymous in this case.

Be careful not to confuse the terms *revenue* and *income*. Revenues are at the top of the income statement and income is at the bottom; net income is revenue *minus* costs and expenses.

Gross margin is calculated by subtracting cost of goods sold from net sales (revenue). This picture shows huge stacks of paper. The revenue from the sale of such paper is quite high. But so is the cost of all the materials needed to make the paper. You will know how much gross profit (margin) one makes in this business by subtracting the cost of goods sold from the sales revenue. When you subtract other expenses, you get the net profit from operations.

Cost of Goods Sold

cost of goods sold
A particular type of expense measured by the total cost of merchandise sold (including costs associated with the acquisition, storage, transportation, and packaging of goods).

gross margin (profit)
Net sales minus cost of goods sold before expenses are deducted.

To calculate how much money a business earned by selling merchandise, you have to subtract how much it cost to buy that merchandise. That cost includes the purchase price plus any freight charges paid to bring in the goods plus the costs associated with storing the goods. In other words, all the costs of buying and keeping merchandise for sale, including packaging, are included in the **cost of goods sold.** Of course you must take into account how much stock or inventory you had at the beginning and end of the period.

When you subtract the cost of goods sold from net sales, you get what is called gross margin or *gross profit.* **Gross margin,** then, is how much the firm earned by buying and selling merchandise before the expenses of operations are deducted.

In a service firm, there may be no cost of goods sold; therefore, net sales equals gross margin. Whether you're selling goods or services, the gross margin or gross profit figure doesn't tell you enough. What you are really interested in is net profit or net income. To get that, you must subtract expenses.

Operating Expenses

operating expenses
The various costs incurred in running a business, including rent, salaries, and utilities, in order to earn revenues.

To sell goods or services, a business has certain **operating expenses.** Obvious ones include rent, salaries, supplies, selling expenses, utilities, insurance, and depreciation of equipment.

After all expenses are deducted, you get what people call "the bottom line," which is net income. It answers the questions, "How much did the business earn?" and "How much of our income will be taxed?"

Net Income

retained earnings
The amount left after a company distributes some of its net income (profit) to shareholders in the form of dividends.

After taxes are deducted, the company may want to distribute some of the income (profit) to shareholders in the form of dividends. The remainder is left in the firm to invest in a variety of other assets and is known as **retained earnings.** Keeping profits increases the value of the firm. Therefore, shareholders (owners) benefit from income whether they receive a share of it in the form of dividends or it is kept in the firm for re-investment.

Pause here and review the income statement in Figure 17–6 until you feel you understand what is involved. Note that **net income** basically equals revenue minus costs and expenses.

net income
Revenue minus costs and expenses.

The Balance Sheet

A balance sheet is the financial statement that reports the financial position of a firm at a *specific date*. It is composed of assets, liabilities, and owners' equity. Note that the income statement reports on changes over a period of time and the balance sheet reports conditions at the end of that period.

The term *balance sheet* implies that the report shows a balance, an equality between two figures. That is, the balance sheet shows a balance: assets versus liabilities plus owners' equity. If you look at Figure 17–7, you will see this.

The Fundamental Accounting Equation

Suppose a company doesn't owe anybody any money. That is, it has no liabilities. Then the assets it has (cash and so forth) are equal to what it owns (equity). The **fundamental accounting equation** is rather obvious. If a firm has no debts, then:

fundamental accounting equation
Assets = liabilities + owners' equity; it is the basis for the balance sheet.

Assets = Owners' equity

This means that the owners of a firm own everything. If a firm has debts, the owners own everything except the amount due others, or:

Assets − Liabilities = Owners' equity

If you add an equal amount to both sides of the equation (you remember this operation from algebra), you get a new formula:

Assets = Liabilities + Owners' equity

If you look at the balance sheet in Figure 17–7, you will note that total assets (in the middle of the page) equal the combined total of liabilities and shareholders' equity, in this case $801,000. This basic accounting equation derives from the double-entry accounting system mentioned earlier. You will recall that because transactions are entered in this way, the numbers on both sides—debits and credits—have to be in balance.

Let us analyze this equation in a little more depth. Where does a firm get its assets? If you think about it for a moment, you will see that there are only three sources:

1. The money the owners invested →	shares issued to shareholders (common stock)
plus	**plus**
2. Profits the company generates →	retained earnings
	= shareholders' equity
plus	**plus**
3. Creditors who have not been paid →	liabilities
= Total sources of assets	= Total assets

Figure 17–7 Classic Cereals balance sheet. Assets = Liabilities + Shareholders' equity. In this case, each side equals $801,000.

CLASSIC CEREALS, INC.
Balance Sheet
Dec. 31, 1993

Assets		
Current assets		
Cash	$ 15,000	
Accounts receivable	200,000	
Notes receivable	50,000	
Inventory	230,000	
Total current assets		$495,000
Fixed assets		
Land	$ 40,000	
Buildings and improvements	200,000	
Equipment and vehicles	120,000	
Furniture and fixtures	26,000	
Less: Accumulated depreciation	(180,000)	
Total fixed assets		$206,000
Other assets		
Goodwill	$ 20,000	
Research and development	80,000	
Total other assets		$100,000
Total assets		$801,000
Liabilities		
Current liabilities		
Accounts payable	$ 40,000	
Notes payable	8,000	
Accrued taxes	150,000	
Accrued salaries	15,000	
Pension fund	75,000	
Total current liabilities		$288,000
Long-term liabilities		
Notes payable	$ 30,000	
Bonds	190,000	
Total long-term liabilities		$220,000
Total liabilities		$508,000
Shareholders' equity		
Common stock *	$ 100,000	
Retained earnings **	193,000	
Total shareholders' equity		$293,000
Total liabilities and shareholders' equity		$801,000

* Invested by owners/shareholders
** Accumulated profits

The balance sheet shows that assets are divided into three categories: (1) current assets such as cash or accounts receivable, (2) fixed assets, and (3) other assets, such as patents and copyrights.

Liabilities are divided into two categories: (1) current liabilities such as accounts payable, and (2) long-term liabilities such as bonds. Shareholders' equity consists of common stock (investment in the company) and retained earnings (earnings not distributed to owners). For businesses that are not corporations, these terms are different.

If you go back to the beginning of this chapter and reread the sections on the "accounts" of accounting (the asset accounts, the liabilities accounts, and so on), you will see that the asset, liability, and owners' equity accounts set up in the ledgers are all part of the preparation for the balance sheet. Review the lists of items in these accounts and you will learn more about what is behind the figures on the balance sheet.

Ratio Analysis

One of the most common and useful methods of analyzing financial statements in greater depth is called **ratio analysis.** This is done by comparing the current year's results with

ratio analysis
A way to analyze financial statements in greater depth by comparing results with the previous year's, the budget, and competing firms' results.

1. the previous year,
2. the budget or plan for the year, and
3. competing firms in the same industry.

Many ratios are used to better understand a company's operations and position. Some of the important ones are reviewed in Appendix D, which follows this chapter.

ACCOUNTING COMPLEXITY

If accounting were nothing more than the repetitive function of gathering and recording transactions and preparing financial statements, the major functions could

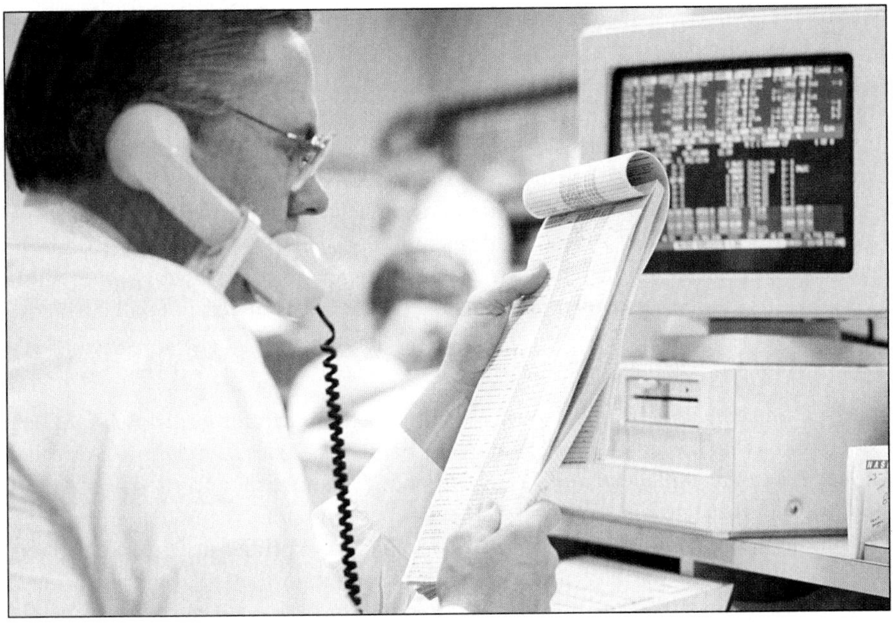

Computers have made the accounting process much faster and easier. Even very small organizations can now enjoy the benefits of computerized accounting systems. As the cost of hardware and software falls, even the smallest firms will benefit from keeping track of accounts on computers (if just for tax purposes).

REACHING BEYOND OUR BORDERS

Accounting Problems When Going International

As you have made your way through this book, you have seen many examples of Canadian companies that have developed important ties beyond our borders. As part of the globalization of business, Canadian companies look to joint ventures and alliances with other companies in the Pacific Rim, Europe, Mexico, and elsewhere. For example, McDonald's Canada Ltd. formed a joint venture with a Russian agency, to operate the largest McDonald's unit in the world, in Moscow. Sometimes Canadian businesses buy out other companies. Bombardier bought the national Mexican railway car construction company in 1992. Smaller companies are also getting involved in this process.

One problem that often arises is how to determine the real value of the foreign company. The starting point is an examination of its financial statements. Have they been prepared on the basis of the same generally accepted accounting principles (GAAP) that are applied in Canada and the U.S. (the two are very similar)? Often there are major differences that make it difficult to determine the real value of the company. Obviously this is very important, especially if you are trying to establish how much you should offer to buy the company or you want to be sure the assets being contributed to a joint venture have the value your partner claims.

Accounting bodies all over the world have been working for many years towards establishing a common set of GAAP through organizations like the International Association of Accountants. It is a major task that is slowly being achieved. ▼

be assigned to computers. In fact, most medium- to large-size firms and many small firms, have done just that. The truth is that there is much more involved.

depreciation
Since assets such as machinery lose value over time, part of their cost is calculated as an expense each year over their useful life.

Take depreciation, for example. **Depreciation** is based on the fact that assets such as machinery lose value over time. Therefore, part of the cost of the machinery is calculated as an expense each year over its useful life. Subject to certain technical rules that are beyond the scope of this chapter, a firm may use one of several techniques for calculating depreciation. However, once a method is chosen, it is difficult to change. Each technique results in a different bottom line, a different net income. Net incomes can change dramatically based on the specific accounting procedure that is used. Accountants can recommend ways of handling insurance, investments, and other accounts that will also affect the bottom line.

Accountants have to make many judgments and decisions regarding the recording of certain types of transactions. For example, when you start your business your sister gives you a computer and printer as a gift to help you on your way. You know that all assets are supposed to be recorded at cost, but how do you record something that has no cost because it is a gift? Or suppose you buy two machines for your factory; one proves useless and ends up quietly gathering dust in a corner. You normally amortize the cost of a machine apportioned over its useful life by charging that portion annually as an expense (depreciation). What do we do about the unused machine that contributes nothing to the annual profit but still has a cost?

Generally Accepted Accounting Principles

These and many more complicated transactions require certain guidelines that help accountants to make proper and consistent decisions. These guidelines are called *generally accepted accounting principles (GAAP)*. They are published in the handbook of the Canadian Institute of Chartered Accountants, along with many other important guidelines. This handbook is the bible of the accounting profession. Bankers, financial analysts, and others also refer to it. From time to time (and after much discussion) it is updated.

MAKING ETHICAL DECISIONS

You are the only accountant employed by a small company, and you have full charge of the books. The company's financial position is weak because of a downturn in the economy. You know that your employer is going to ask the bank for an additional loan so that the company can continue to pay its bills. Unfortunately, the financial statements for the year just ended will not be very strong. You are convinced that no bank will approve a loan increase based on those figures.

Your boss approaches you before you close the books for the year and makes some suggestions for showing higher profits so that he will have a better chance of getting the loan approved. He even suggests that you should find some way of covering your tracks so that the auditors who have to approve the statements will not be aware of the "adjustments."

You know that it is against the professional practice rules of your accounting organization and is a breach of GAAP to do what your boss wants. You try to get him to change his mind but he insists that there is really no choice. He points out that no one knows better than you how desperately the company needs the extra funds. Further, he says, if the loan is not obtained the company will be forced to close and you will be out of a job at a time when jobs are very hard to find, especially for a 55-year-old woman.

You agree with his assessment of how you and the company will fare if the loan is not obtained. What should you do? Do you have any other alternatives beside doing what you are asked to or refusing to do it? ▼

There are about a dozen important accounting principles. Every audited set of financial statements includes a series of notes explaining how these principles have been applied, as well as a report by the auditors that GAAP have been used. This makes it possible for financial statements to be compared from one year to the next as well as from one company to another. Accountants all over the world are working to harmonize GAAP.

THINKING IT THROUGH

Take a look at the table of contents in this book and think about how many of the chapters involve calculation, measurement, recording, and analysis of data. Do you think there are any chapters where the material discussed does not involve accounting? Does this make accounting a critical skill for effective business operations? How about non-profit organizations? Is accounting of equal importance in hospitals, school systems, universities, museums, and government?

CASH-FLOW PROBLEMS

Cash flow is the difference between cash receipts and cash disbursements. One of the greatest problems confronting business is to ensure that there will always be enough cash to meet payments as they fall due. This is a constant challenge for businesses of all sizes. Sometimes very large companies are forced to sell off one or more of their good subsidiaries to raise cash because of recession or other unexpected developments. This is the problem that caused Olympia & York Developments serious difficulties in early 1992. Sometimes, as in the case of Campeau Corp. in the early 1990s, a company is practically destroyed by cash-flow problems. Brian and Sharon Rowan, whom we met at the beginning of the chapter, ran into the same cash-flow squeeze.

cash flow
The difference between cash receipts and cash disbursements.

The problem is most severe with small companies because they often have very few resources to fall back on. We can all understand a company having a cash shortage when it is suffering losses, but what about companies that are doing well? Why should they run short of cash?

There are several reasons why profitable companies have this problem. If they are growing very rapidly, their profits may not be sufficient to finance the greater inventories and accounts receivable they are forced to carry because of increased sales. Or they may be buying a lot of new equipment to increase production to keep up with the increased demand. Growing slowly gives companies a chance of avoiding this problem.

Sometimes a company that is not well managed will tie up too much cash in inventory or let customers delay payments too long. This obviously will put pressure on the cash balance. If you hire an accounting firm before you start a business, it will prepare (with your help) a cash-flow forecast. This is a schedule for one year that shows clearly what the cash situation will be every month, based on your estimate of monthly sales, expenses, terms of credit, and other data. The cash flow can be prepared in three versions—optimistic, pessimistic, and most likely. This equips you to anticipate any scenario, so you can act in accordance with whichever one unfolds and avoid crises. Cash flow will be discussed in more detail in Chapter 18.

SHARON AND BRIAN ROWAN'S SURPRISE

The Rowans (remember them from the beginning of the chapter?) had a different problem. They had no cash-flow problems, so they were surprised when their accountants told them they were incurring losses. How could they feel no cash pressure, a rare occurrence in a new business, while they were losing money? There are several possibilities. Since they started with their large inheritance they may simply have been eating into their original investment. Their bank balance was declining and eventually they would have run into trouble.

Another possibility is that, as a retail store they did not extend any credit, so they were getting paid cash for their sales. At the same time they were getting credit from their suppliers. That gave them a cushion of a month or two of cash income before they had to start paying creditors. This would have caught up with them in a short while.

Finally, they may have stocked up heavily at the start and were now depleting their inventory. This was providing them the cash to pay their bills. Again, they would have soon had to start building up stock and that would have created additional cash pressures.

So we see how businesspeople may be deceived by either cash shortages or surpluses into thinking that their businesses are doing well or not doing well. A proper accounting system and an understanding of the information it yields are essential for a reliable assessment of how a business is performing.

SOME CONCERNS OF THE ACCOUNTING PROFESSION

The Spotlight on Big Business (page 552) highlights a growing concern of accountants about some difficult issues raised by new developments. The new so-called knowledge-based industries and environmental problems have created a whole new set of issues that must be considered if financial statements are to truly reflect the financial position of companies. The troubling questions relate to how to evaluate certain significant intangible assets and some potentially huge liabilities.

As the spotlight notes, how can brainpower, skills, and abilities be valued in dollars? Yet these assests are becoming increasingly important in the high-tech world that so many companies are entering. Similarly, the problem with buying or selling polluted or toxic materials, land, buildings, or other assets, or hazards arising from production processes is that potential buyers, consumers, affected persons, or governments may launch major damage suits. How are such potential liabilities to be evaluated?

A balance sheet is supposed to show all the assets and liabilities of a company at a given date. If important assets and liabilities are omitted, do we have a balance sheet that reflects reality? These are the new concerns of accounting.

CAREERS IN ACCOUNTING

Would accounting be a good career for you? Certain aptitudes are important for anyone who wants to be an accountant.

- An appreciation of accuracy.
- A feel for figures.
- An analytical mind.
- An ability to handle masses of detail without losing perspective.
- A sense of order.

If you have not done well in math in school and don't particularly enjoy working with figures, you probably would not enjoy accounting. A good accountant must also be able to spot inaccuracies and work creatively with numbers, because he or she often works with figures prepared by others. If that sounds interesting to you, you might find accounting a rewarding career.

PROGRESS CHECK

- What three formulas make up the income statement? What is the difference between revenue and income on that statement?
- What is the fundamental accounting equation used to make up the balance sheet? What is "balanced" on the balance sheet?
- What is cash flow? How can a small business protect itself against cash-flow problems before they occur?

SUMMARY

1. Define accounting and explain the differences between managerial accounting and financial accounting.

1. Accounting is the recording, classifying, summarizing, and interpreting of financial transactions that affect an organization. The methods used to record and summarize accounting data into reports are called an accounting system.

- *How does managerial accounting differ from financial accounting?*

  Managerial accounting provides information and analyses to managers within the firm to assist them in decision making. Financial accounting provides information and analyses to managers and to external users of data such as creditors and lenders.

- *What is the difference between a private and a public accountant?*

  Public accountants are independent firms that provide services for a fee to a variety of companies; private accountants are employees of a company. Only public accountants perform independent audits.

2. Many people confuse bookkeeping and accounting.

2. Compare accounting and bookkeeping.

▼ *What is the difference between bookkeeping and accounting?*

Bookkeeping is part of accounting, but only the mechanical part of recording data. Accounting also includes classifying, summarizing, interpreting, and reporting data to management.

3. There are six major classes of accounts in accounting: assets, liabilities, owners' equity, revenues, cost of goods sold, and expenses.

3. Identify and describe the major accounts used to prepare financial statements.

▼ *What are assets?*

Assets are economic resources owned by the firm, such as buildings and machinery. Current assets are converted to cash within a year while fixed assets are relatively permanent and are used to operate the business. Liquidity refers to how fast an asset normally becomes cash. Current assets are thus more liquid than fixed assets.

▼ *What are liabilities?*

Liabilities are debts owed by the organization to others (for example, creditors, bond holders).

▼ *What is owners' equity?*

It is the sum of owners' investments plus profits to date not yet paid out to owners.

▼ *What are revenues?*

Revenues are what is received from the sale of goods or services rendered.

▼ *What are cost of goods sold?*

They are a particular type of expense measured by the total cost of merchandise sold.

▼ *What are expenses?*

Expenses are incurred in operating the business to earn the revenues. They include salaries, rent, and utilities.

4. The primary financial statements provided by accountants are income statements and balance sheets.

4. Understand simple income statements and balance sheets, and explain their functions.

▼ *What is an income statement?*

An income statement reports revenues, costs, and expenses for a specific period of time. The basic formula is revenue minus costs and expenses equals income. (Note that income and profit mean the same thing.)

▼ *What is a balance sheet?*

A balance sheet reports the financial position of a firm at a particular time. The fundamental accounting equation used to prepare the balance sheet is assets = liabilities + owners' equity.

5. Most businesspeople realize the value of using computers to help them with their accounting activities.

5. Describe the role of computers in accounting.

▼ *How can computers help accountants?*

Computers can easily record and analyze data and quickly provide financial reports. Software is available that can continuously analyze and test accounting systems to be sure they are functioning correctly. This software makes regular reporting very easy. Computers can help decision making by providing appropriate information, but they cannot make good financial decisions independently. Accounting creativity is still a human trait.

6. Cash flow is the difference between cash in and cash out.

6. Explain the concept of cash flow.

▼ *Why is cash flow so important?*

Having enough cash at all times to be able to pay bills, salaries, loans, and the like is the first requirement for a business if it is to stay alive. Making a profit is not enough. Many small businesses do not estimate cash flow in advance, and it is one of the main reasons why they fail.

7. Profits and cash are not the same thing.

7. Explain how a business can be making profits and still be short of cash.

▼ *What happens to profits?*

Cash and profits are not the same thing (except for street vendors who have no inventory and no expenses and sell for cash only). Usually when companies sell goods, profits get tied up in additional inventory, accounts receivable, or equipment and are not available to pay bills. This usually happens when companies are growing rapidly. Slow, steady growth allows profits to show up in stronger cash positions.

8. Important assets and liabilities are not being accounted for in financial statements.

▼ *What are these assets and liabilities and why are they not stated on balance sheets?*

Major assets are the skills and education of the employees. Another one is the combined technological knowledge of a company. All of these intangible assets may be more important than a company's tangible assets. Similarly, liability for environmental damage has emerged as a major potential liability for many companies. The problem is that there is no recognized method for evaluating these assets and liabilities.

8. Understand the new concerns of accounting.

GETTING INVOLVED

1. Go to a local business and watch the people recording data in the journals and ledgers. Look over the ledger to see what it contains. Many firms now use computers for these tasks. Visit one that does and compare its ledgers to its journals. Spend some time observing accountants at work—the surroundings, the people, and so on. Report your reactions to the class.
2. Take a sheet of paper. On every fourth line, write one of the following headings: assets, liabilities, owners' equity, expenses, and revenues. Then list as many items as you can under each heading. When you are finished, look up the lists in the text and add to your own. Keep the lists for your notes. As you complete the lists, create a mental picture of each account so that you can understand the concepts behind accounts and accounting.
3. Prepare your own income statement. See how far you can get without looking back to Figure 17–6. Then check the text to see what you have forgotten, if anything. Actually writing down the components does wonders for remembering them later.
4. Prepare your own balance sheet. Remember the simple formula: *Assets* = *Liabilities* + *Owners' equity.* Go back and check your balance sheet against Figure 17–7.
5. Write your own explanation of how small businesses get into trouble with cash flow by expanding too rapidly. Think of several ways a business could avoid such problems. Discuss your thoughts with the class.

PRACTICING MANAGEMENT DECISIONS

Case One Constructing an Income Statement and a Balance Sheet

Stuart Jenkins started Neighbourhood Landscaping Service when he was in high school. As the business grew, Stu hired several of his friends. He is doing well and is now in a position to begin keeping better records. Stu has written down some of his figures, but he doesn't know how to interpret them. He wants to take out a loan and wants to prepare a balance sheet to calculate his financial position. These are his figures:

Assets		**Liabilities**	
Cash	$ 5,350	Money owed bank	$7,500
Truck	13,500	Money owed supplier	545
Accounts receivable	2,400	Money owed for equipment	500
Equipment	4,520	Total liabilities	$8,545
Office furniture	945		
Supplies	550		
Trailer	500		
Total assets	$27,765		

Some other figures Stu hastily put together in no consistent order are:

Income from work done	$74,000
Expenses incurred for trees, shrubs, etc.	22,000
Salaries of helpers (2)	16,000
Advertising	1,360
Insurance	2,000
Office costs (phone, heat, rent, etc.)	8,400
Depreciation on truck	$ 4,000

Stu paid $1,800 for other supplies such as gravel, sand, and slate used for walkways.

Decision Questions

1. What additional information, if any, would you need to construct a balance sheet? Is Stu in a strong or poor financial condition?
2. How much did Stu earn before taxes? Prepare an income statement to show Stu how such a financial statement looks.
3. Stu is unsure of the terminology of accounting. Study his list of figures and names and see if you can find any incorrect usage of terms.

Case Two Where Did Katherine Go Wrong?

Katherine Potter knew a good thing when she saw it. At least, it seemed so at first. She was travelling in Italy when she spotted pottery shops that made beautiful products ranging from ashtrays to lamps. Some of the pottery was stunning in design.

Katherine began importing the products to Canada, and sales took off. Customers immediately realized the quality of the items and were willing to pay top price. Katherine decided to keep prices moderate to expand rapidly, and she did. Sales in the second three months were double those of the first few months. Sales continued to grow during the rest of the first year.

Every few months, Katherine had to run to the bank to borrow more money. She had no problems getting larger loans, because she always paid promptly. To save on the cost of buying goods, Katherine always took cash discounts. That is, she paid all bills within 10 days to save the 2 percent offered by her suppliers for paying so quickly.

Most customers bought Katherine's products on credit. They would buy a couple of lamps and a pot and Katherine would allow them to pay over time. Some were very slow in paying her, taking three months or more.

Towards the end of the year, Katherine noticed a small drop in her business. The local economy was not doing well because many people were being laid off from their jobs. Nonetheless, Katherine's business stayed level. One day the bank called Katherine and told her she was late in her payments. She had been so busy that she hadn't noticed that. The problem was that Katherine had no cash available to pay the bank. She frantically called several customers for payment, but that raised very little cash as only one person was able to pay immediately. Katherine was in a classic cash-flow bind.

She decided to raise prices and refused to make any sales on credit. She started delaying payment on her bills, thus losing the discounts. Then she engaged an accounting firm to review her financial condition.

Their examination showed that she had made nice profits and her overall position was good. Her cash problems were due to the fact that she had allowed customers to run behind in payments and she had built up a lot of inventory that she had paid in full. They prepared financial statements and a cash-flow projection, which showed a good picture.

Based on this information, the bank increased her loan. But it urged her to get after her late-paying customers and reduce her inventory, both of which actions would considerably improve her cash flow. Her accountants had told her the same thing.

Decision Questions

1. Do you see how it was possible to have high sales and profits and still run out of cash? How could Katherine have avoided the problem?
2. Do you think it was wise of Katherine to raise prices and refuse to sell on credit? Will it hurt future business?
3. Was she right to get an accountant at this point? Should she have done so earlier? When?

LET'S TALK BUSINESS

1. Why are college and university students, even business majors, so hesitant to take accounting courses? Would a different approach by colleges and universities be more successful? What should that be?
2. Explain the link between accounting and finance. Do you think you could be a good financial analyst without knowing accounting?
3. Discuss why non-profit organizations need to understand accounting at least as much as businesses.
4. Why are both the balance sheet and the income statement necessary for a proper picture of a company? What is the connection between the two?

LOOKING AHEAD

In Chapter 18, we look at how companies plan their finances and raise funds. We also examine the role of the stock exchange in this connection.

First we look at Appendix D: Financial Ratios. To make proper use of financial statements, further analysis is required. One important type of analysis is called *ratio analysis*. The appendix introduces you to ratio analysis.

FINANCIAL RATIOS: THE LINK BETWEEN ACCOUNTING AND FINANCE

Everyone interested in finance needs to understand basic accounting. What is especially helpful to financial analysis is the use of ratios to measure a company's health. You are familiar with ratios. They are used all the time to measure the success of sports teams. For example, in basketball, the ratio of shots made from the foul line versus attempts is measured. TV announcers say, "Jones is shooting 85 percent of his foul shots, so he is not the one to foul in the final minutes." We judge basketball players by such ratios: 80 percent is good for foul shots, 65 percent is not good. We calculate similar ratios for baseball ("He's batting .300," or 30 percent), football ("He's completed 50 percent of his passes"), and so on. So ratios are not hard to understand or compute, and they give a lot of information about the relative performance of athletes or of businesses. Now let's look at some key ratios that businesspeople use. All the data are obtained from the balance sheet or the income statement.

HANDLING CASH-FLOW PROBLEMS: AVERAGE COLLECTION PERIOD OF RECEIVABLES

We have already noted that a major financial problem of small businesses is poor liquidity or cash flow. In many cases, poor cash flow is caused by not collecting accounts receivable fast enough. Many customers do not pay their bills until they are reminded or pressured to pay. Incentives such as discounts for paying early are often helpful for minimizing collection time. To determine whether or not a business is collecting its receivables in a reasonable period of time, an analyst calculates the average collection period. Unlike the other financial analysis calculations, this one takes two steps. The first step is to divide the annual credit sales by 365 to obtain the average daily credit sales. The second step is to divide accounts receivable by the average daily credit sales (the first step) to get the average collection period in days. For example:

1. $\text{Average daily credit sales} = \dfrac{\text{Total annual credit sales}}{\text{365 days}}$

2. Collection period in days $= \dfrac{\text{Accounts receivable}}{\text{Average daily credit sales}}$

If total annual credit sales were $365,000, then the average daily credit sales would be $1,000:

$$\frac{\$365{,}000}{365} = \$1{,}000$$

If the accounts receivable today were $60,000, then the collection period would be 60 days:

$$\text{Average collection period of receivables} = \frac{\$60{,}000}{\$1{,}000} = 60 \text{ days}$$

CASH FLOW AND CREDIT TERMS

If you collect your accounts in 60 days but pay your accounts in 10 days, you will likely have a cash flow problem. To encourage people to pay more quickly, most companies give credit terms such as "2/10, net 30." This means that if customers pay within 10 days, they can deduct 2 percent from the price. If they don't take advantage of the discount, the total amount is due in 30 days.

Paying within 10 days is advantageous for buyers. Here's why. A 2 percent discount for paying within 10 days means that the company saves 2 percent by paying 20 days early—because the total amount is due within 30 days. Read the last sentence again slowly to be sure you understand. Each year there are 18 20-day periods. Therefore, by paying early (within 10 days) a firm can save 36 percent *annually* (2% × 18). That is why most businesses try to pay their bills within 10 days, if a discount is offered. It is a bargain. Now that you've learned to save money on purchases, let's look at the ratio that measures sales effectiveness.

INVENTORY TURNOVER

A business supply store once asked a consultant why its inventory turnover ratio was so low. The consultant walked through the warehouse and found box after box filled with slide rules, stacked high. These obsolete items were being carried on the books as inventory and lowering the turnover ratio. What signaled the problem was that the owner compared his turnover ratio to the average industry ratio.

A lower than average ratio indicates obsolete merchandise or poor buying practices. A higher than average ratio may indicate an understocked condition, where sales are lost because of inadequate stock, or a very good buyer of merchandise. The faster merchandise moves out, the greater the inventory turnover. The result is greater profit without investing more money in increased inventory. The aim is to have the smallest inventory that can produce the greatest amount of sales. Calculate the ratio to determine inventory turnover by dividing the cost of goods sold by the average inventory for the period. For example, if the cost of goods sold were $160,000 and the average inventory were $20,000, the turnover ratio would be 8. That means 8 times during one year or every 1½ months. This figure by itself is rather meaningless. It has to be compared to industry figures to tell a company how it is doing in relation to competitors. It must also be analyzed to see if it makes sense for that particular type of business. The calculation looks like this:

$$\text{Turnover} = \frac{-\text{Cost of goods sold}}{\dfrac{\text{Average inventory}}{2}}$$

$$\text{Turnover} = \frac{\$160{,}000}{\dfrac{\$23{,}000 + \$17{,}000}{2}}$$

$$\text{Turnover} = \frac{\$160{,}000}{\$20{,}000} = 8$$

MANAGERIAL INFORMATION: GROSS MARGIN (OR PROFIT)

A major concern for all retail merchandising companies is the rate of profit earned on the merchandise sold. If you buy sweaters for $50 and sell them for $120, your markup is $70. That means you have added $70 to your cost to arrive at your selling price. This markup, or gross margin (or gross profit), is usually expressed as a percentage of the selling price.

$$\text{Gross margin rate} = \frac{\text{Gross margin}}{\text{Sales}} = \frac{\$70}{\$120} = .58\text{, or } 58\%$$

If you know the average gross margin rate of your sales from prior years, you can apply that to the sales in any period and get a rough approximation of your total gross profit for that period. For example, merely subtracting your estimated monthly expenses from monthly gross margin immediately tells you what profit or loss you have made.

Similarly, it is easy to calculate your break-even point—how much sales you must do just to cover your expenses. The procedure is a little more complicated for a manufacturing company.

MANAGERIAL INFORMATION: RETURN ON SALES

Each industry has a different rate of return on sales. Such figures are well known in the industry. Therefore, a firm can determine whether or not it is doing as well as other businesses by calculating the return on sales ratio. This involves dividing net income by net sales. If net income were $10,000 and net sales were $200,000, the return on sales ratio would be 5 percent:

$$\text{Return on sales} = \frac{\text{Net income}}{\text{Net sales}}$$

$$\text{Return on sales} = \frac{\$10{,}000}{\$200{,}000} = 5\%$$

A good example of a company that showed a poor return on sales ratio one year was Compaq Computer. It had sales of $300 million but earned only $9 million, a ratio of just over 3 percent. That was about half of IBM's return on sales ratio and 70 percent of Apple Computer's. As a result, Compaq's stock fell from 11 to 3½ in that period. As you can see, investors pay attention to the return on sales ratio. One way to increase the ratio is to increase prices, but Compaq was facing a competitive market and wanted to keep its prices low. Another way is to reduce costs. Shareholders compute return on sales when evaluating a firm (or look up the ratio in business reports). Another ratio they look for is return on investment.

SHAREHOLDER INFORMATION: RETURN ON INVESTMENT (ROI)

Shareholders invest in a business expecting to make a greater return on their money than if they did something else with it, like depositing it in a bank or buying bonds. You can calculate the return on equity (ownership) in a firm by dividing net income by the owners' equity. You are more likely to hear this formula referred to as *ROI,* or *return on investment.* Investment, then, is synonymous with equity. If net income were \$10,000 and shareholders' equity (investment) were \$100,000, the return on investment would be 10 percent:

$$\text{ROI} = \frac{\text{Net income}}{\text{Owners' equity}}$$

$$\text{ROI} = \frac{\$10{,}000}{\$100{,}000} = 10\%$$

SHAREHOLDER INFORMATION: DEBT/EQUITY RATIO

Debt/equity is calculated by dividing total liabilities by owners' equity. Basically, this ratio tells you how much money the company has borrowed compared to other firms in the industry. A high ratio triggers caution among investors. But again, high or low is relatively meaningless unless compared to the average of the same industry.

One year in heavy equipment, the median debt/equity ratio was 0.4, but International Harvester's figure was 5.3, Massey-Ferguson's was 6.1, and Pettibone's was 7.9. All of these firms with high figures were in deep trouble financially. The debt/equity ratio reflected that trouble. If total liabilities were \$150,000 and owners' equity were \$150,000, the debt/equity ratio would be 1:

$$\text{Debt/equity ratio} = \frac{\text{Total liabilities}}{\text{Owners' equity}}$$

$$\text{Debt/equity ratio} = \frac{\$150{,}000}{\$150{,}000} = 1$$

Most consultants feel a ratio greater than 1 is not good, but again that varies by industry. Sometimes debt is a good sign if it means the company is trying to optimize the return to stockholders by assuming more risk.

INFORMATION FOR BANKERS AND CREDITORS: CAN PAYMENT COMMITMENTS BE MET?

Analysts are also interested in certain other ratios. One calculation analysts make is the current ratio.

$$\text{Current ratio} = \frac{\text{Current assets}}{\text{Current liabilities}}$$

This ratio measures a company's ability to pay its short-term debts. A ratio of 1.5 or higher is usually desired. Anything more than 1 indicates the firm's ability to pay all its debts. Less than 1 means that its current liabilities exceed its current assets, so the company cannot pay all its bills.

If we leave inventories out of the above equation, we get a more accurate feel for whether or not a business could quickly pay its current liabilities. Thus, another test is called the *quick ratio* or *acid-test ratio*. This is the supposed acid test of whether a firm is on solid financial ground, short term or not. The formula is:

$$\text{Quick ratio} = \frac{\text{Cash} + \text{Marketable securities} + \text{Accounts receivable} + \text{Notes receivable}}{\text{Liabilities}}$$

Professionals use several other ratios to learn more details about the condition of a business, but this will give you an idea of what ratios are and how they are used. The point is that financial analysis begins where accounting reports end. This appendix, then, represents the link between accounting and finance.

FINANCIAL MANAGEMENT

LEARNING GOALS

After you have read and studied this chapter, you should be able to:

1. Explain the role and importance of finance and the responsibilities of financial managers.
2. Outline the steps in financial planning by explaining how to forecast financial needs, develop budgets, and establish financial controls.
3. Recognize the financial needs that must be met with available funds.
4. Distinguish between short-term and long-term financing and between debt capital and equity capital.
5. Identify and describe several sources of short-term capital.
6. Identify and describe several sources of long-term capital.
7. Compare the advantages and disadvantages of issuing bonds and identify the classes and features of bonds.
8. Compare the advantages and disadvantages of issuing stock and outline the differences between common and preferred stock.
9. Discuss the criteria used to select investments and describe methods of diversifying investments.
10. Explain securities quotations listed in the financial section of a newspaper.

KEY TERMS

blue chip stocks, p. 602
bond, p. 594
buying on margin, p. 603
capital budget, p. 582
cash budget, p. 582
cash-flow forecast, p. 581
commercial paper, p. 590
common stock, p. 600
convertible bond, p. 597
cumulative preferred stock, p. 600
debt capital, p. 586
dividends, p. 598
equity capital, p. 586
factoring, p. 590
finance, p. 580
line of credit, p. 589
maturity date, p. 595
mutual fund, p. 605
operating budget, p. 582
pledging, p. 589
preferred stock, p. 599
principal, p. 595
secured bonds, p. 596
secured loan, p. 589
stock certificate, p. 598
stock exchange, p. 598
trade credit, p. 587
unsecured bonds, p. 596

Stephen Vaughan

PROFILE STEPHEN VAUGHAN FINANCES WITH THE ANGEL ANGLE

While working for Henry Birks & Sons Ltd. in St. John's, Nfld., Stephen Vaughan noticed that university and college grads were snapping up insignia rings. So were athletic teams and even corporations, who awarded them to employees. The custom-made gold and silver rings were a kind of status symbol that showed off the wearer's membership in a select group.

Intrigued by this growing business, Vaughan toured a few factories in Quebec and Ontario. In 1989 he decided to teach himself the art of ring-making and launched his company, Heirloom Insignia Jewellery Inc. "At the time, there was nobody making them in Newfoundland," he says. "The orders were sent to manufacturers on the mainland, and it took them eight to twelve weeks to produce the rings. I estimated that I could manufacture and deliver in four to six weeks."

Having quit Birks, Vaughan canvassed the banks in search of a $20,000 start-up loan. The banks rebuffed him. "They liked my idea, but they didn't like me," Vaughan recalls. "I was 26, had no assets, and was $15,000 in debt because of a car loan and my credit-card spending."

About this time, Vaughan noticed an ad in a local newspaper for the Investment Opportunities Project (IOP), a new city-run program that matched cash-hungry entrepreneurs with investors throughout the province. He approached the manager of the outfit, who assured him that there was a good chance an investor could be found.

Informal investors, known as "angels," range from accountants and dentists to entrepreneurs who have already made their stash. According to a new study by Carleton University business professor Allan Riding, angels are motivated by the desire to make even more money by investing in fast-growing small firms. Riding's survey of more than 250 angels found that their average investment is $110,000 and they aim for a return of 50 percent per year, compounded. They achieve this by selling the shares back to the entrepreneur or to another investor once the company starts making substantial profits and its value increases.

Angels are becoming an increasingly important source of capital for entrepreneurs. Riding estimates that they currently sink $300 million to $800 million a year into small firms. Through the St. John's IOP, Vaughan was given the chance to meet 55 angels. Two of them, both successful entrepreneurs, liked his business idea. In exchange for their $20,000 investment in Vaughan's company, they will receive half the profits made by the time the firm's in the black. Vaughan says Heirloom Insignia Jewellery should hit sales of $300,000 this year and become profitable next year on revenue of $500,000—a remarkable achievement in an ailing economy.

While paying out half the profits sounds steep, Vaughan says the investors don't want to remain as part owners forever. They'd prefer to sell their shares back to Vaughan in a couple of years, making a tidy profit on the increased value of the stock. At that point, Vaughan hopes to entice other informal investors to come on board. He's looking for $70,000 or more next time around, to buy computerized design equipment and to finance marketing campaigns. But he's also looking for expertise. His current investors, he says, injected badly needed funds into the venture, but they are interested only in a three- to five-year project and have little desire to plunge into the day-to-day operations of a small business. "It's a big help, as a start-up entrepreneur, if you can get both capital and know-how from your investor," says Vaughan.

Source: Jerry Zeidenberg, "The Angel Angle," Report on Business, *Globe and Mail,* June 1993, pp. 70–72.

THE ROLE OF FINANCE

An accountant in a company may be compared to a skilled laboratory technician who takes blood samples and other measures of a person's health and writes the findings on a health report (financial statements). A financial manager in a business is the doctor who interprets those reports and makes recommendations to the patient regarding changes that would improve health. Financial managers use the data prepared by the accountants and make recommendations to top management regarding strategies for improving the health (financial strength) of the firm.

A manager cannot be optimally effective at finance without understanding accounting. Similarly, a good accountant needs to understand finance. Accounting and finance, finance and accounting—the two go together like pizza and beer.

Venture magazine recently ran an article citing the mistakes companies make in financing: "Sources for this story couldn't emphasize enough that many companies' financial and money-raising woes come down to inaccurate financial reporting. Young, growing companies need to live and die by the numbers, they say."[1] The message could not be clearer—good finance begins with good accounting.

As you may remember from Chapter 6, financing a *small* business is a difficult but critical function if a firm expects to survive those important first two years. The simple reality is, the need for careful financial management is an essential, ongoing challenge a business of any size must endure throughout its entire life. Financial problems can arise in any organization.

Causes and Effects of Financial Problems

The most common causes of financial problems are:

1. *Undercapitalization*—not enough funds to start or to continue operations. Many small businesses fall into this trap. Starting on a shoestring and a prayer is a good formula for failure.
2. *Inadequate planning and/or control,* which leads to constant unpleasant surprises. Also, inadequate attention to warning signals leads to reduced sales and falling cash flow. A classic example was the way the Big Three auto companies ignored the consumer shift to Japanese cars of better quality and lower prices in the 1980s. Ford and Chrysler are just now recovering and GM is still struggling.
3. *Poor cash flow,* which could be due to any of the preceding causes or other reasons. Granting credit too easily or allowing collections to fall behind can tie up a lot of cash.

In addition, events occur over which you have no control. These are generally changes in the macro environment, the world outside your company and beyond your normal business relationships. New government policies on taxes, interest rates, or imports; fluctuations in Canadian dollar exchange rates with other currencies; inflation or deflation; recession; cross-border shopping; technological developments; and new competitors can all play havoc with the best-laid plans. In Part 1 these issues were discussed in more detail.

Three very large Canadian companies ran into serious trouble in the past half-dozen years because of a big drop in their cash flows. Robert Campeau of Campeau Corp. and the Reichman brothers of Olympia & York have both been mentioned in previous chapters as examples where extreme cash-flow problems caused the collapse of their empires.

A third member of this triumvirate is the giant Edper conglomerate of hundreds of companies, reputed to be the largest such grouping in Canada, controlled by

Peter and Edward Bronfman. Severe cash-flow problems have them selling off companies and adopting other drastic measures to survive.

In all three cases, the companies were in trouble because they had huge debts acquired in various expansions and they were counting on continuous inflation and prosperity to provide enough cash to meet their crushing interest and capital repayment requirements. The recession in the U.S., Canada, and England and the collapse of the real estate market upset all their plans.

One does not have to pursue finance as a career to be interested in finance. Financial understanding is important to anyone who wants to invest in stocks and bonds or plan a retirement fund. In short, finance is something everyone should be concerned with. Let us take a look at what finance is all about.

What Is Finance?

finance
The business function that is responsible for the efficient acquisition and disbursement of funds.

Finance is the business function that is responsible for the efficient and effective acquisition and disbursement of funds. The major preoccupation of finance managers is to develop a financial plan for the amount of funds required and how to obtain them. Without a carefully calculated financial plan, the firm has little chance for survival regardless of its product or marketing effectiveness. Managing finances is the crucial link that makes both production and marketing effective.

You are probably somewhat familiar with several finance functions—for example, the idea of buying merchandise on credit and collecting payment from companies that buy the firm's merchandise or services. Both *credit* and *collections* are important responsibilities of financial managers. The finance manager must be sure that the company does not lose too much money to bad debt losses (people or firms that don't pay). Naturally, this means that finance is further responsible for collecting overdue payments. These functions are critical to all types of businesses but particularly important to small and medium-size businesses, which typically have smaller cash or credit cushions than large corporations. Figure 18–1 outlines the responsibilities of financial managers.

Finally, the finance department has an internal audit division. The internal auditor makes sure company assets are properly controlled and secured, company accounting and financial procedures are carried out, and all transactions are properly recorded. In smaller companies, the internal auditing role is divided between the owners and the external auditors.

Without internal audits, accounting statements would be much less reliable. Regular internal audits offer the firm assurance that financial planning will be effective. We turn next to how financial planning is carried out.

Figure 18–1 What financial managers do. Many of these functions depend on the information provided by the accounting statements discussed in Chapter 17.

- Planning
- Budgeting
- Obtaining funds
- Controlling funds (funds management)
- Collecting funds (credit management)
- Auditing
- Managing taxes
- Advising top management on financial matters

FINANCIAL PLANNING

Planning has been a continuous theme throughout this book. We have stressed the importance of planning as a managerial function and offered insights into planning your career. Financial planning involves analyzing the short- and long-term picture of money flows to and from the firm. The overall objective of financial planning is to optimize profits by making the best use of money. It's probably safe to assume that we all could use better financial planning in our lives.

Financial planning involves three steps: (1) forecasting financial needs, both short and long term, (2) developing budgets to meet those needs, and (3) establishing financial control to ensure the company is following the financial plans. Let's look at the important role each step plays in the financial health of an organization.

Forecasting Financial Needs

Forecasting is an important component of financial planning. (See Figure 18–2.) These plans are not cast in stone. They require annual updating according to results of the current year and new developments that are likely to affect the future. This leads to short-term forecasting, a forecast of revenues, costs, and expenses for a period of one year. The short-term forecast is the foundation for other financial plans and budgets for the year.

Part of this plan is the **cash-flow forecast,** a projection of the expected cash inflows and outflows for a particular period of time. Annual forecasts are broken down into monthly figures to allow for better control of cash. This forecast is based on expected sales revenues and the expected costs and expenses that will be incurred to generate those sales.

cash-flow forecast
A projection of expected cash inflows and outflows for a particular period of time.

The important thing to recognize with all forecasts and budgets is that they are only estimates. Flexibility is required to adjust these figures based on actual results. This means that each month's or each quarter's results lead to modification and updating of forecasts for the rest of the year. Long-term forecasts are then adjusted each year.

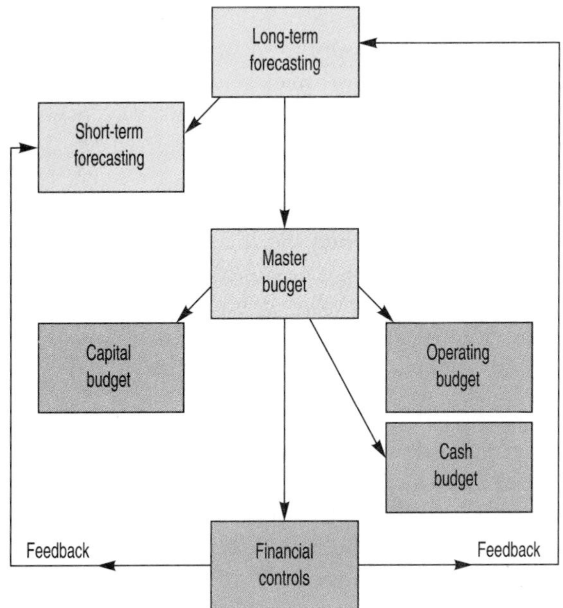

Figure 18–2 Financial planning. Note the close link between financial planning and budgeting.

A long-term forecast is a prediction of revenues, costs, and expenses for a period longer than one year, sometimes 5 or even 10 years into the future. This forecast plays a crucial part in the company's long-term strategic plan. Remember, the strategic plan asks questions such as: What business are we in and should we be in five years from now? How much money should we invest in automation and new plant and equipment over the next decade? The long-term financial forecast gives top management, as well as operations managers, some feel for the income or profit potential of different strategic plans. These long-term projections guide finance managers in preparing annual company budgets and short-term forecasts.

Developing Budgets

A budget is itself a financial plan. Specifically, a budget sets forth management's expectations for revenues and, based on those financial expectations, allocates the use of specific resources throughout the firm. You may live on a carefully constructed budget of your own. A business operates in the same way. A budget becomes the primary basis and justification for financial operations in the firm.

Most firms compile yearly budgets from short- and long-term financial forecasts. This leads to a master budget that has three components:

- An operating budget.
- A capital budget.
- A cash budget.

operating budget
The plan of the various costs and expenses needed to operate the business, based on estimated annual revenues.

capital budget
The spending plan for capital or fixed assets that are expected to yield returns over several years.

cash budget
The projected use of cash during a given period (e.g., monthly, quarterly, or annually.)

An **operating budget** is the plan of the various costs and expenses needed to run or operate the business, based on estimated revenues for the year. How much the firm will spend on supplies, travel, rent, advertising, salaries, and so on, is determined in the operating budget.

A **capital budget** highlights the firm's spending plans for assets that are expected to yield returns over an extended period of time (more than one year.) The capital budget primarily concerns itself with the purchase of such capital or fixed assets as land, buildings, and equipment.

A **cash budget** is based on the cash-flow forecast and projects the use of cash over a given period (for example, monthly, quarterly, or annually). Cash budgets can be important guidelines that assist managers in anticipating borrowing, debt repayment, operating cash disbursements, and short-term investment expectations. Cash budgets are often the last budgets that are prepared.

At this point, it should be obvious to you that financial managers play an important role in the operations of the firm. These managers often determine what long-term investments to make, when specific funds will be needed, and how the funds will be generated. Once a company has projected its short-term and long-term financial needs and established budgets to show how funds will be allocated, the final step in financial planning is to establish financial controls.

THINKING IT THROUGH

Budgets are designed to keep strict controls on spending. An important theme of this book is the need for managers to be flexible so that they can adapt quickly to rapidly changing conditions. This often means modifying previous plans. Do you see any conflict between budgets and such flexibility? How do managers stay within the confines of budgets when they must shift gears to accommodate a rapidly changing world? Which forecasts are more affected by these problems, short term or long term? Why?

Establishing Financial Control

Financial control means that the actual revenues, costs, and expenses are periodically reviewed and compared with projections. Deviations can thus be determined and corrective action taken. Such controls provide feedback to help reveal which accounts, which departments, and which people are varying from the financial plans. Such deviations may or may not be justified. In either case, some financial adjustments to the plan may be made. You will recall reading in Chapter 7 that an important function of managers is controlling. Financial control is one major aspect of this function. After the Progress Check we shall explore specific reasons why firms need to have funds readily available.

PROGRESS CHECK

- Name three finance functions important to the firm's overall operations and performance.
- What does an internal auditor do? Why is it important that this function remain independent?
- What are the three primary financial problems that often cause companies to fail?
- In what ways do short-term and long-term financial forecasts differ?
- What is the organization's purpose in preparing budgets? Can you identify at least three different types of budgets?

THE NEED TO HAVE FUNDS AVAILABLE

Sound financial management is essential to businesses because the need for operating funds never seems to cease. Also, like our personal financial needs, the capital needs of a business change over time. For example, as a small business grows, its financial requirements shift considerably. The same is true with large corporations such as Bell Canada and T. Eaton Co. As they venture into new product areas or markets, their capital needs intensify. It's safe to say that different firms need available funds for a variety of reasons. However, in virtually all organizations, funds must be available to finance specific operational needs. Let's take a look at the financial needs that affect the operations of both the smallest and the largest business enterprises.

Financing Daily Operations

If workers are scheduled to be paid on Friday, they don't expect to have to wait until Monday for their paychecks. If tax payments are due on the 15th of the month, the government anticipates the money will be there on time. If the interest payment on a business loan is due on the 30th, the lender doesn't mean the 1st of the next month. If you habitually pay late, you may be subject to interest and penalties or refusal of future loans. As you can see, funds have to be available to meet the daily operational costs of the business. The challenge of sound financial management is to see that funds are available to meet these daily cash expenditures without compromising the investment potential of the firm's money.

As you may know, money has a time value. In other words, if someone offered to give you $200 today or $200 one year from today, you would prefer to take the $200 today. Why? A very simple reason. You could start collecting interest on the $200 you receive today and over a year's time your money would grow. In business, the income gained on the firm's investments is important in maximizing its profit. For

Charge cards and credit cards serve multiple purposes for small businesses, as you can see from this ad. Like you and me, however, business must be careful about spending too freely. Financial budgeting helps managers control spending.

this reason, financial managers often try to have receipts at a maximum and keep cash expenditures at a minimum, to free funds for investment. It's not unusual for finance managers to suggest that the firm pay bills as late as possible (unless a cash discount is available) and set up collection procedures to ensure that the firm gets what's owed to it as fast as possible. This way finance managers maximize the investment potential of the firm's funds. As you might expect, efficient cash management is particularly important to small firms in conducting their daily operations.

Financing the Firm's Credit Services

Every business knows that availability of credit helps to keep current customers happy and entices other buyers to do business with the firm. In the highly competitive business environment today, it's unlikely a firm could survive without offering credit sales.

The major problem that arises with credit sales is this. As much as 25 percent of the firm's assets could be tied up in accounts receivable. (To refresh your memory, accounts receivable is money owed to a business from customers who bought goods or services on credit. If you refer back to Figure 17–7, you will see that accounts receivable are 25 percent of total assets ($200,000/$801,000 = 25%). This means the firm needs to spend its own funds to pay for the goods or services already provided to purchasers who bought on credit. This outflow of funds causes financial managers to focus a good part of their attention on efficient collection procedures. For example, a firm often provides cash discounts to purchasers who pay their account quickly. Also, finance managers scrutinize old and new credit customers to see if they have a history of meeting their credit obligations on time. In essence, the credit policy of the firm reflects its financial position and its financial policy. Of course, the desire to expand into new markets may also affect credit policy.

SPOTLIGHT ON BIG BUSINESS

Canada's Airlines: A Case of Financial Crash

One of the major stories that dominated Canadian headlines in the early 1990s was the financial mess of Canada's two largest airlines. Both Air Canada and Canadian Airlines International suffered enormous losses in 1991 and 1992 and the haemorrhaging continued into 1993. Their very existence was in question and each sought deliverance through alliances with U.S. airlines. How did they get into such a terrible state?

There were many problems, but the basic cause was the deep, long recession; revenues slid steeply, resulting in huge losses. Both of these companies have large debts from airplane acquisition and big operating expenses, so when cash flow dries up because revenues collapse, they find themselves in serious trouble. It's the classic problem that hits most businesses from time to time: shortage of cash to pay their bills.

How do they cope? Well, they cannot get funds by loans or bond issues because nobody will lend them money now. It's too risky. They cannot raise equity capital because nobody will buy their shares. So they resort to the only methods left: they reduce operational expenses by laying off employees and cutting other costs. They also delay paying their creditors or don't pay them at all, as Canadian Airlines did for a few months in late 1992 and early 1993.

They are not alone. Airline companies all over the world are having problems. Some American companies have gone bankrupt; others are fighting hard to stay alive. ▼

The early 1990s saw many airlines struck with severe financial problems. Canadian Airlines International has struggled to survive through this turbulent time. Many airlines in the United States have already gone bankrupt.

Financing the Purchase of Inventory

As we noted earlier, the marketing concept implies a clear consumer orientation. One implication of this concept is that service and availability of goods are vital if a firm expects to prosper in today's markets. To satisfy customers, businesses are forced to maintain inventories that involve a sizeable expenditure of funds. Although it's true the firm expects to recapture its investment in inventory through sales to customers, a carefully constructed inventory policy assists in managing the use of the firm's available funds and maximizing profitability. For example, an owner of a neighbourhood ice-cream parlour ties up more funds in inventory (ice cream) in the summer months than in winter, since demand for ice cream goes up in the summer. As you may recall from Chapter 9, innovations such as just-in-time inventory reduce the funds the firm must maintain in inventory. Ratio analysis of inventory turnover (see Chapter 17, Appendix D) also helps to prevent inventory from getting too high.

Financing the Purchase of Major Assets

In many organizations, it is essential to purchase major assets such as land for future expansion, plants to increase production capabilities, and equipment to maintain or exceed current levels of output or to reduce costs by modernizing. As you might imagine, these purchases require a large expenditure of the organization's funds. Therefore, it's critical that the firm weigh all the possible options before it commits what may be a large portion of its available resources. (As you may remember, these purchases are referred to as long-term, or fixed, assets.) Financial managers and analysts are called in to provide important insights into the appropriateness of such purchases.

Let's look at an example. Suppose a firm needs to expand its production capabilities due to increases in demand. One option is to buy land and build a new plant from scratch. Other options are to purchase an existing plant, rent a building, or contract out some part of the work. Can you think of financial and accounting considerations that would come into play in this decision?

It's evident the firm's need for available funds raises several questions that need to be considered. How does the firm obtain funds to finance operations and other business necessities? How long will specific funds be needed? Will funds have to be repaid at a later date? What will the needed funds cost? How much profit will the expansion yield? These questions will be addressed in the next section.

PROGRESS CHECK

- Money is said to have a time value. What exactly does this mean?
- Why are accounts receivable a financial concern to the firm?
- Is an efficient account collection plan more important to a small firm or a large corporation? Why?
- What is the major reason organizations spend a good deal of their available funds on inventory?

ALTERNATIVE SOURCES OF FUNDS

Earlier in the chapter, you learned that finance is the function in a business that is responsible for acquiring funds for the firm. The amount of money needed for various time periods and the most appropriate sources of these funds are fundamental questions in sound financial management. We will look at the different methods and sources of acquiring funds next, but first let's highlight some key distinctions involved in funding the firm's operations.

Organizations typically encounter short- and long-term financing needs. Short-term financing refers to the need for capital that will be repaid within one year and that helps finance current operations. Long-term financing refers to capital needs for major purchases that will be repaid over a specific time period longer than one year. We shall explore sources of both short- and long-term financing in the next section.

debt capital
Funds raised by borrowing that must be repaid.

equity capital
Funds raised within the company or from selling shares in the firm.

The other important distinction you should familiarize yourself with involves the different methods of raising capital available to the firm. Specifically, a firm can seek to raise capital through debt or equity sources. **Debt capital** refers to funds raised through various forms of borrowing that must be repaid (debt). **Equity capital** is money raised from within the firm or through the sale of shares (equity) in the firm. Again, we will discuss these two financing alternatives in depth later.

SHORT-TERM FINANCING

The bulk of a finance manager's job is *not* involved with obtaining long-term funds. The nitty-gritty, day-to-day operation of the firm takes up most of the manager's time and calls for the careful management of short-term financial needs. Cash may be needed for additional inventory or some emergency that may arise unexpectedly. As with your personal finances, a business sometimes needs to obtain short-term funds when other funds run out. This is particularly true of small businesses. It's rare that small businesses even attempt to find funding for long-term needs. They are more concerned with just staying afloat until they are able to build capital and creditworthiness. Short-term financing can be obtained in several ways. Sources include:

- Trade credit.
- Family and friends.
- Commercial banks.
- Government programs.
- Factoring.
- Commercial paper.
- Internal sources.

Trade Credit

The most widely used source of short-term funding is called **trade credit.** This means that a business is able to buy goods today and pay for them sometime in the future. When a firm buys merchandise, it receives an invoice (bill) much like the one you receive when you buy something on credit.

trade credit
The practice of buying goods now and paying for them in the future.

Every purchase is made under certain credit terms. The invoice will indicate that payment is due in 30 or 60 days or whatever arrangements have been made. Sometimes terms may read "2/10, net 30" which means that if payment is made within 10 days, a 2 percent discount will be deducted. Otherwise, payment is due in full in 30 days. Figure 18–3 shows when it pays to take discounts.

Sometimes companies that are strapped for cash offer larger discounts, 5 or 10 percent. These clearly mean a big reduction in cost to the purchaser who has the cash to take advantage of such offers.

The decision to take or not to take discounts is often not based on financial considerations alone. If you deal with certain suppliers on a regular basis and have a reputation for paying bills promptly, you will be a favoured customer. This could be very useful whenever you need a special order, a rush delivery, or merchandise that is in short supply. Of course, if you are short of cash, you may not be able to take advantage of discounts.

Where terms of payment are 2/10, N30, 60, or 90, there can be quite a difference between taking the 2% discount versus paying in full in 30 or 60 or 90 days.

		Approximately
2% for 20 days (10 instead of 30)	=	36% per annum
2% for 50 days (10 instead of 60)	=	15%
2% for 80 days (10 instead of 90)	=	9%

If a company is borrowing from the bank at 15% per annum, there is no advantage in earning 15%, a loss in earning 9%, and a big gain in earning 36%. If a company is borrowing at 8%, it pays to take the discount in all cases.

Figure 18–3 Discounts can yield a firm major savings on cost of merchandise purchases.

Family and Friends

A second source of short-term funds for most smaller firms is money lent by family and friends. Because short-term funds are needed for periods of less than a year, often friends are willing to help. Such loans can be dangerous if the firm does not understand cash flow and cannot repay them when promised. As we discussed earlier, the firm may suddenly need funds and have no other sources. It is better, therefore, not to borrow from friends, but instead go to a commercial bank that understands the risk and can help analyze future financial needs.

If you do borrow from family or friends, it is best to be very professional about the deal and (1) agree on terms at the beginning, (2) write an agreement, and (3) pay them back the same way you would a bank loan. If you are lucky, your family or friends who lend you the money might say, "Pay me back whenever you can."

Commercial Banks

It is wise to see a banker periodically and send the banker all financial statements. Remember, though, banks are reluctant to lend money to risky start-up ventures. For new firms, they often insist that short-term loans be backed by collateral (some assets or a guarantee by a third party).

A financial manager may obtain funds from a finance company, but the interest rates are usually higher than from other lending sources. Commercial bank rates are usually lower.

Try to imagine different kinds of businesspeople going to the bank for a loan, and you'll get a better feel for the role of the financial manager. Picture, for example, a farmer going to the bank to borrow funds for seed, fertilizer, equipment, and other needs. Such supplies may be bought in the spring and paid for when the fall harvest comes in. Now picture a local toy store buying merchandise for Christmas sales. The money for such purchases might be borrowed in October and paid back after Christmas. A restaurant may borrow funds at the beginning of the month and pay by the end of the month. You can see that *how much* a business borrows and for *how long* depend on the kind of business it is and how quickly the merchandise purchased with a bank loan can be resold or used to generate funds.

Obviously, if you and your accountant have carefully prepared a cash-flow forecast, you will have fewer surprises. No cash-flow forecast can prevent a drop in sales or the sudden bankruptcy of a major customer. But it does help to alert you to the size of the problem immediately.

There has been much criticism recently of the banks in Canada for their reluctance to make loans to small companies. Figures from the Canadian Bankers Association show that the increase in lending to large corporations from October 1991 to October 1992 was three times as much as to small companies. Because the six largest banks (see Figure 18–4) are responsible for an estimated 80 percent of all loans to small firms, these policies have a major impact on the ability of small business to obtain financing.[2]

David Berch, the president of Cognetics, Inc. has this to say about cash flow:[3]

> Cash flow is a constant issue if you don't go for large outside financing, which we've chosen not to do. You've got a fixed payroll. Everything on the expense side is fixed, and everything on the revenue side is variable. Somebody gets sick and doesn't pay on his receivable, or a salesperson gets lazy and doesn't sell for a couple of months. All of a sudden your cash flow goes to (pot). You find yourself constantly managing cash flow. It's a major issue.

Figure 18–4 Canada's six largest banks*

Company	Revenue (000s)	Assets (000s)
Royal Bank of Canada	$12,199,000	$138,293,000
Canadian Imperial Bank of Commerce	11,388,000	132,212,000
Bank of Montreal	8,847,000	109,035,000
Bank of Nova Scotia	8,420,179	97,660,809
Toronto Dominion Bank	6,138,000	74,133,000
National Bank of Canada	3,713,168	40,044,740

*As of October 1992.
Source: Report on Business, *Globe and Mail,* July 1993.

Can you see why it is important for a businessperson to keep friendly and close relations with his or her banker? The banker may be more willing to lend money in a crisis if the businessperson has established a strong, friendly relationship built on openness and trust. It's important to remember that your banker wants to see you succeed almost as much as you do. Bankers can be an invaluable support to small, growing businesses.

Different Forms of Bank Loans

The most difficult kind of loan to get from a bank or other financial institution is an unsecured loan, a loan not backed by any collateral. Normally, only highly regarded customers of the bank receive unsecured loans. A **secured loan** is one backed by collateral, something valuable such as property. If the borrower fails to pay the loan, the lender may take possession of the collateral. That takes some of the risk out of lending money. **Pledging** is the term for using accounts receivable, inventory, or other assets as security. Other property can also be used as collateral, including buildings, machinery, and other things of value (for example, company-owned stocks and bonds).

secured loan
Loan backed by something valuable, such as property.

pledging
Using accounts receivable, inventory, or other assets as security.

If you develop a good relationship with a bank, it will open a **line of credit** for you, meaning it will lend the business a given amount of short-term funds. The purpose of a line of credit is to speed the borrowing process so that a firm does not have to go through the hassle of applying for a new loan every time it needs funds. The funds are available as long as the credit ceiling is not exceeded. As businesses mature and become more financially secure, the amount of credit is often increased. A line of credit is a particularly good way to obtain funds for unexpected cash needs that arise.

line of credit
The amount of short-term credit a bank will lend a borrower that is agreed to ahead of time.

The Prime Rate

Periodically you will read that the prime rate has been raised or lowered. For most people, that report has little meaning. But for a financial manager, the level of the prime rate is very important. The *prime rate* is the short-term interest rate that banks charge their preferred (creditworthy) customers. Most firms pay more than the prime rate for a loan, but some very good credit risks can negotiate loans at prime. In either case, the prime rate is the base from which many loan rates are calculated.

Government Programs

Elaborate programs of government financing are available. These programs were discussed in detail in Chapter 3.

Farmers often go to the bank to borrow money for seed, fertilizer, and equipment. Careful financial management is critical when farm profits are low and expenses are rising. Bankers can help with finances if given the right information.

Factoring

One relatively expensive source of short-term funds for a firm is called factoring. It works like this: as we know, a firm sells many of its products on credit to consumers and other businesses. Some of these buyers are slow in paying their bills. The company may thus have a large amount of money due in accounts receivable. A *factor* buys the accounts receivable from the firm at a discount (usually advancing 50 to 70 percent of the value of the accounts receivable) for cash. The factor then collects and deducts the amount that was advanced plus its charges and remits the balance to the company.

factoring
Selling accounts receivable for cash.

Factoring, then, is the process of selling accounts receivable for cash. How much this costs the firm depends on the age of the accounts receivable, the nature of the business, the general interest rate level, and the conditions of the economy. Factoring is the most expensive form of financing. It is more common in industries where businesses are under-capitalized and have no other source of funds.

Commercial Paper

commercial paper
A short-term corporate equivalent of an IOU that is sold in the marketplace by a firm. It matures in 270 days or less.

Sometimes a large corporation needs funds for a few months and wants to get lower rates than those charged by banks. One strategy is to sell **commercial paper,** which consists of promissory notes, in amounts from $25,000 up, that mature in 270 days or less. The promissory note states a fixed amount of money the business agrees to repay to the lender on a specific date. The interest rate is identified on the face of the promissory note. Commercial paper is unsecured, so only financially stable firms can sell it. It is a way to get short-term funds for less than bank rates. Since most commercial paper comes due in 30 to 90 days, it is also an investment opportunity. Buyers can put cash into commercial paper for short periods to earn some interest.

Internal Sources of Funds

Just like you and me, a business is wise to get its short-term funds from internal sources as much as possible. There are several ways a firm can generate more cash internally. Often the company accountant works with the other finance people to find such sources of funds. One way is to collect accounts receivable more quickly. Inventory may also be reduced (as discussed in Chapter 9), costs may be minimized, or expenses may be cut. The healthier the balance sheet looks and the better the financial ratios are, the easier it is to borrow outside funds, if necessary, and the lower the interest rate that is charged. A wise accounting/finance team can save a business much money by finding internal sources of funds and freeing them, and by getting external funding at minimal rates (such as selling commercial paper).

PROGRESS CHECK

- If you received terms of 3/10, net 25, exactly what would this mean?
- What is the difference between trade credit and a line of credit at a bank?
- What is meant by factoring? What are some of the considerations for establishing a discount rate in factoring?
- How does commercial paper work? What is the main advantage of issuing commercial paper?

LONG-TERM FINANCING

Financial planning and forecasting help the firm develop a financial plan. This plan specifies the amount of funding that the firm will need over various time periods and the most appropriate sources of those funds. In setting long-term financing objectives, the firm generally asks itself three major questions:

- What are the long-term goals and objectives of the organization?
- What are the financial requirements needed to achieve these long-term goals and objectives?
- What sources of long-term capital are available and which will best fit our needs?

In business, long-term capital is used to buy fixed (capital) assets such as plant and equipment and to finance any expansion of the organization. The revenue generated from these assets is expected to continue over many years, so it will finance the cost of these assets. In major corporations, decisions concerning long-term financing normally involve the board of directors and top management, as well as finance and accounting managers. Sometimes an expert investment banker is included in the decision-making group. In smaller businesses, the owners are always actively involved in seeking all forms of financing.

Initial long-term financing usually comes from three sources: surplus funds, debt capital, and equity capital. This is shown in detail in Figure 18–5. The role of government in financing, especially for small business, is highlighted in the box Spotlight On Small Business.

Surplus Cash Funds

Successful businesses often generate surplus cash over and above their normal operating requirements. All or part of these funds may be available for investment in fixed (capital) assets that the company requires. The finance managers will compare how much interest these funds are earning to how much interest will have to be paid for loans. Usually the loan costs will exceed the revenue from the investments

Figure 18–5 Sources of long-term funds. The three major sources are surplus internal cash funds, debt capital, and equity capital.

Surplus Internal Cash Funds

- Generated from profits and sale of assets and not required for current use

Debt Capital (From:)

- Sale of bonds
- Long-term loans from banks and other financial institutions
- Mortgage on buildings
- Dealer financing of equipment

Equity Capital (Shares Sold To:)

- Current shareholders
- New investors
- Venture capital companies
- Federal Business Development Bank

made with the surplus funds, so the decision is not too difficult. If you are earning 6 percent and have to pay 9 percent to borrow, you save money by using your own funds for new equipment rather than borrowed monies. Sometimes there are other considerations that will lead a company to borrow despite the extra cost.

Debt Financing

A business can achieve long-term financing needs by securing debt capital. Debt capital is funds the firm borrows from lending institutions or acquires from selling bonds (explained later in the chapter). With debt financing, the company has a legal obligation to repay the amount borrowed plus regular interest at fixed dates.

Once a firm is established and has developed rapport with a bank, it can often secure a long-term loan. (For small business, the FBDB is often a good source of such loans.) Long-term loans are usually repaid within three to seven years but may go even longer. For such loans, a business must sign a term-loan agreement, which is a promissory note that requires the borrower to repay the loan plus interest in specified installments, usually monthly. Bonds may be issued for 5, 10, or even 20 years.

A mortgage on land and buildings is a long-term loan that is secured by the property. If the firm does not pay back interest or capital, the property may be seized by the mortgagor and sold to repay the amount owing. Any excess amount is returned to the borrower. Most long-term loans require some form of collateral, perhaps real estate, machinery, or stock. The interest rate for such loans is based on factors such as whether or not there is adequate collateral, the firm's credit rating, and the general level of market interest rates. The rates are usually higher than for short-term loans because of the longer period.

If an organization cannot meet its long-term financing needs from a lending institution, it may decide to issue bonds. Businesses compete with governments to sell bonds. Bonds sold by the federal or provincial governments are risk free because they are backed by the taxing power of governments, which makes them attractive. It also uses up substantial amounts of available investor capital, crowding out corporate bonds. If a firm cannot secure a long-term loan from a lender or issue bonds, it often turns to equity capital.

SPOTLIGHT ON SMALL BUSINESS

The FBDB as the Loan Ranger

For some businesses, the Federal Business Development Bank is "a much-needed oasis in a banking desert." It's not often that an entrepreneur approaches a financial institution for money and walks away with more than twice as much as requested.

So last year, when Grant Bibby, president of Orchid Automation Group Inc. of Cambridge, Ont., asked the FBDB for $400,000 and wound up with $900,000, he was shocked and thrilled. "They told us we needed more money than we thought," says Bibby. "I didn't quarrel with that."

It isn't every 29-year-old who can command enough confidence to secure a $900,000 loan, of course. But Bibby's on to a hot product. Orchid has devised computerized equipment that can change the dies on big metal-stamping machines used by titans like Chrysler in three minutes flat instead of the traditional seven days.

Metal bashers from car makers to appliance firms, intrigued by the Cambridge company's technology, quickly started buying. Two years after its 1988 launch, Orchid boasted sales of $1.1 million in 1990. By 1992, the figure was $5.2 million. Bibby, whose staff now numbers 35, predicts that will rise to $30 million within five years.

In planning for expansion, Bibby has tried to avoid the cash shortages that have traditionally plagued and sometimes killed fast-growing small firms. It isn't easy. Like many businesses, Orchid was started on a shoestring. Bibby's customers, who usually dole out from $100,000 to $1 million for each machine, pay only on delivery. And that comes several months after Orchid has laid out money for materials, engineering, and labour.

In 1991, Bibby recognized that further help from traditional lenders was a non-starter, since they liked their loans to be secured by tangibles such as buildings or machinery. Orchid was leasing its factory space and had already put its existing machines on the line to secure a modest term loan.

Luckily, a colleague mentioned that Bibby might qualify for a new pilot project called the Venture Loan Program, which had been launched by the federal government's FBDB in 1991 and was aimed at businesses three to five years old that were profitable and ripe for expansion.

Venture loans mix elements of a bank loan with techniques used by venture capitalists and, most crucial to Bibby, don't require any collateral. Instead, the FBDB bets on the future earnings of the borrower. "They came in, analyzed our operations, did a 100-page report, and concluded that we would hit our sales and profit goals," says Bibby.

He was even more pleased when the FBDB didn't demand an ownership stake in Orchid, something most venture capitalists would insist upon. "Entrepreneurs hate to give up ownership of their companies," says Francois Beaudoin, president and CEO of FBDB. "They've slaved for years to build what they've got and they don't want to dilute the ownership."

Under the deal he struck with the FBDB, Bibby will repay the Venture Loan over five years, with a 20 percent annual return on the investment for the bank. The payback is a combination of an interest payment and a royalty that's based on the company's revenues. The FBDB justifies its return on the grounds that its government mandate requires it to be self-financing. And while 20 percent is much higher than a standard bank loan (typically the prime rate plus 1 or 2 percent) it's far lower than the 35 to 45 percent expected by traditional venture capitalists. What's more, with the FBDB's $900,000 in its coffers, Orchid has obtained an additional $600,000 from banks at just over the prime rate.

FBDB plans to expand its Venture Loan outlays to $50 million a year by 1995, compared with $6.5 million in 1991. That would make it one of the biggest venture financing operations with a national focus in Canada. "We believe the economic recovery will be based on these small companies," says Beaudoin, "and we want to play a key role."

Source: Jerry Zeidenberg, "Shaking the Money Tree," Report on Business, *Globe and Mail,* June 1993, pp. 73, 74.

Equity Financing

Basically, equity financing refers to issuing (selling) shares or stock of the company. The new owners of shares in the company acquire a piece of the ownership or equity. The firm may offer shares to:

1. Existing owners by asking them to subscribe to additional stock. If the company is doing well, they may be pleased to do so.

2. The public in general through stockbrokers who handle such transactions. This will be necessary if more shares have to be sold than existing shareholders are willing to buy. (This option is not available to private companies.)
3. Venture capital companies. These were discussed in Chapter 6.
4. The Federal Business Development Bank.

Bonds and shares are discussed in detail in the rest of the chapter.

PROGRESS CHECK

- What is the difference between long-term and short-term capital? Do firms actually need both types of funding?
- What are the two major forms of debt financing available to a firm?
- How does debt financing differ from equity financing?
- What are two of the most common forms of equity financing available?

SECURITIES MARKETS

The importance of obtaining long-term funding cannot be overemphasized, because the most common problem facing new companies is starting without sufficient capital. Adequate long-term funding allows a firm to concentrate on operations instead of always looking for funds. It gives company managers a stable base from which to operate.

We now turn our attention to stocks and bonds—equity and debt capital. You will remember from Chapter 5 that public companies can obtain financing by selling bonds and shares to the public at large. This is made possible by the existence of markets—stock exchanges—where stockbrokers buy and sell these securities on behalf of clients. Securities markets are efficient places for carrying out these transactions. Pension funds, insurance companies, banks, trust companies, and companies and individuals with funds to invest (domestic or foreign) constitute a market with a huge appetite for quality securities.

Companies that issue securities to raise funds obtain them when the securities are first sold. All subsequent trading is between buyers and sellers and has nothing to do with the issuing company. This constitutes the bulk of trading on stock exchanges.

DEBT FINANCING THROUGH SELLING BONDS

To put it simply, a bond is a certificate (see Figure 18–6) indicating that the owner has lent money to the issuer of the bond. The company (or government) has a legal obligation to make regular (annual or semi-annual) interest payments and to repay the principal, all on the dates indicated on the certificate. Bonds come in a wide variety, with a terminology to match.

bond
A contract of indebtedness issued by a corporation or government unit that promises payment of a principal amount at a specified future time plus annual interest.

The Terminology of Bonds

A **bond** is a contract of indebtedness issued by a corporation or government unit that promises payment of a principal amount at a specified future time plus annual interest. As you may suspect, the interest rate paid varies based on factors such as the

Figure 18–6 A sample bond certificate from IBM. This is an unsecured and convertible bond (debenture) paying 7⅞ percent interest. It matures November 21, 2004, when the principal amount (or face value) of the bond must be repaid. The bond is convertible to common shares of the company at a fixed amount of shares for each bond. The fine print shows that information as well as the earliest date that the bondholder can exercise that option. The word *subordinated* means that other bond issues rank ahead of this issue if the company gets into financial difficulty. Because this is only a specimen, the amount is not shown. It is normally in multiples of $1,000.

REGISTERED REGISTERED

LESS THAN 1,000 DOLLARS

NUMBER

ZO

7⅞% CONVERTIBLE SUBORDINATED DEBENTURE DUE 2004

CUSIP 459200 AC 5

SEE REVERSE FOR CERTAIN DEFINITIONS

INTERNATIONAL BUSINESS MACHINES CORPORATION

International Business Machines Corporation, a corporation duly organized and existing under the laws of the State of New York (herein called the "Company," which term includes any successor corporation under the Indenture referred to on the reverse hereof), for value received, hereby promises to pay to

SPECIMEN

or registered assigns, the principal sum of

DOLLARS,

on November 21, 2004, and to pay interest on said principal sum semiannually on May 21 and November 21 of each year, at the rate of 7⅞% per annum, from the May 21 or November 21, as the case may be, next preceding the date of this Debenture to which interest has been paid or duly provided for, unless the date hereof is a date to which interest has been paid or duly provided for, in which case from the date of this Debenture, or unless no interest has been paid or duly provided for on the Debentures, in which case from November 21, 1984, until payment of said principal sum has been made or duly provided for and at such rate on any overdue principal and premium and (to the extent that the payment of such interest shall be legally enforceable) on any overdue installment of interest. Notwithstanding the foregoing, when there is no existing default in the payment of interest on the Debentures, if the date hereof is after a Regular Record Date (which shall be the close of business on the May 7 or November 7, as the case may be, next preceding an Interest Payment Date unless the Regular Record Date as so determined would not be a Business Day, in which event it shall be the Business Day next preceding) and before the next succeeding Interest Payment Date, this Debenture shall bear interest from such Interest Payment Date; *provided, however*, that if the Company shall default in the payment of interest due on such Interest Payment Date, then this Debenture shall bear interest from the next preceding Interest Payment Date to which interest has been paid or duly provided for, or, if no interest has been paid or duly provided for on the Debentures, from November 21, 1984. The interest so payable, and punctually paid or duly provided for, on any Interest Payment Date will, as provided in said Indenture, be paid to the Person in whose name this Debenture (or one or more Predecessor Debentures) is registered at the Regular Record Date for such Interest Payment Date. The principal of, and premium, if any, and interest on this Debenture are payable in such coin or currency of the United States of America as at the time of payment is legal tender for payment of public and private debts, at the office or agency of the Company in the Borough of Manhattan, City and State of New York; *provided*, that interest may be paid, at the option of the Company, by check mailed to the Person entitled thereto at such Person's address last appearing on the Debenture Register. Any interest not punctually paid or duly provided for shall be payable as provided in the Indenture.

Reference is made to the further provisions of this Debenture set forth on the reverse hereof, which shall have the same effect as though fully set forth at this place.

Unless the certificate of authentication hereon has been executed by the Trustee by manual signature, this Debenture shall not be entitled to any benefit under the Indenture, or be valid or obligatory for any purpose.

In Witness Whereof, the Company has caused this instrument to be duly executed under its corporate seal.

Dated

International Business Machines Corporation

TRUSTEE'S CERTIFICATE OF AUTHENTICATION
This is one of the Debentures referred to in the within-mentioned Indenture.
CHEMICAL BANK,
as Trustee.
By
Authorized Officer

Attest: John H. Grady, Secretary

By: Chairman of the Board

©IBM

T00000

state of the economy, the reputation of the company, and the rate being paid for government bonds. Generally, once an interest rate is set for specific bonds, it cannot be changed. **Principal** refers to the *face value* of the bond (bonds are almost always issued in multiples of $1,000).

principal
The face amount of a bond.

The company is legally bound to repay the bond principal in full to the bondholder on the bond's **maturity date.** For example, if you purchase a $1,000 bond with an interest rate of 9 percent and a maturity date of 2010, the firm is agreeing to pay you $90 in interest at specific dates each year until a specified date in 2010, when it must repay you the full $1,000.

maturity date
The date the issuer of a bond must repay the principal of the bond to the bondholder.

Advantages and Disadvantages of Issuing Bonds

As a source of long-term capital, bonds offer advantages to an organization. The decision to issue bonds is often based on careful evaluation of these advantages.

- Bondholders have no vote on corporate affairs, so management maintains control over the firm's operations. Remember, bondholders are creditors of the firm, not owners as shareholders are.

- The interest paid on bonds is a deductible expense to the firm's operations, which reduces income taxes.
- Bonds are a temporary source of funding for a firm. They are eventually repaid and the debt obligation eliminated.

However, bonds also have some significant drawbacks.

- Bonds are an increase in *debt* (liabilities) and may adversely affect the market's perception of the firm.
- Interest on bonds is a legal obligation. It must be paid even when the company is incurring losses or short of cash. If interest is not paid, bondholders can take legal action to force payment and seize any assets securing the bond.
- The face value of the bonds must be repaid on the maturity date. This could cause a possible cash shortage for the firm on that date.

Different Classes of Bonds

unsecured bonds
Bonds that are not backed by any collateral.

An organization can choose between two different classes of corporate bonds. The first class is **unsecured bonds** (Sometimes called debentures or debenture bonds.). These are bonds that are not supported by any special type of collateral on the part of the issuing firm. In other words, the primary security the bondholder has is the reputation and credit rating of the company. Unsecured bonds are issued only by well-respected firms with excellent credit ratings. Such bonds do have the backing of all corporate assets not otherwise pledged, but other creditors have an equal claim on those assets.

secured bonds
Bonds backed by some tangible asset that is pledged to the investor if the principal or interest is not paid.

The second class of bonds is referred to as **secured bonds.** These are bonds backed by some tangible asset that is pledged to the bondholder if interest is not paid or principal is not paid back. There are several kinds of secured bonds.

- *First mortgage bonds* are ensured by the company's real assets such as land and buildings. They are the most common of secured bonds and among the most desirable.
- *Collateral trust bonds* are backed by the stock that the company owns and that is held in trust by a financial institution (thus the word *trust* in the title).
- *Equipment trust bonds* are backed by the equipment the company owns. This may include trucks, aircraft, and other equipment that is widely used in industry. A trustee often holds title to the equipment pledged until the bondholders are paid.
- *Zero-coupon bonds* include corporate bonds, municipal bonds, treasury bonds, and even deposit certificates from banks. Instead of making periodic interest payments, issuers sell these bonds deeply discounted from the face value. When the bonds mature, the face value received minus the discounted price paid is the total interest earned. Because they don't actually pay interest yearly, zeros fall more dramatically than other bonds when interest rates rise and they rise more quickly when interest rates fall. They are for investors who do not need the interest cash flow.

As you can see, secured bonds are a relatively safe investment in that the risk to bondholders is reduced. Figure 18–7 lists several kinds of bonds and their descriptions. Not all bonds include the same features.

Bond	Description
Collateral trust	These bonds are secured by the general credit of the issuer as well as the specific property for which it is issued.
Convertible bond	These bonds can be exchanged for another security, usually common stock.
Coupon bond	These bonds have coupons attached; the bondholder submits the coupons to an agent for the payment of interest.
Debenture	These bonds are secured only by the general credit of the firm plus any unpledged assets.
Mortgage bond	These bonds are secured by real property (for example, buildings).
Zero-coupon bond	These bonds pay no interest prior to maturity; the return comes from the difference between purchase price and face (par) value.

As you can see, there are all kinds of bonds available with different risks. There are bonds for every kind of investor.

Figure 18–7 Some bonds available in the market.

THINKING IT THROUGH

Considering the disadvantages and advantages of different forms of raising funds, which method would you adopt if you had to make that decision in your company? How would your decision be affected in a high-interest year? If your company did well? What would you do for short-term financing? For long-term financing? How would you justify your choices?

Special Bond Features

One special feature of a bond issue is a call provision, which lets the issuer pay off a bond prior to its maturity date by *calling* in the bond. Call provisions must be included in the original bond issue so that investors are aware of this clause.

This is a useful feature for the issuer because, if interest rates fall, you can recall the bonds and pay them off with a new issue at a lower interest rate. Normally this right cannot be exercised until several years after the original issue date, as shown on the bond certificate.

There is often a *redemption* feature which gives the bondholder the right to redeem the bond. That means the right to be repaid prior to date of maturity.

A last feature that can be included in bonds is convertibility. A **convertible bond** is one that can be converted into shares of common stock in the issuing company. This can be an inducement for an investor because common stock has the potential to grow over time. When we discuss common stock this advantage will become evident to you.

convertible bond
A bond that can be converted into shares of common stock.

Bonds as an Investment

As an investment, bonds are rather safe. But two questions often bother first-time investors concerning the purchase of a corporate bond. One question is: "If I purchase a corporate bond, do I have to hold it to the maturity date?" No! You do not have to hold a bond until maturity, because bonds are bought and sold daily on securities markets. However, if you sell your bond to another investor, it's unlikely you will get the face value (usually $1,000), since prices fluctuate.

The second question on investors' minds is, "How do I know how risky an investment a *particular* bond issue is?" Fortunately, three companies, Canadian Bond Rating Service, Standard & Poor's, and Moody's Investor Service, rate various corporate and government bonds' degree of risk to investors. Naturally, the higher the risk associated with the bond issue, the higher the interest rate the organization must offer investors. Investors will not assume high levels of risk if they don't feel the potential return is worth it.

Bonds provide an excellent source of long-term financing for the firm and a good investment vehicle for investors. They are a form of debt financing as opposed to equity financing. Let's explore the most common form of equity financing, the issuing of corporate stock.

PROGRESS CHECK

- Why are bonds considered a form of debt financing?
- What is meant if a firm states it is issuing a 9 percent debenture bond due in 2005?
- Explain the difference between an unsecured and a secured bond.
- Why do issuing companies typically like to include call provisions in their bonds?
- What role do the bond rating services play in the bond market?

EQUITY FINANCING THROUGH ISSUING STOCK

As noted earlier, equity financing is another form of long-term funding. *Equity financing* is the obtaining of funds through the sale of ownership in the corporation. There are two different classes of equity instruments; preferred and common stock. We will discuss each after a brief look at the terminology of stock and the advantages and disadvantages of issuing stock as a financing alternative.

The Terminology of Stock

stock certificate
Tangible evidence of stock ownership.

dividends
Part of the firm's profits that are distributed to shareholders.

Stocks are shares of ownership in a company. A **stock certificate** is evidence of ownership. It is usually a piece of paper that specifies the name of the company, the number of shares it represents, and the type of stock it is. **Dividends** are the part of a firm's profits that are distributed to shareholders. Dividends can be distributed in the form of cash or more shares of stock.

Advantages and Disadvantages of Issuing Stock

stock exchange
Market where the securities (shares and bonds) of public companies are traded.

Stock exchanges are markets where the securities (shares and bonds) of public companies are traded. There are some advantages to raising long-term funds via equity financing.

- Because shareholders are owners of the business, their investment never has to be repaid. These funds are therefore available for acquisition of fixed (capital) and other assets.
- There is no legal obligation to pay dividends to shareholders. Note that dividends are payable only when the board of directors declares a dividend out of accumulated profits. In practice, most stable firms declare dividends regularly to keep their shares attractive for investors. For new companies,

normally the firm retains the profits for additional investment and growth for a few years before it begins to pay dividends.

- Selling shares rather than bonds can actually improve the company's financial position because it does not increase the company's debt.

Nevertheless, as the saying goes, "There's no such thing as a free lunch." As you might suspect, there are disadvantages to equity financing as well.

- As owners of the firm, shareholders have the right to vote for the board of directors. As you remember from Chapter 5, the board of directors decides who will manage the firm and what its policies will be. Hence the direction of the firm can be altered through a significant sale of shares. In reality this rarely happens, because most issues add only a small percentage of shares to the total amount outstanding.
- Dividends are not a deduction for tax purposes, while interest on bonds is.
- Management decision making is often tempered by the need to keep shareholders happy. This often forces managers to use short-term tactics to keep earnings up rather than strategies to keep the firm profitable in the long run. Thus the true cost of equity financing may be much higher than is shown on the books of the company.

Figure 18–8 summarizes some important features of equity and debt financing. Let's see how bonds, preferred stocks, and common stock differ. See figures 18–8 and 18–10 for further information on these differences.

Issuing Preferred Stock

Preferred stock gives its owners preference over common shareholders in the payment of dividends and in a claim on assets if the company is liquidated. However, it normally does not include voting rights in the firm. Preferred stock is frequently referred to as a hybrid investment in that it has characteristics of both bonds and stocks. (This can be seen in Figure 18–10.) To illustrate, consider the treatment of preferred stock dividends.

preferred stock
Stock that gives owners preference over common shareholders in the payment of dividends and in a claim on assets if the business is liquidated, but does not include voting rights.

Preferred stock dividends differ from common stock dividends in several ways. Preferred stock is generally issued with a par value, which becomes the basis for the

Preferred Stock Feature	Description
Convertible	The shares may be exchanged after a stated number of years for common shares at a pre-set rate, at the option of the shareholder.
Cumulative	If the dividend is not paid in full in any year, the balance is carried forward (accumulates). The cumulative unpaid balance must be paid before any dividends are paid to common shareholders.
Callable	The company that issued the shares has the right after a stated number of years to call them back by repaying the shareholders their original investment.*
Redeemable	After a stated number of years the investor may return the stock and ask for repayment of his or her investment.*

Figure 18–8 Optional features available with preferred stock.

*If the shares are also cumulative, all dividend arrears must be paid as well.

dividend the firm is willing to pay. For example, if a par value of $100 is attached to a share of preferred stock and a dividend rate of 8 percent is attached to the same issue, the firm is committing to an $8 dividend for each share of preferred stock the investor owns (8 percent of $100 = $8). If you own 100 shares of this preferred stock, your yearly dividend should be $800. Furthermore, this dividend is *fixed,* meaning it does not change year by year. Also, if any dividends are paid, the dividends on preferred stock *must* be paid in full before any common stock dividends can be distributed. Preferred stockholders normally lose their voting rights in the firm in exchange for this preferred dividend treatment.

As you can see, a similarity exists between preferred stock and bonds in that both have a face (or par) value and both have a fixed rate of return. Why not just refer to preferred stock as a form of bond? Remember, bondholders *must* receive interest and be *repaid* the face value of the bond on a maturity date. Preferred stock dividends do not legally *have* to be paid unless the stock is redeemed or called. Nor are the shares usually repurchased (except as indicated in figures 18–8 and 18–10). Both bonds and preferred stock can fluctuate in market price.

cumulative preferred stock
Preferred stock that accumulates unpaid dividends.

One of the more important features of preferred stock is that it is often cumulative. **Cumulative preferred stock** guarantees an investor that if one or more dividends are not paid or only partially paid, the missed dividends will be accumulated. All the dividends, including the back dividends, must be paid in full before any common stock dividends can be paid. For example, as producers of Fiberrific, we may decide not to pay our preferred shareholders the full 8 percent dividend this period in order to retain funds for further research and development. The preferred shareholders must be paid the missing amount the following period before we can pay any dividends to common shareholders. If preferred stock is noncumulative, any dividends missed are lost to the shareholder. Figure 18–9 illustrates how this process works.

Figures 18–8 and 18–10 show some of the features available with preferred stock. If preferred stock does not meet the objectives of the firm or an individual investor, the firm can issue or the individual invest in common stock. Let's look at this interesting alternative.

Issuing Common Stock

common stock
Represents ownership of a firm and the right to vote and to receive the firm's profits (after preferred shareholders are paid), in the form of dividends declared by the board of directors.

Common stock represents ownership of a firm and gives shareholders the right to vote and the right to all of the firm's profits after preferred shareholders are paid. As long as the company exists, these profits can be received only in the form of dividends declared by the board of directors. Shareholders influence corporate policy by electing the board of directors, which selects the management and makes major policy decisions. In general, shareholders' voting rights are based on one vote for each share of stock held. Due to what is called a pre-emptive right, common shareholders have the first right to purchase any new shares of common stock the firm decides to issue to maintain a proportionate share in the company.

Common stock is considered more risky and speculative than either bonds or preferred stock. Remember, common shareholders receive dividends only after both bondholders and preferred shareholders receive their interest and dividends. Also, if a company is forced to cease operations, common shareholders share in the firm's assets only after bondholders and preferred shareholders recover their loans and investments.

Why, then, would investors select common stock as an investment alternative? Because the risk is often accompanied by higher returns. Several investment

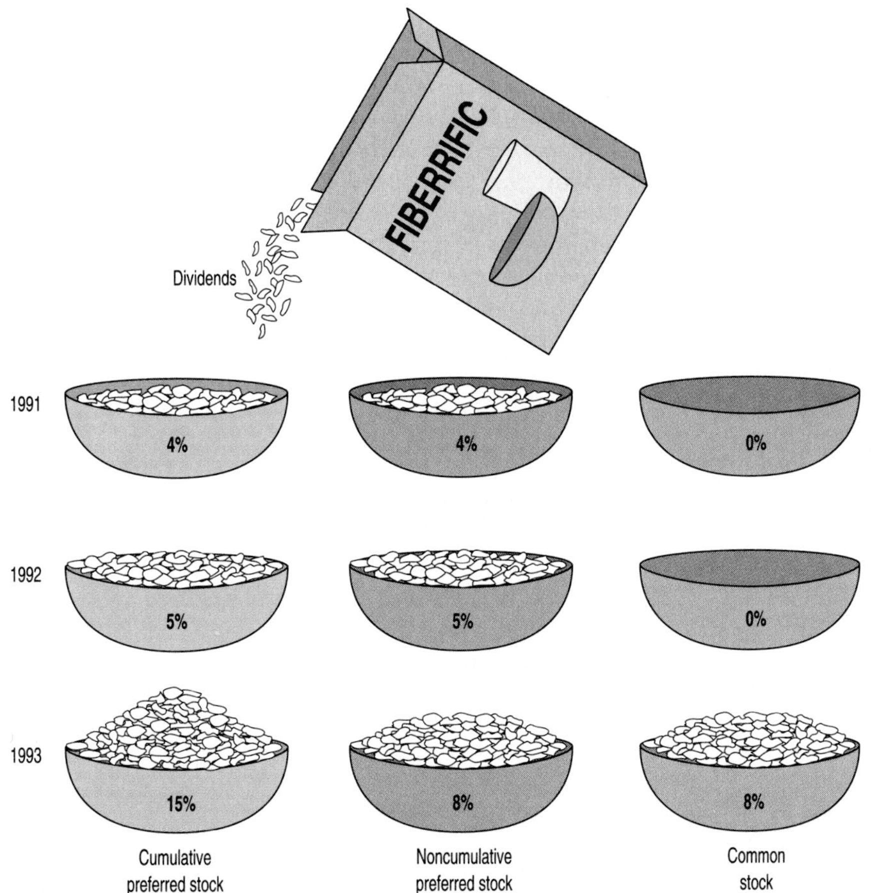

Figure 18–9 The effect of an 8 percent dividend per year, if not paid (or only partially paid) each year. This figure shows what happens when a dividend payment is missed for different classes of stock. With cumulative preferred 8% stock, the dividend for 1991 was 4 percent less than promised. In 1992, it was 3 percent less. That means that the preferred shareholder would get 15 percent in 1993 if the company had the funds available. The way you figure that is 4 percent plus 3 percent plus 8 percent (the 1993 dividend). Noncumulative preferred and common stock get only the dividends allocated. There is no cumulative provision. But note that the preferred dividend carries a fixed rate, which cannot be exceeded, while the common carries no such limit.

Interest or Dividends	**Bonds**	**Preferred Shares**	**Common Shares**
Must be paid	yes	no	no
Pays a fixed rate	yes	yes	no
Deductible from payor's income tax	yes	no	no
Canadian payee is taxable at preferred rate	no	(if company is Canadian) yes	yes
The Stock or Bond			
Has voting rights	no	not normally	yes
May be traded on the stock exchange	yes	yes	yes
Can be held indefinitely	no	often	yes
Is convertible to common stock	may be	may be	not applicable

Figure 18–10 Comparison of bonds, preferred stock, and common stock of public companies.

opportunities are available. For example, an investor may select a growth stock, a stock of a corporation whose earnings are expected to grow faster than other stocks or the overall economy. Growth stocks are often quite speculative and pay rather low dividends, but the potential for growth is strong. Income stocks offer investors a rather high dividend yield on their investment. Public utilities are often considered

blue chip stocks
Stocks of high-quality companies.

good income stocks, as are **blue chip stocks.** *Blue chip* is a term often used to describe stock of a firm that is considered to be of high quality. Investors can even invest in a type of stock called a penny stock, which sells for less than $1 per share. Such stocks frequently represent ownership in mining companies and are often highly speculative. The Vancouver Stock Exchange has many such offerings.

It's important to remember that the value of common stock is very dependent on the performance of the corporation. Common stock is often referred to as participating stock because shareholders participate in the success or failure of the firm. Common stock offers great opportunities but is subject to a high degree of risk, as was evidenced by the major stock market crash of 1987. (Some preferred stock may also have limited participation rights.)

PROGRESS CHECK

- Name at least two advantages and two disadvantages of issuing stock as a form of equity financing.
- What are the major differences between preferred stock and common stock?
- In what ways are preferred stock and bonds similar? In what ways are they different?
- How does an investor benefit by owning cumulative preferred stock as opposed to noncumulative preferred?
- What is the difference between blue chip stocks and penny stocks?

How To Buy Bonds and Stock (Securities)

Bonds and shares of public companies are bought and sold by investors through stockbrokers, who charge a commission on all sales and purchases. Figure 18–11 lists the six largest investment dealers in Canada. These brokers have representatives on the floor of the stock exchanges, where actual trading occurs. That is where a broker's agent with a security for sale on behalf of a client who has given the broker a sell order finds a broker's agent with a similar order to buy.

If you look at the financial pages, where the shares traded are listed daily, you will see that a vast number of shares of many different securities are traded regularly. For example, the Toronto Stock Exchange was trading about 75 to 80 million shares daily in May 1993. See Figure 18–12 for an excerpt of a daily listing.

Several major stock exchanges around the world dominate securities trading. New York, Tokyo, Frankfurt, and London, are such major markets where billions of shares are traded daily. Five Canadian cities have local stock exchanges: Toronto, Montreal, Vancouver, Calgary, and Winnipeg. There are specialized exchanges in

Figure 18–11 Canada's six largest investment dealers.

Company and Year End	Revenue $000	Assets $000
RBC Dominion Securities (Sept. 92)	$690,610	$8,898,999
Burns Fry Holding (Sept. 92)	386,207	3,730,187
Midland Walwyn (Dec. 92)	332,069	933,037
Richardson Greenshields (Dec. 92)	308,615	2,345,151
Bank of Montreal Securities Canada (March 92)	289,695	3,618,163
Nesbitt Thompson Corp. (March 92)	289,285	3,458,517

Source: Report on Business, *Globe and Mail,* July 1993.

major financial centres where trading in commodities, futures, and other activities are carried on. These are complex fields where expert knowledge is required.

Buying Securities on Margin

Buying on margin means you purchase securities by borrowing some of the cost from your broker, who holds them as collateral security until you pay the balance due. In effect the broker, lends you the money and charges you interest. There are provincial regulatory agencies, such as the Ontario Securities Commission, that control all aspects of this industry, including what minimum percentage of the purchase price must be paid in cash. For example, if the current rate is 50 percent

buying on margin
Purchasing securities by borrowing some of the cost from the broker.

Figure 18–12 A segment of the list of trading in the Toronto Stock Exchange, May 26, 1993.

52 Weeks High	52 Weeks Low	Stock	Sym	Div.	High	Low	Close	Chg	Vol (100s)	Yield	P/E ratio
13 1/8	7 5/8	AGF nv	AGF.PRLB	0.40	13 1/8	13	13 1/8	+ 1/8	2	3.05	19.0
5	1 3/8	Aber j	ABZ		4.15	3.90	4.00	− 0.10	802		
16 1/2	12 1/4	Abltlbl-Price	A	0.50	15	14 7/8	15	+ 1/8	24	3.33	
0.40	.085	Acadia Ninri j	ALY		0.27	0.27	0.27	+ 0.02	300		
2.50	1.50	Accord Finan	ACO	0.04	2.60	2.55	2.60	+ 0.10	40	1.45	23.6
2.75	0.10	Accugraph j	ACU.A		2.05	2.00	2.00	− 0.05	82		
8 1/4	4.50	Addands	ACK		7 7/8	7 3/4	7 7/8	+ 1/8	41		21.3
0.75	0.35	Adex Mining	AMG		0.55	0.52	.054		364		
3.50	1.10	Advanced Grv j	AED		2.60	2.50	2.50		200		41.7
25 1/4	24	Aetna	ALLPR.A	1.91	25 1/8	25 1/8	25 1/8	− 1/8	1	7.59	
13 1/4	4.70	Agnico Eagle	AGE	0.10	12 1/4	11 1/4	12	− 1/2	522		48.0
8 5/8	5 1/4	Agra nv	AGR.B	0.16	8 1/8	8	8 1/8		441	1.97	
8 1/4	6	Agra Ind	AGR.A	0.14	7 3/4	7 3/4	7 1/4	− 1/2	5	1.81	
11	9 3/8	Alnsworth Lu	ANS		10 1/8	9 7/8	10 1/4	− 1/8	44487		
5 1/4	2.20	Air Canada	AC		3.45	3.35	3.40	+ 0.05	472		
4.20	0.90	Akitta Dri rv	AKT.A		3.55	3.50	3.50	− 0.05	91		
3.90	1.55	Akitta Driln	AKT.B		3.40	3.40	3.40	− 0.50	35		
20 1/2	12 1/4	Alberta Ener	AEC	0.35	20 1/8	19 7/8	20	− 1/8	282	1.75	37.7
27 1/4	22 1/2	AEC	AEC.PRC	1.94	27	26 7/8	27		11	7.18	
16 1/2	12 2	Alta Nat Gas	ANG	0.68	16	15 3/4	16	+ 1/4	47	4.25	
26 3/8	19 1/8	Alcan	AL	0.30	24 3/4	24 3/8	24 3/8	+ 1/8	8950		
24 1/2	20	Alcan C	AL.PR.E	1.61	21 1/4	21	21 1/4	+ 1/4	51	7.58	
20	16	Alcan E	AL.PR.F	1.44	17 1/2	17 1/2	17 1/2		6	8.21	
5	1.50	Algoma	AFC.PR.A	1.38	4.70	4.40	4.40	− 0.30	140	31.25	
8 1/4	4.80	Allel x	AXB		7 7/8	7 5/8	7 5/8		21		
0.50	0.13	Altal Res	ATI		0.46	0.41	0.41	− 0.02	210		
13 5/8	9 1/8	Amax Gold	AXG	0.08	10 1/2	10 1/8	10 1/8	− 7/8	10		
31	15	Amer Barrick	ABX	0.13	28 3/8	27 3/4	28 3/8		4732		
0.35	0.03	Amer Eagle j	AEO		.335	.315	.335	+ 0.01	36904		11.2
0.35	0.20	Amer Leduc	ARL		0.35	0.35	0.35	+ 0.05	50		
5 1/2	1.17	Anchor Lamin	AKC	0.03	4.85	4.80	4.80	− 0.05	1125	0.63	17.8
24 1/4	8 1/4	Anderson	AXL		24 1/4	24 1/8	24 3/4	+ 1/2	1217		72.8
0.78	0.17	Anthes	All		0.50	0.48	0.50	+ 0.05	95		
14 1/2	11	Arbor	ABO.A		13 7/8	13 7/8	13 7/8	+ 1/4	2		17.3
5 1/8	0.75	Archer	AAZ		4.40	4.25	4.30	− 0.10	46		
37	32 1/4	Argus	AR.PR.D	2.60	33 1/8	33 1/8	33 1/8		1	7.85	
32 1/2	29 1/2	Argus	AR.PR.B	2.70	32	32	32	+ 1	1	8.44	
5 1/8	2.05	Arimetco j	ARX		2.90	2.70	2.85	− 0.09	623		

Annual dividend per share

Highest and lowest price in the last 52 weeks

The symbol for Air Canada used in the stock exchange

$$P/E = \frac{\text{Price}}{\text{Earnings}}$$

If Acklands stock is bought for closing price of 7.875 the price is 21.3 times the 1993 earning per share

Price fluctuations on May 26, 1993: Highest price – 3.45 Lowest price – 3.35 Closing price – 3.40 Change from previous day's closing price was +.05

$$\text{Yield} = \frac{\text{Annual dividend}}{\text{Closing price}} = \frac{.68}{16.00} = 4.25\%$$

If Alberta Natural Gas stock is bought for $16.00 and held for one year there will be a cash income of .68

Number of shares of Alcan Aluminum that traded May 26 – 895,000

Source: Globe and Mail, May 27, 1993, p. B9.

The Toronto Stock Exchange is the major trading centre for stock in Canada. You can visit the exchange yourself and watch the action. There is an excitement there that you might enjoy.

for shares and 10 percent for bonds, you would have to invest a minimum of $4 to buy an $8 share (plus commissions to the broker), and $97 to buy a bond selling for $970.

If the stock or bond drops in price, you will get a *margin call* from your broker. This means that you will have to make a payment to your broker to maintain the margin of collateral protection that the broker is obligated to observe. In this case, the loan cannot exceed 50 percent of the stock value or 90 percent of the bond value.

Personal Situations of Investors

Any type of investing carries some amount of *risk* with it. Some investments are riskier than others. The personal situation of an investor often dictates the type of investment he or she will choose. Important considerations are the age, income, wealth, and philosophy of the investor. A young person with a good income and a daring outlook will be likely to take a higher risk when investing. A retired person will be less interested in risk and more concerned about a reliable, steady flow of income, particularly if he or she has limited funds.

The existence of such a widely diversified market of potential investors lets public companies create varying kinds of securities to raise the funds they need by satisfying a wide spectrum of investor needs. However, the largest buyers of securities are not individuals. They are pension funds, mutual funds (discussed below), banks, insurance and trust companies, stock brokerage firms, and large corporations with surplus funds not immediately required for operations.

Diversifying Investments

A prudent policy for investors is to avoid having all their eggs in one basket. If you place all your money in one stock you have a great deal of confidence in, you are exposing yourself to high risk should you be wrong. Diversify your investment by buying a variety of stocks and bonds that give you a mix of income, security, and growth.

MAKING ETHICAL DECISIONS

You are the chief financial officer of Raven Corp. and have just completed all the preparations for a $50 million issue of preferred stock. The president of Raven has had extensive discussions with the president of Mutual Trust Co., which manages some large pension funds, and Mutual agreed to buy the entire issue for these funds. You are not entirely happy about the future of Raven because of some deep-rooted problems that are not yet public knowledge. They could have a serious impact on Raven's financial position and could even threaten its existence.

A few days later you are having lunch with Kevin, a good friend of yours, who is a manager of one of the pension funds overseen by Mutual Trust. He tells you that his fund will be buying $20 million of the stock issue and he seems quite pleased with this investment decision. You are somewhat uneasy because of your concerns about the long-term viability of Raven.

You are torn between your responsibility to your company and your friendship for Kevin and the possible risk to the pension fund. You know that if it were your own money or the monies of a pension fund you were managing, you would not make this investment. What should you do? What would be the result of your decision? ▼

One way to achieve this goal when your money is limited is to invest in mutual funds. A **mutual fund** buys a variety of securities and then sells units of ownership to the public. It has expert analysts who keep constant watch on the market.

mutual fund
A fund that buys a variety of securities and then sells units of ownership to the public.

Mutual funds let even the smallest investor diversify a portfolio. A wide assortment of mutual funds specialize in acquiring certain types of domestic and foreign securities. This can satisfy the needs of all investors. The Financial Times monthly mutual funds report of May 15, 1993, lists five pages of mutual funds—some 600 in all.

At the same time, by enlarging the market for securities, mutual funds make it easier for public companies to obtain financing for their operations and expansion.

THINKING IT THROUGH

What form of investment seems most appropriate to your needs now? Do you suspect your objectives and needs will change over time? Would investing other people's money be an interesting career to pursue? What are some of the problems stockbrokers or mutual fund managers might face in the course of their jobs? Does it make sense for investors to diversify their investments or would it be more logical to put all their eggs in one basket?

Stock Indexes

Stock indexes measure the trend of different stock and commodity exchanges. Every country with stock exchanges has such indexes. In Canada there are several thousand companies listed on various exchanges and the prices of their shares fluctuate constantly. Some may be rising over a certain period and others may be falling. Some may seesaw up and down. Various indexes have been developed to give interested parties useful information as to significant trends.

In Canada, a commonly used index is the TSE 300, which consists of the weighted average of 300 of the most important stocks listed on the Toronto Stock Exchange. In the U.S. the major (and oldest) index is the Dow Jones Industrial Average—the *Dow,* as it is commonly called. The Dow measures the movements of the shares of 30 of the largest companies in the U.S. that are listed on the New York Stock Exchange. It is an important index that receives worldwide attention.

REACHING BEYOND OUR BORDERS

Kitchener Waterloo Organizes Financing for High-Tech Exports

Case One at the end of this chapter reports the actions of a community group that includes municipal, university, college, and business people to assist certain businesses in their area. The Business Community Program (BCP) was set up to raise funds for high-tech companies that could not raise money through normal channels. Banks would not make unsecured loans to these new companies and there was no security because their products—software and hardware—are knowledge based, not traditional goods.

But the BCP is more than just an investment package. In addition to its financing aspect, the proposed fund will employ experienced managers to provide international marketing assistance to small and mid-sized firms. The need is compelling: Canada's tiny population obliges many technology producers to sell their wares abroad. "You either export or die," asserts Ruth Songhurst, vice-president of marketing for Mortice Kern Systems Inc. of Waterloo, a fast-growing software company that counts on exports for 97 percent of its revenue.

A high-profile marketing executive with connections in foreign climes would provide the expertise that small companies ordinarily can't afford. BCP expects to pay $200,000 for the right person once it gets its long-awaited seal of approval from Ottawa, expected before year's end. This approval is essential for investors to get the tax benefits that would make this high-risk investment feasible. It is something that many industrial countries have done.

Here is a case of a cutting-edge industry being hampered by lack of government action so that it cannot finance the production and export of the kind of products Canada desperately needs to stay in the forefront of modern technology. This is a good example of how government must learn to move much more quickly and adapt to new conditions, as have these companies, if Canada is to provide the necessary knowledge jobs and remain an advanced economy.

Source: Jerry Zeidenberg, "Community Chest," Report on Business, *Globe and Mail,* June 1993, pp. 72–3. ▼

Both of these averages have been carefully designed to give a realistic picture of the results of all trading in their respective stock exchanges each day. They do not work perfectly, but they are usually quite accurate. You can find these and other indexes in the financial pages of your daily newspaper or in the financial papers.

Cycles in the Stock Market and Interest Rates

There are many reasons why the prices of shares listed on stock exchanges fluctuate. A popular stock in strong demand will rise because of that demand. A company that is doing well or is rumoured to be on the verge of being taken over will usually see its stock go up. Certain industries are favoured or out of favour at certain times because they are expected to do well or poorly.

On the other hand, rumours of financial troubles or scandals will often drive a stock down. Some industries, like pulp and paper, are said to be cyclical. That is, they have a few good years followed by some poorer years. Naturally, their stock prices fluctuate in such periods.

Another major cause of stock price fluctuation is that the capitalist economic system undergoes periodic cycles of recession and recovery. These ups and downs are reflected in the general movement of price levels of stocks. The stock market does not move in tandem with the level of economic activity. It does not exactly parallel but rather is thought to predict the cyclical movement of the economy in a particular country.

The level of interest rates in a country also fluctuates. In Canada in the 1980s, interest rates climbed to historic highs. Banks were charging ordinary businesses 22 percent for commercial loans in 1980. In mid-1993, this rate was down to 6 percent. There are complex reasons for such fluctuations. If you are interested in following up on this important topic, consider taking courses in economics.

These fluctuations have a major impact on bond prices and on the interest rate of new bond issues. Preferred share prices are also affected, as is the dividend rate on new issues. If you are going into the market for funding, you must plan carefully to avoid getting caught in a long-term commitment to high dividends and interest costs. That is one reason there is such a variety of vehicles that enable businesses to make flexible financing arrangements.

PROGRESS CHECK

- ▼ What does buying on margin mean? How does it work?
- ▼ What exactly are mutual funds? How do they benefit small investors?
- ▼ What is a stock index? What is its purpose? Can you name a Canadian index? A U.S. index?

SUMMARY

1. Explain the role and importance of finance and the responsibilities of financial managers.

1. Sound financial management is critical to the well-being of any business.

▼ *What are the most common financial problems?*

The most common financial problems are (1) undercapitalization, (2) poor cash flow, and (3) planning and control weaknesses. *Finance* is that function in a business responsible for acquiring funds for the firm, managing funds within the firm (for example, preparing budgets, analyzing cash flow, and planning for the expenditure of funds on various assets.

▼ *What do finance managers do?*

Finance managers plan, budget, control funds, obtain funds, collect funds, audit, manage taxes, and advise top management on financial matters.

2. Outline the steps in financial planning by explaining how to forecast financial needs, develop budgets, and establish financial controls.

2. Financial planning involves short- and long-term forecasting, budgeting, and financial controls.

▼ *What are the three budgets of finance?*

The *operating budget* is the projection of dollar allocations to various costs and expenses, given various revenues. The *capital budget* is the spending plan for capital or fixed assets. The *cash budget* is the detailed cash-flow forecast for the period.

3. Recognize the financial needs that must be met with available funds.

3. During the course of a business's life, its financial needs shift considerably.

▼ *What are the areas of financial needs?*

Businesses have financial needs in four major areas: (1) daily operations, (2) credit services, (3) inventory purchases, and (4) major assets purchases.

4. Distinguish between short-term and long-term financing and between debt capital and equity capital.

4. Businesses often have needs for short- and long-term financing and for debt capital and equity capital.

▼ *What is the difference between short- and long-term financing?*

Short-term financing refers to funds that will be repaid in less than one year; long-term financing is money that will be repaid over a longer period.

▼ *What is the difference between debt capital and equity capital?*

Debt capital refers to funds raised by borrowing (going into debt). Equity capital is raised from within or by selling ownership (stock) in the company.

5. Identify and describe several sources of short-term capital.

5. There are many sources for short-term financing, including trade credit, family and friends, commercial banks, government programs, factoring, commercial paper, and internal sources.

▼ *Why should businesses use trade credit?*

Because it is financing without cost.

▼ *What is a line of credit?*

It is an advance agreement by a bank to loan a specified amount of money to the business whenever the business requires it.

▼ *What is the difference between a secured loan and an unsecured loan?*

An *unsecured loan* has no collateral backing it. A *secured* loan is backed by accounts receivable (called *pledging*), inventory, or other property of value.

▼ *Is factoring a form of secured loan?*

No, *factoring* means *selling* accounts receivable for a fee.

▼ *What is commercial paper?*

Commercial paper is a promissory note maturing in 270 days or less.

6. An important function of a finance manager is to obtain long-term capital.

6. Identify and describe several sources of long-term capital.

▼ *What are the three major sources of long-term capital?*

Major sources of long-term capital are surplus cash funds, debt capital (including dealer financing), and equity capital. See Figure 18–5 for full details.

7. Companies can raise capital by debt financing, which involves issuing bonds.

7. Compare the advantages and disadvantages of issuing bonds and identify the classes and features of bonds.

▼ *What are the advantages and disadvantages of issuing bonds?*

The advantages of issuing bonds include: (1) management retains control since bondholders cannot vote; (2) interest paid on bonds is tax deductible, and (3) bonds are only a temporary source of finance. The disadvantage of bonds include: (1) because bonds are an increased debt, they may adversely affect the market's perception of the company; (2) interest must be paid on bonds; and (3) the face value must be repaid on the maturity date.

▼ *Are there different types of bonds?*

Yes. There are unsecured (debenture) and secured bonds. Unsecured bonds are not supported by collateral. Secured bonds are backed by tangible assets such as mortgages, stock, and equipment. They all have different features.

8. Companies can also raise capital by equity financing, which involves selling stock.

8. Compare the advantages and disadvantages of issuing stock and outline the differences between common and preferred stock.

▼ *What are the advantages and disadvantages of issuing stock?*

The advantages of issuing stock include: (1) the stock never has to be repaid since stockholders are owners in the company; (2) there is no legal obligation to pay dividends; and (3) no debt is incurred, so the company is financially stronger. The disadvantages include: (1) stockholders are owners of the firm and can affect its management through election of the board of directors; (2) it is more costly to pay dividends since they are paid after taxes; and (3) managers may be tempted to make shareholders happy in the short term rather than plan for long-term needs.

▼ *What are the differences between common and preferred stock?*

Common stockholders have voting rights in the company. Preferred stockholders have no voting rights. In exchange for the loss of voting privileges, preferred stocks offer a *fixed* dividend that must be paid in full before common stockholders receive a dividend. Preferred stock has various features.

9. *Investing* means committing capital with the expectation of making a profit.

9. Discuss the personal criteria used to select investments and describe methods of diversifying investments.

▼ *What are the criteria for selecting investments?*

They are (1) risk, (2) yield, (3) duration, (4) age, and (5) income level.

▼ *What is diversification?*

Diversification means buying several different investments to spread the risk.

▼ *How can mutual funds help individuals diversify their investments?*

A *mutual fund* is an organization that buys stocks and bonds and then sells units in the fund to the public. Individuals who buy units in a mutual fund are able to invest in many different companies they could not otherwise do.

10. Explain securities quotations listed in the financial section of a newspaper.

10. Securities quotations are given in the daily papers.

▼ *What information do these quotations give you?*

The stock quotations give you all kinds of information: the highest price in the last 52 weeks, the lowest price, the dividend yield, the price/earnings ratio, the total shares traded that day, and the high, low, close, and net change in price from the previous day. The bond quotations give you similar information regarding bonds.

▼ *What is the TSE 300 index?*

The TSE 300 is the average price of the shares of 300 significant companies traded on the Toronto Stock Exchange. It is reported daily and is the most important indicator of trends in the Canadian stock market.

▼ *What is the Dow Jones index?*

The Dow Jones Industrial Average, a long-established major measuring rod of trends in the American stock market, measures the average price of the shares of 30 very large U.S. companies. It is reported daily and watched by interested parties all over the world.

GETTING INVOLVED

1. Obtain an annual report from a major corporation. Study the balance sheet. Which assets are fixed and what is their value? How much has the company borrowed (look under liabilities)?
2. Visit a local bank lending officer. Ask what the current interest rate is and what rate small businesses pay for short- and long-term loans. Ask for blank forms that borrowers use to apply for loans. Share these forms with your class and explain the types of information they ask for.
3. See if your professor is interested in setting up an investment game in your class. Each student should choose a few stocks and a couple of mutual funds. Each student's selections and trading should be written in a book and the transactions noted. For six weeks, follow the fluctuation in prices. The students with the largest percentage gain at the end win.
4. Go to the library and see what financial newspapers it carries. Look through several issues of at least two of them and report the price of gold to your class.
5. Continue your exploration of the library by looking up the Standard & Poor's or Value Line reports. Bring some photocopies to class and explain the function of these reports.

PRACTICING MANAGEMENT DECISIONS

Case One Community Chest By-Passes Bankers

One after another, the CEOs of 24 high-tech companies stood up and sounded off at a high-level brainstorming session in Ottawa. It was just before Christmas 1991, and they had been invited to tell Harry Rogers, then deputy minister at Industry, Science and Technology Canada [a federal government department], what ailed the advanced technology business. Each executive had the same beef: It was nearly impossible for them to obtain money to expand.

Bankers, they explained, didn't understand the high-tech business, which is brain-rich but asset-poor. Loan officers demanded collateral, such as machines or buildings, before they handed out cash. As a result, high-tech companies, which often produce "invisible" goods such as software, weren't getting the money they needed to keep up with competitors in foreign countries.

The deputy minister understood the high-tech dilemma and called for quick action. "It seemed that something big was going to happen after that," said Larry Zepf, 39, president and CEO of Zepf Technologies Inc. of Waterloo, Ont., a maker of automation equipment for the packaging industry. "But after a few months, it became clear that nothing was going to change. People started to shrug their shoulders and say, 'That's Canada, that's life.' "

But Zepf didn't want to leave it at that. He approached colleagues in the high-tech business, accountants, lawyers, and economic officers in Ontario's technology triangle which includes Waterloo, Kitchener, Cambridge, and Guelph. He also visited academics at the University of Waterloo, the University of Guelph, Wilfrid Laurier University, and Conestoga College in Kitchener to see what could be done.

The result is a proposed high-tech investment fund that is being touted as a model for communities across Canada. Called the Business Community Program [BCP], it's a capital pool that would draw upon local savings—from Main Street investors to large corporations—and plow them back into the region's fledgling technology companies.

Business leaders hope the program will reverse the effects of regional deindustrialization in Southwestern Ontario. "They all wanted to do something to stop their cities from becoming ghost towns," says Zepf. The payoff for the schools, which are generating plenty of high-tech enterprises, is that they get a shot at the money they need to conduct research, development, and marketing.

The idea behind the program is not unique. Other community investment funds exist in Canada, most notably the Community Bond Program that began in Saskatchewan in 1990. But none is so closely connected to universities and municipal governments. Moreover, the BCP contains an innovative tax shelter that allows anyone who locks money into the fund for at least five years, an exemption from paying taxes on the capital gains. "We think we'll be able to attract $100 million to $200 million with this tax break," says Zepf.

Unfortunately, the tax shelter needs federal approval and some bureaucrats are concerned about the capital gains taxes Ottawa would lose, even though they recognize that the fund, in reviving the local economy, could create a new source of tax revenues. "We're considering it," says Robert Dunlop, assistant to industry minister Michael Wilson. "But it's not a minor matter. It requires a change in policy."

Zepf thinks the project will get the go-ahead sooner or later. In 1992 he obtained the backing he needed from four nearby cities and their chambers of commerce as well as the four schools, which have offered to contribute the high-tech and business acumen of their professors and even their presidents. Lorna Marsden, president of WLU and a former Canadian senator, is recruiting investors such as large insurance companies for the fund.

Local professionals like lawyers and accountants, see the fund as a way of rebuilding the local economy and their own businesses. "In the last two years, Waterloo has lost 18 manufacturing companies and 1,200 jobs, and we don't think they're coming back," says Douglas McKenzie, director of economic development for the city of Waterloo. At the same time, he adds, local companies are being restricted from growth, especially in the computer software and hardware sectors.

Decision Questions

1. Is the BCP a good example of the sort of initiative needed to meet today's competitive conditions? Is it a model others should replicate?
2. Do you think the banks are justified in the reasons they give for not helping small business more readily? Should they not be conservative to protect their shareholders' interests? How can they give loans without the usual security they need?
3. Should governments be doing more to help? Why are they so slow to help what seems like a very well-thought out scheme with wide community and business support?
4. Do you think that banks and government have not yet adjusted to the needs of the new technology industries that are so important to Canada's future? What, specifically, would you urge them to do? What attitudes need changing?

Source: Jerry Zeidenberg, "Community Chest," Report on Business, *Globe and Mail,* June 1993, pp. 72–3.

Case Two Bonds or Stock? That Is the Question

In 1963, Carlos Galendez had dreams but very little money. He spent more than 10 years working as a dishwasher and then cook for a major restaurant. His dream was to save enough money to start his own Mexican restaurant. In 1965, his dream finally came true. With a

Small-Business bank loan, he opened his first Casa de Carlos restaurant. His old family recipes and appealing decor helped the business gain immediate success. He repaid his small-business loan within 14 months and immediately opened a second, then a third, location. By 1975, Casa de Carlos was the largest Mexican restaurant chain in the nation.

In 1976, the company decided to go public. Carlos believed continued growth was beneficial to the company, and he felt offering ownership was the way to bring in loyal investors. Nevertheless, he made certain his family maintained controlling interest in the firm's stock. Therefore, in its initial public offering, Casa de Carlos offered to sell only 40 percent of the available shares in the company to investors. The Galendez family kept control of 60 percent of the stock.

As the public's craving for Mexican food grew, so did the fortunes of Casa de Carlos, Inc. Heading into the 1980s, the company enjoyed the position of being light on debt and heavy on cash. But in 1983, the firm's debt position changed when it bought out Captain Al's Seafood Restaurants. Three years later, it expanded into full-service wholesale distribution of seafood products with the purchase of Mariner Wholesalers. The firm's debt increased, but the price of its stock was up and demand at all three operations was booming.

In 1989, Carlos Galendez died. His oldest child, Maria, was selected to take control as chief executive officer. Maria had learned the business from her father. He taught her to keep an eye out for opportunities that seemed fiscally responsible. Unfortunately, in 1990 the fortunes of the firm began to shift. Two major competitors were taking market share from Casa de Carlos, and the seafood venture began to flounder (pun intended). The recession in 1990 didn't help either. Consumers spent less, causing some severe cash problems. Maria Galendez had to decide how to get the funds the firm needed for improvements and other expenses. Banks wouldn't expand the firm's credit line. She considered a bond or stock offering to raise capital.

Decision Questions

1. What advantages and disadvantages of offering bonds to investors should Maria consider?
2. What would be the advantages and disadvantages to the company of offering new stock to investors?
3. Are any other options available to Maria Galendez?
4. If you were Maria, what choice would you make? Why?

LET'S TALK BUSINESS

1. Businesses in the 1990s are trying to raise money by selling stock. During the 1980s, most businesses tried to raise money by selling bonds. What happened to make businesses switch?
2. What are the advantages and disadvantages of raising money by selling stock versus selling bonds?
3. Why would a small business be more interested in selling preferred rather than common stock, if it could?
4. Discuss the risks and opportunities of investing today in stocks, bonds, and mutual funds. Which would you recommend for a college student? Why?
5. Think about what is most confusing about investing and talk it over with the class. See if you can clarify the confusion you and others may be experiencing.

LOOKING AHEAD

Throughout this book, you have seen many boxes on ethical decision making. This issue, along with environmental problems, has become a major concern in Canada and promises to be a leading question in the 1990s. Consequently, we have devoted an entire chapter to a review of ethical and environmental issues. You will find this in Chapter 19.

PART VII

ETHICAL AND ENVIRONMENTAL ISSUES

ETHICS AND THE ENVIRONMENT

LEARNING GOALS

After you have read and studied this chapter, you should be able to:

1. Discuss how business, in the early capitalist period, ignored ethical standards of behaviour.
2. Describe the modern beginnings of business ethics.
3. Understand why ethical issues are so important now.
4. List some important ethical issues.
5. See what business is doing to set and improve ethical standards.
6. Identify what first led to concern about the environment.
7. List some of the major environmental problems.
8. Understand why business tends to see a conflict between a clean environment and competitive ability.
9. Describe the rule of 72 and explain its relationship to growth.
10. Explain how sustainable development has become the major international goal for reconciling growth with environmental constraints.

KEY TERMS

bid rigging, p. 623
corporate social responsibility, p. 617
exponential function, p. 635
laissez-faire capitalism, p. 618
NIMBY, p. 633
organic farming, p. 630
robber barons, p. 617
rule of 72, p. 636
white-collar crime, p. 622

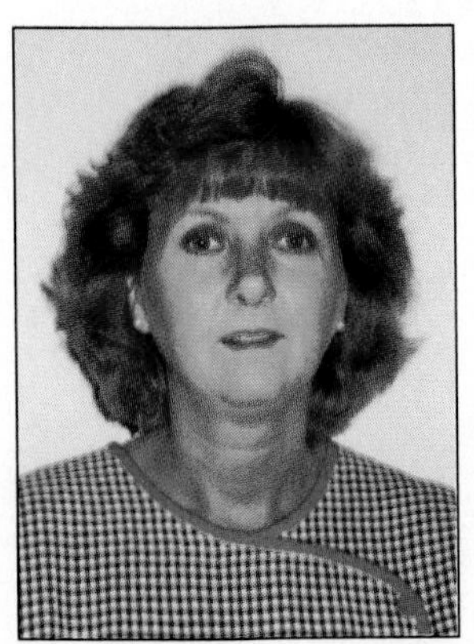
Rose Todorski

PROFILE HOW ROSE TODORSKI BECAME RECYCLING ROSE

"Bell Zeros In on Waste" and "Planning, Education, Teamwork Cut Garbage 97%" shouted the headlines. It was the story of how Rose Todorski, facilities manager at Bell Canada's 12-story Fieldway building at Etobicoke, Ontario, reduced the daily garbage output from 400 to 22 kilograms. Her target is just 3 kg by July 1992. How did she do it? Will she achieve her final goal? To understand what was going on here, we must go back a little bit.

Like many companies in 1989, Bell senior management renewed a corporate philosophy that included a commitment to the environment. That commitment, combined with rising waste disposal costs and an unwillingness to be caught reacting to waste reduction legislation, led Bell's facilities management group to establish a basic recycling program.

After a year of recycling paper, cans, and glass, Fieldway's daily output fell by more than half. But a waste audit found almost 170 kg of paper a day still ended up in the garbage. And while Styrofoam represented little more than 3 kg of garbage a day, it was by volume more than a third of the garbage bags tossed out every day.

Rose Todorski was brought in to achieve the final step, going from about 400 kg of daily waste to 3 kg in one year. She set up a non-management team to help plan and organize an operation that would yield the required results. As a result of the team's advance work, when employees arrived for work on July 2, 1991, they were prepared for the minor revolution that had taken place.

- Plastic cycling bins replaced metal garbage cans. On every desk employees found a plastic coffee mug and a sponge to clean up any spills. In the washrooms, electric hand dryers had replaced paper towels.
- In the cafeteria, china, glass, and stainless steel replaced Styrofoam and plastic. Bulk dispensers of juice, milk, and condiments replaced packages and single servings. Food waste collected in the kitchen and from cylindrical cans on each of the building's floors would be processed in composts beside the company parking lot.
- For any garbage remaining, Bell left behind four beige bins on every floor. A tiny plastic bag was also left on every desk to save trips to the bins and ease the transition. The bag wasn't replaced.
- The result has been a 97 percent reduction in garbage. John Hanson, executive director of the Recycling Council of Ontario, calls the cut phenomenal.

That is how Rose Todorski earned the name *Recycling Rose*. This whole experiment shows what can be done when legislation pushes companies, top management is committed to reducing waste, the proper planning and organization are done, all levels of employees are involved and, finally, it is economically advantageous to change. Bell invested $50,000 in the program and anticipates annual savings of $70,000 in the Fieldway building alone.

Bell plans to expand this program to all of its 120 buildings by the end of the year. It will extend the waste savings concept to include energy conservation.

Source: Case Mahood, "Bell Zeros In on Waste," *Globe and Mail,* May 4, 1992, p. B1.

We will be looking in more detail at environmental issues in the second half of this chapter, but we turn first to business ethics.

ETHICAL BEHAVIOUR IN BUSINESS AND GOVERNMENT

Throughout this book you have seen many comments about the issue of business ethics. Why so much emphasis on ethical behaviour of businesspeople and companies? The reason is that the 1980s saw a rising tide of criticism in Canada (and other countries) of various business practices that many Canadians found unacceptable.

A Brief History of Ethics in Business

The recent criticism of business practices in North America can perhaps be traced back to the 1960s in the U.S., when a young lawyer named Ralph Nader almost single-handedly took on mighty General Motors. He started challenging GM because of its defective Corvair, which had been responsible for many fatal accidents because of sudden, erratic, uncontrollable behaviour.

At first, GM regarded Nader as an elephant might regard a pesky mosquito. Gradually, however, his efforts got more and more support. Despite GM's most strenuous opposition, including hiring private detectives to look for dirt on Ralph Nader's personal life in order to discredit him, GM was forced for the first time in the history of automobile manufacturing to recall cars to correct problems. Now, of course, recalls have become standard procedure for all auto manufacturers. This was perhaps the first important signal of a move towards **corporate social responsibility,** the recognition by corporations that their actions must take into account the needs and ethical standards of society.

corporate social responsibility
The recognition by corporations that their actions must take into account the needs and ethical standards of society.

People have been concerned about business practices for a long time. The advent of the Industrial Revolution at the end of the 1700s led to serious criticism of its drawbacks. (See Chapter 16.) Critics of the new capitalist–industrial societies that emerged in the 1800s in western Europe, Canada, and the U.S. were numerous. Many of them condemned greed and the cruel treatment of workers: harsh and dangerous conditions that caused many accidents, low pay, long hours, child labour, and so on.

These inhumane practices were the subject of many novels that achieved wide acclaim. Charles Dickens in England and later Sinclair Lewis in the U.S. are but two novelists who described and condemned these and other business practices of the day. In Chapter 16 you saw how similar harsh conditions in Canada led to the formation of the union movement and eventually laws banning various unacceptable practices.

A Murky Road to Wealth

The accumulation of large fortunes in the 1800s and early 1900s (before the days of income taxes) was usually aided by many shady if not criminal acts, including the alleged killing of competitors and union leaders. In the U.S., those early, wealthy capitalists were dubbed **robber barons,** a term that became very popular and is still used today. The classic robber baron was John D. Rockefeller, who established a near monopoly in the oil business using power tactics. His huge Standard Oil Co. (from which we get the name Esso, S.O.) was finally forced by the U.S. courts, at the beginning of this century, to split up into a number of companies, each still quite large.

robber barons
Capitalists of the 19th century whose wealth came in part through shady if not criminal acts.

In Canada, one of the most notorious developments occurred during the building of the first railway line to the West Coast in the 1870s and 1880s. This vast project, like most railway construction in North America, was accompanied by many scandals and corruption. This led to the resignation in 1873 of the federal government of Canada's first prime minister, John A. MacDonald. The first scandal involved Sir Hugh Allan. His company (which became the CPR) was given contracts, vast sums of money, and huge tracts of land across Western Canada, often under questionable circumstances. Many men made fortunes, including Donald A. Smith (later Lord Strathcona) and Sir William Van Horne. Similar scandals in the province of Quebec, on a smaller scale, led to the fall of the government of Honore Mercier in the 1890s.

Modern Capitalism

The 19th century saw the emergence of the modern industrial–capitalist system. The economic philosophy that underpinned it was first elaborated upon by Adam Smith, whom we met in Chapter 4. Smith's book *The Wealth of Nations,* published in 1776, gave birth to the concept of **laissez-faire capitalism.** This theory stressed that if left alone and unhindered by government, the free market in pursuit of economic efficiency would provide an abundance of goods at the lowest prices, improving everyone's life. The workings of this "invisible hand" would reward capitalists for their work and financial risks, thus providing jobs for the population and plentiful goods to satisfy human needs and improve living standards.

laissez-faire capitalism
Theory that if left alone, unhindered by government, the free market in pursuit of economic efficiency would provide an abundance of goods at the lowest prices, improving everyone's life.

For some years this seemed to work as Smith predicted. But (as noted in Chapter 4) there were many booms and busts, the economic cycles we now take for granted. There were also the serious problems of poverty, job-related illnesses, the lack of pensions or compensation to workers for the many industrial accidents, and other such problems. Life for the average person was said to be "short, nasty and brutish."

The End of Laissez-Faire Capitalism

The 20th century saw the beginnings of serious attempts to deal with the shortcomings of the capitalist system. In Chapter 3 we saw how Canadian governments were forced to implement a variety of programs to smooth out the rough edges of capitalism and cope with its contradictions of extreme wealth and poverty. Of course, we now take for granted the great productive capacities that capitalism developed, which resulted in greatly improved living standards for the majority of people.

We accept and usually welcome what new technologies make available to us—faster travel, electronic gadgetry and communications, and more—but we also express more concern for human values. Canadian society condemns discrimination in hiring, promotion, or firing; continued high unemployment; poverty; homelessness; and children going to school hungry. We expect solutions. We insist that business managers, company directors, and politicians behave ethically. Activities such as bribery, influence peddling, favouritism, discrimination, and expense padding are denounced. The dumping of wastes and toxic material and many other formerly normal practices are now either severely frowned upon or illegal.

These concerns have also found expression on the international scene. For many years, nearly all countries have supported the sanctions against South Africa because of its official racist policy of apartheid, which kept its black majority in a permanent state of oppression. Canada had laws and policies that banned most dealings with South African government and businesses. Banks and companies that had investments there were severely criticized by shareholders, church leaders, and community groups. Eventually many responded by curtailing or ceasing their activities in that country.

Let us look at some other business activities that have been under attack from various sources as unethical.

SOME QUESTIONABLE BUSINESS PRACTICES

A growing number of "normal" business activities are coming under increasing scrutiny in Canada (and elsewhere) because of their doubtful ethical standards. As society's values are changing, certain practices are now being deemed unacceptable. Let us look at some of them.

Weapons Sales

Many people are concerned about the question of selling military equipment, supplies, and sophisticated industrial machinery and products to brutal dictatorships. In 1991 we witnessed a UN-sponsored attack, in which Canada participated, on Iraq because it had invaded its neighbour Kuwait in 1990 and refused to withdraw. Saddam Hussein, the dictator who rules Iraq, has an extremely unsavoury record and has often been condemned by Amnesty International and other human rights groups.

Despite this fact many countries, including Canada, had sold him billions of dollars worth of military equipment and supplies—including the capability to produce nuclear weapons and missiles. There are many media reports that much military equipment continues to be sold to Iraq by various countries, including the U.S. and Canada. Other countries with odious records send representatives to arms shows in Canada and can pretty well buy whatever they wish from Canadian companies. This is not only a Canadian problem. The UN Office of Disarmament Affairs and other organizations are concerned about the continuing proliferation of arms sold by the major industrial powers.[1]

Atomic Reactors Sold to Romania

Atomic Energy of Canada Ltd. (AECL), a crown corporation, was under heavy fire for having sold our nuclear reactors in the 1980s to the late dictator Nicolae Ceausescu of Romania. These contracts were important to AECL because for years it had been unable to sell any Canadian reactors. It was later learned that the workers who built the massive reactor housings were practically slave labourers. This was a classic example of the pressures businesses and governments face: a badly needed sales opportunity versus a customer who is ethically very distasteful. The question is made all the more complex when competitors in some countries seem to have no ethical standards at all.

Animal Rights

Canada was in the international spotlight in the 1980s because of the annual harp seal hunt in the Gulf of St. Lawrence. A worldwide campaign led by Greenpeace influenced people not to buy coats or other products made of these pelts. Animal rights activists in England and other European countries said the clubbing of the white seal pups was brutal and should be stopped. As a result, an industry that gave much-needed seasonal employment to people in Prince Edward Island and Newfoundland was forced to cease operations. Similarly, trapping by aboriginal Canadians, which provided them with badly needed cash income, was forced to a halt by an anti-fur campaign.

This was a controversial issue in Canada. Most people can see the need for protecting endangered species like leopards and tigers, which have been hunted to near-extinction for their beautiful skins. However, there was no danger of these seals disappearing. The entire fur industry—trapping, manufacturing, wholesaling, exporting, and retailing—has been very hard hit. What do you think of this issue?

The question of hunting seals has come to the fore again because of the serious depletion of the codfish stocks in the Atlantic Ocean off our east coast. This problem is blamed in part on the large increase in the seal population since seal hunting ceased. Seals are known to consume enormous quantities of fish daily. The experts are divided about the facts on this issue.

Animals in Medical Research

The same problem has arisen with new drugs developed by pharmaceutical companies. These drugs are tested on various mammals to see what side effects there are and how dangerous they might be for humans. Animal rights advocates say it is wrong to subject animals to cruel experiments. Pharmaceutical companies ask how they can risk human lives with unproven drugs.

Medical researchers are always experimenting with specially bred small lab animals to advance medical knowledge. Many run into the same complaints from animal rights groups. Should hospitals and research institutes stop working with these small mammals, one of their main sources of medical advances?

Fishing Disputes

Several problems arose regarding large-scale commercial fishing in the Pacific Ocean during the 1980s and 1990s. Many ships used miles-long drift nets that not only catch the fish being sought but also kill large numbers of porpoises and sea birds that dive for fish, get caught in the net, and cannot surface to breathe. These mammoth nets sometimes get detached from their ships and drift freely, trapping all kinds of sea life. It took a lot of pressure over several years from the world community to stop

In the 1980s worldwide attention focused on the seal hunt in the Gulf of St. Lawrence. Greenpeace was actively involved in bringing this issue to the forefront and appealed to people to boycott the products made from the seal pelts.

this practice. The last holdouts, Japan and Korea, finally agreed to reduce or eliminate this form of fishing.

Dolphins caught in the nets of tuna fishermen in the eastern tropical section of the Pacific Ocean are another problem. Dolphins and tuna usually swim together in this area and there is no way to catch tuna without trapping dolphins, who drown. In 1986 an estimated 130,000 dolphins were killed. In 1991 the number was estimated at 25,000. In the U.S., the National Research Council of the National Academy of Sciences and the Fisheries Research Institute see no solution to this problem unless commercial tuna fishing is abandoned.[2] This may affect Canadian fishing fleets.

Executive Compensation

In the U.S., all public companies must file annual reports with regulatory authorities listing the annual salaries of their senior executives so this becomes public knowledge. Canadian public companies are not required to do this, but if they offer their securities (stocks and bonds) for sale in the U.S. they must disclose the same information. It is ironic that Canadians who want this data on Canadian companies have to go to American sources. The Ontario Securities Commission has finally taken a small step in the direction of such disclosures. The Spotlight on Big Business has the story. Many shareholders and other interested parties want to know what senior executives earn and if they have really produced results that justify their high compensation.

Discrimination Against Women

In other chapters, we have discussed how women have been discriminated against in hiring and promotion and how this situation has improved. Companies have changed their policies as federal and provincial governments passed laws banning discrimination of all sorts. Nevertheless, women still earn much less than men for work of equal value. To remedy this situation, governments and companies have agreed in principle to pay equity for women. The Ontario government is the first one in Canada to enact this into law. It has begun making payments to its women employees to make up for past discriminatory salary differentials.

The Quebec Human Rights Commission has recommended a pay equity law that would require all employers to eliminate wage differences based on gender, race, or physical disabilities within four years. If the government adopts this recommendation, Quebec will become the second province with a law applying not just to the public sector but to all employers. The commission president, Yves

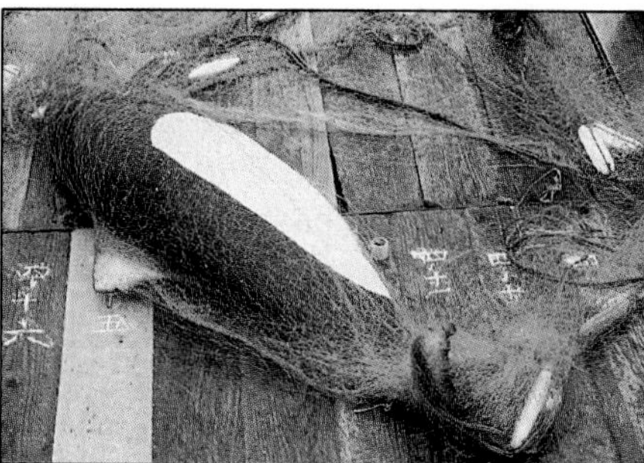

Driftnetting caused serious concern due to the fact that other forms of sea life get caught in the nets and are subsequently killed.

SPOTLIGHT ON BIG BUSINESS

The Big Pay Cover-Up

On the issue of pay disclosure, Ontario's security watchdog has turned out to be a lapdog of the executive suite. Despite pressure from shareholders to match U.S. disclosure standards for senior execs, the Ontario Securities Commission recently opted for a mushy compromise.

While the old system in Ontario merely required companies to report the aggregate compensation paid to all their officers, the revised rules make them divulge the aggregate of their five highest-paid executives. But details of individual salaries need only be divulged if the pay of any one of those individuals exceeds 40 percent of the total.

That's a slight improvement over past practice, which OSC chairman Robert Wright admits was unacceptable. But it stops well short of the U.S. provision: a breakdown of executive compensation for each individual executive. As we have said before, that is the standard the OSC should adopt. While CEOs and their veeps may prefer to keep their individual remuneration a secret, shareholders have a legitimate interest. How can they make an informed judgment on whether a CEO is earning his keep unless they know what his keep is?

Source: Editorial, *Financial Times,* March 16, 1992, p. 30.

Lafontaine, said the pay equity law would reduce the 35 percent gap between men's and women's wages to 15 percent.

Some business associations have already expressed outrage at the report, while unions say they support the proposal. Ghislain Dufour, president of the Conseil du Patronat, Quebec's largest employer group, said his group opposes a pay equity law. Michel Decary, Quebec vice-president of the Canadian Federation of Independent Business, called the proposal a "colossally bad idea."[3]

The federal government, in the March 1991 budget, announced that it would not compensate women civil servants for lack of equal pay for work of comparable value done before November 1990.[4] A *Montreal Gazette* article said that by scrapping the Economic Council and the Science Council, both headed by women, Ottawa had "silenced two of the most outspoken and influential women in Canada." The article pointed out that while women had made gains in the federal bureaucracy in 1991, they were still only 16 percent of senior management.[5]

PROGRESS CHECK

- What issue launched concern about unethical business practices in the U.S.? How was it resolved?
- What was the major business scandal in Canada in the 1800s?
- Can you name some Canadian business practices that were once acceptable but now are perceived as unethical or are even illegal?

White-Collar Crime

white-collar crime
A crime, usually theft, committed by an executive or other white-collar office worker.

Bob Crampton of the Metro Toronto fraud squad has spent many years tracking **white-collar crimes.** These are crimes, usually thefts, committed by executives and other white-collar, or office, workers. Crampton said, "Ethics are a rare commodity in the business community." He quoted Mario Puzo, author of *The Godfather,* who maintains that "behind every great fortune is a crime".[6] This is obviously an exaggeration, but it is often true.

Den of Thieves by *Wall Street Journal* editor James Stewart is about greed run amok in some brokerage firms on Wall Street in the 1980s. A number of major court cases sent brokers to prison and led to some record fines ($100 million in one case) and serious damage to the reputations of some U.S. investment and brokerage houses. A Canadian investment dealer bought 300 copies of this book for its staff so they would learn how *not* to give in to ever-present temptations for the "easy and fast buck".[7]

Price Fixing and Bid Rigging

The Competition Act was passed to ensure that the Canadian marketplace remained fair and competitive. This is vital for the health of the free enterprise system. Companies that conspire to get around that law should be curbed. A recent editorial in the *Financial Times* commends Howard Wetson, director of the Bureau of Competition Policy, for finally applying the law as it was meant to be applied. (The implication is that companies previously engaging in such activities got away with them.)

Canadian Liquid Air Ltd., Union Carbide Canada Ltd., and Liquid Carbonic Inc. pleaded guilty to charges of "conspiracy to fix prices for gases such as oxygen used in hospitals" and were each fined $1.7 million—the largest fines ever imposed under the act. Canadian Oxygen Ltd. was fined $700,000 and a fifth company, Air Products Canada Ltd., will be charged later.

In a previous case, eight companies were charged with **bid rigging,** a secret agreement among competitors to make artificially high bids, for Third World food-aid contracts. After a probe by the competition bureau, four of them were fined a total of $3.25 million. Three of the firms found guilty are among the largest flour-milling firms in Canada: Robin Hood Multifoods Inc., Maple Leaf Mills Ltd., and Ogilvie Flour Mills Ltd. Two other firms later pleaded guilty and received fines proportional to their size. The *Financial Times* editorial condemns this anti-competitive behaviour as being "especially offensive in the sale of medical products or famine aid."[8]

bid rigging
Secret agreement among competitors to make artificially high bids.

THINKING IT THROUGH

In May 1992, a tragic coal mine explosion in Plymouth, N.S., took the lives of 26 men. Accusations were made by members of Parliament and of the Nova Scotia legislature that both levels of government, acting for political reasons, financed the opening of the mine despite warnings from their mining departments that these were dangerous mines with a long record of explosions and deaths. An official inquiry is now being made into the causes of the explosion.

Federal cabinet minister Tom Hockins, interviewed on the CBC, said that economic considerations rather than safety factors led to the mine opening. The area has a persistently high unemployment rate and the mine opening was welcome news despite the known risks. The coal is of high quality.

What would you have done if you had to decide whether to open or not and you were a government official? A company officer?

Drugs and Pharmaceuticals

Newspapers, magazines, and TV programs like "Fifth Estate" on the CBC, and "60 Minutes" and "20/20" in the U.S. have long reported on faulty products produced by pharmaceutical companies who refuse to take the products off the market. These companies spend many years and hundreds of millions of dollars developing and testing new products to make sure they are safe. Every once in a while they slip up, but they are reluctant to withdraw such products because of the heavy investment in R&D, testing, approval, and marketing. They also face many lawsuits and costly settlements from injured users of these products if they admit guilt.

One of the most infamous cases occurred in the 1970s. It involved an intra-uterine contraceptive device called the Dalkon Shield. This IUD caused severe medical problems, including sterility, for many women. For years the manufacturer, A. H. Robins, denied that there were any problems, but ultimately it was forced to withdraw the product and pay substantial court-awarded damages to these women.

An unusual problem has arisen in connection with a possible new drug for cancer. The *Financial Times* reports the following story:

> Taxol, an experimental drug which holds great promise in the treatment of breast and ovarian cancer, is the subject of bitter debate between the drug's developers and environmentalists. "The Forest or the Trees?" (*Individual Investor,* March 1992) looks at how Hauser Chemical Research Inc. of Boulder, Colorado, extracts Taxol from the bark of the Pacific yew tree, which was once simply burned by loggers to get at more valuable firs.
>
> In clinical tests, Taxol has been 30 to 35 percent successful in stopping the spread of ovarian cancer and has few side effects. It could be a bonanza for Hauser and for Bristol-Myers Squibb Co., with which it has an exclusive supply deal. But Taxol is extracted only from the yew's bark, which means that the tree must be cut down. And the yew is native to the same northwest forests where the remaining 500 spotted owls left in the wild survive.
>
> Environmentalists counter that Taxol can be produced from the tree's needles and twigs (albeit more expensively) and that a synthetic form of the drug is just a few years away. They claim Hauser and Bristol-Myers's interest is motivated more by profit than by concern for victims of cancer.[9]

Breast Implants

In March 1992, the giant Dow-Corning Co. announced it was ceasing manufacture of the silicone breast implant used by many women who had had breast cancer surgery. For a couple of years before that, a fierce controversy raged over whether the implant could deteriorate and itself cause cancer. After many statements claiming the implant was perfectly safe, the Minister of Health in Canada abruptly changed her mind and banned it from use in Canada. There is still much controversy about this product.

Asbestos

One of the most famous issues in Canada involves asbestos. For many years, Quebec was one of the largest producers of asbestos in the world. Asbestos has the wonderful quality of being completely fireproof, which seemed to make it a perfect product for building materials, firefighters' clothing, and many other uses. Unfortunately, it was learned that the tiny, invisible asbestos fibres adhere to the lungs and cause asbestosis, which is usually fatal. For years the Quebec CSST (workers' compensation board) refused to acknowledge this as a work-related illness despite the very high incidence of asbestosis among workers and their families in the plants and communities where asbestos was mined and processed. The major companies were American. They fought hard for many years against compensation for workers who died or were laid off due to illness.

Eventually the proof was overwhelming, and by the early 1980s the asbestos industry was almost totally shut down. In the U.S., thousands of lawsuits were launched by workers in various plants where asbestos was used, including the U.S. Navy. There were so many lawsuits that it became an industry in itself. One of the major asbestos companies, Johns-Manville, went into bankruptcy because of all the claims against it. In the meantime, all over Canada, schools and other institutions started tearing out walls, floors, and ceilings that contained asbestos. The total cost in human lives, medical costs, suffering, and building material replacement is incalculable.

Cigarettes

We finish this section with the story of the cigarette. For many years doctors and researchers warned about the dangers of cigarette smoking; lung cancer was killing hundreds of thousands of people annually in Canada and the U.S. Year in and year out, the cigarette manufacturers denied any connection between smoking and cancer. Doctors in white lab coats would appear on TV ads and give their OK on smoking.

It is obvious why the companies refused to yield—cigarettes are the most profitable product made in Canada or the U.S. Governments in both countries were also not keen on giving up the revenue from cigarette taxes. In Canada, taxes make up about 80 percent of the price of cigarettes and provide governments with hundreds of millions of dollars annually.

Finally, the accumulating evidence could no longer be ignored. The actual medical and hospital costs of care for those afflicted with lung cancer and related illnesses were contributing to skyrocketing health care costs. Campaigns warned people of the hazards of smoking, advertising was severely restricted in Canada, and taxes were increased to make cigarette smoking a very expensive habit. A pack a day in 1993 added up to about $2,000 annually.

Cigarette manufacturing and tobacco growing are not illegal, but the continuing decline in consumption of cigarettes has caused tobacco farmers in Ontario and Quebec to seek other profitable items to grow. Tobacco companies diversified into other fields of business activity as they saw the handwriting on the wall. This does not prevent them from continuing to wage legal battles against government restrictions on advertising in a stubborn rear-guard action to protect profits as they withdraw slowly.

An example of this from the U.S. also affects Canada. The U.S. Surgeon General, Dr. Antonia Novello, said that it was time for Joe Camel to "take a hike." Joe Camel is the cartoon character invented in Europe and featured in ads in North America by the R. J. Reynolds Tobacco Co. The problem is that the character appeals to kids. According to the American Medical Association, more young children recognize Joe Camel than Mickey Mouse. Dr. Novello acknowledged that organized medicine does not usually call for the withdrawal of a successful advertising campaign but implied that this issue was so important it had to be done. However, she was rebuffed by R. J. Reynolds, which said that "No linkage has been made between advertising and the consumption of cigarette products."[10]

PROGRESS IN CORPORATE SOCIAL RESPONSIBILITY

Despite all the ethical problems reviewed so far, the fact is that most large companies are concerned about their public image. And many executives are beginning to support the notion of companies acting in a socially responsible way. Many companies have established a department of corporate ethics. This is addressed by a report in *Canadian Business:*

> David Nitkin, founder of EthicScan Canada Ltd. and publisher of *The Corporate Ethics Monitor* newsletter, keeps tabs on the social and environmental performance of 1,500 Canadian companies. He is a consultant to many companies and other organizations, including such giants as Imperial Oil Co., who want to improve their social performance and image. Until recently he would have been dismissed as a nut.[11]

These are encouraging signs that Canadian business has begun a significant change in attitudes and practices. Change is always difficult, particularly when it involves additional immediate costs at a time when international competitiveness is forcing Canadian companies to find every possible way to reduce costs.

We turn now to the impact of environmental issues on business.

THE IMPACT OF ENVIRONMENTAL ISSUES ON BUSINESS

The modern concern with environmental issues traces its beginnings to a famous book, *Silent Spring,* written by U.S. government biologist Rachel Carson in the early 1960s. She had noticed that for several years she had not heard many birds singing in spring. That led to the discovery that DDT, a widely used domestic and commercial pesticide, was a deadly poison that was affecting all wildlife and humans as well. That was the beginning of the serious investigation of how modern technology was affecting our environment.

Nearly everyone is now aware that the physical environment of the earth has been seriously damaged by various activities of human beings. Scientists over a broad range of studies—ecology, genetics, meteorology, botany, chemistry, zoology,—warn us about the serious threats that require prompt action if we are to continue living on this planet. Many international conferences have been held on this topic. Perhaps the most important took place in Brazil in 1992. It was called the United Nations Conference on the Environment and Development (UNCED). See the box, Reaching Beyond our Borders, for the story. Its chairman was Canadian Maurice Strong, who has been an important international figure for many years. He is now CEO of Ontario-Hydro.

In 1972, Strong chaired the Stockholm Conference on the Human Environment, the first international conference to put the *green* agenda on the international stage. Since then, "We've all lost our innocence," said Strong. "I don't think we can wait another 20 years. The Earth has cancer. In the early stages, the symptoms are minimal, but by the time they become acute it's too late."[12]

Trade and Environmental Issues

Former U.S. trade representative Carla Hill, who negotiated all trade matters for her country during much of the 1980s, has said, "I do think that [environmental] issues are going to intersect more and more with trade in this decade, and that we're going to have to analyze them and come up with a multilateral way of dealing with them."[13]

The Sierra Club is a major environmental group in the U.S. and Canada. Its chairman, J. Michael McCloskey, criticized Arthur Dunkel, director general of GATT, as a glaring example of narrow economic thinking. Dunkel said nations can no longer play a role as environmental leaders. He also insisted that agreements

REACHING BEYOND OUR BORDERS

UN Conference on the Environment and Development

After three years of painstaking planning, negotiations, and organizing, the most ambitious conference in history on environmental issues was set for June 1992 in Rio de Janeiro, Brazil. The United Nations is bringing together 160 nations in a massive effort to achieve a breakthrough on proposals to improve the world's environment. The leaders of 116 countries are expected to attend. It is chaired by Maurice Strong of Canada, who says, "Rio will produce more than any other UN conference in history. If Rio does not succeed, it will be the greatest breakdown of all time for the international community and perhaps the beginning of a rich–poor war."

Strong has spent his time in the period leading up to the conference dashing about the world speaking to government leaders of nations rich and poor, developed, developing, and underdeveloped. This huge, almost unmanageable conference seeks to solve the world's greatest environmental problems while reconciling them with sustainable growth that will improve rather than worsen the environment on planet earth. At the same time, it seeks to "alleviate poverty [through] global co-operation—in short, a new economic order."

The conference goal is to "find a way to bridge that divide between wealth and nature, growth and conservation, developed and developing. Summit supporters hope they will steer the world in a new direction, one in which the rich North will consume less while the poor South will produce more."

Strong notes that UN members have approved 98 percent of Agenda 21, a comprehensive 800-page document that outlines how in the next century the world can clean and save its environment. Agenda 21 deals with almost every environmental issue from overpopulation to overfishing.

The problems facing this conference are staggering. Huge sums of money are required if the goals are to be achieved. The rich, developed North says to the poor, underdeveloped South: stop cutting down your tropical forests, stop burning so much coal. You are adding substantially to the greenhouse effect and reducing the earth's ability to absorb carbon dioxide. Malaysia answers: we need space for agriculture for our growing population and we need the money from the sale of our timber. And China says: we cannot afford to convert our 750,000 coal-burning industrial boilers to cleaner methods. "Furthermore," they all say, "you rich Northerners consume too much energy, aggravating the greenhouse effect. You will have to finance us if you want us not to do what we are now doing and what you yourself have done previously."

Strong and others have called for a starting fund of $10 billion (U.S.) of new green funds for developing countries. Negotiators for most Northern countries said $3 billion is more likely.

Source: John Stackhouse, "Canadian on Mission to Save This Planet," *Globe and Mail,* May 2, 1992, p. A1.

concerning ozone depletion, international waste, and endangered species are "possible sources of conflict with the GATT rules." We can see that Dunkel has a different point of view from Hill's. McCloskey went on to state that

> The Sierra club is not opposed to expanded trade but it is opposed to policy that suggests that trade is free of costs to society. Trade agreements can and should become important tools for a more comprehensive form of development, not just narrow economic growth.[14]

The Forestry Industry

One of the most serious environmental hazards is created by the giant pulp and paper industry, which may be the largest employer in Canada. From British Columbia to Newfoundland, they spew their deadly wastes into our rivers, lakes, and ocean bays, causing incredible problems: drinking water is contaminated; aboriginals die from eating mercury-poisoned fish; the population at large is warned not to eat fish often; the rare white beluga whales in the St. Lawrence are dying off, so contaminated that their bodies are handled as highly toxic waste.

Some steps have been taken to improve the situation. Companies have wound down the bleaching process to avoid the use of chlorine. More paper is

Pulp mills have been singled out as major contributors to the level of mercury found in rivers, lakes, and oceans. New technologies are showing some promise in reducing the pollution created by pulp and paper mills.

recycled—we have become familiar with brown envelopes and other recycled paper products. The companies have begun to clean up their operations and waste problems. There are also hopeful signs in new technology emerging to deal with pulp mill sludge. The Alberta Newsprint Co. reported that a $2 million pilot project on the use of effluent sludge as a soil conditioner is showing very good results.[15]

Unfortunately, according to recent reports, mercury pollution has worsened. The *Montreal Gazette* carried a report from the *New York Times:*

> Two decades after the government thought that the problem had been put to rest, mercury is accumulating in fish in thousands of lakes across the United States and Canada, poisoning wildlife and threatening human health. Twenty U.S. states have warned people to limit or eliminate from their diets fish they catch in certain lakes because of dangerous levels of mercury.
>
> Canadian scientists have found elevated levels of mercury in fish caught in 95 percent of the lakes they tested in Ontario. (In Ontario and Quebec, the pulp and paper industry is a major contributor to the problem.) Scientists say the principal source of contamination [in the U.S.] is rain containing traces of mercury from coal-burning power plants, municipal incinerators, and smelters. Other contamination comes from lake and ocean sediments previously polluted by mercury.[16]

The forestry industry, especially in B.C., has run into serious criticism for its rapid depletion of Canada's first-growth forests, which are irreplaceable. A major battle has been fought for some years by aboriginal peoples and environmentalists to save the huge trees hundreds of years old in the Carmanah Valley and Clayoquot Sound in B.C.

This problem does not lend itself to a quick fix. Many large lumber companies, numerous sawmills and thousands of employees work in this industry. Stopping logging operations completely means disaster for the sawmill operators, many of them carrying on family operations that have run for generations. The same scenario looms over the employees engaged in the various components of this industry. What would they do if logging stopped in various areas of B.C.? What would it mean for the local economies? These kinds of problems must be solved soon.

Many environmental groups tried to stop the logging of the Carmanah Valley. One group, the Western Canada Wilderness Committee now has a research station in the valley. The W.C.W.C. was founded to educate the public and promote wilderness values and preservation.

The Canadian pulp and paper industry is also facing some really tough problems. Probably the worst year in the industry's history was 1991, as it lost a staggering $1.5 billion

> at a time when it faces massive spending requirements to comply with new environmental standards. Over the next few years . . . across the country the figure is perhaps as much as $5 billion. As tough as things are for pulp-and-paper makers, these guys had an incredible ride in the last decade. They made billions as prices for pulp and newsprint soared in the roaring '80s.
>
> Greed triumphed over good sense. The companies added new paper machines to meet what they saw as an ever-increasing demand or to keep the other guy from increasing market share. Yes, the investment was massive. But the new capacity came on-stream just as demand began to slow and the public became genuinely concerned about the health of the environment.
>
> If more of the money had gone into pollution control rather than building new machines, the industry would be a lot better off today.[17]

Frank Dottori, chairman of the Canadian Pulp and Paper Association, said the industry was getting a bad rap from everybody and that by the end of 1992 at least 15 mills would be producing recycled newsprint from de-inked paper. Peter Hadekel, business editor of the *Montreal Gazette,* replied that the industry was slow to see the handwriting on the wall. Some 26 states in the U.S. have legislation requiring a minimum amount of recycled content in newsprint. Newspapers form the largest component of waste, causing heavy waste removal and disposal costs. Hadekel also suggested that the pulp and paper industry should spend less time attacking environmentalists as extremists and more time working with them. This is especially important in view of the report on "the ecological catastrophe unfolding across Canada. The pulp and paper industry is by no means the only offender, but it cannot skirt its responsibilities."[18]

Worldwide Deforestation

Vast deforestation has been taking place in Brazil, Borneo, Indonesia, and elsewhere in the world. It leads to soil erosion, since the treeless soil cannot retain water; silting up of rivers downstream; fewer trees producing less oxygen for a growing world population and absorbing less carbon dioxide; logs sinking in rivers and lakes, giving off gases as they decay, which adds to the warming of the atmosphere. Tree planting programs are a partial solution. The solutions are not easy, since many people are trying to survive by clearing forests to farm, raise cattle, or simply earn a living working for logging companies.

Tree planters at work in MacMillan Bloedel's Cameron/Franklin River division, part of the company's Alberni Region operations. Every year, MacMillan Bloedel plants approximately 7 million seedlings on land it harvests. Ninety percent of all MacBlo's working areas of the forest are restocked within three years of harvest, either through replanting or natural regeneration.

Pesticides in Agriculture

A major problem in agriculture is the very extensive, and intensive, use of pesticides and fertilizer as a regular process. David Suzuki, the prominent Canadian geneticist, broadcaster, and writer on environmental issues, points out that after almost a half-century of spraying, not a single insect species has been killed off. Instead, new spray-resistant varieties appear, requiring new and more powerful insecticides, in a never-ending vicious circle. Farmers are locked into ever-rising costs just to stand still in their endless battle against insects.

They also face rising personal health hazards from these chemicals. The CBC reported on March 8, 1992, that farmers in Alberta have been warned not to wear baseball caps during spraying operations. When they perspire, the chemicals absorbed by the hats leach into their scalps, causing a variety of side effects—vomiting, nausea, and other hazards.

Further, the run-off into rivers and lakes causes an accumulation of metals and algae. Fed by fertilizer nutrients, the algae bloom so profusely that they consume all the oxygen, causing fish and all other living matter to die. The algae then produce toxins as they die off.

organic farming
Farming that is done without chemicals.

A significant movement towards chemical-free **organic farming** has developed across Canada, as in other parts of the world. The change is slow, complex, and costly. Organic farming is still a small percentage of total agricultural production. Federal and provincial departments of agriculture have been slow to support this movement, and some people suspect pressure from the giant companies that produce fertilizers and insecticides.

In addition to agricultural run-offs and pulp and paper waste, there is waste from sewage plants. Auto exhausts deposit chemicals on roads and highways that are washed by rain into the seas. A 1978 documentary produced by The New Jersey Network called "Sea Under Siege" shows a miles-long algae bloom. It cites dolphins, full of heavy metals and dioxins, that get cancer and other illnesses as their immune systems weaken and warns of the deadly effect on humans of eating fish and shellfish.

Acid Rain

In central Canada (and the northeastern U.S.), the effects of acid rain from various mills in the U.S. Midwest and Ontario are well known. Thousands of lakes are dead and maple trees have been slowly dying off, threatening the maple syrup industry. When INCO (the International Nickel Co.) sought to overcome the pollution around its large Sudbury operation, it raised its smokestack. This sent the gases higher into the air and the prevailing wind dispersed them much farther east in Ontario and into Quebec.

In general, industry in the U.S., supported by its government, has fought strenuously against reducing its pollution because of the costs involved. In Canada, governments and industry have been trying to work out solutions, but progress is very slow. Companies worry about the substantial costs making them less competitive internationally. Nearly all governments in Canada have passed laws to protect the environment, but they are not pressing large companies too rigorously because of the costs and the recession.

Garbage

Until the late 1970s industries and local governments did not worry too much about the potential problems of garbage. Waste was either buried in landfills or run off into the air or into creeks, lakes, rivers, and oceans. It seemed as if this could continue indefinitely. But we are now faced with two very difficult and unpleasant tasks: the very large costs for cleaning up the problems of the past and the need to change our ways of doing things. The dangers of putting off these tasks are brought home regularly, while industry and government often seem to move at a snail's pace to remedy the situation.

In the summer of 1989, there was a disastrous fire in a poorly managed PCB storehouse near Montreal, forcing the evacuation of an entire small town and damaging agriculture in the region. The following year, two fires of huge piles of old tires, one in Ontario and one in Quebec, burned for weeks, causing serious local pollution. Hardly a week goes by without some sins of the past coming back to haunt us or new ones from current behaviour surfacing.

The Laidlaw Clean-Up

The giant Laidlaw Inc., perhaps the largest waste disposal company in Canada and a subsidiary of Canadian Pacific, was found to have buried hundreds of drums containing hazardous chemicals at a toxic dump it owns in Quebec. After the announcement by the Quebec Department of the Environment, estimates of clean-up costs went as high as $1 billion. Shares dropped in value and the company received very negative publicity.

> All this by-passed the fact that everyone knew the site's groundwater had been contaminated decades before, and remained contaminated thanks to the previous owner, Tricil. Laidlaw set aside what seemed to be a modest $5 million for clean-up costs.

Later president Don Jackson announced that the company had actually spent $5–$10 million to remove the drums and that the site "was far cleaner than when Laidlaw first got involved."

The company said that its clean-up obligations were complete and it was waiting for acknowledgment of that fact by the Quebec government. But, as is the

SPOTLIGHT ON SMALL BUSINESS

Potential Legal Nightmares for Small Businesses

Why are small and medium-sized businesses, in the midst of the serious 1992 recession, spending $900 just to sign up at a Toronto conference on storage and disposal of waste products?

> The potential losses facing business from the mishandling of waste are tremendous. They may require an emission licence, and a conviction for operating without one can bring fines of up to $100,000 a day.
>
> Any company that puffs smoke through a stack on the roof—and that includes restaurants, fast-food or otherwise—may already be breaking . . . regulations and not know it.
>
> Dry-cleaning firms that flush chemicals directly into the sewer system instead of contracting with bona fide waste removal firms may be exposing themselves to heavy fines. The owners or officers of the business might even find themselves hauled off to jail.
>
> A small firm's truck can swerve to miss a rabbit, flip onto its side, and empty its cargo of toxic material, chemicals, or gasoline into a roadside creek, with resulting financial disaster for the truck's owners. The smallest spill—including toxic waste seeping into the soil from defective storage tanks—with the price of clean-up, environmental experts to assess the damage, fees for lawyers and fines, can run up to $100,000, says environmental lawyer Roger Cotton, conference chairman.

And that does not include the large costs of defending against any legal suits brought by any of the surrounding owners.

The pressure is on governments to put teeth into environmental laws and to increase inspections. In 1991, in Ontario alone there were more than 2,000 charges for infractions of these laws. In about a third of them directors, officers, and managers were personally charged.

Unfortunately, insurance is not yet available for this type of problem, which means that all companies, large and small, must consult with waste and storage disposal experts to ensure that they are not breaking any laws.

Source: Claire Bernstein, "Problem of Waste Storage and Disposal Has Even Small Companies Worried," *Toronto Star,* April 6, 1992, p. D3.

case with many other news items, the bad news got more publicity than the good news, so the decline in stock price and the negative image were not reversed.[19]

Clean-ups after Ceasing Operations

The oil companies in Canada had a bad year in 1991 and decided on some drastic steps to reduce their costs. In early 1992 they announced that some 3,000 service stations would be closed in Canada. The cost of making the closed stations safe was estimated at $1 billion to $2 billion.[20]

When the huge Lavalin conglomerate went bankrupt in Montreal in 1991, nobody knew who was going to pay for the cost of shutting down and cleaning up the petrochemical plant it owned in Montreal. It is fortunate that the stranded engineers and employees stayed on without pay to shut down the operation properly to avoid a catastrophe. It looks as though the provincial government, meaning the taxpayer, will be stuck with the cost of the clean-up job.

Contrast this with a case in Alberta also involving a bankrupt company, in this case an oil company. A secured lender, that normally can seize the assets securing a loan, was prevented from doing so in this perhaps historic ruling in Canada. The Alberta Energy Resources Conservation Board ruled that the $200,000 cash that was available to the secured lender must be used to cap the company's oil wells to prevent environmental damage. This landmark case will be watched carefully by all lending institutions in Canada as it makes its way through the legal system to the Supreme Court.[21]

Industrial waste presents numerous problems in regards to its removal and disposal. Many unethical dumping practices have become public through news reports. What do you think is the most practical way to deal with this problem?

Not in My Backyard

One of the major problems with waste—nuclear, ordinary, or toxic—is that nobody wants it. We seem to want the products or processes that produce waste, but everybody says "Not in my backyard" **(NIMBY)** when it comes to disposing of it. All across Canada, any time any level of government proposes to set up some waste storage or disposal facility and hearings are held, the overwhelming response is nearly always NIMBY, regardless of the potential economic benefits and/or jobs that might flow from erecting and operating the facility. We don't mind if our waste is dumped in other provinces or countries—if they will accept it.

NIMBY
Not in my backyard, meaning that people don't want waste disposal facilities in their towns, though they agree that such facilities are needed somewhere.

Obviously, this attitude is neither rational nor practical and offers no long-term solution to waste disposal. Better ways are gradually being adopted. Loblaw's, Ontario's largest food retailer, has been putting money into going green. Vice-president Patrick Carson noted that

> If you want to be successful . . . you have to be realistic, and the reality is that we are living in an environment that is deteriorating. If we make money destroying this planet, we'll have to spend even more money going back to repair.[22]

This lesson is slowly being learned by managers, senior officers, and boards of directors. But all the environmental experts are warning us that we will have to move a lot faster if we are to avoid extremely serious problems in the near future. One solution is to do as Bell Canada did—use conservation to reduce the volume of waste—and save substantial dollars in the process.

Conservation

One effective way to deal with waste is to *use* less, so less waste is created. The amount of packaging per item in supermarkets and elsewhere is being reduced. Furthermore, containers and other packaging are being made biodegradable. The fast-food restaurants have all followed this trend. This does not reduce the volume of waste, but it makes it less threatening to the environment.

Conservation has many more beneficial side effects. More fuel-efficient automotive, marine, and airplane engines reduces demand on the earth's natural resources and transportation and distribution of fuel oils and gasoline. Fewer marine and truck tankers and storage tanks reduce the risk of accidents and spills. Less fuel burned results in less exhaust gas, reducing the warming of the earth by the greenhouse effect.

Electricity consumption is being reduced through energy-efficient kitchen appliances, electric motors, and light bulbs, as well as better-insulated buildings and lower room thermostat and hot-water settings. Hydro and power companies are educating themselves and consumers in conservation methods and offering various incentives. These activities avoid the necessity for costly new hydro-electric projects that would flood vast territories, creating various environmental hazards and encroaching on indigenous peoples' lands and rights.

Hydro-Quebec is still fighting a stubborn battle for new dams despite strong opposition from environmentalists and customers in the northern U.S. states and aboriginal peoples in Quebec whose ancestral lands would be flooded. It has, however, finally gotten serious about conservation efforts.

Ontario-Hydro has suspended new dam projects and will concentrate instead on conservation efforts. It sees this approach as a much less costly way of providing additional power resources without incurring massive debts and damaging the environment.

An example of an efficient and environmentally sound operation is the CBC building in Montreal, headquarters of the French network Radio-Canada. According to the chief heating engineer, this 20-year-old building employs heat from the bodies of its inhabitants plus heat generated by the lights in the TV studios to provide almost all the heating required, with very rare supplementation by a conventional heating system.[23]

All new buildings are now better insulated and have special window installations that reduce heat loss, an important factor in energy consumption in our cold northern climate.

The combined energy-efficient operations of equipment, appliances, buildings, and vehicles have an enormous cumulative effect in reducing the emission of gases that contribute to the warming of the planet by the greenhouse effect. They also reduce other environmental damage.

Ozone

For some time, scientists have warned that the ozone layers in the upper atmosphere have developed holes or are thinning. This poses great risks of cancer because increased amounts of ultraviolet radiation get through from the sun to us. Yet too much ozone in the lower atmosphere causes deadly smog.

The *Globe and Mail,* carrying a news item from the well-respected *Christian Science Monitor* of Boston, notes that California (a forerunner on many environmental issues) has established controls on a wide variety of products that contribute to smog. This includes items like dusting aids, non-stick cooking sprays, charcoal lighter fluid, household adhesives, insecticides, and personal fragrance items. Placing smog controls on these items is expected to cut air pollution in California by the equivalent of one million new cars. Personal fragrance products alone release four tons of volatile organic compounds into the air daily in California.[24]

Environment Canada issues an ozone report every Friday. The first one, issued March 11, 1992, noted that upper atmosphere ozone levels in western Canada were 15 percent below the 1960–1980 average. In the rest of Canada, the figure was 5 percent below that 20-year average.[25] A panel discussion on the CBC that week reported that even if all chemicals contributing to the ozone thinning were reduced to zero immediately it would still take 100 years for ozone levels to return to normal!

Technological Solutions

Some people count on technology as a solution to pollution and other environmental problems. From time to time there are encouraging reports of ingenious ideas that seem to offer some hope. A story in the *Minneapolis–St. Paul Star Tribune* told how engineer Emil Pfender, in his lab at the University of Minnesota, has converted the toxins benzene and acetone into tiny industrial diamonds. He expects to be able to do the same with deadly PCBs as soon as he can solve the problem of handling them safely.[26]

While such advances in science are important, we are a very long way from being able to convert the vast output of waste (toxic or otherwise) into useful substances. It is far more logical to follow the conservation route and start reducing the vast daily outpouring of such products. Conservation has the added advantage of maintaining our resources and natural environment.

The Global Environment

The environmental problems we face in Canada are duplicated all over the world. Typical headlines from Canadian and American newspapers in 1992 read: "Mexico extends restrictions as capital chokes on smog," "Scientists say people, pollution threaten 'rainforests of the ocean,' " "Alps caught in vise between tourism and trucks," "The Sphinx in danger of collapse," and "Why the environment is the issue of our lives."

This small sample indicates the damages caused to the natural environment by the activities of humans. Most of the problems stem from the fact that there has been such an explosion of population and industrial activities that we have gone beyond the capacity of the earth to sustain that growth without suffering serious damage.

The Problem of Endless Growth

All countries, including Canada, believe that growth is a desirable goal. We even worship growth. More plants, more offices, more production, more sales, even more population are all considered positive achievements. In Canada we worry about our population declining because of our low birth rate. Various countries have programs to encourage larger families in order to increase population. Only China has undertaken a serious long-term campaign to control population growth.

David Suzuki points out that it is only in this century that growth has become a normal part of our lives. He quotes University of Colorado physicist Albert Bartlett: "The greatest shortcoming of the human race is our inability to understand the **exponential function.**" It is simply the mathematical description of anything that changes steadily in one direction over a given period of time. Suzuki gives some interesting examples of where that leads to.

exponential function
The mathematical description of anything that changes steadily in one direction over a given period of time.

rule of 72
Divide the rate of increase of any activity into 72 to get the number of years it takes for the result of that activity to double.

The **rule of 72** says that if you divide the rate of increase of any activity into 72, you get the number of years it takes for the result of that activity to double. If the inflation rate is 6 percent, in 12 years prices will double. This holds true whether it is pollution, population, or use of energy that is growing. (You may recall that we first looked at the rule of 72 in Chapter 4.)

The point is that even a small, steady increase can over time have startling effects in one lifetime. A 5 percent inflation rate over a 72-year lifespan would result in gas going from 50¢ to $16 a litre, an $8 movie admission to $256, a $1 soda pop to $32, and a $15,000 car to $480,000! If all of this sounds fantastic, just ask your grandparents if they remember 3¢-per-litre gas, 25¢ movies, 5¢ pop, and $800 new cars.

Suzuki continues:

> It's the same with exponential increase in our use of energy, forests, or ocean resources. Each time total use has doubled, we require more than all that had been exploited in the past up to that point. Yet we continue to demand more. But everything in the universe, including the universe itself, is finite. Nothing in it can grow exponentially indefinitely, for as Bartlett says, "In all systems, growth is a short-term transient phenomenon." Stanford ecologist Paul Ehrlich is more blunt. Steady, endless growth, he says, is the creed of cancer cells and mainstream economists, and the inevitable result is the same for both.
>
> If you look at the history of mankind on this planet, it is only in this century that growth has become such an obvious part of life. On a graph of our numbers—use of food, air, water, soil—the curves are virtually flat for 99 percent of our history. They begin to turn up perceptibly only in the past century; and then in our lifetime, through exponential growth, they leap off the page.[27]

Suzuki's point is clearly demonstrated if we look at population growth. William K. Stevens, writing in the *New York Times,* points out that it took all of human history for world population to reach 2.5 billion in 1950. But it took only 40 more years for that number to double to 5 billion in 1990. If this exponential growth rate of 1.75 percent continues, the population will double again to 10 billion people by the year 2030.

Stevens quotes from a *Beyond the Limits* by Meadows, Meadows, and Randers. Their updated computer simulations indicate that

> if human activity continues as at present, it will "overshoot" the carrying capacity of the biosphere and precipitate a collapse within the next few decades. . . . The new analysis puts more emphasis on the deterioration of the biosphere, says Dennis Meadows. He notes that "Twenty years ago it seemed to us that there was a period out to 2030 or 2040 in which to fashion a sustainable society." Now, he says, it looks as though if a new set of attitudes and policies is not in place in the next 20 years (2012), it will be too late to avoid an eventual collapse.

This same article carries a report from an important business consulting group that denies that there is anything to worry about for the next 100 to 150 years because the market system has repeatedly stretched the so-called finite limits of the earth to become "roughly infinite." But researchers in these fields disagree with this optimistic assessment. They see population and emission increases leading to drastic climate and other changes in the biosphere because of overloading.[28]

Do you recall the book *Small Is Beautiful,* mentioned in Chapter 8? In the 1970s, E. F. Schumacher pointed out the dangers inherent in mindless growth for growth's sake alone. It might be useful to take another look at his ideas.

THINKING IT THROUGH

Do you think that environmental concerns are overstated? Even if they are not overstated, technology has always produced ingenious ways of solving many problems. Why not rely on some new process to take care of pollution, the greenhouse effect, the ozone problem, and the rest?

WHAT IS THE ANSWER?

The problem of business and the environment in Canada is quite complicated. An article in the prestigious *Harvard Business Review* by Charles Hampden-Turner, a senior research fellow at the London Business School and at the Centre for International Business Studies in Amsterdam, addresses the issue globally:

> Environmental clean-up in the United States has been stalled for a decade by a sterile debate about the "costs" of government regulation to economic competitiveness. In Japan, by contrast, government intervened to encourage the development of antipollution technologies. The result: both cleaner industries and a new generation of companies internationally competitive in the emerging global market for these technologies.
>
> The recent Global Environment Charter published by Keidanren (the Japan Federation of Economic Organizations [the most important big business organization in Japan]) last April [1991], calls on Japanese companies to "seek appropriate means for the domestic and overseas transfers of their technologies,

MAKING ETHICAL DECISIONS

In the U.S., there is an influential school of thought that disagrees with the proposition that business should make special efforts to behave ethically. The most prominent member of this school is Milton Friedman, a Nobel laureate and a very influential economist who has advised presidents. He maintains that it's up to government to pass laws that society wants with regards to the environment and ethical behaviour in general.

Businesses, he says, are economic units that must concentrate on making profits. In this way they will produce the greatest benefits for society. This line of thinking harks back to Adam Smith and laissez-faire capitalism. But Friedman does not think governments should keep out. He believes they have a responsibility to govern and business must obey the laws. But it does not have any special duty to engage in ethical behaviour beyond legal requirements.

This way of thinking represents a minority outlook. Most commentators believe that companies have an active responsibility to ensure ethical behaviour of their management beyond the minimum required by law. The success of many ethical mutual funds, which invest only in companies with high ethical standards, shows that there is not necessarily a conflict between behaving ethically and maximizing profits.

What do you think? Throughout this book you have seen various ethical problems, many of them not involving considerations of the law. Often it's a question of doing the right thing versus making bigger bucks. Have you thought about these questions? In the very near future you may find yourself in a management position where you will be facing such choices. How will you respond to some of the issues raised in this chapter?

> know-how, and expertise for dealing with environmental problems." By taking environmental problems seriously, the charter argues, Japanese companies can "foster mutually beneficial relationships between producers and consumers, thereby encouraging the healthy development of the economy".[29]

The difference in attitudes and action between Japanese and American business and governments is clear. In Canada we have a better track record than the U.S., but environmental and community groups generally accuse governments and business of giving mostly lip service rather than being genuinely involved in a serious effort to improve the situation. We also seem to be held back by the concern about the "costs" question and what it will do to our competitiveness. Does the Japanese approach seem a good one for Canada to follow?

Sustainable Development

Another useful input into this difficult area is the concept that emerged from the international conference on the environment in Toronto in 1988. The Brundtland report (named after the Norwegian prime minister who chaired the commission) suggested that sustainable development is the responsible way of the future. Only economic and industrial development that could be sustained over time without damaging the environment should be pursued. Most governments now support this concept in theory, but its implementation is another story. (See Chapter 1 for a more complete discussion of this concept.)

In Canada, we have made a good start by establishing the International Institute for Sustainable Development (IISD). It was set up jointly by the federal and Manitoba governments and is headquartered in Winnipeg. The governments appointed the first three members of the board of directors, who then appointed 12 international members from various countries.

> IISD is an independent, non-profit corporation, funded by the governments of Manitoba and Canada. Its mission is to promote the concept and practice of development which integrates the needs of the economy and the environment

Canada is one of the most beautiful countries in the world. However, in today's global business environment, it is crucial that all countries work together to reduce the negative impact that humans have had on their environment.

> in decision making. The institute undertakes programs and projects internationally and in Canada. IISD is governed by an independent international board of directors.[30]

Business, governments, and labour too are beginning to shift their emphasis from thinking in the short term—profits, jobs, and tax revenues now—to thinking of long-term effects on the environment. It will take a determined effort from everyone concerned to get all these components of decision making pulling in the direction of sustainable development, but we have no choice if we want to maintain a habitable world for ourselves and our children.

In the past few years, many steps have been taken to improve the environment: catalytic converters on vehicles, reduced gas consumption, banning of spray cans that release ozone-depleting chemicals, elimination of toxins like PCBs, and recycling to reduce waste and tree cutting. However, we have not yet made the really hard decisions that must be made.

A RADICALLY DIFFERENT ANSWER

Paul Hawken is an American entrepreneur, cofounder of Smith and Hawken, catalogue merchandisers, and author of *The Ecology of Commerce.* He is at work on another book, *Our Future and the Making of Things.* In both of these books, he has some startling answers for the ethical and environmental issues that face us. He believes that a wholly new approach is required if we are to survive on this planet. He claims that if his suggestions were followed it would:

1. Reduce energy and natural resource use in developed nations by 80 percent within a half-century.
2. Provide secure, stable, and meaningful employment.
3. Be a "self-actuating" system rather than one that is regulated or moralistic.
4. Restore degraded habitats and ecosystems rather than merely sustain them at current levels.
5. Rely on current levels of solar "income."
6. Be fun, involving, and aesthetic.

This may give the impression of some utopian dream but Hawken fleshes out his plan in great detail. He has a 12-point program that proposes a radically different system of government taxation and business operations. Ordinary people will also have to change their way of life. He notes that:

> At present, the environmental and social responsibility movements consist of many different initiatives connected primarily by values and beliefs rather than by design. What is needed is a conscious plan to create a sustainable future, including a set of design strategies for people to follow.

The underlying philosophy of his "design strategies" is that the current systems make destructive commercial and industrial behaviour normal and profitable, and it requires high moral principles to act more responsibly. He would change this around so that irresponsible behaviour would be costly and abnormal, while socially responsible activities would be cheaper and yield more profits for companies. Hawken says, "We need a system of commerce and production in which each and every act is inherently sustainable and restorative."

Some major aspects of Hawken's 12-point program include:

1. Adjusting prices to reflect all costs. This includes proper waste disposal, damage to environment and to people's health, and so on.
2. Total revision of taxation philosophy so that instead of taxing jobs, payrolls, creativity, and real income, it is degradation, pollution, and depletion that will be taxed.
3. Transformation of the way we design products so that most things will be recyclable or biodegradable. This will involve drastic reduction or elimination of the hundreds of chemicals, metals, plastics, dyes, and pesticides that are part of so many products. This is already being done to a certain extent in Germany and Japan with autos and other items.

These are all part of an elaborate scheme that would totally revolutionize how we now function. Hawken insists that we have no choice because even if "every company on the planet were to adopt the environmental and social practices of the best companies . . . the world would still be moving towards environmental degradation and collapse."[31] He is not alone in this belief.

As with ethical issues, important changes in thinking and actions by corporate and government management show an acceptance of greater social responsibility. The new generation of managers emerging from business schools has been alerted to these concerns, so the future looks promising. Are we ready for the kind of changes Hawken is proposing? Do we have a choice?

PROGRESS CHECK

- What is the ozone problem? Why is it so important?
- What is the rule of 72? Why is it useful? Can you give some examples?
- Why is population growth a potential time bomb?
- What is the dominant business outlook in the U.S. on environmental problems, according to Charles Hampden-Turner? Why does he criticize this outlook?

SUMMARY

1. Discuss how business, in the early capitalist period, ignored ethical standards of behaviour.

1. In the 1800s, laissez-faire capitalism was commonly accepted as good and necessary.
   - *Why were ethical standards ignored or so low?*

   It was believed that everyone would benefit from unregulated and unrestricted production and wealth accumulation by capitalists. The evils of this new system were tolerated as being unavoidable.

2. Describe the modern beginnings of business ethics.

2. Prior to the 1960s, there was little real challenge to the ways companies did business. Then something happened in the U.S.
   - *What was the role of Ralph Nader in changing company attitudes?*

   This young lawyer, working almost alone, took on mighty General Motors because of its defective Corvair model. He finally forced them to recall cars for the first time in automotive history.

3. Understand why ethical issues are so important now.

3. A great change has occurred in the attitudes of people.
   - *What are their expectations now?*

   Greater social responsibility is demanded from companies, governments, and their officials.

4. Many important aspects of the behaviour of managers are now under scrutiny.

▼ *What are some of these?*

Some major issues are greed, influence peddling, bribery of officials, expense padding, illegal dumping of waste, price fixing, bid rigging, and excessive executive salaries.

4. List some important ethical issues.

5. In response to changing social attitudes, companies are adopting new standards of acceptable behaviour.

▼ *How are they achieving this goal?*

Most large companies have established a formal structure with a title indicating responsibility for setting and improving ethical standards. They also publicize among their staff a code of ethics that guides acceptable behaviour.

5. See what business is doing to set and improve ethical standards.

6. The change in attitudes regarding the environment started with a book published in the U.S. in the 1960s.

▼ *What was that book and why did it make such an impact?*

Silent Spring by Rachel Carson showed how the numbers of birds had declined sharply. The cause was the insecticide DDT, previously used as a cure-all spray. This led to the birth of the modern environmental movement.

6. Identify what first led to concern about the environment.

7. We are all familiar with a variety of environmental problems.

▼ *What are the most serious, widespread issues?*

Global warming, due to an increase in gases trapped in the atmosphere, is causing the greenhouse effect. Ozone depletion at upper levels and increase at lower levels are other results of certain gas emissions. Pollution of the air, water, and soil is also causing many serious problems.

7. List some of the major environmental problems.

8. There are heavy costs attached to cleaning up problems from the past and just as great costs in changing how industries operate in the future.

▼ *How does this affect competitiveness?*

The concern is that companies that do a good job will incur heavier costs than those in Canada or internationally that do not clean up their act. These additional costs will result in higher prices than those of "dirty" competitors.

8. Understand why business tends to see a conflict between a clean environment and competitive ability.

9. The rule of 72 is a mathematical formula.

▼ *What information does it yield and what is the significance of this information?*

It shows how many years it takes for any steady rate of change to result in a doubling of the results of that change. It is determined by dividing a certain rate of change into 72.

9. Describe the rule of 72 and explain its relationship to growth.

10. Endless uncontrolled growth has led to many of our environmental problems.

▼ *How does sustainable development provide a solution for such problems?*

Planning only as much growth or expansion as the environment can tolerate without deteriorating is the only way to sustain development over the long term.

10. Explain how sustainable development has become the major international goal for reconciling growth with environmental constraints.

GETTING INVOLVED

1. Go to the library and look up the Canadian Competition Act. Take a few minutes to review what it covers and report your findings back to your class.
2. While at the library, check through some recent magazines and newspapers for articles on ethical or environmental questions. Photocopy some that you find important and bring them to class for discussion. Try to determine if there is any trend towards improvement of business attitudes or actions in these matters.
3. Discuss the merits of increased legislation versus self-regulation to prevent deceptive business practices. Which is better in the long run? Defend your position.
4. Where do you see leadership emerging to improve ethical standards in Canada? What can you do to support such leadership?

PRACTICING MANAGEMENT DECISIONS

Case One Ethics in the Road-building Business

Bob Shilo is president of a large, successful road-building company. His old college buddy, Joe Molinari, runs the office of a provincial political party and has a lot of influence with the Ministry of Public Works in the province. Through the years they have had a cozy arrangement. Joe would help Bob get major road construction and maintenance contracts at good prices. In return Bob would regularly make substantial contributions to Joe's party funds.

Bob's son, Gerry, has completed his schooling and has been working in his father's company since graduation. He has spent a few summers during school holidays working with the road crews to get to know the business and is now working in the office.

When he discovers the set-up between his father and Joe he is a bit surprised and wonders if it is a very ethical way of doing business. Bob tells him that every company follows the same practice because it is the only way to get these fat contracts. If he stopped donating handsomely to the party funds, Bob explains, there would be very little business coming their way.

A few days later Gerry is having lunch with a couple of friends. As they talk about their work, the issue of corporate social responsibility arises. He quickly learns that they all face similar problems of ethical behaviour in their companies.

Decision Questions

1. What should Gerry do, go along with the system or try to change it?
2. Suppose his father says it is impossible for one person to change the long-established method of doing business. He refuses to budge. Should Gerry quit and look for another job? What alternatives does he have?
3. How does Gerry know it will be different anywhere else? Should he make a careful search for a company that has a strong ethical code?
4. Can Gerry and his friends work together to try to change the old ways? What can they do?

Case Two Oil Spills and Troubled Waters

Amora Srinivar is a manager in the ethics division of World Oil Corporation. Her job is to ensure that oil is transported with minimum risk to the environment. The company has had some minor spills from oil tankers recently. Investigation showed that ships' officers often drank too much during their long, boring ocean trips. She is growing increasingly concerned that there could be a major ecological catastrophe if nothing is done about the drinking problem.

Srinivar is running into three problems:

1. Drinking is a long-established custom and is hard to change.
2. There is a shortage of qualified captains and other officers for the huge ocean-going tankers.
3. She is not getting much support from her superior. He says that as a woman she is not very knowledgeable in this area, so she tends to exaggerate the risk.

Decision Questions

1. What should Srinivar do? How can she be sure she is right and her boss is wrong?
2. Assuming she is right to be concerned, what alternatives does she have? Should she go over her superior's head?
3. If all else fails, should she go public? If yes, should she leak the story anonymously or make a formal statement? What risks does she run in following either path?

LET'S TALK BUSINESS

1. More and more businesses and individuals are filing for bankruptcy annually. What are some of the potential problems for society of such a trend?
2. Do you feel the laws to promote fair and competitive practices are effective in Canada? What evidence do you have?
3. Do you believe most businesses today are socially responsible? Do you have any evidence to back up your position?
4. How would you describe the ethical environment in Canada today? How important is the role of business in creating that environment?

GLOSSARY

accountability (234) Requirement that workers accept the consequences of their actions and report those actions to their immediate supervisor.

accounting (544) The recording, classifying, summarizing, and interpreting of financial transactions to provide management and other interested parties with the information they need.

accounting system (544) The methods used to record and summarize accounting data.

administered distribution system (381) Distribution system in which all the marketing functions at the retail level are managed by producers.

advertising (414) Paid, non-personal communication through various media by organizations and individuals who are in some way identified in the advertising message.

advocacy advertising (416) Advertising that supports a particular view of an issue.

affirmative action (497) Employment activities designed to "right past wrongs" endured by females and minorities.

agency shop (Rand formula) (521) Workplace in which a new employee is not required to join the union but must pay union dues. This historic formula was devised by Rand.

analytic system (273) Manufacturing system that breaks down raw materials into components to extract other products.

apprenticeship (482) A time when a new worker works alongside a master technician to learn the appropriate skills and procedures.

arbitration (522) The process of resolving all disputes, not only grievances, through an outside, impartial third party.

articles of incorporation (78) The legal documents, obtained from the federal or provincial governments, authorizing a company to operate as a corporation.

assembly process (273) Production process that puts together components.

assets (550) Things of value owned by a business.

authority (233) The right and power to make decisions and take actions.

balance of payments (44) The difference between money coming into a country (from exports) and money leaving the country (for imports) plus money flows from other factors such as tourism, foreign aid, investments, interest, and dividend payments.

balance of trade (44) The relationship of the amount of exports to the amount of imports.

balance sheet (556) Reports the financial position of a firm at the end of a specific period of time. Balance sheet(s) consist of assets, liabilities, and owners' equity.

bartering (51) The exchange of merchandise for merchandise.

benefit segmentation (328) Divides the market by benefits desired.

bid rigging (623) Secret agreement among competitors to make artificially high bids.

blue chip stocks (602) Stocks of high-quality companies.

bond (594) A contract of indebtedness issued by a corporation or government unit that promises payment of a principal amount at a specified future time plus annual interest.

bookkeeping (548) The recording of transactions.

boycott (525) Urging union members and the public at large not to buy a particular company's products or services.

brand (354) A name, symbol, or design (or combination of these) that identifies the goods or services of one seller or group of sellers and distinguishes them from those of competitors.

brand name (318) A logo, word, letter, or groups of words or letters that differentiate the goods and services of a seller from those of competitors.

break-even analysis (367) Process used to determine profitability at various levels of sales.

break-even point (367) The point beyond which a certain quantity of sales results in profits.

brokers (381) Marketing middlemen who bring buyers and sellers together and assist in negotiating an exchange.

bureaucratic organization (238) Organization with three layers of authority: (1) top managers, who make decisions, (2) middle managers, who develop procedures for implementing decisions, and (3) workers and supervisors, who do the work.

business plan (179) A detailed written statement that describes the nature of the business, the target market, the advantages the business will have over competitors, and the resources and qualifications of the owners.

buying on margin (603) Purchasing securities by borrowing some of the cost from the broker.

cafeteria-style benefits (489) Benefit plans that allow employees to choose the benefits they want up to a certain dollar amount.

capital budget (582) The spending plan for capital or fixed assets that are expected to yield returns over several years.

capitalism (110) Economic system in which all or most of the means of production and distribution are privately owned and operated for profit.

capitalist system (105) System in which resources are allocated by consumers and businesses bargaining freely in the marketplace and trading goods and services.

cash-and-carry wholesaler (397) A limited-function wholesaler that serves mostly smaller retailers with a limited assortment of products.

cash budget (582) The projected use of cash during a given period (e.g., monthly, quarterly, or annually).

cash flow (563) The difference between cash receipts and cash disbursements.

cash flow forecast (581) A projection of expected cash inflows and outflows for a particular period of time.

centralized authority (245) Maintaining decision-making authority of the top level of management.

certification (521) The process by which a union becomes the sole bargaining agent for a group of employees. This usually requires a majority vote obtained by secret ballot supervised by an LRB.

channel captain (388) The dominant organization in the marketing channel that gets the other members to work together in a co-operative effort.

channel of distribution (381) Marketing middlemen such as wholesalers and retailers who join together to transport and store goods in their path (channel) from producers to consumers.

check-off (521) Contract clause requiring the employer to deduct union dues from employees' pay and remit them to the union.

closed-shop (521) Workplace in which all new hires must already be union members.

cluster organization (254) A group of people from different functional units who work together on a semi-permanent basis.

collective bargaining (520) The process by which a union represents employees in relationswith their employer.

commercial paper (590) A short-term corporate equivalent of an IOU that is sold in the marketplace by a firm. It matures in 270 days or less.

common market (57) A regional group of countries that has no internal tariffs, a common external tariff, and a coordination of laws to facilitate exchange. An example is the European Community.

common stock (600) Represents ownership of a firm and the right to vote and to receive the firm's profits (after preferred shareholders are paid) in the form of dividends declared by the board of directors.

communist system (106) System in which resource allocation is largely government controlled.

comparative advantage theory (39) Theory which asserts that a country should produce and sell to other countries those products that it produces most efficiently and effectively and should buy from other countries those products it cannot produce as effectively or efficiently.

comparison advertising (416) Advertising that compares competitive products.

competition-oriented pricing (370) Pricing strategy based on all the other competitors' prices.

compressed work week (492) Work schedule made up of four 10-hour days.

computer-aided acquisition and logistics support (CALS) (282) A communication system that allows manufacturers to send design specifications to suppliers over a phone line directly to the machine that will do the work.

computer-aided design (CAD) (280) The use of computers in the design of products.

computer-aided engineering (CAE) (283) The computer-generated design and analysis of products, programming of robots and machine tools, designing of molds and tools, and planning of the production process and quality control.

computer-aided industrial design (CAID) (281) The creation and modification of models with a three-dimensional perspective.
computer-aided manufacturing (CAM) (280) The use of computers in the manufacturing of products.
computer-integrated manufacturing (CIM) (285) Computer-aided design (CAD) combined with computer-aided manufacturing (CAM); it then further integrates CAD/CAM with other corporate functions such as purchasing, inventory control, cost accounting, materials handling, and shipping.
conceptual skills (219) Ability to picture the organization as a whole and the relationship of various parts.
conglomerate merger (155) The joining of firms in completely unrelated industries.
consortium (50) A temporary association of two or more companies to bid jointly on a very large project.
consumer market (326) All the individuals or households who want goods and services for personal consumption.
consumer orientation (315) Finding out what consumers want and giving it to them.
consumer price index (CPI) (130) Monthly statistics that measure changes in the prices of a basket of goods and services that consumers buy.
containerization (393) The process of packing and sealing a number of items into one unit that is easily moved and shipped.
contingency planning (208) Process of preparing alternative courses of action that may be used if the primary plans do not achieve the objectives of the organization.
continuous improvement (293) Procedures designed to ensure and inspire constant creative interaction and problem solving.
continuous process (273) Production process in which long production runs turn out finished goods over time.
contractual distribution system (387) Distribution system in which members are bound to cooperate through contractual agreements.
controlling (206) Checking to determine whether or not an organization is carrying out its plan and taking corrective action if it is not.
convenience goods and services (350) Products that the consumer wants to purchase frequently and with a minimum of effort.
convertible bond (597) A bond that can be converted into shares of common stock.
co-operative (155) An organization owned by members/customers who pay an annual membership fee and share in any profits.
core time (491) The time when all employees are present in a flextime system.
corporate distribution system (387) Distribution system in which all the organizations in the channel are owned by one firm.
corporate social responsibility (617) The recognition by corporations that their actions must take into account the needs and ethical standards of society.
corporation (142) A legal entity with an existence separate from its owners.
cost of goods sold (558) A particular type of expense measured by the total cost of merchandise sold (including costs associated with the acquisition, storage, transportation, and packaging of goods).
countertrading (51) Bartering among several countries and companies.
critical path (286) The longest path a product takes from the beginning of the production process until the end.
crown corporation (73) A company set up and owned by the federal or a provincial government.
cumulative preferred stock (600) Preferred stock that accumulates unpaid dividends.
current assets (550) Cash and assets that are normally converted to cash within one year.
customer-driven (15) Customer satisfaction becomes the driving force that permeates the company.
cyclical unemployment (127) Unemployment caused by a recession or a similar downturn in the business cycle.

debt capital (586) Funds raised by borrowing that must be repaid.
decentralized (14) Decision making is spread downward from the top of an organization.
decentralized authority (245) Delegating decision-making authority to lower-level managers, who are more familiar with local conditions.
delegating (219) Assigning authority and accountability to others while retaining responsibility for results.
delegation of authority (245) Assigning part of a manager's duties to subordinates.
demand (112) The quantity of products that people are willing to buy at different prices at a specific time.
demand curve (112) Line on a graph which shows the relationship between quantity demanded and price.
demand-oriented pricing (370) Pricing strategy based on consumer demand.
demographic segmentation (328) Divides the market into groups by age, sex, income, and similar categories.
departmentalization (244) Dividing an organization's structure into homogeneous departments such as manufacturing and marketing.
depreciation (562) Since assets such as machinery lose value over time, part of their cost is calculated as an expense each year over their useful life.
depression (131) A severe form of recession (see *recession*).
design for manufacturability and assembly (DFMA) (284) A process used to design products with the least number of parts, thus reducing the cost of assembly.

directing (206) Guiding and motivating others to achieve the goals and objectives of the organization.

discretionary income (322) Money available after taxes and essentials for purchase of nonessential items.

disposable income (322) Money available after taxes for purchase of essentials.

dividends (598) Part of the firm's profits that are distributed to shareholders.

drop shipper (397) A limited-function wholesaler that solicits orders from retailers and other wholesalers and has the merchandise shipped directly from a producer to a buyer.

dumping (44) Dumping is the practice of selling products to a foreign country for less than you charge for the same products in your own country.

economics (105) The study of how society chooses to employ scarce resources to produce various goods and services and distribute them for consumption among various competing groups and individuals.

economies of scale (80) The cost savings that result from large-scale production.

electronic data interchange (EDI) (388) Software that enables the computers of producers, wholesalers, and retailers to talk with each other.

embargo (56) A complete ban on all trade or investment.

employee benefits (488) Sick leave pay, vacation pay, pension plans, health plans, and other benefits that provide additional compensation to employees beyond the basic wage.

employee orientation (482) The activity that introduces new employees to the organization, to fellow employees, to their immediate supervisors, and to the policies, practices, and objectives of the firm.

empowerment (14) The leaders of organizations give their workers the freedom, the incentives, and the training to be decision makers and creative contributors to the organization.

entrepreneur (167) A person who organizes, manages, and assumes the risks of starting and operating a business to make a profit.

environmental scanning (321) Analysis of societal forces, economic realities, technological developments, and legal and regulatory conditions.

equilibrium point (112) Point at which supply and demand are equal.

equity capital (586) Funds raised within the company or from selling shares in the firm.

exchange rate (45) The value of one currency relative to the currencies of other countries.

exclusive distribution (404) The distribution strategy that uses only one retail outlet in a given geographic area.

exponential function (635) The mathematical description of anything that changes steadily in one direction over a given period of time.

extrinsic rewards (442) Reinforcement from someone else as recognition for good work, including pay increases, praise, and promotions.

factoring (590) Selling accounts receivable for cash.

factors of production (105) The basic inputs of a society: land and natural resources, human labour, capital, entrepreneurship, and information.

finance (580) The business function that is responsible for the efficient acquisition and disbursement of funds.

financial accounting (546) The preparation of financial statements for people outside of the firm (for example, investors).

financial statements (556) Report the success and position (condition) of a firm; they include the income statement and balance sheet.

fiscal policy (79) The use of taxation to stimulate or restrain various aspects of the economy or the economy as a whole.

fixed assets (550) Items that are acquired to produce services or products. They are not bought to be sold.

flat organization structures (242) Ones with relatively few layers of management.

flexible manufacturing systems (FMS) (284) Totally automated production centres that include robots, automatic materials handling equipment, and computer-controlled machine tools that can perform a variety of functions to produce different products.

flextime plans (491) Work schedules that give employees some freedom to adjust when they work, within limits, as long as they work the required number of hours.

focus group (430) A small group of people who meet under the direction of a discussion leader to communicate their feelings concerning an organization, its products, or other important issues.

foreign subsidiary (48) A company owned by another (parent company) in a foreign country.

formal organization (257) The structure that details lines of responsibility, authority, and position. It is the structure that is shown on organization charts.

form utility (267) The value added by the creation of goods and services using raw materials, components, and other inputs.

four Ps of marketing (319) Product, place, promotion, and price.

franchise (186) The right to use a specific business's name and sell its products or services in a given territory.

franchise agreement (186) An arrangement whereby someone with a good idea for a business sells the rights to use the business name and sell its products or services to others in a given territory.

franchisee (186) A person who buys a franchise.

franchising (186) A method of distributing a product or service, or both, to achieve a maximum market impact with a minimum amount of investment.

franchisor (186) A company that develops a product concept and sells others the rights to make and sell the products.

free-market system (110) System in which decisions about what to produce and in what quantities are decided by the market; that is, by buyers and sellers freely negotiating prices for goods and services.

full-service wholesaler (398) A merchant wholesaler that performs all eight distribution functions.

functional structure (244) Grouping of workers into departments based on similar skills, expertise, or resource use.

fundamental accounting equation (559) Assets = liabilities + owners' equity; it is the basis for the balance sheet.

Hawthorne effect (446) The tendency for a group of people to be more motivated when they know they are being studied and take a more active part in the experiment.

horizontal merger (154) The joining of two firms in the same industry.

human resource management (473) The process of evaluating human resource needs, finding people to fill those needs, and getting the best work from each employee by providing the right incentives and job enrichment, all with the goal of meeting the objectives of the organization.

hygiene factors (453) Factors that cause dissatisfaction if they are missing, but do not motivate if they are increased.

Gantt chart (287) Bar graph showing production managers what projects are being worked on and what stage they are in on a daily basis.

General Agreement on Tariffs and Trade (GATT) (56) Agreement among trading countries that provides a forum for negotiating mutual reductions in trade restrictions.

general merchandise wholesaler (397) A merchant wholesaler that carries a broad assortment of merchandise.

general partner (147) An owner (partner) who has unlimited liability and is active in managing the firm.

generic goods (356) Nonbranded products that usually sell at a sizeable discount from national or private brands, have very basic packaging, and are backed with little or no advertising.

generic names (356) Names of product categories.

geographic segmentation (328) Divides the market into separate geographic areas.

globalization (9) A globally integrated system of production, marketing, finance, and management.

goals (207) Broad, long-term accomplishments an organization wishes to attain.

goal-setting theory (457) Theory that setting specific, attainable goals can motivate workers and improve performance if the goals are accepted, are accompanied by feedback, and are facilitated by organizational conditions.

goods-producing sector (17) Produces tangible products, things that can be seen or touched.

grievance (522) A formal protest by an individual employee or a union when they believe a particular management decision breached the union contract.

gross domestic product (GDP) (124) The total value of a country's output of goods and services in a given year.

gross margin (profit) (558) Net sales minus costs of goods sold before expenses are deducted.

import quota (55) The number or value of products in certain categories that can be imported.

income statement (556) Reports revenues, expenses, and profit or loss during a specific period of time.

independent audit (547) Examination of a company's books by public accountants, to give the public, governments, and shareholders an outside opinion of the fairness of financial statements.

industrial advertising (416) Advertising from manufacturers to other manufacturers.

industrial goods (351) Products used in the production of other products.

industrial market (327) Individuals and organizations that purchase goods and services to produce other goods and services or to rent, sell, or supply the goods to others.

industrial park (270) A planned area in a city where businesses can find land, shipping facilities, and waste disposal outlets so they can build a manufacturing plant or storage facility.

industrial policy (74) A comprehensive, co-ordinated government plan to revitalize the economy and lay out a path for the future.

inflation (129) A general rise in the prices of goods and services over time.

informal organization (257) The system of relationships and lines of authority that develop spontaneously as employees meet and form power centres; it is the human side of the organization and does not show on any formal charts.

information age (7) An era in which information is a crucial factor in the operation of organizations.

information system (254) Network consisting of written and electronically based systems for sending reports, memos, bulletins, and the like.

information utility (326) Informs buyers that the product exists, how to use it, the price, and other information.

injunction (526) An order from a judge requiring strikers to limit or cease picketing or some threatening activity.

institutional advertising (416) Advertising by organizations designed to create an attractive image for an organization rather than for a product.

intensive distribution (404) The distribution strategy that puts products into as many retail outlets as possible.

intermittent process (273) Production process in which the production run is short and the machines are shut down frequently or changed to produce different products.

internal marketing program (433) Marketing program designed to commit employees to the objectives of a firm.

international joint venture (49) A partnership in which companies from two or more different countries join to undertake a major project, or to form a new company.

International Monetary Fund (IMF) (57) An international bank that makes short-term loans to countries experiencing problems with their balance of trade.

Interpersonal skills (219) Ability to lead, communicate, motivate, coach, build morale, train, support, and delegate.

intrapreneur (167) A person with entrepreneurial skills who is employed in a corporation to launch new products; such people take hands-on responsibility for creating innovation of any kind in an organization.

intrinsic rewards (442) Reinforcement from within oneself; a feeling one has done a good job.

job analysis (475) A study of what is done by employees who fill various job titles.

job descriptions (475) Summaries of the objectives of a job, the type of work, the responsibilities of the job, skills needed, the working conditions, and the relationship of the job to other functions.

job enlargement (457) Job enrichment strategy involving combining a series of tasks into one assignment that is more challenging and interesting.

job enrichment (456) A motivational strategy that emphasizes motivating the worker through the job itself.

job rotation (457) Job enrichment strategy involving moving employees from one job to another.

job sharing (489) An arrangement whereby two part-time employees share one full-time job.

job simplification (457) Process of producing task efficiency by breaking down the job into simple steps and assigning people to each of those steps.

job simulation (483) The use of equipment that duplicates job conditions and tasks so that trainees can learn skills before attempting them on the job.

job specifications (475) Summary of the qualifications required of workers to do a particular job.

joint ventures (475) Arrangements whereby two or more companies co-operate for special or limited purposes.

journeyman (482) A worker who has successfully completed an apprenticeship.

just-in-time (JIT) inventory control (276) Arrangements for delivery of the smallest possible quantities at the latest possible time to keep inventory as low as possible.

knockoff brands (355) Illegal copies of national brand-name items.

Labour Relations Boards (LRBs) (520) Quasi-judicial bodies consisting of representatives of government, labour, and business. They function more informally than courts but have the full force of law. They administer labour codes in each jurisdiction, federal or provincial.

laissez-faire capitalism (618) Theory that if left alone, unhindered by government, the free market in pursuit of economic efficiency would provide an abundance of goods at the lowest prices, improving everyone's life.

leadership (214) Creating a vision for others to follow, establishing corporate values and ethics, and transforming the way the organization does business so it is more effective and efficient.

lean and mean (13) The severe process of cutting all possible costs of operations.

ledger (554) A loose-leaf book in which information from accounting journals is entered (posted) into homogeneous groups (accounts) so that managers can find all the information about one type of transaction in the same place.

liabilities (552) Amounts owed by the organization to others.

licensing (47) Agreement in which a producer allows a foreign company to produce its product in exchange for royalties.

limited-function wholesaler (396) A merchant wholesaler that performs only selected distribution functions.

limited liability (147) The responsibility of a business's owners for losses only up to the amount they invest; limited partners have limited liability.

limited partner (147) Owner who invests money in the business, but does not have any management responsibility or liability for losses beyond the investment.

line of credit (589) The amount of short-term credit a bank will lend a borrower that is agreed to ahead of time.

line organization structure (248) Organization in which there are direct two-way lines of responsibility, authority, and communication running from the top to the bottom of the organization, with every employee reporting to only one specific supervisor.

line personnel (249) Employees who perform functions that contribute directly to the primary goals of the organization.

liquid (550) How quickly an asset can be turned into cash.

lockout (524) A drastic negotiating strategy in which the employer locks the premises against the employees.

manageability (233) A system where everyone in the organization knows who is responsible for what, who reports to whom, and what to do when problems arise.

management (206) The process used to accomplish organizational goals through planning, organizing, directing, and controlling people and other organizational resources.

management by objectives (MBO) (457) A system of goal setting and implementation that involves a cycle of discussion, review, and evaluation of objectives among top and middle-level managers, supervisors, and employees.

management by walking around (204) Managers get out of their offices and personally interact with employees and customers.

management development (493) The process of training and educating employees to become good managers and then developing managerial skills over time.

managerial accounting (545) Providing information and analyses to managers within the organization to assist them in decision making.

manufacturing (267) Process of making goods by hand or with machinery as opposed to extracting things from the earth (mining or fishing) or producing services.

marketing (313) The process of studying the wants and needs of others and then satisfying those wants and needs with appropriate goods and services.

marketing boards (94) Organizations that control the supply and/or pricing of certain agricultural products in Canada.

marketing communication system (432) Listening to the market, responding to that information, and promoting the organization and its products.

marketing concept (315) Refers to a three-part business philosophy: (1) a consumer orientation, (2) training of all employees in customer service, and (3) a profit orientation.

marketing manager (319) Plans and executes the conception, pricing, promotion, and distribution of ideas, goods, and services to create exchanges that satisfy individual and organizational goals.

marketing middlemen (318) Individuals or organizations that help distribute goods and services from the producer to consumers.

marketing mix (319) The strategic combination of product decisions with decisions regarding packaging, pricing, distribution, credit, branding, service, complaint handling, and other marketing activities.

marketing research (331) A major function used to determine needs and the most effective and efficient ways to satisfy those needs.

market modification (364) Technique used to extend the life cycle of mature products by finding new users and market segments.

market price (112) Price determined by supply and demand.

market segmentation (328) Process of dividing the total market into several submarkets (segments) that have similar characteristics.

market targeting (328) The process by which an organization decides which markets to serve.

materials handling (394) The movement of goods within a warehouse, factory, or store.

materials requirement planning (MRP) (275) A computer-based operations management system that uses sales forecasts to make sure that needed parts and materials are available at the right place and time.

matrix organization (251) Organization in which specialists from different parts of the organization are brought together to work on specific projects but still remain part of a traditional line and staff structure.

maturity date (595) The date the issuer of a bond must repay the principal of the bond to the bondholder.

mediation (523) The use of a third party to attempt to bring the parties to a resolution of their dispute.

mentors (494) Experienced employees who supervise, coach, and guide lower-level employees by introducing them to the right people and groups and generally act as their organizational sponsors.

mercantilism (54) The economic principle advocating the selling of more goods to other nations than a country buys.

merchant wholesaler (396) Independently owned wholesalers that take title to goods that they handle.

merger (154) The result of two firms forming one company.

middle management (210) Level of management that includes plant managers and department heads who are responsible for tactical plans.

mixed economy (123) All economies that combine free markets with some government allocation of resources.

monetary policy (87) Bank of Canada's exercise of control of the supply of money and the level of interest rates in the country to influence the economy in a desired direction.

monopolistic competition (114) The market situation where there are a large number of sellers that produce similar products, but the products are perceived by buyers as different.

monopoly (115) A market in which there is only one seller.

motion economy (444) Theory that every job can be broken down into a series of elementary motions.

motivators (453) Factors that provide satisfaction and motivate people to work.

multinational or transnational corporation (37) An organization that does manufacturing and marketing in many different countries; it has multinational stock ownership and multinational management.

mutual fund (605) A fund that buys a variety of securities and then sells units of ownership to the public.

national brand names (355) Brand names of manufacturers that distribute their products nationally.

national debt (132) The sum of money the government has borrowed and not paid back.

net income (559) Revenue minus costs and expenses.

net sales (556) Sales revenue minus discounts, returns, and other adjustments made for customers.

networking (1) (285) Linking firms together by making it possible for their computers to talk with one another. (2)(494) Establishing and maintaining contacts with key managers in one's own and other organizations and using those contacts to weave strong relationships that serve as informal development systems.

network marketing (402) Network marketing means that people are recruited to recruit other people until a huge network of salespeople and users is created.

NIMBY (633) Not in my back yard, meaning that people don't want waste disposal facilities in their town, though they agree that such facilities are needed somewhere.

objectives (207) Specific short-term tasks that must be completed to achieve the organizational goals.

observation method (429) Method of collecting data by observing the actions of potential buyers.

off-the-job training (483) Internal and external programs to develop a variety of skills and foster personal development away from the workplace.

oligopoly (115) A form of competition where the market is dominated by just a few sellers.

on-the-job training (482) The employee immediately begins his or her tasks and learns by doing, or watching others for a while and then imitates them.

open shop (521) Workplace in which employees are free to join or not join the union and to pay or not pay union dues.

operating budget (582) The plan of the various costs and expenses needed to operate the business, based on estimated annual revenues.

operating expenses (558) The various costs incurred in running a business, including rent, salaries, and utilities, in order to earn revenues.

organic farming (630) Farming that is done without chemicals.

organizational culture (255) Widely shared values within an organization, reflected in stories, traditions, and myths, that provide coherence and co-operation to achieve common goals.

organizational design (233) The establishment of manageable groups of people who have clear responsibilities and who know how to accomplish the objectives of the organization and the group.

organization chart (241) A visual picture of an organization that shows who reports to whom.

organizing (206) Designing the organizational structure, attracting people to the organization (staffing), and creating conditions and systems that ensure that everyone and everything work together to achieve the objectives of the organization.

other assets (551) Assets that are not current or fixed. This catch-all group includes items such as copyrights and patents.

owners' equity (553) Investments in the company plus all net accumulated profits.

participative management (202) Management style that involves employees in setting objectives and making decisions; democratic and laissez-faire leadership are forms of this type of management.

partnership (142) A legal form of business with two or more owners.

partnership agreement (149) Legal document that specifies the rights and responsibilities of the members of a partnership.

penetration price strategy (369) Method of pricing by which a product is priced low to attract more customers and discourage competitors.

perfect competition (114) The market situation where there are many sellers and buyers and no seller or buyer is large enough to dictate the price of a product.

performance appraisal (484) An evaluation of the performance level of employees against standards to make decisions about promotions, compensation, additional training, or firing.

personal selling (418) Face-to-face presentation and promotion of products and services plus searching out of prospects and providing follow-up service.

PERT (program evaluation and review technique) (286) A method for analyzing the tasks involved in completing a given project, estimating the time needed to complete each task, and identifying the minimum time needed to complete the project.

physical distribution (380) The movement of goods and services from producer to industrial and consumer users.

physical distribution manager (391) The person responsible for co-ordinating and integrating all movement of materials, including transportation, internal movement, and warehousing.

physiological needs (447) The needs for basic life-giving elements such as food, water, and shelter.

picketing (526) The process whereby strikers carrying picket signs walk back and forth across entrances to their places of employment to publicize the strike and discourage or prevent people, vehicles, materials, and products from going in or out.

piggybacking (391) The shipping of the cargo-carrying part of a truck on a railroad car or ship over long distances. This part of its journey results in the total trip having been made in the most efficient manner possible.

place utility (326) Making products and services available in convenient locations.

planning (206) Anticipating future trends and determining the best strategies and tactics to achieve goals and objectives of the organization.

pledging (589) Using accounts receivable, inventory, or other assets as security.

possession utility (326) Making the exchange of goods between buyers and sellers easier.

preferred stock (599) Stock that gives owners preferences over common shareholders in the payment of dividends and in a claim on assets if the business is liquidated, but does not include voting rights.

price leadership (370) Procedure by which all the competitors in the industry follow the pricing practices of one or more dominant firms.

primary data (429) Results from doing your own research.

principal (595) The face amount of a bond.

private accountant (546) An employee who carries out managerial and financial accounting functions for his or her employer.

private brands (356) Products that do not carry the manufacturer's name, but carry the name of a distributor or retailer instead.

private corporations (151) Corporations that are not allowed to issue stock to the public, so their shares are not listed on stock exchanges and are limited to 50 or fewer shareholders.

privatization (73) The process of government selling crown corporations.

process manufacturing (273) Production process that physically or chemically changes materials.

producers' cartels (57) Organizations of commodity-producing countries that are formed to stabilize or increase prices to optimize overall profits in the long run. (An example is OPEC, the Organization of Petroleum Exporting Countries.)

product (317) Any physical good, service, or idea that satisfies a want or need.

product advertising (416) Advertising for a good or service to create interest among consumer, commercial, and industrial buyers.

product differentiation (349) The attempt to create product perceptions in the minds of consumers so that one product seems superior to others.

production (267) The creation of goods and services using the factors of production: land, labor, capital, entrepreneurship, and information.

production and operations management (267) Activities of managers to create goods and services.

production goods (351) Industrial goods such as grain and steel that enter into the final product.

production orientation (314) Business focuses on producing goods rather than marketing them.

productivity (124) The total output of goods and services in a given period of time divided by work hours (output per work hour).

product life cycle (361) The four-stage theoretical depiction of the process from birth to death of a product class: introduction, growth, maturity, and decline.

product line (347) A group of products that are physically similar or are intended for a similar market.

product manager (357) Co-ordinates all the marketing efforts for a particular product (or product line) or brand.

product mix (348) The combination of product lines offered by a manufacturer.

product modification (365) Technique used to extend the life cycle of mature products by changing the product quality, features, or style to attract new users or more usage from present users.

product offer (346) Consists of all the tangibles and intangibles that consumers evaluate when deciding whether or not to buy something.

profit orientation (316) Marketing those goods and services that will earn the firm a profit.

program evaluation and review technique (PERT) (286) A method for analyzing the tasks involved in completing a given project, estimating the time needed to complete each task, and identifying the minimum time needed to complete the total project.

promotion (413) An attempt by marketers to persuade others to buy their products or services.

promotional mix (413) The combination of tools marketers use to promote their products or services.

prospects (419) People who have enough funds and are willing to discuss a potential purchase.

prospectus (90) A document that must be prepared by every public company seeking financing through issue of shares or bonds. It gives the public certain information about the company. It must be approved by the securities commissions of the provinces where these securities will be offered for sale.

protective tariffs (54) Import taxes designed to raise the price of imported products so that domestic products are more competitive.

psychographic segmentation (328) Divides the market by values, attitudes, and interests.

public accountant (546) Independent firm that provides accounting, auditing, and other professional services for clients on a fee basis.

public corporations (151) Corporations that can issue shares to the public, which means that their shares may be listed on the stock exchanges.

publicity (422) Any information about an individual, a product, or an organization that is distributed to the public through the media and that is not paid for or controlled by the sponsor.

public relations (421) The management function that evaluates public attitudes, develops policies and procedures consistent with the public interest, and takes steps to earn public understanding and acceptance.

pull strategy (414) Use of promotional tools to motivate consumers to request products from stores.

push strategy (414) Use of promotional tools to convince wholesalers and retailers to stock and sell merchandise.

quality circle (293) A small group that voluntarily performs quality control activities within the workshop to which they belong.

quality control (290) The measurement of products and services against set standards.

rack jobber (397) A full-service wholesaler that furnishes racks or shelves full of merchandise to retailers, displays products, and sells on consignment.

random sample (430) A sample in which all people have an equal chance of being selected to be part of the representative group.

ratio analysis (561) A way to analyze financial statements in greater depth by comparing results with the previous year's, the budget, and competing firms' results.

rational decision-making model (220) Consists of six steps: (1) define the problem, (2) determine and collect needed information, (3) develop alternatives, (4) decide which alternative is best and also ethically acceptable, (5) implement the decision and (6) determine whether the decision was a good one and follow up.

recession (131) Two consecutive quarters of decline in the GDP.

recruitment (477) The set of activities used to obtain a sufficient number of the right people at the right time to select those who best meet the needs of the organization.

replacement workers (526) Management's name for strikebreakers.

responsibility (233) The obligation of a person to complete a given task.

restructuring (13) The process of reorganizing the structure of companies to make them more efficient.

retail advertising (416) Advertising to consumers by retailers.

retailer (396) A marketing middleman that sells to consumers.

retained earnings (558) The amount left after a company distributes some of its net income (profit) to shareholders in the form of dividends.

revenue (556) The value of what is received for goods sold and/or services rendered.

revenue tariffs (55) Import taxes designed to raise money for the government.

reverse discrimination (497) The feeling of unfairness unprotected groups may have when protected groups are given preference in hiring and promoting.

robber barons (617) Capitalists of the 19th century whose wealth came in part through shady if not criminal acts.

robot (279) A computer-controlled machine capable of performing many tasks.

rule of 72 (636) Divide the rate of increase of any activity into 72 to get the number of years it takes for the result of that activity to double.

safety needs (447) The need for peace and security.

sales orientation (314) Firms focus on promoting their products.

sales promotion (423) The promotional tool that stimulates consumer purchasing and dealer interest by means of short-term activities (displays, shows, exhibitions, and contests, etc.).

sample (430) A representative group of a market population.

scabs (526) Unions' name for strikebreakers.

scientific management (444) The study of workers to find the most efficient way of doing things and then teaching people those techniques.

scrambled merchandising (403) The strategy of adding product lines (to a retail store) that are not normally carried there.

seasonal unemployment (127) Unemployment that occurs where the demand for labour varies over the year.

secondary data (428) Already-published research information from journals, trade associations, the government, information services, libraries, and other sources.

secured bonds (596) Bonds backed by some tangible asset that is pledged to the investor if the principal or interest is not paid.

secured loan (589) Loan backed by something valuable, such as property.

securities commission (90) The official body set up by a province to regulate the stock exchange and to approve all new issues of securities in that province.

selection (479) The process of gathering information to decide who should be hired, under legal guidelines, for the best interests of the individual and the organization.

selective distribution (404) Distribution strategy that uses only a preferred group of the available retailers in an area.

self-actualization needs (447) The needs for achievement and to be all you can be.
self-esteem needs (447) The need for self-confidence and status.
service sector (17) Produces services—like financial, information, marketing, health, recreational, or repair services—not goods.
shopping goods and services (350) Products or services that the consumer buys only after comparing quality and price from a variety of sellers.
skimming price strategy (369) Method of pricing by which the product is priced high to make optimum profit while there is little competition.
skunkworks (167) A highly innovative, fast-moving entrepreneurial unit operating at the fringes of a corporation.
small business (173) A business that is independently operated, not dominant in its field, and meets certain standards of size in terms of employees and annual receipts.
socialist system (106) System in which allocation of resources is done partially by the market (the free trade of goods and services) and partially by the government.
social needs (447) The need to feel loved, accepted, and part of the group.
societal orientation (316) Includes a consumer orientation, but adds programs designed to improve the community, protect the environment, and satisfy other social goals.
sole proprietorship (142) A business that is owned directly, and usually managed, by one person.
span of control (243) The optimum number of subordinates a manager should supervise.
specialty goods and services (351) Products that have such a special attraction to consumers they are willing to go out of their way to obtain them.
staff personnel (249) Employees who perform functions that assist line personnel in performing their goals.
stock certificate (598) Tangible evidence of stock ownership.
stock exchange (598) An organization whose members can buy and sell securities to the public.
strategic alliances (10) Arrangements whereby two or more companies co-operate for a special or limited purpose.
strategic planning (207) Process of determining the major goals of the organization and the policies and strategies for obtaining and using resources to achieve those goals.
structural unemployment (127) Unemployment caused by people losing their jobs because their occupation is no longer part of the main structure of the economy.
supervisory (first-line) management (210) First level of management above employees; includes people directly responsible for assigning specific jobs to employees and evaluating their daily performance.
supply (111) The quantity of products that manufacturers or owners are willing to sell at different prices at a specific time.
supply chain management (388) The overall process of minimizing inventory and moving goods through the channel faster by using computers to improve communications among the channel members.
supply curve (111) Line on a graph which shows the relationship between price and quantity supplied.
support goods (351) Industrial goods such as accessory equipment and supplies that are used to assist in the production of other products.
survey method (429) Direct questioning of people to gather facts, opinions, or other information.
sustainable development (24) Economic development that meets the development needs of the present without endangering the external environment of future generations.
synthetic systems (273) Production processes which either change raw materials into other products or combine raw materials or parts into finished products.

tactical planning (208) Process of developing detailed short-term decisions about what is to be done, who is to do it, and how it is to be done.
tall organization structures (242) Organizations with many levels of management.
technical skills (219) Ability to perform tasks of a specific department (such as selling or bookkeeping).
telemarketing (402) The sale of goods and services by telephone.
test marketing (318) The process of testing products among potential users.
The National Policy (74) Federal government policy imposing high tariffs on imports from the U.S. to protect Canadian manufacturing.
time–motion studies (444) Study of the tasks performed to complete a job and the time needed to do each task.
time utility (326) Making products available during convenient hours.
top management (209) Highest level of management, consisting of the president, vice-president, and other key company executives who develop strategic plans.
total productive maintenance (TPM) (286) Preventive maintenance with total participation of the personnel operating the equipment.
total quality management (TQM) (290) Satisfying customers by building in and ensuring quality from all departments in an organization.
trade advertising (416) Advertising to wholesalers and retailers by manufacturers.

trade credit (587) The practice of buying goods now and paying for them in the future.

trademark (355) A brand that has been given exclusive legal protection for both the brand name and pictorial design.

trade protectionism (45) The use of government regulations to limit the import of goods and services; based on the theory that domestic producers should be protected from competition so that they can survive and grow, producing more jobs.

training and development (482) All attempts to improve employee performance through learning.

truck jobber (398) A small, limited-function wholesaler that delivers goods by truck to retailers.

union shop (521) Workplace in which the employer is free to hire anybody, but the recruit must then join the union within a short period, perhaps a month.

unlimited liability (146) The responsibility of a business's owners for all of the debts of the business, making the personal assets of the owners vulnerable to claims against the business; sole proprietors and general partners have unlimited liability.

unsecured bonds (596) Bonds that are not backed by any collateral.

utility (385) Value- or want-satisfying ability that is added to products by organizations because the products are made more useful or accessible to consumers.

value pricing (370) Offering consumers brand name goods and services at discount prices.

venture capitalist (183) Individuals or organizations that invest in new businesses in exchange for partial ownership of the company.

vertical merger (154) The joining of two firms involved in different stages of related businesses.

vestibule training (483) Training conducted away from the workplace where employees are given instructions on equipment similar to that used on the job.

volume segmentation (328) Divides the market into user categories: heavy, medium, light, and nonusers.

white-collar crime (622) A crime, usually theft, committed by an executive or other white-collar office worker.

wholesaler (396) A marketing middleman that sells to organizations and individuals, but not to final customers.

word-of-mouth promotion (420) Consumers talking about products they have liked or disliked.

World Bank (57) An autonomous United Nations agency that borrows money from the more prosperous countries and lends it at favourable rates to less-developed countries.

CHAPTER NOTES

Chapter 1

1. Danny Kucharsky, *This Week In Business* 3, no. 7, April 7, 1990, p. 13.
2. Shirley Won, "Homing In on New Careers," Report on Business, *Globe and Mail,* April 25, 1992, p. B1.
3. Howard Solomon, "A Quiet Revolution in Finance," Report on Business, *Globe and Mail,* May 5, 1992, p. B24.
4. "From World Trade to World Investment," *The Wall Street Journal,* May 26, 1987, editorial page.
5. Robert Reich, "Who Is Us?," *Harvard Business Review,* January/February 1990, p. 53.
6. The source for the entire section is Gary Lamphier, "Vancouver's New Power Elite," *Financial Times,* June 1, 1992, p. 16.
7. The source for the entire section is ibid.
8. Timothy Pritchard, "Chrysler Changes Tone to Woo Customers," Report on Business, *Globe and Mail,* July 1, 1992, p. B1.
9. All the data in this section are from a series of four articles by Susan Noakes in the *Financial Post,* December 17–21, 1990.
10. *Bank of Canada Review,* May 1992, Table H5.
11. Michael Valpy, "Fate of Manufacturing, a Make-or-Break Crisis," *Globe and Mail,* May 8, 1989, p. A8.
12. Madeleine Drohan, "Service Becoming Canada's New Backbone," Report on Business, *Globe and Mail,* April 16, 1990, p. B1.
13. Nuala Beck, *Shifting Gears: Thriving in the New Economy* (Toronto: HarperCollins, 1992), as reported by Crawford Kilian, *The Province* (Vancouver), reprinted in *The Montreal Gazette,* December 19, 1992, p. B6.
14. All the data in this section come from Ronald Logan, "Immigration during the 1980s," and Gordon Priest, "The Demographic Future," *Canadian Social Trends,* Spring 1991, StatsCan, Cat. No. 11-008E.
15. "Fewer Crossing U.S. Border," Report on Business, *Globe and Mail,* July 15, 1992, p. B3.
16. Most of the material in this section is from *Small Business in Canada: Growing to Meet Tomorrow,* Ministry of Supply and Services, Cat. no. C28-1/2, 1989E and various publications of the Economic Council of Canada.
17. Gordon Pitts, "Stepping on the Quality Ladder," Report on Business, *Globe and Mail,* June 30, 1992, p. B20.
18. Nuala Beck, ibid.

Chapter 2

1. Various publications of External Affairs and International Trade Canada (EAITC), 1990, 1991.
2. *Globe and Mail,* April 10, 1992, p. B7.
3. *Financial Times, Financial Post, Globe and Mail,* March through June 1992, various issues.
4. Donald N. Thompson, "Porter on Canadian Competitiveness," *Business Quarterly,* Winter 1992, p. 55.
5. Alan Freeman, "Manufacturing Exports on a Roll," *Globe and Mail,* April 25, 1992, p. G1.
6. Harvey Enchin, "Competitiveness Not New to Canadians," *Globe and Mail,* May 7, 1992, p. B1.

Chapter 3

1. Canada Communications Group—Publishing, Ottawa.
2. *Financial Post,* "Quebec Inc. Called Model for Canada," March 11, 1992, p. D5.
3. Terence Corcoran, "Enthusiasm Is Brimming at Quebec Inc.," *Globe and Mail,* January 31, 1992, p. B2.
4. Robert Meinbardis, "Why Quebec Inc. Has Got to Change," *Financial Times,* May 4, 1992, p. 1.
5. Joe Bryan, "Delegates Will Seek Way to Untangle Barriers to Interprovincial Trade," *The Montreal Gazette,* February 1, 1992, p. B1.
6. Anne-Marie Tobin, "Algoma Steel Rescued by Employee Takeover," *The Montreal Gazette,* February 29, 1992, p. D3.

7. *Canadian Chemical News,* October 1990, p. 9.
8. *Profits,* Federal Business Development Bank, Autumn 1991, p. 1.
9. James Bagnall, "Can This Man Teach Canada to Compete?," *Financial Times,* December 9, 1991, p. 1.
10. *Annual Report 1990–1991,* National Research Council, and other NRC publications in 1991.
11. *Canadian Chemical News,* October 1990, p. 9.
12. Peter Passell, "Productivity Gain: What, Me Worry?," *New York Times,* October 16, 1992, p. D2.
13. John Godfrey, "Big League Trade," Report on the Nation, *Financial Post,* Winter 1989, p. 26.

Chapter 4

1. *Canadian International Investment Position 1985–1990,* Chart 5, Cat. no. 67-202, Statistics Canada, 1991.
2. John Moynihan, "Tennis Plays the Tax Game: Advantage Monaco," *The Wall Street Journal,* August 2, 1988, p. 20.
3. "Supply-Side Sweden," *The Wall Street Journal,* November 30, p. A20.
4. Mikhail Gorbachev, "Gorbachev Speaks Out on the Roots of Perestroika," *The Washington Post,* December 6, 1987, pp. D1–2.
5. Peter Fuhrman, "The Soviet Economy Is in a Grave State," *Forbes,* October 19, 1987, p. 10.
6. Staff of the International Monetary Fund, "World Economic and Financial Surveys," *World Economic Outlooks,* October 1989.
7. Felipe Ortiz de Zevallos, "Peruvian Democracy on Brink," *The Wall Street Journal,* January 6, 1989, p. A11.
8. William Murchison, "Whatever Happened to . . .?," *The Washington Times,* January 11, 1989, p. F3.

Chapter 5

1. Christi Harlan, "Lawyers Find It Difficult to Break Up Partnerships," *The Wall Street Journal,* October 6, 1988, pp. B1 and B7.
2. Randall Smith, "Merger Boom Defies Expectations," *The Wall Street Journal,* January 3, 1989, p. 8R.

Chapter 6

1. *Starting a New Business in Canada: A Guide for New Canadians* (Federal Business Development Bank, 1990).
2. *Enterprising Canadians: The Self-Employed in Canada* (Statistics Canada, 1988) and *Labour Force Annual Averages, 1990* (Statistics Canada, 1991).
3. *Financing a Small Business: A Guide for Women Entrepreneurs* (Federal Business Development Bank, 1992).
4. *Small Business in Canada, Growing to Meet Tomorrow,* Industry, Science and Technology, Canada, Cat. no. C28 1/2, 1989E.
5. *Small Business,* October 1990, p. 9.
6. Douglas R. Sease, "Entrepreneurship 101," *The Wall Street Journal,* May 15, 1987, pp. 32–35D.
7. *Small Business in Canada, Growing to Meet Tomorrow,* ibid., and other sources.
8. *Small Business,* July/August 1990, p. 48.
9. Meg Whitmore, "Franchising Options for Opportunity," *Forbes,* August 24, 1987, pp. 83–87.
10. *Small Business,* July/August 1990, p. 51.
11. Alan Freeman, "Trade Surplus Biggest Since 1985," *Globe and Mail,* March 19, 1993, p. B9.

Chapter 7

1. Francois Shalom, Groupe Innovation Aims at Management Skills," *Montreal Gazette,* March 2, 1993, p. B2.
2. Alan N. Webber, "What's So New about the New Economy?" *Harvard Business Review,* January/February, 1993, pp. 28–30.
3. Shona McKay, "The New Breed," *Financial Post* magazine, December 1991, pp. 65–67.
4. "Message to Managers: Get Out of Your Offices," *Montreal Gazette,* February 19, 1991, p. D3.
5. Thomas J. Peters, *Thriving on Chaos* (New York: Alfred A. Knopf, 1988).
6. Kenneth Blanchard, *The One Minute Manager* (New York: Berkley Books, 1982).

Chapter 8

1. John A. Byrne, "Is Your Company Too Big?" *Business Week,* March 27, 1989, pp. 84–94.
2. Robert Slater, "GE—How Jack Welch Revived an American Institution," Homewood, IL: Irwin Professional Publishing, 1993, as quoted in *Montreal Gazette,* March 15, 1993, p. F13.
3. As quoted in John Raymond's column, "Worth Repeating," *Globe and Mail,* August 13, 1992, p. B2.
4. Bruce Little, "How To Make a Small Smart Factory," *Globe and Mail,* February 2, 1993, p. B24.
5. Major Rick Charlebois, CMA, "A Trial in Decentralized Decision Making," *CMA Magazine,* June 1992, p. 8.
6. Cathryn Motherwell, "From the Oilfield to the Boardroom," *Globe and Mail,* Classroom Edition, December 1992, p. 14.
7. Jim Clemmer, "How To Make Empowerment Work," *Globe and Mail,* (Classroom Edition), April 1993, p. 17.
8. Lee Iaccoca with William Novak, *Iaccoca: An Autobiography,* New York: Phantom Books, 1984, pp. 152–153.
9. Bruce Little, op. cit.
10. Catherine Motherwell, op. cit.

Chapter 9

1. Peter Drucker, "The Emerging Theory of Manufacturing," *Harvard Business Review,* May/June 1990, no. 3, p. 97.

2. Jay Bryan, "Shrinking Manufacturing Labour Force Isn't Necessarily Bad News," *Montreal Gazette,* March 18, 1993, p. C1.
3. Andrew S. Grove, *High Output Management,* New York: Random House, 1983.
4. Allen Fishman, "Managing Inventory Is Difficult," *St. Louis Post-Dispatch,* March 4, 1991, p. 10BP.
5. Geoffrey Rowan, "New Systems for Planning Can Lead to Production Blunders," *Globe and Mail,* Feb. 23, 1991, p. B5.
6. Patricia Lush, "Just-in-Time Pays Off for the Auto Sector," *Globe and Mail,* February 21, 1990, pp. B1, 4.
7. Michael Schrage, "The Pursuit of Efficiency Can Be an Illusion," *Washington Post,* March 20, 1992, p. F3.
8. C. M. Seifert, "Pratt & Whitney Goes High-Tech at Halifax Plant," *Materials Management and Distribution* 34, no. 3, March 1989, p. 22.
9. Sam Lightman, "Cradle-to-Grave," *Materials Management and Distribution* 34, no. 2, February 1989, pp. 27–28.
10. "GM's Saturn Workers Fire Up for Big Demand," *Washington Times,* February 7, 1992, p. G2.
11. Laura Ramsay, "Robotics Shift Production into High Gear," *Financial Post,* October 27, 1989, p. 14.
12. This was reported in various articles during 1989 and 1990 in the *Financial Post, Canadian Business,* and the *Globe and Mail* Report on Business.
13. Jeremy Main, "Betting on the 21st Century Jet," *Fortune,* April 20, 1992, pp. 102–17.
14. Paul B. Carroll, "Calling Up a Machine to Manufacture a Part," *The Wall Street Journal,* November 4, 1991, p. B1.
15. John Teresko, "Hewlett-Packard," *Industry Week,* November 19, 1990.
16. Tom Werner, "Computers Moving into Manufacturing," *Philadelphia Business Journal,* December 17, 1990.
17. James B. Treece and Patrick Orter, "General Motors: Open All Night," *Business Week,* June 1, 1992, pp. 82–83.
18. Eric Olsen, "Do It Better," *Success,* March 1992, pp. 35–38.
19. John Teresko, "Move from CIM to HIM," *Industry Week,* May 6, 1991.
20. Jerry Flint, "Follow That Ford," *Forbes,* April 27, 1992, pp. 44–46.
21. Tom Hout and George Stalk, Jr., *Competing against Time,"* New York: Free Press, 1990.
22. "Debate: Does the Baldrige Award Really Work?" *Harvard Business Review,* January/February 1992, pp. 126–48.
23. Donna Brown, "Ten Ways to Boost Quality," *Management Review,* January 1, 1991.
24. The comments are from James L. Riggs, *Production Systems,* New York: Free Press, 1987, pp. 614–15; Dr. Riggs's description of Deming's process is from W. Edwards Deming, *Quality, Productivity and Competitive Position,* Cambridge, Mass: MIT University Press, 1982.
25. Riggs, *Production Systems,* p. 615; he quotes from T. Sugimoto, "Present Status and Result of QC Circle Activity in Japan," *Proceedings,* International Conference on Productivity and Quality Improvement, Tokyo, 1982.
26. Charles Garfield, *Second to None,* Homewood, IL: Business One Irwin, 1992, pp. 225–26.
27. D. B. Scott, "Lean Machine," Report on Business, *Globe and Mail,* November 1992, p. 90ff.
28. Catherine Motherwell, "From the Oil Field to the Boardroom," Classroom Edition, *Globe and Mail,* December 1992, p. 14.
29. John Graham, "Watch Those Tiny Trickles—They Soon Become Trends that Change the Way We Do Business," *The CPA Journal,* January 1, 1991.
30. Ronald Henkoff, "Make Your Office More Productive," *Fortune,* February 25, 1991.
31. Julie Moline, "Productivity and Service for the Business Traveller," *Fortune,* April 6, 1992, pp. 39ff.
32. Henkoff, "Make Your Office More Productive," *Fortune,* February 25, 1991.

Chapter 10

1. Tom Peters and Nancy Austin, *A Passion for Excellence,* New York: Random House, 1985, p. 7.
2. Ben Wattenberg, "The Competitive Edge," *Washington Times,* March 3, 1988, p. F3.
3. The American Marketing Association, Chicago, IL.
4. Janet Novack, "We're Not Running the Company for the Stock Price," *Forbes,* September 19, 1988, pp. 41–52.
5. "Granddaddy of Diapermakers Is All Wet," *Business Week,* October 13, 1986, p. 71.
6. John Lynker, "U.S. Suffers from Lack of Listening," *Washington Times,* February 10, 1989, p. 63.

Chapter 11

1. *Canadian Grocer* 104, no. 6, June 1990, pp. 59–60.
2. Yumiko Ono, " 'Waiter, We'll Have Two Coffees and a Couple of Orders of Oxygen,' " *The Wall Street Journal,* March 23, 1988, p. 29.
3. Eric N. Berkowitz, Roger A. Kerin, and William Rudelius, *Marketing,* Homewood, IL: Richard D. Irwin, 1989.
4. "Survey Finds 67% of New Products Succeed," *Marketing News,* Feb. 8, 1980, p. 1.
5. Michael Schrage, "Customers May Be Your Best Collaborators," *The Wall Street Journal,* Feb. 27, 1989, p. A10.
6. Jacquie McNish, "Head of Beverage Unit Tough, Creative, Innovative," *Globe and Mail,* April 19, 1993, pp. B1, B9.

Chapter 12

1. U.S. Department of Agriculture.
2. U.S. Department of Agriculture.
3. An interview with IBM's marketing department, 1992.
4. "EDI in Action," *Business Week,* March 30, 1992, pp. 85–92.

5. Alfred J. Battaglia and Gene Tyndall, "Implementing World Class Supply Management," a paper given to the authors, Feb. 1992.
6. *Rail in Canada,* StatsCan, Cat. no. 52-216, 1990, p. 174.
7. *Retail Trade 1988,* StatsCan, Cat. no. 63-223, Jan. 1991; *Direct Selling in Canada 1989,* StatsCan, Cat. no. 63-218, March 1991; "Merchandising and Services," *Canada Year Book 1990,* StatsCan, p. 17-3.
8. These concepts are based on Jack Nadel, "Cracking the Global Market," *Management Review,* Sept. 1987, pp. 40–43.

Chapter 13

1. Julie Skur Hill and Joseph M. Winski, "Goodbye Global Ads," *Advertising Age,* Nov. 16, 1987, pp. 22, 36.
2. "Selling Tips," *Personal Selling Power,* Jan./Feb. 1989, p. 7.
3. *Small Business* 9, no. 4, April 1990, pp. 30, 32.
4. "Direct Marketing," *Marketing Communications,* Nov./Dec. 1988, p. 34.
5. Regis McKenna, *Relationship Marketing,* Reading, MA: Addison-Wesley, 1991.
6. Charles Garfield, *Second to None,* Homewood, IL: Business One Irwin, 1992.
7. Bill Saporito, "What Sam Walton Taught America," *Fortune,* May 4, 1992, pp. 104–06.

Chapter 14

1. Richard L. Daft, *Management,* Hinsdale, IL: The Dryden Press, 1988, p. 39.
2. David A. Houndshell, "The Same Old Principles in New Manufacturing," *Harvard Business Review,* Nov./Dec. 1988, pp. 54–61.
3. Abraham A. Maslow, *Motivation and Personality,* New York: Harper & Brothers, 1954.
4. Andrew Grove, *High Output Management,* New York: Random House, 1983, pp. 157–80.
5. For more on Theory Y, see Douglas McGregor, *The Human Side of Enterprise,* New York: McGraw-Hill, 1970.
6. Harold Geneen, *Managing,* New York: Avon Books, 1984, p. 17.
7. William G. Ouchi, *Theory Z: How American Business Can Meet the Japanese Challenge,* Reading, MA: Addison-Wesley Publishing, 1981.
8. Harold Geneen, *Managing.*
9. Frederick Herzberg, *Work and the Nature of Man,* World Publishers, 1966.
10. Tom Peters, "Workers' Esteem Tied to Authority," *Washington Times,* Oct. 25, 1988, p. C2.
11. "The Joy of Working," *Inc.,* Nov. 1987, pp. 61–67.
12. "The Joy of Working," p. 66.
13. Martin Yate, "To Serve Customers: Serve Employees," *Personnel,* Dec. 1, 1990; Joseph Weber, Lisa Driscoll, and Richard Brandt, "Farewell Fast Track," *Business Week,* Dec. 10, 1990, pp. 192–200.
14. Tom Peters, "Work Teams Shatter Old Ideas," *Washington Times,* June 23, 1988, p. C2.
15. Martin J. Gannon, *Management,* Boston, MA: Allyn & Bacon, 1988, pp. 256–57.
16. Faye Rice, "Champions of Communications," *Fortune,* June 3, 1991, pp. 111–20.
17. Faye Rice.
18. Barrie McKenna, "Reborn in Rimouski," *Globe and Mail,* July 20, 1993, p. B20.
19. Hugh McBride, "A Corporate Obsession Pays Off," *Globe and Mail,* July 13, 1993, p. B22.
20. Sam Walton, "In His Own Words," *Fortune,* June 29, 1992, pp. 98–106.
21. Alan Deutschman, "The Trouble with MBAs," *Fortune,* June 29, 1991, pp. 67–79.
22. This section is based on John Case, "Why Work?," *Inc.,* June 19, 1988, pp. 25–28.

Chapter 15

1. E. Innes, J. Lyons and J. Harris, The Financial Post 100 Best Companies to work for in Canada (Toronto: HarperCollins, 1990).
2. Brian Dunn, "Human Resources Panel Told Bonuses Don't Work," *Montreal Gazette,* Sept. 21, 1988, p. A3.
3. Joyce Lain Kennedy, "Here's How Today's Employers Hire New Employees," *St. Louis Post Dispatch,* Jan. 6, 1992, p. 14BP.
4. *Canadian Business* 62, no. 8, Aug. 1989, p. 9; *Benefits Canada* 15, no. 2, Feb. 1991, p. 11; *Financial Post,* Jan. 8, 1990, p. 3.
5. "Canadian Women Get Short Shrift, UN Says," *Montreal Gazette,* July 5, 1993, p. C1.
6. Jerry Goldberg, "An Old Girls' Network Aids Female Entrepreneurs," *Washington Business* section of *Washington Post,* July 11, 1988, pp. 1, 32–33.
7. Most of the information in this section is from an interview with LC Consultants, May 17, 1993.

Chapter 18

1. Eileen Davis, "The Root of All Evil," *Venture,* Dec. 1988, pp. 77–78.
2. Jerry Zeidenberg, "The Money Tree," Report on Business, *Globe and Mail,* June 1993, p. 70.
3. "David L. Berch," *Inc.,* April 1989, pp. 38–39.

Chapter 19

1. Linda Hossie, "UN Stymied on Stopping Weapons Sales," *Globe and Mail,* May 29, 1993, p. A7.
2. *Montreal Gazette,* March 14, 1992, p. J6.
3. *Globe and Mail,* March 7, 1992, p. A3.
4. *Globe and Mail,* p. B3.
5. *Globe and Mail,* p. B3.

6. *Financial Times,* March 16, 1992, p. 2.
7. *Financial Times,* March 16, 1992, p. 2.
8. "Gas-Cartel Fines Should Be a Lesson to Others," *Financial Times,* Sept. 23, 1991, p. 34.
9. *Financial Times,* March 16, 1992, p. 31.
10. *New York Times,* March 16, 1992, p. D2.
11. *Canadian Business.*
12. John Stackhouse, "Canadian on Mission to Save the Planet," (New York Times), *Globe and Mail,* May 2, 1992, p. A1.
13. Keith Bradsher, "Trade Official Assails Europe over Ecology," *New York Times,* Oct. 31, 1991, p. D2.
14. "Trade and the Environment," *New York Times,* March 11, 1992, p. D1.
15. Report on Business, *Globe and Mail,* May 4, 1992, p. B2.
16. *Montreal Gazette,* Sept. 21, 1991, p. K6.
17. Peter Hadekel, "Paper Industry Mustn't Use Recession as Excuse to Duck Environmental Issues," *Montreal Gazette,* April 11, 1992, p. D1.
18. *Montreal Gazette,* April 11, 1992, p. D1.
19. Douglas Goold, "Laidlaw Is a 'Green Jungle' Risk," *Globe and Mail,* March 14, 1992, p. B25.
20. Stephen Ewart, "Closing Gasoline Stations Could Cost Billions of Dollars," *Montreal Gazette,* March 14, 1992, p. D7.
21. Claire Bernstein, "Heavy Legal Artillery Now Turned Against Environment Offenders," *Toronto Star,* Dec. 16, 1991, p. B3.
22. *Montreal Gazette,* March 7, 1992, p. D3.
23. Personal interview with A. Delisle, Radio-Canada's chief heating engineer.
24. Report on Business, *Globe and Mail,* March 16, 1992, p. 18.
25. Geoffrey York, "First Weekly Ozone Warnings Issued," *Globe and Mail,* March 12, 1992, p. A1.
26. Jim Dawson, "A Gem of an Idea," *Montreal Gazette,* March 7, 1992, p. J8.
27. David Suzuki, "Only in This Century Has Growth Become Part of Life," *Montreal Gazette,* July 20, 1991, p. J8.
28. "Living on Borrowed Time," *Montreal Gazette,* May 9, 1992, p. K6.
29. Charles Hampden-Turner, "The Boundaries of Business: The Cross-Cultural Quagmire," *Harvard Business Review,* Sept./Oct. 1991, p. 94.
30. *Globe and Mail,* May 1, 1992, p. B24.
31. Paul Hawken, "A Declaration of Sustainability," *Utne READER,* 59, Sept./Oct. 1993, pp. 54–61.

INDEX

G

H

N

T

CREDITS

CHAPTER 1

p. 2, Courtesy of Tourism Vancouver. p. 4, Paul Berman. p. 5, Courtesy of Tourism Vancouver. p. 7, Paul Berman. p. 10, Courtesy of Caterpillar, Inc.; Courtesy of Caterpillar, Inc.; BCL Group; BCL Group. p. 12, Tourism Vancouver. p. 16, Michael Polselli. p. 19, Michael Polselli. p. 22, Michael Polselli. p. 24, Courtesy of Central Louisiana Electric Company; Courtesy of the Georgia-Pacific Corporation. p. 26, Michael Polselli.

CHAPTER 2

p. 34, Michael Polselli, p. 36, Courtesy of Northern Telecom. p. 37, Paul Berman. p. 40, Tim McCabe/Nawrocki Stock Photo. p. 42, Courtesy of Tulleycross Fine Irish Imports. p. 46, Courtesy of Bombardier, Inc. p. 48, Dave Brown/Nawrocki Stock Photo. p. 49, Michael Polselli. p. 53, Mark Snyder/Nawrocki Stock Photo. p. 62, Nawrocki Stock Photo.

CHAPTER 3

p. 70, BGM Photo Centre Limited. p. 72, Courtesy of Gerald Tremblay. p. 74, Michael Polselli. p. 75, Courtesy of Canada Post. p. 82, Michael Polselli. p. 85, Courtesy of Bombardier Inc. p. 87, W.P. McElligott. p. 92, *Newsweek*/John Ficara. p. 94, Courtesy of the Ontario Milk Marketing Board.

CHAPTER 4

p. 102, Michael Polselli. p. 104, Courtesy of the Harvard Office of News and Public Affairs. p. 105, Courtesy Wisconsin Tourism Development; Courtesy Cadillac Motor Car Division; Courtesy of Radio Shack, A Division of Tandy Corporation. Michael Polselli; Michael Polselli; Michael Polselli; Michael Polselli. p. 108, Courtesy of the Chateau Whistler Resort. p. 114, Photography by Voyles. p. 115, Michael Polselli. p. 125, Courtesy of Ford Motor Company. p. 127, Michael Polselli. p. 132, The Bettmann Archive.

CHAPTER 5

p. 140, Michael Polselli. p. 142, Courtesy of Bombardier Inc. p. 144, Michael Polselli. p. 148, Michael Polselli. p. 150, Michael Polselli. p. 156, Courtesy of Farmland Industries Inc. p. 157, Reuters/Bettmann Newsphoto.

CHAPTER 6

p. 164, Michael Polselli. p. 166, Courtesy of Bob Dickie. p. 168, Courtesy of the 3M Company, photo by Mark Joseph. p. 171, Courtesy of Catherine Enright. p. 174, Paul Berman. p. 177, Michael Polselli. p. 180, Michael J. Hruby. p. 182, Michael Polselli. p. 188, Michael Polselli.

CHAPTER 7

p. 200, Michael Polselli. p. 202, Courtesy of Walter Shawlee. p. 205, Michael Philip Manheim/Stock South; Courtesy of Henry Mintzberg. p. 209, Michael Polselli. p. 211, Stephen Green/Nawrocki Stock Photo. p. 212, Photograph by John Thoeming. p. 215, Brownie Harris/The Stock Market. p. 222, Stock Imagery. p. 224, Photograph by John Thoeming.

CHAPTER 8

p. 230, Michael Polselli. p. 232, Courtesy Chrysler Corporation. p. 233, Photo Courtesy Hewlett-Packard Company. p. 237, Courtesy of Bombardier Inc. p. 240, Courtesy United Parcel Service of America, Inc. p. 248, Courtesy of Campbell Soup Company. p. 256, Reed Raestner/Zephyr Pictures; Michael Polselli.

CHAPTER 9

p. 264, Michael Polselli. p. 266, Courtesy of Blaine Hoshizaki. p. 269, Courtesy Bethlehem Steel Corporation. p. 274, Courtesy Amoco Corporation; Courtesy Rockwell International. p. 277, Courtesy Harley-Davidson, Inc. p. 281, Courtesy of Converse, Inc. p. 284, Courtesy Ford Motor Company. p. 296, Michael Polselli. p. 297, Photo courtesy of Hewlett-Packard Company.

CHAPTER 10

p. 310, Michael Polselli. p. 312, Courtesy of Jerry Goodis. p. 314, Michael Polselli. p. 315, Rick Etkin/Scali, McCabe, Sloves. p. 317, Michael Polselli. p. 318, Courtesy Kellogg Company. p. 325, Michael Polselli. p. 326, Michael Polselli. p. 328, Courtesy of Campbell Soup Company;. Courtesy of Campbell Soup Company. p. 334, Courtesy of the Goodyear Tire & Rubber Company.

CHAPTER 11

p. 342, Courtesy of Bombardier Inc. p. 344, Courtesy of Loblaw International Merchants. p. 345, Michael Polselli. p. 347, Courtesy of Bombardier, Inc.; Courtesy of Bombardier Inc. p. 348, All photos courtesy of Oldsmobile. p. 350, Courtesy of Rosignol Ski Company. p. 353, Michael Polselli. p. 354, Coke, Coca-Cola, and the Dynamic Ribbon device are trademarks of the Coca-Cola Company. Permission granted by the Coca-Cola Company. p. 356, Courtesy of Loblaw International Merchants Co's. p. 364, Courtesy Arm & Hammer. p. 366, Courtesy Jaguar Cars, Inc.

CHAPTER 12

p. 378, Courtesy of the West Edmonton Mall. p. 380, Courtesy of JPL International. p. 385, Michael Polselli. p. 386, Courtesy of W.L.

Gore & Associates, Inc. p. 390, Courtesy of Consolidated Freightways, Inc. p. 392, Courtesy of CSX Corporation, photo by John B. Corns. p. 394, Courtesy of United Parcel Service of America, Inc. p. 396, Michael Polselli. p. 399, Michael Polselli; Michael Polselli. p. 401, Courtesy of the West Edmonton Mall. p. 405, Michael Polselli.

CHAPTER 13

p. 410, Courtesy of the Bank of Montreal. p. 412, Courtesy of Jean-Pierre Grenier. p. 414, Courtesy of American Association of Advertising Agencies, Inc. p. 417, Courtesy of the Ontario Milk Board. p. 419, Melanie Carr/Nawrocki Stock Photo. p. 422, Michael Polselli. p. 425, Courtesy General Mills. p. 430, Joseph Jacobsen/Nawrocki Stock Photos.

CHAPTER 14

p. 440, Courtesy of Tourism Vancouver. p. 442, Courtesy of Don Brommet. p. 443, Courtesy of the Montreal Expos. p. 445, Reproduced with the permission of AT&T Corporate Archive. p. 448, Michael Polselli. p. 453, Courtesy of The Limited Stores. p. 462, Michael Polselli.

CHAPTER 15

p. 470, Michael Polselli. p. 472, Courtesy of Herbert Siblin. p. 478, Courtesy of Lake County Placement Office/Bill Kniest Photographer. p. 485, Michael Polselli. p. 487, Courtesy of American Airlines. p. 489, Courtesy of Tourism Vancouver. p. 494, Michael Polselli. p. 495, Michael Polselli.

CHAPTER 16

p. 514, Michael Polselli. p. 516, Courtesy of Alan B. Gold. p. 519, Courtesy Rockwell International. p. 524, Photo courtesy of International Brotherhood of Electrical Workers, Local 213. p. 527, Courtesy of the Bakery, Confectionery and Tobacco Workers' International Union. p. 530, Photo Features Ltd. p. 533, Photograph by John Thoeming.

CHAPTER 17

p. 540, Courtesy Computer Associates International, Inc. p. 542, Courtesy of Leadley, Gunning & Culp International. p. 547, Photograph by Sharon Hoogstraten. p. 548, Photography by Voyles. p. 551, Michael Polselli. p. 558, Gregory Murphy/Nawrocki Stock Photo. p. 561, Stock Imagery.

CHAPTER 18

p. 576, Michael Polselli, p. 578, Courtesy of Stephen Vaughan. p. 584, Copyright 1992 American Express Travel Related Services Company, Inc. p. 585, Michael Polselli. p. 590, Michael Polselli. p. 604, Courtesy of the Toronto Stock Exchange.

CHAPTER 19

p. 614, Courtesy of the Western Canada Wilderness Committee (W.C.W.C.). p. 616, Courtesy of Rose Todorski. p. 620, Courtesy of Greenpeace. p. 621, Courtesy of Greenpeace; Courtesy of Greenpeace. p. 628, Courtesy of the W.C.W.C. p. 629, Courtesy of the W.C.W.C.; Courtesy of the W.C.W.C. p. 630, Courtesy of MacMillan Bloedel Ltd. p. 633, Courtesy of Greenpeace. p. 638, Courtesy of the W.C.W.C.